Politics of the Middle East

Politics of the Middle East
Cultures and Conflicts

Michael G. Roskin
Lycoming College

James J. Coyle
University of San Diego

PEARSON
Prentice
Hall

UPPER SADDLE RIVER, NEW JERSEY 07458

Library of Congress Cataloging-in-Publication Data

Roskin, Michael
  Politics of the Middle East: cultures and conflicts/Michael G. Roskin, James J. Coyle.—1st ed.
    p. cm.
  Includes bibliographical references and index.
  ISBN 0-13-184549-7
  1. Middle East. I. Coyle, James J. II. Title.
DS44 .R745 2003
956—dc22

                                                                 2003025337

Editorial Director: Charlyce Jones Owen
Acquisitions Editor: Glenn Johnston
Assistant Editor: John Ragozzine
Editorial Assistant: Suzanne Remore
Director of Marketing: Beth Mejia
Marketing Assistant: Jennifer Bryant
Prepress and Manufacturing Buyer: Sherry Lewis
Interior Design: John P. Mazzola
Cover Art Director: Jayne Conte
Cover Design: Kiwi Design
Cover Photo: John Dakers/Life File/Getty Images, Inc.
Composition/Full-Service Project Management: Kari Callaghan Mazzola and John P.
  Mazzola
Printer/Binder: Hamilton Printing Company
Cover Printer: Phoenix Color Corp.

This book was set in 10/12 Meridien.

Pearson Education LTD.
Pearson Education Singapore, Pte. Ltd
Pearson Education, Canada, Ltd
Pearson Education–Japan
Pearson Education Australia PTY, Limited

Pearson Education North Asia Ltd
Pearson Educación de Mexico, S.A. de C.V.
Pearson Education Malaysia, Pte. Ltd
Pearson Education, Upper Saddle River, NJ

10 9 8 7 6 5 4 3 2 1
ISBN 0-13-184549-7

Contents

FEATURE BOXES   xv

PREFACE   xxiii

PART I   CULTURES   1

CHAPTER 1
CIVILIZATION AND ITS CRADLE   1

It Comes with the Territory   6
The Lay of the Land   10
Middle Eastern Culture   12
The Importance of the Spoken Word   12
Shared Cultural Characteristics   14
Conclusions   16
Further Reference   17

CHAPTER 2
THE ANCIENTS AND THEIR CONFLICTS   18

The First Cities   19
The Egyptians   19
The Babylonians   20
The Hittites   21
The Assyrians   21
The Phoenicians   22

The Persians   23

The Greeks   25

The Romans   27

Pax Romana   30

The Decline of Rome   30

Byzantium   31

Eastern Weakness   32

The Turks and the Crusades   33

Conclusions   35

Further Reference   35

CHAPTER 3

THE BIRTH OF ISLAM   36

Muhammad   36

Muhammad's Role   40

Birth of Shi'ism   41

The Choice of the Caliphs   41

The Umayyads   43

The Abbasids   45

The Abbasid Caliphate   46

Challenges to Orthodoxy   48

The End of the Arab Empire   49

The Fatimids   52

The Mamluks   52

Iranian Dynasties   53

Conclusions   54

Further Reference   54

CHAPTER 4

THE OTTOMAN EMPIRE   56

The Ottomans   56

The Janissaries   59

The Reign of Sulayman   60

Ottoman Succession   61

Economic Decline   62

The Sick Man of Europe   63

Military Reform   63

The Tanzimat   65

The Committee of Union and Progress   67

World War I   68

Conclusions   69

Further Reference   69

PART II   ARAB-ISRAELI CONFLICTS   70

CHAPTER 5
THE ORIGINS OF THE ISRAEL-PALESTINE WAR   70

Kingdoms and Conquests   71

The Long Diaspora   74

The Rise of Modern Zionism   77

The Rise of Arab Nationalism   79

The Impact of World War I   81

The Mandate   82

The First Arab-Jewish Clashes   84

Conclusions   89

Further Reference   90

CHAPTER 6
THE VERY LONG WAR   91

The 1948 War   91

The Origin of Palestinian Refugees   97

The 1956 War   99

The Six Day War   102

The 1973 War   106

The Lebanon Incursion   108

Conclusions   111

Further Reference   111

CHAPTER 7

IS PEACE POSSIBLE?   113

Sadat's Incredible Journey   114

The First Palestinian Intifada   117

The Second Palestinian Intifada   123

Incompatible Demands   123

The West Bank   130

Jerusalem   131

The Right to Return   132

The Downward Spiral   133

Conclusions   135

Further Reference   135

PART III   THE NORTH   137

CHAPTER 8

TURKEY   137

From Empire to Republic   137

Independence War   138

Independence Tribunals   141

The Free Party Experiment   141

Ismet İnönü   142

The Democratic Party   142

Military Planning   143

Democratic Rule   143

The 1961 Military Revolution   145

New Political Faces   146

The "Coup by Memorandum"   146

Return to Elections   147

The Third Coup   148

The Rise of Refah   149

Military Moves against Refah   151

The Justice and Development Party   152

Conclusions   154
Further Reference   154

Chapter 9
The Kurds   155

Who Are the Kurds?   155
A History of Seeking a Nation   157
World War I and Its Aftermath   159
The Simko Rebellion   160
The Mahabad Republic   160
Soviet Withdrawal   163
The Rise of Barzani   163
The Role of the United States   165
The Kurds in Iran's Islamic Revolution   166
The Iran-Iraq War   167
The Kurdish Break with Iraq   167
The First Gulf War   168
The Kurds in Turkey   169
The Rise of the PKK   169
Turkish Civil War   170
The Capture of Ocalan   170
Conclusions   171
Further Reference   172

Part IV   The Rise of the Oil Kingdoms   173

Chapter 10
Iran   173

The Safavids   173
The Qajars   175
Enter the West   176
The Constitutional Revolution of 1906   178
World War II   181

Shah Mohammed Reza   183

The Soviet Threat   184

Muhammad Mossadeq and Oil   185

Operation Ajax   186

Khomeini's Opposition to the White Revolution   186

Conclusions   189

Further Reference   190

Chapter 11

Saudi Arabia   191

Muhammad ibn Saud   191

Round Two   193

Round Three   194

World War I   195

The Ikhwan   197

Saudi-American Relations   197

Saudi Arabia Enters the World Stage   199

The Fifties   199

Saudi-Egyptian Rivalry   200

Faisal's First Turn   201

The Sixties   202

Faisal's Second Turn   202

The 1967 Arab-Israeli War   203

The 1973 Arab-Israeli War   204

Conclusions   205

Further Reference   205

Chapter 12

Iraq and Kuwait   206

Post-Faisal Iraq   209

World War II   211

The Iraqi Revolution   213

The Coups   215

The June 1967 War   216

Kuwait   217
Conclusions   220
Further Reference   221

PART V   CONFLICTS: THE GULF WARS   222

CHAPTER 13
THE IRANIAN REVOLUTION AND WAR WITH IRAQ   222

The Pressure Cooker   222
The Beginning of the Revolution   223
Khomeini in Paris   224
The Last Imperial Government   224
The First Revolutionary Government   226
Iran's Islamic Constitution   227
The Hostage Crisis   228
The Failed Hostage Rescue   229
Bani Sadr: The Last of the Liberals   230
The Iran-Iraq War   231
The American Tilt   231
U.S. Naval Involvement   232
Saddam Takes the Offensive   233
Constitutional Crisis   234
The Rafsanjani Years   234
The Urge to Reform   235
Reformists Blocked   235
U.S.-Iranian Relations   238
Conclusions   238
Further Reference   238

CHAPTER 14
THE FIRST GULF WAR   240

The Weak American Response   241
The Invasion of Kuwait   244
Kuwaiti Lobbying   245

From Desert Shield to Desert Storm   247

Ground Attack   248

The Rebellions   250

The War over Weapons of Mass Destruction   251

The Clinton Years   252

Conclusions   254

Further Reference   254

CHAPTER 15

THE 9/11 WARS   256

Covert War in Afghanistan   257

The Same War Twice   261

The Conduct of the War   266

The Aftermath   268

The Kurdish Problem   271

The Shi'a Problem   273

The Muslim World after the War   274

Conclusions   276

Further Reference   277

PART VI   ISLAMIC WARS?   278

CHAPTER 16

WHY MIDDLE EAST TERRORISM?   278

Definitions   279

Islamist Terrorists   282

Al Qaeda   283

Relations with Saudi Arabia Gone Sour   285

Bin Ladin's Message   286

Terrorist Attacks   287

September 11, 2001   288

Lessons Learned   289

Conclusions   290

Further Reference   291

CHAPTER 17

A DEMOCRATIC MIDDLE EAST?   292

The Failure of Modernization?   294

A Muslim Reformation?   299

Islam in the West   299

Can Saudi Arabia Democratize?   304

Conclusions   307

Further Reference   308

CHAPTER 18

THE UNITED STATES AND THE MIDDLE EAST   309

U.S. Even-Handedness   310

The Nixon Tilt   311

What Role for America?   314

Kingdom of Denial   316

What Next for U.S. Policy?   320

Islamic Rage and U.S. Response   321

Conclusions   325

Further Reference   325

INDEX   327

Feature Boxes

CHAPTER 1

Key Concepts: The Importance of Getting Civilized   2

Geography: The Great Rift   3

Geography: What Is the Middle East?   4

Cultures: Calendars   6

Geography: Key Features of the Middle East   7

Cultures: Language Groups   8

Religions: What Is Religion?   9

Cultures: Perception versus Reality   11

Cultures: The Arabic Language   13

Cultures: Middle Eastern Layers of Identity   15

CHAPTER 2

Conflicts: Is the Middle East Especially Warlike?   20

Women of the Middle East: Hatshepsut, Iron Lady of Egypt   21

Religions: The First Monotheism   22

Geography: Turkish Straits   24

Cultures: Conquering the Conquerors   26

Women of the Middle East: Cleopatra, Goddess and Ruler   30

Women of the Middle East: The Syrian Empresses of the House of Servi   31

Women of the Middle East: Theodora, Stage Star Turned Empress   33

Women of the Middle East: Empresses Irene, Zoe, and Theodora   34

CHAPTER 3

Religions: Birthplace of Religions   37

Religions: Competing Revelations   38

Cultures: Under the Spell of Arabic   39

Cultures: Arabic Names   40

Religions: The Islamic Calendar   41

Religions: The Constitution of Medina   42

Religions: Hudaybiya   43

Cultures: Family Honor   44

Religions: Shi'a Leadership Philosophy   45

Women of the Middle East: Aisha and the Lost Necklace   46

Religions: Husayn: Martyr or Suicide?   47

Religions: Friday Mosque   49

Conflicts: The Crusades   50

Religions: The Varieties of Shi'ism   52

Religions: Ibn Taymiyah   53

Cultures: Ferdowsi: Nationalist Poet   54

CHAPTER 4

Key Concepts: Praetorianism   60

Key Concepts: Capitulations   61

Women of the Middle East: Hurren   62

Key Concepts: Logistics   63

Conflicts: Vendetta on the Black Sea   64

Cultures: Mullah Nasreddin   65

Key Concepts: A Chronology of Ottoman Pushback   66

CHAPTER 5

Geography: Palestine   71

Religions: The "Promised Land" in the Bible   72

Religions: The Birth of Two Religions   73

Religions: The First or Second Coming of the Messiah?   74

Geography: Everyone Is from Somewhere Else   75

Cultures: Sephardic and Ashkenazic Jews   76

Religions: Israel's Secular Founders   79

Religions: Separate Arab States?   80

Cultures: Cultural versus Material   83

Geography: Politics by Demographic Means   85

Cultures: Thieves in the Night   86

Geography: Partition   87

The United States in the Middle East: Truman Recognizes Israel   89

CHAPTER 6

Geography: Bound Israel   93

Geography: Divided Jerusalem   94

Cultures: "On Wings of Eagles"   95

Geography: Israel's Features   96

Geography: Bound Jordan   98

Geography: Dam Foolish   101

Geography: Territory and Security   103

Peace: Why No Peace in 1967   104

Cultures: Fighting Words   105

Women of the Middle East: Golda Meier   107

Cultures: Israeli Overconfidence   108

Conflicts: The Five Wars of Israel   109

Geography: Bound Lebanon   110

CHAPTER 7

Peace: UN Efforts at Middle East Peace   114

Peace: The UN's First Efforts   115

Geography: Bound Egypt   116

Geography: The Pattern of Israeli Settlements   118

Peace: The Deception of "Atmospherics"   120

Peace: The Killing of Rabin   122

Religions: Iran and the Palestinians   123

Religions: Palestinian "Martyrs"   124

Geography: Jerusalem Internationalized?   125

Peace: Can Diplomacy Work?   126

Peace: Rejectionists on Both Sides   127

Geography: Middle East Irredentism   128

Peace: The Four Great Issues   129

Peace: The Blame Game   133

Peace: Bush's "Road Map"   134

CHAPTER 8

Religions: The Caliphate and September 11   138

Geography: The Population Exchanges   140

Key Concepts: The Six Arrows of Atatürkism   142

Conflicts: The Cyprus Problem   147

Women of the Middle East: Turkey's Tansu Ciller   149

Geography: Turkey and the European Union   150

Women of the Middle East: Merve Kavakci   152

Geography: Turkey, Iraq, and the United States   153

CHAPTER 9

Key Concepts: Nationalism   157

Cultures: Creation Mythology   158

Geography: The Shatt al-Arab Border Dispute   165

CHAPTER 10

Religions: High versus Low Islam   174

Geography: The Name of the Gulf   175

Religions: The Baha'i   176

Religions: Shi'a Hierarchy   177

Religions: Clerics and Politics   179

Women of the Middle East: The Shah's Push for Equality   181

Geography: Bound Iran   182
Geography: OPEC   187
Religions: Khomeini's Political Theory   188
Geography: Twin Pillars in the Gulf   189

CHAPTER 11

Geography: Is Colonialism Only European?   192
Geography: Middle Eastern Strategic Waterways   193
Geography: The Trucial States   195
Geography: Bound Saudi Arabia   196
Religions: The Ulama   198
Cultures: Gap on Pennsylvania Avenue   200
Geography: The Baghdad Pact (CENTO)   201
The United States in the Middle East: The Eisenhower Doctrine   202

CHAPTER 12

Geography: Collapsed Empires   207
Geography: San Remo Conference   208
Key Concepts: Analogies   209
Geography: The Peoples of Iraq   210
Cultures: The Eternal Saladin   212
Geography: Bound Iraq   214
Key Concepts: What Is the Baath?   215

CHAPTER 13

Key Concepts: What Went Wrong in Iran?   225
Key Concepts: Crane Brinton's Theory of Revolution   226
Religions: Can There Be an Islamic Republic?   227
The United States in the Middle East: The Iran-Contra Fiasco   232
The United States in the Middle East: The Downing of Iran Air 655   233
The United States in the Middle East: U.S.-Iranian Signals   236

CHAPTER 14

The United States in the Middle East: CENTCOM   242

Cultures: A Woman Ambassador to an Arab State?   243

The United States in the Middle East: Wobbly George   245

The United States in the Middle East: The United States and UN
  Resolutions   246

Conflicts: Joint Resolutions for War   248

Conflicts: Did Deterrence Work?   249

Conflicts: Gulf War Syndrome   250

Cultures: The In-Law Problem   253

CHAPTER 15

Geography: The "Game of Nations"   257

Geography: Afghanistan and the Gulf   259

Key Concepts: Blowback   260

Conflicts: Did Deterrence Work? Part 2   262

Key Concepts: Bureaucratic Politics   264

Conflicts: Preemptive or Preventive War?   265

Conflicts: Where Are Iraq's Bugs and Gas?   266

Conflicts: Dire and Optimistic Predictions   268

Conflicts: Revolution in Military Affairs   270

Geography: Federalism for Iraq?   274

The United States in the Middle East: U.S. Public Reaction   276

CHAPTER 16

Conflicts: Low-Intensity Warfare   281

Cultures: The Philosopher of Islamism   284

Key Concepts: Micro versus Macro Analysis   285

CHAPTER 17

Key Concepts: Middle East Regimes   294

Key Concepts: Modernization Theory   297

Key Concepts: Civil Society   298

Key Concepts: The Huntington Challenge   300

Religions: Salafiyya   302

Key Concepts: The Praetorian Paradox   305

Key Concepts: The Communications Revolution   306

CHAPTER 18

The United States in the Middle East: Marines in Beirut, 1958   311

Geography: Recognition of Jerusalem   313

The United States in the Middle East: Blown Up in Beirut, 1983   314

Geography: A Unipolar World?   315

The United States in the Middle East: NATO, Not in the Middle East   316

Peace: A U.S. Force for Palestine?   319

Conflicts: Catching Terrorists: No One in Charge   322

Preface

Je ne blâme, ni n'accuse. Je raconte.

—Talleyrand

One of the authors and a daughter recently chanced upon the film classic *Lawrence of Arabia* on television. She was curious: Who were these people? Whom were they fighting? When did it take place? Why were the British involved? This bright young college graduate had never learned anything of World War I in the Middle East and the British-encouraged Arab revolt against the Turks. Indeed, few young (and not-so-young) Americans know anything about this colorful episode and how it influences the Middle East to this day. Few Americans care about things distant in time and place. They tend to consign current conflicts to the realm of mystery and futility: "Those people! They're crazy. Their motives are a puzzle, maybe something to do with their religion. I don't know much about the area, but if our government says we'll have to fight, I guess we'll have to." In the same spirit of ignorant bliss we marched into Vietnam.

The authors aim to acquaint American students with this vital, exciting part of the world, which is very much in the news but not, unfortunately, very much among the courses American students typically take. Moving more and more to the vocational and career-related, few students have the knowledge to make sense of the Middle East. Filling the vacuum, many advocate either strong doses of U.S. military might or isolationism: "We should either nuke 'em or stay out."

Many subscribe to the "none of our business" theory: "If those people want to fight, we should just stand back and let them fight." This school-playground approach to the Middle East leads quickly to catastrophe. One recent president started office with a hands-off policy but was soon forced to become more involved than any of his predecessors. He discovered, as did many American isolationists before him, that we are connected to much of the rest of the world. In the Middle East, especially, we can neither fully stay out nor fully control the region, a frustrating situation. Staying out means letting Middle East conflicts roar out of control until they engulf several countries and damage the region's ability to export oil. When that happens, the entire world economy suffers. America imports relatively little Middle Eastern oil (although the percentage is growing), but a shortfall in production anywhere boosts prices everywhere.

The authors noticed that many works on the Middle East are too specialized and scholarly for a first undergraduate course in the area. With years of experience in college teaching on the region, government service, and journalism, we decided to put together our own textbook, covering Middle Eastern history, geography, and conflicts, including the 2003 Iraq War. That war, by the way, illustrates the interrelated complexity of the Middle East. To understand the 2003 war, one must understand a good deal of the history, geography, and politics not only of Iraq but also of all the neighboring countries. Two areas are especially shortchanged in most textbooks—Turkey and the Kurds—which we try to correct by giving each separate chapters.

Knowledge of geography is especially weak among young Americans, so we include "bounding" exercises throughout the book. This old-fashioned exercise requires the student to recite, from forced recall, countries' boundaries, moving clockwise around the points of the compass. If you do them faithfully, you will be able to locate from memory every country of the region. Memorization makes you smarter (and yes, they will be on the exams).

In recent years the news media have used "Middle East" as synonymous with the Israeli-Arab struggle. When they talk about Iraq or Saudi Arabia, they often say "Persian Gulf." Actually, the two are both Middle East and, although a few hundred miles apart, interconnected. Israel angers the Muslim world and serves as fodder for radical Islamists who would like to take over the Gulf oil states, which already encourage and subsidize Palestinian movements, some of them violent.

Instructors may notice that we interweave much general material in our chapters, everything from praetorianism to bureaucratic politics in Washington. All apply to the Middle East but have wider applicability as well. This is part of our purpose, to build what the French call *culture générale*. Topics in the abstract often become real when introduced in a relevant context. Accordingly, students will learn a great deal beyond the Middle East from this book. The authors thank Cullen Chandler, Mehrdad Madresehee, Robin Knauth, and Steven Johnson of Lycoming College for their valuable comments. We also thank the following reviewers: James L. Lutz, Indiana University–Purdue; Stephen Zunes, University of San Francisco; and Larbi Sadiki, University of Exeter.

The Middle East is full of controversies, and we are aware that our accounts and analyses may anger some readers. In many areas we are likely to be accused of either hostility toward or slavish support of a given cause. We are neither hostile nor slavish; we are simply realists. We look forward to "twining" one letter that calls us anti-X with the next that calls us pro-X. Our purpose is not to take sides but to tell several fascinating, complex stories in an accurate and balanced way. We do not play the "blame game" but recall Talleyrand, who served France before, during, and after Napoleon with equal aplomb: "I do not blame, neither do I accuse. I just tell the story."

Michael G. Roskin

James J. Coyle

Civilization and Its Cradle

Points to Ponder

- What is the difference between culture and civilization?
- What countries does the Middle East include?
- Are civilization and conflict related? How?
- How does water determine much of the Middle East?
- What is a religion?
- Is it valid to characterize whole peoples by culture?
- What is the "oral tradition" and why is it still important?
- Typically, how do Middle Easterners identify themselves?

If markers on our Y chromosomes are telling us the truth, our distant ancestors started to walk northward from their original home in Africa into the Middle East a mere 50,000 years ago. Some stayed in the Middle East while others moved on to populate Asia, Europe, and the Americas.

The Middle East is particularly interesting because the people that settled there, according to most archaeologists, began civilization. This process started when the ice receded, about 10,000 years ago. In the **Neolithic** period humans, after millennia as hunter-gatherers, began staying in one place and cultivating crops they originally found growing naturally. They domesticated grains and animals to become farmers and herders, thereby producing more food than they needed to feed their families. The greater abundance and certainty of food enabled more humans to live in a given area than could hunter-gatherers, and populations grew. From that point until the current historical epoch, most humans have been farmers.

With this shift, however, some humans started the "specialization of labor" and with it social classes. Very early, farmers fought herders over who was to use the land. Genesis 4:1–16 tells us how Cain, the cultivator, slew Abel, the shepherd, an example

---

Neolithic   New Stone Age, transition to settled agriculture and dawn of civilization.

K : *Key Concepts*

THE IMPORTANCE OF GETTING CIVILIZED

All humans carry **culture** with them. Culture does not necessarily mean going to the opera and art museums; it just means the sum total of behavior you have learned: speech, survival skills, and preferences in food, clothing, and religion. Some human behavior is biologically inherited. Biology tells us we must eat, but culture determines what we like to eat. Most of you would walk past a delicious Turkish *döner* in favor of an artificially flavored McCholesterol, because you have learned to like it.

A culture, however, is not necessarily a **civilization**, although some politically correct persons claim so. Civilization is a refined form of culture with cities, writing, fine arts, organized religion and government, manufacturing, architecture, laws, social classes, kings, and war. By now, almost all humans belong to a civilization, but that is a fairly recent thing. The origin of the word civilization is the Latin *civitas*, city. No cities, no civilization. Before cities, it is doubtful that there were any civilizations. Tribes of forest-dwellers or nomads have distinct cultures but probably not civilizations. If they settled down and built cities they would soon have a civilization, which is what ancient Middle Easterners seem to have done first, around 3000 B.C.

of this conflict. Labor became more specialized. An artisan class made shoes, clothing, and implements to be traded for the farmers' and herders' food. To facilitate production and selling, they clustered in towns. Markets—places where people exchange goods—are likely the origin of towns. Towns, because they contained goods, were tempting targets for marauding bands, so towns needed protection and thus began to be built on hilltops and walled. They also needed rudimentary political organization; chiefs turned themselves into petty kings. Jericho, the oldest town yet uncovered, was walled some 8,000 years ago, even before pottery was invented.

With the **Bronze Age** came an "urban revolution." Some towns grew into cities, the cores of ancient kingdoms, which increased complexity. They developed rules and professional magistrates to enforce them, the origins of legal systems. And cities needed to be defended, producing the first professional rulers and their helpers, males who were neither farmers nor artisans but warriors, first to defend their own turf and wherever possible to take someone else's. These rulers became kings and their helpers became nobles, most hereditary, with new lines arising based on wealth and military victories. Together with nobles, scribes, treasury keepers, architects, and poets formed courts to serve the king. In times of war, commoners could be conscripted and armed under the guidance of the nobles, who were either skilled in the arts of combat or lost to those who were.

culture   Learned (as opposed to biological) behavior.
civilization   Highly evolved culture featuring cities, writing, social classes, and complex economic and political systems.
Bronze Age   Beginnings of metal-working about 3,500 years ago.

G : *Geography*

THE GREAT RIFT

One fascinating geological feature of the Middle East is the Great Rift Valley, a giant, jagged crack in the earth's surface formed by two of the earth's plates that moved apart. It extends nearly straight southward from above the Sea of Galilee, down the Jordan River through the Dead Sea, Wadi Araba, and Gulf of Aqaba. Archaeologists believe early humans moved up the Rift Valley through the Middle East and then outward into Asia and Europe. At the Red Sea the rift takes a jog eastward, then another jog southward deep into Africa.

The Jordan Valley contains the lowest spots on earth. The Sea of Galilee is 680 feet below sea level. The Jordan River, entirely below sea level, flows south from Galilee until it empties into the Dead Sea, the lowest place on earth, nearly 1,300 feet below sea level, which explains why it is dead. Water flows in but cannot flow out, because there is nothing lower.

Water leaves the Dead Sea only by evaporation, which is rapid in the dry air and brutal sunshine of the area. Evaporation used to balance inflow, leaving the Dead Sea's level relatively constant. Recently, however, with heavy usage of the Jordan's water, the level of the Dead Sea has been slowly dropping. Left behind in the Sea are the salts and minerals that make bathers extremely buoyant. Sodom and Gomorrah are still sought by archaeologists working by the Dead Sea. They could have drawn their water from small sweet water streams that flow into the Dead Sea to this day. Lot's wife, turned into a pillar of salt as she fled Sodom, might teach today's Middle East peace negotiators something: Don't look back.

Israeli soldiers overlook the harsh landscape of the Dead Sea in the very gully where David hid from Saul. (*Michael Roskin*)

G : *Geography*

WHAT IS THE MIDDLE EAST?

The term *Middle East* is recent and controversial, something that came out of Europe, not from the region itself. The simplest geographical definition is the region where Asia, Africa, and Europe meet. More poetically, it is the "hub of the world island."

Definitions of what it includes get arbitrary. All agree that Iran, which is Muslim but not Arab, is part of the Middle East, but until recently few included the "-stans" (meaning "place of," such as Pakistan, Afghanistan, Uzbekistan, and so on). They are also Muslim but not Arab and generally classified as Southwest or Central Asia even though they are culturally and geographically close to the Middle East. For example, Uzbekistan's Islamic past, architecture, and folkways give it a strong Middle Eastern feel. We will touch on Afghanistan in Chapter 15 because it has great bearing on current problems.

Turkey for a long time was considered the Middle East—Turkey was the core of the Ottoman Empire, which dominated the region for several centuries. But many Turks now insist—sometimes angrily—that they are Europeans and ought to be admitted into the European Union. Brussels is not so sure and has put Turkey on indefinite hold, their indirect way of saying that as part of the Islamic cultural area Turkey does not really belong in Europe. Israel is physically in the Middle East but culturally and politically is largely European.

Europeans used the term "Near East" for the part closest to Europe, the eastern Mediterranean, including Turkey, Egypt, and the Fertile Crescent. They used "Middle East" for the region farther east, around the Persian Gulf, what is now sometimes called Southwest Asia. During World War II, however, Cairo was made the headquarters of the British Middle Eastern Command, and soon most called the entire region the Middle East. You still see some older references to Near East, but fewer and fewer since World War II. Any name you give a region is arbitrary and changeable.

Definitions of the Middle East have changed over time and according to circumstances. In the early 1990s, after the collapse of the Soviet Union and the emergence of independent states in Central Asia, the prestigious Middle East Institute in Washington, D.C., announced that these new states were culturally more attuned to the Middle East than to Russia—and that henceforth they would report on these countries in the *Middle East Journal.*

When the U.S. Defense Department created the Central Command (CENTCOM) to monitor events in the Middle East, it included the countries of Lebanon, Jordan, Syria, and Egypt; Israel, however, was left under the European Command. Today CENTCOM's area of operations has expanded to cover the Central Asian republics of the former Soviet Union and the Horn of Africa but does not include most of North Africa. Until 1974, the State Department included Greece and Cyprus within its European division; Turkey belonged to the Near East and South Asia division. After Turkey invaded Cyprus, however, Washington bureaucrats found it too difficult to coordinate messages between two divisions on the same issue, so they transferred Turkey to the European division. With the stroke of a pen, Turkey joined Europe, and the European division had its first war since the surrender of Nazi Germany in 1945.

For the purposes of this book, we consider the Arab countries of North Africa, the Levant, and the Arabian peninsula, as well as the non-Arab countries of Turkey, Israel, and Iran, to be the Middle East. Due to space constraints, we have not concentrated on North Africa.

Civilization and conflict were born twins. With civilization came organized warfare. Hunter-gatherers could fight other humans when necessary, but that seems to have been rare. Judging from the behavior of primitive peoples recorded more recently, when such bands met they usually traded information about game or pasture, bartered for wives (to guard against inbreeding), and went their separate ways. Humans were few, and the forests and fields were wide, so there was little need for fighting. Some bands developed ritualized warfare in which two clans screamed insults at each other, threw their spears, but seldom hurt anybody.

Nomads, a big evolutionary step up from hunter-gatherers, likewise seldom fought wars. Instead, they raided, either other bands of nomads or the sedentary people who grew crops and lived in settlements. They had no interest in conquering territory; indeed, many had no concept of owning territory. Land was something they passed through while searching for pastures. Quick raids to steal what others had was about as far as they went in warfare. They lacked the numbers, organization, and motivation for conquest. The partially nomadic Mongols might have been an exception here; they developed a large and highly organized state based on conquest. Real war requires states.

Traditional Arab villages of sun-dried bricks have changed little over the millennia. (*Michael Roskin*)

 *Cultures*

CALENDARS

Calendars have evolved, but not everyone likes the new and more accurate ones. The natural calendar, used for most of human history and still used by Jews and Muslims for religious purposes, consists of twelve lunar cycles, each about twenty-nine and a half days long. It was awfully handy—just look up at night—and seemed to be planned by God, but its twelve months come out short of the earth's 365-day rotation around the sun. The Hebrew calendar inserts an occasional thirteenth month, a clumsy thing for telling farmers when to plant. Several lunar calendars were devised in the ancient Middle East. The Muslim calendar has twelve months, some of twenty-nine and some of thirty days, but does not insert an occasional extra month, meaning that Muslim months cycle slowly through the solar year.

Rome started with the lunar calendar but dropped it in favor of one with twelve months, five of thirty days and six of thirty-one, plus poor February, with its twenty-eight days. This was an improvement but not accurate enough, so in 46 B.C. Julius Caesar introduced leap year by making every fourth February one day longer. The Julian calendar was standard for over a millennium and a half, but it accumulated too many long Februaries and by the sixteenth century was ten days off. Advised by the new science of astronomy, in 1582 Pope Gregory XIII ordered that October 5 be called October 15 and that henceforth every year divisible by 400 would *not* leap—February 2000, for example.

The Gregorian calendar was now the world's standard, but not even all Christians accepted it. Protestant and Eastern Orthodox countries smelled a popish plot. England and its colonies did not adopt the Gregorian calendar until 1752, leaving George Washington's exact birthday in some doubt. The U.S. Olympic team nearly missed the revived 1896 Olympiad because they failed to note that Greece was still using the Julian calendar. And the Bolshevik's October Revolution was celebrated every November 7 because Russia in 1917 was still using the old Julian calendar, then thirteen days behind the Gregorian. Calendars are cultural and political symbols. Using the modern Gregorian calendar means giving in to Western ways, something not all Middle Easterners wish to do.

IT COMES WITH THE TERRITORY

Organized warfare comes with the notion of territory and states, which are absent in most hunting and nomadic cultures. The idea of individuals owning land and of states claiming sovereignty over large tracts arrived only with settled agricultural societies. Before that, hunters and later shepherds merely used the land and moved on. Ownership of God's or nature's bounty seemed nonsensical. With agriculture came ownership. You would not willingly cultivate crops if someone else could take them. As John Locke saw, owning land required the invention of government, for that was the only way to guarantee that property was yours. You own land or a car not because you stand guard over them day and night but because pieces of paper filed in a government office say you own them. No government, no property; the two appear simultaneously in history.

G: *Geography*

KEY FEATURES OF THE MIDDLE EAST

Fertile Crescent   Curved swath of arable land from Mesopotamia through Syria and into Palestine. Sometimes includes Egypt.

Nile Valley   Thin band of arable land along Nile River.

Sinai Peninsula   Desert between *Fertile Crescent* and *Nile Valley*.

Asia Minor   Large peninsula bordered by Black and Mediterranean seas; also known as Anatolia and Turkey. Designated Asia Minor by ancient Greeks to distinguish it from main body of Asia.

Levant   Countries of the Eastern Mediterranean.

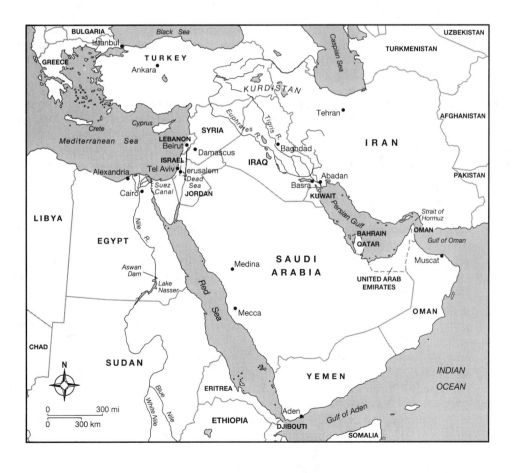

Cultures

Language Groups

Language is not the same as race or biological inheritance. Whole peoples have, after exposure through conquest or migration, learned to speak new languages. Do not confuse language groups with racial groups, a dreadful and deliberate error perpetrated by the Nazis. The Middle East is home to three of the world's several language groups.

Semitic, named after Noah's son Shem, are likely the oldest languages of the region and include Hebrew and Arabic plus Ethiopia's Amharic and Tigrean. Swahili, the *lingua franca* originated by Arab slave traders on Africa's east coast, is a Semitic language. Archaic Semitic languages include Akkadian, Assyrian, and Aramaic, the language spoken by Jesus of Nazareth.

Indo-European is a broad swath of languages stretching across Europe into India. Although many do not sound like it or look like it, Hindi, Iranian, Slavic, Italic, Celtic, and Germanic are branches of Indo-European. The base of English is Germanic (with some Celtic remnants) topped by a thick layer of French (which is from Latin, an Italic language). All big English words were originally French. Finnish and Hungarian are from another language group, Finno-Ugric, and Basque is related to no other language. Although Turkey was for centuries occupied by Indo-European speakers (Greek and Latin), now Iran is the only country in the region that uses an Indo-European language, *Farsi* (Persian), which is written in Arabic characters. Kurdish is an archaic form of Persian.

Turkic languages are spoken in a band from present-day Turkey deep into Central Asia, its place of origin. Turkish was the administrative language of the Ottoman Empire and was thus used throughout the Middle East and Balkans. Turkic languages include Turkish, Tatar, Azeri, Uzbek, and Khazakh. Originally all were written in Arabic letters, but Atatürk moved Turkish to Latin letters while Soviet Turkic languages were written in Cyrillic. More recently, several of them have opted for the Latin alphabet.

Furthermore, the two quickly led to organized coercion. How could a kingdom guarantee land ownership? What would prevent the next marauders from seizing your land? Here is where the role of warrior grew. The king needed his warrior-helpers to safeguard his kingdom and subjects from outsiders. He turned those who fought for him into a nobility and gave them land in exchange for their military services. He also taxed the peasants to pay for the state apparatus. In time—especially after long periods of peace when warriors are little needed—the fighting origins of the nobility faded into symbols. Agriculture, civilization, and warfare were likely born triplets.

Many do not like this close connection between civilization and conflict; some deny that it exists. Surely to be civilized means avoiding conflict. Civilized people settle their disputes in a "civilized" manner. Civilization and conflict are not natural partners but enemies. Would that it were so.

Part of the problem here is confusion between two meanings of "civilization," one abstract and general, the other specific to time and place. The qualities of the first, civilization in the abstract, are indeed refined and gentle, the basis for progress in the arts and sciences. We should all aspire to be civilized in this sense. The second meaning refers to specific civilizations, the entities that started with cities,

R : *Religions*

WHAT IS RELIGION?

A **religion** is a belief system focused on ultimate questions that cannot be empirically verified. Death, for example, is an ultimate question that kept our primitive ancestors in awe and still leaves us uneasy. What happens to you after you die? No one has ever sent back a postcard. Is there a soul that continues after death? Looking at the stars poses ultimate questions: What are they? God's handiwork?

Religion appears with the first humans, and some of the earliest artifacts unearthed in the Middle East are religious figurines, such as pregnant fertility goddesses. Until recently, sex and birth were indeed mysteries. Much of the evolution of human civilization is the development of religious beliefs from primitive nature worship, to divine kings and statues (ancient Egypt), to immortal but human-like gods (ancient Greece), to a single invisible tribal deity (ancient Israel), to a universal being laying down moral commandments (the modern **Abrahamic** faiths). Religion does not explain all of history—often there are important physical factors at work—but it is a major channel of human choices. We cannot make sense of the broad sweep of Middle Eastern history without paying attention to religions.

Some claim there is no clear border between religion and superstition, and indeed many religions have superstitious elements. Superstition, however, is concerned with small things and luck, such as winning the lottery or avoiding trouble, and generally requires only small gestures, such as playing your birthday or bride and groom not seeing each other before the wedding. Superstitions do not ask ultimate questions.

A belief system that can be empirically verified—you can get evidence proving or disproving its tenets—is probably not a religion but a science, discipline, or area of rational discourse. Economics is a social science, for example, although its practitioners hedge their predictions so much ("on the other hand") that they almost ask you to have faith. They typically concern themselves with questions of here and now—how to get the economy to grow or control inflation—rather than ultimate questions.

Secular belief systems—ideologies such as Marxism or nationalism—may argue that they are empirically grounded, but they often fail in practice and do no not focus on ultimate questions. Marxists swore they were following "scientific socialism." These "-isms," however, mimic religions in requiring the faith and loyalty of adherents. Persons strongly caught up in an ideology often exhibit religious-like beliefs. Marxists, for example, whose faith explained everything, had no patience for religion and were devout atheists. Communist parties tried to prohibit members from practicing any religion.

---

grew into kingdoms and empires, and spread their power, language, and often religion far and wide. These civilizations are not necessarily as pretty as civilization in the abstract, as they do much of their work with the sword. It is hard, however, to envision how one could be civilized in the abstract without also belonging to a specific civilization whose actions, especially in dealing with others, may be less than civilized. Thus could English gentlemen of the nineteenth century practice the gentle arts of civilization at home while their forces inflicted the sharp edge of English civilization on Indians, Africans, and Chinese.

---

religion   An unverifiable belief system concerned with ultimate questions.
Abrahamic   The three religions that trace back to Abraham: Judaism, Christianity, and Islam.
secular   Nonreligious.

This dual nature of "civilization" is especially important in the Middle East. Here we see some of the earliest and greatest civilizations, whose achievements we can only applaud. Unfortunately, while they were building these civilizations, they were also nearly continuously at war with neighboring civilizations, a pattern that continues to this day. Civilization is a double-edged sword.

THE LAY OF THE LAND

The prehistoric Middle East that was settled millennia ago must have been a nice region. With an ice age blanketing much of Europe, the region enjoyed a moderate climate. In parts, the soil was good, especially in the great river valleys of the Nile in Egypt and the Tigris and Euphrates in Mesopotamia. Rainfall was more abundant than now, and much of the region was woods and grasslands. Most deserts came later, partly the work of climate change and partly that of humans who too eagerly cut the trees and plowed the grasslands. When Scripture speaks of "wilderness," it probably indicates forests rather than lifeless deserts. One of the most amazing things to see in any desert—whether in the Middle East, Southern California, or Northern Chile—is how it erupts with flowers after rainfall from seeds that have lain dormant for decades. All it needs is rain.

Rains come when moisture-rich clouds, formed over the seas, blow over land and cool. With lower temperatures, the air cannot hold its moisture, so it precipitates out in the form of rain. The surest way for clouds to cool is to rise higher, for the upper levels of the atmosphere are colder than the lower. Mountains are the chief mechanism to do this. Winds push the clouds into mountains, forcing them upward. The coastal range that runs down the eastern end of the Mediterranean can thus generate good rainfall, but other areas of the Middle East are not so lucky, and people had to become clever and redirect some of the water of their great rivers by canals and sluice gates to irrigate many acres. This seems to have begun in Mesopotamia around 6,000 B.C. and is one highly plausible explanation why civilization arose so early in the Mesopotamian and Nile river valleys (and in China's Yangtze valley): They produced more food, but only if kingdoms could build and maintain the irrigation systems. To do this they had to mobilize and direct masses of labor under centralized government. The need to manage water led to the earliest civilizations. Karl Wittfogel advanced a theory of "oriental despotism": The need to manage water resources led to one-man rule.

Another, less powerful, way rain clouds cool is when they blow over green lands, which absorb sunlight rather than reflect it back, as deserts do. Green is literally a cool color. When the forests and grasslands have been denuded by shoddy agricultural practices, the land loses this cooling ability and dries out. Once it turns into a desert, it stays that way until elaborately restored by expensive projects. Environmentalists should take note. In the classic comedy routine of the "Five-Thousand-Year-Old Man," Mel Brooks mentions the "Sahara Forest." His interviewer asks if he means the Sahara Desert. Brooks replies, "Sure, *now* it's a desert." That line may describe what took place in much of the Middle

 *Cultures*

PERCEPTION VERSUS REALITY

Those of us who were raised on television can easily picture the Middle East in our minds: rolling hills of sand, fierce desert winds, emptiness to the horizon. The men are either camel-riding **Bedouin** or bearded terrorists; the women are covered modestly but move with a delicate sensuality.

Some of the images are true, but most of them bear no resemblance to reality. Lose them. The Sahara desert and the Saudi peninsula's Empty Quarter resemble Hollywood's images, except where they are crossed by pipelines, refineries, petrochemical plants, and modern cities. In truth, the Middle East includes rugged Atlantic coastline, deserts, semi-tropical Mediterranean beaches, snow-peaked mountains, over-crowded cities, and modern high-tech industrial parks. The people of the Middle East—male and female—are now mostly urban and include doctors, lawyers, engineers, and political scientists. They wear traditional clothing recognizable in the West from movies such as *Lawrence of Arabia* or *The Ten Commandments*, but they also wear business suits, sports uniforms, and Parisian haute couture.

East: man-made deserts. Irrigation in ancient Mesopotamia slowly built up salinity in the soil, turning it into desert and dooming Sumer.

One great constant of the Middle East is the importance of water. Nomads flocked to it. Civilizations arose by controlling it. Kings conquered for it. In times of sparse rainfall, herders lost their pasture and had to intrude onto farmland, creating terrible conflict. When springs and rivers dried up, as they do periodically, whole peoples had to migrate to new lands, one explanation for the coming of the ancient Israelites to Egypt, where they were enslaved. Even today, control of the aquifer under the hills of Judea and Samaria hampers negotiations between Israel and the Palestinians. The states along the southern shore of the Persian Gulf have exploding populations in part because they can desalinate seawater with their abundant natural gas.

The archeological record does not support the old view that civilization enjoyed **unilinear** growth. The ancient civilizations of the Middle East show spurts of consolidation and growth punctuated by periods of fragmentation and decline. Unified kingdoms expanded their territories; built cities, temples, and palaces; created writing and religion; and provided security for their subjects. Their subjects were not always grateful for these benefits, however, for they were always squeezed for taxes to pay for them. Some theorize that most of the time peasants lived less well under unified kingdoms and disliked their tax-hungry kings. This is one explanation of why all the ancient kingdoms sooner or later broke apart. After some decades of near-anarchy and cultural decline, strong new rulers would conquer the area and set up new kingdoms. Even ancient Egypt shows strong kingdoms followed by

---

Bedouin   Arabic-speaking desert nomads.
unilinear   Progressing evenly and always upward.

chaotic periods of weak governance and then new strong kingdoms. Like many Americans today, not all ancient Middle Easterners liked cities. The Tower of Babel and how it failed is interpreted as criticism of cities in general.

MIDDLE EASTERN CULTURE

Political culture is a valid approach to political science that concentrates on the psychology of whole peoples as the major explanation of why a government takes a particular action. Many view **political culture** with suspicion, however, because in the past it has been abused to justify prejudice and discrimination. Indeed, it is hard to identify commonalities in people as different as the Berbers of Morocco, the Kurds of Iraq, and the Baluch of Iran.

It is important to bear in mind that when describing an individual's culture, we are actually describing the attributes of an **archetype**. All people diverge from this archetype to varying degrees; this is different from a **stereotype**, where one assumes that an individual possesses characteristics shared by all members of a particular group.

Political science has largely avoided accepting the concept that culture can affect the way a person acts. Anthropologists, on the other hand, have always emphasized culture as a major contributor to behavior, and psychologists have joined them. Since at least 1991, the American Psychological Association instructs practitioners to take into account the ethnic and cultural differences of their patients. If the psychologist does not know enough about a patient's culture, he or she should not accept the case. Political analysts, however, when working at the level of analysis on the state level, often deny or downplay crucial cultural influences. What can we say about the cultural characteristics of a people who are spread over two continents? As we will see, the culture has been formed from the social and historical experiences of the people who live in the region. Culture matters, and **Islam** has left a strong cultural imprint.

THE IMPORTANCE OF THE SPOKEN WORD

One of the first things we notice throughout the Middle East is the importance of the oral tradition. Most of the Middle East speaks Arabic as their mother tongue; others have numerous Arab words in their vocabularies. Arabic-speakers have a

---

political culture   The psychology of a nation in regard to politics.

archetype   The perfect embodiment of the characteristics of a particular group. All people diverge from an archetype.

stereotype   The characterization of an individual based on the erroneous assumption that all members of a particular group are alike.

Islam   The monotheistic religion that preaches "there is no God but God, and Muhammad is his prophet." *Islam* means "submission or surrender"; a follower of Islam is a Muslim, one who has surrendered to the will of God.

Cultures

THE ARABIC LANGUAGE

Both Arab nationalists and Western observers speak of Arabic as a *lingua franca* for most of the Middle East. At one level, this is true. In its classical form as written in the **Qur'an**, Arabic is easily recognized by all, but not so easily understood. If you ever read *Beowulf* in high school, the first literary work written in English, you needed a glossary of terms that translated Old English into modern English. The Qur'an is the same way. Qur'anic scholars learn classical Arabic as a separate language from the sort spoken on the Arab street. A Muslim scholar once told one of the authors that the reason Qur'anic Arabic is so different is because the human language was crushed under the weight of God's word.

Similarly, modern written Arabic is the same throughout the Middle East, although some words can have different meanings in different areas. The common, written form is of little use to the hundreds of thousands of illiterate residents of the Middle East, who rely on the spoken word for communication. There is a common form of Arabic known as Modern Standard Arabic, used by newscasters and learned by American diplomats. While most Middle Easterners can understand this form, they have difficulty replying in the same tongue. Diplomatic conversations are occasionally one sided: The American can offer his opinion in modern standard but cannot understand the response he receives in the local dialect. (Given the cultural differences between the conversationalists, it may be questionable that they would understand each other properly even if they were using the same language.)

That leaves the local dialect. Unfortunately, dialects vary considerably. A Moroccan living on the edge of the Atlantic Ocean has a hard time understanding a Syrian or Iraqi. They might not understand each other at all. As technology intrudes further into the Middle East, a common dialect is emerging: Egyptian Arabic that pronounces a "J" as a hard "G." The reason is the popularity of Egyptian-produced soap operas throughout the Middle East. As satellite TV networks such as the Qatar-based al-Jazeera (or is it al-Gazira?) expand their audiences, it will be interesting to see the effect of Gulf Arabic on the dialects in the rest of the Arab world.

real affection for the language that most English-speakers lack for their own tongue. In pre-Islamic times, Arabs developed an advanced form of poetry, and traveling poets were respected members of society. Later, as the Qur'an spread across the region, the language acquired new respect as the medium through which God spoke to his chosen people.

Today, the historical respect for the spoken language is combined with widespread illiteracy. The result is that the spoken word has a powerful effect in the Middle East. Rumors spread quickly and are believed by those who have neither the inclination nor the ability to check facts for themselves. This problem is compounded by government censorship in many countries; the citizenry is aware that the official news is often doctored, and so they are more inclined to accept news they hear "on the street."

Qur'an (or Koran)   Islamic scriptures. Muslims believe it is the Word of God, given to mankind by an angel through the prophet Muhammad. The word *Qur'an* literally means "recitation," because God's word was and is recited.

Countries of the Middle East and their Adult Illiteracy Rates (2000)

Algeria	33.3%
Egypt	44.7
Iran	24.0
Iraq	60.7
Israel	5.2
Jordan	10.2
Kuwait	18.1
Lebanon	14.0
Libya	20.1
Morocco	51.2
Oman	28.3
Saudi Arabia	23.8
Syria	25.6
Tunisia	29.0
Turkey	15.0
United Arab Emirates	23.8
Yemen	>53.6

SHARED CULTURAL CHARACTERISTICS

There are other cultural characteristics in the Middle East that are sometimes re-flected in the politics of the country. Arabs, Turks, and Iranians share the concept of hospitality, where a host acquires merit by providing for a guest. This came out of the desert tradition where, if a host refused to help a visitor, the guest might die of hunger or thirst before finding another benefactor. Hospitality thus became a self-survival mechanism: It was expected that the host would receive equal treatment if the tables were ever turned and he became the traveler. In more recent times, tribal chieftains increased their prestige within the tribe by holding elaborate feasts for their followers. Today, hereditary rulers cement the allegiance of their political allies by including them at feasts at the palace on major holidays.

Despite this great tradition of hospitality, the Middle East also holds a distrust of the foreigner and a reliance on family. This also arose from the desert tradition, where the traveler seeking shelter from the elements could be a noble merchant or a brigand intent on stealing the host's possessions.

Mistrust of people outside the family was reflected in the tradition of in-group marriages; family honor was often protected from outside pollution by marriage be-tween first cousins. This practice is on the wane but by no means extinct today. Un-derstanding of genetic problems that come from first-cousin marriage is penetrating most countries.

 *Cultures*

MIDDLE EASTERN LAYERS OF IDENTITY

1. Family
2. Religion
3. Ethnicity
4. Individuality
5. Nationality
6. Profession

Historically, distrust of people outside of the tribe or family was deepened by attacks of Christian armies against Muslim lands during the Crusades of the eleventh century and again by the perceived attempt of Europeans to rob the residents of their patrimony during the colonial era of the nineteenth and early twentieth centuries. Politically, these cultural traits have resulted in an increased desire to embrace "authentic" movements such as fundamentalist Islamist movements, various nationalisms, and the expropriation of externally owned or controlled assets such as oil companies.

The archetypical Middle Easterner derives his identity from the groups to which he belongs. These groups include family, religion, ethnic group, and region. Traditionally, there is little loyalty to the nation-state because in the vast majority of cases the country is an artificial construct that was imposed on the inhabitants by outsiders (the European colonial powers) less than a century ago. Thus, one could well find someone who identifies as being from Damascus or Aleppo, but it is rare to hear that individual describe himself or herself as a Syrian.

Westerners, Americans especially, highly value individualism. Hollywood glorifies John Wayne, Chuck Norris, Sylvester Stallone—individuals who do it their own way—which is quite different from the Middle East (and Japan), where people prize their group identities.

A similar disconnect can be seen in discussing professions. To Americans, one's job is a large part of identity; it is not just what they do but who they are. In the Middle East, by contrast, employment is merely a means to acquire sufficient wealth to provide for one's family. It is no measure of one's worth, which is calculated by lineage from noble blood. (Almost half the people in the Middle East claim the prophet Muhammad as their ancestor). There is a cultural disconnect when an American president chooses an ambassador who proudly announces that he started from nothing and pulled himself up by his bootstraps through his own entrepreneurial skills. The Americans think they are sending over their best, because the envoy showed initiative and earned a lot of money; the Middle East will welcome him out of hospitality but judge him as beneath them because of his self-admitted lack of noble lineage.

There are, of course, numerous exceptions to this identity schema. Because of the long histories of their lands, citizens of Egypt and Iran have a stronger sense of nationality than is reflected by the archetype. Similarly, Palestinians and Israelis have nationalisms born in part out of their struggles against each other. Many educated Middle Easterners now take great pride in their individual accomplishments, and many of the noneducated share that respect, either because of practical considerations (one respects a doctor who cures a sick child regardless of who his father is), or because of a respect for education that comes from the previously described respect for language.

An unwelcome offshoot to the Middle Eastern reliance on the in-group and suspicion of the out-group is conflict. Outsiders are not necessarily granted the same rights and protections as members of the in-group. Outsiders are fair game, and their goods are forfeit if they lose a fight. On the Arabian peninsula at the time of the Prophet (570–632 A.D.), Arab tribes would raid caravans belonging to other tribes to steal their goods. Further historical precedence for this unequal treatment is the role of the **dhimmi** in Islamic empires: A non-Muslim could live in peace provided he accepted a second-class status, did not participate in certain occupations, did not build a house larger than a Muslim neighbor's, did not attempt to join the military, but did pay a higher tax in return for his exemption from military service.

CONCLUSIONS

While most people would consider the Arabian peninsula and the countries of modern Lebanon, Syria, Jordan, and Iraq as part of the Middle East, once one moves beyond the Arab heartland the definition of the Middle East can change depending on the time and circumstances. As we define the area, it is a land of amazing contrasts, both geographically and socially. It is difficult to make generalizations about such a vast land and diverse population; those generalizations we do make are at best guides to aid in the understanding of the people and are not descriptions of any individuals one might meet.

There is a common culture throughout the Middle East, which has been described as a Muslim or Islamic culture. It arose from the confluence of the history of the region with the cultural mores and religion of most of the area's inhabitants. The region has also experienced a series of conflicts that stretch back into antiquity. As will be seen in the chapters that follow, this culture and conflict has created the politics of the Middle East today.

---

dhimmi   Protected person; non-Muslim living under an Islamic government, required to pay a special tax.

FURTHER REFERENCE

American Psychological Association, "Ethical Principles of Psychologists and Code of Conduct," *American Psychologist* 47/12 (December 1992), 1597–1611.

Andersen, Roy R., Robert F. Seibert, and Jon G. Wagner. *Politics and Change in the Middle East: Sources of Conflict and Accommodation*, 6th ed. Upper Saddle River, NJ: Prentice Hall, 2001.

Bill, James, and Carl Leiden. *Politics in the Middle East*, 2nd ed. Boston: Little, Brown and Company, 1984.

Goldschmidt, Arthur, Jr. *A Concise History of the Middle East*, 7th ed. Boulder, CO: Westview, 2001.

Held, Colbert C. *Middle East Patterns: Places, Peoples, and Politics*, Boulder, CO: Westview, 1989.

Khoury, Philip S., and Joseph Kostiner, eds. *Tribes and State Formation in the Middle East*. Berkeley: University of California Press, 1990.

Lewis, Bernard. *The Multiple Identities of the Middle East*. New York: Random House, 1998.

Long, David E., and Bernard Reich. *The Government and Politics of the Middle East and North Africa*, 4th ed. Boulder, CO: Westview, 2002.

Said, Edward W. *Orientalism*. New York: Random House, 1978.

The Ancients and Their Conflicts

Points to Ponder

- Is the nature of man peaceful?
- Do political units have a natural tendency to expand their territory?
- What have ancient empires contributed to today's Middle East?
- How did ancient Greece influence the Middle East?
- What was Thucydides explanation of war? Does it fit more recent wars?
- When did the Middle East first invade Europe? When did Europe first invade the Middle East?
- Does war promote a nation's strength or its weakness?

There are few direct connections between the ancient empires and today's politics, but there are some indirect connections. First, notice how the earliest civilizations were based on water, specifically those of Egypt and Mesopotamia. The two civilizations were great rivals then, constantly striving for regional predominance, which included control of the coastal caravan route and farming belt of present-day Israel. Egypt and Iraq in recent times have been rivals for leadership of the Arab world. Notice how no civilization lasts forever. Some went for centuries; none were immortal. Notice also how they fought each other. Were (are?) these peoples especially warlike, or not any more than others? In some cases, their long fights so weakened these empires that they were easy prey for outsiders. The Byzantines and Persians bashed each other silly for centuries, making Muslim conquest easy.

At least three modern countries have inherited a proud nationalism from the ancient past: Egypt, Iran, and Israel. In ancient times the small Hebrew kingdoms were simply places to be conquered on an alternating basis by Egypt and Mesopotamia, but by nurturing a monotheistic religion, ancient Judah and Israel put their stamp on humankind. (We will have more to say about ancient Israel in Chapter 5.) These ancient empires were like tides sweeping over a beach, each leaving residues.

THE FIRST CITIES

The first cities appeared about 3,000 B.C. We do not know much about who created these cities, or how or why people chose to live in an urban setting, because there is little by way of a written record much earlier than about 750 B.C. Some stories of earlier times, such as Homer's *Iliad* or the Bible's Book of Kings, were actually written hundreds of years after the events described. As a result, the events described in such books were often dismissed as fictional or allegorical. Indeed, Homer's city of Troy had been dismissed as a writer's fantasy until the German archeologist Heinrich Schliemann uncovered it in 1872.

The cities were primarily located on waterways. Presumably, this was because the inhabitants needed fresh water for drinking and irrigation, and because water transit was cheaper and safer than shipping goods by land. Produce grown in the countryside and transported to the urban marketplace by water could support a city, and the same waterways allowed the cities to initiate commerce with other cities.

By the Bronze Age, three superpowers arose in the Middle East: the Babylonians who built their city where the Tigris and Euphrates rivers run close to each other, the Egyptians in the Nile River valley, and the Hittites who located their capital city on the Anatolian plateau equidistant from tributaries of the Red and Green rivers (Kizilirmak and Yesilirmak). These giants of yesteryear traded among themselves, as evidenced by goods that have been found at archeological sites that were manufactured elsewhere. More importantly, all three superpowers had developed forms of writing; they left written records in cuneiform or hieroglyphs that detailed their trade with one another. The records also show countless invasions and counterinvasions as new city states formed and vied for power and/or independence.

THE EGYPTIANS

The Egyptians arose from their Neolithic ancestors as a self-contained people about 3100 B.C. Protected by vast deserts on either side, the Upper and Lower kingdoms developed in their narrow Nile River valley without the competition of neighboring city-states seeking to invade. It was not until 1750 B.C. that the valley experienced its first invasion. The newcomers were the Hyksos, who may be the "chariot people" who carried the ancient Hebrews into their captivity in Egypt.

The Egyptians had a highly developed social structure, with a royal court, ruling classes, and slave classes. They also built one of the earliest high cultures. They kept accounts on papyrus, sent out colonies, and built irrigation systems to turn barren desert into agricultural land. King Zozer began building the pyramids in 2800 B.C. These giant edifices became symbols of ancient Egypt, and they provided a venue for the Egyptian nobility to demonstrate their many achievements: establishment of a religion with emphasis on the afterlife, mathematical achievements in geometry, architectural greatness, and the development of art and sculpture to decorate the rulers' tombs and temples of the gods. Egypt was conquered by the Assyrians in 670 B.C., and was not to regain its sovereign independence until the revolt of the Free Officers in 1952 A.D., which brought into power Abdul Gamal Nasser.

 *Conflicts*

IS THE MIDDLE EAST ESPECIALLY WARLIKE?

Conflict is not, of course, a phenomenon limited to the Middle East. Although West Europeans have adopted a pacifist stance as a reaction to the destruction of World Wars I and II, the history of Europe and the United States is also a history of recurring conflicts. Mostly, among Westerners, we got our conflicts over with. The Middle East enjoyed long periods of peace—whenever a strong empire ran things—while the West was wracked with centuries of bloody conflicts. In this book we emphasize the causes and effects of conflict in the Middle East because that is the region under study, not because ancient empires, Arabs, or Turks are more inclined to violence than other peoples.

THE BABYLONIANS

The Babylonians originated in **Mesopotamia**, northwest of the Persian Gulf, in the city of Ur (the Scriptural birthplace of Abraham). The inhabitants of the area developed the city-state of Sumer and moved by fits and starts to Babylon—just north of the modern city of Baghdad. In about 2270 B.C., Sargon the Great expanded the kingdom from a small fiefdom of about 6,000 square miles to encompass all of the Fertile Crescent and may even have conquered the island of Cyprus.

Babylon ruled supreme for almost a thousand years. Like its Egyptian counterpart, the Babylonians had a social system that included a ruling class, a military nobility, and a slave class. They also left us with the first recorded legal system: the code of Hammurabi, written about 1700 B.C. The kingdom also gave us the mathematical legacy of dividing a minute into 60 seconds, an hour into 60 minutes, and a circle into 360 degrees. In arts and letters, Babylon produced one of the world's first epic poems, the *Epic of Gilgamesh*. It also produced a religion that included stories of creation and world-destroying floods, similar to the accounts in Genesis.

Egypt and Babylon battled for supremacy of the Middle East on the plains of Syria, but the Egyptians had little to do with Babylon's ultimate destruction. Invading marauders first weakened Babylon's greatness when they swept out of the surrounding mountains in 1677 B.C. and split the kingdom into three. The Hittites, the least known of the ancient superpowers, invaded and destroyed Babylon in 1595 B.C. Although the empire would survive in one form or another for another four hundred years, it had lost its dominant status.

Mesopotamia   (Greek for "between the rivers") Valley formed by Tigris and Euphrates Rivers.

W: *Women of the Middle East*

HATSHEPSUT, IRON LADY OF EGYPT

While much of Middle Eastern history is the story of men, remarkable women had roles in history and politics, primarily before the triumph of Islam. Hatshepsut was one of these individuals. Born into the royal household as a daughter to King Thutmose I in 1508 B.C., she married her half brother and heir to the throne, Thutmose II. After four years, she pushed her husband aside and reigned supreme. Her reign was a brief respite from Egyptian colonial expansion, as she preferred to pursue domestic tranquility. Sadly, these policies were reversed by her successor, who continued the same expansionist policies of her late father.

THE HITTITES

The Hittites were latecomers in the race for ancient supremacy, not arriving on the scene until 1900 B.C. When it came to conquest, the Hittites had an advantage over the Babylonians and Egyptians: The Hittites were a warrior culture. By 1600 B.C., the Hittites controlled all of Asia Minor and began pushing down the Mediterranean coast. In 1595 B.C. the Hittites sacked the city of Babylon, and in 1294 B.C. they defeated the forces of Egyptian Pharaoh Ramses II at the battle of Kadesh. The two kingdoms then divided Syria between them in a peace treaty signed in 1278 B.C.

Although a powerful military force, the Hittites left little behind them. A military nobility ruling over an agricultural society, they used an alphabet they copied from the Babylonians to keep track of their trade and conquests. The Hittites were more interested in improving military chariots than learning to draw or build pyramids. Finally, a minor kingdom in Asia Minor, the Phrygians, destroyed the Hittite cities about 1200 B.C.

THE ASSYRIANS

The Assyrians, another warrior kingdom founded around 2000 B.C., had preserved their independence in the mountain fastness of northern Mesopotamia by geographic isolation and force of arms. With the decline of the previous ancient powers, Assyria began its expansion about 1100 B.C., the time when the **Iron Age** brought stronger and sharper weapons. Assyria reached the height of its power

---

Iron Age   Major advance over Bronze Age, starting about 1000 B.C. in Middle East.

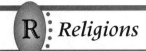

Religions

THE FIRST MONOTHEISM

Some claim Egypt first introduced **monotheism** into human civilization. Well, sort of. In 1375 B.C., Amenhotep IV assumed the throne and decreed that the sun god, symbolized by a disk, was superior to the other Egyptian gods. This was not really the worship of one god. It was also a way of resolving an economic disaster. His predecessors on the throne had emptied the royal treasury. By elevating the sun god, Amenhotep, who renamed himself Akhenaton, refilled the royal coffers with the riches of the priests loyal to the lesser gods, whom most Egyptians went on worshiping anyway. When the old gods were restored by Amenhotep's successor, the money was not returned to the priests. Freud advanced a dubious theory that Moses had picked up his monotheism from Akhenaton's brief experiment.

after replacing its army's bronze weapons with iron. Assyria became an innovator in tactics and weapons design, introducing weapons that would be prominent in Europe throughout the Middle Ages: the battering ram and the siege tower. Assyria became the largest empire in the ancient world, built by its army, the first standing army in history.

Like the Hittites, the Assyrian desire for military power seems to have precluded the empire from much development in the arts and sciences. The kingdom was torn apart by a series of revolts around 728 B.C. until a combined army from the kingdoms of Chaldea and Medea captured and destroyed its capital, Nineveh. The Chaldeans then held sway over the area for the next two hundred years, building the famous "Hanging Gardens of Babylon."

THE PHOENICIANS

The Phoenicians were fishermen and traders who lived in what is today Lebanon. They were little interested in war, and probably could not have prospered in an earlier period. But with the Hittites and Babylonians destroyed, and protected by mountains to the north and east, their only military threat on land came from the Philistines in the north. With the collapse of the naval military threat of Crete (destroyed by two waves of invaders from the Greek mainland around 1400 B.C. and 1100 B.C.), they were free to expand throughout the Mediterranean. Similar to the Hittites and Assyrians, the Phoenicians appear to have borrowed their cultural artifacts from others instead of inventing them indigenously. The West has much to thank the Phoenicians for, however, as it was probably Phoenician merchants who introduced alphabetical writing to the Greeks—thereby allowing Greek philosophy to be recorded and preserved.

---

monotheism   Worship of one god.

Like the Greeks they encountered, the Phoenicians established trading posts that eventually developed into colonies. In 900 B.C., the Phoenicians left the protected waters of the Mediterranean and passed through the Straits of Gibraltar. On the Atlantic side of the Iberian peninsula they established a trading colony at the site of modern Cádiz, Spain. They also colonized the islands of the Mediterranean and much of North Africa.

In 800 B.C., the Phoenicians established Carthage, in what is today Tunisia. This colony soon surpassed the mother kingdom and became a great empire. By 300 B.C., Carthage was the power Rome needed to beat in its ascent to empire. The tales of those battles, recorded in history as the **Punic Wars**, included feats that are still studied in military academies today.

THE PERSIANS

As the Iron Age came to a close, a group of **Aryan** tribes that had migrated from Central Asia onto the Iranian plateau 1,500 years earlier formed their own kingdom: the **Persian** Empire. This last of the ancient empires held sway over the eastern reaches of the known world until they were defeated briefly by Alexander the Great in the fourth century B.C. and by the Arabs in the seventh century A.D.

The Persians had been a subkingdom under the Medes (the kingdom that united with the Chaldeans to destroy the Assyrians) until 550 B.C. In that year, Cyrus the Great revolted against his overlord and established his independence. Over the next twenty years, Cyrus conquered the lands of Asia Minor, Mesopotamia, and the Fertile Crescent. His son annexed Egypt in 525 B.C., and his nephew Darius the Great invaded both India to the East and Europe to the West. This latter event marked one of the most remarkable engineering feats of ancient history: Building a wooden pontoon bridge across the **Dardanelles**, Darius marched an army of 100,000 soldiers into Europe in 513 B.C.

He was defeated by wild **Scythian** cavalrymen in a battle that took place in what is today Romania. When word of Darius's defeat reached the Greek cities of **Ionia**, they rose in revolt. Some of the Greeks destroyed the bridge, forcing the retreating Persian army to make a long march through hostile territory before returning to Asia.

Denied access to Europe, Persia continued to prosper, but the Ionian cities still tried to break free of Persian rule. It took Darius almost eight years to restore order. Denied the ability to march into Europe, Darius now tried a marine amphibious landing near Marathon. There, a force of 40,000 Persian warriors faced a small contingent of Athenians. Badly outnumbered, the Athenians allowed the Persians

---

Punic Wars   Third-century B.C. wars in which Rome vanquished Carthage.
Aryan   Indo-European-speaking tribes who settled ancient Iran and northern India.
Persia   Old name for Iran.
Dardanelles   Southern part of the *Turkish Straits*.
Scythia   Ancient kingdom in present-day Ukraine.
Ionia   Ancient Greek-inhabited area in present-day southwest Turkey.

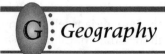

G: *Geography*

TURKISH STRAITS

From ancient times, control over waterways has meant life and death to the kingdoms that vied for power in the Middle East. While the nature of warfare may have changed significantly, the strategic role of water has not. To pass between the Black Sea and the Mediterranean Sea, all military and commercial shipping must pass through the **Turkish Straits**, namely, the **Bosphorus** and Dardanelles, known in ancient times as the Hellespont. No shipping from the Danube River basin or from the countries surrounding the Black Sea (including successor states to the former Soviet Union) can reach the open sea without passing through these waters. As a result, the straits have been considered strategic prizes throughout the centuries. In the twentieth century alone, desire to control the straits led to the Allied invasion of Gallipoli in World War I and strong Soviet pressure after World War II.

Today, thanks to the 1936 **Montreux Convention**, shipping through the straits is internationalized. This uneasy accord is threatened, however, by the prospect of oil tankers bringing millions of barrels of Central Asian oil to market through the crowded Straits in tankers through the Turkish city of Istanbul (estimated population 12 to 15 million) that straddles both sides of the Bosphorus.

---

to break through the center of their lines and then used a pincer movement to close them off. The Persians who were caught were annihilated; others were driven into swamps and killed. While most of the invaders managed to escape back to their ships, the second Persian advance into Europe was halted.

Darius died in 490 B.C. without having achieved his goal of conquering Greece. His son and successor, Xerxes, decided to take up the challenge. This time, the army crossed the Hellespont using two pontoon bridges, while the Persian fleet headed down the Aegean coast toward Athens. Much of the Persian fleet was destroyed, but they were still strong enough to make the Greek fleet withdraw. The Greek army made their stand at the mountain pass of Thermopylae, a clever choice because they were heavily outnumbered (roughly 250,000 to 1,400) and would have had no chance in an open field. After two days of stalemate, a Greek traitor showed the Persians how to bring a force around to the rear of the Greek army. In the fight that followed, 400 soldiers from Thebes deserted. The remaining army, fighting under a Spartan king, died to the last man.

Xerxes did not have long to enjoy his victory; shortly afterward, the Greek fleet used treachery to lure the Persian navy into shallow waters where they could not maneuver. The Greeks had a magnificent naval victory, and Xerxes had to withdraw to Asia Minor so as not to be cut off, leaving behind a garrison force of 60,000. The Greeks defeated this army the following year (479 B.C.), and the Persian advance into Europe was blunted for all time.

Turkish Straits   Strategic waterway that connects Mediterranean and Black Seas.
Bosphorus   Northern part of *Turkish Straits*; Istanbul is on its banks.
Montreux Convention   Treaty opening Turkish Straits to world shipping under Turkish control.

THE GREEKS

Before the arrival of Alexander, there was never a united kingdom of Greece, although the numerous petty kingdoms did manage occasional alliances that allowed them to act—more or less—in a united way against a common enemy. The vast majority of ancient Greek history is the history of internecine squabbles among the petty kingdoms, and they only echoed dimly on the Asian side of the Aegean. Usually, the Greek colonies in Asia Minor became involved only when the fighting included battles against the Persians.

As one might expect from geography, the first Greek colonies in the Middle East appeared about 600 B.C. near the modern city of Istanbul and along the Aegean coast of Asia Minor (the ancient Hellenistic colonies of Ionia). The capital of Ionia was Miletus, which eventually colonized much of the rim of Asia Minor. Some of Miletus' colonies include the modern Turkish cities of Sinop and Trabzon on the Black Sea.

The Greeks gained by the rivalries of the other kingdoms in the East. The remnants of the Assyrian empire granted them preferred trading status in an attempt to check the rising power of the Phoenicians; in return, the Greeks copied numerous advances in shipbuilding from their Phoenician rivals. The Persian defeat of the Lydian empire in 546 B.C. allowed Miletus to expand its influence along the Ionian Coast and learn the coinage of money. At first, the towns expanded under Persian tutelage.

After the Persian army was defeated in Greece in 479 B.C., the Spartans advanced on some of these Persian-controlled Greek cities and conquered **Byzantium**. Greece and not Persia now controlled the Bosphorus. In 477 B.C., the Athenians united the Greek islands in the Aegean and the Greek cities in Ionia that had revolted against Persia into the Delian League, a mutual defense alliance against attack from Persia. Athens soon gained control of the league, and it became an arm of its imperial expansion into Asia Minor. The league's treasury, originally located on the island of Delos, was moved to Athens. League members believed Athens was using the money for its own aggrandizement. When some city-states tried to withdraw from their voluntary confederation, Athens crushed them militarily. Athenian democracy did not apply to foreign policy. Athenian expansionism led to the horrific **Peloponnesian War** against a Sparta-led alliance. One of the best statements on the cause of war in general was penned by a cashiered Athenian general, Thucydides, in his history of the war: "War became inevitable with the growth of Athenian power and the fear this caused in Sparta." Many later Middle Eastern wars can be explained by this formulation.

Much of Ionia remained under Persian control throughout this period. Whether controlled by Persia or Greece, however, the constant fighting and rebellions meant

---

Byzantium   Original Greek town at site of what later became Constantinople and Istanbul; gave its name to *Byzantine Empire.*
Peloponnesian War   Long (431–404 B.C.) conflict between Athens and Sparta; marked end of Athenian greatness.

Cultures

CONQUERING THE CONQUERORS

Persians have a long tradition of eventually coming out on top whenever they are defeated militarily. The Greeks burned Persepolis in 330 B.C., but within a few years the Greeks of Asia were speaking Persian, wearing Persian robes, and writing Persian poetry. The Arabs defeated the Persians in 641 A.D., but within a few years the Muslim armies in Persia were reading poetry by the great Persian poet Ferdowsi. The Turks defeated the Persians in 1503 A.D., but had to import Persian courtiers to run the Ottoman Empire. Persian culture put a strong imprint onto the Middle East and, beneath a layer of Islamic culture, still lives in today's Iran.

that the Ionian cities were cut off from trade or social intercourse with the vast majority of the Persian Empire. Culturally, the Ionian world revolved around Greece regardless of the overlord. In 404 B.C. the Spartans finally defeated Athens with the help of the Persians. As repayment for this assistance, the Spartans delivered all the free cities of Ionia back into the hands of the Persians.

Ten thousand Greek mercenaries defected to the Persian ruler of Asia Minor, Cyrus the Younger. With this foreign army, Cyrus marched to Persia and defeated its king, Artaxerxes. Unfortunately for the victors, however, Cyrus was killed in the battle. The Greeks decided on a leader from their own ranks, and returned home to Thrace. This began another series of Greek-Persian wars, which ended in Artaxerxes dictating a peace treaty in 396 B.C. that gave him final authority over quarrels between the Greek city-states.

Fighting among the Greek states stopped, however, when Phillip of Macedon united them by the sword. His son Alexander, who is known to us as "Alexander the Great," passionately embraced Greek culture and vowed to spread it along with his own power, although by Greek custom he was not Greek. (He was Macedonian, a tribe of northern barbarians.) Alexander took a united Greek army into Asia in 334 B.C. and in three months freed the entire Aegean coast of Persian rule. He marched though Syria, and invaded Egypt. In the ancient capital of the Upper Kingdom, Memphis, the Egyptians crowned him pharaoh. He then founded a city on the Mediterranean and named it after himself, Alexandria. Turning from the pyramids, he conquered the entire Persian Empire. In the process, he convinced the Persians of the barbarity of the West by burning their capital, Persepolis, to the ground. He then marched into India, but his eastward expansion halted just beyond the Indus River when his army revolted. Having united the known, civilized world (except Carthage, which he may have been planning to attack), Alexander died in 323 B.C. at the age of thirty-three.

The Greeks had been interested in conquest, not in administration. As Alexander's armies passed through the Middle East, they left a series of generals to run the newly conquered lands. Other than a handful of their personal guard, however, the generals had nothing with which to run the lands except the administrators they inherited from the defeated Persian Empire. Within a short time, the conquerors had been culturally assimilated into Asian ways.

The next Persian dynasty was the Parthians, followed by the Sassanian Empire. The Sassanians fought a running battle with the West from their founding in 227 A.D. until their destruction by the Arab armies in 641 A.D. Most Western history books fail to record these events, as history for them stopped with Alexander's conquest.

Alexander's descendants immediately began to fight over control of the empire. After fifty years of struggle, the kingdom divided into three: Europe, Egypt and North Africa, and Asia. The Greek general Ptolemy was crowned King of Egypt, and his successors would rule that ancient kingdom until 30 B.C., when they were conquered by the Romans. They turned their capital, Alexandria, into a Greek city and ruled the rest of the country as foreign conquerors.

General Seleucus was given the lands of Asia, and he established a dynasty at Antioch, in northern Syria, his capital. The Ptolemies and Seleucids developed **Hellenistic** culture, which brought Greek architecture and philosophy into the Middle East, with major repercussions. The more religious Jews of Judea disliked the enforced hellenism of the Seleucids—plural gods, male nude wrestling, Greek philosophy—which they regarded as pagan and an affront to the worship of God. From 168 to 164 B.C. the **Maccabees** led a bloody revolt against the Seleucids. Ultimately, the confluence of Greek thought and Jewish faith produced Christianity, according to many scholars.

Over the next hundred years, the various provinces of the East broke away from the Seleucid kingdom until only the lands around the capital remained. These revolts and the fighting against the rebellious provinces kept the Asian kingdom weak until the next conqueror arrived. The Greeks of Europe continued to squabble among themselves until the Romans conquered them.

THE ROMANS

While Rome had been a power on the Italian peninsula, it did not erupt onto the world scene until well after the death of Alexander. As Rome continued to expand its influence, it began to impinge on Carthage's sphere of commercial influence, particularly in Sicily. Like Athens before it, Carthage's main defense was her navy. Control of the seas kept Rome at bay for a number of years, but in 256 B.C. the Romans landed troops in Africa. The Cartheginians destroyed the force, but not before the Romans almost destroyed the capital city. Rome finally defeated Carthage's fleet in 242 B.C., and won Sicily, Sardinia, and Corsica from Carthage as the spoils of the First Punic War.

Hellenistic   Greek culture transplanted into the Middle East by Alexander.
Maccabees   Jewish priestly family who rebelled against Seleucid ruler Antiochus IV in second century B.C.

Having lost much of its empire in the Mediterranean, Carthage turned to Spain to expand. Rome declared war on Carthage, initiating the Second Punic War, when the Carthaginian ruler of Spain, Hannibal, attacked a city that was an ally of Rome. Needing to defend his lands against the Roman army, Hannibal took the initiative, leading his army, including a corps of elephants, across the Pyrenees and the Alps to invade Italy by land from the north. Whenever the Romans launched a pitched battle against the invaders, Hannibal won. The Romans resorted to tactics that would do George Washington well almost two thousand years later: They harried the Carthaginian army but avoided battle until the difficulties of living off the land in a foreign country wore the invaders down. It took sixteen years. Finally, however, Publius Scipio Africanus invaded Africa, and the Carthaginians had to recall their forces from Italy and Spain to defend their capital. Scipio's army defeated Hannibal in 202 B.C., and Carthage surrendered all its lands, except the capital itself and the district around the city.

Rome's next major challenge came from the Seleucid ruler of Syria and Asia Minor, Antiochus III. Seeking to reclaim the glory of Alexander, Antiochus invaded Greece, who turned to the Romans for help. Scipio and his brother entered Asia Minor, and defeated the Seleucids at Magnesia in 189 B.C. The Romans now controlled the shores of the Aegean.

Thoroughly defeated by the Romans, the Carthaginians would not accept defeat by their African neighbors, the Numidians, who lived along the coast of what today is northern Algeria. A Numidian general seized land from Carthage in 155 B.C., and the once great city responded by retaking its possessions by force. This violated the treaty that had ended the Second Punic War, which forbade the Carthaginians from ever taking up arms again. Rome then launched the Third (and final) Punic War by landing 80,000 men to march on the city. The Carthaginians did not believe they had done anything wrong, and they were prepared to open their city to the Romans. Rome did not want peace, however, and so Carthage defended itself two years until it was razed to the ground by the Roman armies in 146 B.C. The population was sold into slavery, and the Romans sowed salt into the fields so they could never produce grain to support a resurrected city. Rome annexed the rest of North Africa in 42 A.D., and it became the breadbasket of the Roman Empire. Using the same strategy the French would later use in Algeria, the Empire relied on Roman settlers to maintain its control. Rome did little to appease the local populace.

With the exception of the Egyptian coast and the feuding Greek city-states, the Mediterranean was now a Roman lake. Following another of the interminable Greek civil wars, Rome signed treaties with each city-state, bringing the peninsula under its domination. Rome's hold on Asia Minor solidified when, in 133 B.C., the king of Pergamon deeded the city to Rome in his will. But the king of the Greek kingdom of Pontus, along the Black Sea in the interior of Asia Minor, challenged Roman might and many rallied to his banner. He conquered Asia Minor, and moved forces into Greece where they were defeated by the Roman army. The Romans now took the offensive, eventually sending Pompey to conquer the Anatolian peninsula and even sign a peace treaty with the king of Armenia in the east. Pompey then seized Syria and Jerusalem, leaving Palestine to be ruled by a descendent

The Altar of ancient Pergamon, a Hellenistic city-state in present-day Turkey, shows the beauty of this late-Greek culture. German archaeologists shipped the altar to Berlin, where it is now displayed. (*Michael Roskin*)

of the Maccabees who was friendly to Rome. Pompey ruled the East to the Euphrates River.

Now it was Egypt's turn. Using the excuse that he was pursuing the rebel Pompey, Gaius Julius Caesar invaded Egypt with 3,000 soldiers in 47 B.C. To curry favor with the new Roman dictator, the regents of Egypt killed Pompey and presented Caesar with his head, preserved in a vat of salt water. Caesar then ordered the regents executed, on the grounds they had killed a Roman citizen—the very Roman citizen Caesar had set out to kill himself. Taking control of Egypt, he then traveled to Asia Minor and defeated another rebel force in the kingdom of Pontus. His victory was so swift that Caesar uttered the well-known phrase, *Veni, Vidi, Vici* ("I came, I saw, I conquered").

Some Roman senators, fearing Caesar's lust for power (not an unreasonable perception) assassinated Caesar in 44 B.C. Several of the conspirators escaped to Asia where they raised an army. Octavian, later known as Caesar Augustus, and his coruler Marc Anthony, led an army that defeated the rebels in Greece. Octavian returned to Italy to claim an empire, while Anthony secured Asia Minor. He then moved to Egypt, where he fell in love—as many know from watching Richard Burton and Elizabeth Taylor—with Egypt's teenage ruler, Cleopatra.

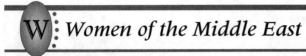 Women of the Middle East

CLEOPATRA, GODDESS AND RULER

Cleopatra was a direct descendent of the Ptolemy dynasty established after the death of Alexander. As such, she was the rightful ruler of Egypt and considered a goddess by many Egyptians. Her fate was to lead a country being conquered by an imperial Roman invasion. To maintain her position, she first made an alliance with Julius Caesar, and she bore Caesar an illegitimate son. Later, she had twins by Marc Anthony. Cleopatra married Anthony in 37 B.C., but the marriage had no standing under Roman law since Anthony was already married. Anthony then declared that Cleopatra's son by Caesar was the rightful ruler of Rome. Taking on Octavian in armed conflict, Anthony's Roman troops deserted the Egyptian cause. Octavian landed in Egypt, and Anthony and Cleopatra committed suicide rather than submit. During their time together, however, it was Cleopatra who decided political and military strategy for her people and for the Roman army led by her consort Marc Anthony.

PAX ROMANA

The Mediterranean basin, including all the lands of North Africa, Asia Minor, and any land capable of cultivation from modern Lebanon to Iran, came under the **Pax Romana**. The lands of the East, pillaged by repeated Roman conquerors, kept their Greek and Oriental complexion and soon recovered. By the end of the first century A.D., the largest city in the Roman Empire outside of the capital itself was Ephesus, less than fifty miles from the ancient Greek Ionian capital, Miletus.

THE DECLINE OF ROME

The East slipped out of Roman hands. The third century A.D. was marked by the rise of the Sassanian empire in Iran, their conquest of a Roman ally, Armenia, and a Persian thrust into Asia Minor. The city of Damascus rebelled against the Romans, and other eastern lands soon joined in. The Roman legions finally regained the upper hand in 273 A.D.

In an attempt to avoid bloodshed after his death, the emperor Diocletian initiated a system of dual emperors, with two emperors-in-waiting (the generals in charge of the armies of the East and West). Diocletian took control of the eastern empire, leaving the West to his co-emperor. Thus began the division of the empire into East and West. The two emperors retired in 305 A.D., and were succeeded by their generals, Galerius and Constantine.

Pax Romana   "Roman Peace," Roman vision of the benefits of their empire; was not especially peaceful.

W : *Women of the Middle East*

THE SYRIAN EMPRESSES OF THE HOUSE OF SERVI

Many are aware that as the Roman Empire declined, its rulers were taken from the Germanic tribes invading Italy. Other non-Romans also wore the purple. In 202 A.D., the North African general Septimus Servus arrived in Rome at the head of an army to claim the throne. Servus was a military man, and his wife made the political decisions. She was a Syrian named Julia Domna.

In 217, Julia's sister, named Julia Maesa, seized the throne in the name of her grandson, a Syrian priest who worshiped a mountain god. Maesa ruled through the grandson for four years, and then for another two years as regent to an underaged successor. When Maesa died, her daughter Julia Mamaea took over for an additional nine years. Roman rule was neither male nor Roman from 202 to 235.

Constantine reunited the empire but moved his capital to Byzantium in 323. As emperor, he declared toleration for all religions, thereby ending the persecution of a small sect of religious fanatics who followed the teachings of a Palestinian carpenter who had been executed many years earlier. Although he was not baptized until his death in 337, he favored Christianity as he believed the "Christian God" gave him victory against his rivals in 312 at the Battle of Milvian Bridge. He presided over the first Church Council in 325, which yielded the Nicene Creed. This established the precedent of considering the emperor both temporal ruler and spiritual ruler of the Church. (In the West, the popes set themselves up as rivals to the Caesars—thus eventually leading to the Western belief of separation of church and state, but only after a millennium of wars on the subject.)

BYZANTIUM

At its height, the Byzantine Empire—more properly, the Eastern Roman Empire—surpassed the glory of Rome. In truth, however, its impact on the East was less than one would expect from a millennium-long empire. Its governmental structure was so stultifying, that the term *byzantine* has come down through the ages to mean a complex and corrupt bureaucracy full of petty schemers.

Its contribution to philosophy was equally paltry. Believing that the writings of "pagan" philosophers such as Plato and Aristotle represented heresy from the teachings of Holy Mother Church, the Empire made it a practice to destroy all copies of the ancients' writings. It even burned the library of Alexandria, the repository of all knowledge of the ancient world. Were it not for some Arab philosophers in Damascus who had taken up the study of Greek philosophy, all trace of Western civilization's intellectual predecessors would have been lost. The main legacy of the Empire was a weakening of both its defenses and those of the Persian Empire, by constant fighting with each other over Syria. This made them both easy prey in the seventh century for the advancing Arab armies.

Constantine the Great founded Byzantium's capital city in 323 and named it after himself. Constantinople was situated in a virtually impregnable position: Surrounded by water on three sides, it had a stout wall protecting its one avenue of approach by land. In a thousand years, the city would only be broached once before its final conquest. Sitting at the mouth of the Bosphorus, the city controlled all transit to and from the Black Sea. In addition, as the Bosphorus was also the narrowest body of water dividing Europe from Asia, it also controlled much of the land trade between those two continents.

While the city could defend itself, it had a difficult time defending the Empire. The first Arab conquests of the seventh century seized two-thirds of the Empire's territory. By 1071, Byzantium consisted of the city itself and some surrounding areas. Everything else was in the hands of the Arabs or the Turks—nomadic tribes from Central Asia who had moved into Asia Minor.

After Constantine, the Western Empire fell into disrepute, as Italy was invaded by wave after wave of barbarians. In the East, the wealth of the Orient was sufficient to buy off the barbarians and send them on to their Western destinations. Constantine's heirs fell to fighting among themselves over title of emperor. In the sixth century, a nephew, Justinian, assumed the throne and attempted to restore the glory of a united empire. Ruling from Constantinople, he reconquered North Africa and parts of Spain. One of his generals killed the last Ostrogoth king sitting in Rome, and he ruled Italy through a representative in Ravenna, a town on the eastern Italian coast. When Justinian died in 565, however, his successors were unable to hold onto the Western Empire.

Although his territorial conquests would not last, Justinian bequeathed two major accomplishments to history. In the libraries, he consolidated the **Corpus Juris Civilis**, a compendium of the laws of the Empire that previously had been located in thousands of court and senate documents. In Constantinople, he constructed the Aya Sophia Cathedral—the largest church in Christendom for a thousand years, which was later converted into a mosque, and is today Istanbul's oldest museum.

Justinian's building program, which made Constantinople the glory of the millennium, almost cost him his throne. Disgusted with the tremendous tax burden imposed upon them to pay for all the construction, the citizens of Constantinople rose in the Nika revolt and crowned another as emperor. Justinian prevailed, however, and launched a massive wave of arrests and executions.

Eastern Weakness

For the next hundred years, the Byzantine Empire was locked in a death struggle with barbarians in the West and with the Persians in the East. The struggles so weakened the Empire it was unable to defend itself when the armies of Islam swept

---

Corpus Juris Civilis   Justinian's massive codification of Roman law, later basis of European legal codes.

W: *Women of the Middle East*

THEODORA, STAGE STAR TURNED EMPRESS

Theodora was the second of three daughters of a Cyprian bear trainer and an acrobat. When their father died, the daughters entered the theater where Theodora won acclaim as a comedienne. She also received notoriety as a prostitute. History records that she not only obliged the members of the upper class who could afford her beauty, but she also bestowed her charms *gratis* on slaves. As Gibbon delicately put it, "Her charity was universal."

She traveled to Africa as the concubine of the new governor but had to make her own way back to the capital when the governor tired of her. She affected the role of a wool spinner, living a virtuous life in a small house. In this role, she met Justinian, at the time still only a senator. The laws of the Empire forbade any member of the Senate from marrying women who had served in the theater, and the noble women of the household rejected any association with the former prostitute. But Justinian prevailed, the law was changed, and he married Theodora.

When Justinian was crowned emperor, he crowned his wife empress and designated her co-ruler of the Roman world. The governors of the provinces had to swear oaths of allegiance to the emperor and to Theodora. Once on the throne, Theodora ruled with an iron fist. She also became famous for her charity and improved roads and hospitals throughout the empire. Her husband claimed that any edicts he issued were actually the result of Theodora's decisions.

When the citizens of Constantinople rose in the Nika rebellion, Justinian was prepared to flee into exile. Theodora, who had worn both the purple and the beggar's robe, told her husband she would rather die an empress than live as a commoner. She gave her husband the backbone he needed to crush the rebellion and stay in power. In 542–543, Justinian was stricken with the bubonic plague and almost died. During his long incapacitation, Theodora ruled as sole Empress of the Eastern Empire. After twenty-two years on the throne, she died while still reigning as Queen of the Orient.

---

out of the Arabian peninsula and captured all the territories outside of Asia Minor. The Empire was further weakened by civil wars over theological questions, such as whether Christ was God and man, or a man with God's nature, or God with man's nature.

THE TURKS AND THE CRUSADES

In 1071, the empire's hold over Asia Minor began to slip. At the battle of Manzikert, Seljuk Turks defeated the imperial army. The Empire shrunk over the next few centuries to the city of Constantinople and some suburbs. The emperor himself was captured and brought before Sultan Alp Arslan. The Seljuk ruler treated the defeated monarch well and released him in return for a ransom and an agreement that henceforth Byzantium would pay tribute to the Turks. When the Byzantine monarch's successor refused to honor the terms of the settlement, the Seljuks seized Asia Minor by force of arms.

W: *Women of the Middle East*

EMPRESSES IRENE, ZOE, AND THEODORA

Emperor Leo IV died in 790, leaving the throne to his ten-year-old son. Leo's widow, Irene, announced she would reign as regent for the young prince. Eventually, she assumed full control by having her soldiers murder her son. She then ruled in her own name an additional five years. A committee of state officials deposed her after it became known that Irene was considering marrying the Western Emperor, Charlemagne, whom most in the East considered an uncouth barbarian unworthy of sharing the marital bed with an empress.

Two hundred years later, two empresses who inherited the throne in their own right ruled the empire. Constantine VIII had no sons, an elder daughter in the convent, and two unmarried daughters in their fifties, Zoe and Theodora, when he died in 1028. While Zoe had the right to rule by blood, it was not considered proper for a woman to sit on the throne. So, shortly before he died, Constantine VIII married Zoe off to an aristocrat who was promptly crowned emperor. Ignored by her husband, Zoe turned her attentions to a man thirty years her junior, Michael. The new emperor died of poison (possibly administered by Zoe), and Zoe married Michael within hours of the death. Michael decided he liked being Emperor, and sent Zoe to a convent. Later, as Michael lay dying, he named his nephew to be the new emperor. The nephew brought Zoe back to the palace to shore up his own legitimacy, but to no avail. The crowds insisted that Zoe and Theodora rule jointly, as direct heirs of the last dynasty, and they did for several years. This did not lead to peace, however, as Zoe and Theodora detested each other. Zoe then married a third time, and the throne passed to Emperor Constantine IX. Now you see why they call it Byzantine.

In 1096, the armies of the First Crusade began to enter and seize Byzantine lands. The Catholic crusaders regarded the Eastern Orthodox faith as heretical and had no trouble robbing and sacking its lands. True disaster struck when the Fourth Crusade besieged Constantinople in 1203 on the justification that the Empire was guilty of heresy because the Eastern Church did not declare allegiance to the pope. In reality, the leaders of the Venetian navy were anxious to recoup the costs of building the army's ships: Venice had insisted on half of all territories the Fourth Crusade took but decided that Constantinople was easier to conquer than Muslim lands. It was the only time in a thousand years that the walls of the city were breeched until the city's final conquest in 1453. The Crusaders looted the city, and much of the art and treasure taken to Venice. The Byzantine ability to hold back the Islamic tide was now fatally wounded, not by the Sultan's scimitar, but by a dagger in the back delivered by Christian rulers.

By 1400, the city was in such danger from the Ottoman Turks that Emperor Manuel II traveled to Europe to beg for help from his brother Christian monarchs. While he was treated like the visiting emperor that he was, none of the European leaders would send him aid. He returned home a happy man in 1402, after receiving word that the Mongols had destroyed the Ottoman armies. This gave the empire a brief respite.

For the next fifty years, the Ottomans battled their way to the gates of the "New Rome." Finally, on May 29, 1453, Mehmet the Conqueror breached the walls of Byzantium with a new weapon, the canon, and extinguished the last vestiges of European government from the Middle East. The Eastern Empire, so concerned with questions about the next life, passed from this life hardly leaving a trace. Nominally, the Empire had lasted a thousand years, but for half of that it was little more than the walled city of Constantinople, henceforth called Istanbul.

Conclusions

For 3,500 years, the Middle East witnessed the rise and fall of a number of empires. From the moment man stopped being a hunter-gatherer and became a cultivator, he began building kingdoms that vied with each other for power: Egyptians, Assyrians, Hittites, Persians, Babylonians, Phoenicians, Greeks, Romans, and Byzantine Greeks. Some of the kingdoms made considerable cultural developments and laid the foundation of Western civilization. Others, more warlike, left no legacy at all. The most developed civilization, the Byzantine, spent its time battling with Persians and debating theology. When it passed from history, few noticed.

Further Reference

Bamban, Robert. *The Military History of Parsiks*. Self-published, 1998.

Brown, Peter. *The World of Late Antiquity, AD 15–750*. New York: Norton, 1989.

Gabriel, Richard. *The Great Armies of Antiquity*. Westport, CT: Praeger, 2002.

Gibbon, Edward. *The Decline and Fall of the Roman Empire*. New York: Penguin Books, 1980.

National Geographic Society, *Everyday Life in Ancient Times*. Washington: National Geographic Society, 1953.

Norwich, John Julius. *A Short History of Byzantium*. New York: Alfred A. Knopf, 1997.

Swain, Joseph Ward, and William H. Armstrong. *The Peoples of the Ancient World*. New York: Harper & Row, 1959.

The Birth of Islam

Points to Ponder

- What are the similarities and differences between Islam and the religions that preceded it?
- What was the Hijra and what does it signify?
- How was the early Muslim community governed?
- How does Islam say a state should be governed?
- What, when, and where were the two great Arab caliphates?
- Does the development of Islamic thought show progress or innovation?
- What is Shi' a and how is it different from Sunni Islam?
- Does Allah demand that Muslims kill Westerners?

MUHAMMAD

Probably more has been written about Muhammad than any man who ever lived. From the beginning, Islamic scholars studied and documented his life as an exemplar for those to follow. European scholars, on the other hand, immediately wrote attacks against Muhammad as the devil incarnate, leading people away from the True Faith to eternal damnation. It therefore becomes difficult after thirteen centuries to get a true and fair picture of him. It is an important exercise, however, in that he is the central human figure in a religion that now has 1.2 billion adherents. It is also important because there is only one goal shared by all Muslims: to follow Muhammad's example. This goal is shared by liberals who want Islam reinterpreted to give greater freedom and democracy, by conservatives who pray for the world's conversion from sin, and by bearded fanatics who, in the name of God, fly airplanes full of innocent people into office buildings filled with other innocent people.

Not much is known about Muhammad's youth. What is known and agreed upon by all is that Muhammad ibn Abdullah was a city dweller, born into a minor branch of a major tribe in Mecca, the Quraysh, in about 570 A.D. His parents died when he was a child, and Muhammad was raised by his uncle, Abu Talib. Arabia at that time was a mix of religions—Jewish, Christian, and pagan. Muhammad

R Religions

BIRTHPLACE OF RELIGIONS

Most people know that the Middle East is the birthplace of the three great world monotheistic religions: Judaism, Christianity, and Islam. In fact, many religions have been born in the Middle East. Once established, it seems almost impossible for a religion to last long without splintering.

Ancient Persia was the birthplace of Mithra and of Mani. Mithra became the cult god of the Roman legions. Many Roman victories were won in his name (even when the empire was nominally Christian) through the fifth century. Mani brought us Manichaeism, a defunct religion that divided the world into good and evil and whose philosophical influence continues to be felt in the West today. The ancient religion of the Persian kings was Zoroastrianism: The leaders of their church were known as Mages, or Magi in Latin. The Three Wise Men whose visit to Bethlehem is celebrated on the feast of the Epiphany were Zoroastrian high priests. Zoroastrians continue to practice their religion in Iran and in India; indeed, Zoroastrianism is a protected religion under the Iranian Islamic constitution. Its followers get a seat in parliament.

Judaism splintered early into those who followed the Pharisees and the Samaritans, who were left in Palestine during the Babylonian captivity. All the early Christian schisms took place in the Middle East, and followers of each of the schismatic churches can still be found in northern Syria and Iraq. Islam preaches adherence to "towhid," Arabic for unity. In reality, Islam is divided between the Sunni and the Shi'a, and each of these movements are subdivided into numerous smaller groupings. Each of these divisions leads to new identities for the faithful.

---

clearly frequented synagogues and churches as a young man and picked up many Bible stories that later appear, somewhat garbled, in the Qur'an.

Some Western sources report that as a child Muhammad had uncontrollable fits and passed out. These episodes caused Muhammad to focus on larger questions than daily living; he became deeply spiritual and began to go into the desert for periods of meditation. It was during one of these periods that he heard the angel Gabriel. Over the years, Gabriel returned many times, seen only by Muhammad, to reveal to him God's words. A modern psychologist might interpret these events as youthful episodes of epilepsy followed by psychotic episodes. A Christian or Jew might dismiss the whole history as a fantasy, since they hold that they already possess God's revelation. To a believing Muslim, however, the words that Gabriel revealed became the Holy Qur'an, the complete revelation of God, unadulterated by man's intervention. In this regard, all Muslims are automatically fundamentalists, because they take the Qur'an literally.

Muhammad and his cousin Ali were raised as brothers. For a long time, Mecca had been a pilgrimage center for all the inhabitants of the Arabian peninsula. They came to venerate the **Kaaba**, and Meccans made money from the adherents of all sects. Muhammad decided, however, that there was only one, true God, and it was to Him whom he prayed.

Kaaba   Ancient meteorite long venerated in Mecca, now focal point of Muslim faith.

R : *Religions*

COMPETING REVELATIONS

Based on the Qur'an, Muslims accept that God gave his revelation to other peoples, including Christians and Jews. "I have sent messengers to all peoples, each speaking in a language to be understood." This is the same revelation that Gabriel carried to Muhammad. For this reason, Muslims accept that Abraham, Moses, Elijah, John the Baptist, and Jesus were all prophets who delivered God's word to the people. Muslims believe that the Old and New Testaments are based on true revelation, but these revelations have been corrupted through human intervention. Either by purposeful fraud, or merely by faulty memory, Christians changed the revelation before recording it. Thus, there are several stories found in both the Qur'an and the Bible, but with subtle differences. Muslims contend that the Qur'anic version is the correct one, unchanged by human intervention.

In both books, the Old Testament and Qur'an, Abraham took his son up the mountain to sacrifice him to God. In the Bible, the child was Isaac, son of Sarah. In the Qur'an, the child was Ishmael, son of Hagar. Both books report that the Virgin Mary married and bore a son named Jesus. In the Bible, Jesus' father was God; in the Qur'an, Jesus' father was human.

There was a wealthy widow in the town, Khadije, who made her money as a merchant. She hired Muhammad to run the business, and the two eventually married. Westerners point to Muhammad's business acumen as evidence of education and sophistication, suggesting that he was not a simple prophet. The Islamic tradition holds that Muhammad was illiterate and incapable of devising a complex new religion by himself. He simply recited God's words. The first word the angel said to him was "Recite," not "Write this down." But if Muhammad could neither read nor write, how could he manage an important trading business?

Khadije supported Muhammad financially for many years and through many difficulties. When the angel Gabriel first appeared to Muhammad, he rushed home and told Khadije. She accepted that her husband had received a divine revelation, and encouraged him in the establishment of his new religion. Khadije holds an important place in Islam, as the first person to whom Muhammad revealed God's word, and the first person to accept his mission of prophecy.

Muhammad began to draw disciples around him. At first, his followers were limited to close friends and family. His cousin Ali was an early convert. Later, he began to attract the Meccan underclass: slaves, tribal clients, second sons. The upper classes decided that Muhammad's teachings of only one God had become a threat to the lucrative pilgrimage trade that was the lifeblood of the city. With the death of his protector, Abu Talib, the leaders of Mecca decided to kill Muhammad.

At the same time, the city of Yathrib, about 200 miles north of Mecca, was in turmoil. Yathrib's inhabitants heard that Muhammad was a fair man and invited him to move to Yathrib to become a judge to hear the complaints of the various tribes. Muhammad accepted. At great risk to his own life, cousin Ali posed as Muhammad and slept in the Prophet's bed as the murderers descended on the

C: *Cultures*

UNDER THE SPELL OF ARABIC

There is no single way to transliterate Arabic into Western languages. If you simply try to record the sounds, some hear them one way, some another. Some sounds in Arabic (and Chinese) are hard to render in English. Some academic disciplines try for a standard **transliteration**, but not all disciplines accept the same one. In America, the most common standard is that of the Associated Press, because it appears in almost all newspapers. The *New York Times*, however, has its own style.

Take something as basic as "the Base," Osama's name for his terrorist organization. The AP calls it *Al-Qaida*, the *Times al Qaeda*. The actual pronunciation sounds like "*ul GUYduh.*" The Arab proper name originally meaning "lord" or "sir" is *Said*, spelled variously *Saed, Sayid, Sayyid, Sayyed,* and *Saeed*. Spaniards are likely to recognize it as the name of their medieval hero El Cid, a Christian knight who served both Moorish and Catholic princes. More than a dozen variations have been counted in the spelling of the dictator of Libya: *Kaddafi, Qadafi, Kadaffy, Gadhafi,* and so on. The Muslim holy book is rendered *Qur'an, Quran,* or *Koran*.

We will try to use the spelling *Muhammad* throughout, but if a Pakistani writing in English spells his name *Mohammed*, who are we to correct him? Scholars may spell the name *Husayn*, but most recognize it as *Hussein*. The media spells it *Osama*; some scholars spell it *Usama*. A leader can be a *shaykh* or a *sheik*. Under the spell of Arabic, one cannot be totally consistent. Even the coauthors cannot agree. We're doing you a favor, because you will face these spelling variations all your life. Get used to them and learn to recognize the variations.

house. When the attackers discovered the ruse, they fled leaving Ali unharmed. Muhammad and many of his followers, meanwhile, slipped out of the city and moved north. The year was 622, and this event—the **hijra**—marks the beginning of the Islamic calendar. Muhammad and his disciples established the first Islamic city-state, and Yathrib changed its name to **Medina**, meaning it was the "city of the Prophet."

Muhammad made a treaty that governed relations between the various tribes. The tribes accepted the Muslims as another tribe, even though it was not organized on the basis of blood ties. The tribes agreed to maintain their separate identities, but to unite into a single polity that renounced traditional blood vengeance in favor of justice administered by Muhammad. The early Muslims accepted Jews as full partners. Later, when some Jewish tribes were expelled from Medina, it was for the crimes of cooperating with the enemy or for disobedience to the Prophet—not because of their religious beliefs. For most of history, Jews and Muslims got along.

transliteration   Rendering a word from one writing system into another.
hijra   (rendered in English as *hegira*) Flight or migration; specifically, Muhammad's move to Medina in 622, the start of the Islamic calendar.
Medina   "City"; specifically, Islam's second holiest city.

Cultures

ARABIC NAMES

Names are important in the Arab world, as a good name is often synonymous with family honor. For most of their history, Arabs did not use family names but were known as sons of their father, **ibn**, such as *Ibn Khaldun*. Arabs still sometimes do not use their given names but refer to themselves as the father of their son, **abu**. If a man named *Ibrahim* has a son named *Hassan*, he will often be known informally as the father of *Hassan*, or *Abu Hassan*. Women are sometimes called mother of their son, **umm**.

MUHAMMAD'S ROLE

As judge, Muhammad was the head of the judiciary; later, as the Medinan tribes converted, he also became head of the executive. There was no legislature, however, because Muslims believed that God had already handed them the only law they needed. Muhammad's practices were recorded as **sunna**, which are also important in Islamic legal and social reasoning. The Medinans gave Muhammad special honor as the medium through whom they learned God's word. They did not consider Muhammad infallible, however. There are several **hadith** in which Muhammad makes a decision and is challenged as to whether he was functioning as prophet or executive. When told that Muhammad was making decisions based on his own logic, the people sometimes made him reverse those decisions.

Over the next decade, Muhammad fought many battles with the Meccans—winning some and losing others. Muhammad was the only founder of a major religion who was also a successful military commander. Islam was always closely connected to the sword. By 629, however, Muhammad signed a truce with the rulers of Mecca, known as the pledge of Hudaybiya. He entered the city on pilgrimage and announced that the Kaaba was a site holy to the one true God. By his words and actions, the pilgrimage trade was saved, albeit transformed into service of the new religion. The following year, Mecca surrendered to the Muslims. Muhammad died in 632, just as his followers were seizing control of the Arabian peninsula.

---

ibn   Arabic for "son of."
abu   "Father of."
umm   "Mother of."
sunna   Traditions concerning the actions of the Prophet; origin of *Sunni*, mainstream Islam.
hadith   Sayings of the Prophet.

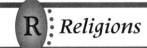

Religions

THE ISLAMIC CALENDAR

In the Middle East, history is judged as taking place either before Muhammad or after Muhammad. The Muslim calendar dates from the Hijra of 622 A.D., when Muhammad and his followers left Mecca to establish an Islamic city-state in Medina. The Middle East of today therefore begins in many ways in the seventh century and not in the two millennium of civilization that preceded it. In the West, the years of the Islamic calendar are sometimes given as A.H. (*anno hegirae*, "year of the hijra"). For example, 1000 A.H. would be 1592 A.D. because each Muslim year is eleven days shorter than a Christian year.

BIRTH OF SHI'ISM

Muhammad's death immediately split the young Muslim community. Abu Bakr, the father of Muhammad's favorite wife Aisha, emerged from the death chamber to tell the assembled multitudes: "Those of you who followed Muhammad, Muhammad is dead. Those of you who follow God, God lives." The elders of the community elected Abu Bakr to be their new leader, or **caliph**, the one who replaced Muhammad in temporal role as leader of the community. No one replaced him in his role as prophet. Muslims believe that since the Qur'an recorded God's revelation whole and intact, there is no need for any future prophet. Muhammad was thus the "Seal of Prophecy." A minority, however, believed that no one could lead the community unless he was related to Muhammad. They turned their allegiance to cousin Ali, who by now was married to the Prophet's daughter, Fatima.

There are even some hadith in which, before his death, the Prophet tells his followers that Ali is his successor. Those who accepted Ali as their leader became known as "Ali's Partisans," which in Arabic is *Shi'aat Ali*. From this term comes the word **Shi'a**, and it is this first succession conflict that marks the great schism in Islam between the **Sunni** and the Shi'a.

THE CHOICE OF THE CALIPHS

The first caliph, Abu Bakr, was chosen by the elders of the community and accepted by the community who swore allegiance to him. After consulting with the learned in the community, Abu Bakr designated his successor, Umar (sometimes

caliph   Successor; specifically, of Muhammad. (Root of *California*.)
Shi'a   Minority branch of Islam that claims Ali was rightful *caliph*.
Sunni   Mainstream and majority branch of Islam.

Religions

THE CONSTITUTION OF MEDINA

The constitution Muhammad devised for Medina was incorporated into Islam, where much persists to this day. There was to be no clear separation between mosque and state, as all believers and their families form a single community, the **umma**. The tradition of family responsibility for violence and harm to others is enshrined in the provision that extended families must provide **blood money** and ransoms for its members. Revenge for the death of a family member was then and is now a prominent motive, as the Israelis have discovered on the West Bank. All members of the umma are expected to fight crime, even if the criminal is a relative.

In a practice that appeared strongly with the 2003 war against Iraq, Muhammad's constitution required the entire umma to stick together against infidels who threaten any members of the umma. In trying to gain Arab allies against Saddam, we were working against Muhammad's intentions. Interestingly, Jews at that time (a large part of the population) were to be treated as members of the community but keeping their religion. Jews and Muslims were to help each other, even with military assistance. This last point held up pretty well until the twentieth century. For most of history, Muslim-Jewish relations were good. Much of Tariq's army that invaded Spain in 711 were Jews.

---

spelled Omar), in a political will. The people, likewise, swore allegiance to him. Umar appointed a council of six men who chose his successor, the third caliph, Uthman. When Uthman died, the people of Medina acclaimed Ali as the fourth caliph.

Note the commonalities in the succession: The first three caliphs were chosen by the community's elders, acting in consultation. This provided the precedent to rely on the learned to decide right and wrong for the community. All four caliphs were then approved by the acclamation of the people, along the lines of the hadith, "My people will never agree on error." The people swore an oath of allegiance, or **bay'a**.

The second caliph, Umar, performed a valuable service. It was he who gathered together all the fragments upon which Muhammad's utterances had been written. Under Umar's guiding hand, the fragments that were identified as being true revelations were compiled into the Qur'an. Umar, and not Muhammad, organized the Qur'an as we know it today. Similarly, Umar discarded those fragments that he and his advisors considered specious.

Ali's predecessor, Uthman, was from another branch of the Quraysh, Muhammad's tribe. He was a descendent of the Prophet's great uncle Abu Sufyan, and thus was from the Meccan aristocracy from whom the early Muslims had fled in 622. Many of the early Companions of the Prophet had difficulty accepting him as

---

umma   Community or a people; specifically, the community of Islam.
blood money   Payment for injury done to member of one family by member of another.
bay'a   Oath of allegiance, binding an individual to obey all the lawful commands of the leader.

Religions

HUDAYBIYA

Within the contemporary Muslim community, Hudaybiya is a controversial matter. The Qur'an gave Muslims a strict order to "command what is good, and forbid what is evil." Dealing with unbelievers was considered an evil act, yet here was the Prophet of God signing an armistice with them. Today, some use this as an example to justify a gentle form of Islam that can coexist with other religions. Others use it as an example that it is permissible to hide your ultimate goal (conquest of the unbelievers) as a means to attain that goal. Deciding which interpretation is correct is an urgent matter on the current world scene.

leader. Eventually, insurgents killed Uthman at the door to his house. When Ali became caliph, he vowed to prosecute his predecessor's murderers, but he never found the assailants. Uthman's family, the Umayyads, launched a full-scale civil war against Ali. The Umayyads enlisted a number of allies, including Muhammad's favorite wife, Aisha. Eventually, Ali was assassinated and the **Umayyad** governor of Syria, Mu'awiyya, claimed the caliphate.

The early caliphs, known as the *Rashidun* or "Rightly Guided," and the Umayyads presided over the incredible expansion of Islam through the Middle East and beyond. In 638 A.D. Muslim armies took Jerusalem, in 641 Egypt, in 642 Iran and Libya, and in 711 part of Spain and India. The Arab general Tarik crossed from Morocco to Spain in 711 and gave his name to Gibraltar, *Gebel al Tarik*, the "Mountain of Tarik." The Muslim advance was halted in Europe in 732 at Poitiers and Tours, only about a hundred miles south of Paris. Muslims controlled all of the Sassanid Iranian Empire and much of the ancient Roman Empire.

THE UMAYYADS

The Umayyads ruled the Islamic world for less than a hundred years (661–749). They lacked legitimacy on several levels. They had obtained power through a civil war against the Prophet's son-in-law, alienating many who had supported Ali's cause.

Mu'awiyyah's son Yazid earned the eternal enmity of the Shi'a by ordering war against the Prophet's grandson, the third Shi'a Imam, Husayn. In fairness to Yazid, Husayn had raised the banner of rebellion against the central government. He gathered his followers into a small army, and moved on the town of Kufa. The Kufans had promised to aid Husayn. Unfortunately for the Imam, however, Yazid had dispatched an army of his own into the area, under General Ubayd. When the residents of Kufa heard the news of the caliph's superior force descending on the

Umayyad First Muslim dynasty, centered in Damascus, 661–749.

Cultures

FAMILY HONOR

Remember our discussion in Chapter 1 about group identities in the Middle East? The primary group from which Middle Easterners derive their identity—and to whom they give their loyalty—is their family. The honor of the family needs to be protected above all else. This means that women must be carefully guarded and kept from any contact with males outside the family. In some countries, women rarely leave the house and then only when escorted by a male relative. Often they must be covered from head to toe lest they tempt lust. A devout Muslim will not shake hands with a woman, as that is a form of sexual contact. Girls go to their own schools, if they are allowed schooling. Sexuality is tightly controlled and restrained in Islam. Adultery may be punished by stoning to death for both man and woman. Forget the image of belly dancers; they are remnants of a pre-Islamic culture now found chiefly in Egypt but forbidden in stricter Muslim countries.

As children reach marriageable age, however, how can a family be certain that the child will choose a partner from a good family? After all, if the spouse is from a family whose honor has been sullied, then the offspring (who are carrying the family name) will not be as honorable. The solution: Marry partners from the one family you know to be truly honorable—your own. Arabs traditionally married their first cousins; this protected the purity of the bloodlines. (In ancient Egypt, the Pharaoh often married his sister for the same reason.) Today, cousin-marriage is still practiced in the area but fading with the spread of knowledge of genetics.

---

area, they barred the gates of the city and refused to allow Husayn to enter. He had to camp on the plain of Karbala, where he was killed in battle in 680.

Many who were not Shi'a, however, also found the method by which the Umayyads came to power distasteful. To escape the plots and machinations surrounding the old capital of Medina, Mu'awiyyah moved the capital to Damascus—the seat of his power. But Damascus derived its economic power from its connections to the Byzantine Empire; now, as an Islamic rival to the Greeks, Damascus was cut off from the trade flows that had been its lifeblood. Mu'awiyyah also tried to win the support of Muslims by initiating a mosque-building program, a strategy that would be pursued any number of times by rulers whose claims were shaky over the next 1,400 years. The Umayyads were responsible for building the Umayyad mosque in Damascus, the oldest Friday Mosque in Islam, and for the Dome of the Rock in Jerusalem.

The Kharijites, Islam's first fundamentalists, also challenged the Umayyads. This group first formed in opposition to Ali, who had tried to compromise with his opponents. The Kharijites took the extreme position that the caliph was charged with executing the law of God—and there could be no compromise over God's law. The Kharijites formed their own community, and claimed that any member of that community could claim to be its leader. As the Umayyads were not members of the breakaway sect, the Kharijites would not recognize the Umayyad claim to the throne. They labeled Umayyad followers as heretics who had strayed from the true faith.

Religions

SHI'A LEADERSHIP PHILOSOPHY

The Sunni are followers of the *sunna*, or "customs," of the Prophet. They are over 80 percent of the world's Muslims. They believe that the first four caliphs were the rightful rulers of the Islamic state. The Shi'a, or partisans, accepted only the fourth caliph, Ali, as legitimate. The Shi'a became a religion of protest, whose leaders became a focal point of opposition to the caliphs. The Shi'a leaders, or imams, usually did not press their claims to the throne, arguing that an illegitimate ruler should still be obeyed rather than risk division and chaos in the community.

Most Shi'a, but not all, claim that the right to rule descended from Ali and Fatima to eleven other direct descendants of Muhammad. Ali and his descendants are known as the Twelve Imams; the Twelfth Imam disappeared as an infant in the tenth century. The Sunni claim that either the Imam died, or possibly was never even born. The Shi'a claim that God would never leave his people without a legitimate leader; thus, the Twelfth Imam was born and then placed into hiding. The Shi'a say that he is still alive today, in this world but not in this time. He will return to restore justice to the world before the Last Judgment Day.

Since the Twelfth Imam is the rightful ruler, and he is still alive, Shi'a religious leaders have traditionally held that any other ruler on earth—including Muslim rulers—are, in a sense, usurpers of the Twelfth Imam's rightful place. This theory was accepted for a thousand years, until Ayatollah Khomeini assumed power in Iran in 1979.

Finally, the Arab conquest of the Persian Sassanids did not sit easily on the Iranian population. While most converted from Zoroastrianism to Islam, that did not mean they accepted the overlordship of Arabs—whom the cosmopolitan Iranians considered ill-mannered louts from the desert with no culture to speak of. Soldiers from the far northeast of the empire, under the leadership of a general named Abu Muslim, rebelled against the impious rulers in Damascus.

THE ABBASIDS

All these groups opposed to the Umayyads united into a single movement, raised black banners as their standard, and marched on the caliph. The last of the line, Marwan II, fled to Egypt in an unsuccessful attempt to save his life. Cleverly, the leaders of the opposition told their supporters that they were restoring the caliphate to the family of the Prophet but never identified which member was their choice. It was only after the armies had triumphed that they announced the new ruler: Abu Abbas. The new caliph was a descendent of the Prophet's uncle Abbas, not of the Prophet himself. Although technically entitled to be called a member of the family since he was a distant relative, the Shi'a felt they were shortchanged and continued to support the claims of their imams.

Following the fall of the Umayyads from power in the East, an Umayyad relative established himself as caliph in Spain. The people of Spain believed that this

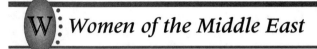 Women of the Middle East

AISHA AND THE LOST NECKLACE

Aisha was the daughter of Abu Bakr, an early companion of Muhammad. The prophet married Aisha at age 9; because Aisha had not reached puberty, Muslims claim that Muhammad raised Aisha as a daughter for three years before consummating the marriage.

Aisha had a sense of humor and was willing to challenge her husband when the occasion warranted it. Aisha was traveling in a caravan when she noticed that her pearl necklace had fallen somewhere. She started to backtrack looking for it. The caravan, not knowing that the Prophet's wife was missing, continued. When the caravan leader realized this, he dispatched a rider to find Aisha. The next morning, the rider brought the missing wife into camp, setting tongues wagging about lost virtue. Remember, no woman must be alone with an unrelated male.

Some of Muhammad's political enemies demanded that he sentence Aisha to death for adultery. The Prophet fell into a troubled sleep as he pondered his wife's fate. The next morning, he announced that the angel Gabriel had appeared in his sleep and gave God's latest revelation: Aisha was innocent of all wrongdoing, and Aisha's detractors should be punished for false testimony. With her reprieve in hand, Aisha joked that God seemed to be in a hurry to fulfill his Prophet's personal wishes.

Umayyad survivor, Abd al-Rahman I, had escaped the fall of their house by swimming the length of the Mediterranean. This second Umayyad caliphate ruled only the Iberian peninsula, but their rule lasted from 756 to 1031, longer than their cousins' in Damascus. Spain under the Moors enjoyed a golden age of science and culture. Muslims, Christians, and Jews lived together unmolested. Moorish learning in Spain eventually returned the ancient Greek classics to the knowledge of the West.

THE ABBASID CALIPHATE

The **Abbasid** caliphate survived in one form or another from 750 until its destruction by the Mongols in 1258. The fact that it survived did not mean that it thrived. Its caliphal title was challenged by the Umayyads in Spain and by the Fatimids, another Muslim dynasty, in Egypt. Further, its control over the central Arab lands weakened in the ninth century when the caliphs came under the control of their military guards. In 945, the Buyids from Iran seized the capital and took over all temporal power. They were succeeded in 1055 by the latest wave of migrants from Central Asia, the Seljuk Turks. In Islamic theory, there is no separation between church and state; from 945 on, however, this separation became a reality regardless of the teachings of the theologians. The caliph was technically the ruler of

---

Abbasid   Second major Muslim dynasty, centered in Baghdad, 750–1258.

R : Religions

HUSAYN: MARTYR OR SUICIDE?

As Muslims accept God as the Creator of all things, including all living beings, they look upon suicide as a grave sin whereby the individual elevates his own choice to destroy God's creation over God's divine plan. By contrast, if a Muslim dies struggling in the way of God, he is a martyr and is promised numerous rewards in Paradise.

Was Husayn a martyr, or did he commit suicide? According to Shi'a teachings, the night before the battle of Karbala, Husayn called his army together. He told them that there would be a major battle the next day, that they were hopelessly outnumbered, and that any who took to the field would probably be killed. Husayn then dismissed all members of his army who had wives, children, or other responsibilities. He ordered the campfires doused so none would see the soldiers who had to leave the camp. When the fires were relit, only Husayn and seventy-two followers remained. Against impossible odds, Husayn the next day fought to the death.

Shi'a faithful throughout the world remember this occasion every year by beating themselves with chains and razorblades to share Husayn's suffering. Passion plays are produced in every Shi'a community where public displays of their religion is allowed. Did Husayn remain true to God's plan by fighting against impossible odds, or did he commit suicide by placing himself in a position where it would be impossible to survive?

the realm, and he held some religious authority. The true rulers, however, were the military commanders who took the title **Sultan**.

Things began well enough for the Abbasids. Abu Abbas seized the throne, and promptly turned on those who had helped him to power but who might challenge him in the future. Abu Muslim and his forces were among the first to die. Using similar logic as their Umayyad predecessors, the Abbasids moved the capital from Damascus to avoid the political scheming of the inhabitants. They moved to the new city of Baghdad in central Iraq between the Tigris and Euphrates rivers. The city was designed to be a fortress, and the new caliphate was soon isolated from the population.

Under the Abbasids, there was a great flowering of Islamic culture. Following the Islamic edict to seek knowledge wherever it is found, Muslim philosophers founded the House of Wisdom in Baghdad. This school housed the only copies of ancient Greek writings to survive the persecution of the Byzantines.

During this time period, the great Islamic jurists codified Islamic law into the four schools of Sunnism: Hanbali, Hanafi, Maliki, and Shafi. In a Shi'a parallel, the Sixth Imam, Ja'afar al-Sadiq, organized the Shi'a school of law, the Ja'afari. In a decision that had tremendous negative repercussions over the centuries, the Sunni jurists proclaimed that by the tenth century all questions had been answered (or

Sultan   Holder of power.

Jerusalem's Dome of the Rock is
one of Islam's holiest sites.
(*Michael Roskin*)

at least the principles for deciding the question had been answered). They declared
the gate of independent reasoning, the Bab al-**Ijtihad**, to be closed. Now there
was only one, standard interpretation, **taqlid**. Shari'a law was now complete.
Thenceforth, jurists would study the **shari'a** and make rulings on questions before
them based on the logic of the tenth century. Some scholars think this closing off
of independent reasoning and interpretation of the Qur'an led to intellectual stagnation in Islamic culture.

CHALLENGES TO ORTHODOXY

The Abbasids also faced a major schism within Sunnism. One of the Abbasid caliphs,
al-Ma'mun, embraced a rationalist interpretation of Islam. This view, known as
Mu'tazilism, held that much of the religion could be understood through the use
of human reason. It also argued that God created the Qur'an, meaning his revelation was not coeternal with him. Al-Ma'mun tried to unite the Sunni and Shi'a by

---

ijtihad   Independent reasoning to interpret the Qur'an.
taqlid   (literally, "emulation") Single, orthodox interpretation of the Qur'an.
shari'a   Codification of Islamic law.

Religions

FRIDAY MOSQUE

In Islam, the day of worship goes from sunset Thursday to sunset Friday. The major prayer service in each city is held at a large, central mosque known as the Friday Mosque. The leading religious figure in the city usually leads the prayers, and offers the prayers of the faithful in the name of the caliph. In modern times, in Iran the role of the Friday mosque has been taken over by Tehran University because it can hold more worshippers than the principal mosque. The prayer ceremony is used to provide guidance to the faithful on the latest political positions of the rulers of the republic.

endorsing the Eighth Imam, Ali al-Rida, as his successor. In the backlash against Mu'tazilism, however, theologians and their followers quickly overlooked al-Ma'mun's choice of successor. Instead, he was succeeded by one who repudiated his predecessor's dalliance with Aristotelian rationalism.

The Abbasids also had to deal with the rise of Sufism, which they frequently persecuted as a heresy. **Sufis** were mystics who sought a personal relationship with God and argued that God hid the true meaning of the Qur'an to all but the initiated. Probably the most famous incident of persecution involved the Sufi mystic Mansur al-Hallaj, whom the Caliph al-Mutaqdir ordered killed in 932. Filled with mystical delight at the union he felt with the divine presence within him, al-Hallaj exclaimed "Ana al-Haq," or "I am the Truth." As truth is a divine attribute, al-Hallaj was accused of blasphemy for calling himself God. Despite persecution, however, Sufism spread throughout the Middle East and Muslim world.

THE END OF THE ARAB EMPIRE

In 1258 Mongol invaders under Hulegu, grandson of Genghis Khan, conquered Baghdad and brutally ended the Abbasid dynasty. He made a pyramid of Arab skulls and ruined the irrigation systems of the region. To this day, Muslims bemoan the Mongol conquest; although they later converted to Islam they were always suspected of hypocrisy. The center of Arab cultural life was shattered just as Europe began to stir in the late Middle Ages. The Seljuks, who had been ruling the empire for two centuries as sultans—and who had reunited the Iranian, Arab, and Anatolian lands under one crown—also went into decline everywhere except in Anatolia, where they continued to press the Byzantine empire. Many believe that the caliphate died in Baghdad with the Mongol invasion; others believe it passed to the Ottomans through the Fatimids.

sufi Muslim mystic sect.

Conflicts

THE CRUSADES

The Crusades represented a short interruption in Islam's dominance of the Middle East. They consisted of a series of military campaigns over almost two centuries, from 1095 to 1291. They were Christendom's counteroffensive against the Muslim armies that had dislodged Christianity from its birthplace.

The first crusade was the only successful one. The French Pope Urban II called it into existence at a council of bishops in the French town of Clermont in 1095. Most of the participants were French or spoke French, so Middle Easterners called them Franks. Today throughout the Middle East the term for foreigner is a derivative of the term Frank: *frangi* or *ferangi*.

The First Crusade took almost five years to reach and conquer Fatimid-controlled Jerusalem, its main target. In 1099, after a five-week siege, the Crusaders took Jerusalem and slaughtered its Muslim and Jewish inhabitants. In those days, Muslims and Jews were united against the barbaric Christians. The Crusaders also took most of Anatolia from the Seljuk Turks who had conquered it from the Byzantines. They spent the next twenty-five years establishing Crusader kingdoms throughout modern Israel, Lebanon, Syria, northern Iraq, and southeastern Turkey. Salah-al-Din, better known as Saladin, a chivalrous Kurdish general, later demolished the Crusaders at the decisive Battle of Hattin in present-day northern Israel in 1187 and quickly retook most Crusader lands, including Jerusalem. The Christian control of Jerusalem lasted less than a hundred years.

The Second Crusade, led by the crowned heads of Europe, was an unmitigated disaster. Most of the army was defeated in Anatolia long before reaching Jerusalem. The Third Crusade included England's Richard the Lionheart and France's King Phillip. One story has it that before a battle Richard asked Saladin what he intended to do. Replied Saladin: "That shall be for thine eyes to see and not for thine ears to hear." While it failed to liberate Jerusalem, the Third Crusade reclaimed Cyprus for Christianity.

The Fourth Crusade degenerated into a sordid fight among Christians. The Doge of Venice agreed to provide the Crusaders with naval transport. When the Crusaders reached Venice they did not have money to pay the Venetians, so they agreed to support Venice in regaining a rebellious vassal Christian city, Zara (now Zadar on the Croatian coast), which had sought Hungarian protection. Already deflected from the goal of reclaiming Jerusalem, the Crusaders sailed to Constantinople to insure the succession of the Western-supported candidate for emperor, Alexius III. For the first time in 900 years, Constantinople was conquered and sacked—not by invading Muslims, but by Crusaders with crosses on their chests. Byzantium was irreparably weakened, and the Crusaders stole most of the treasures of Constantinople. (The horses atop St. Mark's Cathedral in Venice are from Constantinople, as are the relics of the Holy Cross in Rome.)

The Fifth Crusade passed without result, mainly because the Crusade's titular leader, Frederick II, stayed home. When the crusade failed, the pope excommunicated him. Frederick then sailed for the Holy Land, but without papal support. His Sixth Crusade managed to regain Jerusalem through diplomatic negotiations with the ruler of Egypt, the late Salah-al-Din's brother, al-'Adil. Because Frederick achieved this victory while still excommunicated, it led to internecine rivalry among the Christians between supporters of the Church and supporters of Frederick. Jerusalem remained in Christian hands for ten years, as specified by the truce; it then reverted back to the Muslims.

The Seventh Crusade, led by King Louis IX of France, aimed at Cairo instead of Jerusalem. Muslim armies captured the French king, queen, and entire court and held them for ransom. The crusader army was either defeated on the battlefield or executed in captivity. The Eighth and final Crusade did not even head for the Levant but wasted its effort in North Africa.

Left to their own devices and divided by foolish rivalries, the Crusader states in the Levant fell one by one. The Mamluks captured Tyre (present-day Lebanon) in 1291 and drove the last crusaders from Asia. Once again the Holy Land was wholly Muslim.

What can be said of the Crusades? In the West, the movement soon passed into mythology and history books and was largely forgotten. Today in the West, a crusade means to fight for a noble cause, such as a crusade for literacy or to eliminate polio. President George W. Bush called for a "crusade" against terrorism.

Most of the Middle East was horrified at that word; they have not forgotten their two-hundred-year war with Christians. Muslims had learned several lessons from the Crusades: that Christendom in its ignorance opposed the true faith (Islam); that Christians sought to steal Muslim lands and establish military bases on them (never mind that the lands were those which Muslims earlier stole from Christians); and that, contrary to Muslim teachings of tolerance toward other religions, when the Christian armies captured a city they put all Muslims and Jews to the sword. To support this latter point, they often point to Salah-al-Din's behavior when he reconquered Jerusalem: Instead of killing the Christians, he merely sold them into slavery. With these lessons, and with the Arab compression of history into the recent past, the president's words provoked demonstrations in the Middle East. Muslims did not hear an invitation to join a noble cause; they heard a declaration of war on Islam—a war that would result in the occupation of Muslim lands and the death of the Muslim inhabitants.

Ruins of a crusader castle, one of many, could be close to a thousand years old. A nearby kibbutz listed small farm animals in the center as "bears." Secular kibbutzniks cared nothing for the Jewish ban on pork. (*Michael Roskin*)

Religions

THE VARIETIES OF SHI'ISM

Throughout this volume we use the term Shi'a to refer to the branch of Islam that is in the majority in Iran, Iraq, Bahrain, and in Southern Lebanon. This movement is actually more properly referred to as Ithna'ashari Shi'a, or Twelver Shi'ism. The adherents of this religious interpretation claim that Muhammad was succeeded by twelve leaders, or imams. In fact, there have been several Shi'a movements. They are differentiated by how many imams the believers accept. Two groups that still have adherents today are the Zaydis and the Ismailis.

The Zaydis follow the teachings of the son of the Fourth Imam, Zayd bin Ali Zayn al-Abadin. Zayd preached that any descendent of the Prophet, provided he has the ability to rule, is entitled to be the imam of the people. There are few Zaydis left, and they are found predominantly in the highlands of Yemen.

Twelver Shi'a believe that the Sixth Imam, Ja'afar al-Sadiq, had two children: Ismail and Musa al-Kazim. Since Ismail died before Ja'afar, they accept that the younger one, Musa, became the Seventh Imam. The Ismailis disagree, and hold that since Ismail was the eldest son, the Imamate passed through him to his son Muhammad, whom they also identify as the **Mahdi**. There are still a number of Ismailis today, in India. Their head is the international philanthropist and playboy, the Agha Khan.

THE FATIMIDS

The Fatimids were Ismaili Shi'a and the founders of a dynasty that claimed direct descent from the Prophet through his daughter Fatima and husband Ali. For this reason, when the Abbasids began to lose their power in the eighth century, the Fatimids claimed that they were the rightful caliphs of Islam. The Fatimids ruled from Cairo, and they reigned over the ancient lands of Egypt. They built numerous mosques in Cairo, and presided over a major merchant kingdom.

THE MAMLUKS

In 1171 Saladin, liberator of Jerusalem, conquered the Fatimids in Cairo. He founded the Ayyubid dynasty that ruled in Egypt and the former Crusader lands until the mid-thirteenth century. To keep power in a hostile territory, the Ayyubids imported military slaves that would be loyal to the dynasty and that would have no local ties. These military slaves, or **Mamluks**, eventually overthrew the Ayyubids and ruled in Egypt from 1250–1517.

Mahdi   The Rightly Guided One, missing imam some Muslims, especially Shi'a, believe will return at the end of the world.

Mamluk   Arabic for "slave"; Muslim Egyptian dynasty that originated in the army's corps of converted Caucasian slaves.

R⋮ *Religions*

IBN TAYMIYAH

The wars against the Mongols gave rise to one of the most influential political thinkers among Islamic fundamentalists today, ibn Taymiyah. An Iraqi scholar from the Hanbali school of Islam, ibn Taymiyah lived in Damascus as a refugee from the Mongol invasions. When the Mongols caught up with him there, he led the resistance from 1299 to 1304. By this time, Mongols had been in Islamic lands for decades and had converted to Islam. Ibn Taymiyah was faced with the problem of justifying fighting a defensive war against these Muslim invaders, given Qur'anic prohibitions against a Muslim killing another Muslim.

He devised a theory that, even though they said they were Muslims, the Mongols were not true Muslims because their goal was to rule via Mongol law instead of via the Shari'a. Since it was the desire of all Muslims to implement Shari'a, and the Mongols did not implement Shari'a, then the Mongols were hypocrites and could be killed as unbelievers. Any fundamentalist group that advocates killing heads of Islamic states uses the same logic today.

When followers of the blind Shaykh Omar Abdul Rahman assassinated Egyptian President Anwar Sadat in October 1981, they left behind a manifesto justifying their actions entitled "The Forgotten Duty" in which they quoted the writings of ibn Taymiyah at length. Almost a decade later, one of the authors visited Algeria, when it appeared that the local Islamic political party was about to take power. The number-one, best-selling author in every bookstore was ibn Taymiyah. Religion has staying power.

In many ways, the Mamluks saved civilization. After the Mongols destroyed Baghdad, their armies continued to rape and pillage deep into the Arab heartland. The Mamluks sent an army to meet the Mongols in Syria and blunted the Mongol advance. Three centuries later the Ottomans defeated the Mamluks and claimed the caliphate for their own chief.

IRANIAN DYNASTIES

Iran's history throughout this period was one of foreign conquest. The pre-Islamic Sassanids fought Byzantium to a standstill, but the battles drained Iranian strength. So, when the Arab armies invaded Iran in 636, the Sassanid armies fell. The last battle was in 641, the empire crumbled, and Iran became part of the Islamic caliphate.

When the Abbasids moved their capital to nearby Baghdad, Iran acquired considerable influence. The palace was built along Iranian lines, and Iranian courtiers staffed it. Abbasid strength came from the Persian lands to the east rather than the Arab lands of the west. It was a Persian tribe, the Buyids, who deposed the Abbasid caliph of temporal authority in the tenth century. Iran, like the Abbasids, was next invaded by the Seljuk Turks. Between 1055 and 1501, Iran would be divided between Turkish, Mongol, and native families who ruled various parts of the territory.

 *Cultures*

FERDOWSI: NATIONALIST POET

Illustrating the sense of Iranian difference was a new, literary form of Persian that replaced the language of the Zoroastrian Magi. The preeminent scholar of tenth-century Persia, Ferdowsi, composed the *Shahnameh*, a compilation of Persian history and mythology stretching back to the dawn of time. In sixty thousand couplets, Ferdowsi supposedly used less than one hundred Arabic words as he sought to use the new Persian language to the fullest. For a thousand years, Ferdowsi's poem has been an inspiration to Persian nationalists. Using the Persian language to describe Persian themes three hundred years after the Arab invasion, Ferdowsi is seen as a symbol of Iran's ability to persevere despite being conquered by foreigners.

Less well known is the early role Ferdowsi played as a symbol of protest after the 1979 Iranian Revolution. Because he had not used Arabic, the language of the Qur'an, monarchists and anti-clerics embraced Ferdowsi as a symbol of secularism.

CONCLUSIONS

In one form or another, Muslim rulers have held sway in the Middle East from the death of Muhammad until today. According to theologians, the goal of a Muslim ruler is to guide the people under his care to salvation, through his administration of Shari'a law. The most perfect manifestation of this law are the practices of Muhammad as ruler of Medina and later of Mecca.

Despite the myth that the Four Rightly Guided Caliphs ruled over a united Islamic kingdom guided by the Prophet's teachings, in reality the caliphate has been wracked with division from the very beginning. Eventually, the umma divided into several Muslim kingdoms, all claiming to follow the rightful successor to the Prophet. After the dreadful Mongol invasions, the lands of Islam were thrown into chaos. Only a slave army staved off total disaster.

FURTHER REFERENCE

Black, Antony. *The History of Islamic Political Thought*. New York: Routledge, 2001.

Eaton, Charles Le Gai. *Islam and the Destiny of Man*. Albany, NY: SUNY Press, 1985.

Hourani, Albert. *A History of the Arab Peoples*. Cambridge, MA: Harvard University Press, 1991.

Jansen, Johannes J. G. *The Neglected Duty*. New York: MacMillan, 1986.

Nafziger, George F., and Mark W. Walton. *Islam at War: A History*. Westport, CT: Praeger, 2003.

Riley-Smith, Jonathan. *The Crusades: A Short History*. New Haven, CT: Yale University Press, 1987.

Rosenwein, Barbara H. *A Short History of the Middle Ages*. Peterborough, Ont.: Broadview, 2002.

Saunders, J. J. *A History of Medieval Islam*, New York: Routledge, 1996.

Watt, W. Montgomery. *Islamic Political Thought*. Edinburgh: Edinburgh University Press, 1987.

The Ottoman Empire

Points to Ponder

- Can Muslims and non-Muslims live in peace under a single government?
- Why is the culture of the Middle East so similar across national boundaries?
- What are the causes of the fall of the Ottoman Empire?
- What impeded reform of the Ottoman Empire?
- Why did an Ottoman nationalism not develop?
- Are there parallels between the Ottoman decline and today's Middle East?

THE OTTOMANS

The Ottoman Empire was the last Islamic empire and caliphate. Unlike the Arab Umayyads and Abbasids, the Ottomans were Turks. Nonetheless, Muslims worldwide respected the Turkish sultan in his role of caliph. When the caliphate was abolished (by Atatürk in 1924), Muslims felt despair and humiliation. Some, such as Osama bin Laden, still vow to restore an Islamic empire and caliphate. Accordingly, although little-studied in American schools, the Ottoman Empire is important both for what it did and for what it left behind.

At the same time the Moors were slowly being pushed out of Iberia, two Mediterranean peninsulas to the east a new Muslim force was pushing into Europe, the **Ottomans**, a subtribe of the Oguz Turks, the same Turkish tribe that was the progenitor of the Seljuks. Originally, the Seljuks were rulers while the Ottomans were the warriors who protected the land of Islam from the remnants of the Byzantine Empire. The Mongols destroyed the Seljuks as a ruling force in 1293. After their

---

Ottoman   Turkish tribe and later empire in Balkans and Middle East.

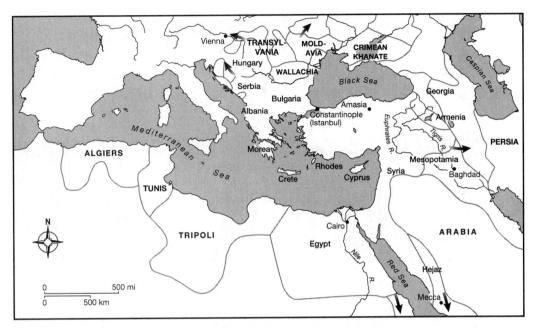

The Ottoman Empire at Its Height, 1683

victory, elements of the Mongols took over most of Iran and ruled it as the Ilkhanid dynasty. Small pockets of Turks remained free of the Mongol yoke. One of these pockets of resistance was in and around the town of Bursa, across the **Marmara** Sea from Constantinople. Freed of Seljuk overlordship by the Mongols, Osman and his family ruled Bursa as a small, independent principality. (Osman, from whom the dynasty derives its name, is the father of the dynasty. It became known as Ottoman in the West due to a mispronunciation of Osman's name.)

Osman and his successors initially bypassed Constantinople and conquered the **Balkans**. The Ottomans beat the Bulgars in 1361 and then beat the Serbian army at Kosovo Polje ("Field of Blackbirds") in 1389, a battle that killed both commanders. This opened the way for the Turks to surge into Hungary's rich Pannonian basin and even on to Vienna, which they besieged twice, in 1529 and again in 1683. All Europe trembled until Polish cavalry under Jan Sobieski drove the Turks back from Vienna in 1683. That was the high-water mark for the Turks in Europe. Thereafter, they were slowly pushed back. It is important to remember that the Ottomans were a Balkan empire before they expanded over the Middle East in the early sixteenth century.

Marmara   Sea between Bosphorus and Dardanelles separating Europe from Asia Minor.
Balkan   Turkish for "mountain"; large peninsula of Southeast Europe that includes Greece, Bulgaria, and Serbia.

Worshippers in the Blue Mosque (also known as the Sultan Ahmet Mosque) of Istanbul, a beautiful early-seventeenth-century edifice in use today. (Michael Roskin)

Before they tried Vienna, with all the Balkans as their empire, the Ottomans had returned to crack open the walls of Constantinople in 1453 with a new weapon, the cannon, enabling Mehmet the Conqueror's triumphal entry into the city they renamed Istanbul. Over the next four and a half centuries, the Ottoman Empire rose to world power but then sunk so low that in 1853 the Russian tsar called it the "sick man of Europe." At its height, the empire stretched from the gates of Vienna in Europe, to Azerbaijan in Asia; it controlled the entire coast of North Africa and all the Arab lands, including the east and west coasts of the Arabian peninsula (but not the untamed center).

The main impact of the Ottoman Empire was probably the protection of the Islamic, Middle Eastern culture that is today spread so uniformly from Morocco to Persia. Before the Ottomans recaptured the Arab lands, they had started to drift apart. There were multiple claims to the caliphate, multiple local rulers, and multiple accommodations with local conditions. The umma had never been so weak. Within fifty years of the Ottoman capture of Constantinople, specifically, in 1492, Muslims were ejected from the Iberian peninsula. Today, while there are Arab influences on Spanish culture, Ottoman culture is very much alive in the foods, clothing, cultural artifacts, and manners of every corner of the Middle East and, to a lesser extent, of the Balkans.

The Ottomans were relatively tolerant of Christians and Jews, who were accorded dhimmi status and protection as "People of the Book." The Turks allowed each religious and ethnic group to rule themselves. Thus, there were Muslim courts, Christian courts, and Jewish courts. Unlike modern America, in the Middle East you stay in whatever ethnic and religious group you are born into. Bloodlines, not free choice, define who you are. Accordingly, under the Ottomans you had to obey the laws of your people and be judged in their law courts. A Muslim could be found guilty of a crime for an action that would be lawful for a Christian, or vice versa. This was known as the **millet** system.

THE JANISSARIES

The center of Mehmet the Conqueror's army was the **Janissary** corps. The Janissaries were mostly Christian boys collected as "blood tax" every few years from the Balkans to serve as slaves in the Sultan's service. Converted to Islam, they were trained from youth to be fighters. This is one reason there is a great deal of Balkan blood among today's Turks. Atatürk himself was of Balkan descent. For centuries, the Sultans used the Janissaries as an all-purpose paramilitary police to run the vast empire. As property of the Sultan, they had no rights. To prevent corruption and nepotism, they could not even marry, as Janissaries might then give legitimate wives and children official and monetary favors. When they were too old to fight, they were released from their service, but new boys were always acquired for the Janissaries from the latest Christian territory the Ottomans captured.

From an early time, the Janissaries wielded significant power at the court, since they controlled much of the weaponry of the empire. Janissaries frequently threw their weight behind competing claimants to the throne, a pattern called **praetorianism**. Some rose to become the Sultan's **viziers**, the day-to-day administrators of the empire. Later, the Janissaries received permission to marry and have legitimate children, who could then inherit their fathers' lands and titles. Sure enough, corruption immediately set in. The Janissaries ceased being a true fighting force and just another part of the ramshackle Ottoman regime.

When Mehmet died, the Janissaries decided which of his children and grandchildren became Sultan. In 1520, Mehmet's great grandson assumed the throne. Crowned Sulayman (often spelled Suleiman) I, his subjects called him Sulayman the Lawgiver because he codified the laws and imperial proclamations that were enforced in the empire. As these laws were written in Arabic script, his lawgiving stature was relatively unknown in the West, who knew him as Sulayman the Magnificent. His reign was the height of the Ottoman Empire.

---

millet   In Ottoman times an ethnic community; in modern Turkish a nation.
Janissary   (from Turkish *yeniceri*, "new soldier") Elite military units of the Ottoman Empire.
praetorianism   After Rome's Praetorian Guard; military takeover of or influence in government.
vizier   Ottoman Sultan's appointed minister.

Key Concepts

PRAETORIANISM

As Rome turned from republic to empire, its emperors appointed a special corps as imperial bodyguards, the Praetorian Guard, which soon became so powerful it could make or break emperors. The guardians took over what they were supposed to be guarding. In modern usage, praetorianism indicates a situation of political breakdown in which no one plays by the rules and all manner of political forces try to grab power by rigged elections, student demonstrations, and nationwide strikes. In this chaos, the military become convinced that they are the only ones who can save the country, so they seize power by military coup. Other groups can sometimes pull coups—radical parties such as Mussolini's Fascists or Muslim fundamentalists as in Iran—but usually the military is the best organized and armed to take over. Praetorianism does not necessarily indicate headstrong or power-mad generals but rather the collapse of political institutions.

Praetorianism became common in Latin America, where weak institutions could not handle social and political stress, so the army stepped in repeatedly. Twentieth-century Europe saw coups in Spain, Portugal, Poland, Greece, and an attempt in France in 1958. Praetorianism arrived in the Middle East with the Ottoman Empire and the military influences on its politics, earlier the Janissaries and later the Young Turks. The Turkish Republic after World War II experienced two outright coups and two additional episodes of strong military influence on the civilian government. Pakistan has had several coups—all designed to save the country from foolish or corrupt elected politicians—and is now ruled by a general. Egypt had one coup in 1952 and power stayed in the hands of a succession of generals. Syria had several coups; its current ruler is the son of an officer who led a coup. The simplest way to explain a coup—perhaps too simple—is that when chaos breaks out, the generals take over.

Sulayman expanded the empire to the west, besieging Vienna in 1529. His desire to increase his holdings derived from several factors: to spread the Muslim faith, to emulate the conquerors of old, and—most of all—to appease the Janissaries with booty from military campaigns. The Viennese withstood a Turkish siege for almost three weeks, after which Sulayman withdrew his forces and returned to Istanbul.

THE REIGN OF SULAYMAN

Although stopped at Vienna from entering the heart of Europe, Sulayman ruled over a kingdom that included the Balkans and most of the Middle East and made the Mediterranean a Turkish lake. Through a series of naval victories, he eliminated Venice's merchant power that had dominated the sea for hundreds of years. His great rival was Charles, the Holy Roman Emperor of Spain and Austria. To hold Charles at bay, he allied himself with the French king, Ferdinand I. It was in making the alliance that Sulayman made his greatest mistake: He granted the French the equivalent of "most favored nation" status. French merchants paid the same taxes on their goods as their Muslim counterparts, while other European merchants paid much higher rates. The treaty of alliance also recognized the

Key Concepts

CAPITULATIONS

The Ottoman government first capitulated to French demands and then to those of other Europeans. The capitulations were signs of growing European strength and Ottoman weakness. No government gives foreigners so many advantages if they can help it. The capitulations did not cause a great burden to the Ottoman government in the sixteenth century, but other European powers used the French precedent to demand similar treatment in the seventeenth to nineteenth centuries. By the time of the fall of the Ottoman Empire, foreigners paid little or no taxes, had immunity from prosecution, and received trade terms from the government that were more favorable than the terms a typical Ottoman subject could get.

The capitulations also stipulated that Ottoman subjects who worked for foreign consulates and trading companies as translators received the same rights as foreigners. This became known as the **dragoman** system, a corruption of the Turkish word for "translator," *turcoman*. Being a translator thus was a road to great wealth and power, and the inequalities in treatment between translators—usually Greek Christians—and the common Muslim Ottoman caused great resentment.

---

jurisdiction of French consular courts over French citizens. Sulayman was the first Middle Eastern ruler to grant **capitulations** to European powers.

In the East, Sulayman's forces fought three campaigns against the Persians, liberating Baghdad from Shi'a control. Finally, in 1555, he signed a peace treaty with the Persians that established the Iranian western border basically where it is today. Sulayman died in 1566, preparing to fight his enemies on a Hungarian battlefield.

OTTOMAN SUCCESSION

Ottoman forces continued to consolidate their hold on the Mediterranean, conquering the island of Cyprus in the years 1570–1572. This caused Venice, Spain, and the Papal States to join forces and launch a combined naval force against the Turks. The two navies met off Greece near the Gulf of Lepanto in late 1571, and the European forces ultimately triumphed. Sulayman had been stopped on land at Vienna; his son was stopped on the sea at Lepanto. Europe remained Christian and outside of Ottoman control. Some peg Lepanto as the turning point for Ottoman power, although Istanbul dismissed it as a minor setback.

The Ottoman Sultans long practiced fratricide to eliminate claimants to the throne. Usually within twenty-four hours of a coronation, the new Sultan would order all his brothers killed. But in 1595, the newly crowned Mehmet III exceeded

---

dragoman   Privileged translator in Ottoman Empire.
capitulation   From Latin *capitula*, chapters; granting of special rights and privileges to Europeans, usually including extraterritoriality (the right to be tried in the courts of one's own country).

W : *Women of the Middle East*

HURREN

Hurren, known in the West as Roxelana, daughter of a Ukrainian priest, became a concubine to Sulayman. She so entranced the monarch that he married her—something no Ottoman Sultan had ever done with a concubine. As Sulayman aged, he turned to his **Grand Vizier** for guidance. This gentleman was Sulayman's son-in-law, married to his daughter by Hurren. It was Hurren who had convinced Sulayman to appoint the man to the post, and Hurren controlled much of the empire through the Grand Vizier. She then convinced Sulayman that his eldest son, borne by another concubine, was plotting to take the throne from the Emperor. Sulayman killed the young man, clearing the path for Hurren's son, Selim the Drunkard, to be crowned emperor on Sulayman's death. For all her scheming, Hurren died before Sulayman, so she did not live to see her son's victory. She is buried next to Sulayman behind his memorial mosque, the Sulaymaniyeh, on the banks of the Golden Horn in Istanbul.

all bounds. He had his nineteen brothers strangled to death, and he threw six pregnant girls from his father's harem into the Bosphorus. The people were outraged at the abuse; from that time on, princes were confined to a "golden cage." Prisoners for life within the harem, they lived a life of unsurpassed luxury.

While more humane on the individual level, it ultimately weakened the Ottoman Empire by leaving a steady supply of rivals for the throne to be manipulated by the Janissaries. And by the time one of these caged princes were placed on the throne, they often knew nothing of the outside world and wanted nothing except to continue the debauched life they had led in the harem. They were easy to manipulate for anyone who wanted to be the power behind the throne, and they were unable to lead or defend Ottoman territories when they came under attack. The following centuries witnessed much bloodshed in the palace, not by command of the Sultan, but by command of the Grand Vizier and/or the Janissaries of various sultans.

ECONOMIC DECLINE

As the Ottoman Empire's growth stagnated and the royal house grew increasingly enfeebled, European merchants discovered America and pioneered routes to the Orient around Africa. This allowed the great trading empires of England and Holland to bypass the ancient, land-based trade routes of the Middle East, precipitating a long economic decline throughout the Ottoman Empire. Europeans mastered the new techniques of war while their countries' economies boomed. Unknown to the Turks, their empire had already entered into a long eclipse.

grand vizier   Sultan's prime minister.

Key Concepts

LOGISTICS

Why could the Ottomans not expand beyond Vienna? Or Napoleon not conquer Russia? The answer: **logistics**. In the Ottoman case, the army was bivouacked in Istanbul. The infantry could not carry enough food with them for their own needs, and the cavalry had the added burden of providing feed for the horses. The army could only march in the summer months, when it could forage for food among the peasants and the horses could find grass. They could only conquer lands as far away as they could travel and return to Istanbul before the end of the growing season. Thus, when Vienna's walls remained standing on October 14, 1529, Sulayman ordered a withdrawal so his army could return to safety before they exhausted their supplies. We will see logistics play a decisive role in other wars.

THE SICK MAN OF EUROPE

The Ottomans suffered a series of military defeats, beginning at the end of the seventeenth century. Beaten by the Austrian Habsburgs, the Ottomans signed the Treaty of Karlowitz in 1699 and surrendered Slavonia, Transylvania, and a large section of Hungary to the Habsburgs. Then the Ottomans lost at the hands of the Russians. Peter the Great and Catherine the Great were determined to expand southward until Russia had a warm water port—one that did not freeze over in winter—and the Ottoman Empire was in the way. These wars continued in one form or another for two centuries (see box on page 64). Russia's great power designs were usually thwarted through the intervention of France, Great Britain, and/or the Austro-Hungarian Empire. In the great game of international politics, however, each time Russia's ambitions were thwarted, it was usually at the expense of the Ottoman Empire.

MILITARY REFORM

In 1805 Sultan Selim III reviewed the military record of the Janissaries and found it lacking. The Janissaries had considerable power because of their control of the arms of the Empire. In addition, they were allied with the Bektasi Sufi order, a powerful and wealthy religious group with direct lines into the palace. The Sultan tried to replace the Janissaries with a "New Army" of infantry and artillery organized along European lines. He also drafted members of the Janissaries into this new army. Fearing a threat to their position, the Janissaries allied with provincial notables and clerical leaders and revolted. They destroyed the New Army and replaced Selim III with his cousin, Mustafa IV.

---

logistics   The supplying of an army.

 *Conflicts*

VENDETTA ON THE BLACK SEA

In Chapter 6 we will consider the long series Arab-Israeli wars. But another series of "vendetta wars" happened much earlier: the long struggle between Russians and Turks over mastery of the Black Sea. For two centuries (1678 to 1878), Tsarist Russia and Ottoman Turkey fought each other in ten wars. By 1566 the Turks nearly surrounded the Black Sea, but by 1812 they had lost its whole northern coast to Russia. They fought for one last time in World War I. There were several underlying causes of these Russo-Turkish wars, and they help us understand the depth and durability of the Arab-Israeli wars.

Religion played a role, although it was rarely the whole cause. When the Turks conquered Constantinople in 1453 and renamed it Istanbul, they also ended the city's importance as the center of Eastern Orthodox Christianity. While Constantinople never had the status that Rome did in Western Christianity, it was still the seat of Eastern Christendom and the center of its religious scholarship. The monks Cyril and Methodius from Constantinople first converted the Slavic peoples to Christianity in the sixth century A.D. Operating out of churches and monasteries on the shores of Lake Ohrid in present-day Macedonia, they taught the newly arriving (from the north) Slavic tribes Scripture, using the Greek alphabet to transcribe it into Old Church Slavonic. This is why the Cyrillic alphabet is used today in Orthodox Slavic countries such as Russia, Ukraine, Bulgaria, and Serbia. Aiding their millions of coreligionists still under Ottoman rule and recovering Constantinople gave Russians a sort of crusader mentality.

Culturally, the Eastern Orthodox peoples conquered by the Turks disliked being ruled—sometimes harshly—by strange people who spoke a strange language. Many Turkish words made their way into Serbian, especially in Bosnia, where heretical Christians known as Bogomils converted to Islam under the Turks. Their descendants are today's Bosnian Muslims and explain the blond, blue-eyed Muslims in Bosnia today. The Orthodox Serbs, on the other hand, over five centuries of Ottoman rule, always dreamed of getting rid of their Turkish overseers. To rob Turks as a *haiduk* ("bandit") was a respected profession in Montenegro, which boasted that the Ottomans had never conquered it. Economically, the Ottomans misruled the Balkans, squeezing them for taxes, stifling industry, and generally keeping them impoverished.

Geography was an important reason for the long feud. Great rivers—the Danube, Volga, and Don—flow into the Black Sea but could not become commercial highways like West Europe's Rhine because for centuries the Black Sea was a Turkish lake. Whoever controls the Turkish Straits controls the Black Sea. That is why Roman Emperor Constantine chose the site for the city of his name, literally, "Constantine's city." With the Ottomans on both sides of the straits, Russian sea traffic could come and go only as the Turks wished; they could tax the traffic or block it altogether. Russian warships could be bottled up in the Black Sea, but friendly warships (such as British and French during the Crimean War of the 1850s) could be let in to attack Russia's soft underbelly. Tsars dreamed of taking Istanbul and the straits to give Russia this vital maritime outlet to the world, although they often cloaked their campaigns with religious goals. After the Communists took over Russia, they had the same dream, for, as Stalin's Foreign Minister Vyacheslav Molotov laconically noted, "A ship passing from the Mediterranean to the Black Sea must traverse the Straits whether the flag on its stern is tsarist or Soviet."

And not to be underrated as a cause is sheer human cussedness, the profound desire to beat the enemy. As an American philosopher noted, "Winning is everything." Sometimes the original or underlying causes are forgotten; all the participants remember is that the enemy is still out there, gloating, and attempting to crush you. Get him or he'll get you. Whatever the causes of the long Russo-Turkish fight, they do not give one grounds for optimism in the Arab-Israeli fight. They teach us, rather, that wars can last for centuries. And each of the Russo-Turkish wars ended in a peace treaty.

 *Cultures*

MULLAH NASREDDIN

Mullah Nasreddin, or Nasreddin Hoca, is a folk figure throughout much of the Middle East. His tales always have a teaching point. The Nasreddin stories always feature the Mullah, a simple country prayer leader, in a ridiculous situation that allows the reader to laugh at himself and learn.

One day in Ramadan (a month of daytime fasting for Muslims), Mullah Nasreddin was very hungry. He forgot it was Ramadan and started to enjoy his breakfast. Neighbors reported him to the Sultan, and he was arrested for breaking Islamic law, the Shari'a. Languishing in his jail cell, he looked out through the prison bars to observe a man drinking wine in broad daylight. Astounded, Mullah Nasreddin asked the man if he was not afraid of arrest. The man replied that, as a Christian, it was lawful for him to drink during Ramadan, even to drink wine, forbidden to Muslims in the Qur'an. "Ah," replied the mullah longingly. "Blessed are you to belong to an accursed race."

Alcohol consumption was not unknown among the Turks. The Ottomans, having run the Balkans as part of their empire for centuries, picked up their Christian Slavic subjects' taste for alcohol and some imbibed but usually kept quiet about it. Kemal Atatürk favored strong drink. In the Middle East and Balkans you can today order *arak, raki,* or *rakia,* and the waiter will know what you mean: brandy.

Mahmut II replaced Mustafa IV in 1807 and, alarmed at the decline in the Janissaries' fighting abilities, asked the units to send a handful of men for Western training. Confident in their position, the Janissaries pursued their usual strategy of ignoring the Sultan's commands. Mahmut had anticipated this reaction, however, and he ordered his artillery units to fire on the Janissaries' barracks, killing many. By 1826, Mahmut abolished the Janissaries, freeing the Sultanate from their grasp. Be careful when you set up an elite group; they may end up running you.

THE TANZIMAT

The reforms of the Turkish government known as the **Tanzimat** began in 1839. The Sultan reorganized the army and gave it more modern equipment. Troops organized in the provinces reported to Istanbul instead of to provincial governors. A reserve force and gendarmerie for keeping peace in the countryside were created. The Sultan introduced (from the Code Napoléon) European family, commercial, and maritime law, reducing the importance of the Shari'a and its clerical protectors. For the first time, non-Muslims had equal status with Muslims. Christians could now serve in the army, own land, and petition the judiciary on the same terms as a Muslim adversary. These rights were granted in the Noble Edict of Gulhane in 1839, and confirmed by the Imperial Edict of 1856.

Tanzimat (Turkish "reorganization") 1839–1876 Turkish reforms.

K Key Concepts

A CHRONOLOGY OF OTTOMAN PUSHBACK

Europe overlaps with the Middle East in the Balkans. The connecting link: the Ottoman Empire, which occupied much of the Balkans for five centuries, giving the colorful region some of the Middle East's foods, architecture, culture, attitudes, and corruption. Since the second siege of Vienna in 1683, the Ottoman Empire steadily lost territory in the Balkans. In a series of wars, the Habsburgs, who ruled Austria from 1278 to 1918 (and Spain from 1516 to 1700) pushed back the Turks in Hungary (including Transylvania), Slovenia, Croatia, and Bosnia. Meanwhile, the Russians pushed the Turks out of Ukraine, Crimea, Romania, and Bulgaria. Key dates are as follows:

1774—Treaty of Kucuk Kaynarci (sometimes spelled Kuchuk Kainarji) gives Crimea and Bessarabia independence and Russia a port on the Black Sea. Russia also gets the right to intervene in the affairs of the Empire to protect the rights of Christians. Russia then annexes the Crimea in 1783.

1798—Napoleon invades Egypt.

1799—Napoleon invades Palestine and Syria.

1802—Napoleon driven out of Egypt by a Turkish-English force led by the Albanian general Muhammad Ali. The Sultan agrees to let him rule Egypt.

1803—Britain begins making treaties with Persian Gulf states.

1829—Treaty of Edirne. Russia gains the mouth of the Danube.

1830—Serbia granted autonomy. France invades the beylik (Ottoman province) of Algeria, nominally part of the Ottoman Empire. At first the French merely want to crush piracy but stay and turn Algeria into a French colony.

1831—Muhammad Ali, Pasha of Egypt and titular vassal of the Empire, invades Syria.

1832—Greece recognized as independent.

1840—Treaty of London. Syria is restored to the Empire, but Muhammad Ali and his heirs are recognized as hereditary rulers of Egypt.

1853–1856—Crimean War. No net gain or loss for the Empire.

1861—Mount Lebanon obtains autonomy.

1878—Russian forces push to the gates of Istanbul and force the Treaty of San Stefano on the Ottoman Empire. In it, Romania, Serbia, and Montenegro obtain their independence. An enlarged Bulgaria under a Russian prince is awarded autonomy, as is Bosnia and Herzegovina. Some eastern Anatolian cities are ceded to the Russians.

1878—Treaty of Berlin tones down some of the Russian gains of the Treaty of San Stefano. Romania, Serbia, and Montenegro retain their independence. The Austrian-Hungarian Empire occupies Bosnia and Herzegovina. Greece obtains some border adjustments. Bulgaria is reduced in size, divided into two provinces, ruled by princes appointed by the Sultan.

1881—France invades the beylik of Tunisia.

1897—Greece aids an uprising on Crete. The Ottomans suppress it but grant the island autonomy.

1908—Austria-Hungary annexes Bosnia and Herzegovina over Serb protests. This plants the seed that started World War I.

1912—Treaty of Ouchy. Italy invades Libya, and the Ottoman Empire cedes it to Italy.

1912–1913—First and Second Balkan Wars. The empire loses, retaining only eastern Thrace in Europe.

By the time World War I started in 1914, the Ottoman Empire retained of its formerly vast holdings only the Fertile Crescent and would soon lose that.

Many opposed such reforms. In 1859, midlevel officers led their troops into the Kuleli incident, an attempted coup. When this failed, a group of Istanbul-based intellectuals calling themselves the Young Ottomans proposed the establishment of a parliament as a way of reuniting the empire and reestablishing Muslim law.

In 1876, Sultan Abdul Aziz attempted to curry British favor by announcing an Ottoman constitution. Conservative theology students rioted, and Abdul Aziz stepped down. Later in the same year, Abdul Hamid II assumed the throne, and asserted his claim to the caliphate of all Islam. Such a conservative move endeared the new Sultan to those who had opposed the Tanzimat, because their position had been threatened by the improved status of Christians. To meet the demands for a parliament, Abdul Hamid II convened the institution in 1877, but dissolved it in 1878, using war with Russia as an excuse.

Meanwhile, the Ottoman Empire went bankrupt. The Sultans traditionally had relied on tax revenues for money, but in 1854 they began borrowing from Europe. At first, they were able to pay back the loans on schedule, but in 1873, amidst a world financial crisis, the Sultan's tax revenues dropped, and by 1881 the empire was bankrupt. In December of that year, in order to receive permission to continue borrowing, he turned over his treasury to the Ottoman Public Debt Authority, a new government department that was staffed and controlled by the European creditors.

Ottoman subjects were outraged at the latest humiliation. They had always been taught to judge the Europeans as inferiors, but now they had equal rights. The Empire was always at war and losing territory to culturally inferior alien powers. Now representatives of these same powers collected taxes. The Ottoman Empire, in both its internal and external weakness, was paying the price for centuries of cultural, intellectual, and economic stagnation.

THE COMMITTEE OF UNION AND PROGRESS

Abdul Hamid II did not trust the military, several of whose leaders trained in the West. He refused to allow the military to modernize, to hold live-fire exercises, or the navy to leave port. He quickly lost any support he may have had in the officers' corps.

In 1889, students of the Imperial Military Medical School formed a secret revolutionary society, the Ottoman Union Society. In 1896, this group planned a coup d'etat, but it was cut short when one of the plotters drunkenly revealed the plans to a senior officer the night before the coup. To escape arrest, many of the society escaped to Paris where they formed the Committee of Union and Progress (CUP), popularly known as the **Young Turks**. In 1907, dissident members of the military in the province of Salonika made contact with Paris, and assumed the CUP mantle. This new group was led by a postal clerk (Mehmet Talat), a major (Ahmet Cemal), and a captain (Enver).

Young Turks   Turn-of-twentieth-century reform movement of Ottoman officers.

The group staged an armed rebellion in 1908 known as the Young Turk Revolution. They called for a restoration of the Constitution of 1906. To maintain the peace, the Sultan agreed to their demands. The CUP then established itself as a guardian council to oversee the actions of the Sultan and his ministers. The CUP won a majority of seats in the new parliament, and the military leadership of the movement used its parliamentary base to control the government.

Within nine months, a countermovement in the military tried to seize power. Calling themselves the Muhammadan Union, a group of officers allied with minor clerics and Sufi shaykhs organized a march on parliament to demand the constitution be abrogated and to return Christians to their status as *dhimmi*. CUP legislators went into hiding.

The real leadership of the CUP, however, was not in Istanbul but in Salonika. They dispatched a relief force that freed the capital. Suspecting that the Sultan instigated the rebellion, the parliament deposed Abdul Hamid in favor of his brother, Mehmet V. The CUP regained power and ultimately led the Empire into the Great War on the side of their ally, Germany.

World War I

World War I in the Middle East was chiefly a British affair. Seeking to guard their "imperial lifeline" and aware of Iraq's oil potential, Britain sent troops from India to fight up the Tigris and Euphrates and Australian and New Zealand forces to Egypt. Britain suffered some reverses, but overall things went badly for the Ottomans, with every general but one suffering military defeats. That one exception was Mustafa Kemal, an Ottoman general who prevented British and Anzac troops from seizing the Gallipoli peninsula, Winston Churchill's bright idea that turned into a catastrophe. The British, pinned down under withering fire, never made it more than a few miles inland. True, if Britain had succeeded in taking this strategic finger of land, it would have strangled commerce between Istanbul and the Mediterranean and possibly knocked Turkey out of the war early.

At British instigation delivered by T. E. Lawrence ("Lawrence of Arabia"), Arabs loyal to the Sharif of Mecca revolted and took out Ottoman forces in northern Arabia, Palestine, and Syria. Russian troops invaded Eastern Anatolia and enlisted the support of the local inhabitants, Russia's coreligionists, the Armenians. This led to one of the most hotly disputed horrors of World War I.

The Ottoman army rounded up Armenians and marched them into the Syrian desert. Turkish historians claim this was a precautionary move to protect its eastern flank from Russian sympathizers. Armenian historians say the population move was an intentional death march, resulting in the death of 1.6 million Armenians. Whichever side is correct, the Armenians disappeared as a people from Anatolia. Those who went into the desert never came back; those who remained behind fled for their lives or fought to the end. This contributed to the Armenian diaspora, much of which came to America.

The Ottomans withdrew from the conflict on October 31, 1918, eleven days before the Armistice went into effect on the Western Front. The Turkish armistice stipulated the victors had the right to occupy any part of the empire if they considered their security to be under threat. The CUP leadership fled the country in a German submarine. Soon five hundred years of Ottoman history would come to an end.

CONCLUSIONS

A traveler passing through the lands from Morocco to Afghanistan finds the intervening countries remarkably alike. The laws are similar, the culture the same, the food identical (except for variations in local spices). All the countries were part of the Ottoman Empire. Some of this holds true for the Balkans as well.

The Ottomans ruled a multiethnic empire and allowed Christians and Jews to live in peace, albeit in an inferior social position. As the empire grew, it expanded as far as logistics would allow it. Istanbul paid little attention to technological or economic innovation or Western advances in weaponry and changes in trade patterns. In effect, it fell asleep.

By the end of the eighteenth century, it was too late to reverse Ottoman decline, and the Empire suffered a series of military defeats and loss of its provinces either to independence or to European colonialists. Finally, in World War I the Ottomans were shorn of all their lands except Thrace and the Anatolian peninsula.

Elements within the Empire tried to reform and modernize in order to survive in the new age. The Tanzimat promised liberty to the people of the Empire, but at the price of granting equality to Christians and Jews. The Young Turks tried to push reform on a reluctant society. Ultimately, the Empire failed because it had never created a distinctly Ottoman identity in the minds of its subjects, as Europe had. It was an **anachronism**.

FURTHER REFERENCE

Goltz, Thomson, ed. *Turkey*, 3rd ed. Boston: Houghton Mifflin, 1993.

Kinross, John Patrick Douglas Balfour (Lord). *The Ottoman Centuries: The Rise and Fall of the Turkish Empire*. New York: Morrow Quill, 1979.

Lewis, Bernard. *What Went Wrong? Western Impact and Middle Eastern Response*. New York: Oxford, 2002.

Merdin, Serif, "Freedom in an Ottoman Perspective" in Heper, Metin and Ahmet Evin, eds. *State, Democracy and the Military: Turkey in the 1980s*. New York: de Gruter, 1988.

Wheatcroft, Andrew. *The Ottomans: Dissolving Images*. New York: Penguin, 1996.

---

anachronism   Something from the wrong time, from a bygone age.

The Origins of the Israel-Palestine War

5

Points to Ponder

- Does the Bible or history give valid title deeds to land?
- How are Judaism, Christianity, and Islam related?
- How did Spain and Germany produce two Jewish cultures?
- What was Herzl's basic argument? Was he right?
- Were Israel's early pioneers secular or religious?
- How did Arab nationalism arise?
- How is fundamentalist Islam at odds with Arab nationalism?
- What did World War I do to the Middle East?
- When and why did Jewish-Arab clashes start?
- What is partition and does it work?

According to Genesis, the Hebrew faith and the land of Israel originated simultaneously, in God's command to Abraham to leave his native Ur of the Chaldees in southern Mesopotamia, then part of ancient Sumer, and move far to the west, to a land God promised to Abraham's descendants for evermore. A more prosaic explanation looks at the ancient pattern of nomadic peoples, who have to lead their flocks to green pastures. Tribes have been traversing the Fertile Crescent for millennia, fleeing drought. Abraham was likely the leader of one such band about 2000 B.C.

Ancient Egyptian records indicate periodic influxes of peoples from the north, also fleeing drought. Among them was Abraham's great-grandson Joseph, along with many other Hebrews, as they were by then known (after the town of Hebron, home and tomb of Judaism's founding patriarchs). After some generations in slavery, in the thirteenth century B.C. Moses led the Hebrews out of Egypt and through forty years of wandering in the desert, which some take as a metaphor for having to replace the old slave generation by a new free generation that was fit to return to the Promised Land, then called Canaan. In a parallel metaphor, God did not allow Moses to enter Canaan but only to glimpse it across the Jordan River.

G : *Geography*

PALESTINE

This little piece of land has had many names: Canaan, Israel, Judah, Judea, and Palestine. This last term originates from what the Greeks named Philistia, a small kingdom on the southern coast between present day Tel Aviv and the Gaza strip. The Philistines were sea traders whose name became synonymous with narrow commercialism. Goliath was a Philistine giant whom David slew with a slingshot.

Fed up with Jewish revolts against them, the Romans in the second century A.D. used the Latin name Palaestina (from the old Greek *Philistia*) and tried to erase memory of Judea by calling it Syria Palaestina, suggesting it was just the southernmost province of Syria. The name Palestine stuck, and the British made it official when they took the area from Ottoman Turkey in World War I. Its Arab inhabitants call it *Filistin*.

KINGDOMS AND CONQUESTS

By now Scripture calls these people Israelites, after the Hebrew *Yiz-ra-el,* "contends with God," suggesting a contentious people. They conquered Canaan and founded the kingdom of Israel with capital and temple high in the mountains, in Jerusalem. Israel's most famous kings were Saul, David, and his son Solomon in the eleventh and tenth centuries B.C. Ever contentious, the kingdom split into Israel in the north and Judah (origin of *Jew*) in the south. Thus weakened, the northern kingdom was conquered by the warlike Assyrians in the eighth century B.C. Judah continued to exist in a weakened condition until Babylonia's Nebuchadnezer conquered it in 597 B.C. and exiled its nobles and priests to Babylon. A majority of the Jews stayed in Canaan but were subject to assimilation into the conqueror's culture and religion.

In Babylonian exile, Jews struggled to keep their distinctive faith alive. To do so, they gave Judaism a written narrative that included emphasis on a Promised Land (see box on page 72), and it has been with the Jewish people ever since. The first **Zionists** were those who followed Ezra back from Babylon in 397 B.C. to reclaim Israel, and revive its religion. Ezra may have brought the first Torah scrolls to Israel and thus started a gradual shift from the old religion that focused on the Temple in Jerusalem to the new Rabbinic Judaism that focused on Scripture (see box on page 73).

In 332 B.C. Alexander the Great led a Greek army through the Middle East as part of his quest for a gigantic empire that would encompass the known world. Curiously, Alexander himself was not Greek but Macedonian, a barbaric kingdom to the north of Greece. With a Greek education—in part tutored by Aristotle—Alexander

---

Zionism   From Mt. Zion in Jerusalem; movement to return to Israel.

R : *Religions*

THE "PROMISED LAND" IN THE BIBLE

The early books of the Old Testament are replete with references to God granting the Hebrews the Land of Israel in perpetuity. In Genesis 11, God commands Abraham to leave his home in Mesopotamia for "a land that I shall show thee." In Egypt, Moses led the Hebrew slaves back to their Promised Land. There are many other such references. Do they prove that Jews have a valid claim to Israel, superseding all other claims?

Some, including Orthodox Jews and Fundamentalist Christians, think the Bible gives Israel to the Jews. Those who believe in the inerrancy of Scripture accept that what God said needs to be carried out today. Others, who think the Bible was written by humans, note that the first five books of the Bible, what Jews call the Torah, were redacted in Babylonian exile from earlier Hebrew religious usages and legends that had likely not been written down in finished form. The redactors aimed to make sure Jews would not forget their religion or their homeland, so they inserted numerous references to "chosen people" with a God-given attachment to the land of Israel. Around 400 B.C. an advance party of Babylonian Jews—the first Zionists—did return to Israel (although many stayed in Babylon) to reclaim it.

Seen in this light, Biblical references to a perpetual Jewish right to Israel are a product of time and place, a powerful man-made narrative to persuade Jews to stay attached to the Land of Israel. Fundamentalists do not like the man-made theory of Zionism any more than they like evolution: The Bible says so, and that takes care of that.

Either way—word of God or man-made—the concept of a people bound to a special land stirs strong emotions that can push people to leave their old homes, set up a new state, and fight for it. Rationalists may dismiss founding narratives of nations and religions as "mytho-poetic legends," but they underrate the power of such stories in motivating humans, who are only partly rational. They also have a great need to believe in things that cannot be empirically verified.

became more Hellenic than the **Hellenes** and sought to spread Greek culture. Although his empire quickly decayed, it implanted a **Hellenistic** overlay on the region in language, architecture, and religion. Under the **Seleucids**, everyone was supposed to act Greek.

Many Jews, however, despised Hellenistic culture as immoral, especially its worship of idols and human rulers. One Jewish priestly clan, the Maccabees, led a revolt in 165 B.C. against the Seleucids and liberated the Temple in Jerusalem. To reconsecrate the Temple they needed a special, consecrated olive oil for the sacred lamps, but there was only one day's supply of it. Miraculously, it burned eight days and nights. Thus when Christians celebrate Christmas, Jews still celebrate Hanukkah, the Festival of Lights, with the mother lighting one more candle each night until eight are burning.

Hellenes   From *Hellas*, "Greece"; the ancient Greeks.
Hellenistic   Late Greek culture spread by Alexander.
Seleucid   Hellenistic kingdom that dominated Middle East 312–64 B.C.

R ∴ *Religions*

THE BIRTH OF TWO RELIGIONS

Two faiths were born out of the Roman occupation of Judea, a time of great religious ferment. Taxation and war had impoverished Judea, and people were eager for spiritual uplift. Judaism was changing rapidly, with new sects and self-proclaimed messiahs springing up. The old faith, centered on the Temple in Jerusalem—rebuilt and enlarged by Herod the Great (a descendant of the Maccabees) under the Romans—drew fewer believers. Some turned to mysticism and withdrawal, such as the Essenes, who left behind the Dead Sea scrolls in caves. Some turned to baptism to mark a new spiritual life.

In this atmosphere, two religions emerged: Rabbinic Judaism and Christianity. The early **rabbis** turned away from the hereditary Jewish priesthood—the *Kohanim* (present-day Cohens)—who ran the Temple, and instead embraced the Torah as the true faith. Discussion of the Torah became the bulwark of the new Rabbinic Judaism, which had one big advantage over the old one: Based on books, it was portable and teachable. Jesus may have learned from the most important rabbi of his day, Hillel. By 70 A.D., as the Romans crushed Jerusalem during a Jewish revolt, the rabbis were carrying Judaism with them throughout the Roman empire. The Judaism of today is Rabbinic Judaism and made Jews "people of the Book."

Jesus of Nazareth was not the only religious figure in Roman Judea preaching a new creed, but he had **charisma** and faithful disciples to spread his word. Jesus never claimed to be anything but Jewish and his teachings are a development of Judaism, but one with a simple, universal message, one much easier to understand and accept than the complexity of Rabbinic Judaism. Jews rarely sought converts; Christians always did. The standard Roman punishment for troublemakers, crucifixion, gave Christianity the indelible symbol it used to slowly and quietly take over the Roman empire from within.

In 64 B.C. the Romans took over what they called Judea from the decaying Seleucid empire. The Mediterranean became a Roman lake, *mare nostrum*, "our sea," as the Romans called it. Rome, its far-flung legions constantly fighting barbarians, kept expanding, and this turned Rome from a republic into an empire. It was just too big and diverse to be ruled by a handful of Roman nobles in the Senatus. Julius started turning himself into an emperor but was assassinated; his great-nephew Augustus became the first Roman emperor. Jesus of Nazareth was born twenty-seven years into the reign of Augustus.

Many subject peoples disliked Roman rule, and the empire was nearly constantly plagued by revolts, in Spain, Germany, and Judea, as the Romans now called it. In Judea the cause was again religious. Some Jews, the **Zealots**, hated the Romans and insisted on their own state and a purified religion. The Zealots—some of the earliest terrorists—killed all who disagreed with them, including more moderate Jews, many of whom did not mind Roman rule. Even then, fighting among Jews weakened and ultimately brought down the Jewish cause. Rome

rabbi Teacher of the Jewish faith, not a priest.
charisma Greek for "gift"; spiritual drawing power, such as that of Jesus.
Zealot Jewish sect opposed to Roman rule of Judea.

Religions

THE FIRST OR SECOND COMING OF THE MESSIAH?

Ancient Israel's priests anointed a new king by pouring olive oil on his head, which became a symbol of elect status. The use of the word **messiah** as a savior from God did not appear in Judaism until the Babylonian exile. There the Jewish tradition developed (but was not clearly stated in the Old Testament) that a descendant of David will come to lead the Jews back to the Promised Land.

For Jews, the messiah is yet to come, and his coming will be closely linked to the recovery of Israel. It is focused on this world, not the next. For Christians, the messiah came two thousand years ago and leads us to eternal peace in the next world. For some Fundamentalist Christians, the founding of the modern state of Israel indicates that the messiah's second coming is nigh. A few Ultra-Orthodox Hasidic Jews argue that Israel should not have been reestablished *until* the messiah appeared; the proclamation of Israel in 1948 was pushing things. Shi'a Islam (see Chapter 3) also awaits a sort of messiah, the *Mahdi*, the last true heir of Muhammad, who will return and save Muslims at the end of time.

was tolerant on religion, and many Roman soldiers came back from the East with new religions, including Judaism, which was spreading within the Roman empire.

Jewish fundamentalists, including Zealots, revolted against Rome from 66 A.D. to 70 A.D. Their remnants fell back to a fortified mountain overlooking the Dead Sea, Masada, where they held out for three years, finally committing suicide rather than be taken prisoner. To celebrate their victory after a long, hard fight, the Romans issued a coin proclaiming *Judea Capta* ("Judea is Captured"). Masada is now a major tourist attraction and symbol of Israeli toughness.

Embers of Jewish revolt in Judea reignited with the Bar Kochba rebellion of 132–135 A.D., crushed by the Tenth Roman Legion, whose motto was "Let them hate me so long as they fear me." This time, Rome leveled Jerusalem and exiled Jews from Judea to distant parts of the Roman empire. By the second century Jews were already in Spain, France, Germany, Italy, North Africa, and elsewhere in the Roman empire as traders and merchants. Thus began the Jewish **diaspora**, which saw Jewish communities throughout Europe, the Arab world, India, and even China. By intermarriage (and other means), Jews took on physical characteristics of the peoples they dwelt among. Today one finds Jews who look just like Germans, Russians, Spaniards, Arabs, and Indians. Jews are united more by belief than by blood.

THE LONG DIASPORA

The Jews' long exile did not erase their hope to eventually return to the Promised Land, a hope renewed almost every time they read the Torah. The Babylonian redactors of the Torah had done their job well. Jews raised their glasses to toast

---

messiah   From the Hebrew *mashiah,* "anointed one," divine savior.
diaspora   Scattering, a dispersed people without their own country.

G: *Geography*

EVERYONE IS FROM SOMEWHERE ELSE

We discussed in an earlier box whether the Bible gives Jews a valid claim to Israel. Posing the question more generally we may ask if any claim rooted in history or religion is valid. What makes any land "ours"? People may have lived there a very long time, but no one has lived there forever. Go back far enough—in some cases, not so far back—and everyone came from somewhere else, and when they got there, they usually found other humans already living there. Sometimes they assimilated them, but often they conquered them.

England, for example, has been conquered by successive waves of Celts, Romans, Angles and Saxons, and Normans. Tribes of wandering Ostrogoths, Visigoths, Vandals, and others washed over Europe, each bumping out previous inhabitants and then often getting bumped out themselves. Americans might not wish to look too closely at the origins of the United States, which were entirely stolen from the Indians. Does anyone seriously propose giving it back?

The ancient Israelites, after wandering forty years in the desert, conquered Canaan, the source of "Joshua Fit the Battle of Jericho." Then Assyrians, Babylonians, Egyptians, Greeks, and Romans conquered ancient Israel. Do any of them have a claim to it? In 639, Arabs spreading their new faith of Islam conquered what had been a Byzantine province, and until the twentieth century their language and culture dominated Palestine, except for the Crusaders' interlude in the eleventh century. Then in 1516 the Ottoman Turks expanded their empire to include Palestine. In 1917 in World War I, the British took it from the Turks and ran it until 1948. Then Zionists proclaimed the modern state of Israel.

So to whom exactly does history give the title deed? Neither history nor religion gives title deeds to any land. Invoking either or both of them simply makes people more adamant and unwilling to compromise and hence prolongs the bloodshed. When it comes to settling claims for sovereignty, history, in the words of Henry Ford, really is bunk.

"Next year in Jerusalem." Keeping this feeling alive was intermittent mistreatment at the hands of their Christian neighbors. There were Jews in most parts of the Roman empire centuries before the various Germanic tribes arrived. But these newcomers soon turned Christian and despised Jews as misguided and dangerous because most refused to convert. (To be sure, millions of Jews did convert to Christianity over the centuries.) At the beginning of the Middle Ages, a nontrivial percentage of Europe's population was Jewish, a percentage that shrank over the centuries. In Medieval Europe, Jews were not rare.

Jewish life in Muslim lands was generally better than in Christian Europe. The Qur'an teaches that Jews and Christians are also "people of the book" and should be treated as dhimmis, "protected people," who had to pay a special tax but were otherwise unmolested. Under the Arabs, Spain reached a cultural high point in which Jews fully participated. While Europe north of the Pyrenees wallowed in filth, Moorish Spain created great architecture (the Alhambra), literature, philosophy, and medical care. Moses Maimonides, born in Córdoba in 1135, wrote (in Arabic) his famous *Guide for the Perplexed*, a philosophical defense of religion in general. In Egypt, Maimonides later became court physician to the famed Saladin, who beat the Crusaders.

Cultures

SEPHARDIC AND ASHKENAZIC JEWS

In Europe, Jews formed two cultural traditions. Those in Spain (*Sefarad* in Hebrew) spoke Spanish but were expelled from Spain in 1492 and scattered around the Mediterranean, including the Ottoman Empire. They continued to speak a fairly good Spanish called Ladino that until recently could be heard in cities such as Istanbul and Sarajevo. They became known as Sepharadim.

Jews who settled at first in the Rhine Valley were called Ashkenazim, from *Ashkenaz*, Hebrew for "Germany." They spoke Middle High German and later moved into Central and East Europe. On top of their German they added Hebrew and Slavic words, producing Yiddish, which is written in Hebrew characters. Most American Jews are of Ashkenazic origin, and most of their ancestors spoke Yiddish, which can still be heard in various cities around the world. I. B. Singer, winner of the 1978 Nobel Prize for literature, was born in Poland but lived in New York and wrote in Yiddish.

The two branches, although based firmly on Torah, also developed different religious traditions and pronunciations of Hebrew. The revivers of modern Hebrew a century ago chose a mostly Sephardic pronunciation as closer to ancient spoken Hebrew, a language that had been liturgical rather than spoken since the third century B.C. At the time of Jesus, Judeans spoke Aramaic, a related Semitic language. Israel today has two chief rabbis, one Ashkenazic and one Sephardic.

During the late Middle Ages, most Jews were expelled from West Europe and went eastward. Jewish cultures that had thrived for a millennium in Spain and the Rhine Valley were destroyed, often violently. The causes were several. The Crusades and Reconquest of Iberia created religious hatred against non-Catholics, including Muslims and Eastern Orthodox Christians. Jews were under constant pressure to convert, and many did.

Another factor in medieval Europe was the fact that Jews were often unable to own land but could loan money at interest, which was prohibited to Catholics. (The Qur'an prohibits Muslims from charging or paying interest.) Jews were a major source of capital. Christian nobles and kings often ran up major debts to Jews, and in the Late Middle Ages took to expelling them rather than paying them. This was the beginning of Yiddish (see box above) and of the concentration of Jews in Central Europe. The biggest single Jewish community was in Poland.

Meanwhile, as Spanish kings reconquered Spain from the Moors (the *Reconquista*, completed in 1492) they ordered all Muslims and Jews to either embrace Catholicism or leave. Portuguese kings did likewise. Some Jewish converts (*Marranos*) continued to secretly practice Judaism in their homes. Those suspected of insincere conversion were tried for heresy, blasphemy, and much else by the Spanish Inquisition, which used torture and burning at the stake to carry out the *auto da fé* (act of faith). The Inquisition even pursued suspect families to Peru, Mexico, and New Mexico, where Marrano families exist to this day. Some families very quietly retained a Jewish identity for centuries, and one can meet Spanish and Portuguese Jews who only recently "came out of the closet."

Most of the Spanish Jews who left sailed to the eastern Mediterranean, where the Ottoman Turks, who were tolerant on religion, recognized the economic benefit of skilled Jewish settlers. "Spain's loss is our gain," was the Ottoman phrase. Thus Sephardic Jews found a home in the Ottoman Empire, which included the Balkans and soon enveloped most of the Middle East.

THE RISE OF MODERN ZIONISM

Jewish life in Central and East Europe, where most of the world's Jews lived after expulsion from West Europe in the Middle Ages, was precarious but possible until the late nineteenth century. Restricted as to residence and profession and suffering occasional violence, Jews built a vibrant cultural life based on the Yiddish language and their traditional religion. They found their niche in the economy as shopkeepers and artisans, seldom as farmers. More educated than most of their neighbors, many could read. They were classic "marginal men," everywhere a minority at the mercy of forces beyond their control. As long as Central and East Europe stayed relatively static and backward (compared to West Europe), they could survive. But when the region awoke in the nineteenth century, their situation worsened, and this laid the foundation for **modern Zionism**.

The belated arrival of capitalism into Central and East Europe brought local Christians into economic competition with Jews, who lost their "niche" status. Napoleon's legions awoke **nationalism** in the region. Having to live under and cast off the French taught nationalism to most of Europe. In fighting to free themselves from French rule, Spaniards, Germans, Russians, and others became nationalistic. Nationalism spread, and by the middle of the nineteenth century Central Europeans rejected rule by empires and longed for their own nation. In the Habsburg Empire (known as Austria-Hungary from 1867 to 1918), Czechs, Hungarians, and others wished to be rid of the Habsburgs. Poland, partitioned between Germany, Austria, and Russia since the 1790s, never died in the hearts of Poles, whose Catholicism was a kind of nationalism for them. During the nineteenth century, nationalism grew until it enveloped all of Europe.

Nationalism can be a progressive force, awakening peoples to unity, independence, modernization, economic growth, and democracy. Unfortunately, it can also be a highly destructive force, leading to racism, intolerance, expansionism, and war. One of the major components of nationalism is hatred of the Other, those who are not like us but who misrule us, exploit us, or rob us. A natural target in much of Europe for these feelings was the Jews, perceived as eternal foreigners. Thus, racial (as opposed to the earlier religious) anti-Semitism appeared in much of Europe during the nineteenth century. Both Jews and Christians started posing

---

modern Zionism   Jewish *nationalism*, founded in late nineteenth century to recover Israel as a Jewish state, secular and socialistic rather than religious.
nationalism   Desire to cast off foreign rule in favor of own state.

the "**Jewish question**," which some Jews answered with their own nationalism, one focused on Palestine. By the 1860s, Jewish writers were proposing a Jewish return to Palestine, and in 1882 the first **aliyah** brought a few Jewish immigrants to Palestine, then under Ottoman rule.

What really galvanized modern Zionism was the trial of Captain Alfred Dreyfus, a Jewish French officer accused in 1894 of selling war-ministry secrets to Germany. On flimsy evidence (some of it forged), he was convicted and sent for life to the infamous Devil's Island penal colony. The Dreyfus Affair, which dragged on twelve years, revealed that France was still split into two camps by the 1789 Revolution. On one side liberals accused the French army of using Dreyfus as a handy scapegoat because he was Jewish. French conservatives and Catholics rallied to the army and denounced all Jews. The two sides battled in print and in the street, and anti-Semitism came into the open. Emile Zola's famous *J'accuse* ("*I accuse*") was penned to support Dreyfus and accuse the generals of a cover-up.

An assimilated Hungarian Jewish journalist, Theodore Herzl, covering the trial for a Vienna newspaper, was horrified at the outburst of anti-Semitism in the most civilized country of Europe. If it could happen in France, he reasoned, it could happen elsewhere. Herzl detected the danger of extreme anti-Semitic nationalism just under the surface in Europe and concluded that Jews would not be safe until they had their own country. In 1897 he organized the first Zionist congress, which began to raise funds to buy land and send Jewish pioneers to Palestine. At that time Herzl predicted that his dream of a Jewish state would be a reality in fifty years. He was off by only one year; Israel was born in 1948.

Zionism started as a minority and romantic movement. Many Jews in Central and East Europe, where conditions were getting bad, immigrated to the United States, only a few to Palestine. Tsarist Russia (which at that time held eastern Poland) contained the largest Jewish population and deflected domestic discontent onto Jews. The people are unhappy? Blame the Jews. The tsarist police encouraged **pogroms** and forged *The Protocols of the Elders of Zion*, a book purporting to reveal a Jewish plot to take over the world (which keeps turning up, most recently in Egypt).

A few religious Jews had long lived in Jerusalem, but at the turn of the twentieth century modern Zionist pioneers arrived in Palestine, whose Turkish governors saw the Jews as a boost to the economy of the poor and thinly populated area. As the earlier Zionists used to say, "A people without a land shall have a land without people." The number of Jewish immigrants was not large, and many soon left the inhospitable conditions for the United States. Few saw the trouble coming from two peoples claiming the same land. Around 1900 Hebrew was revived as a spoken language and displaced Yiddish among the Jewish pioneers. Tel Aviv and the first **kibbutz**, Deganya, were founded by early Zionists in 1909. On the

---

Jewish question   Nineteenth and twentieth century; what should become of Europe's Jews?
aliyah   Hebrew for "ascent" (implying uplift), a wave of Jewish immigration to Israel.
pogrom   Russian for "devastation," murderous anti-Jewish riots encouraged by tsarist police.
kibbutz   Jewish collective farm founded by Zionist pioneers in Palestine.

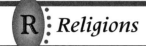

Religions

ISRAEL'S SECULAR FOUNDERS

Many suppose modern Israel was founded on a religious basis, but nearly the opposite is true; Israel's founders and early leaders were **secular** and paid little attention to Judaism. Many were committed to socialism, which in the early twentieth century was riding high in Europe. Their idea was to build not only a Jewish homeland but a socialist one where people would live in equality and sufficiency in a co-operative rather than capitalist economy. This was the foundation of the kibbutz movement and of "Labor Zionism," its strongest branch until the 1970s.

Few early Zionists had religious feelings; most saw themselves as Jewish pioneers establishing a safe haven for Jews from the growing anti-Semitism of Europe. They focused on agriculture, arguing that getting Jews back to the land—and there had been essentially no Jewish farmers for nearly two millennia—was a form of worship far more authentic than prayer and synagogues. Some leftist *kibbutzim* even raised pigs as a tasty and economical source of protein. Most Israelis are still secular, but religion has grown with the influx of new immigrants and recovery of the Old City of Jerusalem, with its religious significance, in the 1967 war. In Israel, religious Jews are the newcomers.

eve of World War I, however, Jews were a small minority in an otherwise Arab Palestine.

Absentee Arab and Turkish landlords, who lived in Beirut and Damascus, owned much of the land of Palestine. They rented land to poor Arab villagers to farm, often for so many generations that the farmers felt the land was theirs. Starting in 1901, the Jewish National Fund purchased land (often at exorbitant prices) from the *effendis* and set up Jewish farms and towns, displacing the traditional Arab tenants. The transfer of land was perfectly legal, but Arab *fellahin* put more faith in personal relationships with leading families rather than in title deeds filed in a government office. In this way, the Zionist pioneers expanded their holdings, but Arabs worried Jews would buy up all the land.

THE RISE OF ARAB NATIONALISM

At about the same time Jews were undergoing a national awakening, so were Arabs. Nationalism, once out of the bottle, spread over the globe. The entire Fertile Crescent had been in Ottoman hands since the sixteenth century, and most Arabs did not mind. The Turks were also Muslims who swore the Arabs were their brothers, and the Ottoman sultan in Istanbul was also the caliph of the Islamic faith, so he enjoyed a double legitimacy, one secular, one religious. There were Christian revolts against Turkish rule in the Balkans, but no Arab revolts against it

---

secular nonreligious; government and daily life little influenced by religion.

 Religions

SEPARATE ARAB STATES?

Islam, in its intertwining of state and religion, presents a permanent problem to Muslim nationalists. The nationalism of the Europeans is built on and vows to strengthen separate states, but Muslims in general and Arabs in particular were never comfortable with the concept of separate nations. Believers should live in one big Islamic community, the *umma*, not divided into nations, which are European concepts, argued strict Muslims. Even in the twenty-first century, Osama bin Laden and his followers hold that nationalism soon turns into the worship of nation, which is a form of idolatry. (American Jehovah's Witnesses argue along similar lines.) Perhaps the *hajj* is the purest expression of this feeling, for there in Mecca all Muslims are brothers and equal, and nationality is unimportant.

Accordingly, every Egyptian or Iraqi or any other Arab nationalist movement meets resistance from devout Muslims who denounce it in favor of a single **pan-Arab** (or even pan-Muslim) entity. Both agree they should cast off foreign domination but disagree over which is more important, nation or Islam? It is for this reason that ambitious Arab leaders cast themselves not just as national saviors but as pan-Arab heroes, destined to unite and lead a new Arab empire. It's not good enough to just head your nation; you must pose as liberator of all Arabs, too. Examples: Nasser of Egypt and Saddam Hussein of Iraq.

Osama and other extremists could opportunistically ally with nationalists such as Saddam Hussein, but ultimately they are at odds. Egyptian Islamists, long suppressed by secular Cairo governments—Nasser kept thousands of members of the Muslim Brotherhood in prison and executed some of its top people—still smolder in hatred that bursts out in such horrors as their 1981 assassination of President Sadat and 1996 massacre of foreign tourists. The struggle between nation and religion, long solved in Christian countries, still destabilizes Muslim lands.

until World War I. Ottoman rule weakened, to be sure. Egypt was ruled by the *mamluks* in the eighteenth century and by the Albanian adventurer Muhammad Ali in the early nineteenth century, but these did not represent a nationalistic revolt against the caliph.

Possibly the seeds for that were planted by the French when Napoleon gunned down the mamluk warriors near Alexandria, Egypt, in 1798. Although soon ousted from Egypt by Britain in 1801, the French had brought a printing press and scholars of Arabic with them. There had been some printing in the Ottoman Empire, but only in Turkish; now Arabs could read newspapers in their own language. The French interlude in Egypt awakened Arab thoughts that a better, freer life awaited them outside of Turkish rule. As in Europe, France triggered Arab nationalism in the Middle East.

Later in the nineteenth century, Arab Christians in Lebanon began a literary revival of Arabic—including a dictionary and encyclopedia—that quickly led to thoughts of an Arab cultural revival. The nationalistic Young Turk movement to reform the Ottoman Empire prompted Arabs into thinking about their own nationalism. Arab

pan-Arab   All Arab lands in one political entity.

civilian and military officers in the Ottoman structure resented that they were not promoted as high as Turkish officers. They started plotting eventual Arab independence from the Ottoman Empire. Just before World War I broke out, the first Arab Congress met in Paris in 1913 and called for Arab autonomy within the Ottoman Empire; Istanbul ignored the demand.

THE IMPACT OF WORLD WAR I

The Great War of 1914–1918 was the seminal event of the twentieth century, the point where it went off the tracks. The war destroyed four empires—the German, Russian, Austro-Hungarian, and Ottoman Turkish. From the ruins of empires flowered the twin evils of Communism and Fascism, both aimed at remaking society into controlled hierarchies by coercive means. An offshoot of World War I, little noticed at the time, was what it did to the Middle East.

Ottoman Turkey, in decay, was courted by Imperial Germany, which had plans to rival Britain in various parts of the world, including the Middle East. One such plan was a Berlin-to-Basra railway that would bring German power into the Persian Gulf. Istanbul, fearing dismemberment by Russia, France, Britain, Italy, and Greece, allied with Berlin. The Turkish army had German weapons and advisors during World War I.

The British, aware of German designs, felt they had to protect their **imperial lifeline** that ran through the Middle East. They were also aware of the oil in the Turkish province of Mosul, which later became northern Iraq. In the **Sykes-Picot** agreement, Britain and France along with Russia and later Italy, planned to carve up the Ottoman Empire after the war. The new Bolshevik government in Russia published its details as a way to discredit the "capitalist" war, and Sykes-Picot was never formally carried out, but Britain after the war got Mesopotamia and Palestine, while France got Syria and Lebanon.

Turkey put up a good fight, inflicting setbacks on mostly colonial British forces in Mesopotamia and **Gallipoli**, until Gen. Edmund Allenby, with help from an Arab uprising, pushed the Turks out of Palestine, taking Jerusalem in December 1917. Paving the way for this uprising were the **McMahon-Hussein letters** exchanged by Britain's Sir Henry McMahon, who ran Egypt during the war, and Sherif Hussein of Mecca. If Hussein would help Britain defeat the Turks—whom many Arabs disliked—the Arabs would get their own independent states, the borders of which were left vague. Britain's liaison and advisor to Hussein was T. E. Lawrence, who had earlier done archeology in the region and whose exploits were turned into the legend of Lawrence of Arabia. The British never told their

---

imperial lifeline   Britain's sea route to India, through the Mediterranean, Suez Canal, Red Sea, and Indian Ocean.
Sykes-Picot   Secret 1916 British-French agreement to carve up Ottoman Empire.
Gallipoli   Ill-fated 1915 British landing near Istanbul.
McMahon-Hussein letters   1915–1916 British pledge to set up Arab states for Arab help to oust Turks.

Arab allies that they had already made the Sykes-Picot deal with France to take the Fertile Crescent for themselves.

British policy also boosted the Zionist movement. The British cabinet, desperate for allies and aware that many Jews lived in Russia (which was dropping out of the war) and America (which was just entering the war), tried to rally Jewish opinion to its cause by issuing the 1917 **Balfour Declaration**:

> His Majesty's Government view with favour the establishment in Palestine of a national home for the Jewish people, and will use their best endeavours to facilitate the achievement of this object, it being clearly understood that nothing shall be done which may prejudice the civil and religious rights of existing non-Jewish communities in Palestine, or the rights and political status enjoyed by Jews in any other country.

Although carefully hedged—it promised no Jewish state and vowed to protect Arab rights—Zionists took it as a charter for their dream. They too had not heard of Sykes-Picot. The next month, Allenby took Jerusalem, and the war ended with Britain in control of the Fertile Crescent. Britain, in effect, had promised the same land, which included Palestine, to three sets of claimants: the Arabs, the Jews, and themselves. Cynical manipulation was always part of imperialism. These incompatible promises laid the groundwork for much of the region's subsequent strife.

THE MANDATE

U.S. President Woodrow Wilson had pushed for the new **League of Nations** but could not persuade the Senate to ratify U.S. membership. Between the wars, the United States slouched into **isolationism**, leaving Britain and France, the other chief victors in World War I, to run the League and give themselves the **mandates** they wished. Under the mandate system, the League assigned former German colonies and Arab Ottoman lands to be supervised by the winners, chiefly Britain and France.

In 1922, Britain formalized its mandates by creating three new entities. It put together the three Ottoman provinces of Mesopotamia—Mosul in the north, Baghdad in the center, and Basra in the south—and called it by its Arab name (since the seventh century) Iraq. In effect, British imperialism invented a new kingdom and placed on its throne one of the sons of Hussein, whom Britain owed for leading the Arab revolt against the Ottomans. In 1932, Britain granted Iraq independence but continued to supervise it through its connections with Iraq's royal family and ruling class.

Balfour Declaration   1917 British support for a Jewish homeland in Palestine.
League of Nations   Interwar precursor to UN.
isolationism   Interwar U.S. policy of no involvement in Europe.
mandate   *League of Nations* grant to World War I victors of temporary supervision over colonies of defeated German and Ottoman empires.

 *Cultures*

CULTURAL VERSUS MATERIAL

Perhaps the greatest issue in the social sciences is whether human behavior originates inside the heads of people or outside in the physical world in which they live. The first camp emphasizes culture—including psychology, religion, and ideology—as the underlying cause. The second emphasizes the material world—including geography, economics, and political structures—as the underlying cause. Max Weber was the great proponent of the cultural school, Karl Marx of the material school. An example of this is the great Arab historian Ibn Khaldun, who in the fourteenth century recognized the impact of climate on the formation of Arab character: The material caused the cultural.

The question is lively and important in the Middle East today. Is the Arab-Israeli struggle one of conflicting cultures—and their cultures are quite different—or conflicting material interests? Do they fight because they embody two different religious psychologies and see the world differently? Or is culture a secondary concern, less important than the fact that there is only one Palestine and both strive to possess it?

On a broader level, intellectuals ask if the current difficulties of Muslim countries stem from religious doctrines that became frozen centuries ago or from foreign conquest and exploitation over those same centuries. Princeton scholar Bernard Lewis spent a lifetime studying the decline of the Ottoman Empire and put most of the blame on a stagnant mentality, one that refused to adapt and modernize, an example of the cultural school. Does this explain the rise of Islamic fundamentalism? Is it the centuries-old fundamentalist doctrines of *salafiyya* that turn Muslims into fanatics? Or is it the enormous numbers of unemployed Muslim youths who find Islamism a convenient outlet for their frustrations? A complete analysis of the Middle East (or anywhere else) must take both cultural and material factors into account and examine how they feed into one another.

At the same time, Britain split its Palestine mandate along the Jordan River and Wadi Araba. To the east, it created the Hashemite Kingdom of Transjordan and placed on its throne another of Hussein's sons. (Transjordan means on the other side of the Jordan River, a creek in U.S. terms.) In 1946, it took the name Jordan. To the west of the Jordan, Britain ran things directly in Palestine on a semi-colonial basis.

Why did Britain want Palestine? Its motives were partly idealistic and partly realistic, and it did not know that it would turn into an impossible problem area, one from which it would have to retreat amidst cries of betrayal from both Arab and Jewish sides. Idealistically, Britain had been fixated on the Holy Land since at least the Crusades. Many English knights participated in the Crusades. To rule over Jerusalem and Bethlehem again in the twentieth century—for the good of all mankind, of course—seemed the fulfillment of English hymns and a sacred trust. Aiding the Zionist cause also appealed to British Protestantism, which read the Old Testament carefully. Britain would facilitate biblical prophecy. There was a bit of romanticism in Britain's motives.

Idealism seldom lasts, however, without realistic backing. Control of Palestine, along with Egypt and Iraq, protected Britain's imperial lifeline and gave Britain control over the major oil fields around Mosul and Kirkuk. Under Sykes-Picot, France had been promised an interest in the area, but Britain rejected French demands. French Premier Georges Clemenceau alluded to the heavy French battle losses in the Great War with his famous phrase, "A drop of blood is worth a drop of oil." He was referring to the very same oilfields of northern Iraq that became important during and after the 2003 Gulf War. One of Britain's projects was a small (12-inch) oil pipeline from northern Iraq through Jordan and across northern Palestine to exit at the port of Haifa (one of the best ports on the eastern Mediterranean), every foot of which ran through British-controlled territory. If things had worked out, Britain would have sat astride the world's most important petroleum corridor. Even the relatively small pipeline and refinery at Haifa were of great help to Britain in World War II. In sum, British motives were religious, strategic, and economic.

THE FIRST ARAB-JEWISH CLASHES

Almost immediately Britain's Palestine mandate was trouble. The Balfour Declaration did not unleash great Jewish immigration to Palestine after World War I—for most of the 1920s it was a trickle—but it was enough to alarm some Palestinian Arabs, who perceived that Jewish land purchases and immigration could eventually turn Palestine into a Jewish state. The first Arab rioting against Jewish immigration flared in 1920 but got bloody in August 1929, when 133 Jews were killed while the British-officered Palestine Police killed 116 Arabs. Governing the Holy Land was no picnic for the British.

With the Nazi takeover of Germany in early 1933 and the takeover of Poland by anti-Semitic colonels in 1935, more Central European Jews turned to Palestine as a refuge. America had passed the Immigration Act of 1924, which incorporated tight national-origin quotas, and was effectively closed to large numbers of Jewish arrivals. In 1933, 30,000 Jews immigrated to Palestine, 42,000 in 1934, and 61,000 in 1935. By 1936, Jews were 30 percent of Palestine's population, and Arabs did not like it. Leading them was the **mufti** of Jerusalem, Hajj Amin al Husseini, appointed by the British in 1921. He soon turned bitterly anti-Jewish and anti-British and was fired in 1937. He spent much of World War II in Germany, urging Muslims worldwide to side with the Nazis.

In 1936 Palestinian Arabs revolted and civil war raged until 1939. Both Arabs and Jews armed themselves, and the British could barely keep a lid on the fighting. The mainstream Jewish self-defense force, the Haganah, became the core of the Israeli army. A militant Jewish organization, the Irgun, rejected compromise in favor of the gun. An even more extreme group, Lehi, practiced assassinations against Arabs and British. Hundreds died on both sides. It was in effect the first Palestinian *intifada* (uprising) against Israelis and a demonstration

---

mufti   Islamic legal authority; issues *fatwas*.

G: *Geography*

POLITICS BY DEMOGRAPHIC MEANS

In 1914, when Palestine was still under the Ottomans, the 85,000 Jews there constituted 12 percent of the small total population of 690,000. In 1933, the Jewish population had grown to 238,000, then 20 percent of Palestine's overall population of 1.2 million. Just three years later, in 1936, the Jewish population had grown to 400,000, then 30 percent of Palestine's population of 1.33 million. Jewish population had increased nearly fivefold from 1914 to 1936, but Palestine's overall population had nearly doubled.

A **demographic** race was underway, fuelled by both immigration and births, that continues to our day. Both Jews and Arabs encourage high birth rates and immigration of their kin with an eye to eventual power. In the late 1930s, when the British largely cut off Jewish immigration, Palestine's Jews practiced "internal immigration," making lots of babies. Now some 5 million Israeli Jews face nearly as many Palestinians (some citizens of Israel, some on the West Bank and Gaza Strip, and some in other countries). Ten million people now wish to live where two-thirds of a million had lived a hundred years earlier.

---

of the impossibility of Jews and Arabs living together in a single state, even one supervised by an outside power. There was a tiny political party, Ihud ("Unity"), composed of some Jewish intellectuals and leftists, that urged a binational state, but they got essentially no Arab takers. Those who now propose a "one-state" solution should reflect on the 1936–1939 civil war.

With Palestine ungovernable, Britain sent the Peel Commission in 1936 to investigate and advise. They came back in 1937 with a **partition** plan that suggested dividing Palestine into a small Jewish territory, a larger Arab territory, and putting Jerusalem under international trusteeship. Some of the Peel ideas turned up in the 1947 UN partition plan, but at the time neither side was interested.

By 1939 World War II loomed, and Britain had extensive interests throughout the Arab world, which Nazi agents were attempting to subvert. To calm Arab anger, London issued a **white paper** that drastically restricted Jewish immigration to Palestine. Only 75,000 were to be allowed in over the next four years, allegedly to not overburden Palestine's very limited "absorptive capacity," a dubious argument. At the very moment Europe's Jews needed a place of refuge, the world closed its doors to most of them. No country wanted Jewish refugees in large number. (Actually, even today no country wants any refugees in large numbers.) The only open port to Europe's Jews was far-off Shanghai, which had a sizable Jewish colony during World War II.

---

demography   Study of population growth.
partition   Dividing a country to keep warring groups apart.
white paper   Major diplomatic statement of policy.

Cultures

THIEVES IN THE NIGHT

A remarkable 1943 novel by Arthur Koestler—better known for *Darkness at Noon*—gives keen insight into the making of a terrorist. In this case an idealistic Jewish leftist, under the pressure of Arab attacks on his kibbutz and British indifference, logically concludes that Jewish terrorism is the only path open. Koestler, a man who tried about everything the twentieth century had to offer, had worked in Palestine and saw such attitudes take shape in the minds of Lehi gunmen. He does not justify terrorism; he merely explains it. Ironically, the pattern fits Palestinian Arabs, too: Under extreme pressure and frustration, terrorism seems logical. Koestler's title is actually from the New Testament ("The Lord shall come as a thief in the night," 1 Thessalonians 5:2).

The Arabs were temporarily mollified, but the Jews were outraged. A few turned to terrorism directed against British immigration policy. Two of Israel's prime ministers, Menahem Begin and Yitzhak Shamir, began their political careers leading respectively the Irgun and Lehi, militant underground organizations with a British price on their heads. "The Germans kill us, and the British don't let us live," was their rationale for turning to the gun and bomb.

The mainstream Jewish community of Palestine, however, saw no choice but to cooperate with the British. Many joined the British army, which gave them the military skills they needed after the war. "We will fight the Germans as if there were no white paper," said Zionist leader David Ben Gurion, "and we will fight the British as if there were no Germans." Few Arabs joined the British army.

With World War II, the Zionist movement lost all patience. Meeting in New York's Biltmore Hotel in 1942, they demanded a Jewish state in Palestine. A mere "Jewish homeland" shared with Arabs would no longer suffice. The liberation of the Nazi death camps in the spring of 1945 confirmed what had been rumored: In what later was called the **Holocaust**, the Nazis had systematically murdered some 6 million Jews while the world stood by doing nothing. Zionist agents organized concentration-camp survivors and smuggled them into Palestine. The British tried to stop the ships, but this just gave them terrible publicity. Irgun and Lehi terrorists in Palestine shot British police and blew up the British headquarters in Jerusalem's King David Hotel.

Exhausted and exasperated, Britain threw the question to the new United Nations in 1947 and announced it would withdraw from Palestine next spring. Meeting in Lake Success on Long Island (because the UN building was not built yet), the UN Trusteeship Council, which inherited the League of Nations' mandates, devised a partition plan that pleased neither side but seemed to provide a way out of the mess.

Holocaust   From the Greek "burnt sacrifice"; Nazi genocide of Europe's Jews in World War II.

G: *Geography*

PARTITION

Everyone agrees that partitioning a country torn by ethnic strife seldom fixes things; usually the conflict continues. Still, when it seems that two communities, religious or ethnic, cannot live together in one state, partition may be the only solution halfway workable. The historical record, however, is grim.

Ireland, 1922—Britain, after misruling Ireland for seven centuries and putting down several Irish uprisings, agreed to an "Irish Free State." But Northern Ireland, with its Protestant majority, stayed British. This did not satisfy the Irish Republican Army (illegal in both Ulster and Eire), which renewed terrorism in the late 1960s.

India, 1947—Britain took India about the time of U.S. independence, but by the 1920s many Indians demanded their independence. Fearing that India would slide over to the Japanese in World War II (some Indians did), Britain promised Indian independence after the war, but some of India's Muslims refused to be ruled by the Hindu majority and demanded their own state. Pakistan was split off, producing 12 million refugees and three wars over Kashmir and East Pakistan (now Bangladesh). The next India-Pakistan war could be nuclear; both have the bomb.

Cyprus, 1961—Britain agreed to leave the eastern Mediterranean island, which it had taken from the Ottomans in 1878, but the Greek Cypriot majority wanted *enosis* ("union") with Greece while the Turkish Cypriot minority wanted *taksim* ("partition"). When Turkey feared a massacre of its kin in 1974, it invaded and partitioned Cyprus.

Bosnia, 1992—As Yugoslavia fell apart, Bosnian Muslims demanded their own state, something that never existed before. Bosnia's Serbs and Croats demanded their own ethnic areas and for a while fought a bloody three-sided civil war that was calmed only by a U.S.-led force in 1995. Bosnia is now effectively partitioned but poor, corrupt, and dependent.

Partition has no success stories. With many Palestinian refugees, five wars, two intifadas, and no solution in sight, it would be hard to call the partition of Palestine a success. Barring a Rodney King solution—"Why can't we all just get along?"—partition is an unhappy last resort.

The 1947 UN partition plan divided Palestine, checkerboard-style, into three Arab patches and three Jewish patches touching at their corners (see map on page 88). Jerusalem was to be an international city belonging to neither. The plan was imaginative but too complex to be carried out. On November 29, 1947, the UN General Assembly voted 33-13 in favor of the plan with ten abstentions. The United States led its European allies and Latin American client states to vote yes. The Soviet Union—seeing a way to oust Britain from the Middle East—led its satellites in East Europe to vote yes. All Arab and Muslim states, Israel's immediate neighbors, voted no. Israel was born with world but not regional approval.

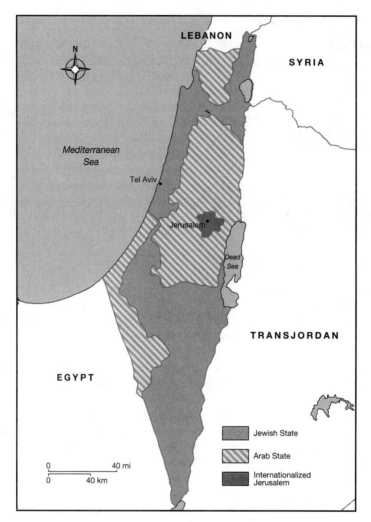

UN Partition Plan, 1947

The Palestine Jewish community was delighted, for this gave them a state, however odd its shape. The Arab community was totally against it, beginning a pattern that continues to this day. The way they see it, Arabs should have to give up zero percent of Palestine for Jews; giving up half was outrageous. In the absence of compromise, only one thing can happen: war. The Arabs lose and the Israelis take more land. This outrages the Arabs more, and they are even less willing to compromise. After a decade or two, this leads to another war, which again the Israelis win, taking even more land and outraging the Arabs still more. In a sick way, they play into each other's hands.

As the last British forces pulled out of Palestine, David Ben Gurion proclaimed the State of Israel on May 14, 1948, and five armies from neighboring Arab states immediately invaded. Israel was born because of and amidst war.

The United States in the Middle East

TRUMAN RECOGNIZES ISRAEL

President Harry Truman extended U.S. **diplomatic recognition** to Israel within minutes of its proclamation, but it was not a sure thing in advance. Recognition, especially by the major powers, is a powerful signal that confirms the sovereignty of a new country and lends it legitimacy. To withhold or withdraw recognition means we wish to have nothing to do with the other country, possibly wish its regime would disappear.

Leading State and Defense Department officials worried (like the British in World War II) that the new Jewish state would enrage Arabs and damage U.S. national interests in the region. State Department **Arabists** especially argued that the Arabs have the numbers, the territory, and the oil, and we should do nothing to anger them.

Truman pondered the issue but decided to recognize, for both political and personal reasons. American Jews, although only a few percent of the population, vote and give money (mostly to the Democrats). As the plain spoken Truman put in 1948: "There ain't many Arab voters in this country." (There are now.) And Truman was up for election that November, which he surprisingly won. Politicians strongly favor whatever gets them elected.

And Truman had an old Jewish friend and army buddy, Eddie Jacobson, with whom he briefly ran a haberdashery in Kansas City in the early 1920s. Jacobson came to see President Truman in Washington and told him emotionally of the suffering of the Jewish people in World War II. Some think the personal connection is what ultimately decided Truman.

CONCLUSIONS

Neither the Bible nor history gives a title deed to land. Abraham, Moses, and the Jews' Babylonian exile sought to claim a New Jersey-sized "Promised Land" that has been called Canaan, Israel, Judea, and Palestine. Crushed and dispersed by the Romans, Jews carried their religion and thoughts of eventual return into nearly two millennia of exile. Jews fared better in Muslim lands than in Christian ones. Bad conditions in Central Europe and France's Dreyfus trial awoke a modern Zionism, secular and socialist, in the late nineteenth century. Jewish pioneers trickled into the Ottoman province of Palestine, but the British interwar mandate over thinly populated Palestine brought more, especially with the rise of the Nazis in Europe.

A parallel Arab nationalism grew in the Ottoman Empire, and the British—seeming to promise the Arabs their own big kingdom—encouraged an Arab revolt against the Turks in World War I. Jewish immigration to interwar Palestine led to a series of Arab Palestinian disturbances, culminating in virtual civil war from 1936 to 1939. The British curbed further Jewish immigration but by the end of

---

diplomatic recognition   Establishment of official relations with another country.
Arabist   Presumably pro-Arab State Department official.

World War II saw that their mandate over Palestine was impossible. They threw the question to the new UN, which voted to partition Palestine into Jewish and Arab states. Jews accepted partition, but Arabs rejected it, leading to Israel's 1948 birth and the first Arab-Israeli war.

Some patterns emerged early and persist. Both sides claim the same small land. Outside powers help set up conflicts. Populations have grown rapidly. Compromise has been hard to find.

FURTHER REFERENCE

Fromkin, David. *A Peace to End All Peace: Creating the Modern Middle East, 1914–1922*. New York: Holt, 1989.

Hilberg, Raul. *The Destruction of the European Jews*, rev. ed. New York: Holmes & Meier, 1985.

Khalidi, Rashid, ed. *The Origins of Arab Nationalism*. New York: Columbia University Press, 1991.

———. *Palestinian Identity: The Construction of Modern National Consciousness*. New York: Columbia University Press, 1997.

Laqueur, Walter. *A History of Zionism*. New York: Weidenfeld & Nicholson, 1974.

Sachar, Howard M. *A History of Israel*, vol. 1, 2nd ed. New York: Knopf, 1986.

Said, Edward. *The Question of Palestine*. New York: Times Books, 1979.

Segev, Tom. *One Palestine, Complete*, tr. by Haim Watzman. New York: Metropolitan, 2000.

Shafir, Gershon. *Land, Labor and the Origins of the Israeli-Palestinian Conflict, 1882–1914*. New York: Cambridge University Press, 1989.

Stein, Leslie. *The Hope Fulfilled: The Rise of Modern Israel*. Westport, CT: Praeger, 2003.

Tessler, Mark A. *A History of the Israeli-Palestinian Conflict*. Bloomington, IN: Indiana University Press, 1994.

Wyman, David. *The Abandonment of the Jews*. New York: Pantheon, 1985.

6

The Very Long War

Points to Ponder

- Are we looking at separate wars or one long war?
- How does Israel bear out what Napoleon said about morale?
- Is there any way Israel could have been born peacefully?
- Has the UN prevented wars in the Middle East?
- Were Israel's 1949 borders indefensible?
- How do Arab and Israeli cultures differ?
- How was 1967 a big but incomplete Israeli victory?
- Could 1973 be considered a "necessary" war? Why?
- Are these wars any of our business?

There are two ways to look at the Arab-Israeli conflict, either as separate wars or as one long war punctuated by occasional cease-fires. Either way, the conflict has no quick or simple solution, and good will among the contending parties is absent. Do not count on a big peace conference to settle things. The crux of the problem is that Israel wishes to exist, while Arabs, especially Palestinians, wish it had never existed. As we considered in the previous chapter, history or Scripture cannot settle these things. Reason and international law do not fare much better.

THE 1948 WAR

Israelis call it their War of Independence; Palestinians call it their Catastrophe. The worst could have been avoided if Palestinian leaders had accepted the 1947 UN Partition Plan and let half of Palestine become the new Jewish state of Israel. Few Palestinians gave this possibility a second thought: All of Palestine was theirs, and they were in no mood to share. Result: They lost even more territory, which Israel gained, a pattern that keeps reappearing. Inability to compromise has created a chronic and endemic Palestinian catastrophe.

The first Arab-Israeli war started as a bigger and worse resumption of the 1936–1939 Palestine civil war, one that the British mandate authorities could barely keep a lid on. After World War II, the lid blew off. Holocaust survivors demanded to be let into Palestine. Jews worldwide demanded a state. The Jewish community in Palestine formed battalions, many of them trained in the British army, and scrounged up weapons. Palestinian Arabs did the same but less effectively. The British, reduced in strength and already committed to withdrawal, essentially stood by as Jewish forces (the Haganah, Palmach, and Irgun) battled several groups of Palestinian irregulars.

The war officially broke out upon Israel's declaration of independence on May 14, 1948, as five Arab states immediately invaded aiming to make Israel disappear. This invasion masked the underlying Israel-Palestine struggle, turning it into a series of wars between Israel and its Arab neighbors with the fate of the Palestinians fading into the background. This was convenient for Israelis but horrible for Palestinians, who over the decades learned that they could not rely on Arab countries to "protect" them. All Israel's bordering neighbors—Egypt, Jordan, Syria, and Lebanon—invaded, plus a contingent from Iraq. The Egyptian army was by far the biggest and greatest threat to Israel, although it turned out that the small British-officered Arab Legion of Jordan achieved much more.

The Arab states emphatically rejected the 1947 UN partition plan (see the previous chapter) and felt it their duty to rescue their brother Arabs, the Palestinians. At the same time, they wanted pieces of Palestine for themselves. As always, motives mixed a little generosity with a lot of self-interest. The Israeli motive was extremely simple: win or die. In Israeli eyes, the recent murder of 6 million of their kinfolk in Europe blended into Arab cries of "Drive the Jews into the sea!" For Israelis, the Arabs were a continuation of the Nazis. (A few German mercenaries fought for Arab armies, which Israelis claimed proved the fascistic-reactionary nature of Arabs. Israeli forces shot German prisoners out of hand.) Israel paid only negative attention to Palestinians. Some Israelis argued then and argue now that there is no distinct "Palestinian" nationality; they were simply Arabs who could be at home in other Arab countries. Few Israelis worried about Palestinian refugees; compared to Israel's survival the point seemed irrelevant. As we shall see, it is highly relevant for any peace settlement.

Informed opinion thought it was a highly unequal match that the Arabs would win. The Arab armies were professional and had been building up weaponry and equipment for years. Many Israelis had been in the Haganah or British army (or both) but had little military hardware. (Ariel Sharon joined the Haganah at age fourteen.) For years, the British had confiscated weapons in an effort to hold down the communal violence in Palestine. Even before the British left, however, Israelis manufactured and imported whatever they could. Some British rifles had been squirreled away. Mortars and Sten guns were machined in small shops. Trucks were armored with steel plates. U.S. war surplus was imported as "scrap metal" and reassembled. Czech rifles were purchased from Europe. Everything was done on a desperate basis.

For soldiers, Israel mobilized most males, welcomed foreign volunteers (many Americans), and quickly trained new immigrants from Europe. It was a strange

G ⁞ *Geography*

BOUND ISRAEL

An old technique will help you learn the region's geography. It is called a "bounding exercise" and requires you to recite from memory a country's adjoining neighbors, starting in the north and preceding clockwise. The directions need be only approximate.

Israel is bounded on the north by Lebanon and Syria;

on the east by Jordan (and the new state of Palestine, when it happens);

on the south by the Gulf of Aqaba and Egypt;

and on the west by the Mediterranean Sea.

It has been proven that memorizing things makes you smarter.

---

mixture: "The air force spoke English, the tank corps Russian, and the infantry Yiddish," Israelis joked. Actually, the backbone of the Israeli army spoke Hebrew. Many officers were born and raised on kibbutzim with a highly nationalist and egalitarian ethos. The Israeli shock troops, the Palmach, were recruited heavily from kibbutzniks. The Hebrew language evolved so fast, with different units developing their own new terms for weapons and tactics, that units had trouble cross-communicating. Holding them together was their high morale and ability to improvise. As Napoleon, himself a great improviser, noted, "In war the moral is to the physical as three is to one."

Arab armies, on the other hand, lacked a sense of desperation: If they did not win, they would simply go home. Officers were from higher social classes than their soldiers, who were treated as inferiors. Officers were not trained to be daring and imaginative. What should have been a quick Arab victory ground to a halt and was pushed back. An Egyptian army was surrounded and cut off in the "Faluja Pocket" along the present Israel-Egypt border. One of those trapped was a young colonel, Abdul Gamal Nasser, who with his fellow officers swore revenge, first against the corrupt Egyptian regime that had got them into this and second against Israel. These formed the core of the Free Officers Movement that did overthrow King Farouk in 1952.

One Arab force did well: Jordan's Arab Legion, set up, trained, and officered by the British. As the mandate ended, the Arab Legion crossed from Jordan and captured most of the West Bank, including several kibbutzim (best known: the Etzion bloc south of Jerusalem, since reestablished) and the Old City of Jerusalem, the walled portion that contains most holy sites. The Jordanian forces got a big advantage when the departing British turned over to them sturdy stone police stations the British had built during the mandate. One of these forts and an abandoned monastery on the Latrun Heights gave the Arab Legion command of the only road

G Geography

DIVIDED JERUSALEM

Jerusalem, cleft by a no man's land (where intruders could be shot by Jordanian snipers), became Israel's capital but stayed divided until Israel conquered the Old City in 1967. Israelis longed to recover the City of David. The only place diplomats and tourists could normally cross directly between Israel and an Arab country was at the so-called Mandelbaum Gate in Jerusalem, on the border of its Jordanian and Israeli halves. It was not one of the biblical gates into Jerusalem; it was simply the street by the house of an unfortunate Mr. Mandelbaum, who lost his home to the 1948 fighting.

Tourists would arrange with their consulates a few days in advance when they wanted to cross. It was normally a one-way trip; if you exited through the Mandelbaum Gate you were not allowed to return through it. An exception was made at Easter allowing Christians living in Israel to visit East Jerusalem, which contains the Via Dolorosa and Calvary, and then return.

No man's land split Jerusalem from 1948 to 1967. (*Michael Roskin*)

Mandelbaum Gate was the only crossing point from Israel into a neighboring country for Israel's first decades. (*Michael Roskin*)

Cultures

"ON WINGS OF EAGLES"

The immigration of the Yemeni Jews to Israel illustrates the cultural differences of the Middle East. Living in medieval circumstances, Yemen's Jews willingly boarded airplanes to fly to Israel, because Scripture promised that they would be born back to the Promised Land "on the wings of eagles." Some cut holes in the roofs of the aircraft for their cooking fires. Once landed in Israel, however, many refused to get into trucks, for there was nothing in the Bible about these lumbering ground creatures.

In a generation, the Yeminites modernized and Europeanized. Their education levels climbed and they served in the military. Especially important was the emancipation of Yemenite women, allowed for the first time to go to schools and jobs. The rapid cultural change of Israel's Yemenite community illustrates what can be done if people are willing to modernize and the context is conducive.

from the coast to Jerusalem, the Jewish parts of which they intended to starve out. With no artillery, Israeli infantry, many fresh off the boat, could not take Latrun, and repeated attacks came under withering fire. Some of Israel's top officers got blooded at Latrun. Twenty-year-old Ariel Sharon, who became prime minister in 2001, was seriously wounded at Latrun. The Israelis managed, however, by fierce fighting and by building a new road up steep, rocky hills, to open a wedge-shaped corridor to western Jerusalem, the bigger and more modern part of the city, largely built and populated by Jews in the twentieth century.

By late summer of 1948 Israel had not only repelled the Arab armies but had taken more territory than the 1947 UN partition plan had mapped out. In a pattern that kept reappearing, Arab adamancy played into the hands of Israelis. If the Arab states had accepted the UN partition plan, Palestinians would have had their own state in 1948, and it would be larger than anything they have been offered since. From an allotted 55 percent of Palestine, by the time the **cease-fire** took effect in 1949, Israel had 77 percent. Should they have given the additional lands back? Israel's answer was terse and negative: You Arabs rejected and violated the UN plan, so you have no claims under it. This left three-quarters of a million Palestinian refugees with nothing and laid the groundwork for the present impasse: What shall become of the Palestinians?

Israel immediately encouraged Jews from all over the world to immigrate, and by 1960 its population was 2.1 million. Soviet Jews were trapped until the 1980s, but some East European countries let their remaining Jews go. Poland, which once had a large and vibrant Jewish minority, saw most of the remaining Holocaust survivors leave. The biggest source of new Jewish immigrants, however, were Sepharadim (see box above) in Muslim countries. Although they had lived in these lands for centuries, Arab governments turned hostile with the birth

cease-fire   Temporary halt in fighting; does not imply a settlement.

G: *Geography*

ISRAEL'S FEATURES

Galilee—The northernmost portion.

Kinneret—The Sea of Galilee.

Plain of Sharon—Coastal strip in center of country.

Negev—Large southern desert.

Haifa Bay—Natural harbor in north of country.

Mount Carmel—Mountains around Haifa.

Samaria—In current usage, northern portion of West Bank.

Judea—In current usage, southern portion of West Bank that includes Jerusalem.

Jerusalem—Ancient and currently claimed capital, high in Judean hills.

West Bank (of the Jordan River)—Judea and Samaria, home of many Palestinians.

Gaza Strip—Area along Mediterranean around city of Gaza, also home of many Palestinians.

Jordan River—South-flowing stream from Kinneret to Dead Sea.

Dead Sea—Large salty lake, lowest spot on earth.

Wadi Araba—("Valley of the Arabs") Depression that continues southward from the Dead Sea.

Tel Aviv—Israel's largest city, on coast in center.

Eilat—Israel's seaport on Gulf of Aqaba.

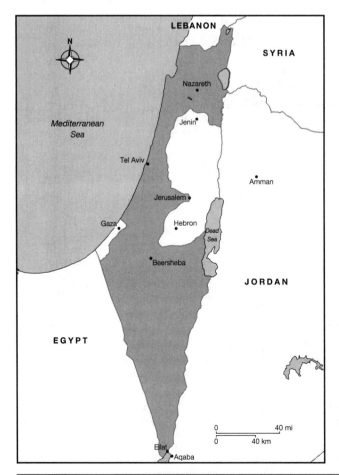

**Israel's 1949–1967
Boundaries**

of Israel. Ancient Jewish communities in Morocco, Algeria, Tunisia, Egypt, Iraq, and Yemen nearly disappeared as their people went to Israel. Immigrants to Israel for the first half of the twentieth century had come almost entirely from Europe. In the 1950s they were heavily from Muslim lands, so that now around a third of Israel's Jews are of non-European origin, and many look like Arabs. (It used to be half, but the wave of immigrants from the ex-Soviet Union tilted the Europeans back into a majority.)

The Origin of Palestinian Refugees

The real losers of the first Arab-Israeli war were some 750,000 Palestinian refugees who fled Israeli-held territories. Israel's standard explanation was that these people left voluntarily and abandoned their properties. They did it, said Israel, because Arab broadcasts told them to temporarily clear out while Arab armies made short work of Israel. They also had the natural human tendency to get out of harm's way.

The truth is that most of them were driven out, sometimes by threats and sometimes by gunfire. The way the new leaders of Israel saw it, Palestinian Arabs hated Israel and would be a permanent **fifth column**, always trying to overthrow Israel. The Arabs had proved even before World War II that they were incapable of living with Jews.

The most deplorable single incident came just before Israel's independence, when full-scale civil war already raged and the British could do nothing to stop it. Some 130 militants from Irgun and Lehi in the early morning attacked the Arab village of Deir Yassin on the western edge of Jerusalem, believing it harbored Palestinian irregular forces. The Irgun killed over 250 Arabs, including women and children. Then Israelis spread news of Deir Yassin, stampeding thousands of Palestinians into flight in fear that they would be next. The Haganah repudiated the Irgun and its bloody tactics but not its purpose of encouraging Arabs to leave. And once they left, even after the 1949 cease-fire, they were not allowed back. Israeli courts declared their property abandoned and sold or gave it to Israelis. Approximately 250,000 Arabs remained in Israel, mostly in remote villages; they were given Israeli citizenship but were under military rule for many years. They now number about 1.2 million.

Palestinians generally fled to the closest Arab land. Most went eastward into the Jordanian-controlled butterfly later known as the West Bank, which was soon incorporated into the Kingdom of Jordan, where it remained until 1967. Most became Jordanian citizens, although many Palestinians disliked the king of Jordan and his Bedouin-based army that seized their West Bank and annexed it to Jordan. Most of Jordan's population was Palestinian; 43 percent still is. Another sizeable group fled into the Egyptian-controlled Gaza Strip, which was never made part of Egypt. Its inhabitants generally did not obtain Egyptian citizenship. The UN Relief

---

fifth column   From Spanish Civil War of 1936–1939, enemy sympathizers and fighters inside one's territory.

G: *Geography*

BOUND JORDAN

Jordan is bounded on the north by Syria;
on the east by Iraq and Saudi Arabia;
on the south by the Gulf of Aqaba;
and on the west by Israel (and the new state of Palestine, if it ever happens).

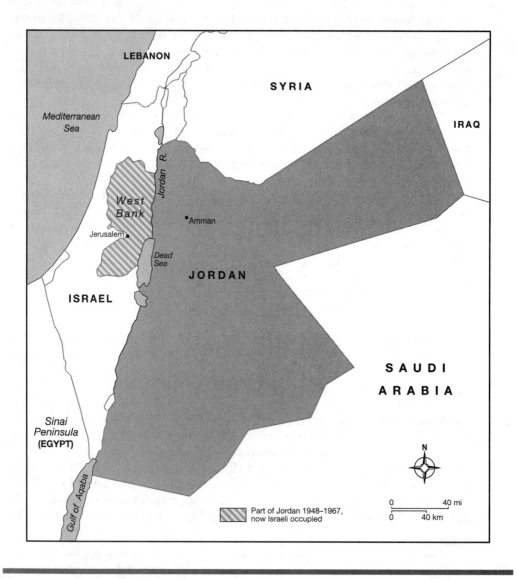

Part of Jordan 1948–1967,
now Israeli occupied

0   40 mi
0   40 km

and Works Agency (UNRWA) provided tents, food, and medical care to those clustered in sprawling refugee camps in several countries. Smaller numbers fled to Lebanon, which offered them no citizenship, and Syria, which did.

Over the decades two trends quickly appeared among the Palestinians, one demographic, the other educational. With no jobs but adequate food, Palestinians had little to do but make babies. For many years the Gaza Strip had the world's highest **fertility rate**; an average woman there bore eight children (now down to six). Replacement rate, at which a population holds steady, is 2.1. With such large families, the Palestinian population soon doubled and doubled again, and now numbers some 5 million. (A century ago, it was around 0.5 million.) Many Palestinians think this is good; it will enable them to destroy Israel and reclaim their land.

Educationally, Palestinians moved rapidly into the twentieth century. Deprived of their farms and small businesses, many saw education as the way up. They are now by far the most educated of all Arabs, and Palestinian doctors and engineers are found throughout the Arab world and even in the United States. Palestinians did much of the skilled work in the Persian Gulf oilfields. Yasser Arafat worked as a petroleum engineer in the Gulf before becoming leader of the Palestinian cause.

For many years, Israel claimed that the crux of the problem was the hostility of Arab states to Israel. If only they could negotiate peace agreements, all would be well in the region. Without the backing of Arab states, Palestinians would soon also compromise with Israel. But state-to-state hostilities are only part of the problem. The underlying problem is the plight of the Palestinians. Egypt and Jordan have signed peace agreements with Israel, but Palestinian unrest has grown. The several Arab-Israeli wars only masked the Palestinian problem.

THE 1956 WAR

Palestinian refugees played a major role in initiating the second Arab-Israeli war. Seething with hatred in refugee camps, some could glimpse their homes across the cease-fire line. Some slipped across the lines to harvest their old orchards. By 1953 they organized bands of *fedayeen*, "self-sacrificers," who shot up Israeli homes and highway traffic, including a school bus. In 1953, after fedayeen murdered an Israeli mother and her two children, Israeli commandos, led by Colonel Ariel Sharon, retaliated by blowing up a Palestinian village in the West Bank, killing sixty-nine. The fedayeen attacks did not diminish; they increased.

In Cairo meanwhile, a 1952 military **coup** ousted King Farouk, whose corrupt rule was blamed for defeat in the war with Israel. Although he did not immediately assume the presidency, the brains behind the coup was Colonel Nasser. When he did take over formally in 1953, he saw himself as the new Saladin (all revolutionary Arab leaders see themselves as the new Saladin) and instituted an ambitious

---

fertility rate   Number of children an average woman bears.

coup   From French *coup d'état*, strike at the state; an extra-legal seizure of power, usually by the military.

program to build a socialist, secular, militaristic Egypt and lead the entire Arab world. (Note how Iraq's Saddam Hussein copied Nasser.) Nasser seized the estates of the rich and redistributed land to poor peasants. He kept almost all industry under state control. There was no democracy; elections were fake. Egypt's large Muslim Brotherhood—a forerunner of Egyptian Islamic Jihad, now part of Al Qaeda—detested Nasser, who kept thousands of them in prison and executed their leaders.

Nasser explained that he was not simply an Egyptian nationalist; he was an Arab nationalist. Egypt, the core of the Arab world, would unite it under his leadership. The Arab world in turn was the core of what came to be called the Third World, and he would play a major role in leading it, too. His associates on the world scene were the leftist neutrals Tito of Yugoslavia and Sukarno of Indonesia. He was hostile to the United States. Although friendly to the Soviet Union, Nasser imprisoned Egyptian Communists. He brooked no opposition, neither Islamic fundamentalists on the right nor Communists on the left.

In the name of pan-Arabism, expansion was important to Nasser, who formed a short-lived union with Syria (1958–1961), called the United Arab Republic. Several such unions have been declared; Qaddafi of Libya was especially eager for them. The idea goes back to the original Islamic notion that all Muslims should live in one umma that is not chopped up into separate nations. Nasser sent Egyptian forces to put down tribal resistance in Yemen, where he used poison gas for the first time since Mussolini used it in Ethiopia in 1935. (Saddam Hussein also used poison gas during his war with Iran.)

Nasser made an old engineering dream his own: a high dam at Aswan on the Upper Nile. The British had built a low dam at Aswan, but a high dam would harness the Nile to irrigate the desert and generate hydroelectricity. The project was terribly expensive. Nasser made an initial feeler for U.S. financing, but Eisenhower's Secretary of State John Foster Dulles, who had no patience with neutralism, turned him down. So Nasser did two things: He threw Egypt into the arms of the Soviet Union, and he nationalized the Suez Canal Company, owned largely by British and French investors. As far as Nasser was concerned, the Suez Company was a last remnant of colonialism; it was built by Egyptian labor and should be run by and for Egyptians. Nasser would use the revenues from Suez transit fees to pay for the dam, and he would get Soviet aid and technical help to build it.

Israel retaliated against the fedayeen with cross-border raids. Many Israelis believe they can gain security only by "teaching the Arabs a lesson." (Israelis are not alone in this approach.) Unfortunately, this produces a never-ending spiral of lessons, what Clausewitz saw as a natural process of **escalation**. In a large retaliation in 1955, Israeli commandos attacked an Egyptian army headquarters in Khan Yunis in the Gaza Strip. (Egypt never annexed the Strip, which is crowded with Palestinian refugees, but did administer it.) The attack enraged Nasser, who immediately purchased massive quantities of Soviet arms, paid for by mortgaging Egypt's cotton harvest for decades.

---

escalation   Tendency for conflicts to intensify, caused by each side trying to outdo the other.

G : *Geography*

DAM FOOLISH

Environmentalists criticize big dams, as do some scientists and engineers and many archaeologists. The Aswan High Dam helps make their case. First, it created big but shallow Lake Nasser behind it. The best such lakes are narrow and deep, to minimize water loss through evaporation. In the hot, dry climate of the Upper Nile, some 30 percent of Lake Nasser's water is lost annually by evaporation. Egypt's ancient prosperity was based on the Nile flooding every year, depositing new, nutrient-rich silt. The Aswan dam retards this process. Species that used to migrate up and down the Nile are now blocked.

Invaluable archaeological treasures were either inundated by Lake Nasser or had to be disassembled and set up elsewhere. (A side benefit of this, however, is that New York, Madrid, and other cities now have ancient Egyptian temples.) Strategically, Egypt has given itself a great vulnerability. In the event of all-out war with Israel (or any country), the Aswan dam would be a tempting target. If it were busted when Lake Nasser was full, it would send a wall of water down the Nile. For a fraction of the enormous expense of the high dam, irrigation could be done by simply pumping water without a dam. But Nasser wanted a showcase project, and the Soviets were happy to oblige him, figuring they were winning an important client state in the Third World.

In 1955, Nasser turned Egypt into a Soviet **client state** to get both arms and engineering for the Aswan dam. Britain and France were furious at having a blue-chip company taken from them and plotted to get it back. They found the perfect partner in **collusion**, Israel, which was alarmed by Nasser's buildup of his newly acquired Soviet weapons in the Sinai. The three countries agreed that Israel would invade Egypt, but just before it reached the canal British and French forces would land to "protect" their canal and keep both Israel and Egypt ten miles distant from it. It was as phony as a three-dollar bill. Eisenhower warned London and Paris against it, but they ignored him. British Prime Minister Anthony Eden (who had studied Arabic at Oxford) thought Nasser was much like Hitler, a dangerous expansionist who had to be stopped early. The French hated Nasser for his help to the Algerian National Front, then fighting to expel France. Unlike today, France in the 1950s was very pro-Israel, seeing Israelis as comrades-in-arms against both Nazis and Algerian nationalists. Israel purchased its jet fighter, the Mystère, from France.

The plan initially went like clockwork. Israel took Egyptian forces by surprise by knocking out much Egyptian armor in Sinai with air strikes, blocking the Sinai's mountain passes by paratroopers, and streaking across the peninsula with its own armored columns in 100 hours. Then British and French paratroopers and marines landed to "save" the canal. They had to fight their way in, and Nasser scuttled many ships in the canal to render it useless. Then the effort bogged down.

---

client state   A weaker state depending on and attached to a major power; not as close as a Soviet satellite state in East Europe.
collusion   Connivance; a seemingly spontaneous activity that has been planned in advance.

Eisenhower, although no friend of Nasser, feared the attack would alienate the entire Arab world. (Note the similarity of French criticism of U.S. actions against Iraq in 2003.) And at the same time the Soviet Union was crushing the 1956 Hungarian uprising. Eisenhower wanted the world's attention focused on this crime; the British and French Suez misadventure distracted the world from Soviet brutality. Ike put pressure on Britain and France to withdraw, and they soon did, angry at the United States. When Washington was angry with France in 2003 for refusing to support us on Iraq, Paris could point to 1956 as a lack of U.S. solidarity in opposing a dangerous foe for common Western interests.

Eisenhower was much more even-handed in his approach to Israel and the Arab countries than later U.S. presidents. He pressured Israel to withdraw from Sinai, and Israel did in the spring of 1957, so the 1956 war netted Israel no territorial gains. Israel was unhappy at the lack of a peace settlement with Egypt but had accomplished some of its goals. It had destroyed much Egyptian equipment in the Sinai so that Egypt was not an immediate threat. Israel **spiked** Egyptian guns at Sharm el Sheik, opening the Strait of Tiran to Israeli shipping. Its southern port of Eilat became its maritime opening for commerce with Asia and Africa. Israel also got some concessions from Washington: The Americans said they would keep the Strait of Tiran open and would support a UN Emergency Force (UNEF) composed of volunteers from several countries to supervise the truce and sound alarms in case of a military buildup. UNEF, however, was to be stationed only on the Egyptian side of the border. Israel thought it had gained something from the Sinai Campaign, but it was temporary.

THE SIX DAY WAR

The eleven years between the second (1956) and the third Arab-Israeli wars (1967) were arguably the happiest and most secure period in Israel's life. There were relatively few Palestinian Arabs within Israel's borders and almost no terrorist attacks or bombings. One could live and travel in Israel freely and safely. The 1949 borders continued, leaving Israel a funny shape. At one point, along the Plain of Sharon, Israel was only ten miles wide between the Jordanian-held West Bank and the Mediterranean. This bothered Israelis, who worried that Israel could be cut in two at this narrow neck by a force invading from the east. As it turned out, this was never a serious threat.

Trouble in 1967 started on Israel's northern border, with Syria, which held the commanding Golan Heights, a chain of hills overlooking Israel's Hula Valley. From time to time, Syrian artillery lobbed shells into Israeli kibbutzim on the valley floor, and Israel fired back. On April 7, after one especially strong Syrian shelling, Israeli jets hit Syrian gun emplacements on the Golan Heights. Syria sent its Soviet-made MiGs into an aerial dogfight with Israel's French-made Mystères. Superior aircraft and pilot skills told the story: Syria lost six, Israel none. Damascus screamed in rage, accusing Israel of massing forces in the Galilee in preparation for an attack on

---

spike   To render an artillery piece useless.

G: *Geography*

TERRITORY AND SECURITY

Many people think territory equals security. That is, the more geographical features under your control, the more secure you are. Gaining land from the enemy means victory and safety. This is not always so, as Clausewitz realized early in the nineteenth century. What matters in war, he wrote, is seldom any particular territorial gains but destruction of the enemy's main forces. Napoleon, whom Clausewitz briefly fought against and later studied, invaded Russia and captured Moscow in 1812. (He did better than Hitler in 1941.) But much of the Russian army was still intact, waiting for the right time. Moscow burned down, and the Grande Armée had to retreat hundreds of miles through the snow, harassed by the Russian army that Napoleon had not broken. Napoleon's overextension deep into Russia led to his defeat and eventually to his downfall.

Additional territory can actually turn into a vulnerability. The United States took the Philippines from Spain in 1898, thinking the islands would give us a splendid presence in East Asia. Teddy Roosevelt, who helped engineer the move, later regretted it, because the Philippines now had to be defended. They were easy pickings for Japan in 1942 (when U.S. forces in the Philippines outnumbered the Japanese invaders).

Israel's seizure of the West Bank in 1967 delighted many Israelis, as it removed the threat of the narrow neck left over from the 1949 borders and gave Israel "strategic depth." Now Israel's main line of defense was the Jordan River, much farther from Israel's population centers. It looked great on a map. But with the West Bank Israel also got some 1.5 million Palestinians, who grew more numerous and angrier over the decades. They launched uprisings and bombings, making life for Israelis far less secure than it had been prior to 1967. Now Israelis must worry about security constantly.

Furthermore, Israel's narrow neck from 1949 to 1967 was not especially vulnerable. All invasions require the massing of forces, and any massing of Arab troops and armor on the West Bank in preparation for an invasion was easily detectable—we're talking about a few miles here—making surprise impossible. Considering current difficulties, Israel's 1949 borders were not so bad.

Syria. Damascus also demanded that Nasser of Egypt, still billing himself as the leader of the Arab world, do something about it. Syria and Egypt were allies, and Nasser began mobilizing his forces. The Soviet Union, patron of both Syria and Egypt, also accused Israel of massing its forces. Israel invited the Soviet ambassador to go to Galilee and see for himself that this was not true. Everything in the Hula Valley, only twelve miles long and six miles wide, can be seen from a hill on its west. The Soviet ambassador refused and repeated the charge. The Soviet Union, trying to enhance its power in the region by championing the Arab cause, deserves much of the blame for the Six Day War that followed.

On May 17, Nasser ordered the UNEF, in the Sinai as peace observers since 1957, to leave, and they did, perhaps too quickly. There were no UNEF observers on the Israeli side of the border. UNEF was never intended or able to impose peace, merely to serve as an alarm bell should either side start massing forces. With UNEF's departure, that function was over and signaled to Israel that Egyptian armor in the Sinai would soon again be a threat, as it had been in 1956. There was speculation that UN Secretary General U Thant could have stalled Nasser a few weeks— for example, by insisting that the UN Security Council debate withdrawing

 *Peace*

Why No Peace in 1967

Rather naively, Israel expected that in the aftermath of the Six Day War the Arab countries would, in the parlance of bygone centuries, "sue for peace." They would say enough of war, agree to some compromises, and sign peace treaties. Instead, meeting in Khartoum, Sudan, on September 1, 1967, the Arab countries passed their famous triple rejection: no recognition of Israel, no peace, and no negotiations.

The problem was that the Six Day War—thanks to the Soviet threat to intervene—ended too soon and was not as decisive as many thought. Israel seized no Arab capitals—Cairo, Amman, and Damascus were far from the fronts at the war's end—or even vital territories. Jordan was hurt by the loss of the West Bank, but Egypt and Syria suffered only humiliation from their losses, respectively, of the Sinai and Golan Heights. Much of the Egyptian, Jordanian, and Syrian armies were still intact if bloodied and were quickly resupplied by the Soviets. The Arab countries did not sue for peace because they did not have to.

If the war had lasted longer and Israel had really crushed the enemy main forces and taken their capitals, then Egypt, Jordan, and Syria would have had to settle. Instead, the war was frozen in midleap, *bellum interruptum*. Instead of peace settlements among the warring parties, the region got UN Security Council Resolution 242. Something similar happened with the 1991 Gulf War, which left Saddam Hussein in power and led directly to the 2003 Gulf War. As Edward Luttwak commented on such situations: "Give war a chance." War is horrible, but a series of incomplete wars is even worse.

UNEF—to let things calm. Some say the Burmese U Thant was too eager to please Nasser, a fellow Third World neutralist who could therefore do no wrong.

Next, on May 22, Nasser declared the Strait of Tiran closed to Israeli shipping. The ship channel passes through Egyptian territorial waters and is easily blocked by mines and shore batteries. Israel did much of its commerce with Asia and Africa through the port of Eilat on the Gulf of Aqaba. Israeli Prime Minister Levi Eshkol asked Washington, which had promised to keep the Strait open in 1957, what it was going to do. President Lyndon Johnson, up to his neck in the Vietnam War, took too long to organize a response. This reinforced Israel's longstanding conviction that it must look after its own security; outside powers are undependable.

For Israel, the final move came on May 30, when King Hussein of Jordan, hitherto extremely cautious, signed a three-country alliance with Egypt and Syria. Hussein may have wanted to stay out of the war but, with a majority-Palestinian population (many of whom wished to overthrow him), felt he had to show solidarity with the Arab cause. (Burdened by the same fears, Hussein, although personally pro-American, gave verbal and some material support to Iraq in the 1991 Gulf War.)

After days of agonizing debate, Israel's government decided to **preempt**. No one was sure it would work, but they were sure they could not wait for the enemy to strike first. On June 5, 1967, Israel launched a textbook-perfect three-front war that stunned the world and soon became known as the Six Day War. (In 1867 Bismarck beat Austria in the Six Week War.) American officers, then bogged down in

preempt   To strike first on the eve of war.

C : *Cultures*

FIGHTING WORDS

Israel picks up Arab radio broadcasts, and many Israelis understand Arabic (many are from Arab countries). The air waves in 1967, especially from Egypt's Voice of the Arabs, were full of rage and promises to erase Israel and Israelis. Much of this was hyperbole; exaggerated rhetoric is part of Arab culture. Leaders especially are expected to use dire accusations and threats; it plays well with the home audience. (Notice how Saddam Hussein in 1991 and 2003 promised to fight to the bitter end.) Nonetheless, in 1967 Nasser swore on the radio that he was ready for war and welcomed it. Some suspect he was bluffing, but the Israelis took him literally and called his bluff. Never bluff.

Israelis, especially those of European origin, are more careful with words, using few of them and weighing their meanings. (Hebrew is a very concise language.) Further, the early Zionist pioneers were fed up with wordy ideologues that talked a lot of theory but could not get off their duff to do anything. They vowed to go heavy on deeds and light on words, building a tough, no-nonsense culture based on hard work and results. (Soviet Communists tried, less successfully, to build a similar culture.)

The very different use of words by the two cultures makes their clashes worse. Israelis take literally the fiery Arab words: "If they say it, they must mean it. When they scream they're going to kill us all, we must take them literally. When we say something, we mean it." Israel, without using a lot of words, then takes forceful military measures, which causes the Arabs to scream even more. Fighting words lead to more fights. In recent years, with the spread of education and modernity in the Arab world, some Arab intellectuals have become moderate and rational in their rhetoric, a hopeful sign of cultural change.

Vietnam, complained in jealousy at the quick, decisive Israeli war, much of it learned at the U.S. Army Command and General Staff College at Fort Leavenworth, Kansas.

First, Israeli jets came in low across the Mediterranean—at one point tailing a commercial jetliner to disguise their presence on Egyptian radar—and destroyed most Egyptian air power on the ground in the first hours of the war. Then Israeli jets knocked out Egyptian tanks in the Sinai, enabling Israeli armor to race to the Suez Canal in two days.

King Hussein of Jordan honored his pledge to enter the war, and Jordanian artillery in the West Bank began shelling Israel. This gave Israelis the excuse to do precisely what they had longed for: seize the Old City of Jerusalem and entire West Bank. A mere three battalions of Israeli paratroopers surrounded East Jerusalem and stormed through it, pausing in awe at the Wailing Wall, the remaining western wall of the last temple. Jordan was effectively out of action, and with little resistance Israeli forces took the rest of the West Bank.

The third phase, on days five and six of the war, was the hardest and bloodiest: straight up the Golan Heights with tanks and infantry against entrenched and bunkered Syrian positions. Time was important, as Moscow promised to send troops to support its Arab client states. Washington passed word to Israel to wrap it up quickly. The dead from the Six Day War: 983 Israelis and 4,296 Arabs. Israel's victory was brilliant but did not lead to peace. The Arabs simply refused to negotiate (see box on page 104).

THE 1973 WAR

The Arabs call it the Ramadan War, for it came during the holy month of Ramadan, when Muslims fast during daylight hours. Israelis call it the Yom Kippur War, for it came when Jews observe their Day of Atonement, one of their holiest. Seculars call it the October War. We will call it simply the 1973 war. Several steps led up to it.

In the aftermath of Egypt's defeat in 1967, Egyptian President Nasser took responsibility for their debacle and "resigned," but that seems to have been a ploy to gain sympathy, for the cheering masses implored him to stay on, and he accepted. Nasser does indeed bear a great deal of responsibility; his decisions made the war inevitable. He had built himself up as the hero of the Arabs and then had to deliver on it. To hide Egyptian shame at having been beaten by the technologically superior Israeli air force, Nasser charged that it was actually U.S. jets that had bombed Egypt during the war. In the face of this preposterous lie, Washington broke relations with Cairo; they were not restored until 1973. Arabs tend to be awfully loose with their words (see box titled "Fighting Words" on page 105).

Nasser died of natural causes in 1970, and power gravitated into the hands of another Egyptian army officer, Anwar Sadat, a far more subtle and clever leader, who reversed some of the consequences of Nasser's mistakes. First, Sadat recognized that Egypt had become much too dependent on the Soviet Union, both for the Aswan dam and for military advice and hardware. By the same token, he recognized that U.S. influence in the region, especially on Israel, was crucial to getting a viable peace settlement. "The United States holds 90 percent of the cards," he used to say, an exaggeration but a welcome corrective to Nasser's anti-Americanism.

Sadat therefore deliberately worsened Cairo's relations with Moscow and improved them with Washington. He found fault (deservedly) with Soviet engineering at Aswan and had European firms complete the project. He at first asked to purchase a vast quantity of Soviet arms and when denied shopped elsewhere. In 1971, he sent Soviet military advisers home, something Washington liked. Sadat put out feelers to President Nixon to get peace talks with Israel going. Unfortunately, neither Washington nor Jerusalem took Sadat seriously. Sadat solved this problem by going to war, after which he was taken very seriously.

To restore Egyptian self-confidence and get taken seriously on the world scene, Sadat had to recover the Sinai peninsula, in Israeli hands since 1967. In holding this vast desert, Israel made what might be termed the "**Maginot Line** mistake": supposing that fixed fortifications, lightly manned, could repel an attack. After victory in 1967, Israel constructed on the east bank of the Suez Canal the Bar Lev Line, named after one of their generals. It consisted of bunkers for observers and weapons and had withstood Sadat's "war of attrition," artillery

---

Maginot Line   French fortifications against Germany before World War II.

Women of the Middle East

GOLDA MEIER

As a child in Kiev, Ukraine, Golda Meier (1898–1978) remembered cowering during a pogrom. Her family immigrated to Milwaukee in 1906, and she went to college there and became a local Labor Zionist youth leader. In 1921 she and her husband went to Palestine to join a kibbutz. By World War II she had become an important leader of the Palestine Jewish community, sometimes guiding underground activities in opposition to the British. She was one of the signers of Israel's declaration of independence in 1948 and was elected to the **Knesset** in 1949. She served as minister of labor from 1949 to 1956, then foreign minister from 1956 to 1966. She helped set up the 1956 Sinai Campaign with Britain and France. Upon the death of Levi Eshkol in 1969, Golda Meier became Israel's prime minister. Accused of lack of preparedness for the 1973 war, she resigned in 1974.

An extremely tough lady, she impressed a wide variety of world leaders, including Henry Kissinger, with her intellect, determination, and get-to-the-point negotiating skills. She admitted that she sacrificed her private and family life to the Zionist cause but said it had to be that way.

duels from 1967 to 1970. It did not seem to require many troops, as any Egyptian attack could be detected in advance, giving Israel enough time to mobilize its forces. The Suez Canal would serve as Israel's moat. Actually, some Israelis warned against relying on the Bar Lev Line and urged using the mountains of Sinai some 200 miles eastward as Israel's main line of resistance. As noted earlier, having more territory does not necessarily make you more secure.

In 1973, the Egyptian army held a series of maneuvers that lulled Israel into thinking the movement of troops and armor were just drills. Egyptian military communications were heavy, but they had been heavy for a long time, so Israel took no special note. The United States, however, did warn Israel about "increased Egyptian communications security," meaning more encrypted messages, a possible tip-off. Apparently Israel was taken by surprise in 1973.

The Egyptian attack across the Suez Canal on October 6, 1973, was daring and well executed, something Israelis thought Egyptians could not carry out. Commandos paddled across the canal at relatively weak spots so that military engineers could cut openings in the sand banks with fire hoses. Pontoon bridges then brought across trucks and armor, which fanned out behind the lightly held Bar Lev Line, capturing it the first day. On the same day, in coordination with Egypt, Syrian (and some Iraqi) forces smashed into the Golan Heights with a huge armored force.

In the six years since 1967, the technological nature of warfare had changed, and Egyptians and Syrians showed they could master it. Microelectronics now

Knesset Israel's parliament.

 *Cultures*

ISRAELI OVERCONFIDENCE

In the 1956 and 1967 wars a victorious Israel became convinced that it had the brains, daring, and skill to trounce its Arab opponents, who were deemed permanently backward in technology and inept and cowardly in war. The only time Arabs fight well is when they are cornered, Israelis used to say; just give them an escape route and they'll take it. Overconfidence in war, as in sport, can be disastrous, as Israel learned in the 1973 war.

What Israelis neglected is that everyone has a learning curve, and that sooner or later Arabs would develop the high-tech skills and bravery under fire the Israelis thought they had a monopoly on. Victory is a wasting asset; it lulls you into thinking you will be permanently victorious.

enabled them to knock out Israeli aircraft and tanks, areas where previously Israel held a big advantage. Israeli losses were larger than before. Israel, of course, immediately mobilized. A large column under the bold General Sharon (later prime minister) crashed through Egyptian lines between the two Bitter Lakes at the southern end of the Canal and crossed to the *west* side of the Canal, trapping the Egyptian Third Army on the east side. Meanwhile, on the Golan Heights Israel and Syria fought the biggest tank battle in history, bigger than Kursk in Russia in 1943. Israel prevailed and pushed the Syrian forces halfway back to Damascus. The losses in 1973 were heavier and narrower than in 1967: 2,838 Israelis killed to 8,528 Arabs. Israel saw that it might not always prevail.

Again, the war stalled, in part because Washington delivered enough munitions to Israel to keep it from losing but not enough to decisively triumph again. Moscow again threatened to intervene, a threat nullified by President Nixon's firm warning not to. In 1973 Washington manipulated cleverly and constructively (see pages 311–312), leading to a military and psychological balance of power between Israel and Egypt. Out of this, with U.S. help, came Sadat's historic visit to Jerusalem in 1977 and the first Arab-Israel peace settlement, between Egypt and Israel in 1979 (see pages 114–117). If you want peace, you must manipulate disputants until they see they have more to gain by negotiating than by fighting. A hands-off approach does not work.

THE LEBANON INCURSION

Some call Israel's 1982–2000 incursion into Lebanon the fifth Arab-Israeli war. It was Israel's messiest and most frustrating military action and ultimately a failure. Israel had been able to beat enemy countries, but it could not fight chaos. At that time Lebanon as a country barely existed; it was more like a Hobbesian war of each against all. Israelis were arrogant to suppose they could fix this. (It

Conflicts

THE FIVE WARS OF ISRAEL

War of Independence	1948–1949	Israel survives Arab invasions and ends up with most of Palestine.
Sinai Campaign	1956	Israel, in collusion with Britain and France, takes Sinai.
Six Day War	1967	Israel takes Sinai and Gaza from Egypt, West Bank and Jerusalem from Jordan, and Golan Heights from Syria.
October War	1973	Israel narrowly beats back Egypt and Syria.
Lebanon Incursion	1982–2000	Israel holds southern Lebanon.

was equally arrogant of the United States to suppose its "peacekeeping" forces in Beirut could bring peace; they were blown up by a suicide truck bomb. See Chapter 18.)

Lebanon (see boxes on pages 311 and 314) had been a delightful but shaky country. After its independence from France in 1943, it aspired to be the Switzerland of the Middle East: rich, neutral, and peaceful. For years, it succeeded. Many wealthy people from all over the Arab world had summer homes in its cool hills. There they could drink, gamble, and do other things not permitted in their home country. Christians, although a minority of the population, ran Lebanon like a southern European country.

But Lebanon could not stay aloof from the troubles of the region. Its Muslim majority was increasingly discontent, especially its rapidly growing Shi'a population, which was also the poorest. In 1958, amidst a small civil war, U.S. Marines landed (see Chapter 18). But starting in 1971, things got much worse. Since 1967, the main headquarters of the Palestinian Liberation Organization had been in Amman, Jordan, where they increasingly acted like a state within a state. The Jordanian army, composed heavily of Bedouin, resented them. Some tried to assassinate Jordan's King Hussein in September 1971. This sparked a bloody showdown between the **PLO** and the Jordanian army, which won and forced the PLO to move its headquarters to Beirut. (This was also the origin of the Palestinian extremist Black September group.) From the south of Lebanon, Palestinians fighters, most of them in Yasser Arafat's mainstream Al Fatah, launched raids and rocket attacks on northern Israel.

The PLO presence accelerated the internal collapse of Lebanon. Lebanese Christians tried to hang on to their old power and privilege, but Muslims turned

PLO Palestine Liberation Organization, formed in 1964, chaired by Yasser Arafat since 1969; leads Palestine Authority; contains several factions, some violent.

G Geography

BOUND LEBANON

Lebanon is bounded on the north and east by Syria;
on the south by Israel;
and on the west by the Mediterranean Sea.

increasingly radical and demanded a new political and economic deal. By 1975 Lebanon had fallen apart as a dozen politico-religious armies battled. Syria took advantage of the chaos to occupy the Bekaa Valley of eastern Lebanon, which it claimed was Syrian territory the French never should have included in Lebanon. Syria still occupies much of Lebanon, supervises its politics, and will likely keep portions of Lebanon.

Some Lebanese Christians started seeing a tie to Israel as their solution and established contacts. Some Israelis started thinking that ousting the PLO and returning Christians to power in Beirut would safeguard their northern border. Both oversimplified an extremely complex situation (as did Washington) and soon made the chaos even worse.

In 1982 Israel's ambassador was shot to death in London by an agent of Abu Nidal, a Palestinian militant who turned into a hired gun (and a "suicide" in Baghdad in 2002, shot three times in the head). Israel was enraged and invaded the south of Lebanon to clear it of the Fatah fighters who routinely shelled northern Israel. Israel called it "Operation Peace for Galilee" and said it would go only about twenty-five miles into Lebanon. At first the Shi'a who lived in the south of Lebanon, who never liked the Palestinians and their disruptions, welcomed the Israelis. Fatah simply pulled back further north, and Israel pursued them, reaching Beirut and shelling its Palestinian and other hostile sections for two months. In August 1982, with help from the U.S. Navy, the PLO left Beirut, its headquarters since 1971, taking some 15,000 PLO fighters with it. Arafat later set up a new headquarters in Tunis. Israel celebrated briefly, but it had just opened a can of worms. Syria held back, not wishing to tangle with Israel. Besides, the more chaos Israel inflicted on Lebanon, the easier it would be for Syria to take it over.

In September 1982 a car bomb killed the leader of Lebanese Maronite Christians, Bashir Gemayel, head of the Phalange militia. The bomb was probably planted by a Syrian agent, but the Phalange took out its wrath on Palestinians. Phalangists charged into the Sabra and Shatila Palestinian refugee camps in Beirut, killing over 1,000 civilians, including women and children. Israeli soldiers did not participate but watched and did nothing, figuring, "Why not let Christians take care of Palestinians for us?" Israel's Defense Minister Ariel Sharon was accused of complicity in the massacre—he had met with Phalange leaders—

but he angrily denied the charge. Israel pulled back but kept a thirty-kilometer "security zone" (about twenty miles) in the south of Lebanon, staffed by Israeli soldiers and local mercenaries.

Israel had not solved its security problem, however. In 1979 radical Islamists had taken over Iran (see Chapter 13) and moved to energize Shi'a coreligionists throughout the Muslim world. Shi'a in Lebanon had long been poor and discontent. They organized the militant **Hezbollah**, which got weapons, money, and guidance from Iran and harassed Israeli forces in the south of Lebanon. Over eighteen years Israel lost scores of soldiers to ambushes, mines, and suicide bombings in Lebanon. Finally, in 2000, Labor Prime Minister Ehud Barak, a former general and Israel's most-decorated soldier but a relative soft-liner, withdrew Israeli forces from Lebanon. Viewed as too ready to compromise, Barak lost reelection to Sharon by a landslide in 2001. In trying to gain security—both in the West Bank and Lebanon—Israel had made itself less secure. War is easy; occupying a hostile land is hard.

CONCLUSIONS

The five Arab-Israeli wars—1948, 1956, 1967, 1973, and the Lebanon incursion of 1982–2000—can be viewed as one long war that never gets settled. The vital national interests of the belligerents are hard to reconcile, and the separate wars never reached definitive defeats or victories. Each war has specific causes, but the underlying cause is that Israel exists, and the Arabs, especially the Palestinians, wish it had never existed.

The real losers have been the Palestinians, roughly five million now. At least two wars, 1956 and 1982, were triggered by Palestinian attacks on Israel. Israel's wars with neighboring Arab states to some extent served to mask the Palestinian question, which is much harder to solve than wars between countries.

A common mistake is to equate territory with security. Israel occupied enemy territory, but the addition of the West Bank and Gaza, with its millions of angry Palestinians, did not make Israel more secure. In two wars, 1956 and 1967, Israel "preempted." When it failed to preempt, in 1973, Egypt breached the Bar Lev Line along the Suez Canal. We have likely not seen the last Arab-Israeli war.

FURTHER REFERENCE

Bickerton, Ian J., and Carla L. Klausner. *A Concise History of the Arab-Israeli Conflict*, 4th ed. Upper Saddle River, NJ: Prentice Hall, 2002.
Herzog, Chaim. *The Arab-Israeli Wars: War and Peace in the Middle East*. New York: Vintage, 1984.

Hezbollah   (also spelled *Hizbullah, Hizballah,* and other ways) "Party of God," armed, radical Shi'a movement, sponsored by Iran.

Milton-Edwards, Beverley, and Peter Hinchcliffe. *Conflicts in the Middle East since 1945*, 2nd ed. New York Routledge, 2003.

Oren, Michael B. *Six Days of War: June 1967 and the Making of the Modern Middle East.* New York: Oxford University Press, 2002.

Pollack, Kenneth M. *Arabs at War: Military Effectiveness, 1948–1991.* Lincoln, NE: University of Nebraska Press, 2002.

Thomas, Baylis. *How Israel Was Won: A Concise History of the Arab–Israeli Conflict.* Lanham, MD: Lexington Books, 1999.

Westwood, John. *The History of the Middle East Wars.* North Dighton, MA: World Publications, 2002.

Is Peace Possible?

Points to Ponder

- Are Americans too optimistic to understand the Middle East?
- Have efforts for peace been insufficient?
- How has the UN worked for Middle East peace?
- Under what circumstances can diplomacy work?
- What do Israelis want from a peace agreement?
- What do Palestinians want from a peace agreement?
- Can the above two be compromised?
- Describe the "downward spiral."

We begin this chapter with the unhappy thought that peace may be impossible. Americans, products of an optimistic society, are uncomfortable with this notion. On the evidence, though, the conflicts and wars between Arabs and Israelis we reviewed in the previous two chapters do not point toward peace. We must put aside three common misconceptions: (1) that the UN has not tried hard enough to settle the Arab-Israeli conflict; (2) that Washington has not tried hard enough to settle the Arab-Israeli conflict; (3) that Arabs and Israelis could settle it if only they would meet together. There have been massive efforts in all three areas. Lack of peace is not from want of trying.

The United States has been involved in Middle East peace efforts from the beginning. U.S. involvement during and after the 1973 October War became especially deep. Secretary of State Kissinger practiced "shuttle diplomacy" by flying tirelessly between Cairo, Jerusalem, and Damascus to arrange cease-fires. For years the State Department has had a top diplomat with rank of ambassador and a staff working full-time on Arab-Israeli peace. U.S. presidents, especially Carter and Clinton, have hosted numerous meetings—often at Camp David, the president's personal retreat in the Maryland mountains—of Egyptian, Palestinian, and Israeli leaders.

And Israel has had numerous contacts with Arab countries—some official, some informal, most of them secret—since its founding. After Egypt's 1952 revolution, for

Peace

UN Efforts at Middle East Peace

1947—UN Partition Plan, Security Council Resolution 181. See pages 86–88.

1948—UN General Assembly Resolution 194 established a "conciliation commission" to settle the first Arab-Israeli war.

1967—UN Security Council Resolution 242 called for Israel to withdraw from its conquests in the Six Day War in exchange for the Arabs making peace. This "land for peace" idea became the basis for all subsequent formulas for settlement.

1973—UN Security Council Resolution 338 called for a cease-fire during the October War and implementation of Resolution 242.

1978—UN Security Council Resolution 425 called for Israel to withdraw from southern Lebanon.

One finds nearly annual UN resolutions on the Middle East. After several iterations, one comes to doubt the effectiveness of UN resolutions, which are often detached from reality. Much the same came of UN resolutions on Iraq: lofty sentiments with no means of implementation applied to strong-willed leaders who have no intention of backing down.

example, Egyptian and Israeli diplomats met secretly in Paris. But a stupid Israeli attempt to bomb the American library in Cairo (to worsen U.S.-Egyptian ties) in 1954, the rise of Palestinian *fedayeen* attacks into Israel, and Israel's retaliatory raids killed this faint possibility. King Hussein of Jordan had repeated personal contacts with Israeli diplomats over the years. Even in the middle of a war, enemies maintain discreet contacts with each other, usually in the capitals of neutral third countries. Please do not say, "If only they could meet." They have met many times. It is not lack of personal chemistry (see box on "atmospherics" on page 120) but inability to compromise what they deem their vital national interests that prevent peace settlements.

Sadat's Incredible Journey

Egyptian President Sadat won much in the October War of 1973. He vindicated his country by showing that Egyptians could fight. He got back part of the Sinai. The world now took him seriously. He reestablished diplomatic relations with the United States and hosted a visit by President Nixon. But he still did not have all of the Sinai, and he did not have peace.

To gain that, Sadat delivered another surprise. In late 1977 Sadat stated that he would be willing to visit Israel. Actually, secret contacts probably began earlier. One story (unconfirmed) has it that Israel's Mosad intelligence service learned of a plot by Egyptian Muslim extremists to kill Sadat. (In 1981, they did.) Israel's new prime minister, Menachem Begin, former Irgun chief and a right-wing hawk, ordered the information be passed on to Cairo, and this began a dialog. Sadat

 *Peace*

THE UN'S FIRST EFFORTS

From its founding in 1945, the United Nations has been deeply involved in the Palestine question. One of the first to make this connection was Ralph Bunche, a black American who studied political science at Harvard and taught it at Howard. During World War II Bunche became a State Department official and worked on setting up the new UN. He saw the need for a UN committee that would handle territories that were not self-governing (in 1945, most of the great colonial empires were still intact) and that would determine how to decolonize these territories. The U.S. delegation was not interested, so Bunche took his idea to the Australian delegation, which was. Bunche built support for and got a UN Trusteeship Council, which inherited the mandates set up by the League of Nations, including Palestine. The 1947 UN partition plan aimed at ending the British mandate in a way that Arabs and Jews could live in peace.

Many UN efforts do not lead to peace. The problem is generally not flawed plans or lack of enforcement mechanisms. The UN has no armed forces or even police; all are on temporary loan (at high salaries) from member countries that wish to participate. The conflict itself may be so deep and bitter that there is no peaceful solution. Debating the issue in the UN puts a diplomatic gloss on the violence but does essentially nothing to get the warring parties to compromise. When—and only when—the sides are ready to compromise, the UN can facilitate contacts, draft documents, and offer stabilization measures, such as truce observers. The UN has no enforcement powers.

As soon as open war broke out in 1948, the UN, still trying to implement its partition plan, set up a Truce Commission and sent mediators to calm the fighting. By that time, with five Arab armies invading, the partition plan was road kill. The chief UN diplomat on the scene, Swedish Count Folke Bernadotte, arranged a **truce** in June that lasted a month, giving Israel time to buy Czech small arms and other weapons. He also recommended changes in the plan, giving all of Galilee to the Israelis and all the Negev to the Arabs. Jerusalem, as envisaged by the original plan, was to remain under international supervision. An Irgun member assassinated Bernadotte for allegedly selling out Israel (he had not). An angry Ben Gurion ordered the Irgun to disband, but none of its members were ever punished. Israel has not been good about cooperating with the UN, viewing it as hostile and pro-Arab.

By late 1948, when both sides were mutually exhausted, they agreed to **mediation** by Ralph Bunche, now a UN official, who invited delegations from Israel and the five Arab countries to the Greek island of Rhodes. The Arabs were so infuriated that they would not meet face-to-face with the Israelis, so Bunche put them on separate floors of the same hotel. He shuttled between floors in what are called **proximity talks**, adding suggestions of his own. He got a series of **armistices** between the Arab countries and Israel in early 1949 and won the 1950 Nobel Peace Prize. Unfortunately, the armistices could not turn into peace settlements, for the underlying problem remained, namely, the Palestinians' situation.

pushed matters along when CBS's Walter Cronkite, the dean of American newscasters, asked Sadat what would happen if Begin invited him to Jerusalem. (The question was likely planted in advance.) Sadat said he'd go. On November 17, 1977, Begin invited and Sadat accepted.

truce   A long cease-fire.
mediation   Neutral third party makes suggestions for compromise.
proximity talks   Close, but not in the same room.
armistice   Stable, longer-lasting *truce*; does not imply a peace settlement.

G : *Geography*

BOUND EGYPT

Egypt is bounded on the north by the Mediterranean Sea;
on the east by Israel, the Gulf of Aqaba, and the Red Sea;
on the south by Sudan;
and on the west by Libya.

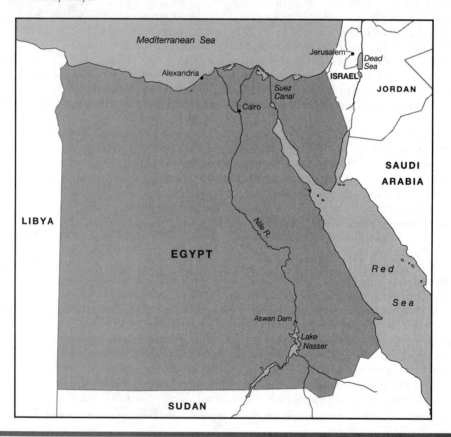

The world was astonished and delighted, for it seemed to herald the beginning
of the end of a series of ghastly wars. Just two days later, on November 19, Sadat
jetted a mere forty minutes to Ben Gurion airport near Tel Aviv and motorcaded
to Jerusalem for meetings with Begin and a speech to the Knesset. The meetings
were awkward and chilly, but they got things rolling. U.S. President Jimmy Carter,
a religious man who dreamed of peace in the Holy Land, in 1978 brought Sadat
and Begin together at Camp David and worked with them long and personally

until they agreed to the first Arab-Israeli peace treaty, signed March 26, 1979, on the White House lawn. Sadat and Begin jointly won the Nobel Peace Prize in 1978, but much of the credit should go to Carter. Egypt got back the entire Sinai. Israel even demolished settlements in Sinai over the violent objections of Israeli settlers. Egypt did not take back the Gaza Strip, which it had never claimed as part of Egypt. A second agreement signed in 1979 vowed to solve the Palestinian problem, but both Israel and Egypt forgot about it. For this reason, many Arabs reviled Sadat for selling out the Palestinians.

Many Israelis had assumed that as soon as Israel had a peace treaty with Egypt, its biggest and most dangerous foe, most of the other Arab countries would quickly follow suit, like a logjam giving way. This did not happen. Each Arab country has its own problems and interests, which may point away from peace with Israel. Anwar Sadat, a man of vision larger than mere nationalism and perhaps the most appealing figure of the twentieth-century Middle East, was gunned down by Islamic extremists in 1981. No one has taken his place in the region. His journey from warrior to peacemaker does not demonstrate that human good will alone can settle a terrible quarrel. It shows, rather, that the proper balances of power and psychologies may enable realistic statesmen to take steps to peace.

THE FIRST PALESTINIAN INTIFADA

The first **intifada**, 1987–1991, seems to have begun largely spontaneously as West Bank Palestinians, seeing their lands eaten away by Israeli settlements and no progress on the diplomatic front, started taking matters into their own hands, initially by throwing rocks, later by shooting. Arafat, in Tunisia, did not instigate the uprising; he reacted only afterward by supporting it. He was not even very aware of what was going on in the West Bank and Gaza Strip, a continual problem with absentee leaders. Many Palestinians came to view Arafat as aging and ineffectual and threw their allegiance to other, far more radical groups, such as Hamas, which started as an Islamic charitable organization but soon turned violent. Ironically, Israel had earlier approved of Hamas as a counterweight to the PLO, figuring that its religious focus was better than the PLO's political focus, an example of what Chalmers Johnson called **blowback** (see page 260).

One of the key ingredients of the Palestinian intifadas is the large numbers of young men willing to die for their cause, their political and religious convictions reinforced by some of the world's highest birth rates. The status of Palestinians had been dangling since at least the 1967 war. In peace talks and accords, the Arab side always insisted on provisions for Palestinian statehood, but the Israelis viewed the clauses as nonbinding and implemented little. Palestinians felt abandoned. Increasingly, militant Islamist organizations such as Hamas, Islamic Jihad, and the Al Aqsa Martyrs Brigade encourage them to die by killing Israelis.

---

intifada   (literally "shaking") Arabic for uprising.
blowback   Supporting a group that later turns against you.

G : *Geography*

THE PATTERN OF ISRAELI SETTLEMENTS

Immediately after the 1967 war, Israel built some settlements in the occupied territories but did little be-yond the **green line** (that demarcated the West Bank and Gaza), thinking they would soon have a peace settlement with the Arabs. A few Jewish settlements were started in the Jordan Valley for security reasons. After the 1973 war, which showed Israel's vulnerability, the Israeli government acquiesced to construc-tion of more settlements in the West Bank. The hawkish **Likud** government took office in 1977 and strongly encouraged Jewish "hillcrest settlements" close to Israel's border. Likud in effect told the world that Israel was in the West Bank to stay. Ariel Sharon was chief architect of the settlement plan. The Labor party has been more cautious, but during the seven years of the Oslo peace process (1993–2000), when Labor governed, the settler population in the West Bank doubled.

From 30,000 settlers in 1984, by 2002 the Jewish population in the West Bank grew to 200,000 in 123 settlements, some of them pleasant towns as big as 25,000. All together—with settlements, securi-ty zones, military areas, and settler-only bypass roads—Israel controls 40 percent of the West Bank. Gaza has seventeen Jewish settlements.

An estimated quarter of the settlers are "ideological," that is, they have political and religious motives for setting up new towns. Typically, a group of settlers, often led by the Gush Emunim (Bloc of the Faith-ful), who argued they were "creating facts on the ground" that God had granted them as Judea and Samaria (they did not use the term "West Bank"), would claim a rocky hilltop of little economic value. With government approval or without, they would quickly set up house trailers for the first occupants. Then they would swiftly build stone-and-concrete row houses, often employing local Arab labor, and sell the homes at bargain prices (starting at $60,000) to Jewish settlers, who got cheaper mortgage rates, lower taxes, and subsidized local government. A majority of the buyers simply wanted affordable hous-ing. For jobs, they commuted to nearby Israel by car, always running the risk of ambush. Settlement growth has slowed in recent years because of the obvious danger of living in the West Bank and Gaza.

Ariel Sharon, then a cabinet minister in charge of the West Bank, had a master plan for Jewish set-tlement of it. First, the settlements would be on hilltops to improve their security and keep watch on the surrounding terrain. Second, also for security purposes, they would form two swaths, one of fewer set-tlers down the Jordan Valley, a second and much more populous one down the Samarian hills near the 1967 border. With scattered Jewish settlements elsewhere, patches of the land in between the two swaths—less than half the total of the West Bank—would be left to Palestinians, who would have local self-governance but not a state. Third, the settlements would tap into the aquifer under the Samarian hills and tie it into Israel's water system. Sharon's map, if implemented, would prevent any territorially co-herent Palestinian state on the West Bank; it would look like a Swiss cheese with many and large holes, connected by roads and "security zones" controlled by Israel.

One can see religious, defensive, hydrological, and territorial purposes to Israeli settlement in the West Bank, but all seem aimed at eventually incorporating it into Israel itself, in effect, recreating Britain's Pales-tine mandate. This idea pleases many Israelis, but the mandate is unworkable and roughly half the in-habitants of an enlarged Israel would be Palestinian Arabs. Any peace plan must take them into consideration.

Palestinians, seeing more of their lands and aquifers taken every year, have turned violent. They mur-der settlers and ambush their road traffic. Settlers go armed and shoot Palestinians they think threaten them, including women and children. The Israeli army patrols and controls most of the West Bank. Many

Israeli soldiers do not like this duty, as it means shooting civilians. Elaborate and expensive fences are being built to stop terrorists from infiltrating areas of Jewish settlements or Israel proper, but many doubt their effectiveness. The fences also cut off thousands of Palestinians from fields, water, and roads, forcing them to leave. Some say the fence will eventually become a border. Several Israeli generals and much public opinion favor removing the most outlying of the settlements as indefensible and drains on military resources. The settlements, originally rationalized as security outposts, have made Israel terribly insecure.

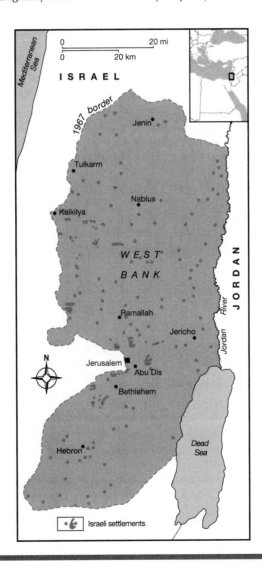

Peace

The Deception of "Atmospherics"

Henry Kissinger, national security advisor and secretary of state in the 1970s, was also a major scholar (Harvard) of diplomacy. He constantly warned against confusing "**atmospherics**" with the substance of negotiations. Statesmen deliberately cultivate atmospherics to build a psychology of acceptance and sway public opinion. Then if things go wrong it will be the other side's fault. The media especially like to note the superficial smiles and handshakes and read into them progress on the talks: "Look, they're getting along great!"

This can be terribly deceptive. The two sides are often miles apart and making little progress, usually the case in Middle East negotiations. One-sided statements released during talks may deliberately raise false hopes as a form of pressure. These negotiators are hard-headed people who have fought long for their cause and are not about to give anything away. They operate under orders from their home governments that allow them little room for on-the-spot compromises. To be sure, nice atmospherics are better than bad ones, but friendly photo-ops at the start of a conference predict nothing.

The first intifada ended after the first Gulf War in 1991. Many Palestinians foolishly pinned their hopes on an Iraqi victory, expecting that Saddam Hussein would then soon liberate them. Some celebrated the Iraqi SCUD missiles that hit Israel (just as some celebrated the 9/11 attacks on America). Iraq's quick defeat in 1991 showed there would be no hope from Baghdad. Now American power and prestige were appreciated in the Middle East. The Gulf War thus opened a window of opportunity for negotiations.

Co-chaired by U.S. President George Bush (senior) and Soviet President Gorbachev (who was barely clinging to power and was about to lose it), Arab and Israeli delegates met in Madrid in the fall of 1991 for two days and agreed on an ambitious agenda. Israel would not accept a separate PLO delegation, but it did accept Palestinians from Jerusalem as part of a "Jordanian-Palestinian" delegation. A major sticking point for Israel: The 1968 Palestine National Covenant called for the destruction of Israel (dropped only in 1998). Nothing of substance was achieved, but many celebrated Madrid as an historic breakthrough. They confused atmospherics with substance (see box above).

By the time Israelis and Palestinians met secretly near Oslo in 1993 for substantive talks, another momentous event had occurred at the very end of 1991: The Soviet Union ceased to exist. Moscow had been the main outside backer of the Arab cause, providing vast quantities of arms, especially to the radical Syrian and

green line   UN manner of marking cease-fire lines by green barrels; in Israel indicates 1949–1967 borders. (See page 118.)

Likud   Israel's main right-wing and currently governing party. (See page 118.)

atmospherics   Pleasant setting and personalities that are presumed to make diplomatic meetings succeed.

Iraqi regimes. Suddenly, the Arabs had no major outside power to support them. Only the United States now mattered. Some Arabs thought it prudent to settle. Together, the two signal events of 1991—the Gulf War and Soviet collapse—changed the power map of the world.

Norwegian diplomats quietly arranged a series of at least fourteen meetings near Oslo where Israeli and PLO representatives made some progress. On September 13, 1993, on the White House lawn, PLO Chairman Yasser Arafat and Israeli Prime Minister Yitzhak Rabin signed a Declaration of Principles on Interim Self-Government for the Palestinians. With President Clinton enveloping both with his arms, the two adversaries shook hands. (As a photo opportunity, it looked much like the 1978 handshake between Begin and Sadat, blessed by President Carter.) Now the two sides halfway recognized each other, a major first step. The whole process, seen as a breakthrough and lasting until 2000, was called the "Oslo peace process." Even Bush's 2003 "road map" was based on Oslo.

Only a little came of Oslo; Arabs and Israelis alike were disappointed with it. U.S. President Bill Clinton sponsored several follow-on talks. The Palestinians got a new **Palestine Authority** (PA) that in 1994 was given control only of Jericho and Gaza. In 1995 Israel signed another agreement in Washington to expand PA control to six additional large towns in the West Bank, totaling about 20 percent of the area. Many Israelis felt Prime Minister Rabin was giving the Palestinians too much, and later in 1995 an Israeli fanatic assassinated him (see box on page 122). After terrorist bombings, **Shin Bet** identified where they originated, and Israeli armor and helicopter gunships retaliated into the PA-controlled towns—the biggest are Qalqilya, Tulkarm, Jenin, Nablus, Ramallah, and Bethlehem—to detain or shoot suspects, search for weapons, and bulldoze houses. Fighting was often heavy, and many civilians were killed. The Israeli incursions, some lasting weeks, encouraged more suicide bombers (who were supported by a majority of Palestinians). The PA really controlled little.

The long-held theory that Arab-Israeli peace should be based on small steps leading up to **final-status** talks must be reexamined. Oslo was a series of small steps aiming at peace but in a few years hit a wall of uncompromisable demands and never got close to final-status talks, which became a euphemism for "the really hard parts," such as borders, status of Jerusalem, and right of Palestinians to return to Israel. Some progress was made in the 1990s, but Palestinians and Israelis were still too far apart for a general settlement. In a last-ditch effort, Clinton called Barak and Arafat to Camp David in 2000. Barak offered extensive concessions, possibly more than his parliament would ratify. Americans called it a good offer. Arafat called it unacceptable. Since then, Israelis and Americans alike saw no point in negotiating with Arafat. The window of opportunity opened by the Gulf War closed, setting the stage for the next, much more dangerous intifada. Israeli-Palestinian talks at Taba on the Red Sea in January 2001 entertained some interesting ideas,

---

Palestine Authority   Interim government of parts of the West Bank and Gaza, began in 1993.
Shin Bet   Israel's domestic security agency. (Mosad does foreign security and intelligence.)
final status   The difficult end goal of the peace process: a Palestinian state and Israeli security.

 *Peace*

THE KILLING OF RABIN

Labor party Prime Minister Yitzhak Rabin, born and raised on a kibbutz and a career soldier, finally saw the futility of warfare and took a chance for peace in the early 1990s. After some diplomatic progress (the "Oslo process"), he shook hands with Arafat on the White House lawn in 1993. Departing from a peace rally in Tel Aviv in late 1995, he was gunned down by a fanatic Israeli law student who viewed any concessions to Palestinians as a sellout of Israel. (He was sentenced to life in prison; Israel currently does not have capital punishment.)

The tragedy extended beyond the death of one courageous leader, as more than a few right-wing Israelis sympathized with the assassin. Some Israelis, perhaps as many as one-quarter, will return no land to Palestinians and want the entire West Bank and Gaza Strip. Although fewer in number and less lethal than Palestinian terrorists, Israeli terrorists are also capable of blocking and reversing attempts at peace. All subsequent prime ministers of Israel are thus on warning that they must not offer Palestinians too much.

but it was held as the second intifada raged and on the eve of Israeli elections. Sharon won and became prime minister, and he always opposed compromise. Taba, touted by optimists as "so close," had no chance of being accepted by either side. The "peace process" was over.

In September 2000, after the collapse of the Camp David talks, Ariel Sharon— head of the hard-line Likud party, then in **opposition**—visited the Haram es Sharif (Noble Sanctuary) in Jerusalem, the plaza around the Dome of the Rock, Islam's third holiest shrine. This area, which Jews call the Temple Mount, overlooks the Western or Wailing Wall, last remnant of the Temple and sacred to Jews. Many fights have erupted because it is so easy for Arabs to throw rocks onto Jewish worshippers below. Sharon wished to show that no part of Israel's capital city is off-limits to Israelis, so he ostentatiously strolled through the Haram with a large security detail. The result was predictable: Muslims expressed outrage at this enemy walking on their site. Sharon's walk triggered but by itself did not cause the second intifada, which grew out of long-standing grievances and the collapse of the Oslo process. Israelis, angry and fearful over the new intifada, turned against the peace-minded Barak government, who lost reelection and was replaced with a new Sharon government in early 2001. The 2003 Israeli elections confirmed the trend by boosting Likud and cutting Labor to its smallest vote ever. Like Americans, Israelis prefer hawks for leaders in time of threat.

The underlying cause was the failure to reach an agreement at Camp David. Arafat had been so unyielding that agreement was impossible. Again Palestinians felt they had no future; their status had dangled unresolved for a third of century—at least since 1967—with no hope for a solution on the horizon.

---

opposition   Political party in parliament that does not support the prime minister.

 *Religions*

IRAN AND THE PALESTINIANS

Iran's Islamist rulers support anything that harms Israel, but Iran does not directly sponsor radical Palestinians. Religion gets in the way. There is no Hezbollah organization among Palestinians, as Hezbollah is Shi'a and Palestinians are Sunni Muslims. The two branches do not like each other. There is a strong Hezbollah among the Shi'a of the south of Lebanon.

Iran does sell arms to Palestinians, a point underscored when the Israeli navy (possibly tipped off by U.S. intelligence) captured the *Karine A* in the Red Sea in early 2002. This small ship carried 50 tons of weapons and explosives Iran had sold, through their Hezbollah clients in Lebanon, to the Palestine Authority. The *Karine A* incident further convinced Washington of Tehran's and Arafat's sponsorship of terrorism.

THE SECOND PALESTINIAN INTIFADA

One of the unexpected consequences of the Israeli pullout from the south of Lebanon in 2000 was that it emboldened Palestinian militants to try something similar. Lebanese Hezbollahis told radical Palestinians that if Hezbollah could harass Israel into withdrawing from Lebanon, Palestinians could harass Israel into withdrawing from the West Bank and Gaza. The Israeli withdrawal from Lebanon set the stage for the second, much larger intifada, which is why some Israelis say they must never give an inch.

Far more Palestinians than Israelis have died in the second intifada, but with suicide bombings—the first was in 2000—the death rates started equalizing. The prospect of taking several Israelis with them appealed to many Palestinians, and there was no shortage of volunteers, even some young women. In the first three years of the second intifada (September 2000 to September 2003), some 2,500 Palestinians and 900 Israelis were killed. The numbers keep growing.

INCOMPATIBLE DEMANDS

Peace deals between states are much easier than ending civil strife within a state. Two relative success stories illustrate the relatively simple problems of ending hostility between states. Thanks to the manipulations of Sadat—a surprise 1973 war and an even more surprising 1977 visit to Jerusalem—plus considerable arm-twisting by President Carter, Egypt and Israel signed the first Arab-Israeli peace treaty in 1979. Jordan followed in 1994. Their demands were compromisable. For example, when Israel gave back the Sinai to Egypt in 1979, it won Egypt's assurance that it would station no major forces there. This was backed up by UN (including U.S.) peace observers who dotted the desert with electronic listening devices to detect any troop movements. Israel could relax about attack from Egypt, use

R ⦙ *Religions*

PALESTINIAN "MARTYRS"

Interviews of young Palestinians who say they are ready to sacrifice themselves show religious and political motives reinforcing each other. Mostly, they show just plain hatred. Many have lost friends and
relatives to Israeli bullets and shells. Many have seen houses bulldozed by the Israeli army. Palestinian
homes, built over many years and with much financial sacrifice, are their prize possessions. All those
interviewed are bitter about the fate of the Palestinians, who have lost more and more of their country.
Their message: "All right, Israelis, you make life unlivable for my people. I make it unlivable for you."
In their eyes, martyrdom empowers.

As their political hatred grows, most also turn rigidly Muslim, more Islamic than their family. Their
mullahs assure them of instant admission to the highest stage of heaven ("Seventh Heaven") for their sac-
rifices, which they do not regard as suicides but as legitimate "martyr operations" against brutal occupiers who seize their lands. They have also seen how relatives mourn but also celebrate sacrificers. Most
Palestinian parents say they are proud of their martyr children.

Some Palestinians now appreciate that killing Israelis only produces a stronger Likud vote and more
hard-line Israeli governments that are less inclined to offer Palestinians their own viable state. The martyrs make things worse, creating the very conditions they deplore.

the Suez Canal, and even send tourists to see the pyramids (no longer advisable for
Israelis). Israel and Egypt never developed warm relations—it was called a "cold
peace"—but it was much better than war.

Jordan, which threatened Israel because the West Bank nearly choked Israel's
narrow neck on the Plain of Sharon, became less of a threat when King Hussein
in 1988 renounced any Jordanian claim to the West Bank, which his grandfather's
army had taken in 1948. This move actually complicated any settlement. Giving
the West Bank back to Jordan would have been relatively easy, and Israel could
have lived with that. Setting up a Palestinian state on the West Bank may be impossible, for many Israelis feel they cannot live with it. Hussein was not giving the
West Bank to Israel in 1988; rather he was indicating that it should be a Palestinian state. At any rate, he was never going to get it back and from now on it would
be an Israeli problem. With the West Bank as kind of a deadly buffer zone between
Israel and Jordan, a peace treaty was not difficult. This too is a "cold peace."

A Syria-Israel settlement is much tougher, as the Golan Heights are a serious
security problem for both sides. Damascus demands back the whole of the Golan
Heights, and Israel is unlikely to give it. When Syria held the Golan Heights before
1967, it shelled Israeli farms. Taking the Heights in the Six Day War was costly,
and Israeli politicians swore to make them part of Israel. On the other hand, Israeli
control of Golan means that its tanks can roll easily into Damascus, only some
forty miles distant. Furthermore, Golan is historically part of Syria, and most of its
Arab inhabitants fled in 1967. Getting back Golan is a question of national honor
that no ruler of Damascus can show weakness on.

Geography

JERUSALEM INTERNATIONALIZED?

An internationalized Jerusalem—advanced by both the 1937 Peel Commission and the 1947 UN partition plan—is not such a bad idea. It would, unfortunately, require reasonable Israelis and reasonable Palestinians. Jerusalem—the City of David to Jews and *al Quds* (the holy) to Arabs—is sacred to all three Abrahamic religions; it contains their sites and shrines and should be open and welcome to pilgrims of all faiths. Jerusalem is an extremely important archeological site and thus a world cultural treasure. More important, putting Jerusalem under international supervision would remove one of the bones of contention between Palestinians and Israelis.

Neither side would accept such an idea; both claim Jerusalem as their own. And what kind of "international" government could supervise this complex, fascinating city? The UN is not equipped for anything like that, and many of its members are weak and corrupt. One possibility: Move the UN headquarters from Manhattan to Jerusalem, which would become a sort of world District of Columbia (not, to be sure, everyone's favorite model of city governance). An international solution for Jerusalem is intriguing but impractical.

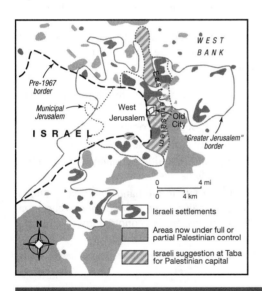

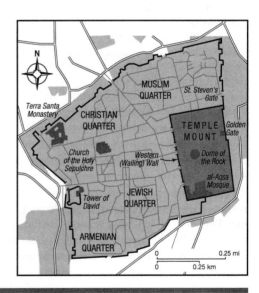

The point is that some conflicts (as with Egypt and Jordan) are compromisable, while others (as with Syria) are not. The Palestine-Israel situation is even tougher, for demands tend to be uncompromisable because they concern the very right of a state to exist. Just because diplomacy worked in one case does not mean it will work in other cases. Americans love to focus on personalities—an appetite fed by the media—and assume that war is caused by mean personalities and peace by nice ones. That is not always the case, although Sadat illustrates how personality can

P : *Peace*

CAN DIPLOMACY WORK?

Diplomacy is widely misunderstood, both by its proponents and its detractors. Some urge, "Give diplomacy a chance!" They see it as a substitute for war. Others scoff at diplomacy as worthless. When necessary, they say, countries must be prepared to go to war. Both sides exaggerate.

At certain times, when two parties to a dispute are willing to compromise, diplomacy that is carried out well can prevent the dispute from getting worse and sometimes solve it. When the two sides have had enough of war, they may be ready for diplomacy. Europe after the Napoleonic wars was ready for diplomacy; this is why the 1815 Congress of Vienna worked and set up a Europe that avoided major wars until 1914. This is what happened with the peace treaties of 1979 between Israel and Egypt and of 1994 between Israel and Jordan. When the time is ripe, diplomacy can work.

But when two sides are far apart over basic issues—the case most of the time in the Israel-Palestine dispute—diplomacy can do little. No amount of smooth diplomacy can bridge the gap between the two on such difficult issues as Jewish settlements in the West Bank, the right of Palestinians to return to old homes in Israel, and Jerusalem as capital of a Palestinian state. Perhaps after some years of bashing each other silly, the two sides will decide it is time to compromise. This situation, however, cannot be wished into existence.

When the time is ripe, there are techniques of **third-party diplomacy** that can help: good offices, mediation, conciliation, arbitration, and adjudication. The first three have been tried for the Middle East, mostly sponsored by America, some by European countries.

Good offices are the most basic third-party diplomacy. A country not a party to the dispute provides a meeting place and security.

Mediation takes the process to the next level. Here the third party suggests compromises.

Conciliation is a more involved mediation in which the third party proposes solutions to the conflict.

Arbitration is much more difficult and happens rarely among nations, and then only on small matters. Here the disputants give their consent to the third party to actually decide the issue.

Adjudication is even harder, as it requires countries to put their fate in the hands of an international court. Sometimes boundary and trade details can be arbitrated or adjudicated between nonhostile countries, but in the Middle East the issues are the life or death of nations, and no country turns its existence over to a court. One cannot extrapolate domestic legal systems onto the world scene.

play a role. Remember, even the "nice" Sadat went to war with Israel in 1973 to break the stalemate. It was his October War that changed the psychological balance of the region and made his subsequent visit to Jerusalem possible. It is not merely problem personalities that make compromise impossible; it is underlying strategic, geographic, and political realities. The world is not one big *People* magazine.

diplomacy   Official contacts between countries.
third-party diplomacy   Neutral country helps settle dispute.

 *Peace*

Rejectionists on Both Sides

"If only Israelis and Palestinians could sit down and talk things through!" say many partisans of peace. Well, persons of good will and high intelligence on both sides have for years tried to talk things over. They sometimes make verbal progress toward settlement but are blocked by the many **rejectionists** in both camps who demand all of historic Palestine. No compromise, no sharing: It's ours!

Graphically, the situation looks like two circles that overlap a bit. Where they overlap is the area where reasonable negotiators on both sides can sometimes compromise. Behind them is a portion of their publics (the white areas) that might go along with a compromise solution of two states, one Israeli and one Palestinian, living side by side in peace. Farther back in their publics, however, are the rejectionists who want the whole of Palestine. Public-opinion surveys—which vary with the latest outrage and the precise wording of the question—suggest close to half of Palestinians and a quarter of Israelis are rejectionists. Both exercise an ultimate veto over any peace process and easily reverse the process by bombings and retaliations. Hard-Line Israelis resisted Barak's "giveaway," and hard-line Palestinians denounced the short-lived Mahmoud Abbas for dealing with Israel at all. The big question for Palestinians and Israelis alike is whether their governments will be tough enough to ignore and control their rejectionists.

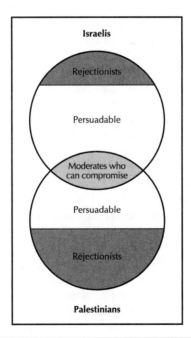

---

rejectionist   Extreme, uncompromising position that rejects a peace settlement and demands everything.

G : *Geography*

MIDDLE EAST IRREDENTISM

When Italian patriots were kicking out foreign rulers and unifying Italy in the nineteenth century they called the parts of Italy still outside their control "unredeemed Italy," *Italia irredenta*, and they aimed to eventually recover them. Foreigners had no right to rule any part of Italy, argued the irredentists. The term caught on especially in the Balkans, where the new little states that emerged from Ottoman rule all sought borders that included their ethnic kin or lands that they once ruled long ago. **Irredentism** is thus closely tied to nationalism. Efforts to build **Greater** Serbia sparked both World War I and wars in Croatia and Bosnia in the 1990s. Efforts to regain Greater Romania led Bucharest to ally with Hitler in World War II. Irredentism is a dangerous force, as it makes exaggerated and unrealistic claims that bring it into conflict with other states that also claim those lands.

We must remember this in dealing with the most difficult problem, that of Israelis and Palestinians. Commentators often focused on the personalities of Israel's Sharon—described as a militarist Arab-hating right-winger—or of the PLO's Arafat—labeled as a rigid and corrupt control freak who quietly encourages Palestinian violence. True, both are hard men, but new leaders will still have extremely difficult issues to resolve and many rejectionists in their respective camps.

If you ask any side in a war what they want, they will all say "peace." That would seem to make peace settlements easy to achieve. When you get them seated at the bargaining table, however, you soon learn that they have additional demands to go with peace. Their demands are always "peace plus." The devil is in the add-on elements, many of which are vital. By the time you elucidate them, you can understand why the two sides are at war. Such is the case with Israelis and Palestinians.

As a first step, the Israelis want immediate cessation of Palestinian violence, especially suicide bombings. Without that, nothing is possible. Then they want (1) all of an enlarged Jerusalem and (2) dozens of Jewish settlements in the West Bank and Gaza, especially those close to Israel's pre-1967 borders. Many Israelis also want to keep the Golan Heights, but theoretically they could be returned to Syria with guarantees that they would stay forever demilitarized. To reach this, however, would require a climate of trust that is utterly lacking.

Most Israelis understand that settlements well east of the green line, housing 35 to 40 percent of West Bank Jewish settlers, would have to be given up. A fair-sized minority of Israelis, however, demand keeping all settlements and building new ones. The unstated goal of some of Israeli rejectionists is to eventually

---

irredentism   Desire to enlarge state to include all lands where it has ethnic or historical roots.
Greater   *Irredentist* end goal.

 *Peace*

THE FOUR GREAT ISSUES

1. *Borders:* What borders will a new Palestinian state have? Nearly the same as the pre-1967 borders of the West Bank and Gaza Strip, or considerably smaller?

2. *Jewish Settlements:* Which ones stay and which have to go? Palestinians will not accept a state fragmented by Israeli towns and roads, a continuation of the present unstable situation.

3. *Jerusalem:* Will Palestinians be able to use even part of Jerusalem as their national capital? If so, which part?

4. *Palestinian Refugees:* How many can return to their ancestral homes inside Israel? Or can they be given material compensation?

turn these areas—minus most of their Arab inhabitants—into a Greater Israel, an unrealistic and dangerous proposition. Accordingly, they want no Palestinian state at all, not even a **truncated** one. Some propose "transfer" of Palestinians to other countries, a euphemism for expulsion and a prescription for even worse bloodshed.

As a first step, Palestinians want an immediate cessation of construction of Jewish settlements in the West Bank and Gaza. Without that, nothing is possible. Then they want (1) a **sovereign** Palestinian state with (2) capital in Jerusalem, (3) abandonment of most Israeli settlements in the West Bank and Gaza, and (4) right of Palestinians to return to their ancestral homes in Israel. This last point simply cannot happen unless Israel wants to commit suicide. The influx of a million or two Palestinians into Israel would severely destabilize and eventually destroy it. Property claims would be insoluble.

A large fraction of Palestinians openly want all of historic Palestine and the destruction of the state of Israel, a mirror image of Israeli maximalist demands. Many Palestinians see violence as the only way to accomplish this and vow to never give up their arms. For them, a peace deal would be simply a stepping stone to the total recovery of all of Palestine. Israeli hawks point to this as reason to give Palestinians little or nothing in peace talks. "If they aim to destroy Israel, why give them a base for attacking us?" they ask.

Hamas, Islamic Jihad, and the Al Aqsa Martyrs Brigade, violent movements to recover all of Palestine, ignore the PLO and its peace negotiations. Said one young Hamas member referring to possible borders: "We don't believe in '67 or '48—it's all our land." Under present trends, Hamas could become more powerful than the

---

truncated   Chopped into pieces.
sovereign   Fully independent, boss on their own turf.

PLO. Hamas wants the West Bank and Gaza integrated into Israel with citizenship for all Palestinians. Very soon, of course, the Palestinians, with a birth rate twice that of Israelis, would outnumber and outvote Jewish Israelis. They would set up "an Islamic state with Islamic law," said one Hamas leader. Needless to say, this is a prescription for civil war, a return to the 1936–1939 fighting on a much larger scale. Clearly **one-state solutions**—notice how they are proposed by both Israeli and Palestinian extremists—will not work.

THE WEST BANK

In hindsight, some Israelis say, it would have been best if the West Bank, with some border rectifications, had soon been given back to Jordan, with perhaps the Gaza Strip thrown in. In the flush of victory in the Six Day War, few could see what an Israeli occupation would lead to. Many expected peace with the Arabs soon, and then Israel would give back most of the West Bank. But peace never came, settlement building took off, and some Israelis started defining the West Bank as part of Israel. More than anything else, the growth of Jewish settlements in the West Bank and Gaza fuels Palestinian rage and terrorism. If peace is to have any chance, settlement building has got to stop and be reversed. Many Israelis reject this notion.

Even in the late 1960s, however, some Israeli intellectuals began to voice concern that Israel would have to chose between being a democracy and being Jewish. If Israel kept the West Bank and Gaza, it would come under pressure to grant more than three million Arab Palestinians Israeli citizenship and the right to vote. If it did not, Israel would not be a democracy. If it did grant them citizenship, the rapidly growing Palestinian population would make Jews a minority by 2010. Most Israelis (like most Americans) do not burden themselves with logic and ignored the dilemma, but these things do not solve themselves. The results, decades later, are the intifadas, terrorist bombings, and Israeli retaliations.

But for a while it worked, say defenders of the status quo. True, at certain times cheap Palestinian labor contributed to a booming Israeli economy that also gave Palestinians more pay and a higher standard of living than they had ever seen. Many built nice homes and sent their children to college. Other factors, however, were more important to Israel's economy: relative peace, computerized high-tech industries, and thriving tourism. In this system Palestinians were confined to low-skilled work in factories, construction, agriculture, and food services. Money by itself cannot buy contentment. Palestinians had been left dangling since 1948, and it got worse in 1967. They were neither Israelis nor Jordanians (although some kept Jordanian passports). No one offered a plausible plan for them, and they had no voice in their future. Their hilltops were increasingly Israeli building sites. It was a prescription for unrest.

---

one-state solution   Making Israel and Palestine a single state with common citizenship.

Some compare Israeli occupation of the West Bank and Gaza to South Africa's infamous **apartheid** that confined blacks to the lowliest jobs, forced them back to their segregated "townships" by sundown, and sent others into rural poverty in "bantustans," territorially fragmented fake little republics that were basically storage bins for cheap labor. The comparison is overdrawn but contains a bit of truth: Israel wants the territories without the Palestinians, so it grants them neither Israeli citizenship nor their own state. The system could not last in South Africa (it was dismantled in the early 1990s) or in Israel, for in both places it depended on the quiescence of the underdogs.

What can be done? First a one-state solution is out. It was tried under the British mandate and blew up. It was tried informally under the Israelis and blew up. Persons of goodwill who still think it is possible are actually proposing permanent civil war. A **two-state solution** is the only one vaguely possible, and it would be difficult.

First, it would involve redrawing borders. At Camp David in 2000, Israel's Barak offered Arafat a Palestinian state on 91 percent of the West Bank. Arafat declined. Shortly before he left office, President Clinton suggested 94–96 percent. No deal, not even a counterproposal. Some observers believe Arafat is incapable of making a major decision, one of the reasons President Bush wanted him replaced. Washington hoped that new PA prime ministers, Mahmoud Abbas and Ahmed Qurei, both named in 2003, would be better peace negotiators than Arafat, but they were hamstrung from the start. Arafat never supported them and radical factions ignored their peace efforts. Israel's Sharon envisions a Palestine state on less than half of the West Bank, territorially fragmented, no presence in Jerusalem, and with Israeli control of its air space. For some calmer Palestinians, Barak's offer of 2000 now looks pretty good.

Some of the largest Jewish settlements in the West Bank are close to the 1967 border and could be incorporated into Israel by drawing the border a few miles further east. Palestinians reject the idea. Other Jewish settlements would either have to be abandoned or live a precarious existence surrounded by a Palestinian state. Israeli settlements in crowded Gaza would simply have to go. Most Israelis say they could accept this, but a militant minority rejects it. Likewise, the portion of the aquifer in Palestine would have to be restored to Palestinian control, an important but often neglected point. Further, some kind of land corridor, approximately twenty-five miles long, would need to connect the West Bank and Gaza Strip, perhaps under Israeli supervision but with Palestinian right of transit.

JERUSALEM

Jerusalem has always been one of the most difficult problems. Israel annexed East Jerusalem in 1967 and proclaimed the city its eternal capital. Municipal borders were enlarged in order to ring the city with Jewish neighborhoods. Now 200,000

---

apartheid   (literally "apartness") South Africa's strict system of elaborate racial segregation, now ended.
two-state solution   Making a separate Palestine on the West Bank and Gaza.

Israelis live in East Jerusalem alone. Arab inhabitants of the Old City are encouraged to depart. Arab homes and apartment houses in the area of the Western or Wailing Wall were cleared away to make a broad plaza for worshippers and tourists. On a purely technical basis, the municipal governance of Major Teddy Kollek did a fine job, transforming Jerusalem into a clean and attractive city of limestone and a tourist magnet. (The legendary Kollek, after twenty-eight years as mayor, was defeated by a right-winger in 1993.) Since 1967, Jerusalem was transformed from Arab to Jewish in character, although 200,000 Arabs still live in Jerusalem.

One of the biggest sticking points for Palestinians is to have their capital in Jerusalem. Yasser Arafat would not yield on this at the 2000 Camp David talks, and it doomed the talks. The Palestine Authority's present administrative offices are in Ramallah, ten miles to the north, but most of them were destroyed by Israeli troops during the second intifada in the early 2000s. Jerusalem is an emotional symbol for both sides.

Could two separate countries have their capitals in one city? (Actually, Nikosia is the divided capital of partitioned Cyprus, but it is a poor model.) It goes against the notion that capitals should be in a nation's **core area**, surrounded by friendly territory. Most Israelis reject out of hand the notion of letting the Palestinians set up a capital in Jerusalem. Some suggest an Arab suburb such as Abu Dis could be designated as part of Jerusalem and serve as a Palestinian capital. This satisfied few on either side. In late 2000 President Clinton suggested that Jewish sectors of Jerusalem be under Israeli sovereignty and Arab sectors under Palestinian sovereignty, not a bad idea if both sides would accept it. There could be an advantage in having two capitals in one city. Potential rioters and terrorists might not wish to harm their own capital city; they might be blowing up their own leaders.

The Right to Return

The right of Palestinians to return to their parents' or grandparents' homes inside Israel also blocks a settlement. It, along with Jerusalem, was one of Arafat's uncompromisable demands that wrecked the 2000 Camp David talks. Why did Arafat stick to a point he knew the Israelis had to reject? Probably because he knew that if he gave in, he would be deposed by more radical Palestinians who have never given up their dream of returning home. Aside from provisions for reuniting divided families—Taba suggested a total of 25,000 Palestinians might be let in—there is little wiggle room on this issue, as Israelis know they would soon be demographically swamped.

---

core area   Territorial heart of a country, often where it originated historically and where it has its capital.

 *Peace*

THE BLAME GAME

Do not play the blame game. It is worthless and just makes things worse. First, it is impossible to accurately assign blame. The historical trail is just too long, complex, and tangled. Should it include the Arab conquest of Spain? The Crusades? The European imperialists? Hitler and the Holocaust? Second, if you do accurately (by your lights) assign blame, how are you going to get the culprit to admit it? Third, when you accuse someone, they just dig in their heels and become more obdurate.

The tragedy of the Middle East (and the Balkans) is that everyone is the aggrieved party, the hurt victims of historical injustice. On this basis, all sides rationalize their moves, even ones that prove self-destructive. In dealing with a problem like the Middle East, effective diplomats soon learn to exclude from their vocabulary words like "justice," "right," and "morality," as the contending parties thunder that they alone possess them. Peace marchers who carry placards proclaiming "No Justice, No Peace" might reflect that both sides pursuing justice makes wars.

Socrates, at the start of Plato's monumental *Republic,* famously asks "What is justice?" He finds the answer in *stability.* Chaos achieves nothing, but Plato's imaginary Republic, by cleverly balancing several elements, would attain stability, and out of that would grow a just and orderly society. Without stability, peace and justice shrivel. Perhaps a philosophical peace marcher will one day carry a placard proclaiming "No Stability, No Hope."

THE DOWNWARD SPIRAL

And what do Israelis want? First and foremost, an end to Palestinian violence, especially terrorist bombings. If the Palestine Authority could guarantee that, they could get many concessions from the Israelis. But they cannot curb violence among Palestinians, many of whom still believe that violence is the only way, the only thing Israel understands. Hundreds of young Palestinians volunteer for suicide bombings. Several groups have either formed within or split away from the PLO because many of its leaders now condemn violence, as did Palestinian Prime Ministers Mahmoud Abbas and Ahmed Qurei. Some Palestinian intellectuals notice that violence merely plays into the hands of Israeli hard-liners. Ehud Barak, who offered major concessions in 2000, was pushed out of office in 2001 elections in favor of hard-liner Ariel Sharon. Palestinian violence shrunk the Israeli peace movement. In Israel's 2003 elections, voters moved to the right; Likud nearly doubled while Labor declined. The intifada just made the Palestinian predicament worse.

From the above it is easy to conclude that peace has little chance. There is one factor that might save it: the realization on both sides that they are caught in a downward spiral that is killing and ruining both. Thousands of lives have been lost in the second intifada alone. The once-booming Israeli economy has slumped. The Palestinian economy has been cut in half; 60 percent of Palestinians live on less than $2 a day. For every Palestinian terrorist act there is a brutal Israeli reprisal, often the "targeted assassination" of a Hamas leader. Said an Israeli colonel in occupied

 *Peace*

Bush's "Road Map"

Even before the Iraq war began, President Bush (junior) promised new U.S. leadership in settling the Israeli-Palestinian quarrel. Bush was forced to do something, as the Arab world was angry at and mistrustful of the United States for its one-sided support of Israel. Bush called it a "road map" to peace.

This list of "to-dos" had actually been drafted and distributed in December 2002 by a "**Quartet**" of the United States, Russia, the United Nations, and the European Union. It was clear that the United States took the lead, but the Quartet made it a worldwide effort and put more pressure on Israelis and Palestinians to settle. Some American prefer **unilateral** U.S. actions, but in diplomacy **multilateral** efforts are often more credible. Quartet sponsorship also shields Washington from charges that it is acting alone.

The road map outlined three phases. First, Palestinians would cease violence and terrorism against Israel, and both sides would declare the other's right to exist. Palestinians would also build the institutions of statehood. Israel would cease building settlements in the West Bank and Gaza and dismantle those built since March 2001. The second phase, which was supposed to take place during the second half of 2003, was to include negotiation of borders and drafting of a Palestine constitution, supervised by international bodies. The third phase, starting in 2004, was supposed to lead to "final status," Palestinian independence and statehood in 2005 and complete withdrawal of Israeli forces. The 2003 road map looked a lot like Oslo and the follow-ons sponsored by President Clinton. Like them, the road map hinted at progress but soon broke down amidst violence by both sides. It was dead within a year.

Nablus: "They will suffer until they understand." After the deaths and humiliations of every Israeli reprisal, there is another Palestinian terrorist act. Some Palestinian rejectionists time their bombings to deliberately ruin peace initiatives. They do not want peace unless they can have everything.

If this keeps going, the next steps are not hard to envision. Israel's cabinet threatened Arafat with "removal," either exile or death. All other countries cautioned against it. Israeli hard-liners—and Benjamin Netanyahu is even tougher than Ariel Sharon—increasingly talk about "transfer," that is, pushing Palestinians out of the West Bank and Gaza. This will quickly turn into full-scale war, and soon neighboring Arab countries will join in. Egypt and Jordan will tear up their peace treaties with Israel. It will be like the 1948 war except with bigger populations and more and better weapons, possibly weapons of mass destruction. Nothing clears the head, it has been said, like the prospect of being hanged in the morning. Perhaps on the brink of mutual destruction, Palestinian and Israeli heads will clear.

Quartet   The four drafters—United States, United Nations, European Union, and Russia—of the 2003 "road map" peace plan.
unilateral   One country acting alone, not in concert with others.
multilateral   Several powers acting together.

CONCLUSIONS

Arab-Israeli peace may be impossible. Whenever you hear, "If only they got together and negotiated," remember that they have met off and on for years, often at peace talks sponsored by the UN, Washington, and others. The UN has been involved from the start. Ralph Bunche mediated the 1949 truce. UN Security Council Resolution 242 in 1967, calling on Israel to trade land for peace treaties with the Arabs, has been the basis for subsequent efforts.

Egyptian President Sadat was a hopeful sign. In late 1977 he visited Israel, paving the way for the first Arab-Israeli peace treaty in 1979, supervised by President Carter. Sadat was assassinated by Islamists in 1981. The 1979 treaty was a "cold peace" and did not tackle the Palestinian problem, which only grew worse. Israeli settlements in the West Bank, few at first, have now taken up much of Judea and Samaria and seem aimed at incorporating most of the territory into Israel. Some Israeli settlers are motivated by religion, but most just want affordable housing. In reaction to the taking of Palestinian lands, the first Palestinian "intifada," 1987–1991, was relatively mild, but the second, starting in 2000, featured suicide bombings and harsh Israeli reprisals. The security fence Israel is building may provide some security but clearly will not solve the problem of the Palestinians, whose status has dangled unresolved since at least 1967.

The 1991 Gulf War opened a "window of opportunity" for talks, which took place in Madrid, Oslo, and the United States, leading to the creation of a Palestine Authority over major West Bank and Gaza cities. At Camp David in 2000, Israel's Barak offered major concessions, rejected by Yasser Arafat, who either could not or would not budge on key issues: (1) the borders of a Palestinian state, (2) rollback of Jewish settlements, (3) Jerusalem as Palestine's capital, and (4) right of Palestinians to return to homes and lands in Israel.

Extremist Palestinian organizations such as Hamas see violence as their only path, and they do not lack for suicide bombers. In turn, Israelis seek security in tough military retaliations and right-wing leadership. The 2003 U.S.-sponsored "road map" came to nothing amidst a downward spiral of violence, which could easily produce another major war.

FURTHER REFERENCE

Aruri, Naseer, ed. *Palestine Refugees: The Right of Return*. London: Pluto Press, 2001.

Carey, Roane, and Jonathan Shainin, eds. *The Other Israel: Voices of Refusal and Dissent*. New York: New Press, 2003.

Etzioni-Halevy, Eva. *The Divided People: Can Israel's Breakup Be Stopped?* Lanham, MD: Lexington, 2002.

Gopin, Marc. *Holy War, Holy Peace: How Religion Can Bring Peace to the Middle East*. New York: Oxford University Press, 2002.

Gordon, Haim, Rivca Gordon, and Taher Shriteh. *Beyond Intifada: Narratives of Freedom Fighters in the Gaza Strip*. Westport, CT: Praeger, 2003.

Jones, Clive, and Emma C. Murphy. *Israel: Challenges to Identity, Democracy, and the State.* New York: Routledge, 2001.

Kimmerling, Baruch, and Joel S. Migdal. *The Palestinian People: A History.* Cambridge, MA: Harvard University Press, 2003.

Peleg, Samuel. *Zealotry and Vengeance: Quest of a Religious Identity Group; A Sociopolitical Account of the Rabin Assassination.* Lanham, MD: Lexington, 2002.

Rubenberg, Cheryl A. *The Palestinians: In Search of a Just Peace.* Boulder, CO: Lynne Rienner, 2003.

Shafir, Gershon, and Yoav Peled. *The New Israel: Peacemaking and Liberalization.* Boulder, CO: Westview, 2000.

Shipler, David K. *Arab and Jew: Wounded Spirits in a Promised Land.* New York: Times Books, 1986.

Survey of Arab-Israeli Relations, 1947–2001. Independence, KY: Europa Publications, 2002.

CHAPTER

8

Turkey

Points to Ponder

- Can democracy flourish in a Muslim country?
- Is there something about an Islamic society that resists modernization?
- Can a traditional country modernize without a dictator?
- Why does Turkey seem to be caught in praetorianism?
- Can a country where the military holds veto power be considered a democracy?
- Is Turkey a Middle East country or a European one?
- Can a country with an Islamist government function as an American ally?

Twentieth-century Turkey has been a permanent tug-of-war between a secular elite, centered in the army and loyal to Atatürk's vision of a modern, European Turkey, and parties with considerable mass support that try to pull Turkey back to Islam. The two streams seriously dislike each other, leaving Turkey, in Huntington's terms (see Chapter 15), a "torn" society: a Westernizing elite on top of a traditional Muslim society, the two continually pulling in opposite directions. The result is episodic military intervention directly in Turkey's politics either as coups or as strong warnings to not undo Atatürk's legacy.

FROM EMPIRE TO REPUBLIC

By the end of World War I, the Ottoman Empire crumbled like the Byzantine Empire before it. Having supported the losing side in the war (Germany), the Ottomans found themselves shorn of all their Arab possessions, all their European possessions except for a small corner of Europe, their capital occupied by the British, their Aegean coast occupied by the Greeks, their Mediterranean coast promised to the French and the Italians. Trying to keep his throne despite the occupation, the Sultan acquiesced to the victorious Allies' demands.

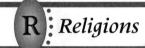

Religions

The Caliphate and September 11

Many rumors surround Osama bin Ladin and the destruction of the World Trade Center in New York. One is that bin Ladin wants to see the caliphate restored and that he chose September 11 as the attack date because it was the anniversary of the Turkish abolition of the sultanate. Not so. The Congress of Sivas met on September 11, 1919, and ratified the National Pact originally approved in Erzerum. But no decision was taken on the caliphate until March 3, 1924, when the Republic of Turkey's parliament abolished the caliphate.

The remnants of the Committee for Union and Progress (CUP) organized guerrilla bands and Societies for the Defense of National Rights throughout Anatolia and Thrace. Sympathizers within Istanbul assisted by smuggling men and materiel through the Allied lines. Mustafa Kemal, the only undefeated general in the Turkish army, became a military inspector in the Ottoman Third Army, giving him a cover to leave the occupied capital and contact nationalist military leaders in the field. The British grew suspicious of him and forced the Sultan to recall Kemal to Istanbul or to resign his commission. At Erzerum, Kemal's resignation crossed the Sultan's edict that he be decommissioned. Despite Kemal's lack of military rank, Erzerum's military commander declared himself still under his command.

The Erzerum Congress, a gathering of **nationalist** leaders, elected Kemal president and formed a National Pact that called for the election of a provisional government within the borders of modern Turkey. The next meeting of the Nationalists was the Congress of Sivas in September 1919, which denounced the sultanate as illegal because its decisions were supervised by occupation forces. The Nationalists vowed to have no further contact with the Istanbul government.

Independence War

While most of the Allies and the Sultan himself limited their actions to condemnations of the Nationalists as rebels against lawful authority, the Greek army tried to seize Turkish territory. The Turkish Nationalist strategy followed the same tactics used by George Washington and the Russians fighting Napoleon and Hitler:

---

nationalist   Movement for unity and independence of nation; in Turkish case, also for repudiation of empire and caliphate.

Avoid a conclusive battle as long as possible, keep the army in the field, and draw out the enemy until his supply lines are over-extended. The expanses of the Anatolian plateau became the Turks' greatest ally. Finally, in August 1921, the Greeks reached the Sakarya River, a mere fifty miles from the new Nationalist capital of Ankara. The Nationalist parliament made its president, Mustafa Kemal, commander of the Nationalist army, and it defeated the Greeks. The Nationalists were too exhausted to follow up and had to wait almost a year to regain their strength to push the Greeks off the mainland, which they did on September 9, 1922. The Greeks set fire to Izmir (Greek: Smyrna) as they departed. The Allies signed an armistice with Kemal one month later.

The Nationalists still did not control the old Ottoman capital of Istanbul. While the rest of Anatolia answered to the new Grand National Assembly in Ankara, Istanbul still answered to Sultan Vahit-ed-Din and the British occupation authorities.

The Nationalist representative to the peace conference, Refet Bey, traveled to Lausanne via Istanbul. Refet stopped by the palace, swore religious devotion to the caliph, and declared preservation of the caliphate a Nationalist goal. Refet said nothing about the Sultan's political claims. Vahit-ed-Din appealed to the British occupiers to support his demand that the Turkish delegation to the conference be composed of Nationalists and monarchists. When the British announced they would remain neutral on questions of Turkish internal affairs, Vahit-ed-Din knew he had lost and left Istanbul on a British warship on November 17, 1922. The Grand National Assembly elected Vahit-ed-Din's cousin, Abdul Mejit, as caliph. The Assembly recognized the last of the Ottomans as the religious leader of Islam but reserved political power to itself.

On July 24, 1923, the **Lausanne** Peace Conference concluded with the signing of a treaty between the new government of Turkey and the Allies. The Grand National Assembly, the governing body throughout the War of Independence, dissolved itself. The country held partly free elections (many political opponents of the Nationalists were banned as candidates).

The Second Grand National Assembly was sworn in. The Allies withdrew from Istanbul as Turkish troops entered on October 2, 1923. Fearful of Ottoman palace intrigues and anxious to avoid having to deal with the Istanbul merchant classes and their allies in the old, imperial elite, Mustafa Kemal rewarded Ankara for supporting the Nationalists by declaring it the country's capital. Twenty days later, October 29, 1923, the Grand National Assembly declared Turkey a **republic**, and elected Mustafa Kemal as president.

In 1924, President Kemal announced—somewhat deceptively—the revival of a pure Islam untainted by politics. As a first step, he had the parliament abolish the caliphate, the office of the Shaykh al-Islam, and the Ministry of Religious Affairs. The caliph and his family were put on a train to Switzerland and forbidden to return. Kemal was clever at making his reforms look conservative. In a series

---

Lausanne   (Swiss town) 1923 treaty ending World War I with Turkey.
republic   Government without a monarch; in Turkish case, also repudiation of Ottoman Empire.

G : *Geography*

THE POPULATION EXCHANGES

In a parallel to the difficulties of partition (see Chapter 5), population exchanges are another hellish solution in situations where ethnic groups cannot live together. In 1923 Greece and Turkey agreed to an exchange of populations. Greeks in Turkey (where they had lived for two and a half millennia) were to go "back" to Greece; Turks in Greece (where they had lived half a millennium) were to "return" to Turkey. In the months that followed, families who had lived on the same land for centuries were uprooted and moved to a country they did not know. Massive death and impoverishment resulted. One Smyrna Greek refugee who made good: Aristotle Onassis, who kept on going to Argentina.

The decision for expulsion was not based on bloodlines, where the family originated, or language; it was entirely religion. Christian Orthodox Turks (yes, there are some) were sent to Greece, and Muslim Greeks were sent to Turkey. Is religion and ethnicity the same thing in the Middle East?

of "reforms," he turned Turkey from empire to republic and, symbolically, moved its capital from Istanbul to Ankara.

The government closed the religious schools and confiscated the assets of the religious charitable foundations, the Awqaf. They then closed the Shari'a courts, declaring that secular law (the Swiss civil code) was to rule in questions of family law. These steps alienated the religious and conservative elements of society from the new republic, and they have been that way ever since. Unlike America where secularism is separation of church and state, in Turkey (and many other lands) secularism means the subjugation of church to state. The Directorate of Religious Affairs, an arm of the central government, assumed control of all mosques, mausoleums, Sufi lodges, and other religious institutions.

Having deprived his religious-based rivals of their power base, Mustafa Kemal moved against his rivals in the army. He announced a "generals' coup" and forced the "coup plotters" to resign. He also ordered his military aide and army chief of staff to resign from parliament, establishing the precedent that active-duty military officers would not serve in parliament.

Kemal's supporters called themselves the Peoples' Party and later the Republican Peoples' Party. A group of his fellow Nationalists broke ranks in parliament over the population exchanges with Greece, in which thousands of people died. They formed an opposition party, the Progressives. They saw themselves as a loyal opposition, but it was inevitable that a group openly contesting the authority of the government became a magnet for monarchists, tribal chieftains, religious leaders—all those members of the former elite who had been disenfranchised by the Nationalists. The Istanbul newspapers flocked to the new party, calling for a restoration of the caliphate as the basis of traditional legitimacy for a new government.

INDEPENDENCE TRIBUNALS

Things turned nasty when the Kurds revolted, supposedly in support of the Progressives. The Turks, Republican and Progressive alike, were appalled and denounced the revolt. The Progressives even supported the government in declaring martial law. The government took advantage of the opening, however, by having parliament let the cabinet suppress any organization deemed **reactionary**. To enforce the law, the government established Independence Tribunals, who closed the opposition party. In 1926, in Ankara and Izmir, several members of the failed party were tried and executed for fomenting rebellion. Many of the Imperial generals in the opposition were spared, but they had learned their lesson. It would be many years before any military officer led an active opposition movement.

In November 1925, Kemal issued an edict mandating the wearing of hats with brims and outlawing the fez that could be worn while praying. (A brim kept a pious Muslim from touching his forehead to the ground, part of the Muslim prayer.)

The Third Grand National Assembly (1927–1931) completed Kemal's religious program. The parliament **disestablished** Islam as the state religion, making Turkey a **secular** republic. The assembly also ordered use of the Latin alphabet in place of the Arabic/Ottoman script. This far-reaching change meant that within a generation few educated Turks could read four hundred years of Ottoman thought. For these changes, Kemal—better known as Atatürk—is considered the first great reformer of what we now call the Third World.

THE FREE PARTY EXPERIMENT

Mustafa Kemal, despite authoritarian tendencies, liked things to look democratic. He interpreted any attempts to create an independent opposition as hostile. To create a loyal opposition he set up a contrived Free Republican party. The experiment lasted three months. Kemal had anticipated a kind of debating society. Instead, the disenfranchised former elite and their followers flocked to the new party, which began as a parliamentary faction but quickly opened branches throughout the country. The Free party leader was met with Islamic banners and demands for the repeal of many of Kemal's reforms. The party leader, loyal to the Republic, dissolved his party rather than allow the controversies to hurt the government. Not all Turks liked Kemal's reforms.

Six weeks later, a religious riot broke out in the town of Menemen. During a religious celebration, Sufi clerics called for a return to Islamic law and Arabic. One of the clerics killed a military officer, and the army opened up on the rioters with machine guns. Newspapers blamed the Free party for the outburst, despite the fact that the party had already ceased to exist.

---

reactionary   Extremely conservative, trying to return to bygone ways.
disestablish   Breaking tie between state and former official religion.
secular   Nonreligious.

Key Concepts

THE SIX ARROWS OF ATATÜRKISM

In 1931, the Republican Peoples' party platform outlined the six principles that would eventually be incorporated into the Turkish constitution: republicanism, secularism, nationalism, populism, **statism**, and revolutionism. To some extent, each of these principles still guides the Turkish state elite. Turgut Özal introduced the free market into the Turkish economy in the 1980s, abandoning the statism that had retarded economic growth. Secularism is under siege by **Islamist** parties today, and Kurdish revolutionaries challenge republicanism. The Turkish military, defenders of Atatürk's legacy, still live by these six arrows.

ISMET İNÖNÜ

Mustafa Kemal died in Istanbul on November 10, 1938. In death, he was given the name Atatürk, Father of the Turks. Ismet İnönü, a Nationalist general who had served many years as Atatürk's vice president, won support of the military's chief of staff and became president. İnönü kept Turkey neutral throughout most of World War II, but the defense ministry increased its share of the budget from 30 to 50 percent, and the size of the army ballooned from 120,000 to 1.5 million. The government tried to tame inflation through a series of price controls, devices that always fail. Rampant inflation, shortages, the black market—and the repressive measures to control them—made the Ankara government and the leading party unpopular. To ensure a place in the postwar United Nations, Turkey declared war on Germany only in February 1945.

İnönü, a democrat, announced in 1945 that Turkey needed an opposition party. He consulted with the military and got their approval to preserve the democratic order. Allowing an opposition may have been done to provide a safety valve for the frustrations of the Turkish people, built up during the siege economy of the war years. Turkey's democracy also strengthened its claim to join the new United Nations and to enlist Western support against Turkey's threatening neighbor, the Soviet Union. In 1947, as part of the Truman Doctrine, the United States did precisely that.

THE DEMOCRATIC PARTY

Like İnönü, Celal Bayar was a member of the Young Turks and Republican Peoples' party and a former vice president under Atatürk. Bayar combined forces with Adnan Menderes, a large landowner who opposed land reform. The Land Reform

---

statism National government owns main industries and leads economy.
Islamism Islam turned into a political ideology or party.

Bill, passed in January 1945 by İnönü's government, had driven a wedge between the rural-based landowners and state-centered bureaucrats.

The two registered the Democratic party (*Demokrat Parti*, DP) in early 1946 and quickly gathered support in the countryside, from those who blamed the Republicans for repression of Islam, from people hurt by inflation and shortages, and opponents of land reform. The Republicans tried to counter DP popularity, and in 1947 called for the repeal of the Land Reform bill.

The Republicans also competed with the Democrats for the religious vote and for the first time allowed foreign exchange for pilgrims for the hajj to Mecca. They allowed the teaching of Islam in public schools on a voluntary basis and allowed Ankara University to open a Faculty of Divinity, which graduated the first religious personnel trained in Turkey in over a decade. They authorized the reopening of Sufi tombs and shrines, and offered Turkish citizenship to displaced Muslims if they immigrated to the country.

The public was convinced, however, that Republican rule meant secularism and Democratic rule a return to Islam. Actually, the Democratic leadership was as firmly committed to secularism as Atatürk's party. DP leaders ousted a group of Islamists in the summer of 1946 and vowed that they would honor the secular basis of the state. To maintain their hold on power, the Republicans called for snap elections in 1946, to not give the Democrats time to organize. The Republicans captured 396 of 466 seats in parliament.

MILITARY PLANNING

As the Democratic party gained, military officers in Ankara and Istanbul organized as early as 1946 to monitor the political situation. They suspected the DP would abandon Atatürk's path. In 1947, a political discussion group was organized at the Istanbul Staff College, which by 1949 sounded out generals about a military coup. In public, the army vowed to respect election results.

At the funeral of the long-serving minister of defense in April 1950, the government arrested twenty-five mourners for reciting the Qur'an in Arabic. This created a voter backlash against the Republicans, and a month later the Democrats won 53.4 percent of the popular vote, giving them 408 of the 487 seats in parliament. Ismet İnönü was taken by surprise that the public had not rewarded his party for introducing democracy into the political system. For the first time in Turkish history, power passed peacefully to an opposition party.

DEMOCRATIC RULE

The Democrats did not trust the bureaucracy they inherited, particularly the military supporters of former general Ismet İnönü, who was now leader of the opposition. The Democrats purged the military by retiring senior officers, a move supported by junior officers trained in the United States, who believed their promotion prospects were being hindered by less well-trained superiors. Prime Minister Menderes' antipathy to the officer corps was legendary and mutual. In 1954, he said he could run the army with reserve officers, a blow to officers' already weakened morale. With high inflation and low wages, by 1956 one-third of all commissioned officers had resigned, citing inadequate income.

The DP got support from the religious public. They legalized the use of Arabic in the Muslim call to prayer, and within twenty-four hours the entire countryside returned to the practice. A month later, the Democrats approved broadcasting the Qur'an over state radio. Religious education was made mandatory. During the Democrats' stay in office, an average of 1,500 new mosques a year opened. In December 1950, the regime allowed the largest public prayer service in a quarter century, on behalf of the Turkish troops in Korea, where they fought gallantly and took heavy casualties. The Democrats reintroduced public piety in a ceremony to which the military could not object. Turkey was turning part way back to Islam.

Despite its reputation as the party of religion, the Democrats did not stray too far from the secularism of the Turkish constitution. In 1951, Tijani Sufis went on a rampage, smashing statues of Atatürk. The new government was quick to respond, arresting the order's leader. Similarly, in January 1953, the government banned the Nation party (*Millet Partisi*) for political use of religion. Followers of the banned party reorganized into the Republican Nation party and held onto five seats in parliament. To eliminate them, the Democrats gerrymandered the conservative district that had voted for the five candidates. The Democrats did allow one change that had a profound impact on the future of religion in Turkey, the opening of eleven additional Muslim seminaries. Designed to provide Turks with indigenous prayer leaders, these schools later fostered an Islamist challenge to the political center.

By 1957, with the Turkish economy again in recession, the bureaucracy and armed forces withdrew their support as their buying power declined. The party also lost many intellectuals, who began to listen to Republican complaints that the Democratic party used religion for political purposes. The DP, born as an opposition movement, now attempted to silence opposition. As early as 1953, they ordered the government to confiscate most of the Republicans' assets, claiming they had been illegally acquired with public funds during the single-party period. In 1956, they got laws allowing them to suspend newspapers for publishing "false" news, to approve all newspaper advertising in advance, to ration newspaper print, and to prohibit newspapers from covering subjects deemed to be "of an offensive nature." They amended the Law on Elections so a candidate rejected by his party could not change parties in the general election and forbade opposition parties from uniting by running a joint list.

In 1955, the DP played the nationalist card by allowing a limited "spontaneous" student demonstration in Istanbul after a bomb exploded near the Turkish consulate in the Greek city of Salonika. As slum dwellers joined the students, however, it turned into unlimited attacks on Greeks and the wealthy. (In 1961 the courts acquitted DP officials of responsibility for the riots.) The police, who had been ordered not to intervene, took no action. To restore public order, the Democrats turned to the military and declared martial law in the major cities.

Once the military had been invited to participate in politics, it was hard to get them back to the barracks. Dissident military officers sought the views of Ismet Inönü about a coup. Most Turkish officers still admired and followed Inönü, but the DP government of Menderes feared him and tried to keep him isolated. Praetorianism (see box in Chapter 4), the tendency for military takeovers, tends to become a chronic, self-reinfecting endemic illness. Catch it once and you'll get it again.

THE 1961 MILITARY REVOLUTION

On the morning of May 27, 1961, Turkish radio told the nation a military coup had ended Democratic party rule to prevent civil strife. Thirty-eight junior officers, led by General Cemal Gürsel, formed a National Unity Committee (NUC) to lead the country. The **junta** abolished party structures and suspended party activities. A new constitution established a National Security Council of top generals to advise the government on security issues.

The NUC abolished the Democratic party and charged former government officials with treason. The trials that followed kept the party in the eyes of the public throughout the period of military rule and were a public relations disaster. Judges dismissed many of the charges against the Democrats for lack of evidence. The public perceived other charges as petty. The senior officers hanged Prime Minister Menderes and two colleagues.

To maintain and protect the military hierarchy from the junior officers in the NUC, the generals who were not involved in the coup organized the Armed Forces Union. Throughout 1961 and 1962, the Union warned politicians not to return to the pre-coup policies that had so disrupted the country. The Union lobbied in support of the death sentence for Adnan Menderes, fearful that if he lived he might regain power and put the junta on trial.

In June 1961, the Union reached the height of its influence. Fearing a NUC plan to purge the armed forces of Union members, the Union sent jet fighters to buzz Ankara and demanded their members be protected. The NUC caved in and established the independence of the traditional military hierarchy from the governing junta. The mixing of governing and military roles is always one of the weak points of military takeovers. Like the Brazilian generals a few years later, the Turkish generals had to decide whether to be an army or an administration.

Civilian political activity also began to pick up. A coalition of industrialists, shopkeepers, landowners, peasants, religious reactionaries, and Western-oriented liberals formed the Justice party in 1961. The party's platform called for "justice" for the imprisoned DP members. The junta allowed elections in October 1961, but only after forcing participants to sign a "National Declaration" supporting the legitimacy of the coup. The Republicans were the only major party to survive the

---

junta   (from the Spanish) Group, usually of military officers, that governs after a coup.

coup and received 36.7 percent of the vote. The upstart Justice party won 34.7 percent, with many of their successful candidates still in jail cells because of their previous DP activities. Inönü formed a coalition government that included members of the Justice party. The government collapsed after less than a year, and President Gürsel turned to Justice to form the new government.

One coup tends to lead to another. The head of Ankara's War College attempted another coup and came within minutes of arresting the government. He was forced to resign from the army, and the Armed Forces Union was broken. The same man tried again in 1963, but this time he was executed.

New Political Faces

Suleiman Demirel led the Justice party into the October 1965 elections, which it won, and for the first time a European-type left-right cleavage entered Turkish politics. The Republicans moved away from its role as party of the state toward a more radical platform. The Democratic party, now under another name, returned to power. Alpaslan Türkes, who was part of the 1961 military coup, took over the Republican Peasant's National party in 1963 and infused it with Turkish nationalism. In 1969 he changed the name to the Nationalist Action party. He declared that Islam was an integral part of Turkish nationalism and sponsored a paramilitary group known as the Gray Wolves. In 1969 Necmettin Erbakan's National Order party arrived. An avowed Islamist, Erbakan said the country could only reclaim its past glory by turning back to the Islam that it had abandoned over the previous half century.

The "Coup by Memorandum"

Right and left clashed in the streets, with left-wing terrorists battling right-wing Gray Wolves. The government invaded campuses to crush student radicals. As violence grew, groups within the military began plans for a new military intervention. The General Staff handed the prime minister a memorandum demanding he halt violence or face military intervention. Demirel immediately resigned. Turks called it the "coup by memorandum."

Violence continued, and in 1971 the National Security Council declared martial law in eleven provinces. After the Turkish People's Liberation Army killed the Israeli consul in Istanbul, the military arrested over 5,000 alleged leftists. In the general anti-leftist mood of the era, the Workers party was closed but the Gray Wolves were allowed to operate more or less freely. Note that this was a time of radical leftism in many countries, including Germany and Italy. The military also closed Erbakan's National Order party for bringing religion back into politics. Erbakan opened a new party, the National Salvation party but did not call for an Islamic state, only one that furthered traditional Turkish culture and its Islamic components.

 *Conflicts*

THE CYPRUS PROBLEM

Until 1960 Cyprus had been a British colony with a Greek majority and Turkish minority. After years of guerrilla warfare by Greek Cypriots aiming at union with Greece, Britain granted the island independence only if it would not join Greece. Greek Cypriot militants did not give up; some murdered ethnic Turks.

In 1967, Turkey threatened to intervene to protect the Turkish minority that lived mostly on the northern side of the island. President Johnson warned the Turks that NATO would not cover them if they did, and the Turkish military shelved their plans. Many Turks never forgot their abandonment by the Americans. In 1974, a Greek-inspired coup in Cyprus brought the Cypriot National Guard to power, and it proclaimed the island a part of Greece. Faced with this, Turkish Prime Minister Ecevit ordered Turkish intervention to protect Turkish Cypriots. They captured 40 percent of the island, which declared itself the Turkish Republic of Northern Cyprus. No government recognized the new republic except Ankara. Cyprus stays split today.

The United States suspended all military aid to Turkey. Turkish intellectuals, who already felt abandoned by U.S. threats in 1967, concluded that the West was aligning against Muslim Turkey to support the Christian Greeks. This provided the psychological and cultural foundation on which Erbakan built his political movement.

A further Cyprus problem threatens. The Republic of Cyprus (the south) is set to join the European Union (EU) in 2004. Since the other EU governments recognize the Republic as sovereign over the entire island, Turkey would be an illegal occupier. This will block Turkey's own effort to join the EU, which requires unanimous approval—meaning the Republic of Cyprus could veto Turkey's admission.

The new government changed the constitution to give the military an institutional method to voice its recommendation through the National Security Council. The 1971 intervention failed to resolve the conflicts in Turkish society because it did not convince a single major group or party that the military should have intervened. Civilian officials grew frustrated at operating under the implied veto of the generals.

RETURN TO ELECTIONS

In 1973, voters elected Bülent Ecevit and his Republican Peoples' party. This was not, however, the party of Atatürk. Ecevit abandoned the statist perspective and converted it into a center-left party. Ecevit's party received 33.5 percent of the vote, surpassing Demirel and the Justice party's 29.5 percent. Ecevit entered a governing alliance with Erbakan and the National Salvation party, whose Islamists demanded unsuccessfully making Friday, the Muslim sabbath, part of the weekend, that the government forbid tourists from entering Turkey, and that female police officers and customs officials wear longer skirts. Islamism, however, was now part of Turkish politics and grew.

Capitalizing on his popularity following the Turkish invasion of Cyprus, Ecevit resigned as prime minister and called new elections. The president, however, deferred elections and asked Suleiman Demirel to organize a new coalition. The Justice party therefore formed the new government with the Nationalist Action party and Türkes' Nationalist Order party, which took advantage of their control of the interior ministry to infiltrate the security forces with Gray Wolves.

Over the next five years, weak coalition governments alternated, and they could do nothing to stop increasing left and right violence. Even the security forces divided into left and right factions, which arrested their ideological opponents. Prime Minister Ecevit, fierce opponent of the 1971 military intervention into politics, was forced to declare martial law "with a human face." From the military's view, this meant continued civilian interference in military activities that prevented them from carrying out their jobs. When Demirel again assumed power, he abolished the martial law, but it was too late to appease the military. When you have a mess, you get coups.

THE THIRD COUP

With an average of twenty Turks a day killed in political violence, on New Year's Day 1980 the general staff issued a 1971-style warning. On September 12, 1980, the military again took over, and much of the public was relieved. The National Security Council had a retired admiral form a government of nonpartisan **technocrats**, including six retired military officers, who took orders from the Council.

The generals blamed the politicians for the state's gridlock and arrested all of the country's senior politicians, disbanded the parties, and dismissed mayors and municipal councils. The Council ruled via regional and local commanders. To break the terrorists, the military conducted mass arrests, and military tribunals condemned 3,600 people to death (although only fifteen sentences were actually carried out).

A constitutional assembly wrote a new constitution, in use today. To win support of religious Turks, it made religious education compulsory in primary and secondary schools. In March 1983, Ankara authorized the return to civilian rule, but pre-coup parties and politicians were banned. The Council approved three parties for the scheduled elections. The party least associated with the military, the Motherland party under the former Deputy Prime Minister for Economic Affairs Turgut Özal, won 45 percent of the vote (and a majority of parliament) from a populace weary of taking orders from the army. The junta resigned on December 6, 1983, and the third military intervention in twenty years was over.

The new parliament called for a referendum that overturned the ban on precoup politicians and parties. In 1991, Suleiman Demirel was reelected as the head of his renamed party, the True Path party. When Demirel was elected president

---

technocrat   Nonparty official appointed on basis of technical, usually financial, skills.

W : *Women of the Middle East*

TURKEY'S TANSU CILLER

Tansu Ciller was a female economics professor with limited government or party experience. After graduate school in the United States, she became the youngest professor in modern Turkish history. Intensely disliked by traditional faculty members for her imperial style, the chiefs of her True Path party united behind her because they thought they could control a woman.

The party elders misjudged her. She was tough. Through speculation in Turkish and American real estate, Ciller had amassed a fortune estimated at $50 million to $100 million. Unusually, Ciller did not assume her husband's last name. Instead, Ciller's father made the groom change his name, so that the Ciller family name would not die out (as Ciller has no brothers). Ciller bucked thousands of years of tradition, and her time in office marked Turkish modernization.

following Özal's death by heart attack in 1993, True Path had a new leader, Prime Minister Tansu Ciller (pronounced Chiller), a woman who had only two years of parliamentary experience.

THE RISE OF REFAH

While Turkey won praise for choosing a female prime minister, things were different at the local level. In 1994, Necmettin Erbakan's newest effort, the Refah (Welfare) party, captured city governments in Ankara and Istanbul, shocking the secular establishment. The lower-middle class, many of them rural villagers, had moved to the cities without changing their Islamic orientation. The party also captured twenty-nine other major cities, and 400 smaller towns. Two-thirds of the population of Turkey now lived under Islamist municipal governments.

The secularist military and Refah were on a collision course. Erbakan announced the inevitability of the "Just Order," code for an Islamic state. In 1995 the General Staff warned against "reactionary" trends, the term the military used for the Islamists. Refah captured 21 percent of the popular vote and a plurality of seats in parliament. Much of their vote came from southeastern Turkey, home of an armed Kurdish rebellion. The government had banned Kurdish political parties, and many voters supported Refah simply to protest the ban. Others protested the rampant corruption of the centrist parties. Secular parties formed a shaky coalition and kept Refah out of the government, despite its parliamentary plurality. Then Erbakan struck a deal with Ciller of the True Path party to form a new coalition with Erbakan as prime minister. Turkey now had an Islamist chief of government, and the army did not like it.

Erbakan was cautious toward the army. He wanted the United States out of the Middle East but let the U.S. Air Force continue to use the important Incirlik air base

Geography

TURKEY AND THE EUROPEAN UNION

Is Turkey in the Middle East or in Europe? Secular Turks are adamant that Turkey belongs in Europe, but Brussels and Islamist Turks are not so sure. The **European Union** (EU) doubts Turkey's economic and democratic credentials, and although it will not say so in public, doubts that a Muslim country belongs in the EU. Turkish Islamists want to preserve its traditional Muslim character. The 2.1 million Turks now in Germany have voted with their feet to join Europe.

Only two countries with Muslim populations have ever applied for EU membership, Morocco and Turkey. Brussels said that Morocco was not a European country. Brussels did not reject Turkey's application but delayed it forever with a variety of reasons: Turkey must liberalize its politics, improve its economy, and clean up its (at times brutal) human-rights record. Many Turks believe former German Chancellor Helmut Kohl gave the real reason when he said Europe was a Christian club that would never accept a Muslim country.

Turkey first applied for EU membership in 1959 and signed an "association" agreement in 1963 that cut tariffs between Turkey and the EU. In 1970 the EU set up a **customs union** with Turkey, to be implemented over twenty-five years. In 1987, however, Prime Minister Turgut Özal applied for full EU membership. The EU Commission took thirty months to respond and said the fuller unification of present members took precedence.

In 2000 the EU announced accession dates for twelve of the thirteen applying states. The odd man out, as usual, was Turkey. The Christian former-Communist countries of East Europe were good Europeans; Muslim Turkey was not. Many Turks began to suspect they never would be.

to enforce the no-fly zone over northern Iraq. Erbakan removed Islamist officers from the military because they violated Turkish military law. He even let the military improve relations with Israel in a series of military cooperation and training agreements.

On the other hand, Erbakan tried to reinforce his Islamist credentials in foreign policy. He ostentatiously first visited his Muslim neighbors of Iran, Libya, and Egypt. In Iran, he thumbed his nose at the United States by signing a $23 billion deal for Iranian gas, less than a week after a new U.S. law ordered sanctions (unenforceable) for those who did business with Iran. In Libya, Erbakan urged Libya to pay the debt it owed Turkish construction companies, but Qaddafi lectured Erbakan publicly on Kurdish rights and the need for a Kurdish homeland. In Egypt, there were no Turkish flags at the airport for the welcoming ceremony, an insult the Turkish military noted.

European Union   Federation of most European states with main institutions in Brussels; began as Common Market in 1957.
customs union   Pact providing same external tariffs for members.

At home, Refah sought to change the national education system, giving greater rights to Islamic seminarians. They also attempted to place the General Staff under the defense ministry, and thus under the Islamist government's control. Refah parliamentarians sought to cut the military budget by a half billion dollars to protest the continuing expulsions of Islamists from the military.

MILITARY MOVES AGAINST REFAH

The army wanted the Islamist government out but was divided on a coup. They were especially incensed at the Iranian ambassador urging a Turkish audience to support an Islamic revolution. In 1997 the General Staff told the government to repudiate Refah's ideology, asserting the threat from Islamists to the Turkish state was greater than any external threat. In return, some Refah members urged withdrawing from the government.

As they had earlier agreed, Tansu Ciller was supposed to become prime minister in 1997, but Turkey's president rejected the swap and named the chief of the Motherland party. Now out of power, Refah's supporters protested violently in the streets. Accused of fomenting Islamism, in early 1998 the Constitutional Court banned Refah and barred seven leaders, including Erbakan, from all political activity for five years. Refah parliamentarians and other officials kept their positions, but as independents. Some Refah members had already organized another party, the Fazilet (Virtue) party.

The state continued to pressure Islamists. Istanbul mayor Recep Tayyip Erdogan (pronounced "Erdowan") went on trial for reading an Islamist poem that called for the liberation of the oppressed from the rule of "Pharaoh." The State Security Court ruled the speech was an incitement to hatred based on religious and racial differences, and Erdogan was jailed and banned from public office. The centrist government fell in late 1998, accused of awarding bank privatization to friends, the latest in a long line of scandals touching centrist prime ministers. Corruption is one big reason Turks often vote for Islamist parties, which are relatively clean and deliver welfare measures.

In 1999, Turkish security forces captured the leader of the Kurdistan Peoples party (PKK), Abdullah Ocalan (pronounced "Ojalan"), who had been hiding in the Greek ambassador's residence in Kenya. The Turkish public held Ocalan personally responsible for over 30,000 deaths from the long PKK insurrection. The arrest gave Bülent Ecevit's caretaker government a tremendous boost in public support, and his Democratic Socialist party won the most votes in the 1999 elections. Second place went to the Nationalist Action party. Fazilet drew only 15 percent of the vote. The electorate had heeded the military's warnings to not return Islamists to power. The electorate's message, however, was neither pro- nor anti-Islamist; it was for clean government.

Ecevit formed an alliance with the right-wing Nationalist Action party but faced Turkey's second economic crisis in ten years (the first was under Ciller in 1994), a crisis that continues today. They brought Kemal Dervis, a technocrat economist who worked for the World Bank, back from Washington to lead an economic recovery

W: *Women of the Middle East*

MERVE KAVAKCI

In 1999, as the new parliament was sworn in, Fazilet member Merve Kavakci entered the chamber covered with an Islamic headscarf in violation of parliamentary dress codes. It was a brave, symbolic step, as no woman had entered the General Assembly with a headscarf since Atatürk. She was driven from the floor amidst cries of "Shame, shame!" from secular deputies. Kavakci was stripped of her parliamentary seat on a technicality, because she had also become a U.S. citizen and had thus surrendered her Turkish citizenship. The incident showed the continual bitterness between secularists and Islamists.

team. Dervis and his team failed but did win a law bringing Turkey into alignment with EU laws. In 2002, parliament abolished the death penalty and legalized teaching and broadcasting in a language other than Turkish (meaning Kurdish).

Now in opposition, Fazilet began to show internal divisions over getting Erbakan out of jail or keeping distant from him in order to avoid being shut down as a continuation of the Refah Party. In 2001, the Supreme Court banned Fazilet as a focus for illegal Islamist activities.

THE JUSTICE AND DEVELOPMENT PARTY

As usual, a new Islamist party took the place of Fazilet. The Justice and Development party (AKP), led by the reformers Abdullah Gül and Tayyip Erdogan, took a conciliatory tone with the secular establishment, saying it was culturally conservative but committed to a secular state. The 2002 elections swept the AKP into power. The previous coalition parties, as well as all opposition parties except the Republican Peoples' party, failed to reach the 10 percent national threshold and therefore did not receive a single seat in Parliament (despite the fact that 46 percent had voted for them). For the first time since 1987, one party had a parliamentary majority, and for the first time since 1954 parliament had a two-party system.

Although Erdogan was leader of the AKP, he was ineligible to sit in parliament because of his conviction for inciting religious hatred as a Refah party leader. Abdullah Gül became prime minister with the understanding that he would soon turn the office over to Erdogan. In late 2002, parliament amended the constitution to restore the rights of those banned for ideological crimes, such as Erdogan. In 2003, Erdogan won a seat in a by-election in a conservative town and a week later was named prime minister. Gül became foreign minister. The new government declared their three main priorities were joining the EU, improving relations with the West, and increased regional cooperation. Turkey's strategic relationship with Israel was unchanged despite the Islamist character of the new government.

G : *Geography*

TURKEY, IRAQ, AND THE UNITED STATES

Turkey has had problems with its border with Iraq going back to the founding of the Turkish Republic. Under the Ottomans, Iraq had simply been three Ottoman provinces. The Treaty of Lausanne awarded the oil-producing cities of Mosul and Kirkuk to Iraq, then under British supervision. Turkey objected strongly, and some Turks have kept Turkish claims to these oil fields alive. In addition, Turkey asserts a right to protect the Turkic minority of Iraq, the Turcomans, 2 percent of Iraqis.

Turkey also has national security reasons to watch northern Iraq. Having fought a murderous Kurdish insurgency for fifteen years, Turkey opposes any independence or autonomy for Kurds in Iraq for fear of creating a safe haven for Turkish Kurdish insurgents and an example for Turkish Kurds to resume their struggle.

When Iraq invaded Kuwait in August 1990, Turkey joined most of the world in condemning it. Turkey allowed coalition aircraft to fly from the NATO airbase at Incirlik. Turkey also agreed to the U.S.-led economic embargo of Iraq, cutting the crucial oil pipeline into Turkey and costing Turkey billions of dollars in trade and transit revenues. President Turgut Özal relied on promises from President Bush (senior) of massive economic aid, but the U.S. Congress only passed a fraction of it. Turkey felt it had given America much and gotten little in return.

Following the Gulf War, Iraq's Kurds rebelled against Saddam Hussein at America's instigation. The U.S. military stood by and did nothing while Saddam destroyed the rebels, and half a million Kurds fled into Turkey. Alarmed at both the costs of caring for these refugees and at the security situation created by an influx of Kurds (who possibly sympathized with Turkish Kurdish rebels), the Turks agreed to a no-fly zone in the north of Iraq. That way, Iraqi Kurds would stay in Iraq.

Every six months for the past decade, the Turkish parliament has reluctantly renewed permission for U.S. warplanes to patrol northern Iraqi skies from Incirlik. Ankara did not like the way Iraqi Kurds took advantage of the relative peace to establish a northern Kurdish zone independent of any central authority in Baghdad or Ankara. Again, it might give Turkish Kurds ideas. In 1991, however, Turkey did not participate in the invasion of Iraq. They massed troops along the border, giving Iraq a potential threat to defend against, but Turkey did not actually fight.

In 2002, President Bush (junior) asked Ankara to let us stage the U.S. Fourth Infantry Division's invasion of Iraq from Turkey. Washington promised $6 billion in outright grants and $24 billion in concessionary loans. The Turkish General Staff wanted to accept and even send Turkish troops into Iraq to keep the Kurds under control, a deployment of Turkish troops that required parliamentary approval. The new government would go along with this if the UN authorized it, but when the UN deadlocked the Turkish parliament refused to authorize either the U.S. transit or use of Turkish troops.

At first, the Turkish public applauded parliament for preserving Turkish honor: "We cannot be bought for a bribe, no matter how large." When the public began to realize it had lost major financial aid, a voice in the future of Iraq, and the goodwill of its primary Western ally, Turkey granted U.S. forces overflight rights. With the Iraq War underway, the Fourth Infantry Division pulled its equipment out of Turkish ports and sailed through the Suez Canal to enter Iraq from the south. Parliament granted the United States permission to use Incirlik to bomb Northern Iraq, earning about $1 billion in grants and $5 billion in loans. But Turkey had lost U.S. aid and goodwill. U.S.-Turkish relations are still good but not what they used to be.

Conclusions

Turkey is a case study in the difficulty of modernizing a Muslim country. Turkey is the first Islamic country to attempt modernization and has not fully succeeded. Significant elements resist. Generals who had earlier tried to modernize the Ottoman Empire founded the Republic of Turkey with one of its own as first president, Atatürk, an authoritarian reformer, who led the country on a secular, Western course. His successor, Ismet Inönü of the Republican Peoples party, democratized Turkey by legalizing opposition parties, some of which tried to roll back Atatürk's reforms, leaving Turkey "torn" between a Westernizing elite and Islamic mass parties. Turkey seems to be permanently praetorian.

In 1950, the Democratic party came to power and tried to disenfranchise the Republicans and their military supporters. This triggered the 1960 coup. Having tasted power, military officers tried twice more in the 1960s to overthrow the government. In 1971, they threatened a coup if the government did not improve security, and the government resigned. In 1980, the military intervened again, to restore security to the streets.

In the 1990s, a series of Islamist parties took power, either in coalitions or on their own. The current AK party is run by Islamist reformists. While an Islamist government cooperated with the United States in the Gulf War, the current party did not. As the country struggles to come out of the worst depression in sixty years, it turned down a major U.S. aid package rather than assist the second Bush administration to invade Iraq.

Further Reference

Ahmad, Feroz. *The Making of Modern Turkey*. New York: Routledge, 1993.

Henze, Paul B. *Turkey and Atatürk's Legacy*. Haarlem, Netherlands: SOTA, 1998.

Heper, Metin, and Jacob M. Landau, eds. *Political Parties and Democracy in Turkey*. New York: I. B. Tauris, 1991.

Lewis, Bernard. *The Emergence of Modern Turkey*, 2nd ed. New York: Oxford University Press, 1968.

Pope, Nicole, and Hugh Pope, *Turkey Unveiled: A History of Modern Turkey*. New York: Overlook Press, 1998.

Zurcher, Erik J. *Turkey: A Modern History*. New York: I. B. Tauris, 1993.

The Kurds

Points to Ponder

- Are the Kurds a separate nationality?
- Can one nationality have several languages?
- Should all nations have their own state?
- What has prevented the Kurds from establishing a state?
- If Kurds establish a state in one country, what will be the effect on Kurds in other countries?
- Is it right for nationalist movements to constantly switch allies in order to get powerful supporters?
- Is this region especially full of violence and betrayal, or no worse than many others?

Largely forgotten, the Kurds have been a long-smoldering problem that took on new urgency with the two wars against Iraq. Should these strange, divided people have their own country, or should they be content to be citizens of other countries? To answer these questions, we have to understand the concept of nationalism.

WHO ARE THE KURDS?

The Kurds are approximately 25 million people who live where Turkey, Syria, Iraq, Iran, and Armenia nearly meet. They have no country of their own and never did. They have usually been divided and do not form one single ethnic group. The biggest concentration of Kurds is probably Istanbul, home to some 3 million Kurds.

The ancestral home of the Kurds is in the mountainous region where these five countries come together, a land of plateaus and mountains, many with peaks over 10,000 feet. Even the cities are at altitudes over 4,000 feet. Winters are extremely cold; snow isolates many mountain villages. The harsh climate and terrain breed self-reliant people used to hardship. The same conditions produce social isolation and difficulties in communication.

155

The Scattered Kurds

The Kurds speak a variety of dialects. the two most common are Kurmanji and Sorani—Indo-European languages related to Iranian. The third dialect (known as Macho-Macho by the Kurds, Zaza by the Turks, and Gurani by the Persians) is not linguistically related to the other two. Kurmanji and Sorani reflect a common origin, but there are numerous differences between them. Kurmanji has gender and case endings; Sorani does not. Differences in pronunciation often make the languages mutually unintelligible. The Kurmanji-Sorani divide reflects an underlying cultural chasm. Kurmanji speakers are organized more along tribal lines, whereas the Sorani are more urbanized. Written Kurdish also varies with the countries Kurds live in. In Iraq and Iran, Kurdish uses a modified Arabic script, in Armenia a Cyrillic one, and in Syria and Turkey a Latin script.

While most Kurds are Sunni Muslims, some are Shi'a or Christians. Most Kurds are tolerant of religious minorities. Some Kurds believe in sects that most orthodox Muslims reject, such as the Yazidi and the Ahl al Haq or Ali Allahi. Even among the traditional Sunni Kurds, many are members of Sufi religious orders, primarily the Qadiri or the Naqashbandi.

Kurds are divided among nomadic tribesmen, sedentary tribesmen, and city dwellers. Traditionally Kurds have looked to the nomads as their real fighters. Feuds between tribes often interfere with nationalist aspirations. Even when tribal chiefs support a nationalist movement, other tribes oppose it out of tribal rivalry. Kurds do not have a long written history; instead they have a rich body of folklore. The bulk of Kurdish literature is poetry, transmitted orally.

Key Concepts

NATIONALISM

As we discussed in Chapter 5, nationalism is the belief that a people ought to govern themselves with their own state. The basis for this feeling can be language, ethnicity, religion, or ideology. Nationalism often emphasizes the greatness and unity of one's people and a dastardly Other, those who are not like us but occupy us, misrule us, oppress us. Nationalism can be very negative and nasty.

Ethnic nationalists look at physical appearance, common ancestry, common language, and common religion. Few nations are ethnically pure, as you always find mixed marriages, immigrants, emigrants, contrived histories and ancestries, and converts into or out of the religion. Nationalism based on ideology accepts a variety of people who believe they are part of the nation. Self-identification is what matters here. We are Americans because we wish to be, not because of common ethnic origins. Few countries are like that. The Kurds, divided by dialects, have trouble defining themselves as a nation based on purely ethnic criteria. Do they have sufficient self-identification to form a nation on ideological grounds?

A HISTORY OF SEEKING A NATION

Ancient Sumerian records describe a people called Gutu, or Kuti, who held the middle Tigris region between 2400–2300 B.C. These could have been early ancestors of the Kurds, as could the Kardukhia who lived on the Armenian plateau between the ninth and sixth centuries B.C. Other possible ancestors are the Cyrtii, first mentioned by Polybius in 22 B.C. as rioters among the troops of the governor of Media.

By the fourth century A.D., Armenians gave the name Kerchkh to the region northwest of Lake Urumiyeh, and they referred to the residents by the same name. When the Arabs conquered the area in 644–656, they called the inhabitants Kurds. Between 951 and 1096, numerous Kurdish dynasties ruled in Eastern Turkey, Western Iran, and Azerbaijan. The Kurdish general Salah-ad-Din, better known as Saladin, defeated the Crusaders, recaptured Jerusalem, ruled over central Arabia, and reconquered Fatimid Egypt for the caliphate.

In 1501 Shah Ismail founded the Safavid dynasty in Iran and tried to convert his subjects to Shi'a Islam. Many of the Sunni Kurds migrated out of Iran and into the Ottoman Empire, especially after the battle of Chaldiran (1514) when the Turkish Sultan Selim the Grim defeated the Persian Shah. The Sultan established a series of five independent Kurdish principalities on the border to act as a buffer. Iran followed suit. The last of these semi-independent emirates lasted until 1865. During the reign of Shah Abbas the Great (1585–1628), many Kurds left their traditional heartland forever. To protect his borders against invading Uzbeks and Turcomans, the Shah transferred several Kurdish tribes from the western borders of his kingdom to the far northeastern corner of Khorasan. These tribes were Shi'a Kurds and gave their loyalty to the Shah of Iran rather than the Sunni caliph in Istanbul.

Cultures

CREATION MYTHOLOGY

Persian creation mythology is found in the Shahname; Kurdish creation mythology is in the Sharafname. Much of the creation is the same in both accounts, suggesting a common ancestry. The differences emphasize group attributes in which Kurds take great pride.

The fifth king in the Pishdadides dynasty of Iran was Zohhak, son of Jamshid. Zohhak had a peculiar illness in which serpents grew from his shoulders. To assuage this malady, Satan advised Zohhak to apply the brains of young men to each of the shoulders. Zohhak accordingly ordered the execution of two youths daily. In the Persian version, this practice continued until a hero killed Zohhak.

In the Kurdish version, the executioner took pity on the intended victims and only sacrificed one youth. The executioner then mixed the brains of the one victim with the brains of a sheep. As for the youths who were saved, they were forced to escape and hide in the most inhospitable mountains in the country, where they multiplied and became the original Kurdish people. Thus, this creation story emphasizes the oppressed nature of the Kurds, and their ability through cunning and perseverance to survive.

In the nineteenth century, nationalism began to stir among Turks. Emir Badr Khan of Botan began to unite Kurds in a single state. He struck his own coins and the Friday prayer was said in his name—both signs of sovereignty. In 1843 and 1846, Badr Khan sent expeditions against his Nestorian Christian neighbors, but the Ottomans, under European pressure, forced his surrender. Badr Khan was exiled to Canada and later to Damascus, where he died. Some Kurdish historians consider him the father of Kurdish nationalism.

In 1872, the Persian government demanded that the Kurds pay taxes to the central government. They refused, claiming that in 1836 the Shah had let them pay whatever taxes to their own leader, Shaykh Taher. The Persian government sent an army to collect the revenues. Shaykh Taher, head of the Naqashbandi order in the region, had died, but his son, Shaykh Ubaydallah, saw his authority was being challenged and appealed to the Ottoman Sultan for protection. The Shaykh also sent a small force to the Russo-Turkish war of 1877–1878; in recognition, the Ottomans appointed him commander of Kurdish tribal forces, bolstering his claim of leader of the Kurdish lands. With little Ottoman help, the Shaykh decided Kurds could rely only on themselves.

The Treaty of Berlin ended the war and obligated the Ottoman government to protect Christian Armenians from Kurds. Ubaydallah interpreted this as a European guarantee of Christian ascendancy in Kurdistan. Hearing the Armenians were to get an independent state around Van, Ubaydallah stated he would never permit it, even if he had to arm *women* to stop it!

In 1879, Kurds from the Haraki tribe plundered a village, and the Ottomans retaliated against them. In response, Ubaydallah launched an armed uprising against the Turkish government. The insurrection, under command of his son Abdul Qadir, was easily put down, and the Shaykh bowed to the central government. In 1880,

Persian troops crossed the border and killed or kidnapped some young Kurds. In retaliation, the Shaykh attacked Iran and threatened to set up an independent Kurdish kingdom. He attacked with 80,000 soldiers and, joined by Iranian tribesmen, reached Tabriz before being repulsed. The Ottoman government tired of Ubaydallah's attempts at a Kurdish kingdom. In 1882 Ubaydallah sought Russian support for yet another Kurdish movement. Weak political movements seek help everywhere and anywhere. Istanbul soon heard of it and deported the Shaykh and his tribal chiefs to Mecca.

To guard against another Ubaydallah, in 1890 Sultan Abdul Hamid II established the Hamidiye, cavalry regiments of native tribesmen. They had to provide their own weapons and horses, and the tribal chieftains were made unit commanders. The Hamidiye continued in one form or another until the establishment of the Turkish Republic. Local residents remember these units with revulsion, because the tribal leaders used them to oppress all in the area not allied with them.

WORLD WAR I AND ITS AFTERMATH

Allied pronouncements after World War I fueled nationalist aspirations among Kurdish leaders, as they did worldwide. Woodrow Wilson in his 1918 "Four Principles" speech said territorial settlements at the upcoming peace conference should be based on national self-determination. At Versailles, Wilson's Fourteen Points seemed to tell Kurds that the Western powers would look favorably on an independent Kurdistan. Point twelve specifically said that in the Turkish portions of the Ottoman Empire, other nationalities should be assured an opportunity for autonomous development. Point fourteen called for the establishment of the League of Nations to protect the political independence and territorial integrity of great and small states alike. Britain, less enamored with nationalist rights than Wilson, suggested a Kurdish buffer state between Turkey and Mesopotamia.

The allies met at Versailles to negotiate a peace. The Kurds sent a delegation as a national minority that had been guaranteed independence by the Fourteen Points. But, as usual, the Kurds could not maintain a united front. In November 1919, several Kurdish chieftains under Turkish influence telegraphed the conference protesting plans to separate them from Turkey, especially if the new entity would be under a foreign mandate, namely Britain as the mandatory power of Iraq. Britain had no intention of turning oil-rich Mosul province over to an independent Kurdistan. It kept Mosul as part of the new country of Iraq it was setting up.

Nonetheless, the allies signed the Treaty of Sèvres on August 10, 1920, and the Ottoman, British, French, Italian, and U.S. governments ratified it. Article 62 provided for the establishment of a Kurdish autonomous area within Turkey, and pointed out that the Turkish border could be redrawn if necessary to fulfill this commitment. Article 64 said that if the Kurds then petitioned the League of Nations for independence and the League accepted the petition, Turkey would recognize the independent country and renounce all claims to its territory.

It looked like the Kurds had international recognition for a country of their own, but that recognition had been granted by the Ottoman representatives. When the Atatürk's Nationalist forces took over Turkey, they refused to recognize the treaty, claiming that the Sultan was under the pressure of foreign occupation. Atatürk demanded the treaty be renegotiated, and the new treaty, the 1923 Treaty of Lausanne, avoided all mention of an independent Kurdistan. What the Kurds thought they had won was snatched away from them.

THE SIMKO REBELLION

The leader of the Shakak tribal confederation was Ismail Agha Simko, husband of Shaykh Ubaydallah's granddaughter. Simko, an opportunist, first achieved prominence during the Iranian Constitutional Revolution of 1906. Originally aligned with the constitutionalists, he switched to the monarchists. As a reward, the Iranian government appointed him subgovernor of the district of Qotur. During World War I he fought as a Russian ally against Turkey and later against the Russians to defend Iranian territory from their occupation. In 1918, he personally shot the Assyrian Christian pope, Mar Shimun XIX, in the back to eliminate the Assyrians as a political or military threat. By the end of the war, Simko was the only power in the Turkish-Iranian border area. By July 1922 he appointed both tribal leaders and governors for the area.

Simko's rebellion was less a nationalist uprising than a bid for personal control. In July 1922, in British-ruled Iraq, another Kurdish ruler decided to join in Simko's revolt. In an attempt to obtain British support for his own movement, Simko opposed the Iraqi revolt and convinced the other Persian tribes to deny the Iraqi movement any support. In August 1922, the Iranian government sent its Cossacks against Simko, defeating him decisively and forcing him into exile.

Reza Khan Pahlavi pardoned Simko in 1924, paving the way for Simko's return to Iran. In 1926, Simko again tried to regain leadership of the Kurdish tribes. This time, the Turks and Iranians combined forces and worked jointly against him. When the Kurds retreated across the Turkish border, the two armies encircled, disarmed, and interned Simko. In 1929, the Iranian government again invited Simko to return. Immediately, tribal chieftains gave him obeisance. Before he could reorganize, however, the tribes betrayed Simko to the Iranian government, which killed him in an ambush. The tricky Simko is a dubious Kurdish national symbol.

THE MAHABAD REPUBLIC

World War I gave Kurds their first chance at nationhood; World War II gave them a second. After Hitler turned on his ally Stalin in 1941 and invaded the Soviet Union, the allies supplied the Soviets heavily through Iran. In August 1941, the British took control of southern Iran and the Soviet Union took over the northern part of the country. Both agreed to evacuate six months after the end of the war. The central part of the country, including some Kurdish territory, fell between the two zones, an area that achieved de facto autonomy. Barely a third of Iranian Kurds fell inside the borders of this area.

In the absence of government authority, the Kurdish tribes began to reassert themselves and establish independent principalities. In the town of Mahabad, middle-class Kurds replaced Iranian government employees. With Soviet permission, Tehran appointed the chief of the Dehbokri tribe governor of the region, but the leaders of other tribes did not accept him. In August 1942, the Iranians appointed Seif Qazi to the position, the son of a Sunni religious leader and ally of Ismail Simko. Iran was attempting to hold itself together.

Stalin played his own game, namely, expanding Soviet power in the **Caucasus** by detaching Iran's Kurdish and Azeri areas and amalgamating them into his own Soviet Kurdish and Azerbaijan republics under the name of ethnic unification. Some say Stalin's attempt at this was the opening shot of the Cold War. In November 1941, the Soviets took several important Kurdish leaders to Baku in Soviet Azerbaijan for meetings that convinced them that the USSR would support a Kurdish republic. Later Kurdish chiefs in Western Iran submitted a petition to the Soviets, requesting freedom for the Kurds in their national affairs. Meanwhile, a secret Kurdish nationalist society, Komala, formed and called for political and cultural autonomy within Iran but ultimate unification of all Kurdish lands into an independent state.

The Tehran government lost control of the area in May 1943, when Kurdish townspeople stormed a police station to obtain arms. An Iranian army detachment set out to restore order, but the Soviets stopped it on the pretext that the troop movement would upset the balance of military forces in the region. By 1944, Soviet political agents were situated throughout Northwest Iran, centered on the Soviet Consulate in Rezaiyeh. In 1944, Komala affirmed its unity with groups seeking Kurdish independence in other countries and asked the pro-Soviet Qazi Muhammad to join them, although some feared he would quickly draw the group's power into his hands—which is exactly what he did.

In 1945, the Soviets convinced the Qazi to accept leadership of the Komala and also invited the group to use the Soviet cultural center in Mahabad as headquarters. Komala changed its name to the Kurdish Democratic party, and went from a clandestine party to an open party that many Kurdish leaders joined, convinced that the party's goal was democracy. But the Soviets had other plans—namely, to use it as a front to grab another country. Qazi Muhammad and 105 Kurdish notables signed a democratic-sounding party program that may have been drawn up under the direction of the Soviet consul in Rezaiyeh. Qazi Muhammad denied the party was Communist but recognized the USSR as a true democracy and worthy of emulation. Setting up such "democratic fronts" was the standard Soviet technique for slowly taking over parties and governments in other countries.

Caucasus   Mountains between Black and Caspian Seas, home to a bewildering variety of peoples.

In September 1945, a Kurdish group returned to Soviet Azerbaijan where they were promised everything: military and financial support for independence and positions at the Baku Military College for Kurdish military cadets. Except for some light arms, none of the promised aid arrived. The Soviets also purchased the Kurdish tobacco crop as an indirect form of financial support. The Tehran government, of course, was furious at the dismemberment of Iran. The United States, which had replaced the British in southern Iran, complained that the Soviets had not evacuated six months after victory in Europe. Some historians once saw the continued Soviet presence in northern Iran as what turned President Truman against Stalin and thus started the Cold War, a view now discarded.

On December 17, 1945, the Kurdish Republicans raised their flag in the Kurdish area of Iran. Men who had served in the Iranian army were recalled into a new Kurdish army. In January 1946, Qazi Muhammad formally declared the establishment of the Mahabad Republic, named after the local town. For protection against Tehran, the Republic turned to the tribes. Some, but not all, at first agreed to support the experiment but soon abandoned it in favor of Tehran. Many tribes did not support the nationalists because they had a historical hatred of Russians and regarded the Kurdish republic as a Russian creation. The communist orientation of some of the nationalists such as Qazi Muhammad disturbed traditional leaders. In addition, many tribal leaders had good relations with Tehran for decades.

With Iranian Kurdish tribal support insufficient, the republic accepted the help of an Iraqi Kurdish leader, Mullah Mustafa Barzani. The Barzani tribe was the most loyal defender of the republic, but in the end they also negotiated with Tehran through the Americans. The Barzanis had entered Iran in late 1945, before the Republic had been announced, en route to the Soviet Union to seek Soviet help for Iraq's Kurds.

Soviet and Kurdish aims frequently clashed. Stalin wanted to speed up the secession of neighboring Iranian Azerbaijan and its union with his Azerbaijan SSR. The Soviets were worried, however, that the Mahabad Republic, led by members of the middle class and tribes, could become a nucleus for a Western-style democracy instead of a Communist state. By February 1946, Soviet unhappiness with the Kurdish Republic was clear. Stalin hated what he did not control.

The Mahabad Republic introduced measures to attract support of the Kurds. It allowed the use of Kurdish national dress, previously banned by the Shah. It established universal elementary education, with textbooks in Kurdish. Using a printing press probably supplied by the Soviets, they issued a Kurdish-language newspaper, a periodical, and two literary magazines. Barzani was named "marshall" of its armed forces.

The Kurdish republic never formally declared independence from Iran because its backers, the Soviets, were not willing to burn their bridges with Tehran by supporting such a move. The Kurds themselves recognized that Tehran would oppose with force the creation of an independent Kurdistan but hoped Tehran would accept an autonomous Kurdish region within Iran. The republic also had problems with its neighbor, the other Soviet creation, the Azerbaijan Republic, as both claimed the same territories.

SOVIET WITHDRAWAL

On May 9, 1946, a year after the war's end, the Soviets withdrew the last of their troops from northern Iran and the Iranian central government moved troops against the breakaway republics. Qazi Muhammad realized he had to negotiate with Tehran if he wanted to preserve any Kurdish gains. Iranian Prime Minister Qavam proposed that Iranian Kurdish lands be combined into a single province to be directed by a governor general, probably the Qazi himself. Qazi sought the advice of the Soviet Embassy, which told him not to, so Qazi never agreed to Qavam's proposals.

The Azerbaijan Republic fell to Iranian forces first, and the Kurdish tribes turned against the Kurdish government. Qazi Muhammad surrendered Mahabad on December 14, 1946—eleven months after having announced the creation of the republic there. Mullah Mustafa Barzani tried to convince Qazi Muhammad and the rest of the government to flee, but they refused. Iran hanged the Qazi, his brother, and cousin for treason.

Within a few days, all traces of the Mahabad Republic had been erased. The government forbade the teaching of Kurdish. Iranian soldiers destroyed Kurdish books in the Mahabad public squares. Kurds who had been active in the movement hid any compromising documents. The Kurdish Democratic party was banned, but continued as a clandestine organization. Barzani escaped to Iraq and then passed into the Soviet Union where he would remain in exile until 1958. His stay in the USSR earned him the title, "the Red Mullah" and the rank of Soviet general.

THE RISE OF BARZANI

Amidst the confusion of the 1958 Iraqi revolution, Mullah Barzani went back to his tribal homelands. Based on his military reputation, his role as defender of Mahabad, his Soviet backing, and his lack of competition, Barzani was immediately recognized by Kurds in Iran and Iraq as their leader. Barzani treated Iran as his guerrilla army's hinterland. The Iraqi army blockaded Iraqi Kurdish territory, but neither Iran nor Iraq had the power to close their border. This let Iraqi Kurds escape the blockade and import the materials they needed. Iranian Kurds sent provisions, clothing, tents, arms, and munitions. To ensure that aid continued, Barzani established a network of contacts throughout Iran and appointed a close aide as leader of the Iranian Kurdish Democratic party. Many Iranian Kurds were so convinced of Barzani's role as nationalist leader that they moved to Iraq, some to fight alongside the Barzani forces.

As usual, the Kurds were split. Mullah Barzani clashed with Ibrahim Ahmad Jalal Talibani for the leadership of Iraqi Kurds in the summer of 1964. Barzani sought support from Iraq's historical enemy, Iran. The Shah provided Barzani money, weaponry, and intelligence. The Shah believed he could use the Iraqi Kurds as leverage in his boundary dispute with Iraq over the **Shatt al-Arab**.

Shatt al-Arab   "River of the Arabs," confluence of Tigris and Euphrates that flows fifty miles to Persian Gulf.

In return, Barzani promised to maintain peace in Iranian Kurdistan. He told Iranian Kurds that with the Shah's help they could get Kurdish **autonomy** in Iraq first, so in the interest of Kurdish nationalism the Iranian Kurds should "freeze" their anti-Tehran activities. Many Iranian Kurds were outraged at this backdown, and some broke with Barzani. About a hundred Iranian Kurdish fighters in Iraq returned to Iranian territory, where the central government arrested and shot them. Barzani's fighters even assisted the Shah's police in their efforts. This is a sharply divided nationalist movement.

Baghdad in 1966 protested to Tehran over the support it was providing Iraqi Kurdish rebels. Barzani saw the Shah as his only support and in 1968 even killed Iranian revolutionaries who were trying to transit Iraq into Iran. Their bodies were turned over to Iranian authorities as proof of Barzani's fealty. The Shah in return sent Iranian troops across the border to support Iraqi Kurds in 1969. Worried, Baghdad sent a secret delegation to Tehran to negotiate. The Iranian prime minister toyed with the Iraqis, refusing to admit Iran's complicity with the Iraqi Kurds, but claiming inability to control the border.

In 1970 Baghdad and Mullah Barzani signed a peace accord and autonomy agreement committing the ruling Baath party to recognize that Iraq had two peoples, Arabs and Kurds, and to give Kurds a role in government. The Shah was furious at this switch, but he was a realist. In 1972 he renewed contact with Barzani because the Soviet-Iraqi Friendship Treaty alarmed him. The Shah feared encirclement. Israel had informal but good relations with Tehran (the Shah did not want to publicly recognize Israel) and sent arms captured in 1967 to the Kurds in Iraq via Iran. Notice how countries and political movements are highly opportunistic: They ally with whomever they think will further their cause. The United States does it, too.

By July 1972, Barzani was receiving heavy weapons from Iran and had begun broadcasting from Iran. Washington approved of this renewal of Iranian-Barzani contacts. President Nixon, like most U.S. presidents, saw Iran as an anti-Soviet ally and Iraq as a Soviet client. The 1970 accord fizzled, and by 1974 Iraqi forces had several military successes against the Kurds. In reaction, Iran aimed artillery fire into Iraq from Iranian territory. In February 1975 Iran sent 400 men and twelve 155mm howitzers into Iraq to protect Barzani's forces with two other artillery batteries in reserve. Fire was not very precise, and the Iranian soldiers quickly learned to fear Iraqi airpower. To protect their military assets, the Iranians sent the Iraqi Kurds surface-to-air missiles. Quietly, in the Kurdish region, Iraq and Iran fought, years before Iraq's 1980 invasion.

While Iran provided enough support to allow Barzani to continue his battle against overwhelming Iraqi military force, he did not provide enough to let the Kurds win. The Shah opposed Iraqi Kurdish autonomy for fear of the precedent spreading to Iranian Kurds, precisely the same fear that Turkey has. As the Shah was providing Iraqi Kurds with military support, he was violently suppressing his own Kurds. As early as October 1972, the Shah sent word to Iraq that he would assure peace among the Kurds if Iraq gave Iran part of the Shatt al-Arab.

---

autonomy   Partial independence.

G ⋮ *Geography*

THE SHATT AL-ARAB BORDER DISPUTE

The border between Iraq and Iran was first settled in a 1555 treaty between the Ottomans and the Persians. With the British in charge of Iraq, the 1937 Iran-Iraq treaty set the border along the river's eastern edge, placing the entire Shatt solely under the control of Iraq. Iranian navigation was only with Iraqi permission. Iran wanted the border redrawn, to run along the **thalweg**, the midpoint of the deepest channel in the river.

Iraq gave in and signed the Algiers accords on the Shatt boundary on March 6, 1975. Both sides agreed to discontinue support to the others' Kurdish populations, and the river frontier was to run along the thalweg. That evening, Iran withdrew its artillery back to its border. The following morning, Iraq systematically bombed Kurdish forces. After a week of aerial massacre, Baghdad let Kurds either submit or flee to Iran. Mullah Barzani and his tribe crossed into Iranian territory to await a chance to fight another day. The Shah, having gotten the border he wanted, cynically sold out the Kurds who had counted on him. In this region, betrayal is a way of life. An old Kurdish saying: "The Kurds have no friends."

THE ROLE OF THE UNITED STATES

The United States had no national-security interests in the Kurdish question. Because the United States wanted to build up Iran as its major ally in the region, to protect the Persian Gulf from Soviet encroachment, Nixon agreed to provide Barzani help. The support had to be covert. If it became public, our NATO ally Turkey—itself facing a Kurdish separatist movement—would be furious. The United States followed the Iranian lead in providing the aid and in making sure the aid was insufficient for the recipients to actually succeed in their quest for independence. The U.S. House's Pike Commission later remarked that even in the context of covert action it was a cynical enterprise. News reports said the commission quoted a "high government official" (supposedly Henry Kissinger) who defended himself and his policies: "Covert action should not be confused with missionary work."

According to press accounts, the United States subsidized the Shah's efforts to the tune of approximately $12–16 million. U.S. aid probably began in the 1960s. In 1971–1972, National Security Advisor Henry Kissinger (for more on this office,

---

thalweg   (German "valley path") Line drawn along the deepest part of a valley or river, often used as a ship channel and boundary.

see Chapter 15) rejected Kurdish requests for funds, but the administration reversed itself after Iraq signed its friendship treaty with the USSR. The United States halted the aid again when the Iraqis signed the 1975 Algiers accords.

THE KURDS IN IRAN'S ISLAMIC REVOLUTION

The Soviets and Iranians, cutting deals of their own, abandoned the Kurds. The Soviets wanted Iraq as a client state, and the Iranians wanted a better border in the Shatt. So Barzani switched sides again, this time to the United States. Actually, every step in gaining and shifting allies that Barzani made was rational. Americans tend to get sentimental and want to keep allies. Mullah Mustafa Barzani died in 1979 at Walter Reed Army Hospital in Bethesda, Maryland. He had become acquainted with columnist William Safire, who continued to support the Kurdish cause in the *New York Times*. Barzani's sons, Idris and Masoud, took over leadership of the movement. The Barzanis called their group the Kurdish Democratic party of Iraq (KDP) and got Iranian support.

In Iran, the Kurds sympathized in general with the growing opposition to the Shah. The Kurds felt the monarchy had crushed and betrayed them. Iran's Kurds, however, were not active during 1978, as the Iranian Revolution was an urban phenomenon. As it grew, though, Kurdish tribes seized the lands the Shah had appropriated from their chiefs in the 1963 White Revolution (see Chapter 10). The Kurds established local committees to manage their own affairs, the only way to maintain law and order with no central government. When the Islamic Republic was declared, many Kurds joined it. In the Bazargan government, the ministers of foreign affairs and labor were Kurds, as was the assistant army chief of staff. The leader of the Iranian Kurds, Ahmad Kazem Qassemlu—newly returned from exile in Europe—appealed for Kurdish autonomy but to no avail. By September 1979, the Kurds were in armed opposition to the new Islamic government.

The Supreme Leader of the Islamic Revolution, Grand Ayatollah Ruhallah Khomeini, refused to recognize the existence of a separate Kurdish minority and labeled the Iranian Kurdish Democratic party as agents of America. The government annulled the election of Kurdish delegates to the new parliament, despite the fact they received 80 to 85 percent of the votes in their area. Their leader, Qassemlu, was elected to the Assembly of Experts that wrote a constitution for the Islamic Republic, but Khomeini banned his participation. At first, Kurds tried to fight the central government, but the Iranian military easily overcame them. By late 1979, the Kurds turned to guerrilla warfare. The Islamic revolutionaries in Tehran rejected Kurdish cease-fire proposals.

The Barzani brothers, driven by their hatred of the Baathist regime of Saddam Hussein, allied with the Iranians. Tehran did not use the Barzanis to fight Iraq but to pacify their fellow Kurds in Iran. The Barzanis played upon tribal and linguistic ties to split the Kurds and to deprive the Iranian Kurdish Democratic party of many of its followers. Iranian Kurdish leader Qassemlu tried to negotiate another cease-fire, and Iranian President Hassan Bani Sadr appeared ready to accept. The head of the Islamic Republican party, Ayatollah Muhammad Beheshti, overlooked the fact that the Iranian army was collapsing in the provinces and insisted on continuing the war against the Kurds.

By May 1980, Tehran sent Rashid Jahruquiri, an Iranian Kurd who was cooperating with them, to close the road along the Soviet border to insure the rebellious Kurds would receive no support from that direction. Rashid was unsuccessful, and the Iranians sent the 64th Division to do the job. By the end of June 1980, the cities of Kordestan Province had returned to normal, and Kurdish rebels either surrendered or returned to the hills. The war degenerated into night raids.

THE IRAN-IRAQ WAR

The Iraqi army invaded Iran on September 22, 1980 (see Chapter 13). With active Iraqi military assistance, Kurds opened a northern front against the Iranians while the Iraqi regular army fought in the south. At a time when Iran needed every soldier in the southwest province of Khuzistan, the Kurds tied down at least a quarter of Iran's army. In 1981 Tehran offered to recognize oppositionist ethnic groups if they would lay down their weapons. The Kurds doubted the offer and continued fighting.

Iran's Kurds aligned themselves with the Mujahidin-e Khalq (People's Warriors), a cultist Islamic-Marxist organization that had originally supported but then broke with the Islamic Republic. The alliance did not provide the Kurds, however, with sufficient military power to challenge the central government. In May 1982 Iranian forces militarily destroyed the Iranian Kurdish Democratic party. Qassemlu went into exile and was negotiating for Kurdish autonomy with an Iranian delegation in Vienna when he was assassinated, probably by the Iranian negotiators. Dr. Sadeq Sharafkandi then took over but was assassinated in Berlin in 1992. Tehran conducted a bloody "war in the shadows" with its opponents for several years.

THE KURDISH BREAK WITH IRAQ

Kurds on both sides of the border took advantage of the Iran-Iraq war to further their cause. In Iraq, the head of the Patriotic Union of Kurdistan (PUK) attempted to negotiate with Baghdad. Saddam Hussein, desperate for peace in the north while he battled Iran, agreed to a Kurdish autonomous region that included the oil city of Kirkuk. The deal collapsed, however, when Turkey brought pressure on Baghdad so that Turkey's own restive Kurdish population would not demand similar treatment.

With the collapse of the negotiations, Iraqi Kurds resorted to armed resistance to Saddam. But Saddam was not governed by any rules of civilized warfare and launched the al-Anfal campaign that used poison gas against his Kurdish citizens, supervised by Saddam's cousin, Ali Hasan al-Majid ("Chemical Ali"). The most horrible case was in the village of Halabja, where up to 50,000 Kurds died from air-dropped gas. In a three-day period, the Iraqi military dropped conventional bombs, mustard gas, Sarin, Tabun, and VX on Iraqi Kurds. The United States, then supporting Iraq out of anger with Iran, said and did nothing. In 2003 we went to war with Iraq allegedly over these same chemical weapons. Consistent U.S. opposition to any chemical weapons would have set a standard for moral clarity. Halabja was only the latest in a long line of Baathi efforts to eliminate Kurdish opposition to their rule, going back to 1963 when the Baath first took power in Iraq.

THE FIRST GULF WAR

In August 1990 Iraq invaded Kuwait. After a U.S.-led coalition drove the Iraqi army out of Kuwait, President Bush (senior) urged the people of Iraq to rise up and overthrow Saddam. The Shi'a in the south and Kurds in the north responded and began seizing control. Bush did not back the rebellion, however, and Iraqi forces easily and bloodily put down the Shi'a rebellion. Then the Iraqi army turned north, and half a million Kurds fled into Turkey.

The Turkish General Staff was appalled. Not only did they worry about the cost of the refugees to their weak economy, they were concerned that the new Kurds would strengthen their own, indigenous Kurdish rebellion. Ankara demanded that the coalition put the Iraqi Kurds back into their own land. The United States established a northern, no-fly zone above the 36th parallel under UN Security Council Resolution 688. Deprived of their airpower, Baghdad could not defeat the armed Kurdish militias, known as *peshmerga* ("those who stand before death"). The Iraqi Kurds left Turkey to live in their own homes and receive humanitarian aid. Since the March 1991 implementation of the no-fly zone, the Kurds living above the 36th parallel have been free of Baghdad's control. They established an autonomous region with its own government and parliament, supposedly democratically elected. Their finances are from customs tolls, collected at the crossings with Turkey and Iran.

In reality, the region is governed by an uneasy alliance between two factions: Talibani's PUK and Barzani's KDP (which crossed back into Iraqi Kurdistan during the first Gulf War). Idris Barzani died in 1987, and Masoud Barzani ruled the KDP as Mullah Barzani's sole surviving son. The KDP controlled the northern, tribal regions of the autonomous zone while the PUK derived its strength from the zone's southern cities.

The parliament, the Kurdistan National Assembly, was chosen in 1992 elections under international observers, and most believe the election itself was free and fair. The results, however, were never announced because it could have destabilized the new Kurdish regional government if one faction held sway over the other. KDP and PUK leaders decided to divide the parliamentary seats 50-50, with five of the 105 seats going to Christians.

The new government organized itself around the March 1970 Autonomy Agreement the Kurds had negotiated with Saddam Hussein. The prime ministership and cabinet were divided between the two factions. In 1994 fighting broke out between the KDP and PUK over customs revenues. The main collection point was the Habur Gate between Iraq and Turkey, located in KDP-controlled territory.

Barzani was taking a share for his followers before turning the revenues over to the Kurdish government. Talibani wanted a more equal division, and armed conflict erupted. In 1996, during a cease-fire, they established two administrations: a KDP administration in Irbil, and a PUK one in Sulaymaniyeh. The area remained divided until October 2002, when the two factions again united in anticipation of a U.S. invasion of Iraq. These two groups have been intense rivals for over thirty-five years. Kurds do not easily unite into one movement.

THE KURDS IN TURKEY

The Kurds of Turkey, the biggest group of Kurds, were not affected by rivalries between the great powers or between Iran and Iraq. Compared to their cousins across the borders, Turkish Kurds had it pretty good: They were full citizens of the Turkish Republic, and many of their notables advanced to the highest levels of Turkish government. There were scores of Kurdish members of parliament and of the cabinet and prominent party officials. Even the former president of Turkey, Turgut Özal, was rumored to have a Kurdish mother. To achieve these positions in Turkish society, however, a Kurd had to fully identify with Turkey—at the expense of a Kurdish identity. As a Turkish citizen, one could achieve much. Those who emphasized Kurdishness, however, by demanding Kurdish cultural or political autonomy, would be jailed as separatists. Turkey means to hold together as one country.

THE RISE OF THE PKK

Abdullah Ocalan (sounds like "Ojalan") founded the group that eventually became the Kurdistan Workers' Party (PKK) in Ankara in 1974. Ocalan had been one of many students caught up in the left-right violence that tore Turkey apart in the 1970s (see Chapter 8), and served prison time for leftist activities. The group resembled many of the left-leaning organizations at the time, composed of intellectuals who applied Marxism to the Kurdish question in Turkey and hot-blooded youths who spread propaganda and fought other leftists. In 1978, Ocalan established the PKK with a central committee to direct the struggle. As did many liberation movements that Vietnam inspired in the Third World, Ocalan declared the method for achieving Kurdish rights was guerrilla warfare.

In 1980, the Turkish military seized power to stop left-right violence and arrested thousands of activists, most of them from the left. They hit the PKK heavily, and imprisoned several members of the Central Committee. Ocalan, known as Apo, escaped to Syria, whose government provided him with a safe villa in Damascus, a Mercedes, and security protection. The Syrian government considered the PKK a strategic resource to force Ankara to abandon plans to dam the Tigris and Euphrates Rivers and to prevent Turkish cooperation with Israel. Ocalan also sought relations with Iraqi Kurds, but ultimately they were at cross-purposes and opposed each other.

TURKISH CIVIL WAR

PKK armed insurgents established camps in Iraq south of the Turkish border from which they attacked southeastern Turkey. To counter them, Ankara organized a "village guard" system that paid and armed loyal villagers to keep out the PKK. These village guards soon became the primary target for the PKK. Schools, a symbol of central government authority, were also a major target. At its height, the PKK claimed 10,000 to 15,000 armed fighters. Ankara evacuated some villages either because they were too distant to protect or because they were suspected of giving aid to the guerrillas. Commandos trained in counterterrorist operations operated in Kurdish areas, and locals accused them of brutal tactics against noncombatants. It was a very nasty war.

The Turkish government also tried to win Kurdish hearts and minds. Recognizing that the southeast was underdeveloped and that poverty fueled the terrorists, Ankara instituted a major project to build dams on the headwaters of the Tigris and Euphrates Rivers that would irrigate fields and generate electricity for industrial development. The theory was that employed Kurdish males would not "go to the mountains" and join the rebels. In 1991, the government lifted its ban on the use of the Kurdish language in homes and unofficial settings. Kurdish remained illegal in schools, government offices, or political campaigns.

The PKK did not limit its activities to the military field. In October 1991, its allies in the Social Democratic party broke with the party, and organized an ethnically Kurdish political party, the People's Labor party (HEP). Eighteen Kurdish nationalists were elected to the Turkish parliament. They arrived on the floor dressed in Kurdish national colors and insisted on taking their oath of office in Kurdish instead of in Turkish. The parliament voted to strip seven of the newly elected members of their parliamentary immunity, and they were eventually jailed for advocating separatist activities.

The PKK established foreign chapters in Europe to raise money from Kurds living abroad (often using extortion, threats, and robbery), drug smuggling, and to spread PKK propaganda that was accepted uncritically by European leftists. The PKK even had its own television station, MED-TV, broadcast from Britain. PKK propaganda efforts were so successful that in 1995 the European Union parliament gave a jailed Kurdish parliamentarian, Leyla Zana, its human rights award.

THE CAPTURE OF OCALAN

By the late 1990s the Turkish General Staff decided to end the Kurdish rebellion once and for all. It massed units of its 600,000-man army on the Syrian border and told Damascus that if they did not expel Ocalan, Turkey would invade. Turks and Arabs do not like each other. Syria expelled Ocalan, who traveled through many European countries, which kept it quiet. In November 1998, Ocalan requested political asylum in Italy. Turkey, Italy's NATO ally, pointed to the outstanding INTERPOL arrest warrant for Ocalan, charging him with the responsibility for 37,000 deaths. Washington supported Turkey's demands. Rome did not want to oppose allies, but many Italians wanted to protect a "freedom fighter." In January 1999, the Italians put Ocalan on an airplane and informed the allies they had no knowledge where he had gone.

Finally, in February 1999, Turkish intelligence located Ocalan in the Greek Embassy in Nairobi, Kenya. Embassies are not supposed to do that. Ocalan was traveling on a Greek Cypriot passport. In a daring raid, Turkish commandos captured Ocalan and smuggled him out of Kenya. When Apo realized he was in the hands of Turkish authorities, he denounced his comrades and offered to be a Turkish government penetration agent against the PKK. Unhappily for Apo, the Turks filmed the entire event and broadcast it to the world.

Apo's supporters were not discouraged and demonstrated in sixteen European cities. Turkish courts found Apo guilty of murder and incitement to murder. His sentencing was postponed while Apo made public calls renouncing violence. He asked his followers to lay down their arms. The PKK at first said they would hold off any armed attacks as long as their leader remained alive; if Turkey executed Apo, the PKK would renew its terrorism strategy. As an armed force, the PKK was finished.

In February 2000, the mayor of Diyarbakir and twelve other Kurdish leaders were arrested for aiding the PKK. Evidence of their crimes included their organizing a protest against Turkey's attempts to extradite Ocalan from Italy in 1999, something that would have been in the common interest with the PKK. They were sentenced to four years in prison.

As for Apo himself, he eventually got a death sentence, but it was never carried out. In 2002 Turkey ended its death penalty to meet criteria to enter the European Union. Ocalan now faces a life in prison. The PKK renounced violence as a tactic forever and changed its name to KADEK. There is some evidence to suggest that KADEK cadre members have renewed low-level terrorist attacks in Turkey.

CONCLUSIONS

The Kurds have always suffered two insurmountable obstacles. First, they never had a unified kingdom and are divided along lines of dialect, tribe, and nation of residence. Their factions often fight each other. Second, in the game of international politics, regional powers have always used the Kurds as a pawn. They used the Kurds to fight battles and then ditched them when their interests shifted. No one ever took Kurdish wishes and aspirations seriously. This has left the Kurds an angry and unpredictable force in the region.

Kurds have occasionally risen up for autonomy or independence whenever the great powers stalemated one another, leaving some room in which the Kurds could maneuver. Ubaydallah and Simko managed to gain power when the Turks and Persians balanced each other; Qazi Muhammad had limited success when the Russians and Persians were at loggerheads. The Iraqi Kurds recently achieved some autonomy when allied airpower kept Baghdad at bay, but Ocalan's rebellion never had a chance since there were no powers to oppose Ankara in southwest Turkey.

The Kurds have made it clear that they want to rule themselves. What is less certain is what form this self-government should take, how large an area it should encompass, and how a Kurdish government could support itself economically. Some Kurds think the oil fields of Kirkuk could give them an economic basis, but the United States is no more willing to let that happen than were the British between the two World Wars. Until someone can unite the various Kurdish factions, they will continue to fight among themselves. Similarly, until the countries of the area are comfortable with a Kurdish entity, history has shown the Kurds have little chance of success.

FURTHER REFERENCE

Arfa, Hassan. *The Kurds: An Historical and Political Study*. New York: Oxford University Press, 1966.

Bidlisi, Sharaf Khan. *C'heref-nameh, ou, Fastes de la Nation Kourde*, tr. from Persian and commentary by François Bernard Charmoy. Westmead: Gregg International Publishers, 1969.

Bruinesen, Martin van. *Agha, Shaikh and State*. Utrecht: Ph.D. dissertation, 1978.

Eagleton, William, Jr. *The Kurdish Republic of 1946*. New York: Oxford University Press, 1963.

Ghareeb, Edmund. *The Kurdish Question in Iraq*. New York: Syracuse University Press, 1981.

Imset, Ismet G. *The PKK: A Report on Separatist Violence in Turkey*. Ankara: Turkish Daily News Publications, October 1992.

Izady, Mehrdad R. *The Kurds: A Concise Handbook*. Washington, D.C.: Taylor and Francis, 1992.

Kutschera, Chris. *Le Mouvement National Kurde*. Paris: Flammarion, 1979.

Latham, Aaron. "Introduction to the Pike Papers," *Village Voice*, February 16, 1976, 70–92.

More, Christiane. *Les Kurdes Aujourd'hui: Mouvement National et Partis Politiques*. Paris: Editions L'Harmattan, 1984.

Nikitine, Basile. *Les Kurdes: Etude Sociologique et Historique*. Paris: Imprimerie Nationale Librairie C. Klincksieck, 1956.

Olson, Robert. *The Emergence of Kurdish Nationalism and the Sheikh Said Rebellion, 1880–1925*. Austin: University of Texas Press, 1989.

CHAPTER

10

Iran

Points to Ponder

- What is the difference between "high" and "low" Islam?
- What is the origin of the Baha'i faith?
- When did Europeans first arrive in the Persian Gulf?
- Describe the Shi'a hierarchy. What does it resemble?
- How were the Pahlavis "modernizing tyrants"?
- Who took over Iran in World War II? Why?
- What did Stalin try to do in northern Iran?
- Who was Mossadeq and what did he try to do?
- What is OPEC and what does it attempt?
- Who was Khomeini and what was his political theory?

The Arabian peninsula has a number of independent Arab countries, most of which were invented by the British as they were protecting their sea lane to India. These include Yemen and what used to be called the Trucial States—United Arab Emirates, Bahrain, and Qatar. Each of these countries has a fascinating history, and many play important roles in the area. The UAE is an international transit point and major trading center. Bahrain was one of the first places in the region to produce oil. Qatar is the current headquarters for U.S. CENTCOM forces in the area. Yemen at one time was a quasi-ally of the Soviet Union and housed a unique school of Islamic thought.

In discussing the Persian Gulf since World War II, however, the major players are the oil states of Iran, Saudi Arabia, Iraq, and Kuwait.

THE SAFAVIDS

At the end of the thirteenth century, a Sufi order sprang up in north-central Iran known as the Safavids. Within two centuries, it had spread throughout the Turkic world. Its leaders sought political power as well as spiritual influence. The Safavids were originally a Sunni order, but the majority of its followers were

R : *Religions*

HIGH VERSUS LOW ISLAM

The Islam of textbooks is sometimes referred to as "High Islam." It is the religion of the learned, with a thousand years of rules and regulations, historical interpretations, and judicial rulings. Many Muslims find High Islam a rather dry faith that does not fill needs for an inner spirituality. Enter "Low Islam," namely Sufism, which we mentioned in Chapter 3 in connection with the Abbasid Empire. Rather than concentrate on the God of 99 names (such as "The All Powerful," "The Great," "The Merciful"), Sufism concentrates on manifestations of God in hearts of individuals. It is a creed of love and a desire for oneness with God through extinction of one's self.

Sufism is a powerful, mystical movement within Islam. High clerics condemn it because it incorporates pre-Islamic themes and rituals into Islamic ceremonies. Most Sufis belong to religious orders that trace their origins back to the original companions of the Prophet. Sunni orders often cite Abu Bakr while Shi'a orders often cite Ali as the ultimate source of the "hidden knowledge," which they pass onto their followers. The largest Sufi orders are the Naqashbandi, the Qaderi, the Bektasi, and the Sanussiya.

Turkic tribesmen who looked for salvation through the Prophet's son-in-law, the Imam Ali. In 1501, the Safavid Shaykh Ismail captured Tabriz in Persia and declared himself **Shah**. He also declared that his kingdom would embrace Shi'ism as the official religion. It has often been debated whether Ismail took this move because he truly embraced Shi'a doctrine or if he wanted to differentiate himself and his movement from the Ottomans ruling the Anatolian plateau immediately to the west. Whatever the reason, Ismail believed his own propaganda and declared himself the "Shadow of God on Earth."

By 1509, the Safavid Empire ruled all Iran. The Ottomans invaded Iran and defeated the Safavids in 1514 at the battle of Chalderan. The borders established in the peace treaty have held, with only minor (sometimes nasty) variations, as the dividing line between Turkey and Iran for almost six hundred years.

The greatest Safavid ruler was Shah Abbas. Prior to his coronation in 1588, the kingdom had begun to disintegrate because most Iranians were Sunni Muslims who did not accept the Shi'ism of the Safavids. Iran is an empire in the true sense of the word because it is composed of many ethnic groups under the rule of one executive. Within Iran are Persians, Azeri Turks, Kurds, Baluch, Uzbeks and other nationalities. As we saw with the Kurds, when central authority is weak these ethnic groups tend to drift away and rule themselves. Through force of arms, Abbas reunited his empire and established strong central government.

Shah   Persian for "king."

G: *Geography*

THE NAME OF THE GULF

Even the name of the Persian Gulf is disputed. Known for centuries as the Persian Gulf—which Iranians like—Arabs say it should be called the Arabian Gulf. (There is already east of the Gulf of Oman an Arabian Sea that blends into the Indian Ocean.) One of the authors, working on AP's World Desk long ago, sent out a story from an Arab Gulf emirate that called it the "Arabian Gulf"—and quickly got an angry response from AP's Tehran bureau. The Shah of Iran ordered his diplomats to walk out of any meeting that did not call it the Persian Gulf. At stake was not just a name but an understanding as to who was the dominant power in the region.

When the Americans entered the region in the late 1980s, Pentagon briefers began to refer to the Arabian Gulf in an effort to win Arab support, despite the fact that the official name recognized by the U.S. government was the Persian Gulf. To sidestep the issue, the Department of State began to refer to the water as just "the Gulf," an unsatisfactory solution because you cannot be sure to which gulf spokesmen are referring. Washington has yet to come up with a solution, and each department calls the Persian Gulf whatever works.

Shah Abbas was the first Iranian ruler to invite British troops onto Iranian soil. Portuguese merchants had established an outpost on one of the islands near the Strait of Hormuz, and Abbas did not have the naval power to oust them. He invited the British, rivals with the Portuguese in India, to do it. This opened the door to British influence over time on both sides of the Persian Gulf, as the British recognized the importance of the Gulf to their control of India.

Abbas's successors could not hold the kingdom together. Raised in the harem with little training for governance, they soon faced fissiparous tendencies, halted briefly by Nader Shah, who reunited the empire at the beginning of the eighteenth century. Nader is most famous for raiding India in 1738 and seizing the Peacock Throne that he brought back to Iran. It has been there ever since. With Nader's death in 1747, however, the kingdom resumed breaking into smaller units ruled by military commanders.

THE QAJARS

At the end of that century, one of the military commanders managed to reunite the country. He was Mohammad the Eunuch, better known as Shah Mohammad Agha, a member of the Qajar tribe. He started the Qajar dynasty that ruled Iran through the nineteenth century. Shah Fath Ali succeeded Muhammad Agha and presided over two disastrous wars with the growing Russian power in the north. In 1813, Iran signed the treaty of Golestan and in 1828 the treaty of Turkmanchai, both ceding to the Russians Iran's claims in the Caucasus.

R ⋮ *Religions*

THE BAHA'I

Every hundred years or so, a messianic movement rises in Islamic territories. In the 1840s, it was Mirza Ali Muhammad of Isfahan. He accepted Shi'a teachings that there would be no more prophets after Muhammad and that the twelfth Imam was hidden. Mirza Ali Mohammad claimed that he was the gateway (*bab* in Arabic) to the twelfth Imam. The Shi'a religious hierarchy suppressed his teachings and persecuted his followers. The leading clerics in Iran were supreme leaders to their followers and disliked a new figure whose claims would place him above them. The government did not want anyone claiming to rule as spokesman for the Imam. The Bab's followers revolted; he was arrested and condemned to death.

After Mirza Ali Mohammad's execution, Mirza Husayn Ali Nuri took over the movement and called himself the Glory of God, Baha' Allah. His followers named themselves after this title, the Baha'i ("those who are part of the Glory"). Mirza Husayn claimed to be the Mahdi, the individual who would come at the end of the world to prepare mankind for the Second Coming. Traditional Muslims, Sunni and Shi'a alike, condemned Mirza Husayn and his followers as heretics. Under official sanction, Mirza lived in exile in Acre, Palestine, from where his religion spread worldwide.

ENTER THE WEST

The Qajars are not remembered fondly in Iran. They were corrupt and let Western influences penetrate the land. The Qajars received official subsidies from the British to keep the sealanes to India open and keep the Afghans off balance so they could not attack the **Raj**. When they ran short of money, the Qajars sold "concessions," monopoly rights to a particular Iranian commodity. It began in 1872 when Naser al din Shah sold Iran's mineral rights (except gold, silver, and some precious stones) to Baron Paul Julius von Reuter for 60,000 pounds and a percentage of the revenues. Other concessions to the British included the right to print banknotes and run shipping and roads. The Russians got the telegraph concession, road-building contracts and a monopoly on Caspian fishing. The imperial competition between Britain and Russia often led to concessions granted to one and then cancelled when the other protested, to be settled by whichever government offered more money or bigger threats. The wishes of the Iranian people were never considered. To many, the Qajars were no more than puppets of the infidels.

The biggest flareup was the Tobacco Rebellion of 1891–1892. Naser sold the rights to market the Iranian tobacco crop to a British major in return for a bribe, a payment to the state, and a percentage of future revenues. The Iranian clergy spread the rumor that the Christian British handling of the crop made it religiously impure. Smoking tobacco, beloved in Iran, was thus damned because a

Raj   British India.

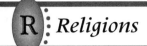

Religions

SHI'A HIERARCHY

Traditional Shi'a Islam has no single religious authority that rules supreme in matters of faith and morals, like the pope in Catholicism. Rather, there are a number of senior clerics, each free to agree or disagree with the other clerics. Their rulings are binding on all Shi'a who follow that particular cleric. These clerics, in descending order of importance, are as follows:

Grand Ayatollah—literally, the "Word of God." Grand Ayatollahs are teachers with religious students following them, but they also have the rank of *Marja'ye Taqlid*, meaning source of emulation. These learned men must make religious rulings based on the primary sources in Islam, using their own judgment. All Shi'a are supposed to follow the teachings of a living Marja'. Times and circumstances change, and so the Marja' needs to constantly reinterpret Islamic law. Since a dead man cannot reinterpret the law, when a Marja' dies his followers are supposed to change their allegiance to another Marja'. A Marja's rulings are no longer binding after his death and need to be reaffirmed by a living Marja'. There can be anywhere from one to ten Grand Ayatollahs at any one time. One achieves the rank of Grand Ayatollah by acclamation of one's followers.

Ayatollah—Slightly lower in importance than a Grand Ayatollah, they number in the hundreds. Ayatollahs have the equivalent of a Ph.D. in Islam and, after long study in seminaries, have to write a dissertation accepted by their professors. Grand Ayatollahs are always Ayatollahs first.

Hojatollah—literally, "Sign of God." These men, numbering in the thousands, hold the equivalent of a master's degree in Islam.

Alem or *Mullah*—one who is educated in Islam, the equivalent of the parish priest or minister in Christianity.

This hierarchical structure, familiar to Catholics (think cardinal, bishop, priest), has no equivalent in Sunni Islam. While the Sunni tradition has a special place for those who study their religion, any male can legally lead prayer in a mosque. This is based on the opening verses of the Qur'an, the *Fatiha*, that Muslims repeat several times a day at prayer. In these verses, Muslims acknowledge that they are creatures of God, and no one stands between a Muslim and God. In Shi'ism, however, sacerdotal roles are reserved for the mullahs alone.

Muslim would be ingesting impure materials. When British agents arrived in Iran to handle the new concession, **bazaars** across the country closed in a general strike, and the mullahs issued a **fatwa** forbidding the use of all tobacco. The boycott brought the Shah to his knees, and he cancelled the concession. Once the Shah had been proven vulnerable, a wave of street protests began, culminating in the Shah's assassination in 1896.

bazaar Persian for "market."
fatwa Muslim religious ruling.

Despite his personal corruption, Naser had been committed to modernizing Iran. He copied his neighbors to the west, the Ottomans, who were trying their own reforms in the *tanzimat*. Naser did the same, reintroducing sciences to the school curriculum, creating a civil service, and modernizing the army. One of his reforms was the creation of a Russian-style Cossack brigade in 1879. This light cavalry drew many of its members from Central Asia. Naser's successor was Muzaffar Shah, who had learned from his predecessor the easy way to raise money. In 1901 he sold the concession to explore for and exploit petroleum in the southern half of the country to an Australian financier, William Knox D'Arcy. He drilled for and found oil, the oil that allowed the British navy to convert from coal to oil.

THE CONSTITUTIONAL REVOLUTION OF 1906

While the Tobacco Rebellion showed the people of Iran that they could force their ruler to change an economic policy, the first mass challenge to Qajar rule was the 1906 Constitutional Revolution. Pressure had been growing in the bazaar for a year, marked by strikes and violence, as the *bazaaris* sought a voice in national politics and the cancellation of foreign concessions.

Almost like the 1978–1979 upheaval, events were precipitated by a funeral and overreaction by the government. The police arrested a local cleric who had delivered a sermon critical of the government; his students launched a demonstration at the police station. The police shot one of protesters; the next day after the funeral, the Cossack brigade beat all who attended as they exited the mosque. Outraged at this breach of religious etiquette, all the clerics in the capital exited en masse for Qom, an Iranian Shi'a holy city, vowing not to return until the Shah instituted political reform. In sympathy, the bazaar closed and the country as a whole went on strike.

The protesters then took refuge in the garden of the British Embassy. In the end, over 10,000 Iranians crowded into the diplomatic compound. After some weeks, the Shah agreed to the creation of a parliament. Political groups organized throughout the country, elections were held, and in October 1906 Iran's first National Assembly opened its doors. It immediately wrote a constitution, which the Shah signed, making the National Assembly answerable only to the people of Iran. The Shah dropped dead five days later and was succeeded by his son, Muhammad Ali Shah, who wanted to rule in the old, imperial manner. With Russian encouragement, the Shah and his government ignored the parliament.

In 1907, the parliament passed the Supplementary Fundamental Laws, based on the Belgian constitution and limiting royal authority. The Shah refused to sign. Vast crowds of protesters took to the streets, and the prime minister was assassinated. Over 100,000 people attended the funeral. Appalled at the assassination and frightened by the size of the protests, the Shah retreated and signed the laws.

The Shah struck back the following year. Backed by tribal elements and a senior cleric, he declared he could not support constitutionalism because it was alien

R ⋮ *Religions*

CLERICS AND POLITICS

Traditional Shi'a political theory encourages clerics to avoid politics, but their political involvement began long before the 1979 Iranian Revolution. The Tobacco Rebellion would never have succeeded without Ayatollah Behbahani issuing a fatwa forbidding tobacco. Similarly, the leaders of the Constitutional Movement included Ayatollahs Behbahani, Tabatabai, and Nuri. The Shah felt strong enough to move against the reformers only when Ayatollah Nuri defected from the Constitutionalists and threw his support behind the monarchy. Shi'a clerics have not been perfectly apolitical.

to Islam. He directed the Cossack Brigade to open fire on parliament. Many of the parliamentarians fled to the Ottoman Embassy; those who did not were arrested. The Shah had completed a coup against his own government.

While the Shah controlled Tehran, the rest of the country revolted against his arbitrary attack on the people's representatives. Fighting ended only when the Shah's foreign bankers ceased providing him funds to pay his tribal supporters and the Cossacks. Many of the senior clerics in Qom supported the constitutionalists against the Shah. The Shah's supporters left him when their checks bounced, and he abdicated, taking refuge in the Russian Embassy. His son, a child of twelve, assumed the throne.

The second National Assembly opened in November 1909, but it was too late. Without strong guidance from the palace, the country slid into anarchy. As always in Iran, when the central government is weak, the outer provinces and the tribes pulled away and started to rule themselves. Ottoman, British, and Russian troops seized various parts of the country as the Great Powers sought positions in advance of World War I. In the south, the British were particularly active in arming tribes who opposed the central government. The British were motivated by a desire to protect "their" oil fields and route to India.

In the north, the Russians also supported tribes fighting the central government. While this policy began under the tsars, the Bolsheviks continued after the Russian Revolution of 1917. The Soviets supported the "Jangal Movement," a group that established a Soviet Republic of Gilan on the southern shore of the Caspian Sea. They even sent Red Army troops to prop up their puppet government.

In 1919, the government signed the Anglo-Iranian agreement, which guaranteed the British a monopoly to sell the government weapons and provide Iran all its military and civilian advisors. The opposition enlisted the new Soviet government to help fight the ever-increasing British control of the government, and they allied with the Gilan republic.

In the middle of all this, the Cossack Brigade flexed its muscle. Its leader, the illiterate Colonel Reza Khan, marched on Tehran. Reza got the support of the police and gendarmerie and in 1921 overthrew the government (but not the Shah). The new government signed a friendship treaty with Moscow, which gave the

Soviets the right to intervene in Iranian affairs if something threatened Soviet security. The treaty also cancelled the 1919 Anglo-Iranian treaty and pledged that Iran would never be used to launch an attack against the Soviet Union. The Soviets, in turn, withdrew their forces from Iranian soil. Without their support, the Gilan republic collapsed.

By 1926, Reza had convened a parliament that deposed the last of the Qajars, Ahmad Shah, while he was on one of his frequent trips to Europe. The parliament, in turn, crowned Reza the new Shah of Iran. The leading opponent to this move was a parliamentarian with royal blood from the old regime: Dr. Muhammad Mossadeq, educated at Paris's prestigious Political Science School. Wishing to give his newly founded dynasty a link with Iran's imperial past, Reza Khan took the name of the ancient language of Iran, Pahlavi, as his family name. Reza's blood was quite ordinary, but he liked to pretend to continue two and a half millennium of Persian monarchy.

Once crowned, Shah Reza Pahlavi embarked on a massive modernization campaign. He decided that the path to modernization was not to follow the liberal democracies of the West but rather to emulate the totalitarian regimes that had begun to sweep Europe. He abolished political parties, closed presses, outlawed trade unions, and broke the power of the tribes to oppose the central government. He also built thousands of miles of railroads and paved highways, enlarged the military, and streamlined the bureaucracy by eliminating the thousands of hereditary positions in the provinces. He replaced them with a centralized hierarchy, staffed by graduates of the new schools and universities he created. Like Atatürk, he was a modernizing tyrant.

Pahlavi shared Atatürk's views that Islam held his country back. He did what he could to limit the role of the mullahs in the public sphere. He abolished Shari'a courts, seized traditional lands controlled by religious institutions, and established a secular court system based on European legal codes. He also eliminated clerics from government positions and the parliament.

Pahlavi wanted to change not just the economy but the whole society. He ordered men to wear European-style hats in place of more traditional or ethnic headpieces, and he ordered women out of the veil. (Atatürk did the same, but by leading parliament to pass laws.) In Mashad, this led to massive protests and the takeover of the Shrine of the Eighth Imam by the opposition. Traditionally, Iranians recognized the concept of sanctuary, which is why the opposition had taken over the gardens of the British legation in 1906. Mosques and religious shrines were places of sanctuary, just as cathedrals were in medieval Europe. Shah Reza, however, ordered troops from Azerbaijan to invade the Shrine and kill or wound the protesters.

Pahlavi's opposition to the religious and his support of women's rights are exemplified by a supposedly true story. The Shah's mother visited the main mosque in Tehran where the Imam berated her for entering the building uncovered. Returning to the palace, the mother reported to her son what had happened. Enraged, the Shah personally went to the mosque and beat the Imam severely with a walking stick. The majority of Iranians were conservative, and the Shah's efforts to modernize the country usually met public opposition. The Shah relied more on his army and security forces to rule instead of the support of the populace.

W: *Women of the Middle East*

THE SHAH'S PUSH FOR EQUALITY

With the Constitutional Revolution of 1906, Iran was on its way to establishing a liberal democracy. The Pahlavis reversed this course in favor of rapid modernization. In one respect, however, the Pahlavis were ahead of most of the Middle East: advancing the role of women.

Reza Shah moved slowly and did not try to change the superior role of men in Shari'a family law. He did, however, allow women to advance socially. He opened the universities to them, forbade gender discrimination, and outlawed the **chador**. To set an example, in 1935 he ordered government officials fired if their wives wore the chador. It was a major step that the ayatollahs tried to reverse after 1979. Women traditionally wore the chador, usually black, anytime outside the house. It is still used in Afghanistan and on the Arabian peninsula. Muslim jurists in the tenth century declared that the Qur'an prescribed the chador so that women would conceal their "adornments." In fact, use of the chador probably began in Damascus before Islam to protect the expensive clothing of rich women when moving through the dust and grime of fifth-century streets.

WORLD WAR II

In the late 1930s the clouds of war gathered over Europe and Asia. Almost too late, Britain, France, and some small countries allied against the growing Axis powers of Germany, Italy, and Japan. In August 1939, Germany signed a Non-Aggression Pact with the **Soviet Union**; a secret protocol divided East Europe between the Germans and the Soviets. A week later, Germany invaded Poland and started World War II with no Soviet protest. Indeed, Stalin was in on the deal and took the eastern third of Poland.

Joseph Stalin, leader of the Soviet Union, played down Adolf Hitler's hatred of Communists—a hatred Hitler explained in his autobiography *Mein Kampf* ("My Struggle"). Hitler's 1939 pact with Stalin was intended to be very temporary, although Stalin had trouble understanding that. Once Hitler conquered most of Europe, he ordered the *Wehrmacht* to invade Russia in Operation Barbarossa in June 1941, the largest invasion in history.

In Britain, Prime Minister Winston Churchill was both thrilled and frightened by events. Germany now had a two-front war, something the German General Staff had long predicted would lead to their ultimate defeat. Churchill looked at the Soviet Union's size and the millions that could be mobilized into its Red Army and proposed that Britain seek an alliance with the formerly hostile giant. Justifying this stand, he told critics that if Hitler invaded hell, he would give favorable mention to Satan in the House of Commons.

---

chador   Persian for "tent"; women's head-to-foot garment.
Soviet Union   Communist Russia and some adjoining republics, 1922–1991.

G ⋮ *Geography*

BOUND IRAN

Iran is bounded on the north by Armenia, Azerbaijan, the Caspian Sea, and Turkmenistan;
on the east by Afghanistan and Pakistan;
on the south by the Gulf of Oman and Persian Gulf;
and on the west by Iraq and Turkey.

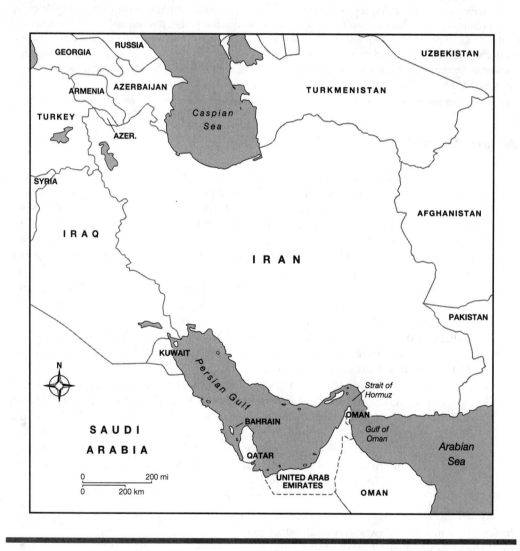

These developments made Iran important. Britain had long been unhappy with Shah Reza's preference for Nazi Germany. (Actually, German agents in Iran had also been active during World War I.) As the British fleet was powered by Iranian oil, the British landed troops in Southern Iran to protect their energy source. In addition, now the Soviet Union was an ally and had to be supplied. Nazi armies blocked all routes through Europe, so the British set up a supply corridor through Iran.

British and Soviet troops invaded Iran in August 1941. The British seized the south, the Russians the north, leaving a narrow band that included the capital in the hands of the Iranian government. The Iranian army tried to halt the invasion, but fled the battlefield and deserted in a matter of days. The government fell, and the new prime minister negotiated in secret to remove the Shah. The British, on their part, began a propaganda campaign against the Shah to encourage members of parliament and others to jump on the victors' bandwagon and condemn the Shah.

SHAH MOHAMMED REZA

The final straw was the Soviet army. The Russians began to move on Tehran, and Reza Shah knew there was nothing he could do to avoid capture. He abdicated in favor of Crown Prince Mohammed Reza Pahlavi, a Western-educated youth (Swiss boarding schools) without any government experience. Reza Shah sailed into exile like many of the Maharajah's of India, aboard a British battleship. He died in South Africa in 1944.

The new Shah was aware that he had neither domestic nor international allies. His best path to survival was to win over as many supporters as possible. He turned much of his administration over to American advisors, who by early 1942 had generally replaced the British in southern Iran. He then concentrated his attention on the Iranian army, which had deserted during the allied invasion but was still the most powerful element in Iran. He also pledged full cooperation with the Allies and even hosted the 1943 Tehran Conference, where Roosevelt, Stalin, and Churchill outlined measures for ending the war and carving up Europe afterward. Significantly, the Allies decided to hold the conference in the Shah's capital city before they asked him, and they did not allow him to participate. The Allies allowed him only to pose for pictures with the world leaders at the end of the summit.

With the heavy hand of Reza Shah removed, groups that had been held down by the central government revived. New newspapers gave intellectuals a voice. In politics, Mohammed Mossadeq, who was briefly jailed for opposing the Pahlavis and who spent the last fifteen years in seclusion on his estates, returned to parliament in November 1941. The parliament, or **Majles**, began to reassert itself after fifteen years as a rubber stamp. Political parties, including the Communist Tudeh party, organized and/or surfaced from the underground.

Majles   (also *majlis*) Arabic for "meeting, convocation, or audience." In Saudi Arabia, princes' local meetings; in Iran, national parliament.

In parliament, Mossadeq picked up where he had left off years before: opposing the unlimited power of the Pahlavi monarchy. The opposition recognized that Mohammed Reza's power depended on the military, so they unsuccessfully attacked the military's privileges. When workers in Isfahan revolted several of the oppositionists returned to the royalist fold out of fear of the masses.

THE SOVIET THREAT

The conventional story of the Cold War is that it began in Europe in 1946 or 1947 as Stalin turned East European countries into obedient satellites. Some argue that it began months earlier, in Iran. In August 1944, Iranian Prime Minister Muhammad Sa'id gave oil concessions in the southern sector to a consortium of American and British oil companies. The Soviets in October in turn demanded oil concession in the zone they occupied. When the prime minister played for time, the Soviets offered to drop their demands if the Shah replaced Sa'id with someone who was not anti-Soviet. After Sa'id's downfall, Iran stumbled through a series of political crises and prime ministers, none of whom could unite the country.

Moscow and London (later Washington) had agreed to evacuate Iran within six months of the end of the war in Europe. We did and they did not. Some see this as the opening round of the Cold War. The Soviets had not abandoned their desire for a piece of northern Iran and its oil. In September 1945, Ja'afar Pishevari established the Democratic party of Azerbaijan and called for the province's autonomy from Tehran. Pishevari, an old Iranian leftist ideologically attuned to the Soviet Union, coordinated his actions with Soviet representatives such as the Soviet consul and military advisor in Tabriz and Rezaiyeh and shadowy figures of the Soviet intelligence apparatus. In addition to Pishevari, the Soviets encouraged the Kurds to establish the Mahabad Republic (see Chapter 9).

To protect their ally and further their aims in northern Iran, the Soviets interposed military forces between Tabriz and Tehran. The only way the central government could reassert its authority in the area would have been to fight through the Red Army. U.S. President Harry Truman issued an angry ultimatum to Moscow to withdraw or face a hostile America. Whether this was the start of the Cold War and whether Truman's threat was effective are still controversial.

The latest prime minister, the wily Ahmad Qavam, in March 1946 negotiated a Soviet withdrawal by seeming to grant the Soviets' demand for the northern oil concession. Qavam noted that the Iranian constitution required parliamentary approval to grant such a concession, and the Majles was in recess. He promised to get parliament to pass the concession. In fact, the oil concessions were worthless. No one ever had or has found oil in northwest Iran. Once the Soviet troops were out, the Shah's army moved in and crushed the Azerbaijani and Kurdish Republics. The Majles refused to grant the oil concession. Some historians say it was Qavam's craftiness that got the Soviets out of Iran, not Truman's warning.

Iran's parliament continued frozen among squabbling factions, leaving the Shah as the only power on the national scene. In February 1949 the Shah was shot and wounded at Tehran University. Taking political advantage of the incident, the Shah declared martial law and cracked down on opponents. After eight years in the shadows of others, the Shah followed his father's footsteps and reclaimed the country with his military and security forces.

MUHAMMAD MOSSADEQ AND OIL

In June 1950 the government submitted its proposals to parliament for the revision of the 1933 Anglo-Iranian oil agreement. Oppositionists claimed that the Anglo-Iranian Oil Company (AIOC) was a state within a state, paid too small a percentage of the profits (somewhat over 20 percent) to the government, and did not pay enough taxes. Some radicals demanded nationalization of the AIOC, arguing the Iranian oil belonged to the nation and not to a British corporation. The hot question brought yet another prime minister through the revolving door. Prime Minister Razmara tried to lead the bill through the Majles but was assassinated in 1951 in Tehran's Friday mosque. Parliament passed a law nationalizing the oil company as Muhammad Mossadeq, the fiery nationalist and crowd manipulator, emerged as prime minister in May 1951. A hypochondriac, when in trouble Mossadeq retreated to his sickbed and was often interviewed in pajamas.

Mossadeq led a patchwork alliance of nationalists, leftists, and some religious leaders, united in their opposition to royal power. One of his major allies against British power was Ayatollah Abdul Qassem Kashani, who appealed to the conservative masses in his efforts to restore Shari'a law to Iran. The Mossadeq-Kashani marriage was one of convenience, but an effective one. The group was known as the National Front.

The British refused to recognize the legality of the nationalization. Oilmen from around the world pressured their governments to refuse to accept Iranian oil. They were afraid of the precedent: If the Iranians could nationalize oil, what would the Arabs and Venezuelans do? The AIOC said they would sue any company that accepted Iranian oil for receiving stolen goods. The British navy steamed into the Persian Gulf to threaten Iran with possible invasion, and British diplomats condemned Iranian actions in the UN. Mossadeq accused the British of interfering in the domestic affairs of Iran and ordered British diplomatic posts closed. The royalists secretly sided with the British but did not have the strength to oppose Mossadeq openly.

Mossadeq upped the ante by appointing a new war minister the Shah would not accept. Mossadeq resigned, releasing a letter to the public protesting the Shah's interference in the workings of government. The National Front called for strikes that the Shah tried to put down with military force. When he failed to halt the protests, he turned back to Mossadeq and asked him to form a new government.

Mossadeq sought revenge. He seized royal lands, confiscated royal charities, reduced the palace's budget, demanded that the military report to him as head of government instead of the Shah, and isolated the Shah in his palace. He ruled the country with a series of emergency powers he obtained from parliament. Mossadeq brooked no opposition, disbanding the upper house and forcing the lower house to resign. In establishing his rule, Mossadeq lost the support of many in the National Front, including the religious wing.

OPERATION AJAX

Mossadeq had risen to power claiming the Shah had usurped the constitution. Now the Shah tried to use the constitution against Mossadeq. In August 1953, a colonel of the Imperial Guard tried to deliver a royal decree firing Mossadeq, but Mossadeq's home was surrounded by military loyal to him. Faced with his total lack of control in the country, on August 17 the Shah fled to exile in Baghdad and then to Rome, never expecting to return.

London was alarmed with the loss of the AIOC and took its concerns to Washington, which viewed Iran in Cold War terms as a Soviet takeover target. The Communist Tudeh party, after all, was among Mossadeq's supporters. Eisenhower's militant anti-Communist Secretary of State John Foster Dulles had no trouble seeing a Communist threat in Iran, and neither did his brother, Director of Central Intelligence Allen Dulles. Ousting Mossadeq became a top Washington priority in 1953. Some now wonder if the Communist threat was that great or if Mossadeq was merely an Iranian nationalist.

Two days after the Shah fled, British and American agents implemented "Operation Ajax," a secret plan to restore the monarchy. CIA Near East Director Kermit Roosevelt (Teddy's grandson) arrived with a suitcase containing $1 million and spread dollar bills throughout the slums of South Tehran, buying a demonstration that chanted "Long Live the Shah!" Meanwhile, military coup plotters loyal to the throne attacked Mossadeq with tanks. They captured the prime minister, and the Shah returned to Iran. Backed by his military, the Shah arrested his political foes and crushed those who opposed him in the streets. Muhammad Reza Pahlavi had regained his throne with the military he had so assiduously cultivated.

Back in power, the Shah cancelled the nationalization of the oil companies that had started the whole crisis. He did negotiate a new deal that split the oil revenues equally between the government and the oil companies, a giant boost in Iran's take. In the end, the Shah was as big a hawk on Iran's oil as Mossadeq.

The Shah ruled through the 1950s without any real opposition. He tamed parliament by dividing it into two parties—but both loyal to him. He increased the size of the military and created SAVAK, his brutal intelligence and security service. He had the support of traditional clergy and recaptured Ayatollah Kashani's support when the Shah released him early from prison.

KHOMEINI'S OPPOSITION TO THE WHITE REVOLUTION

Like his father, the Shah believed in modernization. He launched a **"White Revolution"** (as opposed to a Bolshevik-type Red Revolution), which included land reform. This limited reform alienated large landowners and the clergy by nationalizing their holdings for redistribution to peasants. Traditionalists in

---

White Revolution   Major reform program controlled by the monarchy from the top down.

G : *Geography*

OPEC

With plenty of oil coming on line in the 1950s and 1960s, world oil prices were low. To boost their revenues, several oil countries founded **OPEC** in 1960 to keep oil prices up by limiting production. With headquarters in Vienna, OPEC negotiates members' production quotas to try to keep production low enough so that prices stay up. OPEC is not just an Arab organization. It has several Latin American and African members. Some major producers—Russia, the United States, Mexico, Canada, and Norway—are not OPEC members.

OPEC got noticed when the 1973 Arab-Israeli war (see Chapter 6) prompted Arab producers to cut the flow of oil, creating a worldwide economic slowdown but increasing fivefold the price they got for oil, from about $2.25 a barrel to $11. Furthermore, Gulf producers rewrote their deals with the oil companies to give themselves some 90 percent of the revenues. Now the oil companies worked for their host countries as their technical and marketing agents. Staggering sums of oil revenue flowed into the Gulf countries. In 1979, with the turmoil created by the fall of the Shah, prices again climbed, to over $30 a barrel.

In the long run, OPEC cannot permanently set world quotas or prices. All producers' cartels eventually leak. Nonmembers do not obey and even some members, strapped for cash, cheat by quietly producing more than their quotas. In times of crisis OPEC may tighten quotas and boost prices, but the quotas soften after the crisis passes. In the short term, however, OPEC can cause disruption, as in the U.S. **"stagflation"** of the 1970s.

1963 mobilized the population into a series of demonstrations in Iran's major cities, which the Shah crushed with the army, as usual. Paratroopers dropped on the holy city of Qom. Handing over land deeds personally to some peasants were great photo opportunities for the Shah, but the land reforms did little good. The peasants' small new holdings, unsupported with loans, training, or marketing infrastructure, netted them little. Much of the land for redistribution was taken from traditional Islamic foundations, earning the Shah the hatred of the mullahs.

In the meantime, Iran did modernize, but in a way that undermined the Shah's regime. The Shah had always favored higher prices for oil, and Iran had been a big supporter of OPEC. In effect, the Shah nationalized Iran's oil much like Mossadeq tried to do. Awash with petroleum revenues, the Shah hatched grandiose plans for a rich, modern Iran that would not get distracted by democracy. Ties with the United States were strong. Tens of thousands of Iranian students attended U.S. universities, and thousands of U.S. contractors and advisors worked in Iran. The

---

OPEC   Organization of Petroleum Exporting Countries, a producers' cartel aimed at keeping up oil revenues.
stagflation   Slow economic growth plus inflation; came in 1970s from high oil prices.

Religions

KHOMEINI'S POLITICAL THEORY

Recall that the Shi'a in Iran believe that the world's rightful rulers were the Twelve Imams, direct descendants of the Prophet through his daughter, Fatima, and his son-in-law, Ali. The twelfth Imam did not die but is hidden, still in the world but not in time. Since the true ruler of the world is still alive, any temporal government is usurping the rightful position of the Imam. Some clerics theorized that it was acceptable to support these temporal governments if the government protected the Islamic lands and tried to shepherd the citizenry toward salvation. This support did not imply, however, that the usurping regimes were legitimate.

Enter the Ayatollah Khomeini, who turned twelve hundred years of Shi'a theory on its head. Khomeini noted that no one had seen or heard from the Imam in a thousand years, and it could easily be another thousand before he was seen again. He also reasoned that neither God nor the Imam would want Muslims to be without guidance. He concluded that the only people who were qualified to guide were those who understood the faith fully: the clergy who spent their lifetimes studying the Qur'an and other religious texts. If one cleric could be found who epitomized Muslim learning and virtue, he should rule an Islamic Republic. If that cleric could not be found, then a committee of clerics could rule. The theory for the committee was that even though no cleric alone might possess all the qualities, each would have some of the necessary qualities. The clerics could band together, making sure that all the qualities were represented in the group. This concept, rule by those who knew Islamic law, became known as the "Guardianship of the Islamic Jurist."

Shah bought much U.S. military equipment, a point that rankled opponents, who thought he was spending too much on the military. A journalist once asked the Shah if he could become a figurehead monarch, like the king of Sweden. "I'll become like the king of Sweden," replied the Shah, "when Iranians become like Swedes."

The 1960s brought a new voice to the opposition, one previously unnoticed. Ayatollah Ruhallah Khomeini had criticized the Shah for a number of reasons and had tried to mobilize his students against the crown. His arrest in 1963 sparked demonstrations in Qom. In 1964 he denounced the Status of Forces Agreement, whereby U.S. soldiers in Iran would be tried in an American military court rather than an Iranian court. To Khomeini, this was much like the hated capitulations that the Qajars had agreed to as they sold the country to Europeans.

The Shah sent Khomeini into exile. In 1965 Khomeini started teaching at a seminary in the holy Shi'a city of Najaf, Iraq (historically far more important than Qom). Khomeini attracted a large following both for his political views and his learning in Islamic mysticism. During his years of exile, he developed a new political theory, that of **Velayat-e Faqih.**

Velayat-e Faqih   Guardianship of the Islamic Jurist.

G : *Geography*

TWIN PILLARS IN THE GULF

When the world's leaders met in Tehran in 1943, they assigned responsibility for maintaining peace in the Middle East to Britain, long the regional power. Britain was too weak for its traditional burdens and in 1968 announced it could no longer supervise the Persian Gulf. As the British retrenched, the Shah of Iran sought to fill the void in the Persian Gulf. Days before the British were to grant independence to the oil sheikdoms on the Arabian side of the Gulf, the Shah ordered his troops to seize the islands of Abu Musa and the Tunbs near the strategic Strait of Hormuz.

President Richard Nixon recognized the important role the Shah could play in keeping the Soviets out of the region. He announced that Iran, along with Saudi Arabia, would be the "twin pillars" of U.S. security policy in the Middle East. The Nixon administration approved the sale to Iran of the most advanced weaponry in America's arsenal. The Shah, loaded with oil dollars, could afford it.

To protect their new protégé, the United States supported Iran in its dispute with Iraq. The United States provided covert assistance to the Shah's allies in Iraq, the Kurds, and discontinued the aid when the Shah and (then) Iraqi Vice-Premier Saddam Hussein signed the Algiers Accords, in which the two promised to settle all outstanding differences, split the Shatt al-Arab between the two countries, and not interfere in the internal affairs of the other. The United States and the Shah were very close, perhaps too close.

Khomeini and his followers recorded audiocassettes condemning the Shah and his government. These cassettes were smuggled into Iran and passed hand-to-hand in the mosques and bazaars. SAVAK monitored this flow, arresting those who were most active. This underground communication, popular among Iran's lower classes, escaped the notice of foreign diplomats, including the U.S. Embassy. The stage was thus set for the Islamic Revolution of 1979.

CONCLUSIONS

The smaller emirates along the southern shore of the Persian Gulf are interesting and important, but the main action centers on the oil giants of Iran, Saudi Arabia, Iraq, and Kuwait. Iran differs from Arab lands not only in language and culture, but also in religion. The Safavid takeover of Iran in 1501 made Shi'a the official faith, and its mullahs, more hierarchically organized than their Sunni counterparts, gained a certain political role. In the early seventeenth century, the British presence began in Iran and grew as the corrupt Qajar dynasty sold numerous monopolistic "concessions" to British business, all of them resented by the Iranian people.

In the early twentieth century, with Tehran's rule in decay and a Russian sphere of influence in the north and a British one in the south, an illiterate cavalry officer, Reza Khan, seized power and crowned himself Shah. Both Pahlavi shahs were modernizing tyrants, but more dictatorial than Ataturk. World War II made Iran an important transportation corridor into the Soviet Union and brought Soviet domination in the north and British (later U.S.) domination in the south. This began the massive U.S. involvement in Iran and support for the Shah as one of the "twin pillars" to block Soviet power in the Gulf region. When populist premier Mossadeq tried to oust the Shah and the British oil company, the CIA ousted Mossadeq in 1953. Oil prices, bolstered by OPEC, brought Iran new wealth. As the Shah modernized, however, he also alienated much of the population, especially the Shi'a clergy and Ayatollah Khomeini, who eventually brought down the regime in 1979.

FURTHER REFERENCE

Bakhash, Shaul. *Iran: Monarchy, Bureaucracy, and Reform under the Qajars, 1858–1896*. London: Ithaca, 1978.

Banani, Amin. *The Modernization of Iran, 1921–1941*. Stanford, CA: Stanford University Press, 1961.

Bill, James A. *Iran: The Politics of Groups, Classes, and Modernization*. Columbus, OH: Merril, 1972.

Binder, Leonard. *Iran: Political Development in a Changing Society*. Berkeley, CA: University of California Press, 1962.

Cottam, Richard W. *Iran and the United States: A Cold War Case Study*. Pittsburgh: University of Pittsburgh Press, 1988.

———. *Nationalism in Iran*. Pittsburgh: University of Pittsburgh Press, 1979.

Kinzer, Stephen. *All the Shah's Men: An American Coup and the Roots of Middle East Terror*. New York: Wiley, 2003.

Lenczowksi, George. *Russia and the West in Iran, 1918–1948*. Ithaca, NY: Cornell University Press, 1949.

Mackey, Sandra. *The Iranians: Persia, Islam, and the Soul of a Nation*. New York: Dutton, 1996.

Yergin, Daniel. *The Prize: The Epic Quest for Oil, Money and Power*. New York: Simon & Schuster, 1992.

Yu, Dal Seung. *The Role of Political Culture in Iranian Political Development*. Brookfield, VT: Ashgate, 2002.

Zahedi, Dariush. *The Iranian Revolution Then and Now: Indicators of Regime Instability*. Boulder, CO: Westview, 2001.

Saudi Arabia

Points to Ponder

- How did a religious alliance bring al-Saud to power?
- What are the strategic waterways of the Middle East?
- Since when has Arabia been "Saudi"?
- Why did the Saudis and Hashemites mistrust each other?
- How old and deep is the U.S.-Saudi relationship?
- How did Nasser jolt the Arab world?
- What are the weaknesses of the Saudi monarchy?
- How could Saudi Arabia live with U.S. support for Israel?

There are great and deep rivalries among Arabs. The rise of the House of Saud illustrates some of this complexity. The al-Saud had been trying to rule the peninsula for two centuries; the present kingdom is their third effort. Back in the 1740s, the Arabian peninsula was a desolate place. The east and west coasts were ruled by the Ottoman Empire, and the protector of Mecca and Medina was the Sultan in Istanbul. The south coastline and the desert interior were tribal and independent, probably because the blowing sands had no apparent economic value.

MUHAMMAD IBN SAUD

In Najd, the north-central part of Arabia, in a small hamlet near what is today Riyadh, in 1744, a tribal chieftain cast his lot with a local preacher. Their alliance ultimately founded a kingdom and has repercussions into the twenty-first century. The chieftain was Muhammad ibn Saud, ruler of a small clan in the town of Dar'iyya. The preacher was Muhammad ibn Abd al-Wahhab, a man obsessed with the unity of God, the basic tenet of the Islamic faith: "There is no God but God." Wahhab took this message to an extreme not practiced in other lands. Wahhab

G : *Geography*

IS COLONIALISM ONLY EUROPEAN?

Anything that goes wrong in the Middle East is often blamed on colonialism. Many Algerian intellectuals, for example, blame their country's murderous political strife on the French colonialists, who robbed and ruined Algeria. Intellectuals throughout the Middle East repeat the simplified story, often substituting British for French.

Is colonialism only a European phenomenon? A Turkish royal house hundreds of miles away controlled the coasts of the Arabian peninsula. Turks, ethnically very different from Arabs, sent governors from Istanbul, collected taxes, and kept the peace. Some Turks even settled in Arab lands. Ottomans ruled for the benefit of the **metropole**, rather than for the benefit of the local population. The Ottoman Empire was a colonial empire, but it was a Muslim empire, and that often justifies it in the Middle East.

said that a sinner places himself as either the equal to God or superior to God's will, implying that a sinner was declaring himself a god. Wahhab therefore argued that anyone who did not practice Islam as he described it was a heretic to be thrown out of the community and/or killed.

Such a radical interpretation might never have caught on in the luxury of the ancient capitals, but it found an audience in the unremitting heat of the Arabian desert, where nomads and farmers found the harshness of this interpretation a reflection of the harshness of the world in which they lived.

In 1744, Saud and Wahhab signed an agreement to support one another. It is not quite certain why Saud agreed to sponsor the preacher and his rigid creed; one must assume that Saud believed in the preacher's message. Saud backed the preacher with the arms of his tribe; Wahhab provided the motivating ideology. Within a generation, this band of holy warriors had conquered half the peninsula. In 1801, a Saudi raiding party reached Karbala in Iraq and ransacked the tomb of Husayn. This was fair game for the warriors, since the Shi'a, in their eyes, were worshipping Husayn and the Imams instead of God alone.

The Saudi forces even captured the cities of Mecca and Medina briefly but were unable to hold them. The Ottoman Sultan ordered his Albanian viceroy in Egypt, Muhammad Ali, to retake the towns in the name of the caliph. This was the beginning of the end for the first Saudi kingdom. Members of the al-Saud clan began to squabble among themselves over position and were unable to unite against Muhammad Ali's forces. Eventually, the viceroy attacked Dar'iyya itself in 1818, and the leading member of the al-Saud was taken to Istanbul and beheaded. The family's first bid for supremacy had failed.

---

metropole   The home or central country of an empire.

G : *Geography*

MIDDLE EASTERN STRATEGIC WATERWAYS

The Middle East contains at least four maritime choke points, narrow waterways of great strategic value. Two of them are at corners of the Arabian peninsula but not under Saudi control. Closing any of them would damage the world economy. They are as follows:

Strait of Hormuz—The narrow entrance to the Red Sea is less than forty miles wide, the channel for supertankers less than half that. Most of Japan's oil passes through Hormuz. Iran is to the north; U.S.-friendly Oman is on the south.

Bab al Mandab—Arabic for "Gate of Tears," it is the narrow southern entrance to the Red Sea. Unstable Yemen is on its east.

Suez Canal—Completed in 1869, it is not quite as important as it once was, as supertankers are too big for it.

Turkish Straits—Connecting the Mediterranean and Black Seas, the Straits, now crowded with merchant shipping, were long a Russian goal but are now internationalized.

How strategic are they? When Turkey did not allow the U.S. Fourth Division to invade Iraq from Turkey in 2003, it had to move its equipment quickly through Suez, the Bab, and Hormuz. In addition, the Tiran Strait, entrance to the Gulf of Aqaba, is strategic for Israel and Jordan.

ROUND TWO

The fate of the al-Saud now became intertwined with the fate of the Ottoman Empire and Muhammad Ali. Once the viceroy had declared victory over the al-Saud, Muhammad Ali left the peninsula. Almost immediately, the Saudis reclaimed much of the territory they had previously held. Fighting for supremacy within the tribe continued, however, and ultimately brought the tribe down a second time.

Meanwhile, Muhammad Ali realized that the reason the Sultan had asked for his help was because the Albanian controlled the strongest army in the Ottoman Empire. With a small jump in logic, Muhammad Ali realized the Sultan needed him, but he didn't need the Sultan. So in 1834 Muhammad Ali renounced his allegiance to the Ottomans and set out to conquer his own kingdom. On the peninsula, this meant again subduing the al-Saud. This time, however, Muhammad Ali did it with diplomacy. He brought a rival claimant to the al-Saud leadership with his army and forcibly placed him on the throne. Muhammad Ali then became the military arm of the al-Saud family's ambitions.

The European powers knew the Ottoman Empire was decaying, but they were not ready to dismember it and decided in favor of the status quo. They forced Muhammad Ali to return to Egypt but guaranteed him that his family would be the hereditary rulers of Egypt (but as vassals of the Ottoman Sultan). In 1841, the last of the Egyptian troops left the peninsula and the rival claimants to al-Saud leadership resumed fighting among themselves. For a brief period, the family was able to maintain control, but as Ottoman subjects. In the end, weakened by internal dissension, they were defeated by the al-Rashidi clan in 1886. These Arab rivals were loosely allied with the British on the Persian Gulf coast. The Saudis tried to reclaim their land in 1891, but the military defeat was so decisive that the family had to flee to Kuwait to avoid capture and possible death. The Rashidis could not capture Kuwait (although they tried) because the ruler of Kuwait had a treaty with the British. The British navy defended Kuwait City against Rashidi attack with an artillery barrage.

ROUND THREE

Much has been made of the events of January 1902, when Abd al-Aziz ibn Saud began the third and successful conquest of the peninsula. As an ally of Emir Mubarak of Kuwait, Abd al-Aziz continued his family's quarrel with the Rashidis. In one popular account, Abd al-Aziz slipped into Riyadh with sixty men. Under a full moon, he personally led his men up the walls of Riyadh castle, holding his bared scimitar between his teeth, and battled the governor of Riyadh in a sword duel to the death. This Hollywood story may not be totally accurate. More probably, Abd al-Aziz and his men ambushed the governor. The Saudis were victorious in the skirmish, and the people of Riyadh rallied to the cause of the al-Saud, whom they regarded as their religious and legitimate rulers.

The peninsula saw fierce fighting over the next few years. The Ottoman Empire aided the Rashidis, believing the Saudi attacks were British-supported efforts to seize control of the new German-built Hijaz railroad, which carried pilgrims from the Levant to Mecca. (Lawrence of Arabia helped blow it up in World War I, and it has never been repaired.) Abd al-Aziz defeated the Rashidi but swore allegiance to the Sultan and was appointed governor of the Arabs.

The Saudis still did not control the peninsula. In the western **Hijaz** the Sultan appointed a member of the Hashemite dynasty, who could trace its lineage directly to the Prophet, to be the **Sharif** of Mecca. Sharif Husayn had pure blood, Ottoman backing, and possession of the holy places. The Hashemites and the Saudis were headed for conflict; the peninsula was not big enough for two leaders with ambitions of conquest.

The Ottomans did not oppose Saudi rule in the eastern part of the peninsula and Hashemites in the west, because both were nominal subjects and paid taxes. The Saudis, however, wanted the other Ottoman-backed power, the Hashemites, out. To obtain leverage against the empire, Abd al-Aziz approached the British on

---

Hijaz   Western area of Arabian peninsula, holds Mecca and Medina; sometimes spelled *Hejaz*.
sharif   Prince or chief, a descendant of Muhammad (not the origin of our sheriff).

G: *Geography*

THE TRUCIAL STATES

As early as 1820 the British (through its Indian colony) signed treaties with the various **shaykhs** who ruled along the southern shores of the Persian Gulf. Collectively they were known as the Trucial States, named after the 1853 Perpetual Maritime Truce they signed with Britain and each other. The British wanted suppression of piracy that threatened shipping to India; the shaykhs wanted British support against local rivals. Depending on the era, these rivals included the Saudis, the Hashemites, the Ottomans, and/or smaller neighbors. In 1869, treaties formalized this arrangement. The British guaranteed the shaykhs protection in return for the shaykhs giving Britain control over their foreign relations. Britain assigned Political Officers to Kuwait, Qatar, Bahrain, and the six emirates that eventually united into the United Arab Emirates (Abu Dhabi, Dubai, Sharjah, Ajman, Umm al Qaiwan, Fujaira, Ras al-Khayma).

In Muscat, the British had a consul, indicating British acceptance of a more independent status for the Sultanate of Oman. The British also granted formal protectorate status to the port of Aden, an essential port for fuel and supplies on the long voyage to India. The British were concerned only with the foreign policies of the rulers and played little or no role in the internal government of the sheikdoms, which gave the British a good reputation in the region. Goods sold in the Trucial States today, from refrigerators to underwear, are still more likely to be imported from Great Britain than from any other country.

numerous occasions and proposed an alliance similar to British treaties with the coastal powers. For a decade before World War I, however, the British refused to deal with Abd al-Aziz ibn Saud.

WORLD WAR I

Once the war broke out in 1914, the British rushed to obtain an alliance with ibn Saud against the Ottomans and their allies on the peninsula, the Rashidis. This treaty gave him British recognition as ruler of the provinces he held in return for Saudi guarantees not to attack the Trucial States and not to sign any treaties without British permission. This latter clause was standard in British treaties with all Arab countries.

Of note, Ibn Saud did not agree to join the war as a British ally. To weaken Germany's ally, the Ottomans, the British relied on another Arab leader, Sharif Husayn of Mecca. The Sharif and his sons, encouraged by British agent T. E. Lawrence, led the Arab revolt that brought the Hashemites into modern Jordan, Syria and Iraq. Abd-al-Aziz considered British agreements with his enemies, the Hashemites, a betrayal of the relationship he thought he had with the British.

---

shaykh (literally, "old man") Arab chief. More commonly spelled *sheik*, but pronunciation is closer to "shake" than "chic."

G: Geography

Bound Saudi Arabia

Saudi Arabia is bounded on the north by Jordan, Iraq, and Kuwait;

on the east by the Persian Gulf, Qatar, and the United Arab Emirates;

on the south by Oman and Yemen;

and on the west by the Red Sea and Gulf of Aqaba.

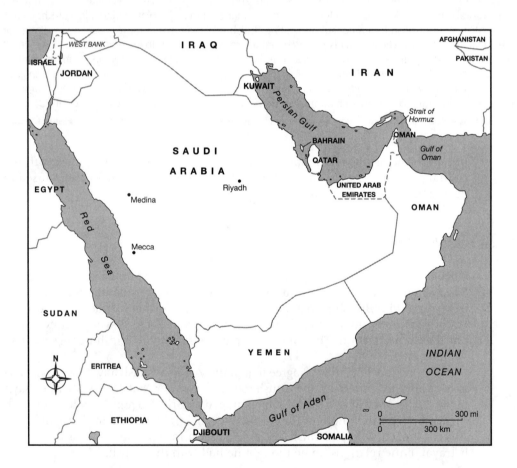

The Ikhwan

It took almost twenty years for the Saudis to win British backing; even then, the Saudis would never be Britain's closest allies. Ibn Saud felt that the British had been responsible for too many betrayals. In the meantime, Abd-al-Aziz used the same ideology as his forefathers to unite the tribes under his banner: Islam as interpreted through the teachings of ibn Wahhab. Rival tribal forces could never defeat his troops, known as the **Ikhwan**, but they were no match for the British army.

The last of the Rashidis surrendered to ibn Saud in 1921, and the Ikhwan captured the peninsula between the mandate territories in the north and the Trucial States in the east and south. The British-backed Hashemites remained the only other rival for power on the peninsula. Sharif Husayn, with an overdeveloped opinion of his own importance and unwillingness to compromise, soon alienated his British overlords. By late 1925, the Saudis had evicted the Hashemites from the peninsula. When Abd-al-Aziz attacked the Hashemite stronghold of the Hijaz, Sharif Husayn's sons—whom the British had made kings of Jordan and Iraq—were prevented from coming to his aid by British instructions to maintain neutrality in the conflict.

Abd-al-Aziz controlled the territory he sought but still had to face internal challenges to his power. The problem with using an ideology to motivate troops is that ideologies often have no limits. Ibn Saud had unleashed the Ikhwan as holy warriors to battle unbelievers, meaning those who practiced Islam in a slightly different manner. But there were still "unbelievers" in Iraq, Jordan, and among the Hijazis who had been ruled by the Hashemites. Ibn Saud tried to make the Ikhwan stop raiding British-controlled territory and in his newly conquered territory of the Hijaz, so the Ikhwan declared him an apostate. Ibn Saud took to the field, and in 1929 defeated an Ikhwan revolt. Those members of the tribal levies who surrendered were resettled; others escaped to Iraq and submitted to Hashemite authority. Abd-al-Aziz proclaimed that tribal chieftains were not trained to interpret Islam, a function reserved to the **ulama**. This edict would lead to the religious authorities eventually controlling not only religious activities in the kingdom, but also the judiciary, education, and much of the police powers of the state.

Saudi-American Relations

With the British government supporting the Hashemite kingdoms of **Transjordan** and Iraq, ibn Saud sought to balance the British. When American businessmen approached him in the early 1930s looking for petroleum in his realm, he found

---

ikhwan   Arabic for "brothers or brotherhood." In Saudi context, tribesmen who spread Wahhabi Islam by the sword. In Egypt, used for extremist Muslim Brotherhood.
ulama   (literally, "learned men") Muslim scholars as a whole; sometimes spelled *ulema*.
Transjordan   Original name of British-created Hashemite kingdom in the Palestine mandate territory east of the Jordan River.

R ⋮ *Religions*

THE ULAMA

Islam has no clergy with sacerdotal duties as has Christianity. It does have an important group of scholars responsible for interpreting religious law. These are the ulama, Arabic plural for *mu'alim*, meaning "one who is knowledgeable in the science of religion."

the counterweight he was seeking. Not only did the oilmen promise money for his depleted treasury, they also held out the possibility of U.S. backing. America was especially good because it was far away. Seeing all the problems he had over the years with Britain on his doorstep, ibn Saud calculated that if he let any power into his country, it would be one that could not intervene easily. Washington was in no hurry to deepen a relationship with ibn Saud; President Franklin D. Roosevelt had an understanding with London that the Middle East was in Britain's sphere of influence.

Ibn Saud signed a deal with Southern Oil of California in 1933, which found oil in commercial quantities in 1938. The revenues did not really flow until after World War II. SOCAL had promised royalties of roughly $1 per barrel of oil. Abd-al-Aziz existed on revenues from the hajj, on British subsidies, and on the limited oil payments. With World War II, all his sources of revenue were strained. Ibn Saud looked everywhere for income, recognition, arms, and a counterweight to Britain. He concluded arms deals with Mussolini's Italy and Nazi Germany, and signed a treaty of friendship and trade with Japan. Washington saw that an assured source of foreign oil was a national-security interest and agreed to provide the Saudis with money under the Lend-Lease Act, even though the Saudis were not in the war.

With World War II, Saudi Arabia became really important. By 1945, the United States saw that its future economic health would rely in large part on access to Saudi oil. FDR understood that Saudi oil was important enough for a personal meeting with ibn Saud. In February 1945, following the Yalta Conference to divide up postwar Europe, FDR met the king aboard the USS *Quincy* in the Great Bitter Lake in the Suez Canal. It was a triumph of American diplomacy and cemented the "special relationship" that bound the United States and Saudi Arabia for the rest of the twentieth century. The bedrock of the relationship: The United States wanted access to the oil, and Saudi Arabia wanted to sell it to us. FDR also assured the king that the United States had no territorial desires in the area.

The only discordant note was when FDR tried to sell Abd-al-Aziz on the establishment of Israel. FDR eloquently described the plight of the Jewish people and the Nazi genocide. Ibn Saud was sympathetic and recommended that the allies award the Jews the best German lands but would not agree to a Jewish state in an Arab and Muslim area. After all, he pointed out, why should Arabs have to pay for crimes committed by Germans? FDR promised to consult the king before taking any actions that would impact negatively on the Arabs, a promise that died with FDR less than a month later.

The British, not wishing to be cut out, insisted that Prime Minister Winston Churchill also meet with the king, a meeting that turned into a disaster. The Americans had been scrupulous in observing Muslims' rules and regulations so as not to offend their royal guest. (FDR even hid in his private elevator when he needed a cigarette.) Churchill insisted on his usual after-dinner cigar and brandy in front of Abd-al-Aziz. Instead of promising consultations as the Americans had, Churchill demanded ibn Saud's cooperation on Palestine as a price for the subsidies Britain had paid him for the previous twenty years. When the king did not acquiesce, Churchill showed how little he understood of the Arab world by mentioning to an aide that the al-Saud family should be grateful for the aid the British had provided the Hashemites, the Saudis' old enemies.

SAUDI ARABIA ENTERS THE WORLD STAGE

In 1945, Britain established the Arab League in Cairo to give the Arabs a united voice in world politics. Ibn Saud was wary of it because it might give too much voice to the Hashemites. His foreign policy was always to check the Hashemites. In 1947 he sent his son, Crown Prince Saud ibn Abd-al-Aziz ibn Saud, to Washington. Shortly afterward, the United States voted for the partition of Palestine, opposed by all Arab countries. The Hashemite kingdoms demanded that the Arabs stop selling oil to any country that supported the "Zionist" resolution. King Saud sent a message to President Truman affirming his opposition to the UN resolution but advising that he would not allow his Hashemite rivals to embroil him with a conflict with his good friend, the United States. To strengthen his hand against the Hashemites, he opened relations with Syria and Egypt. Embarrassingly, the only victorious Arab army against Israel was that of Hashemite Jordan. The Saudi king asked the United States for a treaty, but Washington gave him only a military assistance agreement, which effectively brought Saudi Arabia into the U.S. strategic orbit.

THE FIFTIES

Abd-al-Aziz died in 1953 at the age of 77. He had founded the third Saudi realm over most of the Arabian peninsula, defeated his enemies the Rashidis and the Hashemites, and made deals that brought great financial wealth. Now it was the turn of his son, Saud, who was as devoted to Islam as his father was. He paid to renovate the mosques in Mecca and Medina and abolished the taxes that pilgrims had to pay on the hajj. He reasoned that God had given him oil and that was all the money he needed. Saud was captivated by Egypt's new President, Gamal Abdul Nasser. Nasser's heady rhetoric called for Arab unity and social justice. Saud even followed Nasser's lead in establishing contact with the Soviet bloc for an arms deal.

Saud's alignment with Nasser was based on the family's old rivalry with the Hashemites. Britain, with the support but not the participation of the United States,

Cultures

GAP ON PENNSYLVANIA AVENUE

The Saudi crown prince's 1947 Washington visit illustrates the cultural gap. As the usual honor for foreign dignitaries, he stayed at the official guesthouse, Blair House, across Pennsylvania Avenue from the White House. (Truman resided there while repairs were made to the White House a year later.) It is a charming Federalist red brick building, furnished with early American antiques. Americans think Blair House is beautiful and historic, but the crown prince was furious at what he thought were shabby lodgings. He demanded to know what he or his father had done to be insulted with rooms full of old furniture. Wasn't his country important enough to warrant new furnishings?

organized the Baghdad Pact. King Saud opposed it because he believed the British were creating an alliance that gave his Hashemite rivals supremacy in the Middle East. Instead, he aligned with Egypt in an effort to stop the growth of Hashemite influence.

SAUDI-EGYPTIAN RIVALRY

Saudi-Egyptian amity could not last; the two are culturally and politically vastly different. Saud realized that Nasser was costing Saudi Arabia money, influence, and power. In 1955, military officers in Ta'if plotted to kill the king, just as the Free Officers in Egypt had overthrown their monarchy. Saud responded by recruiting a Royal Guard from among the Ikhwan his father had resettled a quarter century ago. This tribal force persists to this day as the National Guard, headed by Crown Prince Abdallah.

The big break came in 1956, when Nasser nationalized the Suez Canal without consulting his Saudi allies. This triggered the 1956 Arab-Israeli war, which closed the Suez Canal and deprived Saud of revenues from oil that ordinarily passed through it (then 40 percent of the country's output). Because Saud had signed a military alliance with Egypt (he thought it was against the Hashemites), he was forced to support Nasser and grant him basing rights. Saud even broke diplomatic relations with its longtime ally Britain. Despite his public support of Egypt, Saud seethed. He believed Nasser had deceived him into joining an alliance that put him on a collision course with the European powers. He also was upset at the loss of oil revenues.

Most alarming, when Nasser visited the Kingdom, Saudi subjects turned out by the thousand in spontaneous demonstrations. Saud saw a threat to his throne and vowed to oppose any additional incursions by Nasser. Saud's opportunity came in 1957, when King Hussein of Jordan dismissed his pro-Nasser government. Saud sent reinforcements to help the Jordanian king against pro-Egyptian elements. The two monarchs established a "Royals Alliance" against Nasser that finally buried

G Geography

THE BAGHDAD PACT (CENTO)

The 1950s were the height of the Cold War in which the United States and the Soviet Union regarded international relations as a zero-sum game where countries were traded like playing cards. Every card held by one side was one less for the other. The superpowers looked at the Middle East, like other parts of the world, as a playing field for their rivalry.

Eisenhower's Secretary of State John Foster Dulles wanted to unite the world in a series of anti-Communist alliances. Copying the North Atlantic Treaty Organization (NATO) in Asia, he created the Southeast Asia Treaty Organization (SEATO). To stop Soviet expansion into the Middle East, he organized the Central Treaty Organization (CENTO)—an anti-Soviet, Middle East coalition that would keep the Soviets from fulfilling their age-old ambition of obtaining a warm-water port to their south. Neither SEATO nor CENTO was ever worth much.

Egypt's Nasser, through his position in the Arab League, lined up opposition to CENTO. When the League rejected CENTO, the only country to join it was Iraq, still under British influence. The United States did not participate in CENTO because Ike believed it would overextend U.S. commitments in an area that was not America's traditional responsibility. Instead, Britain fulfilled its usual role as guarantor of security in the Middle East.

CENTO's five member countries were Britain, Turkey, Iraq, Iran, and Pakistan, the so-called "Northern Tier" of countries blocking Soviet penetration into the Middle East. They signed the mutual defense treaty in the Iraqi capital of Baghdad, earning them the name "Baghdad Pact." After the Iraqi revolution of 1958, Baghdad withdrew from the Baghdad Pact, leaving Britain and only non-Arab countries in CENTO.

the enmity between the Hashemites and the Saudis. Washington, which had been alarmed at the king's flirtations with Nasser's anti-U.S. Arab nationalism, again regarded the Kingdom as an ally. The king visited Washington and renewed military cooperation.

FAISAL'S FIRST TURN

King Saud tried to buy a revolution in Syria, which in 1958 had joined Egypt in an experiment of Arab nationalism, the United Arab Republic. The Saudi covert action ended badly, embarrassing the Saudis and the king, who may have suffered a nervous breakdown. The sons of Abd-al-Aziz, Saud's brothers, met in council and transferred governmental authority from the king to a regent, Crown Prince Faisal. The regent ruled two years and concentrated on reform of the state bureaucracy.

Faisal decided he could not defeat Nasser but could appease him by distancing himself from his British and American allies and withdrawing his troops from Jordan. In 1958 Arab nationalists inspired by Nasser overthrew the Iraqi monarchy, the United States stood by, and Britain was unable to protect the monarchy it had created and nurtured. The safe bet was on Egypt.

The United States in the Middle East

THE EISENHOWER DOCTRINE

President Dwight Eisenhower obtained a joint congressional resolution allowing the president to use military forces to protect the independence of any state in the Middle East threatened by international communism. Eisenhower invoked the doctrine only once, to send troops into Lebanon in 1958 (for more, see Chapter 18). In reality, there was no Communist threat, but a spat between an outgoing Lebanese president and an incoming candidate who was supported by Nasser.

The United States invoked the new Eisenhower doctrine to justify landing Marines in Lebanon to prop up the government there. The real goal of the 1958 action was to show the countries of the region that America was prepared to oppose expansion by Nasser. King Saud supported Egypt in its opposition to the Beirut landing, but Nasser's propaganda offensive against monarchies continued. Ultimately, traditionalists cannot work with radicals.

THE SIXTIES

Saud returned to power in 1961 and continued Faisal's policies of appeasement. He did not renew the U.S. lease on the important Dhahran airfield. He joined Egypt in providing troops to oppose Iraq's efforts to annex Kuwait. Even then, Baghdad claimed that Kuwait never should have been broken away from Iraq.

A military coup in Damascus in 1961 brought to power officers who withdrew Syria from the United Arab Republic. Feeling betrayed, Nasser called on the Arab world to rebel against their governments so that Arab unity could proceed. Saud could not countenance this and again aligned the Kingdom with the Western powers and built up Saudi armed forces.

In 1962, a military coup overthrew the traditional ruler of Yemen, the Imam Muhammad al-Badr. When a civil war broke out in Yemen, Egypt sent a military force to support the new, socialist government. Egyptian troops—who reportedly used poison gas in Yemen—thus got a toehold on the Arabian peninsula and may have had designs on Saudi territory. Dissident Saudi princes flocked to Cairo, and some military aircraft defected to the Egyptians in Yemen. King Saud suffered a nervous breakdown, and the Council of Ministers again bestowed authority on his brother Faisal.

FAISAL'S SECOND TURN

Faisal now acted as king, not as regent, and supported the Imam in Yemen by providing military aid, but, not wanting to tangle with Egypt directly, sent no troops. He also turned to the United States and Britain for assistance. Washington promised to protect the kingdom against direct Egyptian attack but would not intervene in Yemen. Even when Egyptian jets attacked Saudi border towns, the United States did not react because the Kennedy administration was trying to woo Egypt. Britain, by contrast, began to provide aid immediately.

Faisal built up his National Guard, and the British increased their presence in the area. Nasser concluded he could not win in Yemen and agreed to UN arbitration and to a summit meeting with Faisal. In 1964 this caused one of the greatest crises in modern Saudi Arabia. A rested King Saud returned from abroad and demanded to lead the Saudi delegation. Faisal and his other brothers did not recognize Saud's authority. The Royal Guard loyal to Saud surrounded Faisal's palace while the National Guard loyal to Faisal surrounded Saud's. The brothers turned to the ulama, which decided that Saud should lead the delegation as he was still the country's king, but Faisal should continue to run the country because of Saud's ill health. Saud, claiming his health had been restored, tried to dismiss Faisal. The dispute continued for eight months with military standoffs and arrests of royal brothers. Finally, in November 1964, the ulama issued a fatwa that stated Saud had been deposed as king, and that King Faisal reigned in the Kingdom of Saudi Arabia. Saud then moved to Cairo to oppose his brother, under the sponsorship of Nasser. Some fear there could be another Saudi succession crisis.

THE 1967 ARAB-ISRAELI WAR

Faisal immediately moved to consolidate power. He abolished the post of prime minister and made the Council of Ministers purely advisory. To balance the Nasser-controlled Arab League, in 1964 Faisal formed the Organization of the Islamic Conference. Just as the al-Saud had used religion domestically to prop up its legitimacy, now al-Saud used it internationally.

Saudi Arabia played no role in the 1967 war. Israel's defeat of Egypt forced it to withdraw its broken army from Yemen, where tribal loyalists again tried to dislodge the republicans and failed. In nearby Aden, leftists founded the People's Democratic Republic of Yemen (PDRY), whose goal was to unite with the Yemen Arab Republic against the Saudis. The new rulers turned to the Soviet bloc for military help. Egypt had been replaced by the Soviets on the toe of the Arabian peninsula. Yemen unified in 1990 and became, by some accounts, the only Arab Communist country.

In Oman, the Saudis had supported a long-smoldering rebellion in Dhofar province that now burst into flames, supported by leftist elements from the Yemens. By 1970, rebel troops were at the palace doors in Muscat, capital of Oman. The British convinced Qabus ibn Said, the British-educated son of the sultan, to depose his father so the military could respond effectively to the rebel offensive. Faisal did nothing to help the young sultan, who eventually asked Iran to intervene.

This could have led to increased rivalries with the Shah but did not. The King of Saudi Arabia and the Shah of Iran reached an informal understanding whereby the King's sphere of influence extended to water's edge, while the Shah could guarantee the safety of shipping in the Persian Gulf. This became important after Britain withdrew from the Gulf in 1971, and America began to look for someone to police the area. They found the Saudi-Iranian partnership workable, and President Richard Nixon declared his support for the "twin pillars" of stability in the Gulf.

The Soviets moved to counter the U.S. foray into Gulf politics by signing a treaty of friendship in 1972 with Iraq, turning Iraq into a dangerous and well-armed client state. With the backing of a superpower, Iraq invaded Kuwait in 1973, the second time in twelve years that it tried to lay claim to the country. Saudi Arabia immediately responded by sending troops to support Kuwait in its battle, and the Iraqis quickly withdrew. Iraq's 1990 invasion was its third attempt to grab Kuwait.

THE 1973 ARAB-ISRAELI WAR

Ever since Abd-al-Aziz met FDR in 1945, American support for Israel has irritated U.S.-Saudi relations. King Faisal opposed Israel, and it was only his antipathy to Nasser that prevented the Saudis from doing more in 1967. By 1973, however, things had changed in the Middle East. Nasser died of a heart attack in 1970, and Anwar Sadat took over. Sadat traveled to Riyadh to consult with the Saudi king and told Faisal of his plan to renew the war with Israel. He got both Saudi financial pledges and a Saudi agreement to use the oil weapon.

Egypt and Syria launched their attacks on October 6, 1973 (see Chapter 6). As Israel quickly used up its munitions, the United States airlifted supplies directly to the front lines. The Saudis interpreted this as direct American intervention on behalf of the Israelis—this after President Nixon had given his assurance that he wanted to see a peace based on Resolution 242 (see Chapter 7). Faced with what Faisal doubtlessly saw as a personal betrayal, he and the Arab nations of OPEC declared an embargo on oil sales to any country that supported Israel. In December 1973, OPEC (see page 187) quadrupled the price of oil. For the first time OPEC worked as a unit and actually set the price of oil. OPEC, founded as a defensive cartel to keep oil prices from dropping, went on the offensive.

The embargo hit the world oil market at precisely the wrong time. Europe and Japan depended heavily on Arab oil, and the United States could not make up the shortfall as it, too, relied on imports. In economic terms, there was no "elasticity" in the market. Even a few-percent shortfall kicked prices to the sky. As Americans tasted rationing, gas lines, and odd-even fill-up days, the Europeans abandoned Israel and the United States. Some date the U.S.-European split over the Middle East to 1973.

The Saudis ended the boycott against the United States in March 1974. After both sides adjusted to the new relationship between the powers, they signed a Saudi-American military cooperation agreement in June. The Americans agreed to provide security assistance in return for Saudi pledges to work to guarantee American energy supplies. The Saudis could have sold large quantities of oil on the open market and driven the price back down. Many in the Kingdom were concerned that the high cost of crude would drive consumer countries to develop alternative fuels. In the end, the king allowed the new prices to stand, and Saudi oil revenues jumped 330 percent. America tried to regain the money it was sending to the Kingdom for oil by selling the Saudis modern armaments.

In 1975 King Faisal was assassinated by his nephew for unknown reasons. Crown Prince Khalid was crowned king. The elder in the family, Muhammad ibn Abd-al-Aziz, decided that Fahd should be the crown prince, and two princes in the middle were passed over. Succession was thus determined by the family elder and not by the king of the country.

When Egypt signed its peace treaty with Israel in 1979, it immediately became a pariah state to the rest of the Arab world. Washington asked the Saudis to support the peace treaty, something the king rejected. This forced the Saudis to unwillingly side with the rejectionist front: Palestinians, Iraq, and Syria. The United States sought to maintain its special relationship by agreeing to separate the Arab-Israeli conflict from the rest of its dealings with the Kingdom. This awkward compartmentalization could only work as long as there was a common enemy to unite the two countries. The Iraqi invasion of Kuwait in 1990 brought the two together for a while, but the demise of the Soviet Union at the end of 1991 brought a very different Saudi-U.S. relationship.

CONCLUSIONS

Arabia became Saudi starting with the 1744 alliance of a tribal chief, Saud, and a fundamentalist preacher, Wahhab. It took three attempts, but finally in 1925 the al-Saud evicted their last rivals, the Hashemites. Saudi-U.S. relations have been long and deep, starting with U.S. oil developers in the 1930s. FDR met with the king in early 1945. Although Israel was an irritant, the two countries needed each other: their oil for our security protection. Initially impressed by Nasser of Egypt, the Saudis soon learned that conservative regimes must fear revolutionary ones. With the 1973 Arab-Israeli war, OPEC quadrupled oil prices making the Kingdom very rich and, as we shall see in Chapter 18, likely beginning its destabilization.

FURTHER REFERENCE

Aburish, Said K. *The Rise, Corruption and Coming Fall of the House of Saud*. New York: St. Martin's Press, 1995.

Esposito, John L. *Islam: The Straight Path*. New York: Oxford, 1991.

Helms, Christine Moss. *The Cohesion of Saudi Arabia: Evolution of Political Identity*. Baltimore, MD: Johns Hopkins University Press, 1981.

Holden, David, and Richard Johns. *The House of Saud: The Rise and Rule of the Most Powerful Dynasty in the Arab World*. New York: Holt, Rinehart & Winston, 1981.

Howarth, David. *A Desert King: Ibn Saud and His Arabia*. New York: McGraw-Hill, 1964.

Lacy, Robert. *The Kingdom: Arabia and the House of Saud*. New York: Harcourt Brace and Jovanovich, 1981.

Miller, Aaron David. *Search for Security: Saudi Arabian Oil and American Foreign Policy, 1939–1949*. Chapel Hill, NC: University of North Carolina Press, 1980.

Iraq and Kuwait

Points to Ponder

- When and why did Britain conquer Iraq?
- Is the British experience in Iraq a good analogy with the present situation?
- How did Iraq get its king? What royal house was he from?
- What was the Baath party? What was its ideology?
- What are the population groups of Iraq?
- Why do "Saladin figures" arise in the Arab world?
- Was Kuwait always independent or part of Iraq?
- Did Britain invent both Iraq and Kuwait?

World War I brought Britain into what it then called Mesopotamia for two reasons. First, the Ottoman Empire sided with Germany in 1914, and, second, London knew of Mesopotamia's oil potential. Forces from Britain's Indian Army landed on the Faw peninsula at the head of the Persian Gulf in 1914 and soon took Basra (which British troops took again in 2003). They moved rapidly up the Euphrates Valley (as U.S. forces did in 2003) and by the fall of 1915 tried to take Baghdad, but a Turkish counteroffensive pushed them back to Al Kut on the Tigris, where, after a 140-day siege, the British surrendered in April 1916. In March 1917, however, British forces took Baghdad and in November took Mosul, so that by the end of World War I they held all but the north of what was now called Iraq, after the old Arabic name.

In a parallel to the 2003 Iraq War, victorious British General Stanley Maude in 1918 proclaimed that Britain, having liberated Iraq from foreign (Turkish) rule, intended to return control to Iraqis. Iraqi nationalists for some time had opposed Ottoman rule. Indeed, the British-sponsored Arab Revolt of 1916 had encouraged Arab nationalism against the Turks. These Iraqis therefore bitterly resented the "mandate" over Iraq that Britain had given itself. Britain ran Iraq like a colony, staffed with experienced British and Indian administrators from India. Initially, no Iraqi administrators were appointed.

G : *Geography*

COLLAPSED EMPIRES

The collapse of an empire always leaves a terrible political mess behind, like a vacuum that many rush in to fill. World War I collapsed four empires—the German, Austro-Hungarian, Russian, and Ottoman— leaving a wide swath of chaos and instability from Central Europe, through the Balkans and Middle East, and into Asia. When you collapse a political entity in war you must always ask what will come after it. In Europe, the collapse of the German, Austro-Hungarian, and Russian empires led straight to communism, Nazism, and World War II. It was, in the words of E. H. Carr, "the twenty years' crisis."

What it left behind in the Middle East might be termed "the hundred years' crisis." Ottoman power was out, but British and French power could not bring stability. Local nationalists opposed them and strove constantly to oust them. The new states set up by the imperialists had ancient roots but only a weak sense of themselves as modern states. Britain virtually invented a modern state called Iraq out of three Ottoman provinces. Boundaries were open to question and drawn mostly by the British and French. The British, over Iraqi objections, allowed a separate Kuwait to continue. The French took Syria's Bekaa Valley and made it part of Lebanon. Empires may be bad, but what comes after them can be worse.

Compounding the problem was the fact that at the end of World War I the triumphant Arab armies of Hashemite Prince Faisal were in Damascus. With British promises and encouragement, they had pushed the Turks out of much of northern Arabia and Syria. Now they turned to the British and demanded what they had been promised in the 1915–1916 Husayn-McMahon correspondence: self-determination for the Arabs in the lands they conquered. In March 1920 the Syrian National Congress proclaimed Faisal their king. The only problem was that Britain had also promised Syria to the French in the Sykes-Picot agreement, a deal that was confirmed at the San Remo Conference in April.

French forces in Lebanon hesitated in pressing their colonial claims until Faisal accepted the Syrian kingship. The French considered this move a direct threat to their interests, especially since Faisal was considered a British ally. The French commander marched on Damascus and deposed the king in August 1920. The French then escorted Faisal to Palestine and to the protection of his British masters.

In the lands of the Tigris and Euphrates, a British army of 130,000 men kept order as they waited for a new British mandate to be established. When the Syrians proclaimed Faisal king, however, it inspired officers of the Arab army to proclaim Faisal's older brother, Abdallah, king of Iraq. The British did not recognize this Arab move for self-government. Probably triggered by the April 1920 announcement of a British mandate over Iraq, Arab nationalists rebelled in Mosul in July, and the rebellion spread down the Euphrates Valley. The British response was fierce and, after a few months, successful. In what Iraqis call the Great Iraqi Revolution of 1920 and the British call the Iraq Revolt, British Royal Air Force bombers and reinforcements from India killed some 8,450 rebels with a loss of over 400 British and Indian troops killed. The British public soon disliked the cost of men and money in Iraq.

G : *Geography*

SAN REMO CONFERENCE

This conference of victors, held April 19–26, 1920, is not as famous as some of the postwar conferences because most of its decisions were ratified in August in the Treaty of **Sèvres**. The purpose of the meeting in San Remo, Italy, was to abolish the Ottoman Empire and to divide up its lands. The countries at the conference to decide the face of the Middle East for the next century were Britain, France, Italy, Belgium, Japan, and Greece. The United States was not in attendance, so there was no voice urging a settlement based on Wilson's Fourteen Points, which stressed self-determination. Similarly, neither Turkish nor Arab delegations were present. The people whose future was being decided were not just silent but absent from the table. Imperialists did those kinds of things.

The conference awarded Syria and Lebanon to France, which had interests in the area dating back to the Crusades. It gave Palestine (including Transjordan) and Iraq to the British. Sykes-Picot originally indicated a French role in the oil region of Mosul, but the British decided to keep it for themselves. To buy-off French objections to the British getting the Iraqi oil fields, the conference also awarded France 25 percent of Iraqi oil. Most of these deals were ratified as new League of Nations "mandates" two years later. (For more on mandates, see Chapter 5.)

The San Remo Conference followed British desires in uniting the Ottoman provinces of Mosul, Baghdad, and most of Basra into the new country of Iraq. A small portion of Basra province that had not been under direct Ottoman control, the Emirate of Kuwait, was left outside the new entity, although Iraq always claimed it belonged to Iraq. The Europeans had created Iraq, but the Iraqi revolt of 1920 showed that its inhabitants did not want European rule. Since the British had ruled out Abdallah as king (he was chosen by the people without British prior consent), they had to devise another way to run the country.

A meeting of British government and colonial administrators in Cairo in March 1921 switched kings. It made Abdallah the king of Transjordan and made Faisal, whom the French had kicked out of Syria, king of Iraq. In those days, Britain invented countries and kings. In Iraq, the British held a plebiscite on the choice of Faisal. Before the vote, the British arrested and deported General Sayyid Talib, a rival claimant to the throne. With no other candidates to oppose him, Faisal received 96 percent of the vote.

Iraqi nationalists by now hated the British; they wanted full independence. Then, as now, Iraq was hard to pacify. Young Saddam Hussein was raised by his uncle in an atmosphere of intense anti-British hatred. The king, put on the throne by Britain and with no family roots in Iraq, found it hard to crack down on Iraqi nationalists. He could not risk losing his standing as an authentic Arab war hero by being perceived as too close to his British colonial masters. Britain decided to

Sèvres   1920 peace treaty in which Ottoman Empire gave up non-Turkish territories.

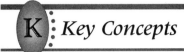

Key Concepts

ANALOGIES

Most of our reasoning, especially in the social sciences, is by **analogy**, but such reasoning is often flawed and misleading, as no two cases are ever exactly alike. Looking at unruly Iraq after the 2003 war, some journalists eagerly seized on the 1920 Iraq Revolt against the British as an analogy and warning. There were points of comparison. In both, new victors proclaimed their intention of liberating Iraq but stayed as occupiers. Local nationalists disliked the previous regime (respectively, Ottoman and Saddam) but also disliked Western occupiers. In the interests of speedy restoration of order, both British and Americans brought in outside administrators and attempted to name outsiders as leaders, and this fostered even more nationalistic anger. In both cases, irregular guerrilla-type raids were met with tough retaliations, mass arrests, and searches of homes.

But there are several elements of **dysanalogy**. The United States sought no mandate, colony, or prolonged occupation of Iraq. All Americans, especially soldiers, wished to be out as quickly as possible. The Pentagon had a friendly exile, Ahmad Chalabi, in mind as interim leader but named him as one among many in the face of Iraqi rejection. In 1920 the Kurds, hoping for their own country, opposed the British. In 2003, the Kurds, hoping for autonomy, supported the Americans. One element that holds up is the persistence of Iraqi nationalism. Beware of overly facile analogies. Every time we see two historical events compared we must ask, "Do the elements of analogy outweigh the elements of dysanalogy?"

forgo the mandate it had been promised and protected its interests in Iraq by a treaty. The treaty provided for the same role that Britain would have played under a mandate; that is, Britain provided advisors at all levels of the Iraqi government, and Iraq agreed to sign no treaties without British consent. Iraqi nationalists realized this was indirect British control but took solace in the thought that they had prevented the British from imposing a formal mandate. Indeed, these fledgling steps toward independence culminated in 1932, when Iraq was admitted as a full member of the League of Nations. Through the local ruling elite, Britain was still influential in Iraq.

POST-FAISAL IRAQ

King Faisal's personal reputation kept Iraq's factions together. In 1933, however, Faisal died and was succeeded by his inexperienced twenty-one-year-old son, King Ghazi. The new king lacked the leadership skills (and interest) of his father, so the political forces in the kingdom split into pro- and anti-British camps. The pro-British camp was led by the most famous of the pre-war politicians, General (later Prime Minister) Nuri al-Said.

---

analogy Finding that one case is like another.
dysanalogy Finding that one case differs from another.

G: *Geography*

THE PEOPLES OF IRAQ

Iraq is mentioned in the *hadiths* of the Prophet as an area near the southern Tigris and Euphrates, so Arabs have since the seventh century called it Iraq. But British colonial administrators in Cairo invented Iraq's modern borders in 1921. In so doing, they united groups of people under one government that had little in common, Iraq's weakness ever since.

The three Ottoman provinces had reported to three different governors; there was no geographic unity among the units for hundreds of years. The people within the provinces were also quite different from one another: Ethnically, about 80 percent of the people of Iraq today are Arab and 20 percent Kurds. From a religious viewpoint, an estimated 60 percent of Iraq is Shi'a, while some 38 percent are Sunni. Less than 20 percent of the population is Sunni Arab, but they have always held political power, whether under Ottomans, British, Hashemite kings (who were Sunni), or Saddam Hussein.

The population is divided roughly along the lines of the old provinces: The Shi'a Arabs are concentrated in the former province of Basra (although many live in Baghdad as well), the Sunni Arabs live in the former province of Baghdad, and the Sunni Kurds live in the former province of Mosul, but there is a good deal of overlap and mixing.

There is also a scattering of Greeks, Iranians, Assyrians, Turcomans, Orthodox Christians, Jacobite Christians, devil worshippers, and Jews to make the mix more interesting. Finally, about one-sixth of the country is tribal, whose followers owe their allegiance to a tribal chieftain—usually a distant relative as tribes are large, extended families that united for self-protection over the years.

Iraqi histories often talk of "the nationalist movement." Such movements in the Middle East always start among intellectuals; mass actions come later when the educated classes incite the people for whatever cause on any particular day. With so many different claims to loyalty, one has to ask whose nationalism the Iraqi nationalist movement was espousing? Mostly it means that of the Sunni Arab minority.

The country acquired new importance to the British as World War II loomed. Iraq was strategic, and in 1930 the Iraqi government signed a treaty granting the British access to air bases in the south, and basing rights for ground forces in the north. In the same year, Iraq began producing oil in commercial quantities. Soon a small (12-inch) pipeline carried some of this oil from Iraq through Transjordan to the port of Haifa in Palestine, all of it under British control. As the British pushed to increase their role in the Baghdad government, the anti-British camp pushed harder as well.

The tension led to a series of five coups from 1936 to 1941. The king continued to reign unopposed; the coups were aimed at the cabinet and the political rulers of the country. The monarchy changed hands in 1939 when King Ghazi died in an automobile accident and left the throne to his four-year-old son, Faisal II.

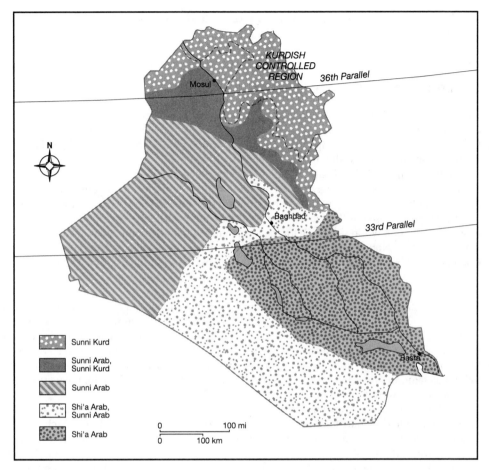

Iraqi Demographics

WORLD WAR II

In 1941, pro-German former Prime Minister Rashid Ali al-Gailani returned to power in a military coup. He had already shown his colors by welcoming such prominent pro-Nazi leaders as Hajj Amin al-Husayni (see page 84) to take refuge from the British authorities in Palestine. The British could not countenance an Iraq aligned with Germany and invaded the country. After some brief fighting, they returned Faisal II to the throne, and he ruled the country until the revolution of 1958. Because he was so young, his uncle Abdallah ruled as regent until 1953.

The first Arab-Israeli war had an impact on Iraq, as it did on all the countries of the Middle East. The Iraqi people responded to Israeli independence with anti-Western riots and anti-Jewish pogroms. Most of Baghdad's ancient

 *Cultures*

THE ETERNAL SALADIN

The Muslim, specifically Arab, world seems to need a Saladin from time to time. As we considered in Chapter 3, Saladin was the chivalrous twelfth-century Kurdish general who beat the Crusaders and ruled Egypt. Saladin, although of Kurdish origin, is an ikon among Arabs: the hero who unified us and kicked out the Europeans. Because the Arab world continued to suffer the same problems—fragmentation and foreign dominance—a charismatic Saladin figure has been an intermittent phenomenon.

Nasser of Egypt seemed to have had a Saladin image of himself even before he led the 1952 coup that eventually made him Egypt's permanent president. Through the 1950s and 1960s, he used heroic references to himself as the man who would unify the Arabs and expel the foreigners. He saw his mission as the Arab world searching for the right man to liberate it, him. Most of the Arab world hero-worshipped him. Notice how even conservative Arab regimes—such as Saudi Arabia's discussed in Chapter 11—were initially drawn to him even though he represented a threat to their monarchies. They liked the way he stood up to the West, although they did not want to be overthrown. Automatically, the West had to oppose Nasser.

The latest Saladin figure was Saddam Hussein of Iraq. Rationally, many Arabs knew he was a brutal dictator, but emotionally they could not help admiring the way he stood up to the United States. Almost all Arabs favored Saddam in the 2003 Iraq War; hardly anyone spoke against his tyranny. Saddam played the same themes as had Nasser: Unify the Arabs and kick out the West. Across the culture gap, we had trouble understanding the overwhelming Arab support for Saddam. To us, he was a tinhorn dictator. To Arabs, he was the latest manifestation of the spirit of Saladin. We were not just fighting Saddam; we were fighting history.

Another historical pattern showed up recently. Egypt and Mesopotamia have always been rivals, in competition to dominate the Middle East. They may have the same goals, but each wants to lead. Nasser made Egypt the leader; then Saddam Hussein tried to do the same for Iraq. With America watching Iraq, where will the next Saladin figure emerge? Osama or a follower in Saudi Arabia? We can be sure of two things about him: He will claim to be unifying the Arabs, and he will be anti-United States.

Jewish community—some two and a half millennia old—left. The Iraqi government also cut the oil pipeline that connected northern Iraqi oilfields with Haifa, costing the Iraqi treasury millions in lost revenues until alternative export routes could be developed.

Much as they had done in Greece, Turkey, and Iran, the Soviet Union took advantage of the unrest in Iraq. The Soviet embassy ran a series of operations designed to increase the prominence of its proxy, the Iraqi Communist party. The arrest of a number of Communist leaders reinforced in the eyes of the palace the need for strong ties with Britain, even though the rise in Iraqi nationalism caused by the first Arab-Israeli War made the British position untenable. To avoid running afoul of Iraqi public opinion, in 1947 the British withdrew all their troops in the country that were left over from World War II, leaving their only presence at two air bases.

Control of the Baghdad government fluctuated between the pro- and anti-British forces throughout the early 1950s. By 1955, Britain's ally Nuri al-Said was back in power, and Nuri agreed to join the Baghdad Pact (see page 201). He made Britain pay a price, however. In return for joining the Baghdad Pact, Nuri got cancellation of the Anglo-Iraqi Treaty that kept Iraqi foreign policy hostage to Britain's approval. The Arab League, under the sway of Egypt's Nasser, condemned Nuri's agreement to cooperate with the British, and most Arab countries sought to isolate Iraq.

In 1956, Nasser became the hero of the Arab world (and on the streets of Baghdad) because of his successful opposition to the British, French, and Israeli invasion of the Suez Canal. In 1957, Crown Prince Abdullah and four former Iraqi prime ministers met with King Saud ibn Abdul Aziz during the latter's visit to Washington. The two sides agreed to bury the generations-old enmity between the Hashemites and the Saudis, so that they could work together to defeat Nasser's popularity among their own populations. Iraq then sought to federate with the other Hashemite monarchy in the region, Jordan, to create a counterbalance to the United Arab Republic of Egypt and Syria. The Hashemite federation was even shorter than the Egypt-Syria union; the Iraqi Revolution ended it in 1958.

THE IRAQI REVOLUTION

On July 14, 1958, Brigadier General Abdul Karim Qasim (sometimes spelled *Kassem*) overthrew the Iraqi government. The young King Faisal II, Crown Prince Abdullah, Prime Minister Nuri al Said, and all members of the royal family that could be caught were executed. The new deputy prime minister, Colonel Abdul Salam Muhammad Arif, traveled to Damascus to sign a cooperation agreement with Nasser, ending Iraq's role in the anti-Nasser coalition. Premier Qasim also signed a treaty with Nasser's superpower patron, the Soviet Union, thus cutting Iraq's long ties with its founding power, Britain. Shortly thereafter, Qasim threw Colonel Arif into prison on charges of plotting a coup.

Iraq divided between supporters and opponents of Nasserism. The Communists took advantage of the stalemate between the two forces to stage a comeback. The government of Premier Qasim allowed the Communists as a counterweight to the Nasserists. When a group of Communists marched on the northern city of Mosul in March 1959, however, the garrison, manned by Kurds, took advantage of the unrest and revolted. It was a brief fight, and the garrison was soon defeated by a combined force of government troops and armed Kurdish tribes. The Communists then tried to take advantage of the situation themselves and launched a pogrom against the middle class in the city.

The Communist forces of Iraq were strengthened further by the arrival the following month of Mullah Mustafa Barzani in the north (see Chapter 9). He and his followers had been living in the Soviet Union ever since fleeing there following the collapse of the Mahabad Republic in 1946. Following their success in terrorizing Mosul, the Communists moved on Kirkuk in July of 1959. It was their high-water mark.

G: *Geography*

BOUND IRAQ

Iraq is bounded on the north by Turkey;
on the east by Iran;
on the south by the Persian Gulf, Kuwait, and Saudi Arabia;
and on the west by Jordan and Syria.

Qasim realized that the Communists were too great a danger to be used against the Nasserists, and he brought them under control before they could seize power. He arrested the leadership, purged popular organizations and unions of Communist members, and turned back toward the West. He made an arms purchase from Britain in 1959 and signed cultural agreements with the United States in 1960.

Qasim had no supporters in the country except the military. On the international front, he soon isolated himself just as he had done domestically. He nationalized most of the assets of the Iraqi Petroleum Corporation, which was British controlled and operated. In retaliation, the oil multinationals moved their investments to other countries in the region and denied Iraq the benefits of any increases in oil revenue. Qasim then took on the rest of the Arab world by laying claim to Kuwait. Britain sent forces to defend the newly independent country. Saudi troops later replaced British troops there. When the Arab League welcomed Kuwait as a full member, a combined unit of the Arab League replaced the Saudi contingent.

K : *Key Concepts*

WHAT IS THE BAATH?

Like its more famous contemporary, Nasser's Egyptian Arab nationalism, the **Baath** party advanced a socialistic, pan-Arab philosophy. Sorbonne-educated Syrian intellectuals founded the movement in the 1940s. The two most famous were a Sunni Muslim, Salah al-Din al-Bitar, and a Greek Orthodox Christian, Michel Aflaq. At a time when fascism was riding high in Europe and World War II renewed European intervention in the Middle East, these and other thinkers proposed a party that combined nationalism with socialism. (Aflaq had learned Marxism while in Paris.) They believed the only way for Arabs to control their own lives was the rebirth (*Baath* means "rebirth or renaissance" in Arabic) of a united Arab nation. The Baathis eventually seized control in Syria and Iraq. Since there could only be one Arab nation that included both countries, the governments of these countries were referred to as "regional commands." Nationalist rivalries continued even in the pan-nationalist movement: The Baath party in each of the states claimed that they were the National Command, and the other state was a regional command. They established competing claims for leadership of the movement.

The Baath is a secular ideology, seeking to unite Arabs of all religions. (This was probably the influence of the Christian Aflaq, who would have had no place in a movement based on Islam.) Despite its secular principles, it accepted Islam as the highest manifestation of the Arab culture. Some see Baathism as a kind of Arab fascism. The Baathis organized themselves into clandestine cells until they seized power through military coups in both countries. At present, Baathism stands for nothing clear.

THE COUPS

On February 8, 1963, the Baath party in Iraq overthrew the Qasim regime and took power for the first time. They shot Qasim and proudly displayed his corpse on television. The Baath in Syria seized power a month later. The two commands of the Baath party tried to negotiate unity with Egypt, since all three countries were now supposedly committed to Arab unity. But Nasser believed the Syrians had deceived him during the aborted United Arab Republic. He supplemented his negotiations with attempts to overthrow the Baathists and replace them with his own people, and the negotiations fell apart. Arab unity, much commented upon in the Arab press from the 1930s to the present day, had been shown to be unfeasible in 1961 and now in 1963. The fiction would continue a number of years, however, as the three countries continued to periodically negotiate and sign various bilateral and multilateral unity agreements. None ever came to fruition. The trouble with Arab unity is that several countries want to lead it.

The leader of the Iraqi coup was Colonel Abdul Salam Arif, the same individual who had helped Qasim achieve power and who was imprisoned as his reward. Arif ruled as both president and as chairman of the Baath Revolutionary Command

Baath   Arab Socialist Renaissance party; came to power in Syria and Iraq.

Council (RCC). Arif did not like having to rule by committee, and he staged a second coup in November 1963 to eliminate the RCC. The only tie to the party in the new government was the powerless vice president, Baath party member General Hassan al-Bakr. The vice president kept only his honorary title three months before resigning.

THE JUNE 1967 WAR

President Arif died in a helicopter crash on April 13, 1966. His brother, General Abdul Rahman Arif, promptly succeeded him and presided over a period of relative peace and prosperity. The Six Day War with Israel in June 1967 shattered the calm. Although the war did not last long enough for Iraqi troops to actually engage in battle with the Israelis, Israeli preemptive strikes wiped out the entire Iraqi air force. This provided the Soviet Union with an opportunity to expand its influence in the area, as Moscow promptly replaced all the destroyed aircraft with newer models. This act of friendship was followed by a number of economic, political, and military agreements between the two countries, and visits by high-level Soviet and Iraqi officials to each other's capitals.

On July 17, 1968, the Baath returned to power through another coup. Washington was briefly reassured by the overthrow of the Arif regime that had become so friendly with the Soviets. American discomfort increased, however, when two weeks later all pro-Western members of the coup were dismissed. The RCC transformed the country into a single-party state and rapidly solidified their hold over the instruments of power. The leader was General Hassan al-Bakr, the former vice president. Al-Bakr, in turn, appointed a distant cousin to be his vice premier, a Baathi enforcer named Saddam Husayn (spelled in the media as *Hussein*).

The new government's foreign policy was guided by a desire to improve the regional position of the country rather than by an ideological compass. It fought with the Baath government in Syria over the Syrian construction of a dam, which reduced the flow of Euphrates river water into Iraq. Iraq also alienated Syria by building a pipeline through Turkey that, in effect, recognized Turkish control of Iskenderun—an area Syria still claimed was part of the Syrian homeland under its old name of Alexandretta.

The Baathis completed the break with Britain by nationalizing the rest of the Iraqi Petroleum Company. It also joined the Rejectionist Front along with other hard-line countries such as Syria and Libya, which were allies of the Palestine Liberation Organization. The Front opposed any recognition of Israel or negotiating peace with it. Iraq hosted the Baghdad summit of 1978, which condemned Egypt for negotiating a separate peace with Israel. As a leading source of instability in the Middle East and a leader in the movement opposed to Western influence, Iraq continued to deepen its ties with the Soviet Union. Iraq and the United States had no diplomatic ties from 1967 to 1984.

As for relations with Iran, Iraq had been fighting a low-intensity conflict with Iranian surrogates (the Kurds) from 1970 to 1975 (see Chapter 9). Saddam Hussein estimated that the Iraqi army lost 16,000 in the fighting and another 60,000 wounded. Nonetheless, he signed the 1975 Algiers accords bringing stability to Iraq's northern territories and eastern border. The southern border remained a point of contention, however, as Baathists renewed Iraq's claims to parts of Kuwait. This time, Baghdad did not seek to justify its claims on history but on Iraq's strategic needs since the lands it coveted controlled the approaches to the strategic Iraqi port of Umm Qasr.

On July 17, 1979, President al-Bakr stepped down after eleven years in office and appointed his cousin Saddam to succeed him. The new president ruled over a country that many economists judged was so advanced that it might soon surpass the economies of such European countries as Spain and Italy. Economic growth was not Saddam's primary ambition.

KUWAIT

Kuwait has a short history, as it has existed as an independent state for only about forty years. The current aristocracy (known as the *Utub* or "wanderers") arrived in Kuwait via Basra around 1750, having been previously driven out of Qatar. At the time, the area was titularly part of the Ottoman Empire. There were two wealthy tribes among the migrants: the al-Khalifa that controlled the lucrative pearl industry, and the al-Jalahima that owned the boats. The economics of the situation made conflict between the two tribes inevitable. To arbitrate the competing claims, tribal chieftains elevated a third tribe to run the government, the al-Sabah, who have ruled (and mostly owned) Kuwait ever since. The al-Khalifa migrated out of Kuwait in the 1760s, and eventually became the ruling family in Bahrain. The al-Jalahima also left at the same time and were a threat to the al-Sabah for a number of years.

KUWAIT'S BRITISH CONNECTION

The British East India Company traditionally used the Ottoman port of Basra as a transshipment point in the northern part of the Gulf, but they frequently turned to Kuwait as an alternate when politics kept them out of Basra. As an example, when Persians besieged Basra in 1775–1779, the British used Kuwait as an alternative. They returned to Kuwait in 1793–1795 when local anti-British sentiment heated up in Basra. Again in 1821, when the British were in a dispute with Ottoman authorities, they removed themselves to Kuwait.

While the various members of the al-Sabah valued their British connection, they were not willing to surrender their independence to maintain it. Instead, the family played the British off against the Ottomans. In 1838, Shaykh Jabir I accepted to his court a representative of the Egyptian Pasha, Muhammad Ali, who was on the Arabian peninsula to reestablish Ottoman control of the area that had been conquered by the al-Saud. The Egyptians withdrew in 1840, but the Shaykh's willingness to accept the caliph's Egyptian representative cemented his good relations with the Ottoman Empire.

In 1856, the British offered to switch their port permanently from Basra to Kuwait; Kuwait would gain shipping fees but would have to sign the usual British treaty surrendering rights of the Shaykh to make foreign treaties or to cede any land without prior British approval. The Shaykh refused the terms and in 1862, when British merchants began using Kuwait as a port of call, he closed the harbor to them. This allowed the traditional Kuwaiti merchant class to maintain their monopoly on shipping in Kuwait and was perceived favorably by Ottoman authorities in Basra.

In the 1860s the Ottomans insisted that Kuwait was a part of Basra province and tried to enforce their claims. Istanbul even dispatched naval vessels to impose its will militarily. In reply, the Shaykh notified Istanbul that the inhabitants were prepared to abandon Kuwait and migrate elsewhere rather than accept Ottoman supremacy. The governor of Basra supported the al-Sabah, and the Ottomans dropped their efforts to enforce their claims.

As the Ottomans moved against the second Saudi kingdom, Shaykh Abdallah II realized the two warring powers were squeezing him. To protect his de facto independence, in 1871 he accepted the Ottoman title of governor of the subprovince of Kuwait. Abdallah II had preserved his ability to operate, but at the cost of formally recognizing his position as an official of Basra province of the Ottoman Empire. Iraq later used Kuwait's Ottoman connection to demonstrate that Kuwait rightfully belongs to Iraq. Kuwait emphasizes that it was never Ottoman-ruled or part of Ottoman-administered Iraq, and thus Iraq has no historic claim to it.

MUBARAK

Mubarak I founded the modern al-Sabah dynasty in 1896 with the help of two of his sons, Jabir and Salim. Since Mubarak's death, rule of Kuwait has alternated between the descendants of these two sons. Mubarak did not come to power cleanly. After his eldest brother Abdallah II died, the second in line was Muhammad I. Muhammad and younger brother Jarrah teamed up to run the country, and appointed Mubarak head of the military, keeping Mubarak with the troops in the desert, far from the palace. There are reports that Mubarak traveled that year to Bushehr in Persia and met with a British political agent. Whether this unconfirmed report is true or not, Mubarak went to the palace and, with the help of his two sons, assassinated Shaykh Muhammad and his brother Jarrah. He then seized control of the government.

Mubarak I presided over Kuwait during its most defining moments. In 1897, the Ottomans renewed the title it had bestowed on Mubarak's brother, governor of the subprovince of Kuwait. They insisted on Turkish rule of the subprovince, and Mubarak I turned to the British to act as a counterweight. In a secret agreement in 1899, the British finally got the Kuwaiti shaykh to sign the usual trucial agreement, cementing Kuwait's position into the British colonial system.

Armed with British defense guarantees, Mubarak launched a campaign against the al-Rashidis, who were closely aligned with the Ottomans. Mubarak lost the battle but won the war. Even though he was militarily defeated in 1901, Mubarak earned an alliance with the al-Saud family, who also opposed the Rashidis. (The al-Saud were living in exile in Kuwait, and they launched their third conquest of the peninsula from Mubarak's palace.)

WORLD WAR I

In 1913, the British betrayed their Kuwaiti allies in an effort to keep the Ottomans from joining the German side in the upcoming war. They acknowledged the Ottomans' claim that Kuwait was part of the Ottoman Empire and agreed to allow an Ottoman political officer to be assigned to Kuwait. Before the official could reach his new post, however, World War I broke out and the Ottomans joined it alongside the Central Powers.

Britain declared Kuwait an independent shaykhdom under British protection. Kuwait was unable to take advantage of its new status, however, because Mubarak I died in 1915, and his successor supported the Ottomans. As a result, the British blockaded Kuwait for the length of the war. At the same time, the Kuwaitis were fighting off the Saudi Ikhwan who advanced from the desert.

At the end of the war, the British Resident responsible for the Persian Gulf, Sir Percy Cox, convened a conference in 1923 that established the borders of modern Kuwait. Because no exact border could be created in the desert between Kuwait and Saudi Arabia, the parties agreed to the establishment of a neutral zone. Should any natural resources ever be discovered in the large, empty land of the zone, it would be divided between the Saudis and the al Sabah. With peace restored, the British then defended the Kuwaitis against the continuing raids of the Ikhwan.

In December 1934 the Gulf Oil Corporation and the Anglo-Iranian Oil Corporation signed a joint agreement with Kuwait establishing the Kuwaiti Oil Company. In 1935, this new entity discovered oil, guaranteeing that Kuwait would become one of the richest countries in the world and holder of the world's fourth-largest oil reserves. The oil company began exporting crude in 1946. Kuwait followed the lead of other Arab oil-exporting states and nationalized the industry by 1977.

In 1938, Kuwait became the first country on the Arabian peninsula to convene a Legislative Assembly. The British Political Officer and Kuwaiti reformists forced the Shaykh to accept this innovation. The fourteen-man Assembly elected the future Shaykh Abdallah III as its leader, but the ruling Shaykh Ahmad I assembled his supporters and closed the legislature after only six months.

The 1956 Suez Canal crisis enflamed anti-British emotion among young Kuwaitis. In 1958, Britain's major allies in the region, the Iraqi royal family, were overthrown and executed. Kuwaiti nationalists began to agitate against Britain's preferential status in the shaykhdom. To appease the critics, in June 1961 Shaykh Abdallah III ended the Anglo-Kuwaiti Defense Treaty of 1899. He declared Kuwait an independent country and joined the Arab League.

Barely before the ink could dry on the declaration, Iraqi President Qasim renewed the old Ottoman claims. Qasim said that since Kuwait had been a subprovince of Basra, and Basra was now part of Iraq, Kuwait was also legally a part of Iraq. Ironically, Qasim's attempts to subvert Abdallah III's independence had the opposite effect; by providing an outside enemy to rally against, it solidified the role of the al-Sabah family as defender of the country's independence.

First British, then Saudi, and finally an Arab League military force deployed to Kuwait to protect its sovereignty. Iraq never agreed to delineate its border with Kuwait, and in the 1970s renewed its claims on two areas of Kuwait that controlled the access to the Iraqi port of Umm Qasr, the island of Warba and the Bubiyan peninsula.

In 1962 Abdallah III approved a constitution that limited the powers of the royal family, established a National Assembly that opened in January 1963, and guaranteed equality to all Kuwaiti citizens. (One catch: Kuwaiti citizenship is limited to its original families. Most of the people who work in Kuwait are descended from more recent immigrants and cannot become Kuwaiti citizens.) The elections produced a bloc of strongly anti-Western nationalists that kept the country in political turmoil. By 1967, there had been a strong backlash against the oppositions, and elections brought a solid, pro-government grouping into the Assembly. By 1976 however, Abdallah's successor, Shaykh Jabir III, decided that the Assembly was producing results contrary to the country's national interest, and he ordered the body closed. It was reconvened in 1981, with a number of religious conservatives among its members.

As the oil revenues continued to expand the country's production capabilities, the Kuwaiti population proved too small to run the country. The government accepted massive waves of immigrants, the majority Palestinian, to live and work in the country. These new inhabitants had no rights to remain in the country and no chance of ever obtaining citizenship, but they had the ability to make excellent money they would never earn in refugee camps. By 1990, the original Kuwaiti population was a minority in the country.

In foreign policy, once Britain announced its withdrawal from the Persian Gulf, the Kuwaitis tried to straddle the Cold War divide. It sold its oil to, and made most of its purchases from, the West. At the same time, however, it opened diplomatic relations in 1970 with the Soviet Union and with the People's Republic of China.

CONCLUSIONS

The countries of Iran, Saudi Arabia, Iraq, and Kuwait assumed their current forms in the early twentieth century. Their previous histories were, for the most part, a succession of murders, coups, and military conquests. What unites four disparate countries are oil, the Persian Gulf, oil, Islam, and oil. Did we mention oil?

With the exception of Iran, which has a history and civilization stretching back thousands of years, none of the countries would have been anything more than minor tribal principalities without the black gold. Once the countries produced commercial quantities of petroleum, they were integrated into the world economy and became strategic interests first of Britain and soon of the United States. As the British lion lost strength in its old age, the Americans assumed more of the responsibility of maintaining the peace in the Gulf. All the countries have a history of achieving their current borders through armed clashes. It is thus no surprise that fighting among the countries continued into the twenty-first century.

FURTHER REFERENCE

Batatu, Hanna. *The Old Social Classes and the Revolutionary Movements of Iraq*. Princeton: Princeton University Press, 1978.

Crystal, Jill. *Kuwait: The Transformation of an Oil State*. Boulder, CO: Westview, 1992.

Farouk-Sluglett, Marion, and Peter Sluglett. *Iraq Since 1958: From Revolution to Dictatorship*, rev. ed. New York: Palgrave, 2001.

Khadduri, Majid. *Independent Iraq, 1932–1958: A Study in Iraqi Politics*. New York: Oxford, 1960.

———. *Republican Iraq: A Study in Iraqi Politics Since the Revolution of 1958*. New York: Oxford, 1969.

———. *Socialist Iraq: A Study in Iraqi Politics Since 1968*. Washington, D.C.: Middle East Institute, 1978.

Marr, Phebe. *History of Modern Iraq*, 2nd ed. Boulder, CO: Westview, 2003.

Miller, Judith, and Laurie Mylroie. *Saddam Hussein and the Crisis in the Gulf*. New York: Times Books, 1990.

Pavis, Timothy J. *Britain, the Hashemites and Arab Rule, 1920–1925: The Sherifian Solution*. Portland, OR: Frank Cass, 2003.

Rush, Alan. *Al-Sabah: History and Genealogy of Kuwait's Ruling Family 1752–1987*. Atlantic Highlands: Ithaca Press, 1987.

The Iranian Revolution and War with Iraq

13

Points to Ponder

- Was the Iranian Revolution bound to happen?
- Could the right reforms have headed off Iran's revolution?
- Did President Carter hasten the Iranian Revolution?
- How could a country dependent on a superpower break away from it?
- Is Iran a theocratic state, a democratic one, or a hybrid of the two?
- What is the role of the United States in Iran today? What should it be?
- Who is now in charge in Iran?
- Could Iran have another revolution?

THE PRESSURE COOKER

The United States was distracted in the 1970s by the resignations of the vice president and president, the unhappy end of Vietnam, and the 1973 October War. Nixon had posited the Shah as the gendarme of the Gulf and had sold him over $10 billion of advanced weaponry paid for with increased oil wealth from the price run-up of the 1973–1974 oil embargo (see Chapter 10).

In January 1977 Jimmy Carter began his presidency with an evangelical Christian streak that made human rights a pillar of U.S. foreign policy. Some argue that foreign policy has to be amoral and pay little attention to human rights; trying to make it moral opens cans of worms. Oblivious to such perspectives, Carter named Iran as a country that had to improve. Some Iranians took heart from Carter's emphasis on human rights. Iran was indeed a dictatorship that crushed opposition and dissent, often physically through its security service, the dread SAVAK. Deeply Islamic Iranians hated the secularization, and *bazaaris* hated being pushed out by larger modern firms. Furthermore, the big oil revenues ignited an inflation that melted salaries.

Some say that Carter persuaded the Shah to relax his repression, and that caused all that followed. Others say the Shah was reforming anyway to secure his son's succession to the throne. Either way, in May 1977 Washington signaled its approval of these changes by selling the Shah F-16s and AWACS planes. Congressional criticism of the sale sent the Shah a different signal that some elements of the U.S. government were reconsidering its support of him.

In November 1977 the Shah visited the White House. Sixty thousand Iranian students demonstrated in Lafayette Park across from the White House. As President Carter welcomed his royal visitor, police fired tear gas to disperse the demonstrators. The fumes drifted over the White House lawn and both leaders retreated into the White House with tears in their eyes. The TV image was of two world leaders fleeing from the wrath of their people. Six weeks later Carter visited the Shah in Tehran where he toasted the country (and by extension the monarch) as an island of stability. American Ambassador William Sullivan reported that the Shah was elated by what seemed to be Carter's renewed support.

Opposition to the Shah among secular groups grew in 1977. Groups such as the Tudeh (Communist) party and old supporters of Muhammad Mossadeq revitalized their networks. The real revolution began, however, in the opening days of 1978.

THE BEGINNING OF THE REVOLUTION

Specifically, on January 7, 1978, the government-run *Etella'at* newspaper condemned the Ayatollah Ruhallah Khomeini, then in exile in Iraq, and all clerics who opposed the Shah. The accusations were nutty, but Khomeini's students, friends, and followers in the seminary city of Qom were horrified. On January 9, 1978, the clerics organized a demonstration march in Qom. Police opened fire killing several. Iran's leading cleric who had not been opposed to the monarchy, Ayatollah Kazem Shari'atmaderi, condemned the Pahlavis as anti-Islamic.

Following Shi'a custom, a mourning ceremony takes place at the burial and another forty days later. At that time demonstrators in Tabriz attacked theaters, bars, and anything that could be considered a symbol of the Shah's new Iran. This cycle of violence followed by renewed violence every forty days continued until February 1979.

On August 19, 1978, a fire broke out at the Rex cinema in the southern oil town of Abadan killing almost 500 people. It was Ramadan and the Shah's supporters immediately blamed the religious opposition who had been setting fires to movie theaters throughout the country. The opposition called it a "Reichstag fire" set by the regime itself to place blame on its critics. In early September the religious opposition organized two demonstrations to celebrate the end of Ramadan, the Muslim month of daytime fasting. The gatherings were illegal but police did not interfere. Emboldened by the regime's timidity, the opposition called for a general strike. The Shah imposed martial law, in spite of the liberalization he had been promising. The next day, September 7, 1978, thousands gathered in

Tehran's Jaleh Square and refused to disperse. Troops opened fire killing from 100 to 1,000. The country was now racked with daily protests and strikes.

Iranian intelligence reported that the mastermind behind the opposition was Ayatollah Khomeini, whom the Shah had exiled to Turkey in 1964. Khomeini had been living in the Iraqi Shi'a shrine city of Najaf where he used Shi'a pilgrims to smuggle his sermons into Iran. The Shah had enough and asked the Iraqis to expel Khomeini. The French gave the Ayatollah refuge in a Paris suburb.

KHOMEINI IN PARIS

The Shah thought he had won a victory, but he was wrong. Paris's distance did not hurt Khomeini's ability to communicate. He simply recorded his anti-Shah sermons and phoned them to Iran, where his followers recorded them on cheap cassettes and played them in mosques nationwide. Simple technology eluded the Shah's communications monopoly.

The Shah's plan was to work with the secular opposition of former Mossad-eqists in the National Front, sharing some power with them and breaking them away from Khomeini. Then, he believed, moderate religious leaders would support the new government. Front leaders went to Paris for Khomeini's consent to the Shah's offer. The implacable Ayatollah rejected the compromise, and the secularists stayed with him. The incident showed that the secularists had already subordinated themselves to the religious fanatics. Many later regretted it.

To restore order in the rapidly deteriorating situation, the Shah established a military government on November 6, 1978. Each province got a military governor, and demonstrators retreated in fear. At the same time, the Shah arrested leaders of his intelligence service and some of his political allies in order to try to appease the angry crowds. (These officials were still in jail when the revolution delivered them to the executioners.) He also continued to try to negotiate with the National Front. Khomeini and his followers interpreted these moves as acts of desperation—they were—and ordered the opposition to redouble its efforts.

THE LAST IMPERIAL GOVERNMENT

The Shah finally convinced Shahpour Bakhtiar, French-educated and a longtime member of the National Front who had served as a member of Mossadeq's cabinet, to lead a civilian government. Bakhtiar assumed power as the last imperial prime minister on December 27, 1978. In his New Year's address he promised the creation of a social-democratic society. Bakhtiar did what he could. He dissolved the hated SAVAK and appointed secular nationalists to head the ministries. He

Key Concepts

WHAT WENT WRONG IN IRAN?

Twenty-five years after the revolution the Shah's supporters still debate whom to blame for his fall. Some use 1953 as a model and argue that U.S. intervention could have saved the Shah. Others look at the Huyser mission and see a deep U.S. conspiracy to dump the Shah. Western analysts point to economic and educational change and rising expectations. Others just claim that Iranians wanted a change in government. Deprived of democratic means, they turned to revolution.

More puzzling is why the Shah equivocated in his response to this challenge. Early on, he saw he would either have to crack down by military means or liberalize to survive in power. Instead of choosing one strategy and sticking with it, he vacillated between the two. We now know that the Shah was dying of cancer, but no one in Washington was aware of it. Fatigue, mood swings, and weakened cognitive abilities from medications hurt his ability to make firm decisions.

The Shah still relied on his American ally for guidance but did not know that Washington was deeply divided between the National Security Council and the State Department as to what to do. Secretary of State Cyrus (a Persian name) Vance would applaud the Shah's plans to liberalize while National Security Advisor Zbigniew Brzezinski would call him and tell him to be firm. The Shah's policies depended on whom he had last heard from. (For more on "bureaucratic politics" in U.S. foreign policy, see Chapter 15.)

was naive in failing to understand that as a secularist appointee of the Shah he would soon be dumped by the Islamists.

U.S. General Robert Huyser then visited and possibly made things worse. Soon Iranians realized that it was Huyser and not Ambassador Sullivan who had Carter's ear. Huyser tried to convince the Iranian military that their longstanding ties with the Pentagon remained intact regardless of what events transpired in Iran. Acting on orders, Huyser encouraged Iran's military to support the new government and not rebel or flee. Since then, many monarchists claimed that Huyser had been sent to convince the military to side with the opposition, thereby guaranteeing the return of Khomeini. Huyser did encourage the military to open communication with Khomeini—something Washington had not done itself until it was too late.

On January 16, 1979, the Shah left Iran. The night before he went to the imperial cemetery and dug up the remains of his father, Reza I. He boarded the royal jet accompanied by his entire family, untold millions in cash, and his father's remains, indicating he did not expect to ever return.

Headlines screamed, *"Shah Raft"* ("The Shah has gone."). Everyone anticipated the return of Ayatollah Khomeini. Bakhtiar, fearing what would happen if Khomeini returned, closed the airports. Khomeini ordered his followers into the streets until Bakhtiar reopened the airports. On February 1, 1979, Ayatollah al-Ozma Ruhallah Khomeini returned to Iran aboard a chartered Air France jet to rule Iran, not as king but as Imam or Supreme Leader.

Key Concepts

CRANE BRINTON'S THEORY OF REVOLUTION

In 1938 Harvard historian Crane Brinton explained how revolutions unroll in a similar pattern. *The Anatomy of Revolution* has stood the test of time and closely fits the Iranian Revolution. Brinton saw the following stages:

1. The old regime loses legitimacy. Intellectuals especially lose faith in it. Curiously, this often happens when the economy is *improving*, a point made a century earlier by Tocqueville on the French Revolution.
2. Antiregime groups coalesce. Some political problem cannot be solved, such as forming a new government. Rioting breaks out, but troops cannot quell it. The old regime departs because it knows it is finished.
3. At first, moderates take over and institute reforms, but they have neither the power nor the guts to crush the real revolutionaries, who hold them in contempt.
4. Extremists push the moderates aside and bring the revolution to a frenzied high, punishing enemies and "immoral" people in a reign of terror. Purity becomes the law of the land. France had Robespierre, Iran Khomeini.
5. People cannot stand the revolutionary purity for long; they get fed up with rule by extremists. Brinton called this stage **Thermidor** after the French revolutionary month in which Robespierre was guillotined. Brinton likened it to a cooling down after a fever. It indicates the revolution is over.

In 1938 Brinton virtually predicted how the 1979 Iranian Revolution would unroll. He found a logic to revolutions that is still valid.

THE FIRST REVOLUTIONARY GOVERNMENT

Bakhtiar's opposition credentials were impeccable, but accepting a post from the Shah doomed him in the eyes of Khomeini. The Ayatollah ignored Bakhtiar, and soon fighting broke out between noncommissioned air force officers loyal to Khomeini and the Imperial Guard. The generals ordered the army into the barracks and declared their neutrality in the political struggle taking place. Bakhtiar and his cabinet had no choice but to resign because no one would listen to them. Bakhtiar hid and then fled into exile to promote resistance to Iran's Islamist regime. For that he was stabbed to death in 1991 in his suburban Paris home.

Thermidor   A calming down after a revolutionary high.

Religions

CAN THERE BE AN ISLAMIC REPUBLIC?

Is there such a thing as an Islamic Republic? Islam holds that sovereignty belongs to God alone, but in a republic sovereignty resides in the people. The Iranian Constitution tried to make these two concepts work together. The result is a mishmash that, with complex additional screening bodies, keeps the Iranian government incoherent.

Iran's constitution says that power comes from God and resides in God's chosen one, the Imam. But laws are made by a parliament that is elected by the people. But the Assembly of Experts can overturn the laws if they are deemed un-Islamic. But if a law is declared un-Islamic and the parliament wants it anyway, then the issue is resolved by the Expediency Council. So, at that point, is the law the will of the people? Is the law Islamic? What is the law? One suspects that Islamic governance is unworkable.

Khomeini appointed another old National Front hand, Mehdi Bazargan, as his prime minister. Khomeini's victory was almost complete, and the monarchy was officially declared overthrown on February 11, 1979. Each year Iran commemorates the eleven days from Khomeini's arrival on February 1 to the abolition of the monarchy on February 11 as the "Days of the Dawn."

IRAN'S ISLAMIC CONSTITUTION

The United States had little influence on the Iranian Revolution. Iranians were determined to master their own destiny and repudiate American influence. Khomeini played the Tehran political scene like the clever revolutionary he was. Lenin had nothing on Khomeini. For example, secular intellectuals liked Western thought and supposed religious revolutionaries could not run Iran. In February 1979, Bazargan picked a cabinet of secular oppositionists much like himself and the first president of the Islamic Republic, Abol Hasan Bani Sadr. They congratulated themselves on cleverly manipulating Khomeini's supporters into putting right-thinking people like themselves into power instead of people they considered clerical reactionaries.

Nothing was further than the truth. Revolutionaries, as they often do, created structures parallel to those of the state, working around Bazargan's official government. Revolutionary committees sprang up next to the police, and the Revolutionary Guard competed with the military. Revolutionary courts condemned monarchists to death and seized the properties of those who fled. The clerical supporters organized the Islamic Republic party (IRP) and prepared for electoral battle.

Under orders from the ruling Revolutionary Council, Bazargan organized a referendum on March 31, 1979, in which 98 percent of the voters supported establishing an Islamic Republic. Bazargan then appointed a committee of his fellow moderates to draft a new constitution along West European socialist lines. Under Khomeini's guidance, hard-liners reworked the document, making the key office the *Velayat-e Faqih* ("Leadership of the Islamic Jurist"; see page 188), a role intended for its author, Ayatollah Khomeini. The constitution centralized power in this Supreme Leader and made the directly elected president much weaker. Supreme Leader Khomeini was entitled to these powers because of his unique qualifications as the religious and political leader of the country.

In January 1980 Iranians elected a president. The clerics in the IRP chose the ideologically pure Jalal ad-Din Farsi, but he was disqualified from running only weeks before the election. The IRP rushed a substitute candidate onto the lists but not in time. Moderate forces supported Bani Sadr, who had returned to Iran aboard the same jet as the Ayatollah. Bani Sadr won with 70 percent of the vote. The educated moderates again congratulated themselves for controlling the direction of the revolution.

Despite the constitutional limits on his position, Bani Sadr believed his electoral margin gave him the authority to govern. He pledged to eliminate the revolutionary bodies. Khomeini swore in the new president two months before the first parliament was elected; he also gave Bani Sadr other duties such as commander in chief of the armed forces and head of the Revolutionary Committee. The Ayatollah seemed to realize that authority was escaping his control and he needed to get it back. He soon found the perfect opportunity.

THE HOSTAGE CRISIS

After twenty-five years there is still no hard evidence that Ayatollah Khomeini or members of the government instructed radical students to seize the U.S. Embassy or knew about it in advance. It really doesn't matter, as once the students seized the embassy, Khomeini embraced the hostage taking and made it a cornerstone of his policy. Now he would dump Bazargan and break all ties with Washington.

The embassy had been taken before. Three days after the monarchy had been abolished students overran the embassy, taking the ambassador and other diplomats hostage. On that occasion Khomeini sent representatives to convince the students to let the diplomats go. So ingrained was the belief that the embassy was a "nest of spies" planning a counterrevolution that the students never left the embassy compound. For the next nine months American diplomats had to enter their own embassy through checkpoints manned by armed revolutionaries.

The revolutionaries believed that the Americans would repeat their 1953 covert action that had brought the Shah back. They feared any American contacts with the Shah. In fact, such contacts were not going well. Tehran had warned Washington that there would be serious problems if the Shah or his family were admitted to the United States, and President Carter feared for the safety of Americans still in Iran. As a result, the contacts usually consisted of the Shah's people reminding the Americans that he was an invited guest and the Americans responding that this was not the right time.

Only in October 1979 did the Shah tell Washington that he had been battling cancer for five years and needed treatment in the United States. President Carter felt he could not deny medical treatment to an old U.S. ally. The Shah flew to New York for medical treatment. Many knew it was only a matter of time before the embassy was seized again.

On November 1, 1979, demonstrators massed around the embassy to protest America's support for the Shah. Iranian police protected the compound and brought the protest under control. The diplomats inside breathed a sigh of relief, believing the worst was over. On November 4, "students" who followed a revolutionary cleric, Hojjatollah Islam Mohammed Musavi-Khoeniha, attacked the embassy again, and the police let them in. It appears that the students did not plan to take the diplomats hostage or hold the embassy for long. They saw their actions as preventing the United States from overthrowing the revolution and as an expression of anger at America admitting the Shah. They did not attempt an Islamic justification, as the Muslim tradition since the time of the Prophet was to protect the emissaries of foreign lands to the House of Islam. Basically, they poured out all their hatred of the Shah on the country that had helped him for decades.

Once the press swarmed around the embassy, the militants realized they had a good thing. They found documents describing contacts between the embassy and moderate Iranian officials. This gave them power to denounce their political opponents as spies. Ayatollah Khomeini embraced the militants as "Children of the Revolution" and the hostage crisis was on.

The crisis caused the downfall of two governments. Unable to convince the militants to honor international law and release the Americans, after two days the Bazargan government resigned. For 444 days America watched nightly as the militants humbled its self-image and reputation. In the end it cost Jimmy Carter reelection. The militants did not, however, kill their hostages.

THE FAILED HOSTAGE RESCUE

The Shah completed his treatment and returned to Mexico in December 1979. The Americans asked for the hostages' release since the original reason for the seizure no longer existed: The Shah was not in the United States. The militants replied the crisis would continue until the United States delivered the Shah and his rumored wealth to Iran. Even when the Shah died in 1980 in Cairo, the hostage crisis continued. The militants added demands for apologies and for refunds on loan payments. Clearly diplomacy was not the answer.

Carter felt paralyzed. In April 1980 he ordered a daring hostage rescue effort of the kind that works in movies. The secretive Delta team was to helicopter into the middle of Iran and snatch the hostages. One thing after another went wrong. A helicopter rotor ripped a cargo plane, killing eight, and the mission was aborted. Some feared that if Delta had actually got into Tehran, the hostages would have been killed. The militants claimed that God himself had intervened to stop the American invasion and protect His Islamic Republic.

Secretary of State Cyrus Vance was kept out of planning the operation because he never would have approved. When he learned of it, he told Carter he would stay in office until the April 24 rescue operation but would resign immediately afterward. He was replaced by Senator Edmund Muskie. Now Carter was politically wounded and was voted out of office in November 1980. The conservative former governor of California and movie star Ronald Reagan won and was not shy about using military force. Khomeini saw the hostages no longer did him any good and released them precisely as Reagan was being inaugurated. Iran broke every rule in the diplomatic book and suffered when Iraq invaded later in 1980, for now it had no powerful friends or protectors.

BANI SADR: THE LAST OF THE LIBERALS

President Abol Hassan Bani Sadr was the last of the secular moderates in office. When the Bazargan cabinet resigned over the hostage crisis, Bani Sadr's status was not affected. He was protected because he had worked with Khomeini in Paris, and Khomeini had personal affection for him. Bani Sadr, however, was determined to reassert his authority over that of the revolutionary institutions and ran afoul of the IRP and its clerical supporters. He tried to resolve the hostage crisis because it hurt Iranian diplomacy, but this cost him Khomeini's backing.

The parliament controlled by the IRP thwarted his every move. Cabinet nominees were rejected and policy proposals turned down. After the Iraqi invasion, he retreated into his role as commander in chief, which gave him a platform to attack his critics. He criticized revolutionary figures for corruption, torture, misuse of power, and violating the constitution. These liberal positions won Bani Sadr the support of the Mujahidin-e Khalq, a strange Islamic-Marxist cult that had served the revolution but was being pushed out. In June 1981, parliament impeached Bani Sadr by a vote of 177 to 1 with 13 abstentions. Bani Sadr and the head of the Mujahidin, Masoud Rajavi, fled for their lives to Paris. The last of the liberal secularists had left the Iranian political scene.

Days later the Mujahidin bombed the headquarters of the IRP. Two months later they destroyed the prime minister's offices, killing the president, prime minister, head of the National Police, and others. This was the closest the Mujahidin ever came to power. In the resulting crackdown, the Mujahidin and the Tudeh were crushed or fled into Iraq. Iran had essentially no more domestic opposition.

The Iran-Iraq War

The Islamic Revolution declared that it was not just against the Shah but was world-wide, against "global arrogance," "corruption on earth," "world-devouring imperialism," all meaning the United States. For several years they encouraged Shi'a communities to overthrow their "illegitimate" rulers. Shi'a opposition groups in southern Iraq, Bahrain, Kuwait, and Lebanon were supported by Iran, as were many fundamentalist Sunni groups, especially Palestinian.

Saddam Hussein was enraged at the Iranians telling his subjects to revolt. He also had some old scores to settle with Iran: the thousand-year Arab-Iranian conflict, Iranian support for Iraqi Kurdish groups, and the Shatt al-Arab border, which was forced on him. Saddam was also greedy; the southwest of Iran is inhabited by ethnic Arabs and has much oil. Saddam believed that the Iranian military had been destroyed by the revolution, leaving "Arabistan" (*Khuzestan* in Persian) easy pickings.

Iraq attacked September 22, 1980, and advanced rapidly. Iran's clergy unleashed their ideology and promised hundreds of thousands of youths eternal paradise for defending Islam. Untrained and unarmed, they charged Iraqi lines in waves. Bearing plastic keys symbolizing admission to heaven, they rushed willingly into mine fields. The clerics emptied Iranian jails of the Shah's military commanders, promising them freedom for their military service. Losses were staggering. By May of 1982 the Iranians had repelled the Iraqi invasion, but Khomeini ordered the army to invade Iraq. He said he would settle for nothing less than the overthrow of Saddam Hussein.

By mid-1983 Iran had made some inroads. Iraq retaliated by launching a "war of the cities" in which Saddam lobbed SCUD missiles at Tehran. By 1987 the Iranians besieged Basra. In the north, Iran encouraged the Barzani Kurds to rebel. Saddam responded with the al-Anfal campaign: genocide of Kurds by poison gas (see Chapter 9).

The American Tilt

No one in Washington liked Saddam, but believing the old Arab dictum that "the enemy of my enemy is my friend," America tilted toward Iraq in the hope of stopping Iran, a dangerous revolutionary power that had held our diplomats hostage. We let rage dominate instead of clear thinking. In 1982 the United States removed Iraq from the list of state sponsors of terrorism despite the fact that Saddam sheltered Abu Abbas and numerous other Palestinian terrorists. We lent Iraq money and shared intelligence. In 1984 Washington restored diplomatic relations with Baghdad, a move we later regretted. Soon there were American diplomats and advisors in Baghdad. Some American officials were proud that we were weaning Iraq away from its dependency on the Soviet Union.

🎵 *The United States in the Middle East*

THE IRAN-CONTRA FIASCO

The Reagan White House, hoping to get U.S. hostages back from Hezbullah in Lebanon and improve relations with Iran, offered Iran some obsolescent U.S. missiles. Using Iranians and Israelis as middlemen, they sold some Hawk missiles and other arms to Iran. The money would then secretly fund the Nicaraguan *contras*, who were supposed to be fighting communism. Congress, suspicious of the contras' inactivity, had ended U.S. funding. By law, all funds taken in by the Federal government must go to the Treasury, and none can be expended without Congressional appropriation. Anything else is an illegal "slush fund." Iran-Contra broke several laws. Although Reagan did not plan the operation, he approved of it retroactively in a Presidential Finding in January 1986.

It was a hare-brained scheme that career professionals would have warned them against. Instead, the White House used dubious middlemen who claimed to have connections in Tehran but could not pass a lie-detector test. The operation was run by the National Security Council, which is not supposed to run any operations. Marine Lt. Col. Oliver North, enthusiastic but naive, was in charge. By the time the middlemen skimmed off their percentages, the contras got little.

Much worse, in October 1986 Iranian officials who were opposed to cooperation with America leaked news of the deal to a Lebanese newspaper. The White House was embarrassed; it had broken its own law against trading with the enemy. If the United States could do it, why not the French or Japanese? One U.S. gift brought with the U.S. arms: a bible with an inscription from the president. Apparently no area expert explained to the NSC that Muslim fanatics do not much care for Christian bibles. Another American president looked foolish because he had tried to improve relations with Iran.

The Lebanon hostages were finally released when neither Hezbullah nor Iran got any further benefit from holding them. The last, AP newsman Terry Anderson, was released in December 1991 after six and a half years. Beware of dealing with Iran.

U.S. NAVAL INVOLVEMENT

Gulf Arab states, especially Kuwait and Saudi Arabia, gave Iraq generous loans, making them belligerents in Iran's eyes. Iran fired missiles at Kuwait City and hunted Kuwaiti oil tankers, many of them carrying Iraqi crude. Actually, Iraq had been attacking ships calling on Iranian ports for months. In early 1987 Kuwait sought international protection for its shipping fleet and Washington let them fly the stars and stripes. Soon the U.S. Navy protected the "American" ships by escorting them in armed convoys from the Gulf of Oman outside the Strait of Hormuz and then across the Gulf. Mines—some of them 1908 models sold to Iran by tsarist Russia—were the biggest worry. They were simple, cheap, and effective, and the U.S. Navy, intent on high-tech, had little mine-sweeping capability.

The United States in the Middle East

THE DOWNING OF IRAN AIR 655

On May 17, 1987, an Iraqi jet fired a French-made Exocet missile into the USS *Stark* in the Gulf, killing thirty-seven American sailors. Baghdad claimed it was a mistake and the Reagan administration quietly accepted Iraq's apology, although many questioned if the attack was truly an accident. Slowly the United States was drawn into a naval war in the Gulf. One cannot be a little bit involved in the Gulf any more than one can be a little bit pregnant.

Increasingly U.S. and Iranian gunboats shot at each other. We were in a low-level but escalating war with each other. After an Iranian missile hit a reflagged Kuwaiti tanker, Navy SEALs blew up an Iranian oil platform in the Gulf that was rumored to be a launching point for raids.

On July 3, 1988, a scheduled civilian Iranian jetliner was flying across the Gulf over a U.S. destroyer, which thought it was another attack like the *Stark*. Misreading all signals that showed Iran Air 655 looked nothing like a warplane, panicked crewmen on the USS *Vincennes* shot it down with a missile, killing all 290 aboard. In dangerous situations, your mind plays tricks with you. The United States apologized and offered compensation to the families. Many Iranians believed the shoot-down had been deliberate, a U.S. signal that the war would increasingly hurt Iran. It was not, but it may have persuaded Iran to end to war.

SADDAM TAKES THE OFFENSIVE

In 1986 Iraq turned to chemical weapons. With Iranian troops threatening Basra, Iraq's second-largest city, Saddam ordered gas to push the Iranians back. The United States said nothing. Iran may also have used some chemical weapons, but not as many. Thus Washington acquiesced to the introduction of **weapons of mass destruction** (WMD) in the Gulf and in the world. In 2003 we went to war with Iraq over alleged WMD.

Finally, during four months in 1988 Iraq won four major battles. Their chemical weapons unnerved the Iranians who fled en masse. Ayatollah Khomeini finally recognized that his dream of overthrowing Saddam would destroy his revolution, so he accepted a UN cease-fire resolution, stating he would rather drink poison. Khomeini never spoke in public again and died in June 1989 at age 89.

The Iran-Iraq War ended August 20, 1988, after almost eight years. Conservatively, about 233,000 died; ideological estimates range as high as a million, two-thirds of them Iranians. A huge Tehran cemetery, with a blood-red fountain, commemorates the fallen, many of them teenagers. The war ended with the troops at nearly the original border. A horrible war had ended in the **status quo ante bellum**.

---

weapons of mass destruction   The NBC weapons—nuclear, bacteriological, chemical, or "nukes, bugs, gas."
status quo ante bellum   Latin for the "situation before the war."

CONSTITUTIONAL CRISIS

In January 1988, with the war sill on, Ayatollah Khomeini reversed fourteen hundred years of Shi'a jurisprudence with a statement that the Velayat-e Faqih was so important that its protection was a higher duty than any other. Since the Velayat-e Faqih ruled over a true Islamic State, and everything such a state did was correct, then the Islamic state could overrule any aspect of Islamic law that stood in its way. Only Khomeini had the power to make such an un-Islamic statement.

Khomeini used his new power in February 1988 to create the Expediency Council. The Islamic Republic had long been paralyzed; the conservative Council of Guardians vetoed laws from the more liberal parliament as contrary to Shari'a. Khomeini declared that an Expediency Council would resolve disagreements between the two bodies.

Khomeini's death the following year put the country into a constitutional crisis. The constitution said that the Supreme Leader had to be a preeminent theologian; if no one individual possessed all the qualities for leadership then the position should be held by a council. No single theologian was found acceptable in 1989. President Ali Khamenei was considered an Ayatollah but the Qom Theological Seminary had never approved his dissertation. The regime found a hundred-year-old cleric in Qom, Ayatollah Araki. The Council of Experts declared that Araki was the country's new *marja'*, "source of emulation," whom Iranians were to obey. Araki said to continue to follow the teachings of Khomeini and accept Ali Khamenei as the Supreme Leader.

Khamenei took Khomeini's old position but lacked Khomeini's status. The Speaker of the parliament, Ali Akbar Hashemi Rafsanjani, was elected the new president. Over the next eight years Iran underwent an ideological battle largely ignored in the West. Many prominent lay thinkers and clerics began to second-guess the revolutionary leadership; in their opinions the ruling clerics had usurped the rights of the people. They did not challenge the Islamic Republic but claimed they wanted to put the revolution back on the right course. This group's leader, Ayatollah Husayn Ali Montazeri, once Khomenei's likely successor, was stripped of his position and placed under house arrest for expressing doubts. These relative liberals supported the 1997 election of Muhammad Khatami as president.

THE RAFSANJANI YEARS

For many years Hashemi Rafsanjani was considered the most powerful man in Iran. A pragmatist and deal maker, he got cooperation among competing factions when he was Speaker of parliament. He was in the middle of the Iran-Contra dealings with America but kept on good terms with conservatives. In 1989 he was elected president. His economic policies were a disaster. Khomeini had come out of the war without having borrowed a single penny from any foreign power; Rafsanjani now sought to buy some popularity and stimulate the economy through deficit spending. The country went on a consumer spending binge that led to inflation and big international debts. Rafsanjani also presided over the so-lidification of conservatives in power. In his second term parliamentary elections returned a conservative majority, although party identification is not permitted. After the presidency Rafsanjani became head of the Expediency Council. Unpopular, in 2000 he placed thirtieth out of thirty seats from Tehran in the parliament. Rafsanjani refused the seat and stayed in the Expediency Council.

THE URGE TO REFORM

Muhammad Khatami was elected by mistake; had the Council of Guardians known that they were getting a relative liberal—by Iranian standards—they would never have allowed him to run. They have the power to bar candidates who are not sufficiently Islamic and used this to keep anyone out of the political scene who did not support a hard line. In 1992 the Council unseated forty-five incumbent members of parliament, including government ministers, for insufficient revolutionary fervor.

In 1997 the hard-liners' man was Ali Akbar Nateq-Nuri. The system was fixed to guarantee Nateq-Nuri victory. To maintain a facade of legitimacy and to split any opposition vote, the Guardian Council approved three other candidates to also appear on the ballot. Two of them had close ties to the hard-liners. The third was a weakling cleric, a former minister of culture who left to run the National Library: Muhammad Khatami. The hard-liners did not care for Khatami's moderate politics, but he had revolutionary credentials, was a family friend of Supreme Leader Khamenei, and was a direct descendent of the Prophet, entitled to wear a black turban.

Tapping a growing desire for reform, Khatami came from out of nowhere to become the leading candidate. He never was a liberal; "cautious reformer" is more accurate. The regime's bully boys, the Ansar-e Hizballah, tried to halt the Khatami express. These groups of youths—misrepresented as students or as spontaneous defenders of the revolution—traveled in government buses to harass pro-Khatami rallies. Pro-Khatami newspapers were shut down and Khatami campaign offices closed. Khatami was even denied permission to campaign in some cities. Khatami followers tried to work as poll watchers but were blocked by the police. It all made Khatami more popular.

Iranians flocked to the polls, believing they had been offered a choice for the first time since the revolution. Khatami won two-thirds of the votes. Two years later, 70 percent voted for Khatami allies in parliament. It looked like the beginning of moderation and reform. In 2001 Khatami was reelected with 70 percent.

REFORMISTS BLOCKED

Khatami should have known that he could not get even mild reforms. Ever since the attempts of Bani Sadr, it was obvious that the president had no real power. Hard-liners controlled the judiciary and the key ministries, and had the Supreme

The United States in the Middle East

U.S.-Iranian Signals

Consider the positive signals Washington and Tehran have given each other: In 1990–1991 Iran remained neutral in the first Gulf War and even kept many Iraqi aircraft sent to Iran for safekeeping. Iran could have made some mischief but did not.

In 1998 President Khatami told an American television reporter that he supported cultural exchanges, and Secretary of State Madeline Albright invited the Iranians to seek normal relations.

In 1999 the United States eased sanctions on Iran. Now American companies would be able to sell food and medical items to Iran. In 2000 Washington allowed importation of Iranian caviar, pistachios, and carpets, albeit with high tariffs. In May 2000 the World Bank approved its first loan to Iran in seven years. The United States did not veto it.

In September 2001 the Iranian people held candlelight vigils in sympathy for 9/11. In October, when the United States began its retaliation against Afghanistan, Iran said it would help U.S. pilots who came down in Iran. President Khatami condemned Osama bin Ladin and the 9/11 murders. Iran stayed neutral while the United States drove the Taliban from power. (To be sure, Iran had always disliked the Sunni Taliban, who persecuted Afghan Shi'a.)

In 2001 at the UN General Assembly the Iranian foreign minister and U.S. secretary of state met and shook hands, a symbolic step.

In 2002 U.S. Senator Joseph Biden (D-Delaware) proposed the Senate Foreign Relations Committee meet with Iranian parliamentarians. Tehran did not oppose it.

In 2003 Iran remained neutral in the second Gulf War. President Khatami called for renewed ties with the United States.

But positive signals have always been offset with negative ones: Iran was neutral in the 1991 and 2003 Gulf Wars but condemned U.S. attacks on a Muslim country and wants American forces out of the region. In 1993 newly elected U.S. President Clinton announced a policy of "dual containment" of both Iran and Iraq. In 1995 he signed an executive order banning trade with Iran.

Leader on their side. Khatami's initial election brought a brief flurry of political and press freedoms. Numerous intellectuals took advantage of the opening to begin newspapers and magazines attacking the regime from different angles. Some published details of the 1998 murders of political dissidents by the intelligence ministry, probably with the approval of the highest levels of government. The Supreme Leader dismissed the minister of intelligence and declared the killings were a rogue operation. Khamenei ordered the arrest and trial of the lead perpetrator, who allegedly committed suicide in jail, but there was no way to confirm it.

Soon the judiciary closed all the newspapers and imprisoned editors and writers. President Khatami could not stop the imprisonment of his closest political ally, the mayor of Tehran, Gholam Hossein Karbaschi. People hoped that parliament would support the new president, but when it formed a committee to investigate abuses in government, Supreme Leader Khamenei declared the targeted offices were direct extensions of his own and outside the purview of parliament. Khatami, whatever reformist intentions he may have had, was blocked at every turn.

In June 1996 Saudi Hizballah truck-bombed Khobar Towers, an American barracks in Saudi Arabia, killing nineteen U.S. soldiers. Iran was suspected immediately, and in June 2001 a federal grand jury confirmed the bombers had Iranian support.

In August 1996 Congress passed the Iran-Libya Sanctions Act, punishing any company doing business with the terrorist countries. Europeans denounced and ignored the U.S. law. Net impact: Europeans and Japanese make money trading with Iran while U.S. firms are frozen out.

In March 2000 Iranian hard-liners heard a speech by Secretary Albright as an admission of U.S. guilt but demanded a formal U.S. apology.

In October 2001 Supreme Leader Ali Khamenei condemned U.S. air strikes on Afghanistan as part of America's plan to dominate the Middle East. After the Taliban's fall, Iran began to support groups opposed to the U.S.-backed Afghan interim government.

The same month Iran resumed purchase of Russian arms. Russia had ceased the sales during the Yeltsin era because of American pressure.

In January 2002 President George W. Bush (forty-third president; his father is George H. Bush, forty-first president) in his first State of the Union Address condemned Iran as one of the Axis of Evil. This shocked Iranians, especially reformers, who had hoped to improve relations.

In January 2002 Israel captured the *Karine A* carrying fifty tons of weapons from Iran's Revolutionary Guard to the Palestinian Authority.

In May 2002 and in May 2003 Supreme Leader Ali Khamenei condemned suggestions that Iran renew negotiations with the United States.

In May 2003 Washington accused Iran of harboring al Qaeda militants who planted bombs in Saudi Arabia. American accusations that Iran is building nuclear weapons have increased over the years. In sum, hints of improvement have not changed the underlying hostilities of hard-liners on both sides.

Khatami drew much of his support from young Iranians. Voting age is sixteen. After a spurt of births (now curbed), over half of Iranians are under twenty-five. Most Iranians today have little or no memory of the Shah, the Islamic Revolution, or the battles of the older generation. Now they are fed up with Islamic fanatics telling them how to run every aspect of their life. They like democracy and the United States. Iranians showed a mass outpouring of spontaneous sympathy for America after 9/11. They are Muslim but want the mullahs in mosques, not in government. Increasingly, mullahs agree. Mullahs who run Muslim economic foundations called *bunyads* have become corrupt and rich. Anything can touch off a student protest, for example, the closing of newspapers or arrest of critics. The regime immediately attacks with toughs who beat them and police who arrest them, often on campus. This does nothing to quiet discontent, which may someday boil over into revolt.

In his second term, Khatami was a defeated man. Iranians despaired that he or anyone else could give them freer, happier lives. The ballot having done them no good, they stopped voting as an act of protest, and turnout plunged. Half in jest, some urged the United States to liberate Iran. With all their efforts at reform blocked, some parliamentarians threatened mass walkouts, and Khatami threatened to resign the presidency. Either would severely damage the already shaky **legitimacy** of the political system. Many believe another revolution is close in Iran.

U.S.-IRANIAN RELATIONS

Americans and Iranians talk about reestablishing diplomatic relations, but Tehran's hard-liners denounce any contact with the "Great Satan," meaning us. President Khatami hinted at a dialogue with the American people (not with the government), but nothing came of it. When one of the countries signals an interest, the other spurns it. This then proves to hard-liners in the first country that the other side is incurably hostile.

CONCLUSIONS

In 1978 Iran was America's closest ally in the Middle East; a year later Iran was America's greatest enemy. A group of clerics and secular liberals overthrew the monarchy, but the Islamists outsmarted the secularists and established an Islamic Republic under the charismatic rule of Ayatollah Khomeini. Since Khomeini's death, most Iranians want freedom and democracy, but they are constantly blocked by an Islamist elite, which holds effective power even if reformists are elected to high office. The United States and Iran appear no closer to renewing relations.

FURTHER REFERENCE

Abdo, Geneive, and Jonathan Lyons. *Answering only to God: Faith and Freedom in Twenty-First Century Iran*. New York: Henry Holt, 2003.

Al-Suwaidi, Jamal S. *Iran and the Gulf: A Search for Stability*. London: I. B. Tauris, 2002.

Bakhash, Shaul. *The Reign of the Ayatollahs: Iran and the Islamic Revolution*. New York: Basic Books 1984.

Bill, James A. *The Eagle and the Lion: The Tragedy of American-Iranian Relations*. New Haven: Yale University Press 1988.

Ganji, Manouchehr. *Defying the Iranian Revolution: From a Minister to the Shah to a Leader of Resistance*. Westport, CT: Praeger, 2002.

---

legitimacy   Feeling among people that the regime's rule is rightful.

Hoveyda, Fereydoun. *The Shah and the Ayatollah: Iranian Mythology and Islamic Revolution*. Westport, CT: Praeger, 2003.

Keddie, Nikki R., and Eric Hooglund, eds. *The Iranian Revolution and the Islamic Republic*. Syracuse, NY: Syracuse University Press 1986.

Sick, Gary. *All Fall Down: America's Tragic Encounter with Iran*. Harrisonburg, VA: Penguin Press 1987.

14

The First Gulf War

Points to Ponder

- Can Americans and Middle Easterners understand each other?
- Is there any validity to Iraq's claims to Kuwait?
- Why did the United States stop the 1991 war unfinished?
- Was Saddam deterred in 1991?
- Should the United States have finished off Saddam in 1991?
- How effective were UN resolutions in curbing Iraq?
- Did U.S. intervention in the Gulf bring democracy to any Gulf state?

With the long Iran-Iraq War over the United States maintained its watch on the threat of Iranian-sponsored Islamic fundamentalism. Some in Washington hoped that Iran and Iraq would be so busy watching each other they would not bother anyone else, but Saddam Hussein had other ideas. For the Arab Gulf states, Iraq had been their "Defender Against Persian Aggression," and they had loaned him vast sums. Now the oil shaykhdoms wanted to get back to making money and began to pump oil to pay for the last war. Both Kuwait and Iraq exceeded their OPEC quotas, driving down oil prices. Arab potentates also demanded that Saddam begin to repay his war loans.

Willie Sutton once said he robbed banks because that's where the money is. Saddam eyed his neighbor Kuwait for the same reason. Iraq had some unclear historical claims to Kuwait, but the stronger draw was the multibillion dollar Kuwait Development Fund. With considerable forethought, the rulers of Kuwait had planned for the day the country no longer had oil and had been depositing a portion of the oil revenues into the fund for future generations. Just as American corporations eye a company with liquid assets for takeover, Saddam eyed Kuwait for takeover.

He prepared the way with a series of excuses. First, he demanded that the Arabs forgive his war debt, which Iraq had paid with the blood of its soldiers. Next, he accused Kuwait of cheating on its OPEC quota, pretending Iraq had not. Kuwait naturally denied the charges and continued to produce as before. Finally, Saddam accused Kuwait of stealing Iraqi oil by "slant drilling" in the Rumaila oilfield, which is split by their boundary. He said that oil wells on Kuwait's side of the border were drilling diagonally and taking the oil from Iraqi soil. In 1990 he threatened military action if Kuwait did not cease its activities and reasserted Iraq's old claims that Kuwait was a province of Iraq. He began massing Iraqi army troops along the Kuwaiti border.

THE WEAK AMERICAN RESPONSE

The United States was never close to Saddam even during the war when they cooperated against Iran. Saddam distrusted every offer of help from the Americans, convinced it was a Trojan horse that would lead to his destruction. Similarly, Americans could not warm to a merciless dictator who made his way to the top by murdering political opponents. They could work with such a man, but he never got an invitation to the White House. Mistrust breeds miscommunication, and that leads to misunderstanding.

When the first Bush administration took office in January 1989, policymakers realized that Iraq had emerged from the recent war as the most powerful country in the Persian Gulf region. They sought a working relationship with Saddam through "constructive engagement," a policy that mixes cooperation with suggestions for change that Washington also used with the Soviet Union and South Africa. By the end of the year the administration concluded the policy was not working—Saddam would not budge—and Washington discussed how to reverse course and reduce contacts with Iraq.

By July 1990 U.S. intelligence had noticed the Iraqi troop movements. Washington was split as to whether this was merely a bargaining tactic with the Kuwaitis or if it was a military exercise. They checked with their Middle East allies: Egyptian President Hosni Mubarak, Turkish President Turgut Özal, Saudi ambassador to Washington Prince Bandar, and many other regional leaders. They were unanimous that the troops were a part of Saddam's bargaining strategy. No one believed Saddam was preparing to invade. After all, it was the end of the twentieth century, and countries just didn't invade one another anymore, right?

On July 25, 1990, U.S. Ambassador April Glaspie met with Saddam personally. Ambassador Glaspie was a career foreign service officer, fluent in Arabic and schooled in diplomatic compromise and making harsh messages palatable to the recipients. Like the State Department as a whole, she thought Saddam was angling for a better oil-drilling arrangement with Kuwait and did not comprehend that he intended to seize Kuwait. She told Saddam that U.S. interests in the region were important, and we would not stand by if Saddam threatened those interests. Unfortunately, Saddam heard only her mild wording that Iraq and Kuwait should negotiate their differences. Then she left on vacation.

The United States in the Middle East

CENTCOM

When the first Gulf War crisis began, CENTCOM was a paper tiger headquartered in Tampa, Florida—thousands of miles from its operational area. At that time CENTCOM was only a command and planning unit and had not a single combat soldier assigned to it. Contingency plans called for CENTCOM to borrow combat units from other theaters of operation. CENTCOM's commander, General Norman Schwarzkopf, was a blustery old warrior who had been given a preretirement job in Florida. He was renowned for a fierce temper. Few liked working for him because of his mercurial personality.

In 1980 President Jimmy Carter created the Rapid Deployment Joint Task Force in response to the Iran hostage crisis. The Pentagon signed a basing agreement with the Sultanate of Oman and the local headquarters for the task force was established there. At the beginning of 1983, with the Soviet occupation of nearby Afghanistan and the continuing Iran-Iraq war, President Ronald Reagan replaced the task force with the more permanent CENTCOM. The command had to be situated in Florida because none of the Gulf countries were willing to allow their territory to be used as an American military base. It was—and still is—a peculiar situation where we were trying to defend countries that did not wish to be defended.

Saddam should have reversed his mobilization, but he did not take the American warning seriously. The United States had never before deployed troops in the Middle East in sufficient number to stop his invasion, and no major U.S. forces were in the Gulf now anyway. A credible deterrence would have required many U.S. troops and ships in the Gulf. Otherwise a warning sounds like a bluff. In addition, Kuwait was not a close U.S. ally. It had always been stubbornly independent and hosted the largest Soviet legation in the area. Kuwaiti princes frequently opposed U.S. policies and were highly critical of the Saudis for being so close to the Americans. It was not credible that the United States would put its forces in harm's way to protect one of its loudest critics.

The other explanation is that Saddam believed he had U.S. approval to invade Kuwait. When Saddam tried to engage Ambassador Glaspie with his complaints about Kuwaiti violation of Iraqi borders with slant drilling, Glaspie replied that the United States had no opinion on inter-Arab conflicts such as Iraq's border disagreement with Kuwait. This was completely in accord with the State Department's position. In Washington spokeswoman Margaret Tutweiller told the press that the United States had no defense treaty or security commitment to Kuwait. Diplomatically, Tutweiller and Glaspie gave the correct answer, that the United States did not want to be the hegemonic power in the Gulf and would rely on Iraq and Kuwait to negotiate between themselves without U.S. supervision.

Cultures

A Woman Ambassador to an Arab State?

The U.S. ambassador to Baghdad in 1990, April Glaspie, was bright, tough, and an expert on the Middle East. But Arab culture does not accord women equality. Men do the work of the world; women stay home and raise children. Out of politeness, many Arab states agree to a woman ambassador from America, but do they respect her? A special problem comes with a cold-blooded murderer like Saddam Hussein. Could any woman ambassador deliver a tough warning that he would understand?

The American answer has been that diplomats and soldiers overseas are images of America, which gradually and with much struggle has moved toward racial and gender equality. We must show the world a true picture of America, not an America of white male supremacy. Such a picture also encourages gender equality in the host country. Female U.S. soldiers in Saudi Arabia in 1990–1991—driving vehicles, working with men, even giving orders—were noticed by Saudi women, some of whom broke the law and started driving. Saudi authorities soon put a stop to that. If a host country tells us they do not want our women soldiers or diplomats, should we give in to them?

This is not a simple problem. American and Arab cultures are very different. Should we stay sensitive to Arab culture and send no women, or should we stay true to what America stands for? Would Saddam have listened more carefully in 1990 if an American male ambassador had delivered a warning? How about someone like tough, barrel-chested Deputy Secretary of State Richard Armitage, a former Navy officer and high Pentagon official? Different jobs require different types of people.

Saddam heard a different message because he was asking a question the American diplomats had not heard: Do you really care if I take Kuwait? Saddam came away from the meeting understanding that the United States would really not care. Glaspie returned to the embassy convinced that she had defused an international crisis, and she cabled Washington that tensions would now be reduced.

To be on the safe side, the United States offered to send fighter planes to the Gulf to show Saddam that American allies also were capable of marshalling forces. Unfortunately, none of the Arab countries except the United Arab Emirates (UAE) would accept an American military presence. The root of the problem was that there was no U.S. military presence in the Gulf to deter Saddam because the Arab governments of the region refused to invite the Americans in. No credible forces, no deterrence.

By July 28, the Pentagon changed its mind when it realized that there were too many Iraqi troops for a bluff, and they did not seem to be exercising. To make matters worse, Iraqi armored carriers and missile launchers were being taken out of storage and sent to the front line. Chairman of the U.S. Joint Chiefs of Staff Gen. Colin Powell contacted Gen. Norman Schwarzkopf at U.S. Central Command (CENTCOM) and told him to make contingency plans for the defense of Kuwait.

THE INVASION OF KUWAIT

Saddam concentrated 100,000 troops on the Kuwaiti border and on August 2, 1990, ordered them to seize Kuwait. Within hours they had taken Kuwait City and were approaching the border of Saudi Arabia. Saddam announced that his occupation of Kuwait was temporary and that he would soon withdraw. It was only later in the crisis that he announced that Kuwait had returned to the Iraqi motherland forever.

Washington was worried on a variety of fronts, but the most serious concern was for the free world's supply of petroleum. Since World War II, every American president had acknowledged that unfettered access to Gulf oil was an important U.S. interest. Saddam had owned 20 percent of the world's known oil reserves before the invasion; now he had Kuwait's reserves. He also had shown that he could militarily crush any Arab country that opposed him. OPEC would now be nothing more than an extension of Iraq's foreign ministry.

There were other American concerns. A primary one was the concept that an aggressor should not invade a neighboring country and grab its natural resources. President Bush (senior) thought of Munich in 1938 and how appeasement of Hitler had led to World War II in 1939. Arabs in the region pointed to Israel's occupation of the West Bank. Why, they asked, did the United States not support nonaggression in the case of Israel?

The Saudis were equally concerned but from a different perspective. The king and his council feared that Saddam would not be content with his seizure of Kuwait and might order his troops to invade Saudi Arabia. The Kingdom's oil fields, after all, were not that far from Kuwait's.

Not wanting to create a panic, President Bush (senior) maintained his normal schedule and flew to Aspen, Colorado, to give a speech with British Prime Minister Margaret Thatcher while Washington worked on the problem. A first step was to go to the United Nations and obtain support from the international community for any actions they would take. The UN condemned the aggression and ordered an embargo on Iraqi oil. Turkey cut its pipeline and the American navy blockaded the Gulf. Saddam was cut off from his buyers except through Jordan, where the 60 percent of the population of Palestinian origin considered Saddam a hero for defying the West. The anger of the street allowed Jordan's King Hussein no choice except to align his small kingdom with Iraq.

Bush and Thatcher discussed options in Aspen. Some reports say the Iron Lady persuaded the president to oppose the Iraqi invasion, but more likely she merely reinforced decisions Bush had already tentatively made. When he returned from Aspen, Bush told the press that he would not allow the invasion to stand.

General Powell met with the Saudi ambassador, Prince Bandar, in Secretary of Defense Dick Cheney's office to request Saudi permission to base American troops there. Bandar said the Kingdom would welcome the intervention but only if they could count on America staying the course. After America's withdrawal from Vietnam and Lebanon, the Saudis did not want to align against their powerful northern neighbor and then be left stranded. The American team outlined their plan to place 100,000 soldiers in the Kingdom, and Bandar saw it was a commitment that

The United States in the Middle East

WOBBLY GEORGE

Saddam Hussein decided early on to test whether UN sanctions meant anything. On August 26, 1990, an Iraqi tanker approached U.S. Navy ships in the Gulf. To determine if the tanker was carrying oil, the Americans would have to stop it and board it for inspection. If the Iraqis put up resistance a shooting war would have commenced on the spot. The Bush team wavered and recommended the American cordon pull back to give diplomacy time to work. Maybe one of our Arab allies could convince Saddam to turn the ship around. Or maybe we would determine that the ship had no oil. Or maybe we could follow the ship until after it left the Gulf because boarding there would be easier.

Bush spoke with Prime Minister Thatcher to get her consent to move the blockade. The Iron Lady of Downing Street told the president, "Look, George, this is no time to go wobbly. We'll do it this time, but we can't fall at the first fence." The allies stopped the ship, but the story, in amplified form, made Thatcher appear as the real spine in the alliance.

could not be easily reversed. After consulting with his uncle the king, Bandar said that if the Bush administration sent a delegation to Saudi Arabia the king would agree to America's planning. Cheney was immediately dispatched, and the next day King Fahd formally requested American assistance to defend his kingdom. Operation Desert Shield was born.

The Army flew the 82nd Airborne Division to the Kingdom, but it was just a trip wire, telling Saddam that if he invaded he would be fighting the American army. In reality, the 82nd was almost defenseless against Saddam's tanks, which would have run through the lightly armed Americans with ease. Under pressure of time, the U.S. Army had to ignore one of its rules: Never send light against heavy. This did give the Americans time to build up in the Gulf and ultimately reach a half million men and women with heavy weapons.

A number of people tried to mediate the crisis, including Soviet President Mikhail Gorbachev. At the same time, President Bush began building a coalition against Saddam. Before it was over, Arab countries such as Saudi Arabia, Egypt and even Syria would join the Americans against their fellow Arab ruler. Egyptian President Mubarak commented that the world that he had known and worked for all his life, that of Arab unity, had ended.

KUWAITI LOBBYING

The Kuwaiti government, now in exile but still in control of billions of dollars, moved to help the American public make up its mind to support the U.S. deployment. Under the deceptive title "Citizens for a Free Kuwait" Kuwaiti officials hired the blue-chip public relations firm Hill and Knowlton for $11 million. As part of

The United States in the Middle East

THE UNITED STATES AND UN RESOLUTIONS

The UN was on America's side in the first Gulf Crisis. The Security Council passed a number of resolutions condemning Iraq and detailing what the international community expected. When the First Gulf War finally broke out, Washington said it was acting in fulfillment of UN Resolutions, and the world community agreed. In the second Gulf War of 2003, Washington made the same claims—and none of the resolutions on Iraq had been revoked—but many European powers condemned U.S. actions. These are some of the UN Security Council resolutions dealing with Iraq:

August 2, 1990—SC660—Condemns invasion of Kuwait and demands Iraq withdraw.

August 6, 1990—SC661—Imposes economic sanctions on Iraq.

November 11, 1990—SC678—Gives Iraq until January 1991 to withdraw and authorizes "all necessary means" to implement SC660.

April 3, 1991—SC687—Calls for destruction of all chemical and biological weapons and all missiles with a range greater than 150 kilometers and creates **UNSCOM** to inspect for these weapons.

April 5, 1991—SC688—Condemns Iraq's repression of civilians.

August 15, 1991—SC707—Asks for unfettered UNSCOM and International Atomic Energy Agency (IAEA) inspections

October 11, 1991—SC715—Demands Iraq accepts UNSCOM and IAEA inspectors unconditionally.

October 15, 1994—SC949—Demands Iraq cooperate fully with UNSCOM and withdraw troops it deployed to Kuwaiti border.

June 12, 1996—SC1060—Condemns Iraq's refusal to cooperate with UNSCOM inspectors.

June 21, 1997—SC1115—Condemns Iraq's menacing actions against UNSCOM helicopters.

November 12, 1997—SC1137—Condemns Iraq's violations of previous resolutions.

December 17, 1999—SC1284—Orders Iran to grant immediate and unconditional access to new **UNMOVIC** inspection teams (replacing UNSCOM).

November 13, 2002—SC1441—Declares Iraq "in material breach" of previous resolutions. This is the seventeenth time the Security Council (including permanent members Russia and France) had demanded that Iraq disarm. Saddam ignored all these resolutions.

the effort, the daughter of the Kuwaiti ambassador to Washington appeared before Congress, claiming to be a refugee who had personally observed Iraqi soldiers throwing babies onto hospital floors to steal their incubators. It was a fabrication, but Kuwait later justified its actions by stating that the big picture was correct. What was the problem with a little embellishment? Lying and wars are natural twins.

UNSCOM   UN Special Commission to inspect Iraq for WMD following the 1991 Gulf War.
UNMOVIC   UN Monitoring, Verification, and Inspection Commission, 1999–2003.

Kuwait need not have gone to such extremes. Saddam's actions were bad enough. He seized thousands of civilians in Kuwait and in Iraq and deployed them to strategic sites as human shields. He finally released the helpless noncombatants when he realized their presence would not stop the United States and his holding them was hurting rather than helping his international image.

FROM DESERT SHIELD TO DESERT STORM

By mid-October 1990, U.S. deployments to the Gulf had reached the level that the Pentagon had projected was needed to protect Saudi Arabia from attack. General Powell traveled to Riyadh to outline plans for an offensive against the Iraqi occupiers of Kuwait. Upon Powell's return, President Bush ordered the Pentagon to double the number of U.S. forces in Saudi Arabia. The White House had made its decision to remove the Iraqi army from Kuwait. They began negotiations at the UN, and the Security Council in November authorized "all means necessary" to remove Iraq from Kuwait.

There was only one problem: No one had asked Congress. While Secretary of State James Baker flew to Geneva in early January for a meeting with Iraqi Foreign Minister Tariq Aziz, Bush realized he could not order troops into combat without congressional approval. Bush did not seek a declaration of war, and Congress, which was split on the issue, would likely not have passed it. On January 12, 1991, the Congress narrowly gave the President the authorization he was looking for—a joint resolution authorizing the president to use U.S. combat troops to eject the Iraqis from Kuwait.

The UN imposed deadline of January 15 came and went as world tension climbed. On January 17, 1991, U.S. jets began attacks on Iraq. Bombs and cruise missiles rained on Baghdad and other high-value targets for more than a month. Saddam responded with SCUD missile attacks on Americans in Saudi Arabia and on nonbelligerent Israel. Saddam hoped that Israel would respond by jumping into the fray, thereby alienating the Arab members of the coalition. He believed that if the Arabs withdrew support from the United States, the Iraqi army could sustain a war of attrition until the United States tired of conflict and withdrew.

Saddam's plan could have worked too well. Most Israelis (and CNN) expected poison gas. A flight of three Israeli jets appeared on U.S. radar headed for Baghdad. We had to assume they carried nukes and begged Israel to call them back, promising we would take care of the problem and defeat one of Israel's greatest enemies without Israeli intervention. We also promised an aid package and rushed Patriot missiles to Israel to shoot down incoming SCUDs. They were ineffective but a psychological boost. An important U.S. persuader: electronic Friend or Foe Indicator (FFI). Without the proper FFI, an Israeli jet stood an excellent chance of being shot down by the allies as an Iraqi warplane. Israel decided to wait out the conflict.

Conflicts

JOINT RESOLUTIONS FOR WAR

Congress has not passed or seriously entertained a declaration of war since December 1941. Indeed, very few countries have. Declarations of war may be passé in the modern world, where presidents move fast but need flexibility. Instead of declarations of war, presidents get Congress to pass joint resolutions, bills of identical wording passed by both houses allowing the president to take specified military steps overseas. Although milder than a declaration of war, a joint congressional resolution, when signed by the president, has force of law. They do not require the president to go to war; they merely let him if he thinks the situation warrants it.

The Cold War saw several joint congressional resolutions, but the 1964 Tonkin Gulf Resolution came back to haunt Congress. President Johnson asserted that North Vietnam had attacked U.S. destroyers in the Tonkin Gulf, which was not the whole story. Congress quickly and obediently passed a joint resolution authorizing LBJ to use the military in Southeast Asia, thinking he would not really go to war. It was just a warning to North Vietnam. But LBJ did use it to take America to war. It was perfectly legal but infuriated Congress.

Since then, Congress has been cautious, now understanding that a joint resolution is the functional equivalent of a declaration of war: You pass it, you got yourself a war. Accordingly, in both the 1991 and 2002 Gulf crises, Congress debated its joint resolutions with some care and passed them knowing they would take us to war. Some critics say we should return to declarations of war, which leave no doubt in anyone's mind that we are going to war.

For the only time since World War II the United States and Soviet Union were on the same side of an international conflict. There are many reasons why the Soviets were willing to cooperate in an American attack against a Soviet ally. The Berlin Wall fell in 1989, signaling the end of the Soviet empire, and the United States was emerging as the sole superpower. It was in Moscow's interest to cooperate with the new **hegemon**. Soviet leader Mikhail Gorbachev was also piqued by Saddam's unwillingness to accept Soviet advice. James Baker was in Siberia with Soviet Foreign Minister Eduard Shevardnazde when Iraq attacked Kuwait. With the two already sitting at the same table, it was relatively easy to issue joint statements condemning aggression.

GROUND ATTACK

On February 24, 1991, after thirty-eight days of air attacks, the allied ground attack began. Within four days the Iraqis were defeated and fleeing Kuwait. Troops on the sole road north, the "Highway of Death," became sitting targets

---

hegemon   Leading or dominant power.

Conflicts

DID DETERRENCE WORK?

Many analysts believe the Cold War did not explode because of mutual **deterrence**. With both sides loaded with nuclear weapons, neither dared use them. Does deterrence work after the Cold War? Some say it did work in the 1991 Gulf War. Saddam had weapons of mass destruction (namely, chemical) but did not use them on Israel or on U.S. forces because he knew both would not hesitate to nuke him.

Saddam tried to goad Israel into entering the Gulf War, thinking it would break up the alliance. He fired forty conventional-explosive warheads at Israel. Many missed and none did much damage. Why did he not shoot chemical warheads at Israel? He was capable of it, but he knew how Israel would react: with nuclear weapons, of which Israel reportedly has some 300. Saddam wanted Israel in the war, but not in that way. Deterrence worked. Some say we should have considered the possibilities of deterrence against Iraq in 2003.

---

for U.S. airpower. General Powell grew uneasy at the slaughter and convinced the president and General Schwarzkopf to offer a cease-fire. Powell noted that with the liberation of Kuwait the United States had met its and the UN's war aims. Saudi Arabia and other U.S. allies did not want a wider war. A unilateral U.S. conquest of Iraq would have saved the world much trouble later. Fully 60 percent of Saddam's Republican Guard, his best units, escaped, and his real pillar of support, his security police, were intact. *Bellum interruptum* again. When the magnitude of the mistake sank in, Washington vowed to never let Saddam off the hook again.

Withdrawing from Kuwait, Saddam's army, full of hatred, set fire to Kuwait's oil fields and befouled Gulf waters by opening the oil taps. There was little or no military purpose to this wanton ecological destruction, which actually changed the weather for a time.

The generals from the allied and Iraqi sides met at Safwan inside Iraq and negotiated a cease-fire. Not wishing to humiliate the Iraqis further, there was no demand that Saddam personally sign the cease-fire accords. This oversight gave Saddam the ability in later years to say he had never agreed to the arrangements. As a defensive measure, the allies forbade the Iraqis the use of aircraft over the country. The Iraqi generals pointed to the destruction of the country's infrastructure and asked the allies for permission to use helicopters so that they could administer distant provinces. Schwarzkopf soft-heartedly agreed, leading to a humanitarian disaster.

---

deterrence   Preventing an attack by inducing fear of retaliation.

Conflicts

GULF WAR SYNDROME

Thousands of American soldiers returned home from the war complaining of blinding headaches, rashes, and nerve problems. The symptoms were more than psychological, such as posttraumatic stress disorder; they were physical.

A number of theories tried to explain the malady: exposure to depleted uranium in U.S. antitank rounds, smoke from oil fires, immunizations against biological agents such as anthrax, or desert mites. One interesting possibility: Saddam may have ordered chemical and biological weapons buried along the lines of expected allied advances. As allies destroyed enemy fortifications they would unknowingly release the toxic materials. After much analysis, no single explanation is accepted as solid.

THE REBELLIONS

Throughout the war and after, President Bush (senior) urged the people of Iraq to rise up and overthrow their brutal government. Thinking that the humiliated and weakened Saddam would soon be overthrown by his own people was one reason Bush did not press the war further. But the Americans were not in contact with members of the various ethnic and religious groups in Iraq, and the president didn't realize he was putting a match to a tinderbox.

In the south of Iraq, members of the Shi'a majority rose in rebellion; in the north the Kurds pursued their age-old demands for an independent homeland. The Iraqi army rallied and with air support from the Schwarzkopf-approved helicopters brutally put down the uprising in the south. Tens of thousands died while American troops in the area did nothing. The Americans were in a peculiar position. The Shi'a were harkening to the U.S. president's call but the American soldiers were honoring a cease-fire their commanders had signed. Since the Iraqi army was attacking its own citizens and not allied troops, they were not violating the cease-fire, and the Americans' hands were tied. Some American help for the Shi'a might well have gotten Saddam overthrown, and it would have been the just and moral thing to do.

Saddam next turned to the rebellious Kurds, but they did not wait for extermination; after all, they had survived Saddam's genocide in the 1988 al-Anfal campaign. Many fled across the border into the mountainous wastelands of Turkey, seriously discomforting the Turkish government, which realized it was now responsible for humanitarian aid. The refugees had no food, clothing, or shelter; they would die if Turkey did not give costly assistance. Turkey was losing millions in transit fees because of the closed Iraqi pipeline and other trade. Worse, Turkey was in the middle of putting down an insurgency by its own Kurds; the Turkish general staff feared the refugees included guerrilla fighters who would join the Turkish conflict. The Turks demanded the international community help.

Britain's new prime minister, John Major, proposed a safe haven in northern Iraq, and the UN did establish such a safety zone north of the thirty-sixth parallel. The United States added its support, ordering Iraq to withdraw its military from the area. Protected by American guns, the Kurds reversed the flow and returned home. Eventually the United States and Britain created "no-fly" zones over the northern and southern thirds of Iraq.

THE WAR OVER WEAPONS OF MASS DESTRUCTION

For the next decade Saddam delayed and obfuscated in a desperate attempt to both stay in power and preserve his military capabilities. The crown jewels in his arsenal were his weapons of mass destruction (WMD), both planned and existing. While it is no longer certain whether Saddam had any of these weapons by late 2002 (or even early 2003), Saddam did everything he could to protect them for as long as possible. By the time he did allow destruction of some of his WMD, his long record of deceit meant he could never produce sufficient proof of cooperation to assuage the Americans.

Following the creation of UNSCOM to supervise destruction of Iraqi WMD, Saddam ordered his scientists to hide anything pertaining to the WMD program. He then declared some of his chemical weapons to the UN and denied having a biological program. Later, when confronted with proof that he was lying, Saddam said the research was for defensive military purposes.

By June 1991 Saddam's troops fired into the air to prevent UNSCOM inspectors from examining Iraqi trucks carrying nuclear-related equipment. In September inspectors from the UN's International Atomic Energy Agency (IAEA) discovered files documenting the Iraqi nuclear weapons development program, leading to a four-day standoff as Iraq tried to prevent the inspectors from taking a copy of the documents with them.

In March 1992 Iraq confirmed it had some ballistic missiles and chemical weapons, but the numbers declared were suspiciously low. Saddam said the Iraqi military had destroyed most of the materials themselves the previous summer, instead of turning them over to the UN.

In July 1992 an inspection team tried to enter the Iraqi agriculture ministry in search of archives on the banned weapons programs. The Iraqis prevented the inspectors from entering for seventeen days until they gave up. Emboldened by their success in defying the UN, the Iraqi military began to make military incursions into the northern protected zones.

Iraq also denied UNSCOM permission to fly into the country using its own aircraft. Had Saddam won this point, UNSCOM would have needed to fly in Iraqi airplanes, effectively ending the "no-fly" zones. Instead of agreeing to the Iraqi demands on his last full day in the White House, President Bush (senior) launched Tomahawk missiles into Baghdad. Iraq relented and the inspections continued. One suspects that Bush senior regretted not finishing the job, which fell to Bush junior.

THE CLINTON YEARS

Bill Clinton was elected on a platform that emphasized domestic politics. He accused outgoing President Bush of being too involved with international affairs. Every new American president who announces he is giving priority to domestic problems is destined to be deeply involved in foreign affairs. For the next eight years Clinton tried to avoid taking decisive action in Iraq, but sometimes he had no choice in the matter.

Saddam was a vindictive ruler, and in the Middle East all politics is personal. When former President Bush visited Kuwait in April 1993, Saddam tried to take revenge on the American he blamed for his defeat. He sent an assassination team to Kuwait to kill Bush, but the Kuwaiti security service uncovered the plot and arrested the would-be assassins. In response, Clinton ordered a cruise-missile attack on Iraqi intelligence headquarters in Baghdad. In the typical Clinton fashion of half-measures, he had the attack take place at night when the headquarters building was empty. Clinton had begun to replace action with symbols of action.

Meanwhile the skirmishes with the weapons inspectors continued. Saddam refused to allow them to install cameras at missile engine test grounds until they threatened to leave the country. Saddam tested Clinton's resolve by again marshalling his forces on the Kuwait border but backed down when the UN Security Council demanded it. Then, in July 1995, Saddam admitted he had an offensive biological weapons program but denied he had weaponized any materials.

In November 1995 UNSCOM intercepted a shipment of Russian gyroscopes headed for Iraq. Likely use: missile guidance. In December UNSCOM drained the Tigris and uncovered additional missile components. In May 1996 UNSCOM destroyed Iraq's main biological weapons production complex.

Saddam then ended the limited cooperation he had been providing. When inspectors wanted to search a sensitive site, Iraqi troops prevented them. When an inspector tried to take pictures out of a helicopter, an Iraqi military officer assaulted him. UNSCOM later videotaped Iraqi officials burning documents and dumping materials into a river while they sat at the front gate of a facility waiting for permission to enter.

In September 1997 UNSCOM was again denied permission to visit a "food laboratory." One of the inspectors sneaked in through a rear entrance and observed several men running out with suitcases. The inspector grabbed one of the suitcases from the fleeing men and found it full of logbooks documenting Iraqi efforts to create illegal bacteria and chemical compounds. The books came from the Special Security Office, so the inspectors headed to that facility for a surprise inspection. Iraq refused them entry. Following additional UN pressure, Iraq admitted it had been producing VX nerve gas as recently as May 1997.

Saddam changed tactics to split the allied coalition. He noticed that a number of countries such as France, Germany, and Russia were interested in establishing commercial relationships and reasoned it wouldn't take much to strip these countries away from the United States. His first gambit was to pledge total cooperation with weapons inspectors but only if the UN no longer sent any Americans as

Cultures

THE IN-LAW PROBLEM

Husayn Kamil and his brother were married to Saddam's daughters and knew about Saddam's weapons programs. Trying to make new lives for themselves, in August 1995 they fled to Jordan with their families. There Husayn Kamil gave UN inspectors directions to his farm in southern Iraq where the inspectors exhumed details of the Iraqi military and nuclear weapons programs. The UN was startled to find that Iraq was less than a year from the development of a working nuclear device. It was a major black eye for Saddam.

Kamil was the toast of Amman for several months, but when his brief fame was over he realized he had no future outside Iraq. He tried to join the Iraqi opposition, but they said he had blood on his hands and would not take him into their ranks. In February 1996 Husayn received a message from Baghdad that all was forgiven. Saddam invited him to come home and promised no punishment. Against the advice of everyone around him, Husayn trusted his father-in-law and he returned to Baghdad.

That same night members of the Kamil clan surrounded the home where Husayn was staying. Saddam's daughters were seized and whisked away to a presidential compound, never to be seen in public again. Husayn and his brother were tortured and beaten to death. Saddam said it was an honor killing by the family that he had nothing to do with. Actually, honor killings are part of Muslim culture, but it was clear that Saddam ordered them murdered. From that time on, no one believed an "all was forgiven" message from Baghdad. Like his model Stalin, whom Saddam carefully emulated, personal cruelty went with tyranny.

members of the teams. Rather than comply, in November 1997 UNSCOM withdrew from Iraq. When they returned two weeks later, Saddam refused to allow them to inspect his many presidential palaces.

By 1998 the Gulf was again on the verge of war. After six years of Saddam's antics, Britain and the United States began plans for military intervention. Faced with such resolve, Saddam resumed cooperation with weapons inspectors, even opening up several of the presidential palaces. In August Tariq Aziz certified that Iraq was now free of weapons of mass destruction and demanded the inspections cease. In light of the U.S. inability to find evidence of WMD in the 2003 war, Aziz may have been telling the truth. But after all the lies, no one believed him. Iraq then expelled the teams on October 31, 1998.

Clinton had to do something no matter how much he wanted to avoid a Middle East war. He ordered air strikes on Iraq but cancelled the order when Iraq agreed to allow UNSCOM to return. Actually Britain and the United States waged a low-scale bombing campaign against the Iraqi air defense system throughout the entire decade. New planned air strikes were to have been more extensive than the "routine" bombings Iraq had been absorbing. A month after the UNSCOM inspectors returned to Iraq they pulled out again because of Iraqi noncooperation. The UN evacuated its other aid workers and the United States and Britain launched four days of bombings.

Rather than pretending to cooperate as Iraq had previously done countless times, this time Iraqi Vice President Taha Yassin Ramadan announced it would no longer cooperate with UNSCOM. Saddam had picked his time perfectly. Three of the five permanent members of the UN Security Council called to lift the oil embargo on Iraq. Instead of punishing Iraq for failing to cooperate, Russia, France, and China wanted to reward Saddam. The UN created UNMOVIC as a replacement for UNSCOM, but Saddam refused to cooperate. The stage was set for the arrival of George W. Bush, who finished what his father started.

CONCLUSIONS

Writers often refer to the American-Iraqi conflict of 1990 and 1991 as the First Gulf War. It might be more appropriate to consider the conflict as the opening skirmishes in a thirteen-year war that only ended when America took the whole country in 2003. We will call 1991 the Gulf War and 2003 the Iraq War for the sake of clarity.

There were good reasons to defend Kuwait from Iraqi aggression, not least Kuwait's oil reserves. There were morally compelling reasons for the United States to intervene in the Balkans earlier than it did or in Rwanda, but in the Gulf, American security interests were at stake; they were not in the other conflicts.

The United States tried to win the 1991 war but allowed it to end halfway through, not wanting to lose American lives to invade Iraq and overthrow Saddam with little help from allies or the UN. Besides, Washington figured Saddam would soon be overthrown. Instead, his security police shot thousands who tried. Both Republicans and Democrats have engaged in wishful thinking on Iraq.

Saddam Hussein actively developed chemical, biological, and nuclear weapons, constantly deceiving UN inspectors. He had no compunction against using such weapons, as he showed in the Iran-Iraq war. In many ways, whether we find evidence of these programs is immaterial: Saddam's behavior throughout the 1990s clearly demonstrated that once the United States let up the pressure and the international inspectors went away, he would have resumed his programs. One could not really deal with Saddam in any humane, rational way.

FURTHER REFERENCE

Fürtig, Henner. *Iran's Rivalry with Saudi Arabia between the Gulf Wars*. Reading, UK: Ithaca Press, 2002.

Hamza, Khidhir, with Jeff Stein. *Saddam's Bombmaker*. New York: Simon & Schuster, 2000.

Khadduri, Majid, and Edmund Ghareeb. *War in the Gulf, 1990–1991: The Iraq-Kuwait Conflict and its Implications*. New York: Oxford, 1997.

Little, Douglas. *American Orientalism: The United States and the Middle East Since 1945.* Chapel Hill, NC: University of North Carolina Press, 2002.

Mottale, Morris M. *The Origins of the Gulf Wars.* Lanham, MD: University Press of America, 2001.

Public Broadcasting System. *Frontline: The Gulf War. Oral History.* <www.pbs.org/wgbh/pages/frontline/gulf/oral.html>.

The 9/11 Wars

**Points
to
Ponder**

- If Bush senior had done things differently in the region, would it really have mattered?
- What was the "game of nations"? Are we playing it now?
- Is Afghanistan inherently anarchic? Why then not just leave it alone?
- Was it right to connect Iraq to 9/11?
- Were Iraqi weapons of mass destruction ever a real threat?
- How was the plan of the 2003 war brilliant but risky?
- Do U.S. high-tech military advantages guarantee U.S. victories?
- Is federalism right for Iraq? How could it fail?
- Will the United States be in the Gulf a long time?

The U.S.-led war with Iraq in 2003 grew out of two projects that were left unfinished by the administration of the senior Bush—Afghanistan and Iraq—as well as the terrorist attacks of 9/11, which unleashed a torrent of American emotion eager for revenge. Without the terrorist attacks of 9/11, the junior Bush would not have been looking for enemies to punish. If senior Bush had finished what we started in Afghanistan and Iraq, we might not have had enemies there. The problem goes deeper than Bush senior; it was America as a whole that did not wish to get deeply involved in this difficult and dangerous region. Unfortunately, the Persian Gulf does not give us much choice about getting involved.

Both Afghanistan in 2001 and Iraq in 2003 were very much a result of the terrorist attacks of 9/11, which produced American anger that had to go somewhere. President Bush claimed that Iraq had sponsored terrorism against the United States, and most Americans believed it. Patient police work to catch terrorists was not enough for the American public. Bush, with Texas twang and simple sentence structure, connected with mass emotions in a way that intellectual leaders seldom do. With this, Bush junior led a public and a Congress that were eager to be led. Complexities and doubts came later, and the patient police work is still needed.

G : *Geography*

THE "GAME OF NATIONS"

In the nineteenth century, Britain and Russia played what came to be known as the Great Game of Nations in the lands between the tsarist empire and the British Raj of India. The Russians aimed to push south, enrolling Persia, Afghanistan, and Tibet in their **sphere of influence**. The British in India aimed to stop them by keeping these borderlands at least neutral buffer zones if not in the British sphere. Decades of treaties, intrigues, espionage, and armed expeditions by the Russians and British gave Kipling the setting for *Kim*.

In the First Afghan War (1839–1842), the British in India, fearful of anarchy and Russian influence in Afghanistan, marched in with 12,000 troops to install a pro-British king in Kabul. The old king, though, in 1841 led an uprising of outraged Afghans, and in early 1842 the British agreed to leave. The Khyber Pass, the gate to India, was just ninety miles away, but they never made it. Afghan tribesmen picked them off in the rugged terrain. According to legend, only one British survivor, a surgeon, staggered back alive. Britain tried to subdue Afghanistan twice again, in the Second Afghan War (1878–1880), and Third (1919), at which point Afghanistan achieved full independence, and Britain, badly burned, left it alone. Wrote Kipling of the British fighting in Afghanistan:

> When you're wounded and left on Afghanistan's plains,
> And the women come out to cut up your remains,
> Just roll on your rifle and blow out your brains,
> And go to your Gawd like a soldier.

In 1907, Britain and Russia agreed to let each other establish spheres of influence in Persia, the Russians in the north and the British in the south. Afghanistan was to remain neutral, in neither sphere, and it did until the Communists took over in 1978. The Soviets in the 1980s might have learned something from the earlier British experience: Afghanistan is not hard to get into, but it can be deceptive, trapping and slowly decimating occupiers. Will the lesson also apply to Americans?

COVERT WAR IN AFGHANISTAN

Afghanistan is one of the poorest countries in the world and one of the last we wish to be involved in. Afghans, still tribal in organization, do not like being ruled by anybody, especially foreigners. In 1747, Afghanistan broke from the Persian empire and became independent. Afghans tolerated a weak, traditional monarchy because it left them alone. The long reign of King Muhammad Zahir (1933–1973) is remembered as a time of peace and prosperity. Modernization changed Afghan society, producing a class of educated young Afghans impatient

sphere of influence   Area where imperial power holds sway.

for reform. A coup overthrew the king in 1973, and Afghanistan has been in turmoil ever since. In 1978, a Communist coup took power and sought help from Moscow. Most Afghans hated the Communists and started an insurrection against them; by 1979 it was nationwide. The Soviets knew the situation was bad but could not let a dependent Communist regime go down the drain, so they intervened directly and massively into what turned out to be a major mistake that contributed to their demise.

In late December 1979 Soviet troops landed at Kabul airport, immediately shot the president (a Communist, but from the wrong faction) and his family, and installed a Communist president more to their liking. Soviet troops soon numbered 120,000 (some 15,000 were killed) but they could not subdue the Afghan *dushmani* ("bandits"), as they called them, even with exceedingly brutal tactics that wiped out whole villages. Some 3 million Afghans fled to Pakistan and another 2 million to Iran. From camps in Pakistan, *mujahedin* with equipment supplied by the U.S. Central Intelligence Agency, training by Pakistan's ISI (Inter-Services Intelligence agency), and money from Saudi Arabia made forays back into Afghanistan to harry mercilessly the Soviets and their Afghan puppet troops. Volunteers came from all over the Muslim world, especially from Saudi Arabia. Encouraging them with money and guidance was a quietly charismatic Saudi fundamentalist, Osama bin Laden.

Tipping the balance, in 1986 the rebels got American shoulder-fired, surface-to-air Stinger missiles. Soviet helicopters fell at the rate of one a day and soon learned to keep their distance. From then on, the Soviets were on the defensive and pulled out entirely by early 1989, the same year their East European satellite system collapsed. Many Soviet soldiers returned embittered and drug-addicted. Some peg the Afghan misadventure as the exhaustion of the Soviet Union, which collapsed at the end of 1991.

On the world scene, the Afghan war cost the Soviet Union friends and influence, especially in the Muslim world. Moscow's attempts at relaxing tensions with the United States were wrecked by the invasion. U.S. President Jimmy Carter declared that he "learned more about the Soviets in one week" than he had in all previous years. He began a U.S. arms buildup (often attributed to Reagan), cancelled grain sales to the Soviet Union, and pulled the U.S. team out of the 1980 Moscow Olympics. Covert U.S. aid to the Afghan rebels was a natural U.S. move. The Soviets had gotten themselves into a vulnerable situation, and we would make it worse, draining them and getting back at them for their massive aid to North Vietnam. In international relations, turnabout is fair play.

Indirectly and never openly claiming it, the United States won in Afghanistan. We made some vague promises of aid to the anti-Communist mujahedin, but when their several tribes started fighting among themselves we walked away from and forgot Afghanistan. It seemed so remote and unimportant as the Cold War ended. These problems do not solve themselves, however, and Afghanistan descended into complete chaos and anarchy presided over by local "warlords," who obeyed no central authority.

(G) Geography

AFGHANISTAN AND THE GULF

Bound Afghanistan:

Afghanistan is bounded on the north by Turkmenistan, Uzbekistan, and Tajikistan;
on the east by China (tiny) and Pakistan;
on the south by Pakistan;
and on the west by Iran.

In 1979 Washington saw that the Persian Gulf region could soon be in very hostile hands. The anti-U.S. Islamists of Ayatollah Khomeini in Iran were bad enough. The Soviet takeover of Afghanistan late that year made things worse. Soviet bases in the south of Afghanistan put Soviet airpower a mere 300 miles from the Strait of Hormuz, a strategic waterway through which flows much of the world's oil. Moscow's thumb was or soon could be on the world's petroleum throat. Washington could not let this stand. Geography rather than ideology explains both Soviet and U.S. motives.

Afghanistan is important for another geographical reason. It bordered the Soviet Union (now it borders the ex-Soviet **Central Asian** republics of Turkmenistan, Uzbekistan, and Tajikistan), where live Muslims related to the peoples of Afghanistan. If the **mujahedin** beat the new Communist regime, they would spread their militant Islam into the rapidly growing and not completely reliable Soviet Muslim population. The successor republics have this same problem today. This explains why Russian and Central Asian governments helped the United States knock out the Taliban in 2001. Geography sometimes produces common interests between previously hostile countries.

In late 1994 the **Taliban** movement of students trained in Saudi-financed fundamentalist schools in Pakistan and supplied by the ISI moved into the chaos and took over most of Afghanistan. The Taliban were mostly Pushtuns of the south, and other Afghan commanders fought them, slowly retreating back into the northeast corner of Afghanistan. Basically, Pakistan's military invented the Taliban to stabilize their northern neighbor. No one likes chaos on their borders. Another reason: A stable Afghanistan could be a corridor for a natural-gas pipeline from Central Asia to Pakistan. The United States did not much care what happened in Afghanistan.

That is, until terrorism started hitting American targets. The same Osama bin Laden who had fought to oust the Communists from Afghanistan turned bitterly anti-American by 1991. In 1990, Saudi Arabia had invited U.S. forces onto its soil to mass for the 1991 Gulf War. Attacking a brother Arab country was bad enough

---

Central Asia   Ex-Soviet region between Caspian Sea and China.
mujahedin   Muslim holy warriors.
Taliban   (Persian for "students") Fundamentalist movement that took over Afghanistan in the 1990s.

K ⦂ *Key Concepts*

BLOWBACK

Berkeley political scientist Chalmers Johnson coined the term "blowback" in his 2001 book of that title. His point was that often when we think we are manipulating the forces of history by aiding a group or country, we get burned. We thought we had similar or compatible interests with the group and could use them to achieve our goals in the region. But they accept our help only on a temporary and opportunistic basis. Their agenda is power for themselves, not the promotion of U.S. interests. "Blowback" describes the Middle East quite well. Other political scientists have called it "unforeseen consequences."

A prime example is U.S. aid to the Afghan militias who fought the 1979 Soviet occupation of their country. We were delighted to get the Soviets bogged down in an unwinnable Afghan war. But the Afghan freedom fighters fought each other. Some were anti-American. None said thanks. Out of the chaos the Taliban seized most of Afghanistan and instituted a hostile, repressive regime, supported by and home to Osama bin Laden. Afghanistan blew back in our face. U.S. help to Iraq in the 1980s blew back in our face. Careful whom you help in the Middle East.

---

for Osama, but allowing U.S. troops to remain on sacred Muslim ground after the war was unforgivable. Osama aimed his jihad against us and anyone cooperating with us, namely, the House of Saud. Osama had never been a U.S. ally and had no contact with Americans during the Afghan struggle. He had merely made temporary common cause with us when it was useful for his ultimate purposes. Islamic fundamentalists can be highly opportunistic.

Osama, expelled from Saudi Arabia in 1991, set up shop in Khartoum, Sudan, where he helped a Muslim fundamentalist regime consolidate power. Accusing Osama of anti-U.S. terrorism, the United States pressured Sudan to expel him in 1996. Osama went to Afghanistan where he helped the Taliban take over most of the country. Al Qaeda fighters became the most effective element of the Taliban armed forces. On August 7, 1998, al Qaeda bombers simultaneously blew up the U.S. embassies in Kenya and Tanzania. U.S. Navy cruise missiles hit one of Osama's training camps in Afghanistan, but he had already departed. You cannot do everything with airpower.

Instantly, 9/11 was pegged as an al Qaeda project, and Washington demanded that the Taliban turn over Osama and his top lieutenants. The Taliban head of Afghanistan, Mullah Muhammad Omar, refused, claiming to be innocent of any wrongdoing. The Taliban had a serious weak spot: They had not fully taken over Afghanistan. In roughly the mountainous northeast tenth of the country, anti-Taliban forces, the Northern Alliance, still held out under the command of the charismatic Ahmad Shah Massoud. As a favor to Omar, shortly before 9/11 Osama sent two al Qaeda suicide bombers posing as TV journalists to kill Massoud, supposing that would end the Northern Alliance. Instead, it energized it.

U.S. Special Forces used this opening and within days were inside Afghanistan, working with local anti-Taliban forces. Their chief weapons were radios and global positioning systems, with which they could pinpoint Taliban positions for air strikes launched from U.S. bases and aircraft carriers in the Gulf. Many Afghans had grown to detest the fanatic Taliban—who forbade music, radio, TV, and flying kites while forcing women to wear head-to-toe bags and men to grow beards—and soon other groups joined in (some changed sides). By December, the Taliban were defeated. The bold operation involved few U.S. forces or casualties. Unfortunately, follow-up—always a weak spot in these operations—was weak, and most al Qaeda and Taliban leaders, including Osama, slipped away, most of them across the border to the mountain wilds of the Northwest Frontier Province of Pakistan, a tribal area where government writ does not run and Westerners are not permitted.

World support for U.S. actions in Afghanistan was strong, and antiwar movements were small. Sympathy for 9/11 was genuine, and no one had a good word for the Taliban, who had made themselves isolated and detested. They had just blown up ancient statues of a gigantic Buddha carved into a mountainside. (Before Islam, Buddhism had been prominent in Afghanistan.) Pakistan and Saudi Arabia, the sponsors of the Taliban, broke relations with them. Even Iran approved, as the Sunni Taliban and Shi'a Iranians have no love for each other, and the Taliban had killed Shi'a Afghans. Russia, facing its own problems with a Muslim breakaway movement in Chechnya, arranged for U.S.-bases in Uzbekistan and Tajikistan. The UN cheered what America was doing.

Afghanistan, as usual, is still lawless and untamed. The Taliban and al Qaeda have quietly regrouped and attack foreign peacekeepers. The Afghan warlords are as bad as ever, corrupt mini-tyrants who rob and repress their provinces. A U.S.-approved president, Hamid Karzai, educated in India and English-speaking, took office, but few outside of Kabul answer to him. Opium-poppy cultivation, suppressed by the Taliban, has returned. It is Afghanistan's one sure moneymaker. A massive foreign-aid program is needed to lift Afghanistan out of its misery. Some criticized the Bush junior administration for not paying enough attention to the rebuilding of Afghanistan. Many Afghans who welcomed liberation now despair that little good has come of it. Afghanistan could again become a haven for terrorists.

THE SAME WAR TWICE

According to several accounts, **neo-conservatives** in the Bush administration (for more on neo-conservatives, see Chapters 17 and 18) approached the White House within days of 9/11 to point at Iraq as a source of terrorism as bad as Afghanistan. Furthermore, Iraq had weapons of mass destruction. They also argued that eliminating Saddam would restart Israel-Palestine peace talks. Israelis would feel more secure, and Palestinians would see no hope coming from Iraq or anywhere else. The 1991 war with Iraq had opened a window of opportunity; another war would do the same. President Bush decided on war with Iraq by December 2001 but kept plans vague.

---

neo-conservative   Rediscovery of tough-minded foreign policies, including use of force, often by ex-liberals.

C Conflicts

DID DETERRENCE WORK? PART 2

If Saddam was deterred from using WMD in 1991, could we have used deterrence—some preferred the term **"coercive diplomacy"**—on Iraq instead of invasion in 2003? One of the debates leading up to the 2003 war was whether our nukes would deter his gas and bugs. Saddam was evil but not stupid, argued some experts, so we could keep him bottled up without going to war. Not so, a former CIA expert on Iraq argued: Saddam was an undeterrable risk-taker. He invaded both Iran and Kuwait heedless of consequences. Deterrence requires rationality, and Saddam often seemed irrational.

The Iraq War was not a good test case for deterrence or coercive diplomacy and did not settle the debate. In a sense it did work: Massive U.S. power had deterred Iraq from attacking anyone since 1991 or in using WMD in 2003. By the time we invaded, we found neither bugs nor gas. But when did Iraq get rid of them and why? We know Iraq had chemical and biological weapons in 1991 and was working on nuclear. UNSCOM had overseen the demolition of some of them in the early 1990s, but the Bush junior administration argued Iraq had hidden much from UNSCOM and resumed work in all three areas.

If the claims of some Iraqi scientists are correct, Iraq dumped its remaining WMD only days before the March 19 invasion, suggesting that deterrence worked but only on the eve of war, when the U.S. forces were already massed. Up to that point, Saddam was likely either thinking of using his WMD or was bluffing that he would. But with war very close, Saddam found himself in a trap of his own making. After years of calculating that WMD had a certain utility, he (probably suddenly) realized that he had to either (1) use his WMD and get nuked in return; (2) let his WMD get discovered, thereby proving U.S. claims that he had them; or (3) dump his WMD and fight a conventional followed by a guerrilla war. The only rational choice is the last one. Saddam, it turns out, was a deterrable risk-taker, but only when it was too late to avoid war.

Saddam should have demolished his WMD weeks earlier in front of UN inspectors: Dump, but notify. But then he would have given up using them for deterrence or bluff. When he saw that we were not deterred, he had to dump them. Iraq was a poor test case because the weapons and fears were **asymmetrical**. Deterrence now works only when both sides have nukes, which induce mutual fear. Bugs and gas, especially against prepared forces, do not counterbalance nukes. If Saddam eventually got nukes, that might have been a test case of deterrence, one we may face with Iran and North Korea.

Ironically, the peace community used to denounce deterrence during the Cold War because it threatened to destroy the world. It was an evil, power-centered doctrine that must be replaced by disarmament. U.S.-Soviet deterrence was not completely stable and could have broken down under the stress of the 1961 Berlin Wall crisis and 1962 Cuban missile crisis. As war with Iraq loomed in 2002 and 2003, however, many doves found deterrence highly preferable to invasion. "Give deterrence a chance," they urged. Deterrence may still work, but we now see it requires not only the weapons themselves but rational doctrines developed over the years in tension with a rational opponent. During the Cold War, Americans and Soviets had learned to "play the game." Saddam never did; other would-be possessors of WMD should be warned that WMD can do them more harm than good, getting them into wars they would rather avoid.

---

coercive diplomacy   Using threat of force to get a country to change its policy.
asymmetrical   Unbalanced, especially in military strengths.

At that time another factor moved Washington: the first known attack with biological weapons. One week after 9/11, mysterious letters containing anthrax were mailed to various parts of the United States, including Capitol Hill. Five died from the anthrax, which was in the form of a highly refined powder, something allegedly beyond the capacity of al Qaeda to produce. It had to have come from the biological-weapons program of some government. Czech security police reported that the Egyptian leader of the 9/11 hijackers, Muhammad Atta, met in Prague that summer with a senior Iraqi intelligence official. Did Iraq supply Atta with a sample pack of anthrax to try out in America? The claim, based on one witness in Prague, is now doubted but at the time added to U.S. suspicions of Iraq.

Some press accounts saw a split in 2002 between a hawkish Defense Department and a dovish State Department. That may have been, but it appears that neither camp influenced Bush, as he had already decided on war. In December 2001 speechwriter David Frum was instructed to incorporate a justification for war in the president's State of the Union address, and on January 29, 2002, President Bush called Iraq, Iran, and North Korea the "axis of evil," his first public indication that he was preparing for war.

In contrast to the U.S. toppling of the Taliban in Afghanistan, most of the world did not support Washington on Iraq. Many felt the U.S. accusations of major, ongoing Iraqi programs of WMD or Iraqi sponsorship of terrorism were exaggerated and unproved, certainly not a valid basis for war. London's International Institute of Strategic Studies, for example, thought Iraq was capable of producing WMD but probably had little on hand. Within a year of 9/11, world sympathy and support for America largely dried up.

This bothered Bush little. Always inclined to unilateralism, President Bush made it clear that, unless Saddam came clean fast on his WMD, we would go to war with a "coalition of the willing," meaning mostly Britain, whose prime minister, Tony Blair, went out on a limb to support Bush. British public opinion, like all of West Europe, was heavily against the war. Some detected behind Bush's stance the hawkish voice of Defense Secretary Donald Rumsfeld and his neoconservative deputies, but Bush had already reached his own decision on war and merely let State and Defense play at policy debate.

More-moderate and internationalist Secretary of State Colin Powell—once the Army's top general who had also urged caution on Bush senior before the 1991 war with Iraq—urged that we first make the case in the United Nations to try to gain multilateral support. Powell was one of the few top Bush appointees who fought in Vietnam, an experience that convinced him the case for any war must first be overwhelming, and then the war must be pursued with overwhelming force. In Vietnam, we failed to do both. Generals, who have to actually deliver their soldiers' lives, are among the most cautious about going to war. The Pentagon's hawks on Iraq were all civilians, many with no military service.

In 2002 both Bush and Powell made persuasive speeches to the UN, which had set up a new program, UNMOVIC, to make sure Iraq had gotten rid of its WMD. In the early 1990s, after the Gulf War, UNSCOM had supervised the destruction of some Iraqi weapons. Iraq claimed it had not reactivated these programs and had no weapons of mass destruction. By 1998, however, UNSCOM,

 *Key Concepts*

BUREAUCRATIC POLITICS

Studying foreign-policy decisions as the result of bureaucratic politics enjoyed brief vogue in the early 1970s. One influential article claimed to show that squabbling among agencies resulted in the U.S naval blockade of Cuba in 1962. (More recent research shows that President Kennedy was in command at all times and that bureaucratic infighting had little to do with his decision.) The 2003 Iraq War recalled some of the bureaucratic-politics theory. True, the war brought a sharp break between the State and Defense Departments, but President Bush directed policy.

The conduct of foreign relations used to be in the hands of the secretary of state, but during the Cold War the initiative drifted to the **National Security Council** (NSC), a 1947 creation that has as much power as the president wants to give it. Under Nixon, national security advisor Henry Kissinger built the NSC into the center of foreign policy, easily eclipsing State, which was then headed by a pleasant lawyer, often the case. In 2003 Bush centralized our Iraq reconstruction efforts in the NSC.

The Department of Defense (DOD) also took on foreign-policy functions. Indeed, it is difficult to separate security policy from foreign policy. DOD gives crisp, clear answers while State voices doubts and ambiguities. Another factor: DOD has billions of defense dollars to spend, millions in almost every Congressional district. State has little to spend, and that is in Washington and overseas. State has no natural domestic constituency; Defense has a big one. Since Eisenhower's strong-willed Secretary of State John Foster Dulles, that office has shrunk in importance and influence compared to DOD and the NSC.

Colin Powell looked like an effective secretary of state, and he did his best to keep foreign-policy primacy in State, where many foreign-service officers know the Middle East well. They know how complex and difficult it is and so tend to be cautious (as is the CIA). Defense, especially under forceful and blunt-spoken Donald Rumsfeld, prefers simplicity to complexity, a style suited to President Bush. Rumsfeld and his neo-con deputies took the initiative on Iraq policy. The best Powell could do was delay the war a bit until he could place the matter before the UN and our allies. He had little success, and Defense proceeded with a brilliant war but a flawed aftermath. State was the clear loser in 2003.

Rumsfeld thought he could handle postwar Iraq on the cheap and on his own. State argued that its Agency for International Development, with experience in disaster relief in coordination with charitable nongovernmental organizations (NGOs), should run postwar reconstruction. NGOs do not like working with the U.S. military because they fear losing their neutral status. State Department officials believe Iraq's postwar chaos was in part the result of State being pushed out of the planning by Defense. The incident raises the question of whether the United States is too bureaucratically fragmented to handle nation-building.

---

frustrated by noncooperation and deception by Baghdad, left Iraq, and suspicions remained of secret and mobile weapons labs. UNMOVIC was likewise frustrated from the cat-and-mouse game with Iraqi authorities. UNMOVIC was never intended to search out hiding places, merely to verify that WMD had been destroyed. If Saddam wished to avoid war, he should have cooperated fully with

---

National Security Council   White House body to coordinate and oversee defense and foreign policies.

C : *Conflicts*

PREEMPTIVE OR PREVENTIVE WAR?

One of the minor debates on the Iraq War was whether it was a preemptive or preventive war. The difference is one of time pressure. If war is nigh and you are sure the other country is ready to strike you, then you may wish to preempt them by striking first, as Israel did in 1967. In the eyes of much of the world, this may be justifiable.

A preventive war has a longer time frame. You see a problem coming up with a hostile country, but it is not an urgent threat. You decide to attack anyway, on the theory that you are heading off a worse war later. Launching a war to prevent a war is dubious and wins no world sympathy. It may start precisely the big war you wished to prevent. Bismarck, Germany's nineteenth-century unifier, called preventive war "suicide from fear of death." After the Iraq War, few characterized our invasion as preemptive, as Iraq had been in no condition to attack anybody.

UNMOVIC. Baghdad's continual lying had made unbelievable its claims that it had no more WMD.

In the UN, debate centered on whether the United States could legally go to war without further UN sanction. The UN **Security Council** had passed seventeen resolutions over twelve years on Iraq, starting with Resolution 660 condemning Iraq for invading Kuwait in 1990. One resolution after another demanded that Iraq cease building and eliminate its WMD, but Iraq evaded, lied, and misled UN weapons inspectors. UN resolutions looked less than resolute. In November 2002, it passed Resolution 1441 declaring that "Iraq has been and remains in material breach" of the previous resolutions. That is all we need, declared the Bush administration. Others—including France, Russia, and China, who sought to balance U.S. power—have veto rights on the Security Council and claimed 1441 did not give Washington legal authority to go to war. Neither were they prepared to pass a war resolution, a rare thing over the life of the UN: Korea in 1950, Iraq in 1991, and Afghanistan in 2001. A descendant of the Republican isolationist tradition that never liked the UN, Bush said the UN could not block U.S. military action that, he argued, was preemptive self-defense. By the fall of 2003, however, the Bush administration was asking for UN help.

The White House made weapons of mass destruction its main reason for going to war with Iraq and easily won a joint resolution from congress in October 2002 authorizing war. Ending Iraqi sponsorship of terrorism was second. Some say human rights should have been our first goal, namely, ousting a fascistic dictatorship that murdered and tortured hundreds of thousands and impoverished the entire country. Instead, it was usually mentioned in third place.

Security Council   Fifteen-member UN body assigned to keep the peace. (Do not confuse with *National Security Council*.)

Conflicts

WHERE ARE IRAQ'S BUGS AND GAS?

President Bush, Vice President Cheney, and Secretaries Rumsfeld and Powell repeatedly stated that Washington had solid evidence that Iraq had many weapons of mass destruction. U.S. intelligence professionals said there was no solid evidence, only **rumint**. In 2002 and 2003 UN inspectors found no WMD, but Iraq could not account for what had happened to them. Likely sites were empty and deserted. Iraqi officials said they had ended their weapons programs. But Iraq is the size of California and has many hiding places. It was also a brutal police state where everyone lied. The most damning evidence against Iraq was that it earlier had such weapons and used them in the Iraq-Iran war, both against the enemy and against its own Kurds, whom it suspected of disloyalty. One could not presume good will or honesty on the part of Baghdad.

No WMD were found in Iraq after the war, only some facilities for producing them. The chief U.S. reason for the war was undermined. Intelligence officials said the administration hyped and distorted rumors of Iraqi WMD and terrorism links to gain public and congressional support for a war. A special Defense Department team had been set up to reinterpret ambiguous evidence to make the case for war. It reminded some of the 1964 Tonkin Gulf incident, when President Johnson sold Congress unclear reports that North Vietnamese PT boats had attacked U.S. destroyers; Congress quickly authorized war in Vietnam but later regretted it. Two mobile labs found in Iraq after the war were possibly for production of simple biological agents such as anthrax, but no anthrax was found.

What had happened to Iraq's WMD? There are many unanswered questions. Were they destroyed sometime between the 1991 and 2003 wars? But then why did Saddam behave so deceptively with UN inspectors? He should have welcomed them. WMD might have been carefully hidden. But months after Saddam, surely someone who knew about them would snitch. Why did Iraq not use them in the war? Perhaps they were afraid of massive U.S. retaliation. Why were thousands of chem-bio suits, gas masks, and antidotes to nerve gas found by U.S. forces? Do they indicate the Iraqi army was getting ready to use WMD? Or were they on hand for defensive purposes only? Iraq knew that the United States possesses no chemical or biological weapons; perhaps that explains why the chem-bio suits were in storage and not distributed to the troops. How old were these materials? Recent or left over from a previous war?

Some Iraqi scientists asserted that their last WMD had been destroyed just days before the 2003 war and others had been sent for years to Syria, also ruled by a Baath party. Damascus denied it, but Damascus denies everything, including providing a haven for Saddam's relatives, selling arms to Iraq, sponsoring terrorism, and controlling Lebanon like a colony. Whatever the explanation, U.S. troops never got to use their chem-bio suits, which were strapped to each soldier's leg.

THE CONDUCT OF THE WAR

U.S. and British war planners faced two obstacles. Saudi Arabia, the launching ground in the 1991 Gulf War, would not consent this time. Domestic Saudi opinion strongly opposed it (see pages 316–320). The biggest loss was Turkey, which had been helpful in 1991 but refused in 2003 to let U.S. forces launch from Turkish soil,

---

rumint   Derisive CIA term for intelligence based on rumors.

even with a $6 billion U.S. aid offer. Turkey demanded $32 billion. It was perhaps fortunate that the whole aid/bribery process failed, as it demeaned both countries. Turkish public opinion did not want war either, and an Islamist party had just been voted into power. Other Gulf states (Oman, the United Arab Emirates, Bahrain) supported the U.S. position, but only Kuwait and Qatar allowed use of their territories to mount an invasion of Iraq. U.S. and British ground forces massed and trained in little Kuwait in late 2002 and early 2003.

The U.S. plan of commanding General Tommy Franks was bold but risky. Starting with the first bombing of Baghdad on March 19, U.S. mechanized forces, both Army and Marines, moved rapidly up the Euphrates valley, taking out Iraqi troops who wished to do battle but not delaying to secure cities or even their **lines of communication**. The British took Basra, the largest city of the south. U.S. forces reached the ring of Iraqi Republican Guards around Baghdad in a mere two weeks. "We executed faster than they could react," said a U.S. officer. Only the need to refuel slowed U.S. columns as they sped up highways and across desert.

There were two risks to this strategy. The first was that this long line of communication, little defended, would be easy prey for Iraqi fighters—both army and civilian militias—that had been bypassed but were still intact. They could cut off our rapidly moving spearhead. Most military commanders are cautious about overextending and thus inclined to go slow to make sure their LOC are secure. Franks gambled that stay-behind Iraqi forces would not be much of a threat, and he was right. It was no walk-through, and some Iraqi units fought fiercely, but they were totally outclassed by superbly trained high-tech U.S. soldiers with great mobility, communications, artillery, and airpower.

The second risk, widely predicted, was that Saddam would set up urban warfare in Baghdad, a sprawling metropolis of 5 million. He did not. Some suggest Saddam feared that soldiers would find it too easy to slip away in a big city or feared a military coup. The U.S. advance was so swift that Iraqi generals did not have time to adjust their defenses. The taking of Baghdad only three weeks after the war began was almost unopposed. On April 9, 2003, a U.S. Marine tank pulled down a big statue of Saddam Hussein in the center of Baghdad before cheering Iraqis. After that, it was just mopping up. The main-unit fighting part of the war lasted less than a month.

Unfortunately, we still did not know at that time what had happened to Saddam Hussein. Several attempts to kill him with **precision guided munitions** (PGMs) had missed. The superstrong bunkers under his numerous palaces appeared to have been unused. Instead of getting trapped underground, he preferred anonymous safe houses scattered around Baghdad, from which he seems to have departed shortly before we took the capital. His sons (killed in a firefight in Mosul in July) fetched $1 billion dollars—even those who hate America prefer dollars—from the national bank. Several of Saddam's relatives made it to Syria and Jordan. Many suspect he is alive and using his cash to direct Baathists to foment uprisings against the Americans. Attacks aimed at making Iraq ungovernable—including truck bombs at UN offices and a Shi'a mosque—followed someone's instructions.

---

lines of communication   (LOC) routes by which an army moves, supplies itself, and communicates.
precision guided munitions   Smart bombs.

Conflicts

DIRE AND OPTIMISTIC PREDICTIONS

Critics, both foreign and domestic, of the U.S.-British war against Iraq offered numerous dire predictions about the conduct of the war:

- Without the United States simultaneously invading from Turkey in the north, the attack was crippled from the start.
- Without being able to launch from Saudi Arabia, as in 1991, the Iraqis will keep us bottled up near Kuwait.
- Iraqi forces were too well dug in for airpower to take them out.
- The "elite" Republican Guard divisions are really good, and this time Saddam will use them instead of pulling them back as in 1991.
- Saddam will use his chemical and biological weapons.
- We will have to take Baghdad in long and deadly urban warfare, which negates our superior firepower.
- There will be massive civilian casualties.
- Saddam will blow up Iraq's oil fields, producing a monumental economic and ecological disaster, as he did in Kuwait in 1991.

After a few days of fighting, more dire predictions came:

- U.S. armored columns raced too quickly toward Baghdad, bypassing enemy concentrations and exposing our overextended lines to harassment and cutoff.
- Iraqi militias and Saddam loyalists will fight a long guerrilla war against us, making Iraq another Vietnam.

In short, the war was going to be hell, predicted numerous critics, journalists, and armchair generals. These wrong predictions were more statements of political opposition to the war than military analysis. The planning and conduct of the war were brilliant. Some predictions on the fighting, to be sure, were foolishly optimistic: It would be a "cakewalk." The U.S. strategy of "shock and awe" would collapse the regime in a week. A coup would overthrow Saddam. Whole Iraqi divisions would surrender, as they had

THE AFTERMATH

Military planning was superb, but there was little planning for what was to come afterward. Armed forces do nation-destroying, not nation-building. A month after victory, Congress charged that they had seen no administration plan for postwar Iraq. Critics, including active and retired U.S. generals and diplomats (such as George F. Kennan, founder of our Cold War "containment" policy), had warned about the difficulties of the war's aftermath but had been brushed aside. The assumption was that occupation would be easy and short, and peace would bring a federal democracy to Iraq. An interim Iraqi government was to take over most in 1991. Saddam's control over his army was too strong for that, but it turned out not to matter; U.S. forces rolled over Iraqi positions. Few Iraqi soldiers surrendered; most just went home, which was fine with us. Roads were littered with discarded uniforms.

Some dire predictions of dangerous political consequences, however, were more solid than the military predictions:

- The Arab and possibly Muslim world will hate America.
- Moderate Arab regimes, such as Saudi Arabia, will come under fundamentalist attack.
- Thousands of young Muslims, enraged by the war, will join al Qaeda for terrorist acts against us.

Relating to the war's aftermath in Iraq, some of Washington's predictions proved overoptimistic:

- All Iraqis hate Saddam and will welcome us as liberators.
- Massive evidence of Iraqi WMD and sponsorship of terrorism will be uncovered.
- Iraqi civil administration, courts, police, firefighters, and hospitals will be intact and immediately resume work.
- There will be little lawlessness and looting.
- U.S. food and medical aid will arrive quickly.
- Electrical, water, and sewage systems will keep functioning.
- Full oil production will quickly resume and pay for Iraq's reconstruction.
- Returning Iraqi exiles, whom we have groomed for the job, will be accepted by Iraqis as their leaders.
- Iraqis will quickly and cooperatively form a democratic, federal Iraq.
- The Shi'a majority of Iraq will be moderate and reject Iranian influence.
- We will not become occupiers but will soon be out of Iraq.

In sum, predictions were a mixed bag. Those predicting a long and difficult war were wrong, but some predicting a stable, peaceful aftermath were naive about the complexities of Middle Eastern culture and politics. As you read this, we are likely still dealing with the effects of the war throughout the region. Clausewitz, the great Prussian theorist of war, noted long ago that war is the closest human activity to gambling. You simply cannot know its outcome in advance.

civil functions by the end of May, but amidst civil disorder it had to be postponed, and we became occupiers for an indefinite time period. It was not what we had wanted or expected.

Initially, retired U.S. general Jay Garner—who had a good reputation among the Kurds for helping them in the early 1990s—was named as a temporary administrator. But with little staff and money, he tried to let Iraqis sort things out themselves. They did not, and a U.S. civilian administrator, L. Paul Bremer, soon replaced him with a deeper and longer mandate but one still short of money. Iraqi leaders long opposed to Saddam and encouraged by General Garner were meeting to set up a national assembly leading to a provisional authority when Bremer

Conflicts

REVOLUTION IN MILITARY AFFAIRS

For some years U.S. defense thinkers had discussed the electronic **"revolution in military affairs"** (RMA) that was supposedly changing the art of war, mostly to our benefit. Command, control, communications plus intelligence (C3I) added computers to become C4I. Spy satellites, signal intercepts, instant radio and e-mail communication, global positioning, and many other high-tech marvels had given U.S. armed forces a big lead. Other armies, even those of NATO allies, lagged twenty or more years behind us. PGMs enable us to knock out much of the enemy's brain in the first hours of a war, leaving him blind and confused. In the 1991 Gulf War, only one U.S. jet in five could bomb a target sighted by laser; twelve years later, all could. In 1991 only 9 percent of our bombs were precision-guided; in 2003 two-thirds were. Front-line U.S. combat vehicles now have computers.

RMA helps explain the quick U.S. victories over Iraq in both 1991 and 2003. But does it give us an advantage in all situations? Most officers are cautious (their civilian masters less so). Anywhere an enemy can hide—in forests, mountains, cities, or among friendly populations—can negate PGMs. Iraq was nearly perfect terrain for us. Recalling the difficulties of Vietnam, American officers in 1991 joked: "We do deserts; we don't do jungles." Low-tech opponents can sometimes bypass high-tech armies. Al Qaeda hid in caves in the Tora Bora Mountains, then sneaked into Pakistan at night without ever being detected. (They likely bribed soldiers on both sides of the border.) Some of Saddam's militia attacked U.S. convoys from small pickup trucks, although they did little damage and were quickly destroyed. Baathist believers still tried to start a guerrilla uprising against U.S. and British oc-cupiers months after the war.

told them it would have to wait. They were disappointed. We had promised them democracy. The U.S. dilemma was that to honor this pledge we might have to let Iraq slide back into anarchy or takeover by extremists. To not honor it for some time risks the growth of anti-U.S. extremism. A U.S. occupation government lasting several months seemed to be in order, but what if it lasted years?

Things immediately went wrong as the entire Iraqi infrastructure collapsed. Many water systems were damaged or shut down. In the south, bottled water had to be trucked in for thirsty Iraqi civilians. The civilian and police apparatus, high-ly centralized and under the tight control of Saddam's Baath party, evaporated. Monumental looting broke out, most by impoverished citizens, some by criminal gangs, but later as deliberate sabotage. With no plans and underestimating the sit-uation, U.S. soldiers were assigned to guard only a few buildings. Most other build-ings nationwide—including the national museum housing priceless ancient artifacts, the oil industry, hospitals, even a radioactive nuclear storehouse—were looted and left in ruins. Government records that might demonstrate Iraq's WMD and spon-sorship of terrorism were destroyed. It was a botched job.

---

revolution in military affairs   War becoming high-tech.

Mass anger leaped out after thirty-two years of ironclad dictatorship. Now Iraqis could show their feelings, and short tempers flared in the streets. Anything could start a shouting match, some with Americans as the targets. Feeding this was the discovery of mass graves of Saddam's victims. Relatives picked them over in a frenzy of grief, hoping to recover the remains of loved ones for proper Muslim burial. With Saddam likely still alive and attempting to come back, and Baathists still bombing and shooting, how could we reassure Iraqis of protection? We had assumed that only joy would leap out after liberation, but feelings were mixed and often focused on daily survival. Said one Shi'a farmer: "Money was OK under Saddam. Freedom was not so good." He called Saddam a "so-so" president.

Two important specialties were not in the Pentagon's combat plans: military police and civil affairs, which you need to run a country. These units are almost entirely in the reserves, to be mobilized only when needed. The Pentagon focuses on its combat branches, as it must; MPs and civil affairs were an afterthought. In actuality, they should have been one day behind our combat troops, who are not trained and should not be used for police duty. To do so invites catastrophe. MPs, civil affairs, and certain engineering units could have immediately imposed law and order, got local administration running, and restored water and electricity. Instead, only a few arrived and weeks later, after the situation had deteriorated. Conflicts like Afghanistan and Iraq need the quick establishment of domestic order. If you are not prepared to follow up, do not go in.

Many Iraqis, to be sure, were delighted to be liberated. They had cowered in fear for decades. Crowds bashed at the toppled statues of Saddam and cheered the Americans. Within a month, though, complaints and shootings replaced cheers. Used to the government providing everything—jobs, food, medical care, pensions, schooling, police—Iraqis expected the Americans to provide everything. That was not possible and not our intention. Americans thought that Iraqis were being unreasonable. Iraqis, with no other means of support, felt that they had been made desperate by the American takeover. Many disliked Saddam, but he had built their world, which America had just demolished with nothing to put in its place. With no GIs speaking Arabic, the situation begged for misunderstandings. Most Iraqis regard Americans as occupiers.

THE KURDISH PROBLEM

Iraq's regions brought special problems. Like Russia's regions, Iraq's harbor breakaway tendencies. Recall that Iraq is a relatively new country that Britain set up after World War I, joining together the old Turkish districts of Mosul in the north, Baghdad in the center, and Basra in the south, a somewhat artificial creation that has only the Tigris and Euphrates Rivers in common. The British, under a League of Nations mandate, intended to run Iraq and profit from its oil. The Kurds in the north (see Chapter 9) were never happy about being included in Iraq and asked the League to give them their own country. Britain put a quick stop to that. With about 20 percent of Iraq's population, at times Kurds have revolted and fought running civil wars with Baghdad (and with neighboring Turkey). Fearing the Kurds favored Iran in the Iran-Iraq war, Saddam repeatedly gassed forty-nine Kurdish villages in 1988. Mothers died trying to shield their children from the toxic fumes. By gas and executions, Saddam killed some 100,000 Kurds in 1988. Thundered the Iraqi general in charge: "I will kill them all with chemical weapons! Who is going to say anything? The international community?" The United States soon learned of the atrocities but did nothing. U.S. claims to be fighting Iraq's WMD in 2003 would have been more persuasive if we had opposed them consistently.

The 1991 Gulf War won Iraq's Kurds some autonomy. As Saddam's army moved in to kill Kurds after we let him survive in office, we warned him to keep out of the mountainous area in the northeast of the country where Kurds either lived or had fled to. In fear of their lives, Kurds fled their homes in the mostly Kurdish cities of Mosul and Kirkuk, which Saddam then repopulated with Sunni Arabs who would be loyal and grateful. (When Israelis do such things, Arabs call it a crime against humanity.) In harsh conditions, Kurds survived only with U.S. air cover and aid shipments. Saddam's army learned to keep back and send no aircraft into the "no-fly zone" north of Kirkuk.

The hardy Kurds adjusted to their unfortunate circumstances and even prospered and enjoyed their autonomy. Astride the main highway from Iraq into Turkey, Kurds made money from the trucks smuggling oil north and merchandise going south. Left to govern themselves, Kurds produced a kind of democracy and are now the only Iraqis with experience in democracy. Unfortunately, the area is divided between two Kurdish parties—the Kurdish Democratic party (KDP) and Patriotic Union of Kurdistan (PUK)—that dislike and sometimes shoot at each other, a standard problem in Kurdish history. During the 2003 war, U.S. airborne dropped in to help the Kurds liberate Mosul and Kirkuk and take out a Kurdish al Qaeda branch. The Kurds are generally pro-American, our best friends in Iraq.

But how to merge their quasi-autonomous Kurdistan into Iraq? Some Kurds said they could live with a federal Iraq, provided they get an enlarged area that includes oil fields and plenty of self-governing rights. Militants, however, still dream of an independent Kurdistan, something they have fought for off and on for a century. With control of the cities of Mosul and Kirkuk and oil fields, they would have a comfortable economy. Turkey gets hysterical at the mere mention of this, as it would encourage Turkish Kurds to demand autonomy or even union of the southeast quarter of Turkey with the Iraqi portion to make a large Kurdistan. (Iran fears the same thing among its Kurds.) Turkey had just ended a fifteen-year civil war that cost 30,000 lives to crush the PKK, the Kurdish Workers party, which sought to separate from Turkey. Ankara is not about to let this war reignite and tried to send Turkish forces into Iraq to make sure Kurds there got no ideas. For a time during our Iraq War, we feared a war within a war in northern Iraq between Turks and Kurds, one of the reasons for sending U.S. airborne to the Kurdish region. We told the Turks to keep out—since they did not let us use Turkish territory for the war, we could speak firmly—and they did. The Turkish-Kurdish problem is still a danger point.

THE SHI'A PROBLEM

The other problem is in roughly the southern half of Iraq, occupied mostly by Shi'a, who form 62 percent of Iraq's population but have always been short-changed in political power and wealth. The Ottomans, British, Hashemite monarchy, and Baathists all favored the Sunni Arabs of the center of Iraq, now a mere 16 percent of the population. Most Shi'a did not like Saddam, and some admired the Shi'a fundamentalist government in neighboring Iran after its 1979 revolution. Shi'a clerics found refuge from Saddam in Iran, but for 1,300 years the historical and religious heart of Shi'a has been not the holy city of Qum, Iran, but the holy Iraqi cities of Najaf and Karbala, which see Qum as a rival and upstart. Furthermore, Iraqi Shi'a are still Arabs and do not wish to be ruled by Iranians, who may be coreligionists but speak a strange language. Iraqi Shi'a fought in Saddam's army against Iran in the 1980s and did not rise up against him.

When the 1991 war was over, however, they did rise up and might have won with even a little U.S. help. Much of their territory had been liberated by U.S. and other coalition forces in 1991, and President Bush senior at first encouraged Iraq's Shi'a (and Kurds) to overthrow the brutal Saddam, which many were glad to do. Bush was mistaken in thinking the weakened Saddam would soon be overthrown with no help from us. Saddam had lost part of his army, but his great strength was never his army; it was his security police and Baath party, which were intact and kept him in power. Washington got second thoughts about the uprising when Iran-based Shi'a fighters infiltrated the south of Iraq to spread Islamic revolution. Opposed to Iran as much as to Iraq, we did not attempt to stop Saddam's Baath party members and security services from executing many thousands of Shi'a, including their top clerics, on mere suspicion of disloyalty. It is for this reason that Iraqi Shi'a now severely mistrust the Americans and want us to leave. Never tell people to revolt against tyranny unless you are prepared to help them all the way, a lesson we should have learned from the Hungarian Revolution of 1956. After the 2003 war, mass graves of Saddam's Shi'a victims—bound, blindfolded, and shot in the head, some of them children—were found in several places.

Iraq's Shi'a are motivated by several impulses and contain several factions, including armed militias. Their leading clergy returned in 2003 from exile in Iran, many of them imbued with the precepts of Islamic revolution and calling for "Islamic democracy." But they were still Arabs and did not want to be junior partners to Iranian clerics. Some suggested an Islamist government in which Sunni and Shi'a would be equally at home. Some Shi'a clerics cooperated with the Americans; others denounced them as infidels. Some, like moderate Kurds, indicated they could live in a federal Iraq, but others want to be masters of their own land. One project they sought was to reflood the vast marshes where the Tigris and Euphrates flow together and where many of their ancestors, the so-called "Marsh Arabs," had lived for centuries. Saddam, to crush the Shi'a revolt, drained these marshes, turning them into desert. Iraqi Shi'a will not consent to a Baghdad regime run yet again by Sunni Arabs. They want and have the votes to get a Shi'a-run government. It would be a fine irony if the Iraq War led to elected ayatollahs.

G: *Geography*

FEDERALISM FOR IRAQ?

Americans like **federalism** and think it is the natural solution to many political problems. There is nothing natural or easy about federalism. To work, it must be carefully crafted and balanced. A federal system may contain **particularistic** cultures, but they cannot be totally different from one another. Major differences in language, religion, or economics often lead to breakaway movements, as in Quebec, India's Punjab, and Croatia. All three Communist federal systems collapsed after their respective dictatorships were lifted: the Soviet Union, Yugoslavia, and Czechoslovakia. Even the United States split in two in the 1860s.

A successful federal system requires loyalties and responsibilities divided and balanced between the subunit and the central capital. If the subunits have too much autonomy, the system turns into a **confederation** and usually then falls apart, the fate of Yugoslavia. If the center has too much power, the system turns **unitary** with the subunits as little more than administrative conveniences, as in Stalin's Soviet Union. Federal institutions, such as the U.S. Senate or German Bundesrat, must give not too much and not too little representation to states.

Can federalism work in Iraq? Considering its particularistic differences—Kurds in the north, Sunnis in the center, and Shi'a in the south—federalism sounds like a solution. But are their differences too great? Are there sufficient overriding loyalties to Iraq as a whole, an Iraqi patriotism? Actually, many Sunni Arabs claim to be Iraqi patriots because they view Iraq as "their thing," with themselves its natural leading element. Kurds and Shi'a do not share this feeling and are more inclined to seek a weak federalism, which can fall apart. Too much power in Baghdad, however, could reignite the **center-periphery tensions** of Kurds and Shi'a against the center that have plagued Iraq for all its existence. There will be no easy federal solution for Iraq.

THE MUSLIM WORLD AFTER THE WAR

The war lost America most of its Arab friends. Arab intellectuals—some of whom studied in the United States and have relatives here—used to see a positive U.S. influence in moving their societies to freedom and democracy. With the Iraq War, they ceased defending America. Actually, Arabs admire American freedom and democracy, which are widely studied by educated Arabs; they just oppose

federalism   Division and balancing of powers between central government and autonomous divisions, such as U.S. states and German *Länder*.

particularism   Regional feeling that its culture is distinct and must be preserved, as in Texas and Bavaria.

confederation   Extreme form of federalism with subunits able to override the central government, as in the U.S. Articles of Confederation or the southern Confederacy.

unitary   System that concentrates most power in the nation's capital with little autonomy left to territorial subdivisions.

center-periphery tensions   Resentment of outlying areas against rule by the nation's capital.

U.S. policy, especially support for Israel. Intellectuals are important; they gradually steer society by their ideas and respected positions in law, education, science, and communications. The loss of Arab intellectuals is a long-lasting price America must pay for the Iraq War.

The neo-conservative advocates of the 2003 Iraq War understood that the Muslim world would not like the U.S. invasion of Iraq. One indication was the hundreds who volunteered from all over the Arab world for a jihad to defend Iraq. (Some are still coming.) As in 1991, the **Arab street** erupted with anger at the United States beating up a brother Arab country. But, the neo-cons argued, this anger will quickly fade in 2003, as it did in 1991. They were right, but it left a residue of bitterness that will likely last. Once again, Arabs and Muslims had been humiliated by the Christian West. Many Arabs felt the Americans were arrogant, crowing at the ease and speed of their victory. We see ourselves doing a difficult job for the sake of our national security and to rid the world of a terrible dictator. We are disappointed that more people do not thank us.

Without paying any attention to the rightness or wrongness of either side, Arabs feel that every time we win, they lose, a feeling that goes back to the *Reconquista* and Crusades. Arab regimes killing their own citizens is either ignored or excused. Hafez Assad, Syria's brainy and brutal dictator, leveled the northern Syrian city of Hama with artillery fire in 1982, killing some 20,000 Syrians, to crush a fundamentalist uprising. Few Arabs said anything; Syria is hard to govern and needs a strong hand at the top was the excuse. Saddam Hussein killed some 500,000 Muslim Iranians and 300,000 Muslim Iraqis, but few Muslims said anything; even Tehran condemned the U.S.-led attacks on Iraq in both 1991 and 2003. Facing the West, Islam displays a solidarity that they ignore when attacking each other. If we do it to ourselves, it is because the other side is not truly Muslim. If outsiders do it to us, they are the new crusaders trying to destroy Islam.

One moderate Arab intellectual said it was not the "Arab street" that worried him; it was the "Arab basement," the places out of sight where enraged youths concoct plots and bombs. Al Qaeda, a very loose-knit organization, does not publish membership statistics, but Islamist volunteers infiltrated Iraq after the war and made it the terrorist center Bush had vowed to overthrow. Al Qaeda's terrorist activities did not disappear. Al Qaeda-related bombings in Saudi Arabia and Turkey told the world that it was alive. One al Qaeda cell was reported operating in Iran, a Shi'a country that previously had not supported the Sunni al Qaeda. A Kurdish al Qaeda affiliate, Ansar al Islam, was holed up in the north of Iraq on the Iranian border. Its members fled into Iran as Kurdish and U.S. forces moved in on them in 2003.

Will the hostility of the Muslim world hurt the U.S.-led hunt for terrorists? Some countries, such as Saudi Arabia, suddenly discovered they had an incentive to join the hunt before al Qaeda overthrew them. But other Muslim countries quietly discovered that they could calm domestic unrest and gain respect in the Muslim world by dragging their feet in the hunt for terrorists. Yemen, an al Qaeda playground, promised cooperation with U.S. officials but let suspects in the *Cole*

Arab street   Shorthand expression for public opinion in Arab countries.

⑤ *The United States in the Middle East*

U.S. PUBLIC REACTION

The ultimate test of a foreign policy is its acceptance by the American people. As usual, going into the 2003 Iraq war, public opinion was hesitant and divided, preferring to act with the UN and allies. But the Bush administration, utilizing the feelings of hurt and anger from 9/11, did an excellent job convincing Americans that invading Iraq was necessary and right. Support for the war, President Bush, and the U.S. military was over 70 percent. It was an emotional and patriotic time.

The morning after, however, produced doubts and lower support numbers. What hurt was the inability to find WMD or terrorism links plus the thought of a long and costly U.S. occupation of Iraq. By late August 2003, more Americans had been killed after the war than in it, mostly by ambush. Total costs were estimated at $200 billion, far higher than imagined. Continued terrorist strikes made some—including Democratic presidential hopefuls—say we had concentrated on the wrong target. We should have been pursuing Osama and al Qaeda rather than Saddam and Iraq. The real nuclear danger was North Korea and Iran, not Iraq. Leaks that intelligence had been cooked caused more doubts.

One principle is clear in U.S. foreign policy: Americans hate long wars. (Actually, Sun Tzu said 2,500 years ago: "No one ever benefits from a long war.") Related to this is another principle of U.S. foreign policy: American public opinion is **volatile**. Initially, most Americans support their president on foreign policies, including the use of force overseas. But if fighting goes badly or lasts long, they change their minds. Two-thirds of Americans supported the Vietnam War when it began in earnest in 1965; two-thirds opposed it three years later. Bush wants to speed up "Iraqization" before the 2004 election.

bombing escape. Some governments work both sides of the street, with one ministry cooperating with the United States while others help terrorists hide and ply their trade. Pakistan never combed through its lawless northwest looking for Osama and his associates, who almost certainly were (and still are) there. Al Qaeda affiliates conduct a terror campaign in Kashmir to help Pakistan win it from India, and Pakistan does not want this shadowy relationship revealed. Cracking down on al Qaeda could cost Pakistan its best terrorists. Remember, Pakistan's ISI set up the Taliban and possibly aided al Qaeda in Afghanistan. Al Qaeda is not despised everywhere.

CONCLUSIONS

9/11 led a vengeful United States into two wars, one in Afghanistan in 2001, the other in Iraq in 2003. Both were problems left over from the administration of Bush senior. Al Qaeda was headquartered in Afghanistan, whose fundamentalist Taliban regime refused to turn its leaders over to us. America had great world support in taking out the Taliban, which was done quickly and cheaply by Special Forces helping local anti-Taliban fighters. Afghanistan, however, is still untamed.

---

volatile   Rises and falls quickly.

In late 2001 Bush junior, bolstered by neo-conservatives, decided to also take out the tyrannical regime of Saddam Hussein in Iraq. During 2002, as his plans became clearer, most of the world parted company with the United States. Many did not believe that Iraq's alleged WMD or ties to terrorism warranted a war. The UN Security Council had condemned Iraq many times but refused to authorize war, so Bush proceeded unilaterally. After the war, no gas or bugs were found in Iraq.

The U.S.-led Iraq War itself was brilliant and quick, but the aftermath was an unanticipated mess. All authority collapsed and vast lawlessness and looting broke out. A projected federal democracy was put on hold. The Kurds and Shi'a (a majority of Iraqis) have special grudges that make it difficult to hold Iraq together. Saddam loyalists and *jihadi* infiltrators made U.S. soldiers their targets. More Americans were killed after the war than in it. American enthusiasm for a long U.S. occupation of Iraq declined with the mounting expenses and casualties, and Bush ordered the quick transfer of governing powers to Iraqis to minimize the issue before the 2004 elections. Many wondered if the result would be a democratic Iraq.

FURTHER REFERENCE

Braude, Joseph. *The New Iraq: Rebuilding the Country for Its People, the Middle East, and the World.* New York: Basic Books, 2003.

Clark, Wesley K. *Winning Modern Wars: Iraq, Terrorism, and the American Empire.* New York: Public Affairs, 2003.

Cordesman, Anthony H. *The Iraq War: Strategy, Tactics, and Military Lessons.* Westport, CT: Praeger, 2003.

Johnson, Chalmers. *Blowback: The Costs and Consequences of American Empire.* 2nd ed. New York: Holt, 2004.

Kristol, William, and Kaplan, Lawrence. *The War over Iraq: Saddam's Tyranny and America's Mission.* San Francisco, CA: Encounter, 2003.

Pollack, Kenneth M. *The Threatening Storm: The Case for Invading Iraq.* New York: Random House, 2003.

Shawcross, William. *Allies: The U.S. and Europe after Iraq.* New York: Public Affairs, 2003.

CHAPTER

Why Middle East Terrorism?

16

Points to Ponder

- Why is terrorism so difficult to define?
- Who counts as a terrorist?
- Can conventional military force stop terrorism?
- Is there anything within Islam that justifies terrorism?
- What are the origins of al Qaeda?
- Who was Sayyid Qutb and what was his influence?
- What are the "micro" and "macro" levels of analysis?
- Did al Qaeda really serve its cause by its 9/11 attacks?

We've all heard that one man's terrorist is another man's freedom fighter. Terrorism is a currently popular subject, but it is a tricky one. The more you analyze it, the more it eludes you. In 1942 the leader of the Irgun movement, Menachem Begin, combined his organization with remnants of the Stern gang who had escaped from prison to launch a series of attacks against the British presence in mandate Palestine. The Stern remnants, now called Lehi, included such figures as Yitzak Shamir. They launched a series of assassination attempts against British officials. Begin, however, did not want to be perceived as hindering the British war effort against the Nazis. He ordered Irgun to attack only British civilian targets in the area.

The war ended, but the British did not leave fast enough. Begin's group bombed Jerusalem's King David Hotel, where the British had a headquarters in one wing in 1946, killing ninety-one, including fellow Jews. Shamir, at one time under a death sentence, ordered the killing of British policemen. Both Begin and Shamir eventually became prime ministers of Israel. Were they terrorists or freedom fighters?

If we accept that the Jewish leaders were freedom fighters struggling for an independent Israel and were forced to use unconventional tactics against a larger occupying force, how were they different from Palestinians who launch attacks against Israeli targets today? If Begin and Shamir were not freedom fighters but terrorists, does their involvement in legitimate politics after the creation of the state of Israel remove the terrorist label? If so, can Hezbollah officials join the Lebanese parliament and no longer be considered terrorists? Some have. Does it really matter to the United States that their diplomatic partners did or did not engage in terrorist acts fifty years ago? After all, didn't George Washington use unconventional warfare to help found the United States? American patriots did some nasty things to Tory loyalists.

In 1994 a Jewish immigrant doctor from Brooklyn opened fire with an automatic rifle on Palestinians praying in the Tomb of the Patriarchs in Hebron on the West Bank. The worshippers were civilians in a holy site that Muslims and Jews had shared for years. Enraged Palestinians killed the immigrant, Baruch Goldstein, on the spot. Who committed terrorism, Goldstein or the worshippers? Israeli settlers have since erected a shrine to Goldstein's memory.

In 1995 ultra-Orthodox rabbis ruled the withdrawal of Israel Defense Forces from the West Bank would violate Jewish sacred law. Further they ruled that peace talks with the Palestinians were endangering Jewish lives, and because Prime Minister Yitzhak Rabin encouraged the talks he was a traitor to his people. Benjamin Netanyahu, a future prime minister, accused Rabin of being outside of Jewish traditions and values, and of threatening the Jewish homeland. The unstated conclusion to such ideas was that the death of such a traitor to the Jewish people would be religiously sanctioned. Yigal Amir, a devout Jew and law student, decided he had to remove Rabin's threat to the existence of Israel and assassinated him at a peace rally in 1995. Was Amir a terrorist?

The purpose of raising these questions before moving to the question of Islamist terrorism is to point out the difficulty of dealing with the concept of "terrorism." Lord Cornwallis would surely have considered George Washington a terrorist if the term had been invented. (It actually came out of the French Revolution some years later). Today he is the father of the country. What does it all mean if we are to build a unified theory of terrorism?

DEFINITIONS

There are as many definitions of terrorism as there are people trying to define it. If one assembled all the UN documents of the last thirty years dealing with the issue, one would have over 1,800 pages and still not have a single definition. The U.S. government defines terrorism in Title 22 of the U.S. Code Section 2565f(d): Terrorism is the "premeditated politically motivated violence perpetrated against noncombatant targets by sub-national groups of clandestine agents, usually intended to influence an audience." International terrorism involves citizens or the territory of more than one country; a terrorist group is any group practicing international terrorism or that has significant subgroups that practice international terrorism.

Let's examine each aspect of the definition. There appears to be little controversy over what constitutes violence, although one could quibble over whether psychological violence qualifies for the definition. If Palestinian demonstrators at the federal building in downtown Los Angeles counterdemonstrate against Jewish demonstrators and they raise their arms in imitation of suicide bombers on the West Bank, have they engaged in terrorism?

The violence has to be premeditated and politically motivated. Thus an impulsive action by a lone gunman to commit "suicide by cop" by spraying the El Al counter at Los Angeles International Airport was not considered terrorism. His motive was personal rather than political. But where does that leave the Palestinian bomber who decides to seek revenge for the killing of a family member? His motivation is also personal and not political. Is it terrorism?

To count as terrorism, the violence must be perpetrated on noncombatants. If perpetrated on soldiers in wartime, it resembles war. This raises the question of whether a state of war exists. The French Resistance in World War II quickly learned to avoid taking on the German army; they concentrated on "spreading a thin film of terror" (in the words of Bernard Fall, who aided them) between French citizens and the Germans and their Vichy puppet government so as to make France ungovernable. As such, they mostly killed fellow French civilians who collaborated with the Germans. In 2003 partisans of Saddam did the same to Iraqis who cooperated with the Americans. When Hizballah attacked the U.S. Marine barracks in Beirut in 1983, were they attacking combatants or noncombatants? The Marines were there for peacekeeping. When supporters of al Qaeda drove a boat full of explosives into the USS *Cole*, was the American warship a combatant or noncombatant? It was not on war duty, and we were in no war at the time.

The violence is perpetrated by subnational groups, usually by clandestine agents. This definition gives a pass to the military forces of nation-states, the holders of the monopoly on the exercise of power. Iraq dispatched clandestine agents to assassinate former President Bush in Kuwait in 1993. Was it terrorism or simply an act of war? (For terrorism as type of warfare, see box on page 281.)

If a subnational group such as the Kurdish Democratic party sent clandestine agents to sabotage Iraqi military facilities in the 1970s, was it terrorism? If so, how is it different if the same group committed the same sabotage in 2003 in support of U.S. Operation Enduring Freedom?

The violence is almost always designed to influence an audience, what the old anti-tsarist Russian anarchists called "propaganda of the deed." Killing one official may be unimportant except to arouse the masses. Terrorists above all want to be noticed in the hope of rallying others to their cause. A terrorist strike that draws no media attention is almost worthless.

Terrorism often resembles crime, but the former is intensely political and the latter not. The goal of a terrorist is the overthrow of a hated political authority. The criminal just wants money. To be sure, in Colombia crime and politics overlap. The leftist rebels and right-wing paramilitaries may have started with political motives, but now both profit so much from the drug trade that the political goals take second place. Both sides call each other terrorists. The United States sees the drug traffic as crime but quickly got involved in fighting Communist-type guerrillas. The for-profit war in Colombia will be difficult to end; there is simply too much money to be made.

Conflicts

LOW-INTENSITY WARFARE

One way to define terrorism that avoids some of the complexities and ambiguities is simply to see it as a type of low-intensity warfare. We can array warfare on a spectrum or scale. At the top is all-out warfare between countries, with uniformed soldiers, much equipment, massive destruction, and essentially no limits. World Wars I and II are examples. Not all wars are total; some are confined to one area. The United States and China fought in Korea but not outside of Korea. Some wars have only a little at stake. Argentina and Britain fought a brief, undeclared war over the Falklands (Malvinas, if you prefer) in 1982 but did not attack each other's homelands. It simply was not worth it.

Smaller than that is **guerrilla** warfare. Guerrilla is simply Spanish for "little war" and was first used in the early nineteenth century as Spanish patriots, civilian "partisans," strove to expel Napoleon's legions. Faced with a much stronger occupying power, the partisans (often with British help) resorted to irregular tactics. The opening stages of guerrilla struggles are often insurgencies, a group trying to overthrow a hated political authority. The Pentagon calls this "low-intensity warfare" and instituted "counterinsurgency" tactics to oppose it. The Green Berets in Vietnam are examples.

It is here that we get to terrorism. Typically, an insurgency starts with and continues acts of terrorism. A small group of believers robs a bank, shoots police, or bombs a main street. They hope the hated political authority overreacts by arresting, torturing, and shooting many people. The more they do, the more recruits for the insurgents' cause. Tito's *Partizani* deliberately killed German soldiers in Yugoslavia during World War II, knowing the Germans would kill a hundred locals for every dead German, thus producing hundreds of German-hating new Partizani. The terrorist practices a kind of jujitsu, using the larger mass of the opponent to trip himself. We might see terrorism as entry-level warfare. Once the terrorists' political commitments become rooted in a population, they are hard to root out.

An international terrorist group is any group or subunit of the group that practices international terrorism—involving citizens or territory of another country. According to this definition, American militia groups, the Unabomber, and the Ku Klux Klan do not qualify as international terrorist groups because their activities involve the citizens and territory of only one country. When Syrian Muslim Brothers launched attacks against the government of Hafez al-Asad, it consisted of Syrians fighting in Syria. Terrorism?

Some commentators have tried to avoid the definitional problems, quoting a Supreme Court justice on pornography: "I may not be able to define it, but I know it when I see it." This is a cop out. Terrorism is an action that the government decides to label as terrorism. Once the action carries the label it can be condemned outright and participants can receive extra punishment when they are caught. Terrorism is not a legal concept but an emotional one—regardless of Title 22 or its equivalent in other countries.

---

guerrilla   Irregular small-unit, hit-and-run warfare.

Accordingly, had the British triumphed in mandate Palestine, the state authority would have labeled Begin and Shamir terrorists. The British left, and the Israeli state approved their actions. Cornwallis may not have liked Washington, but the Americans loved him. Depending on who wins the struggle, Palestinian militants who are now called terrorists will either maintain their appellation or be exonerated by future generations.

ISLAMIST TERRORISTS

In the Middle East nonstate fighters are usually grouped into three categories: Palestinian, Hezbollah, and al Qaeda. While the first two categories are important in their own right, our focus here will be on al Qaeda.

Palestinian groups include Hamas, Palestinian Islamic Jihad, the Al Aqsa Martyrs Brigade, Black September, Popular Front for the Liberation of Palestine, and others. Those who are motivated by Islam include the first three of these. These groups are of vital importance to the state of Israel since they are fighting to wipe out the Jewish state. They have killed a number of Jewish combatants and even more Jewish noncombatants.

To Western states such as the United States and Britain, these groups are important largely because they threaten an ally. The Palestinian groups have not targeted citizens of Western states, but some fear they will turn to attacks against Westerners. Some already have. Black September attacked the Jewish athletes at the 1972 Munich Olympics and did not stop to ask if the security guards were German citizens. Six months later, the same Black September, an offshoot of Yassir Arafat's PLO, assassinated the U.S. ambassador in Khartoum, Sudan. Palestine Liberation Front terrorists threw Leon Klinghofer (in his wheelchair) off the *Achille Lauro* in 1985, knowing he was an American. In 1997 a Palestinian gunman opened fire on people on the top of the Empire State Building in New York City. We may not be immune from Palestinian terrorism.

Many victims of Palestinian suicide bombings have been citizens of Western countries or dual citizens. Al Qaeda began its anti-American crusade because of anger over American support of the group's first target, Saudi Arabia. The same logic chain could eventually lead Hamas or Palestinian Jihad into targeting any supporter of Israel.

Lebanon is the home of Shi'a-related Hizballah or the "Party of God" (often spelled *Hezbollah*). Until September 11, 2001, Hizballah had killed more Americans than any other terrorist group. Hizballah destroyed the American embassy in Beirut, used truck bombs on the U.S. Marine and French barracks, and kidnapped and tortured U.S. and U.K. citizens throughout the 1980s. Ronald Reagan struck the colors and ran off the beaches of Lebanon. Then in the Iran-Contra scandal (see Chapter 13), we provided Hizballah's principal supporter (Iran) with some weapons to fight Iraq. After that, Hizballah had no reason to target Westerners.

Hizballah maintains a terrorist arm sometimes called the Islamic Jihad Organization and a military structure in the south of Lebanon. Hizballah politicians insist they are not a terrorist group but a Lebanese group opposed to Israeli occupation. This claim is questionable, since Israel unilaterally withdrew from Lebanon in 2000. Hizballah members sit in the Lebanese parliament and Hizballah hospitals and clinics aid the Shi'a population. When the Syrians give them permission, Hizbal h will gladly ambush an Israeli patrol or lob missiles into northern Israel.

AL QAEDA

The "Mother of all Islamist Terrorist Groups" is al Qaeda or "The Base." It was founded in the killing fields of Afghanistan. At least 15,000 Islamists from around the world converged on the Soviet-occupied Central Asian country to wage holy war against the infidel. The son of a Saudi millionaire, Osama bin Ladin paid for many of the warriors' travels. He input the names of his co-jihadists into a computer database, thus giving birth to the name of his organization.

Bin Ladin was a scary figure to the West. The scion to a fortune, he voluntarily relinquished a life of wealth to live in a cave in Afghanistan. He may have been trying to reject his father, who appears to have had little time for his seventeenth son (of over fifty children). Osama's mother divorced his father long ago and because of this is not considered part of the bin Ladin family. This must have placed Osama's own position within the clan in question. The father died in a plane crash when Osama was ten.

A playboy older brother, Salim, took over as head of the family; Osama retreated into piety. He began to study the works of Sayyid Qutb and other philosophers who condemned the role of the West in Islamic affairs.

When the Soviets invaded Afghanistan in 1979, bin Ladin became a fund-raiser for the jihad against them. He visited Afghanistan in the early 1980s, importing construction equipment to help the opposition. He set up a series of guesthouses throughout Pakistan for the warriors en route to the jihad. During their time in these hostels they were indoctrinated with bin Ladin's own interpretation of Islam. He settled into Peshawar, Pakistan, in 1986. In Afghanistan, he came under withering Soviet fire at Jaji. He and his followers retreated after taking heavy losses, but somehow he convinced his fellow jihadists this was a victory.

Much has been written about how the American government supported bin Ladin during this period, but this is inaccurate. According to press reports, the American support to the opposition was funneled through Pakistan's Inter-Services Intelligence agency (ISI), and the United States had no say where its money and weapons went. The Pakistanis favored Gulbuddin Hekmatyar despite the fact that his philosophy made the Iranians next door look liberal. Osama would work with Hekmatyar but not under him. Bin Ladin didn't need the American aid; he was already the nexus for Islamist contributions to the jihad. The Kingdom of Saudi Arabia also supplemented bin Ladin's efforts. The head of Saudi intelligence believed he had the young Saudi under control. Air Saudia gave 75 percent discounts to all Arabs seeking to fight in Afghanistan.

Cultures

THE PHILOSOPHER OF ISLAMISM

Egyptian writer Sayyid Qutb (1906–1966) has had a hypnotic influence on a long generation of Islamic fundamentalists. A thinker in the salafi mold (see page 286 and Chapter 17), Qutb (pronounced "CUT-eb") is credited with inventing **Islamism**, at least among Sunnis. Born in Cairo, he had memorized the Qur'an by age ten but then went to a modern college. He knew both traditional Islam and Western socialism and tried to synthesize them. Only Islam, he wrote in the 1940s, can deliver social justice. In the late 1940s he earned a master's degree at the Colorado State College of Education but hated America for its sexual permissiveness. So much for understanding through student exchanges.

A brilliant intellectual and powerful writer, Qutb in large part was reacting against the encroachment of Western thought in the Muslim world. He emphasized that Western wealth, philosophy, and science had only made humans unhappy. Only by fusing them with traditional Qur'anic teaching would humans find happiness. The splitting of faith and reason, God and science, was a Christian error the West had inflicted on the world, leading to confusion and madness. The solution was to return to the Qur'an, reconstitute the Muslim caliphate that Atatürk had terminated in 1924, and restore shari'a as the legal system. Martyrdom was a perfectly acceptable method for this end.

Qutb was the leading theorist of Egypt's important Muslim Brotherhood, who found Nasser a dangerous secularist and tried to assassinate him. In retaliation, Nasser outlawed the Brotherhood and jailed its members, including Qutb, whom Nasser had hanged in 1966. Qutb's brother fled to Saudi Arabia where he taught Islamism to a student named Osama bin Laden.

The Soviets withdrew from Afghanistan in 1989. Islamists never accorded any importance to U.S.-supplied Stinger missiles, Chinese military support, and the collapse of the Warsaw Pact for reasons having nothing to do with Afghanistan. Instead, they incorporated the Soviet withdrawal into their founding mythology. Islamists believed they had single-handedly caused one of the two world superpowers to retreat under their fire. Having been successful once showed it should not take much to make the other superpower, the United States, also retreat from Muslim lands.

With the Soviets out, the Islamists had no reason to remain in Afghanistan or Pakistan. They had come from all corners of the Arab world: Algeria, Libya, Egypt, Saudi Arabia, Yemen, and other countries. They now returned to their home countries. Some retired from military activities but most spread the Islamist message in their home territories. In some cases, they infiltrated and took over preexisting groups; in others they organized from scratch. These "Afghan Arabs" were a transnational group that might be called the Afghan Veterans of Foreign Wars. They stayed in touch with one another, shared training and techniques, and counted on one another when traveling. Whenever an Afghan Arab landed in a country he had the names of fellow jihadists with him whom he knew could give him food, shelter, and operational assistance.

Islamism   An extreme form of Islam turned into a political ideology.

Key Concepts

MICRO VERSUS MACRO ANALYSES

In the shock of 9/11, many Americans sought to explain its "root cause" as poverty. It is the desperately poor who do such things; the long-term solution is alleviation of poverty. Neo-cons dismissed this notion as typical of liberals who suppose that more "programs" will cure malignant evil. Neo-conservatives quickly pointed out that most of the 9/11 murderers were middle-class and educated. In the neo-con perspective, the cause of Islamic extremism is Islam.

The two sides in this debate tended to talk past each other. For sound analysis of the motives of suicide bombers and other terrorists, at least two things need to be sorted out. First, the "level of analysis" has to be settled. Are we talking about the **micro** level, which looks at individuals, or the **macro** level, which looks at whole countries? Macro approaches note that suicide bombers come from undemocratic countries with enormous birth rates and slow economic growth, producing many unemployed and discontented young people. This suggests the suicide volunteers are angry and frustrated, and the cure is economic growth and political democratization. Micro studies, on the other hand, look at individual suicide bombers and find that many are educated, not poor, psychologically normal, and show no despair or sense of "nothing to lose." If the micro picture is true, poverty has little to do with suicide bombings. This "micro-macro gap" has been with the social sciences a long time, although some try to bridge it. We cannot assume that individual behavior and attitudes explain the behavior of millions of people, and vice-versa.

The next analytical problem is the bundling together of unlike cases. Palestinian, Lebanese, Saudi, Egyptian, and other killers have different motives and socioeconomic profiles. Interviews of Palestinian "martyrs" do not explain the 9/11 terrorists, who in turn do not explain Moroccan suicide bombers. In contrast to the 9/11 Saudi killers, the 2003 Moroccan bombers were poor and uneducated. One size does not fit all. A political scientist needs both micro and macro approaches and must separate out the various countries involved. Each has a different political situation, and each creates extremists with different motives. Beneath the several factors producing martyrs, the one consistent point they have in common—and here the neo-cons are right—is the passionate embrace of Islam.

RELATIONS WITH SAUDI ARABIA GONE SOUR

On August 1, 1990, the "godless regime" of Iraq's Saddam Hussein invaded Kuwait and many believed threatened Saudi Arabia. Bin Ladin flew to Riyadh with an amazing offer: to defend the kingdom with his jihadists, relieving the king of the need to turn to the West for help. After defeating the Soviet Union, Osama thought it would not be too hard to beat Iraq.

Instead, the house of al-Saud turned to the guarantor of their security ever since Abdul Aziz met FDR in 1945—the United States of America. Bin Ladin was appalled; according to tradition the last words of the Prophet before he died were

---

micro   Looking at the close-up picture of individuals.
macro   Looking at the big picture, usually a whole country.

"No two religions in the land of the two holy places" of Mecca and Medina, now taken to mean the entire Saudi peninsula. Now the royal family that was pledged to uphold Islam in the Kingdom was violating the Prophet's dying edict. Bin Ladin's analysis was supported by dissident clerics in the Kingdom. Spurned by a royal family he now perceived as hypocritical puppets of the West, starting in 1992 he openly encouraged overthrow of the Saudi government. He left the Kingdom for the Sudan before he could be arrested.

In Sudan he invested his millions in a variety of business pursuits and opened terrorist training camps. Since he remained loudly anti-Saudi, in 1994 the Kingdom stripped him of his citizenship. The bin Ladin family, whose fortune was wholly dependent on the House of al-Saud, publicly disowned their renegade member. Bin Ladin was an international pariah.

As the terrorist training came to the attention of Western powers, the United States pressured Sudan to expel their guest. In 1996 bin Ladin declared war against the United States and returned to the familiar territory of Afghanistan, where he provided training and operational assistance to groups in fifty-five countries who accepted his message.

BIN LADIN'S MESSAGE

Osama's message of hate has had a number of targets over the years. His teachings are firmly anchored in the fundamentalist Islamist interpretation of Islam, what is called the **salafiyya** (see page 302). Originally he and his movement concentrated on removing the Soviet Union from Afghanistan. His theory was that the Soviets, whose official ideology included atheism, were godless infidels who had taken Muslim lands by force. Since the Dar al Islam (House of Islam) was under attack, it was the individual duty of all Muslims to oppose the Soviet occupation.

After the Soviets withdrew from Afghanistan, Osama's ire fell on the House of Saud and other rulers of Islamic lands who were not sufficiently pious in his eyes. Osama looked at two different standards: the personal piety of the ruler and the efforts of the ruler to implement shari'a law in their countries. If political leaders did not meet his personal standards, they became targets of his anger. In the case of Saudi Arabia, bin Ladin believed the rulers were impious personally and a danger to Islam for inviting a non-Muslim army into the Kingdom. He vowed to overthrow the House of Saud.

At this point in the development of his theory Osama's thinking concentrated on making already Islamic countries more Muslim. He maintained contact with fellow jihadists in other countries who were fighting to overthrow their own governments for being insufficiently Islamic. He turned his attention to the United States because of America's presence in the Middle East and because he believed

---

salafiyya   "The way of the forefathers," reactionary doctrine of alleged pure Islam, basis of current Islamic fundamentalism. Adjective: *salafi*.

the "heretic" governments he opposed were propped up in power by American military might. His opposition to the United States was in a sense "nothing personal." His opposition to America was merely a necessary step to his real goal: the removal of the house of Saud.

It was just a short step in deepening his theory to see the United States as the principal threat to Muslims worldwide. He then declared it was all Muslims' duty to kill Americans anywhere they could be found. Bin Ladin's conversion into an anti-American fanatic was complete.

Interestingly, bin Ladin originally did not show much interest in the Israeli-Palestinian conflict. In 1998, forming a "Coalition Against Crusaders, Christians, and Jews," he merged his al Qaeda organization with the Egyptian fundamentalist groups Gama'at Islami (sometimes spelled *Jamaat Islami*) and Egyptian Islamic Jihad. Their leader, Egyptian physician Ayman al-Zawahiri, soon became Osama's second in command. Zawahiri brought the Egyptian opposition to Israel into the equation. Bin Ladin subsequently declared Muslims had to fight against the United States and Israel both to rid the world of the evil regimes and to defend their faith.

Neither bin Ladin nor Zawahiri are Islamic clerics; they do not hold the title of *mufti* and are therefore not entitled to issue binding religious edicts, fatwas. For religious justification, bin Ladin relied on radical clerics on the fringe of Islamic thought to issue fatwas supporting his positions. By 2000 he relied on the leader of the Afghan Taliban, a religiously undereducated activist named Mullah Omar, to provide the legitimating religious rulings. In return, bin Ladin encouraged his followers to accept Omar as the caliph for Muslims worldwide. Religious justification, blind hatred, and access to technology, money, and weapons were a potent mixture.

TERRORIST ATTACKS

Al Qaeda's handiwork is well known and so we will review it only briefly here. In 1992 they conducted three bombings in Yemen and targeted American servicemen attempting to bring aid to Muslims suffering from hunger and deprivation in Somalia. Then when American intervention in Somalia deepened in an attempt to bring food and peace in that benighted corner of Africa, bin Ladin sent trainers to teach the Somalis how to shoot the tail assembly of helicopters with shoulder-fired missiles. The result, as shown in the book and movie *Black Hawk Down,* was the death and capture of American servicemen. Weeks later President Clinton ordered American troops out of Somalia. Bin Ladin had learned that military opposition could make the Soviets withdraw from Muslim lands and that the same tactics could make the United States withdraw as well.

In the United States a group of followers of the Egyptian blind Shaykh Abdul Rahman tried to blow up the World Trade Center in New York City in 1993 with a van bomb. The blast killed six people and injured 1,000. The leader, Ramzi Yusef, was a nephew of leading al Qaeda organizer Khalid Shaykh Muhammad. The same group also had plans to destroy the Statue of Liberty, the Empire State Building, and the tunnels connecting Manhattan to New Jersey.

Ramzi escaped to the South Pacific where he continued his terrorist planning. In 1994 and 1995 he planned the assassination of Pope John Paul II during his visit to Manila, bombings of U.S. and Israeli embassies in the area, midair bombings of trans-Pacific jetliners, and the assassination of President Clinton during a visit to the Philippines. According to press reports, police captured him when he had accidentally set fire to his kitchen while mixing ingredients for a bomb.

In 1995 a car bomb destroyed the front of the National Guard building in Riyadh, Saudi Arabia, killing five Americans and two Indians. The Saudis arrested and beheaded four of their fellow countrymen for the crime. Three of the four admitted to having fought in Afghanistan, one in bin Ladin's own group.

On August 7, 1998, suicide bombers drove trucks full of explosives into American embassies in Nairobi, Kenya, and Dar-es-Salaam, Tanzania. The two bombs separated by hundreds of miles exploded within 9 minutes of each other. Planning for the bombings had taken five years. The bombs killed 224 and injured thousands, most of them local Muslim Africans.

On January 1, 2000, al Qaeda tried to bring in the new millennium with simultaneous attacks on tourist sites in Jordan and at the Los Angeles International Airport. Law enforcement authorities foiled the attacks before they could take place. An alert U.S. Customs official—yes, using physical profiling—spotted the suspicious driver on a ferry from British Columbia to Washington State.

Two days later in Yemen, a group of fanatics tried to pilot a rubber boat full of explosives into the side of the USS *The Sullivans*. The overloaded boat sank under its own weight. The Americans never even knew they had been targeted. Ten months later, the same fanatics tried again. Having dried out their explosives and patched their boat, they drove it into the USS *Cole*, killing seventeen American sailors and almost sinking the warship. In the aftermath of the attack, the Pentagon ceased using the port of Aden as a refueling point. Bin Ladin had won again.

September 11, 2001

On September 11, 2001, the world we had known for generations ended. Al Qaeda terrorists armed with box cutters and led by Egyptian Muhammad Atta hijacked four American airliners. They did not try to smuggle weapons or explosives on board but used the planes' fuel as bombs. Two planes destroyed the World Trade Center, killing almost 3,000 and causing billions in damage. Citizens of eighty countries, many of them Muslim, died in the attack. It was Britain's greatest terrorist tragedy as well as America's. A third plane crashed into the Pentagon, killing 180. The fourth plane high over Pennsylvania turned toward Washington, D.C. Passengers who heard on their cell phones of the fate of the other planes rushed the hijackers. The plane crashed and all died. Their valiant sacrifice prevented the plane from killing possibly hundreds or thousands more had it reached its target in the nation's capital.

In retaliation, an angry America invaded Afghanistan, deposed the Taliban government, and killed hundreds of al Qaeda supporters (see Chapter 15). Many of the leading members of al Qaeda were killed or captured. The two at the top, bin Ladin and al-Zawahiri, escaped and may be hiding in the tribal territories in Pakistan's lawless Northwest Province.

On May 12, 2003, al Qaeda launched a wave of bombings inside Saudi Arabia. Three car bombs detonated simultaneously inside residential compounds where foreign workers stayed. At least twenty-nine foreigners were killed, including seven Americans. Bin Ladin's actions delivered three messages simultaneously: They had not been defeated, they could operate inside the capital city of their enemies, and they had not abandoned their goal of driving Americans out of the Kingdom. One of the compounds was the residence of Vinnell Corporation employees who trained the Saudi National Guard. Four days later fourteen suicide bombers killed twenty-nine people in five explosions in Casablanca, Morocco. The targets included a Jewish center and the Belgian consulate. Moroccans associated with al Qaeda had attacked the foreign presence in a distant corner of the Dar al-Islam.

Over the past fifteen years there have been hundreds of terrorist attacks and attempts. Some, such as shoe-bomber Richard Reid and José Badillo, were al Qaeda associates who were stopped. Others had nothing to do with this international terrorist conspiracy but were motivated by their own causes. Clearly the United States and Western Europe remain targets of bin Ladin's wrath.

LESSONS LEARNED

There are a number of lessons to be learned from the terrorist attacks described above. The most important is that bin Ladin does not give up. He tried to take down the World Trade Center in 1993; he returned and finished the job in 2001. He tried to sink a U.S. warship in Yemen in January 2000; he succeeded in October. He tried to drive Americans away from supporting the Saudi National Guard in 1995 and returned to the target in 2003.

He likes to show his reach by organizing simultaneous attacks on multiple targets. The targets themselves are usually symbolic but may also have secondary importance as economic targets. Finally, bin Ladin has no compunction in shedding Muslim blood.

The United States may have the most powerful army in the history of the world, but its military prowess has been unsuccessful in removing the terrorist threat of Osama bin Ladin and his supporters. The country is currently engaged in a long twilight struggle with the terrorists, employing the country's law-enforcement and intelligence organizations. Numerous arrests of al Qaeda supporters throughout Europe show that in what the Pentagon called the "Global War on Terror" (GWOT) the United States still can count on allies that opposed its 2003 invasion of Iraq.

The arrests are a good sign: We have had a number of successes in the GWOT. They are also a bad sign: Despite the arrests, al Qaeda has no trouble recruiting. Many flocked to Iraq to fight the U.S. occupation. "The Base" no longer has its safe haven in Afghanistan, and in many ways the organization has been decapitated. While this may hurt the organization's ability to coordinate, it also makes it harder to root out its component parts. Al Qaeda is not a monolith; it is more like a holding company comprised of a number of independent organizations that have come together for economies of scale. Take away the corporate headquarters as the allies did in Afghanistan and the component organizations still function.

Harvard's Jessica Stern called al Qaeda **"protean"** for its ability to adapt itself according to circumstances and opportunities. It has no formal structure, headquarters, or membership. That is why searching for al Qaeda's links to any particular country—Afghanistan or Iraq—is frustrating. Even if some connections were found—and no clear al Qaeda links were found in Iraq—al Qaeda has already vanished like the mist. It was a bit like searching for the communists' elusive Central Office for South Vietnam (COSVN). U.S. forces in Vietnam supposed it must be a sort of bamboo Pentagon, but it was likely little more than a commander and two radios, ready to move in moments. We never found COSVN.

Al Qaeda is motivated by a number of grievances, some reasonable, some not. There is poverty and suffering in the Islamic world. Israel exists and is at war with elements in the Palestinian territories. Many Islamic rulers pay little attention to the needs of their people or the precepts of their faith. American troops are posted in more Islamic lands than ever. But even changing these conditions cannot guarantee an end to terrorist attacks. The demographic bulge in Muslim lands produces millions of angry young men, who easily fall into salafi beliefs.

Western governments actively support many of the conditions opposed by al Qaeda for legitimate reasons of national interest, such as U.S. support for Saudi Arabia. Bin Ladin and his people hope that terrorist attacks will convince the West that the price they pay to pursue these interests is higher than the benefits received. When that happens, they reason, the West will withdraw as it did in Vietnam, Beirut, Somalia, and Yemen. The questions for policymakers: How important is the Middle East to Western interests? Is the occasional terrorist attack (no matter how horrific) a price we are willing to pay?

CONCLUSIONS

There are terrorists of all stripes and persuasions. In the Middle East there are people who have committed "terrorist" acts who are now national leaders. There are others who sit in jail because of their national aspirations. For the United States the most serious form of international terrorism is Islamist terrorism as practiced by the followers of Osama bin Ladin.

Al Qaeda got its start in the Islamic struggle against the Soviets in Afghanistan. While it received no direct U.S. support, America must take at least part of the blame for creating the climate that allowed al Qaeda supporters to prosper. Similarly, in Saudi Arabia the royal family protests that they, like the United States, are victims of Islamist terrorism rather than supporters of it. Yet, like the United States, the Saudis have to take some of the blame by allowing an extremist interpretation of Hanbali Islam to spread.

---

protean   Able to change shape and assume many forms.

There will be no victory in the Global War on Terror, no parade when the troops come home. This is a war being fought in the shadows, and it will continue as long as there is Islamist hatred. For that hatred to subside, Islam may have to undergo a reformation that makes its values compatible to the modern, democratic values of the West. We consider this possibility in the next chapter.

FURTHER REFERENCE

Bergen, Peter L. *Holy War, Inc.* New York: Touchstone, 2002.

Bowden, Mark. *Black Hawk Down.* New York: Signet, 2002.

Hoveyda, Fereydoun. *The Broken Crescent: The "Threat" of Militant Islamic Fundamentalism.* Westport, CT: Praeger, 2002.

Ismael, Tareq Y. *Middle East Politics Today: Government and Civil Society.* Gainesville, FL: University Press of Florida, 2001.

Kepel, Gilles. *Jihad: The Trail of Political Islam.* Cambridge, MA: Harvard University Press, 2002.

Rubin, Barry, and Judith Colp Rubin, eds. *Anti-American Terrorism and the Middle East: A Documentary Reader.* New York: Oxford, 2002.

Smith, Charles D. *Palestine and the Arab-Israeli Conflict,* 4th ed. Boston: Bedford/St. Martins, 2001.

Stern, Jessica. *Terror in the Name of God: Why Religious Militants Kill.* New York: HarperCollins, 2003.

Stout, Chris E., ed. *The Psychology of Terrorism,* 4 vols. Westport, CT: Praeger, 2002.

Williams, Paul. *Al Qaeda: Brotherhood of Terror.* Indianapolis, IN: Alpha, 2002.

A Democratic Middle East?

Points to Ponder

- Is democracy a real prospect for the Middle East?
- Which Middle East countries are the most democratic? Which are the least democratic?
- Why do some countries fail to modernize?
- How did Huntington's "clash of civilizations" challenge optimists?
- What is "modernization theory," and does it fit the Middle East?
- Do Muslim immigrants in Europe become culturally European?
- What is "civil society" and can America promote it?
- What is *salafiyya* and why is it enjoying an upsurge?
- What forces are hitting Saudi Arabia now? Can democratization save it?

As the clouds of the Iraq War gathered in 2002, some of the neo-conservative hawks who supported war included among their reasons a chance to democratize the Middle East. Knocking out the Saddam regime, they argued, would not only curb weapons of mass destruction and terrorism but also allow the United States to set up a democracy that would in turn encourage democracy in other Middle Eastern countries. Iraq would be a demonstration project for the entire region. America would reform the Middle East.

Many found this optimistic scenario highly improbable if not outright impossible. Iraq and indeed most of the region is far from ready for democracy, the critics claimed. Until recently, the Republicans themselves had scoffed at the Clinton administration's policies of "enlargement of democracy" and "nation-building" as muddle-headed "international social work." Indeed, good conservatives ought to scoff at the notion of redoing society. The long-standing conservative view is that societies change themselves; efforts to speed up or guide this process of change are dangerous meddling, whether practiced by liberals or Leninists. But the proponents of democracy for Iraq were not conservatives; they were neo-conservatives, people from liberal backgrounds who

Traditional Arab transport plods past an Israeli kibbutz, an outpost of modern farming methods. Israeli culture, essentially European, moves fast. Arab culture moves slow. (Michael Roskin)

rejected the **relativism** and pacifism that had made their home in the Democratic party. Traditional conservatives are skeptical of activism; neo-conservatives like muscular intervention. The two strands coexisted uneasily among Republicans.

Can the United States implant democracy in Iraq or anywhere else? Those in favor point to Germany and Japan after World War II as examples of successful democratization. Skeptics say this is a false analogy because Germany and Japan were industrialized countries with educated populations who had some democratic experience between the two world wars. The Nazis and Japanese militarists had discredited themselves; many citizens hated them and welcomed democracy. In postwar Germany and Japan, democracy did not start from scratch.

The Middle East, on the other hand, has historically never known democracy. Its governments have been **authoritarian**, either traditional monarchies or personalistic dictatorships. Only Israel is a stable democracy, but it was brought from Europe by Jewish settlers with a democratic political culture. Turkey is an unstable democracy; its elected governments operate under an implied military veto. Turkey has had four military coups since World War II. Lebanon looked like a democracy for much of the postwar period, but it was a contrived system based on a set allocation of political positions among its many religions, what is called **consociational democracy**. The Middle East looked like poor soil for growing democracy.

---

relativism   View that there is no absolute morality, that social and political questions are complex and ambiguous.
authoritarian   Nondemocratic governance.
consociational democracy   Power-sharing among groups at the executive level.

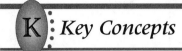

MIDDLE EAST REGIMES

Nothing is simple in the Middle East, and descriptions of the region's regimes require many qualifications. First, we should distinguish between "loose" and "tight" authoritarian regimes. The former permit a little freedom; the latter are control freaks. Saddam Hussein's Iraq was a **totalitarian** regime, because his Baath party attempted to control everything, aided by a terroristic police apparatus. Nominally, Syria is also run by a Baathist party, but it is little more than a vehicle for personalistic rule, currently by the son of the previous dictator. Israel and Turkey are both parliamentary democracies, but Israel's is stable and Turkey's is not.

Iran's regime is the hardest to classify. It has some of the institutions of democracy and some of **theocracy**. Its parliament and president are elected, but from a limited slate supervised by top Muslim clerics, who also veto efforts at liberalization. Iran probably has the greatest democratic potential of the region. The emir (prince) of Qatar has embarked on democratization by permitting an elected assembly and freer media.

Freedom House in New York does annual surveys, rating countries for both "political rights" and "civil liberties" by giving 1 for most free and 7 for least. The average of these two are shown for 2002 along with FH's classification of "free," "partly free," and "not free." (See table at end of box on page 295.) Jordan rated "partly free" because it was improving. Among FH's worst nine—scoring 7 in both categories—for 2002 were Iraq, Libya, Saudi Arabia, and Sudan.

The prevalence of authoritarian regimes should not be surprising or mysterious. The great German sociologist Max Weber a century ago explained **charismatic** authoritarian systems as characteristic of the painful transition from traditional to modern societies. At this in-between stage, traditional **legitimacy**, such as those of monarchs, has broken down, but modern "rational-legal" legitimacy, such as those of democracies, has not yet been established. In this time of weakness, powerful personalities seize power by coup and keep power by their security police, control of mass media, and rigged elections.

THE FAILURE OF MODERNIZATION?

Many analysts of the Middle East see its problems as failures of modernization, a view that has been around for centuries and voiced by some Muslim intellectuals. A thousand years ago, Muslims were far ahead of Christian Europe, but about five hundred years ago the balance began to shift. Europe was rapidly modernizing and the Ottoman Empire was not. The 1571 naval battle of Lepanto, in which a joint Venitian, Spanish, and Austrian fleet defeated an Ottoman fleet, was a sign that power was shifting. At the time, when the Ottoman Empire was

---

totalitarian   Regime that attempts to control everything and remake society; more thorough than *authoritarian*.

theocracy   Rule by priests.

charismatic   Able to sway masses by strong personality.

legitimacy   Mass feeling that regime's rule is rightful.

Country	Type	Executive	FH Rating
Algeria	military dictatorship	permanent president	5.5 not free
Bahrain	traditional monarchy	hereditary prince	5.0 partly free
Egypt	loose authoritarian	permanent president	6.0 not free
Iran	Islamist semi-democracy	powerless president	6.0 not free
Iraq (pre-2003)	totalitarian	charismatic dictator	7.0 not free
Israel	parliamentary democracy	elected PM	2.0 free
Jordan	traditional monarchy	hereditary king	5.5 partly free
Kuwait	traditional monarchy	hereditary king	4.5 partly free
Lebanon	consociation (Syrian-supervised)	president	5.5 not free
Libya	tight authoritarian	permanent president	7.0 not free
Oman	traditional monarchy	hereditary prince	5.5 not free
Pakistan	military dictatorship	changeable president	5.5 not free
Qatar	modernizing monarchy	hereditary prince	6.0 not free
Saudi Arabia	traditional monarchy	hereditary king	7.0 not free
Sudan	Islamist dictatorship	permanent president	7.0 not free
Syria	tight authoritarian	hereditary president	7.0 not free
Tunisia	one-party dominance	permanent president	5.5 not free
Turkey	parliamentary democracy	elected PM	4.0 partly free
United Arab Emirates	traditional monarchy	hereditary princes	5.5 not free
Yemen	tight authoritarian	permanent president	5.5 not free

at its peak, the Ottomans dismissed Lepanto as a minor setback. The Turks dominated the Mediterranean and Black Seas, the Middle East and Balkans, and twice besieged Vienna.

More decisive pushbacks of Ottoman power came in 1683 when they failed to take Vienna for the second time and the 1699 Treaty of Karlowitz, which freed Hungary, Transylvania, and the northern part of Yugoslavia from Ottoman rule. In 1878, a Russian army neared Istanbul. By the time World War I began, the Ottomans held only a little corner of Europe (which still belongs to Turkey).

Why could the Turks not respond to these defeats by modernizing their society and beating the Europeans at their own game? Increasingly, Ottomans themselves asked this question, and demands for reform stirred the Empire in the late nineteenth century. In 1908 the Young Turk movement of military officers (one of them: Mustafa Kemal, later known as Atatürk) attempted to reform and modernize the Empire. They were only partially successful because key elements of the Empire did not wish to become like Europe. The Ottoman Empire was old, complex, carefully balanced, and based on an Islamic legitimacy in which the temporal ruler, the sultan, was also the spiritual ruler, the caliph (successor to the Prophet). Serious modernization would rip this structure apart.

Instead, the Ottomans embarked on halfway and half-hearted modernization. "We will copy the Europeans in some things," decided the Ottoman elite, "but preserve our overall traditional system." This was not possible, as partial modernization leaves the job undone. The Ottomans, for example, could modernize their military with Western-type weapons and uniforms. But a modern army needs an industrial base to make the weapons. This means factories, workers, capitalists, engineers, and transportation networks. You need an educated officer corps to organize and train the army. This means universities and military academies. In short, you cannot become just a little bit modern; you have to go all the way, which the Turks refused to do.

By way of contrast, starting with the 1868 Meiji Restoration Japan embraced thorough modernization. So secure are Japanese in their Japaneseness that they did not fear Western ways. In one generation, Japan went from traditional to modern, copying the West in everything from industry and education to medical care and naval warfare. Why could the Japanese do it and not the Turks? The answer in part is cultural. Japan had long imported foreign culture—for example, Buddhism and Confucianism from China—but always bent and shaped it to suit Japanese needs. Japanese religions are vague, flexible, and no barrier to modernization, the opposite of the rigidities of Islam. Shintoism and Buddhism have no single book or doctrine and can mutate without limit. Japan's emperor was a living god for Japanese, but he was largely a figurehead and neither a sultan nor a caliph. Japanese did not fear that modernization would erase their culture; indeed, it was only by modernizing that Japan could preserve itself. Japan's ability to modernize is rare, however. Adaptability and flexibility like that is so far found only in East Asia.

In economic terms, the countries of the **Gulf Cooperation Council**—Kuwait, Saudi Arabia, Bahrain, Qatar, United Arab Emirates, and Oman—enjoyed spectacular growth since World War II, based either on oil or servicing the oil-producing countries. Current projections give the Gulf states about a hundred years as major oil producers. Within living memory, they went from camels and kerosene lamps to glittering high-rises and e-trading. Since 1960, GCC population has risen sixfold, the fastest growth in the world, partly through the world's highest birth rates and partly through massive immigration from poorer countries bordering the Indian Ocean. The net effect of this has been to keep per capita GDP stagnant—in some places declining—as population growth eats up economic growth.

Political, social, and religious modernization did not keep pace with economic growth. We see here that there is nothing automatic about modernization. Derided earlier as "tribes with flags," the GCC countries are all hereditary monarchies, some of them (Kuwait, Qatar) toying with notions of democracy. All these monarchies claim to be in touch with their people through the *majlis*, local meetings open to all males in which the visiting prince dispenses advice and money to individual pleaders. Charming, but hardly democracy.

Gulf Cooperation Council   (GCC) Loose grouping of monarchies on southern shore of Persian Gulf.

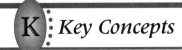

Key Concepts

MODERNIZATION THEORY

Modernization theory, a broad-brush term that traces back at least to Hegel, argues that all facets of a society hang together as a package. If you change one important element, you soon change everything else. For example, when you bring manufacturing into an agricultural society, you also bring urbanization, education, higher standards of living, and mass communications, as well as shifts in customs, tastes, and expectations. After some decades of such changes and much turmoil, the traditional society becomes modern. The transition phase is called **modernization**, and it is a tumultuous and risky time when nations frequently break down into authoritarianism.

At a certain point during this process, demands for democratization rise. Countries with **per capita GDPs** below $5,000 have trouble establishing democracies, but ones with per capita GDP of $6,000 or higher ("middle-income countries") usually establish democracies. Attempts at democracy in poor lands tend to fail as populist **demagogues** or military officers turn themselves into authoritarian rulers. Democracy seldom takes hold in poor countries. India is an interesting exception; neighboring Pakistan with its alternating civilian and military rulers is more typical of the Third World. Middle-income countries, however, have large and educated middle classes, and they form the bases of democracy. Demagogues do not fool middle-class citizens, who reject demagogic promises and vote for moderate politicians with feasible programs. Most middle-income and richer countries are stable democracies. As Taiwan, South Korea, Brazil, and Mexico achieved middle-income status, they turned from authoritarian to democratic.

If modernization theory is accurate, it will be some time before the Middle East is ready for democracy. Most countries are still poor. Some oil kingdoms have high per capita GDPs, but they are based on an accident of nature, not on the slow and arduous growth of industry. Their incomes are badly distributed, with few rich and many poor people. They have a fake middle class that depends on government jobs and handouts and lacks the autonomy and interest groups of a real middle class. Noneconomic factors also work against Middle Eastern democracy. Regional, ethnic, and religious differences rend many lands in the region.

And modernization theory might be wrong. Some cultures resist becoming modern. Their religions may reject modernity. And under certain circumstances modernization might lead not to democracy but to vicious and well-armed dictatorships. Some modernize but resist becoming democratic. Malaysia, 60 percent Muslim, enjoyed rapid economic growth—from poverty in the 1960s to a middle-income $9,000 per cap by 2000—but grew *less* democratic, declining in the FH rating from "free" to "partly free." Those who crossed Malaysia's president got in bad trouble. (If modernization theory is correct, Malaysia should soon become a democracy.) Fareed Zakaria reminds us that elections can produce "illiberal democracy," a majority vote to silence dissent, repress others, or march to war.

The U.S. effort to democratize Iraq has an uphill struggle. Many say that it will not work, that the best we can hope for is a moderate and rational authoritarian regime, one that stresses stability and economic growth, a "kinder, gentler Saddam." Free elections in Saudi Arabia, Egypt, and other countries would bring radical Islamists to power, and they would not be democratic: one man, one vote, one time. We may prefer traditional monarchs or pragmatic dictators to elected Osamas. Elections do not automatically equal democracy.

---

modernization   The process of shifting from traditional to modern.
per capita GDP   Sum total of what is produced in a country in a year, divided by population; a measure of prosperity.
demagogue   Politician, often *charismatic*, who manipulates masses with deceptive promises.

Key Concepts

CIVIL SOCIETY

Philosophers have recognized for centuries that what makes any society work is only partly government institutions such as kings, parliaments, and officials. A large part depends on the associations that form in the large area between family and government: clubs, religions, businesses, even informal networks of neighbors and coworkers talking with each other. Scottish philosopher David Hume called these "the little platoons of society." This **civil society** is widely believed to be the foundation for stability and democracy. Pluralistic habits grow out of associations not controlled by government. Can the United States promote civil society, or is it something that each country must develop itself?

If civil society is undeveloped or has been deliberately crushed by a dictatorship, order and democracy will have rough going. Totalitarian systems, such as Stalin's, extend state power over civil society and carefully control it. No church, club, or business is free; all are run or supervised by the single ruling party and its dictator. It was neglect of this factor that tripped us up in post-Soviet Russia. We supposed that once the Communist regime was ousted, a happy, prosperous, and democratic Russia would quickly emerge. Instead, lawlessness and decline led to the quasi-authoritarian regime of President Putin. In contrast, Poland, which had a civil society—much of it centered on its defiant Roman Catholic Church—emerged quickly from communism to a market economy and democracy.

Saddam, who modeled himself after Stalin, likewise stomped out civil society in Iraq. All religions were controlled, most of the economy was state-owned, and his Baath party supervised everything. Saddam's regime even penetrated the family and neighborhood. Relatives and neighbors learned to say nothing political; the other person might be an informer. Iraqis learned to trust no one, an attitude still present. When the Saddam regime collapsed, it left behind little civil society to promote order and democracy. It left a vacuum. One of the few Iraqi organizations that could partly fill this vacuum was the Shi'a clergy. In several cities, including Shi'a areas of Baghdad, mullahs, exuding natural authority and organizational skills and backed up by armed and angry militias, took over and ran hospitals, charities, and city cleanup.

You cannot fill anarchy with democracy. It will be tumultuous, unstable, and soon taken over by an authoritarian regime, some of them worse than others. We were mistaken about post-Saddam Iraq, just as we had been about Russia. We supposed that law, order, and democracy spring up spontaneously once you remove the totalitarian regime. They do not. They need first the patient cultivation of civil society. Pollsters can actually measure this by asking a cross section of citizens if they think most people can be trusted. If this is high, you have a civil society. This is likely to take some decades, as it tends to grow with rule of law and the economy. If neither grow, stable democracy is unlikely.

Many Arab intellectuals now accept the urgent need for their societies to modernize. Several of them coauthored a UN study, *The Arab Human Development Report 2002*, which found declining economies, lagging science and technology, widespread illiteracy, suppression of women, and no political freedoms, elections, or media. The GDP of Spain exceeds that of all twenty-two Arab countries combined, including oil producers. These Arab states currently have a combined population

civil society   Associations, some informal, between family and state and the pluralistic values that come with them.

of 280 million (about the same as the United States), but by 2020 it is projected to reach between 410 and 459 million. Many Arab thinkers recognize that something must be done, and soon.

A Muslim Reformation?

How important was the Protestant **Reformation** to the history of the West? Most thinkers rank it high; some (such as Max Weber) posit it as the underlying element of Western modernization. While it is hard to prove which caused which, Luther's nailing of his ninety-five theses to the church door came closely in time with capitalism, absolutism, scientific and technological innovation, and the strong state. One of the elements that contributed to the Reformation was printing—Gutenberg's Bible (in German) appeared in 1455—which enabled large numbers of Europeans to read Scripture for themselves. Hitherto, reading the Bible (in Latin) was generally reserved for Roman Catholic priests. With Scripture newly available through printing, readers could quickly see that much of what they had been taught as sacred was not found in the Bible. Parts of Catholic practice could thus be discarded, and worshippers felt they were reaching a Christianity that was truer to its written sources.

Islam has never had a reformation. For a millennium it has been essentially frozen. Groups have branched off from Islam (Druze, Alawites, Baha'is), but they have not influenced mainstream Islam. The two great branches of Islam, Sunni and Shi'a, have no quarrel over the Qur'an or basic tenets of the faith. Their quarrel is over who was the legitimate successor to the Prophet.

Scholars point out that originally Islam did permit independent, rational interpretations of the Qur'an (*ijtihad*), but between the ninth and eleventh centuries these were eliminated in favor of a single, orthodox interpretation (*taqlid*, literally "emulation"). With this, intellectual rigidity blanketed the Muslim world. The Arab inheritors of the philosophy and science of ancient Greece failed to develop it further. The brilliant Islamic civilization—whose architecture is still magnificent—that was far ahead of Europe in 1000 A.D. found itself overtaken by 1600, although it did not know it.

Islam in the West

One of the remarkable movements since World War II has been the massive influx of Muslims into West Europe and to a lesser extent into North America. Unlike the Moors who swept through Spain and into France in the eighth century or the Ottoman Turks who swept through the Balkans and into Central Europe in the fifteenth century, these Muslims come in peace as immigrants looking for work. Including illegal immigrants and temporary visitors, some 14 million Muslims now

---

reformation   The modernization of a religion, often based on original texts.

Key Concepts

THE HUNTINGTON CHALLENGE

Harvard political scientist Samuel P. Huntington jolted both academics and policymakers with a 1993 article in *Foreign Affairs*, "The Clash of Civilizations," later expanded into a book. Huntington saw several **civilizations**, most of them based on religion, which is a major component of culture:

Western—Formed from Western Christianity (Catholic or Protestant), with European and North American branches.

Slavic/Orthodox—Formed from Eastern Christianity, such as Russia and Serbia.

Islamic

Sinic—East Asian countries of Confucian background, such as China and Korea.

Hindu—India as a separate civilization.

Japanese—Borrowed much from the Sinic and the Western but a separate civilization because it bent everything it borrowed.

Latin American—Mostly Catholic, but an odd blend of European, Native American, and North American influences.

African

Huntington sometimes included Buddhist, such as Sri Lanka and Thailand, as a civilization, but it consists of few countries and they show little solidarity among themselves.

Within a civilization, countries can generally understand and get along with each other. Between civilizations, though, misunderstanding is frequent and sometimes hostile. Huntington argued that the Cold War had covered over these tensions, but with the Cold War over they had come out with renewed vigor and were now the main dynamic of world politics. Not all civilizations clash; Latin American civilization gets along reasonably well with all the others. Huntington's theory explained why Poland, the Czech Republic, and Hungary turned quickly to democracy and market economies while Russia, Ukraine, and Bulgaria did not. The former, mostly Catholic, were returning to their roots in Western civilization while the latter, mostly Eastern Orthodox, resisted adopting Western patterns.

live in West Europe, roughly 4 percent of the population. (France, with 5 million, is 7 percent Muslim.) Some observers suggest that keeping the Muslims in Europe calm is one reason European governments are critical of Israel and the U.S. war on Iraq.

Demographically, the reason for this influx is not hard to see. Europe has low fertility rates. Italy's and Germany's rates are among the lowest, around 1.2 babies per woman, not nearly enough to maintain their populations, which requires a replacement rate of 2.1 babies per woman. Women in Muslim countries

civilization   In Huntington's theory, a large area of shared culture based mostly on religion.

The real problem, wrote Huntington, is Islamic civilization, which clashes with most of the others: "Islam has bloody borders." As he was writing, a three-sided civil war in ex-Yugoslavia set Catholic Croats, Orthodox Serbs, and Bosnian Muslims against each other, a perfect illustration of Huntington's theory, which fit many other areas: Russians against Chechens, Indians against Pakistanis, Israelis against Palestinians, and Americans against Islamic fundamentalists.

Not everything fit Huntington's theory. Muslim countries also fought each other, as did Iraq and Iran through the 1980s. In 1990 and 1991, the West made common cause with several Muslim countries as they expelled Iraq from Kuwait. Even in 2003, America got cooperation from some Persian Gulf countries. Increasingly, Europe and the United States quarreled over everything from the Iraq War to beef imports and capital punishment. NATO was hollowed out until it became a paper alliance. American thinkers had long explained U.S. culture as a repudiation of Europe, not an extension of it.

Huntington's challenge was to the sometimes glib assumptions that after the Cold War a single, happy world would emerge. Francis Fukuyama (perhaps trying to be provocative) wrote of the "end of history": After communism there are no ideological alternatives to capitalist democracy. Thomas Friedman of The *New York Times* became a prophet of **globalization**, proclaiming as inevitable and wonderful the free flow of goods, capital, and information that would uplift poor countries and unify the globe. Fukuyama and Friedman foresaw a "universal" culture that is a lot like America. Actually, globalization is an old vision, going back to at least the optimistic Victorians of the nineteenth century, a vision that collapsed in World War I.

Huntington's challenge was also to the sometimes glib "nation builders" of both the Clinton and the junior Bush administrations, who supposed democracy could be set up just about anywhere, even in Iraq. A civilization that is culturally at odds with the West does not strive to become like the West; it rejects the West: "We are not like you and do not wish to become like you." As American and British forces liberated Iraq, many political views appeared among Iraqis. Only a few intellectuals, some of them returning from exile in the West, proposed democracy. The biggest single political current was among the Shi'a majority of Iraq, many of whom embraced an Islamic fundamentalism imported from their Shi'a brethren in Iran. Perhaps the best chance for democracy was among the Kurds of the north of Iraq, who had enjoyed an autonomous existence for a decade, with some of the trappings of democracy, although one characterized by clan loyalties and strong leaders. And more than a few Iraqis, especially Sunni Arabs, harkened to the stability of the brutal Saddam regime. "At least then we had jobs and electricity," was their cry. Growing a democracy in Iraqi soil will be difficult. Huntington warned us in advance.

often have six to eight babies. In general, people in advanced industrialized countries have few children; people in poor countries have many. Europe's population is aging fast, with many people on pensions (which often start in the fifties in Europe), too few earners to pay for the pensions, and too few hands to do the grimy and less-desirable work. Europe created a partial population vacuum while Muslim lands created a population pressure of too many young people and too few jobs. Like the wind, migration blows from high-pressure areas to low-pressure ones.

globalization   The world becoming one big, capitalist market.

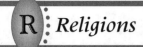

Religions

SALAFIYYA

Rather than a reformation, Islam has undergone a series of reaffirmations. Under stress—such as the Mongol invasion and more recent Western pressure—Islamic society tends to seek salvation by returning to a strict interpretation of the Qur'an. For centuries, certain Sunni Muslim thinkers have articulated the doctrine of *salafiyya*, and it has been present ever since as a puritanical criticism of many Muslim rulers. (Salafiyya is not present in Shi'a Islam, which has its own brand of fundamentalism. Salafis despise Shi'a as a pagan renegade movement.) Al Qaeda is a salafi movement.

Salafis emphasize that Islam, starting with the Prophet, had to fight both idolatry and hypocrisy. Muhammed faced pagan beliefs and false Muslims from the beginning. Worship of anything but Allah—such as pre-Islamic practices, the modern nation-state, material possessions—is idolatry. Those who claim to be Muslims but just use Islam to gain or retain wealth and power are hypocrites. (See discussion of Taimiyya on page 53.) This includes most current Muslim governments. And these twin dangers constantly beset Islam, so salafis must be forever on guard against them and willing to engage in jihad to stop them.

Salafis such as Osama ideologically despised Saddam Hussein's Iraq, for it was the most secular Arab state and preached nationalism—"Hooray for Iraq!"—which is a form of idolatry. Neither do salafis really like Palestinian nationalism, for it tends to worship Palestine rather than Allah. This religious divide does not prevent salafis and nationalists from cooperating opportunistically with each other, so al Qaeda could have worked with Iraq. Destruction of Israel and liberation for Palestine were not at the top of Osama's list; he included them more recently as devices to mobilize angry Muslims. Accordingly, al Qaeda is willing to make temporary and ad hoc alliances with a vast variety of Muslim movements that it really does not approve of. Once salafiyya wins, it will break and discard these idolatrous nationalisms and construct a single community of Islam, as the Prophet intended.

Crusaders, Zionists, and the United States—which is pagan and corrupt—are all terrible threats to Islam and must be crushed. Even worse are Muslim rulers who go along with and seek favor from the Americans, such as Egypt's Sadat (assassinated in 1981) and the House of Saud, which only pretends to be pure. Actually, the founding doctrine of Saudi Arabia was the 1744 alliance of the Saud family with the Wahhabi branch of salafiyya, an alliance that eventually unified the Kingdom in 1932. In return for Wahhabi support, the Kingdom teaches salafiyya in its own schools and funds Wahhabi schools in other Muslim lands, especially in Pakistan. True salafis such as Osama bin Laden are not fooled by this outward show of piety, however, and struggle to bring down the hypocritical House of Saud.

In the case of Britain and France, the influx started as a remnant of imperial policies that allowed the "natives" of their respective empires to live and work in Britain and France. Pakistanis came to Britain and Algerians, Moroccans, Tunisians, and others to France. Germany, without colonies since World War I, needed labor beyond the Italians, Spaniards, and Yugoslavs it had admitted since the 1950s and found an abundant supply in Turkey. In every case, it is jobs that pull immigration, just as American jobs draw millions from south of the U.S. border.

Many Europeans do not like the influx of chiefly Muslim foreigners. They never got to vote on it but are often the losers from the increase in crime and changes in laws, schools, and neighborhoods to accommodate the newcomers.

France, which prides itself on uniform education standards, angrily debated *"l'affaire du foulard"* ("the question of the headscarf"): whether Muslim girls could wear the traditional *hijab* to school. Female hair is just too sexy, argue strict Muslims. All children must dress the same, argue the French. Americans may think this argument is meaningless, but what happens in a U.S. school when a child refuses to recite the Pledge of Allegiance? We all have our national rituals and symbols, and those who do not accept them irritate us.

With resentment of Muslims growing, every country of West Europe has at least one angry anti-immigrant party such as the National Fronts of Britain and France, the National Republicans of Germany, the Freedom party of Austria, the list of Pim Fortuyn (assassinated) in the Netherlands, the Flemish Bloc in Belgium, the Danish People's party, and Italy's Northern League and National Alliance. They draw a nontrivial 10 to 20 percent of the vote. Mainstream European politicians got the message and have steadily choked off immigration until it is now quite restrictive throughout West Europe, although tens of thousands of illegals still sneak in.

Some suppose that Muslims living in West Europe (and the United States) will serve as spark plugs for modernization and moderation back in their home countries. Immigrants, like those who flocked to the United States generations ago, will pick up the new, largely secular culture of pluralism and democracy plus money-making skills and transmit them by visits and remittances to their relatives back home. We should be careful of this analogy. European culture, especially in the crucial area of religions, is similar to American culture, so European immigrants did not have to cross a big gap in America. The language may have been different, but the churches were the same. Large numbers of German and Italian immigrants in America, furthermore, did not dissuade their home countries from turning fascist.

Islam has a very big gap to bridge with Western culture. First, Muslims are not supposed to live outside the *dar es salam*, the "house of peace," meaning the great community of Islam. The outside world, the *dar al harb*, "the house of war," is ignorant and dangerous. Historically, Muslims might visit it for business but not stay. Muslims residing in Europe came only when the great European empires brought them in as sailors, students, and workers from their colonies in the nineteenth century. Large numbers came only in the twentieth century, especially after World War II. If they had jobs and good money at home, few Muslims would settle in Europe.

There is evidence of religious rethinking among Muslims in West Europe. How else can you live there without making some accommodation to the prevalent secular culture? Muslims in Europe and America have to emphasize tolerance for themselves and this has introduced the broader notion of tolerance for all. Iran's current President Muhammad Khatami, for example, served earlier in Hamburg's Islamic Center; he professes to be open to Western ideas of freedom. Some Muslim clerics in West Europe have started to articulate new ideas that could contribute to an Islamic reformation.

But there is greater evidence of a **bounce-back effect**, of young Muslims in Europe becoming more Islamic than their parents ever were. Anthropologist Ernest

---

bounce-back effect   Reversal of views and values from those held previously.

Gellner, who taught in London, was among the first to explicate the trend, which occurs almost automatically among people brought into a new and very different culture. It is a psychologically confusing ordeal; those undergoing it lose their sense of identity: Who am I? Uprooted from their Islamic culture back home, they have not joined European culture. Many Europeans dislike and discriminate against them. They cannot feel wholeheartedly British or French even if they are educated and employed, and many are not. Muslims in Britain have three to four times the jobless rate of white Britons. America may have an easier time of integrating Muslims, as we are all descended from immigrants and generally tolerate diverse cultures. Until recently, Europe has been a source of emigrants, not a goal of immigrants.

The upshot is that some young Muslims in West Europe identify as Muslims first and only and throw themselves into the Islamic fundamentalism preached in several mosques throughout Europe. One can find the children of Pakistani immigrants in Britain, clothed and educated exactly like other young Britons, who suddenly around college age become super-Muslims—bearded, clothed in body-length shirts, learning Arabic, and plotting to kill Westerners, especially Jews. The leader of the Pakistani Islamist gang that slit the throat of *Wall Street Journal* reporter Daniel Pearl (and distributed a video of it) in 2002 was born and educated in Britain, as was the suicide bomber of a Tel Aviv jazz club in 2003. In England one can attend celebrations of 9/11. Said one Muslim youth in England: "We should all get together and kill all the Jews." All of the recruitment and planning for 9/11 took place in Germany among Arab (chiefly Saudi) students, who became fundamentalists *after* living in Germany for some time, not before. Gellner was right: Living in the West can make Muslims more Islamic.

Accordingly, do not count on cross-cultural familiarization to lead to understanding and toleration. People from Muslim cultures are both intrigued and shocked at Western culture. They recognize its economic and technological superiority, but they deplore its lack of humane and spiritual values. Where we see freedom and individualism, they see materialism and sexual debauchery. In Muslim eyes, we have nothing to teach them about morality, for we utterly lack it. Muslims in Europe or America may like their higher incomes but deplore the erosion of family and religious values that anchor their lives. Getting to know you does not necessarily mean getting to like you.

CAN SAUDI ARABIA DEMOCRATIZE?

Saudi Arabia could soon be a problem as difficult as Iraq or Iran. Saudi Arabia modernized—or halfway modernized—but rejected any democratization. Iran had done the same, creating the massive discontent that brought down the Shah in 1979. Oil wealth, especially the price jumps of 1973 and 1979, enabled the House of Saud to buy off threats and problems. Saudi youths learned Wahhabi Islam in school and then went to college—all paid for by the regime—and given sinecure jobs. Now there are not enough such jobs; you cannot put everyone on the government payroll. Manual labor is done by imported workers from Egypt, Pakistan,

K Key Concepts

THE PRAETORIAN PARADOX

As we considered in Chapter 8, praetorianism is the tendency for military takeovers. We may be building such a situation in Iraq. One of the main American efforts was to train a new Iraqi army and police. If we succeed, they will be the only effective forces in a chaotic and fractured Iraq. Power will almost automatically flow into the hands of their leaders. To restore order, these leaders will have to be dictators and not flinch at tough measures. Nice guys do not govern countries like Iraq; they are soon overthrown by those more ruthless. The net impact of U.S. training may be to install a new dictatorship, which may bring a kind of stability to Iraq but will hardly be democratic.

This process has happened before, in the U.S. interventions in Central America and the Caribbean early in the twentieth century. The U.S. Army or Marines would govern chaotic countries like Nicaragua for some years while training a local national guard. Upon departure, we would turn power over to the head of this national guard, and he would become the new dictator. Anastasio Somoza, for example, based on the Nicaragua National Guard, set up a hereditary dictatorship that lasted from 1937 to 1978. The United States did not mind the Somoza dictatorship, which was better than chaos. When it fell, however, the Communist Sandinistas took over. In Iraq, we may find a Somoza solution perfectly acceptable.

---

even the Philippines at one-third the cost of Saudi labor. Over half of the Saudi workforce is foreigners.

One of the world's highest rates of population growth—an amazing 4.1 percent a year from 1960 to 2000—rapidly tripled the Saudi population to 23 million, and now young Saudis (a majority are under eighteen) are unemployed and bored. The outlets available to American youths—girls, drinking, rock music, and movies—are forbidden in the Kingdom. Salafiyya grows because it is one of the few things to do.

Saudi per capita GDP plunged from a peak of $24,000 in 1980 to $10,000 currently, and it is maldistributed in favor of the 5,000 or so princes, the product of multiple and rotating wives. Each prince gets an allowance of at least several thousand dollars a month; some get millions a year. Many use their princely connections to get huge commissions on business deals and government contracts; corruption is rife. The royal family passes out wealth in the form of jobs and charity to supporters and petitioners, a medieval arrangement. Little noticed are the large numbers of poor people in Saudi Arabia; the oil boom passed them by. The Kingdom is not nearly as rich as it once was—the Saudi budget has been in deficit since 1991—and can no longer buy off discontent, which grows rapidly.

As Samuel Huntington pointed out in his magisterial 1968 *Political Order in Changing Societies*, modernizing monarchs create hatred against themselves and doom their own regimes. The educational and economic improvements they foster make them utterly out of date. Generously handing out money, a traditional form of power in the Middle East going back centuries, no longer buys loyalty.

K : Key Concepts

THE COMMUNICATIONS REVOLUTION

A new and highly influential mass medium marked the 2003 war that was not present for the 1991 war: *Al Jazeera* ("The Island") satellite television. Heretofore, Arab mass media—all television and radio, most newspapers—had been rigorously state controlled, delivering only what reinforced the regime, often by deflecting discontent onto the United States and Israel. Regime brutality and corruption were never mentioned. In 1996 Al Jazeera, based in Qatar and funded by its emir, went on the air with news and views controlled by no government. Satellite technology overleaps ground stations and goes right into homes via a little dish antenna. Al Jazeera's frank, modern news coverage resembles that of an American network; many of its staff learned their trade with the BBC Arabic service.

The United States came to detest Al Jazeera for its anti-U.S. slant, especially after 9/11, when it became Osama bin Laden's medium for his taped appeals for jihad. Like most Arabs, Al Jazeera was pro-Iraq in the 2003 war; we charged that they distorted reporting. Al Jazeera says it covers the news professionally, everything from Israeli repression in the West Bank to the toppling of the Saddam statue in Baghdad with cheering Iraqis kicking it. Millions of Arabs watch Al Jazeera, the only free Arab medium and by far the Arab world's favorite news source. Iraqis saw on Al Jazeera the rapid progress of U.S. forces, and many decided not to fight for a lost cause.

We must put aside our anger at Al Jazeera to ask what its long-term impact will be. Communications are an important factor in modernization and democratization. Informing viewers and listeners of a better, freer life undermines authoritarian regimes. The United States supported Radio Free Europe and Radio Liberty, CIA fronts that broadcast accurate news into, respectively, East Europe and the Soviet Union. Today, we still support Televisión Martí, which does the same for Cuba. The East German Communist regime could never gain full legitimacy with most of its citizens able to receive uncensored TV broadcasts from West Germany and West Berlin.

If Al Jazeera pushes corrupt, dictatorial regimes to clean up their administration and opens the door to democracy a crack, it will be doing a great service to the region. Like most Arab intellectuals, Al Jazeera is going to criticize the United States. Get used to it. If we persuaded Qatar to close or control Al Jazeera, what kind of a statement would that make about press freedom? We have no way to stop the critical coverage and comments of Al Jazeera, but it is also a catalyst for the kind of changes we want in the region. Nobody promised that a free press reports only nice news.

Young Saudis feel little gratitude to the royal house that has funded their college educations; they feel resentment and bitterness at those who have all the wealth and power of the country. How could an educated person remain loyal to a corrupt and secretive medieval regime? Properly channeled, these relatively recent demands for greater political and economic equality could form the basis of a democratic transition. Left to fester, they feed only revolution—in the Saudi case, possibly Islamist rage of the sort that ripped apart Iran.

In modern Europe, only figurehead monarchies, such as those of northwest Europe, survive. They long ago gave up power to parties and parliaments; now their monarchs are more like official greeters. No Middle Eastern monarch has made the transition to democracy, although the emir of Qatar may be attempting it now. Instead, some have already been overthrown with a variety of bloody and dictatorial results. Since the 1950s, Huntington noted, monarchy has been overthrown in Egypt, Iraq, Libya, Ethiopia, and elsewhere. He virtually predicted the fall of the Shah of Iran. Is the Saudi court, ensconced in palaces and Spanish villas and surrounded by obsequious courtiers, immune to this logic?

In 2003 Crown Prince Abdullah, the day-to-day ruler who is likely to take the throne on the death of the ailing King Fahd, said he would offer cautious steps leading to democracy in Saudi Arabia. The steps sounded as if they were well thought-out, calculated to slowly bring the masses of Saudi citizens into political participation. But shortly after the 2003 Iraq War and al Qaeda bombings that killed twenty-five in Saudi Arabia, Abdullah ordered editors who discussed modernization and democratization to stop criticism of Wahhabism. One top editor was fired. Senior Saudi clerics had just complained to Abdullah, and he acceded to their demands. The incident illustrates the Saudi dilemma: They must modernize but are not willing to take on the conservative forces, which have much to lose from modernization. Such a choice is perilous, because democratizing amidst seething revolutionary discontent is like opening the lid of a hot pressure cooker: It blows off. "We're the most conservative country in the world," said one Saudi prince. Can they change? A gradual Saudi transition could set the course for other such transitions in the Middle East. Its failure could ensure tumult and U.S. military involvement for decades.

CONCLUSIONS

The 2003 war was supposed to establish democracy in Iraq and encourage it throughout the Middle East, but critics saw this as unfeasible. The region has known little democracy and currently ranks low in Freedom House's ratings. Some see the problem as a cultural failure to modernize. Even Turkey has not been able to overcome Islamic resistance to modernization. Democracy needs a large, educated middle class, lacking in the Middle East. Islam has never had a reformation, which could contribute to modernization and democratization; instead it has emphasized rigidity and *salafiyya*. Huntington's "civilizational theory," which sees an Islam hostile to most other civilizations, rejects optimistic predictions of globalization and democratization.

Muslim immigrants in West Europe could theoretically serve as a bridge to modernization, but some of them become more Islamic than ever. Independent TV such as Al Jazeera, with criticism of Arab regimes and the United States, has brought a communications revolution. Saudi Arabia used to be able to buy off discontent, but an exploding population and great income inequality have set the stage for Islamist upheaval. No Middle Eastern monarchy has made a transition to democracy or even tried to, raising the possibility of revolution.

FURTHER REFERENCE

Ajami, Fouad. *The Dream Palace of the Arabs: A Generation's Odyssey*. New York: Vintage, 1999.

Baer, Robert. *Sleeping with the Devil: How Washington Sold Our Soul for Saudi Crude*. New York: Crown: 2003.

Barlas, Asma. *"Believing Women" in Islam: Unreading Patriarchal Interpretations of the Qur'an*. Austin, TX: University of Texas Press, 2002.

El-Nawawy, Mohammed, and Adel Iskandar. *Al-Jazeera: How the Free Arab News Network Scooped the World and Changed the Middle East*. Boulder, CO: Westview, 2002.

Gerges, Fawaz A. *Islamists and the West: Ideology vs. Pragmatism*. New York: Cambridge University Press, 2004.

Gerner, Deborah J., ed. *Understanding the Contemporary Middle East*. Boulder, CO: Lynne Rienner, 2000.

Hashmi, Sohail H., ed. *Islamic Political Ethics: Civil Society, Pluralism, and Conflict*. Princeton, NJ: Princeton University Press, 2002.

Hunter, Shireen T., ed. *Islam, Europe's Second Religion: The New Social, Cultural, and Political Landscape*. Westport, CT: Praeger, 2002.

Huntington, Samuel P. *Political Order in Changing Societies*. New Haven, CT: Yale University Press, 1968.

———. *The Clash of Civilizations and the Remaking of World Order*. New York: Touchstone, 1997.

Mandaville, Peter G. *Transnational Muslim Politics: Reimagining the Umma*. New York: Routledge, 2003.

Murden, Simon W. *Islam, the Middle East, and the New Global Hegemony*. Boulder, CO: Lynne Rienner, 2002.

Rubin, Barry, and Judith Colp Rubin, eds. *Anti-American Terrorism and the Middle East*. New York: Oxford University Press, 2002.

Sachedina, Abdulaziz. *The Islamic Roots of Democratic Pluralism*. New York: Oxford University Press, 2001.

Viorst, Milton. *In the Shadow of the Prophet: The Struggle for the Soul of Islam*. Boulder, CO: Westview, 2001.

The United States and the Middle East

Points to Ponder

- When did America become deeply involved in the Middle East?
- What did the Soviets try to do in the Middle East? Did they succeed?
- How and why did Lebanon twice draw in U.S. Marines?
- When did U.S. policy shift from even-handed to pro-Israel?
- How did Kissinger rig the results of the 1973 war?
- Is Jerusalem widely recognized as Israel's capital?
- What is the influence of the Christian Right on U.S. policy on the Arab-Israel dispute?
- Is the U.S.-Saudi relationship stable and reliable?
- Can America steer clear of the Middle East?

The United States has long had contact with the Middle East, but until World War II the connection was weak and intermittent. Europe, Latin America, and Asia mattered far more. President Jefferson sent America's first overseas military expedition "to the shores of Tripoli" in 1805 to stop piracy against U.S. merchant ships in the Mediterranean. (It did not stop.) Tripoli, in present-day Libya (there is another Tripoli in Lebanon), was then nominally part of the slowly decaying Ottoman Empire, with which the United States developed trade relations. The Ottomans permitted American missionary activity, but only among the Christians of the empire. Muslims are not permitted to exit the faith; **apostasy** is punished by stoning to death. American schools and colleges in Istanbul, Beirut, and Cairo educated many future leaders of the region, all of whom stayed Muslim. (The Mormons, who proselytize almost everywhere, do not send missionaries to Islamic countries.)

U.S. interest in the region grew with World War II, and for several reasons. The British had oil contracts with Iraq and Iran sewn up decades earlier, but the immensity of the Saudi oil fields became clear during the war, and here the United

---

apostasy Abandoning a religion.

States was in on the ground floor, establishing a close relationship with the ruling House of Saud even under President Franklin D. Roosevelt. As soon as Germany invaded the Soviet Union in 1941, Britain and Russia acted on their 1907 agreement (which Iranians always hated) to chop Iran in two, Russia in the north and Britain in the south. The United States soon took over from the British and turned Iran into a major supply corridor for the beleaguered Soviet Union. After the war, the United States made Iran the main element of its anti-Communist containment policy in the region.

U.S. EVEN-HANDEDNESS

The Holocaust and birth of Israel also forced the United States to pay attention to the Middle East. Before World War II, this had been a British and French sphere of influence. Troubled by guilt over having done little to save Jews from the Holocaust, America firmly supported the new Jewish state, even to the point of antagonizing Britain, by mobilizing votes in the UN in 1947 and by Truman's instant recognition of Israel in 1948. The United States also sold surplus World War II tanks and trucks that Israel used for decades. Israel's standard tank in 1973 was a U.S.-made Sherman, first produced in 1942 but refitted by the Israelis with a bigger gun (105mm) and engine into a "Super-Sherman."

Truman, however, upon the advice of the Arab-leaning State Department, kept a polite even-handedness in the Arab-Israeli dispute. Eisenhower was cool toward Israel as he tried to minimize Soviet influence in the region. The Cold War and fear of losing the Arabs to communism kept U.S. policy in rough balance; we could not be especially pro-Israel. Ike was angry at the 1956 British-French-Israeli attack on Egypt and told them to clear out. Johnson was too bogged down in Vietnam to take much of an interest.

At its birth, Israel defined itself as neutral in the Cold War. Israel was founded by socialists—or at least they thought they were—and many still harbored warm feelings toward the Soviets as brothers in arms against the Nazis. Moscow recognized Israel just a few minutes after Washington did. Stalin was not pro-Israel but merely saw a way to get the British out of the Middle East. The paranoid Stalin decided he could not trust Jews—he called them "rootless cosmopolitans"—and unleashed a wave of anti-semitism in the Soviet Union and its East European satellites, where Jews were sent to prison or the gallows, making some Israelis doubt and then oppose the Soviet Union.

After Stalin died in 1953, his flamboyant successor, Nikita Khrushchev, began courting the **Third World**. In 1955 he signed up Egypt as a client state, the first of several in the Arab world, and Israel rethought its neutralism, by then seriously at odds with reality. The neutrals of the Cold War—led by Nehru of India, Sukarno of Indonesia, and Nasser of Egypt—declared solidarity with the Arabs and accepted the Arab line that Israel was an outpost of Western imperialism. In 1967

Third World   Asia, Africa, and Latin America.

U_{S}: *The United States in the Middle East*

MARINES IN BEIRUT, 1958

The U.S. Marines blown up in their barracks in Beirut, Lebanon, in 1983 (see box on page 314) marked the second time they had been there. Almost forgotten was the Marines' first visit in 1958. Eisenhower had hoped to improve relations with Nasser by opposing the 1956 Israeli-British-French invasion of Egypt, but Nasser did not reciprocate. Instead, Nasser became more radical, expansionist, and pro-Soviet. To some American specialists, it looked like Nasser was helping the Soviets gain control of the Middle East. This was not the case—communism and Nasserism were two very different things—but the Cold War produced great oversimplifications.

In 1958, Lebanon experienced a constitutional crisis and major breakdown, a harbinger of the total breakdown that was to come in the 1970s. Lebanon had gained its freedom from France in 1943 on the basis of power balancing among a dozen religions in what was called the National Pact, with Christians having more power than Muslims. The presidency, for example, was always in the hands of a Maronite Christian (the local branch of Roman Catholicism). The basis of the National Pact was an out-of-date census that had counted more Christians than Muslims. By the late 1950s, with the Muslim birth rate far exceeding that of Christians, Muslims were in the majority and demanded a bigger slice of power.

Following the 1956 war, President Camille Chamoun came under fire for not breaking relations with Britain and France. He was also accused of manipulating elections. Lebanese Muslims, discontent at being shortchanged in power, rebelled in early 1958 and smuggled in arms from a sympathetic Syria, which had just joined Nasser's short-lived United Arab Republic. Washington, fearing a Soviet plot to destabilize the region and gain clients, landed U.S. Marines in Beirut in 1958. Nothing special happened, the Marines soon left, and the National Pact was restored. The relatively minor incident marked the first U.S. intervention with troops in the Middle East and the beginning of deeper U.S. involvement.

the Soviet Union—which helped start the Six Day War (see page 103)—and its satellites (plus Yugoslavia) all broke diplomatic relations with Israel, and Israel turned staunchly anti-Soviet.

THE NIXON TILT

In 1973 President Richard Nixon greatly deepened U.S. involvement in the region, and on Israel's side. Previously, Washington had been rather hands-off in Arab-Israel wars; now it was hands-on. First, Nixon warned Moscow not to intervene in the October War and backed it up by putting U.S. forces on heightened status. Nixon delivered a credible deterrence threat in 1973, and the Soviets heeded it. He also sent U.S. warships to the Eastern Mediterranean.

Modern warfare consumes munitions at an incredible rate, making logistics extremely important. Israel in 1973 soon ran short but was resupplied by rapid U.S. airlifts. Defense Minister Moshe Dayan told the Knesset, "We are firing shells this afternoon that we didn't even have in the country this morning."

But Nixon and his national security advisor Henry Kissinger, who had just also become secretary of state, played a trickier game than merely supporting Israel. When Israel was in trouble, U.S. munitions flowed quickly to Israel, some from U.S. stores in Germany, others from stateside, in massive airlifts. But when the tide of battle reversed and Israel was winning, U.S. munitions dried up. Using a "good-cop-tough-cop" routine, Kissinger told the Israelis that he was trying to get more airlifts while Defense Secretary James Schlessinger said that we had no more to spare. It was a gimmick to restrain Israel from another victory.

Kissinger was no expert on the Middle East (he specialized on the Soviet nuclear threat), but he had a fine feel for power, from his massive Harvard dissertation on post-Napoleon Europe and its manipulation by Austrian Prince Metternich. You do not reach peace directly (the pacifist mistake), but by first balancing power so the two sides have an incentive to talk. If Israel simply wins again, saw Kissinger in 1973, it will be 1967 all over again—total Arab rejection of any talks. So, in 1973 neither side could totally win nor totally lose; there had to be a psychological balance. This allowed Kissinger to shuttle (on Air Force One) between Cairo, Jerusalem, and Damascus, hammering out cease-fires that separated the parties by demilitarized zones. These formed the basis of subsequent Egyptian-Israeli talks that led to peace.

The 1973 war also marked the beginning of an open split between the United States and its European allies on the Middle East. The United States was getting deeply involved in the Middle East, but Europe emphatically wished to stay out. In 1973 Germany objected to the use of U.S. bases and munitions in Germany to resupply Israel. These bases were strictly for NATO purposes and the United States had no right to use them for anything else. By the same token, Portugal objected to the use of U.S. bases in the Azores to refuel the U.S. aircraft resupplying Israel. The 1973 war thus marks an issue that came to a head by the 2003 war. By treaty, NATO has nothing to do with the Middle East, although Washington wishes it did. NATO's inability to expand its role from European defense to a Western security community that speaks with one voice even outside of Europe made NATO irrelevant in the twenty-first century.

With the U.S. tilt toward Israel in 1973, the United States and Israel recognized their mutual interest in opposing Soviet power, which at that time looked quite threatening. The shift also marked a partial reversal of alliances in domestic U.S. politics. At least since Franklin D. Roosevelt, most American Jews had been Democrats, a constituent block of the Democratic party. With Nixon, however, some American Jews shifted to the Republicans. (During the nineteenth century, most American Jews had been Republicans; things change.) Jews were now middle class and many were turned off by ultraliberals in the Democratic party. They feared the growth of Soviet power and worried about Israel's security. Some Jewish intellectuals became neo-conservatives and served Republicans in Washington.

By the time the junior Bush took office in 2001, the Republicans were more pro-Israel than the Democrats had ever been. Protestant evangelicals and fundamentalists, a large portion of the Republican electorate, had turned pro-Israel. Fundamentalists read the Bible literally, and it states that God gave this land to the

G : *Geography*

RECOGNITION OF JERUSALEM

The United States, like most nations, does not officially recognize Jerusalem as Israel's capital, even though it houses Israel's parliament and chief executive offices. (But not its defense ministry, which remains in Tel Aviv, farther from potential attackers. Germany for the same reason left its defense ministry in Bonn when it moved its capital to Berlin in 1991.) Only Costa Rica and El Salvador have their embassies in Jerusalem.

The U.S. **embassy**, like most, is in Tel Aviv, although a **consulate general** in Jerusalem handles much contact. Officially, the United States still designates its consulate general there as "Jerusalem, Palestine," perhaps the last remnant of the 1947 UN partition plan. In order to avoid recognizing Israel as sovereign in Jerusalem, American staffers in the consulate general are accredited to no host government, an unusual situation. The United States also has no formal defense alliance with Israel, although many refer to Israel as a U.S. ally. Security relations are close but have never been formalized into a treaty.

Jews for eternity. Starting in the 1960s, fundamentalist authors (often citing the Books of Daniel and Revelation) wrote that the rebirth of Israel heralded Christ's second coming, and this view, encouraged by Israel, took over the Christian Right, who are now more pro-Israel than some Jewish Americans.

America has a natural affinity for Israel as the only stable democracy in the region. (Turkey is a democracy but a shaky one, beset by Islamists on one side and its military on the other.) Democracies favor other democracies and disfavor dictatorships. Israel for years has been the largest recipient of U.S. foreign aid, some $3 billion a year. Egypt is in second place with about $2 billion, mostly in food. (Historically, the biggest recipient was South Vietnam.)

Is America's strong support of Israel a good or bad thing? As the result of long-building trends in U.S. politics, it really cannot be helped. It does some good in that it tells Israel's enemies that America will not permit Israel's destruction, so they should abandon such illusions and settle. It perhaps backs Israel too much, however, in letting Israel expand its settlements in the West Bank and Gaza, which only increases tension and blocks any peace deal. If Palestinians come to see America—as Anwar Sadat of Egypt did—as the player holding most of the cards in the Middle East, our friendship with Israel could ease both Palestinians and Israelis into a peace settlement. To play this role, we will have to be powerful and friendly but even-handed. It will be America's greatest challenge.

---

embassy   Diplomatic representation of one country to another, usually a house in the host country's capital.

consulate general   A diplomatic post of lesser status and more limited functions than an *embassy*.

U.S. *The United States in the Middle East*

BLOWN UP IN BEIRUT, 1983

President Reagan's Secretary of State George Shultz, new to the job and with little knowledge of the Middle East, thought he understood the region and believed the United States could play a constructive peacemaking role. By 1982, Lebanon was in ruins, its territory rent by a dozen politico-religious militias and occupied by Syria and Israel. Along with France and Italy, the United States sent peacekeeping forces to try to calm Beirut. U.S. Marines went ashore, backed up by a battleship. Congress in effect rescinded its **War Powers Act** by giving Reagan eighteen months to use these forces, because they were "not involved in hostilities." But they were.

The trouble with trying to keep peace in a civil war is that you are quickly driven to take sides. Then the other side hates you and shoots at you. In this case, the United States drew close to the Lebanese Christians and found itself the target of Lebanese Muslims. In retaliation, we fired huge (but inaccurate) naval shells onto Muslim positions. We were up to our necks in a war but did not want to admit it. There were warnings. A widely respected (and pro-Arab) American scholar, Malcolm Kerr, president of the American University of Beirut, was gunned down outside his office. In April 1983 a car bomb demolished the U.S. embassy in Beirut, killing more than sixty.

Then, in October 1983, a Hezbollah suicide driver crashed a Mercedes truck loaded with dynamite into the barracks of sleeping U.S. Marines at Beirut airport, killing 241. (The French peacekeepers were likewise bombed.) America was shocked, and Reagan swore we would not "cut and run," but we did. Too late came the realization that you cannot play peacemaker in the midst of an ongoing civil war, a lesson that still was not learned when West Europeans attempted to do it in Bosnia a decade later.

WHAT ROLE FOR AMERICA?

The junior President Bush—specifically, his national security advisor, Condoleeza Rice—entered the White House saying not much could be done about the Israel-Palestine struggle; we should just be friends with Israel and advance no special peace initiatives. American diplomats and even presidents had worked long and hard on the "peace process" only to see it fail. We were too involved in the Middle East and should distance ourselves from it. We cannot fix it, so we should stop trying.

It was a plausible notion, but then came 9/11 and everything changed. We learned that the Muslim world was seething in anger at America, and one of its main complaints was unlimited U.S. support for Israel. Many Palestinian militants display pictures of Osama bin Laden and the World Trade Center. By the Iraq War in 2003, the Arab world was against the United States. While fighting the war, Bush proclaimed that as soon as we won we would get to work on the Israel-Palestine question with a "road map" for a settlement. Soon Bush's involvement in the Middle East resembled that of Clinton. We may want to stay out, but the Middle East does not let us.

War Powers Act   1973 U.S. law to limit president's use of troops overseas.

G : *Geography*

A UNIPOLAR WORLD?

How is power distributed around the world? Many political scientists described the Cold War as **bipolar**. After the demise of the Soviet Union in 1991, the situation is not so clear. Some see a **multipolar** world dominated by several blocs, including the United States, West Europe, China, and Japan.

But most neo-conservatives (see page 292) see the world as **unipolar**: The United States has so much power that it can and must do what needs to be done. Only we have the economic and military power to balance and stabilize an otherwise tumultuous and dangerous world. Historically, a stable world has required a stabilizer, such as Britain in the nineteenth century. If we do not lead, no one will. The unipolar view of the world underlays some of the unilateralism of the Bush junior administration (see page 134): Try to lead others, but act alone if need be. According to the neo-cons (and many others), the European Union and UN can be relied upon for nothing.

There are many criticisms of the unipolar-unilateralist view. It is at odds with the much older conservatism of the Republican party, which tends toward isolationism, not involvement in distant lands. As such, there were disagreements inside the Bush administration and among Republicans in Congress over the unipolar view. It assumes that we have enough power to stop aggression and chop evil axes throughout the world. This in turn assumes that the American people and Congress have the money and patience to sustain major overseas military involvement. A short crusade rallies the American people, but a long war costs reelection. Consider the effects of Korea on the 1952 election and Vietnam on the 1968 election. It disregards the difficulties and complexities of areas like the Middle East. Do we have sufficient expertise in these areas? Are the experts listened to? It assumes that we can get along without allies or even sympathy from the rest of the world. Going it alone long enough could really leave us isolated.

The Bush about-face illustrates the gigantic question of how involved we should be in the Middle East. Clearly, a hands-off policy begs for an explosion. Trouble in one spot can quickly boil over into trouble in several places. Too much is at stake. But a hands-on policy also begs for trouble. The two Beirut visits by U.S. Marines illustrate how we can get involved in other people's civil wars (see boxes on page 311 and page 314). A major American presence, especially military, can anger local populations. (This happens in South Korea and Japan as well.) We really do have a different culture and like to spread it. One culture inserted into another irritates the host culture. Even a simple thing like female U.S. soldiers driving in Saudi Arabia in 1990 and 1991 unsettled the Kingdom: Many Saudi women, yearning to be a little freer, copied it, but Saudi authorities, fearing change, banned American service women from driving. Like Saudi women, they had to be covered from head to toe and sit in the backseat.

---

bipolar   World dominated by two major powers, the United States and Soviet Union.
multipolar   World divided among several power centers.
unipolar   World dominated by one superpower.

ⓤⓢ *The United States in the Middle East*

NATO, NOT IN THE MIDDLE EAST

The first casualty of the Iraq War, even before the bombs dropped, was NATO. Unable or unwilling to expand its scope into the Middle East, it became a zombie alliance, a dead treaty walking. NATO performed admirably for forty years (1949–1989). It first made Stalin less frightening and let European economies and self-confidence recover.

NATO also gave America the legal and moral structure with which to defend West Europe while giving West Europeans the excuse to avoid defending themselves. From its beginning, NATO was plagued by imbalance, with the United States spending more on the defense of Europe than the Europeans did. Starting with Truman, all presidents complained that our European partners had to do more in their own defense. What hit NATO in 2003 was years in the making. The end of Communist regimes in East Europe in 1989 and demise of the Soviet Union in 1991 made explicit what had long been implicit: What good is this alliance?

It could be very good, if it could redefine itself, in Samuel Huntington's terms, as Western civilization with a sense of solidarity and mission to defend itself against barbarism. But Huntington erred, many now agree, in posing the West as a single civilization with European and North American branches. Seymour Martin Lipset, with much better empirical grounding, emphasized the cultural differences between Europe and the United States.

Europeans complain that American politicians are cowboys, too quick to see threats and charge out to run the world. But it is equally true that Europeans, with some exceptions, are too immersed in welfare-state pacifism to venture outside their Continent. A Swiss friend told one of the authors years ago, "You know, Europe is so drenched in blood from centuries of warfare that Europeans really won't fight again. They've had it with wars."

More importantly, the interests of the United States and West Europe were never identical—they were complementary—and in 2002 they rapidly diverged over the Middle East. Americans and Europeans simply did not see the Middle East the same way. Washington sees a region on the brink of chaos that

KINGDOM OF DENIAL

Iraq and Iran are important, but Saudi Arabia is far more important to us in the Middle East. Saudi Arabia sits atop the world's biggest pool of oil, one quarter of all proven reserves, and supplies one-sixth of U.S. oil imports. (Our biggest supplier: Canada.) The United States and Saudi Arabia are strongly interdependent, and in recent years both turned scared. The traditional Saudi regime, now revealed as unstable, could collapse as quickly as the Shah's did in 1979. The problem has been years in the making but can be papered over no longer.

No one has been stupid or shortsighted in U.S.-Saudi relations. All decisions were rational. Washington did what it had to do for good reasons, and so did Riyadh (the Saudi capital). U.S. support for the Kingdom was an absolute necessity during the Cold War. We knew they were not Jeffersonian democrats, but we also knew that overthrow of the House of Saud would bring a far worse regime, a Mossadeq (see page 185) times ten. The House of Saud disliked America as a non-Islamic cultural threat and supporter of Israel, but only the Americans could offer we must stabilize—to halt terrorism, to ensure the flow of oil, to foster democratization, and to reach an Israel-Palestine compromise. Europeans see a dangerous region that outside intervention can only destabilize. They see Israeli intransigence as the barrier to peace. American public opinion is pro-Israel, European sharply anti-Israel. Some suggest Europeans are burying their guilt over their World War II actions and inactions by denouncing Israelis as fascists. Americans see Israelis as fellow believers and fighters against terrorism. No amount of diplomacy can bridge these different perceptions.

Ironically, the only time NATO invoked Article 5 of its 1949 founding treaty ("attack on one . . . attack on all") was when a tentacle of the Middle East reached out and wounded America on 9/11. A German AWACS plane took a few turns around the Northeast, a little photo op that may be the only time Europe will ever come to the defense of America. And Iraq was very much about 9/11, which changed the psychology of America. We suffered it; the Europeans did not. America was angry; Europe was not. America was deeply involved in the Middle East; Europe preferred to leave the region alone.

Some analysts see the differences as naturally arising from the fact that America is now the most powerful nation on earth while Europe has only modest power. Powerful countries stride forth to remake the world to their liking; weak powers hunker down, hoping trouble passes them by, and criticize the strong nation for arrogance and misuse of power. For decades, especially since Vietnam (where the Europeans were right), European intellectuals have criticized American foreign policy. A few just plain hate America, a hatred that leaped out again with the Iraq War in 2003. Official Washington used to take their criticisms with forbearance, determined not to let it harm the Atlantic alliance. A few sarcastic peeps about feckless Europeans came from Henry Kissinger, Zbigniew Brzezinski, William Cohen, and Capitol Hill. In 2003, however, Washington criticized back, loudly and openly. What a few realists muttered for years in academic journals and op-ed pieces were now heard from the highest levels. Secretary of Defense Donald Rumsfeld was the most caustic ("Old Europe"), but the White House and State Department did not disavow his remarks. Europe and America now see the Middle East very differently and probably cannot act in concert on it.

---

the Kingdom military security. In return, rich Saudis (including the royal family) parked an estimated half trillion dollars in the United States. Pulling out some of their billions from U.S. banks and investments helped bring down the value of the dollar in 2003. It was hard to tell if they were showing their opposition to the U.S. war with Iraq or merely diversifying their holdings. Top Saudis know they are incredibly rich but dangerously weak. The Washington-Riyadh partnership was a level-headed marriage of convenience that worked for half a century.

It can no longer work and is coming apart. First, the Cold War is over. Problems subsumed under the struggle against communism now come into the open. For decades we managed to be simultaneously pro-Saudi, pro-Iran, pro-Jordan, pro-Egypt, pro-Turkey, and even pro-Israel. All fit under the containment blanket, now rudely jerked away.

For decades apologists (some paid by the Saudi embassy) assured us that the Kingdom was firmly built on traditional legitimacy and a contented population. With essentially no news coverage, it was hard to confirm or refute this picture. One got only hints of trouble, all of it denied by Saudi officials. Some observers say the beheading of a Saudi princess (with a sword) in the late 1970s for premarital sex was a cover-up for widespread un-Qur'anic behavior among the royal family. (Her commoner lover was not beheaded; he was simply shot.) French special forces were required to dislodge the Saudi extremists who took over Islam's holiest site in Mecca in 1979. Saudi troops could not do the job, so the regime requested French help but kept the whole operation quiet. In 1990, the Saudi government waited three days before allowing the mass media to report on Iraq's invasion of Kuwait. This is a frightened regime.

9/11 brought us face-to-face with the reality that Americans and Saudis have parted company. In Internet chat rooms Saudis show deep hatred for the West and praise for 9/11 and al Qaeda. In a survey done by Saudi intelligence, 95 percent of educated Saudis supported Osama bin Laden. Some American observers now posit the Saudis as false friends or covert enemies. The Bush administration, like all previous Washington administrations, was restrained in its comments on the Saudis, but the U.S. Congress and media grew increasingly critical. The Saudis simply lied and denied that fifteen of the nineteen skyjackers were Saudis. Some Saudis still say it has not been proved. If they admitted that most of the 9/11 murderers were Saudi, they would be admitting that there is revolutionary rage in the Kingdom, a fact they do not want to face. Riyadh was slow and lazy in investigating the Saudi friends of Osama bin Laden or Saudi "charity" funds for al Qaeda. They knew what they would find and did not want to find it, for that could trigger the very revolution they wish to prevent. Best to keep some things quiet, was the Saudi response; we'll solve this in our own way. But the old way of denying unrest while quietly buying it off is no longer feasible and merely telegraphs fear and weakness.

U.S.-Saudi relations became strained over the issue of terrorism in the mid-1990s. Saudi police caught and quickly executed the 1996 bombers of the Khobar Towers but did not allow U.S. officials to interrogate the suspects. Some U.S. officials suspect the Saudis feared the suspects would name names to U.S. interrogators, and some of those names might be highly placed Saudis. American officials were outraged but said nothing. The U.S. embassy and State Department blandly reassured us of Saudi cooperation and friendship, and no U.S. official said a critical word in public about the Saudis, for that might undermine the regime. Finally, in 2003, the U.S. ambassador to Riyadh charged that we had warned about terrorist bombings weeks in advance, but the Saudis had not beefed up security. It was the first official, public U.S. rebuke to the Saudi government. The Saudis denied they had received any U.S. requests for improved security.

Recent al Qaeda bombings in Saudi Arabia indicate the Osama network is alive and well in the Kingdom, apparently immune from what the Saudis claim is a thorough and well-informed **mukhabarat**. Saudi security police did uncover a cache of 800 pounds of explosives and many weapons in May 2003 but let the nineteen terrorists—all trained in Afghanistan or Chechnya—slip away to bomb three sites simultaneously the next week. Some fear the Saudi security police have been infiltrated and compromised by al Qaeda sympathizers.

---

mukhabarat   Arabic for "security police."

P ⋮ *Peace*

A U.S. FORCE FOR PALESTINE?

Some observers of the Israel-Palestine impasse suggest that the only way to get peace is for American peacekeepers to enforce it. America, they argue, is the only country with the prestige to make it work. Third parties enforcing cease-fires is fraught with peril. With the best of intentions, you can easily get caught up in somebody else's civil war, as we have seen in Lebanon and Bosnia.

The United States has excellent relations with Israel but not with the Palestinians. Even if we tried to be totally neutral, we would be perceived as favoring Israel, just as Lebanese Muslims perceived us as favoring the Christians. Soon we would be shot at. The United States has contributed small numbers of personnel to peacekeeping missions after Arab-Israel cease-fires. For years after the 1973 war, Americans maintained electronic listening devices in the Sinai that would have revealed any troop movements. This helped stabilize a cease-fire that was already agreed to.

A basic problem is that peacekeeping does not work until and unless both sides have reached a cease-fire that both are ready to observe. You cannot "enforce" a cease-fire without yourself entering the fighting. Several European battalions in UNPROFOR attempted to keep peace in Bosnia from 1992 to 1995, where there had been no cease-fire. As a result, they were arrested, shot at, and ignored, especially by the Serbs. In one particularly horrible incident at Srebrenica in 1995, outnumbered Dutch peacekeepers turned over Bosnian Muslim refugees to Serbian forces, who promptly shot more than 7,000 men and boys into mass graves. UNPROFOR had extremely restrictive **rules of engagement** that let them shoot back only if they were directly fired upon. Their home governments did not want them involved in a war. If the Dutch had fought at Srebrenica, they would have been breaking orders. After all, they were there to keep the peace.

Later in 1995, after the Serbs had suffered military reverses (thanks to U.S.-sponsored arms shipments and training), all parties agreed to a cease-fire at Dayton mediated by top U.S. diplomat Richard Holbrooke. Then 20,000 heavily armed U.S. forces as part of a 60,000 man NATO Implementation Force (IFOR) with "robust ROEs" got compliance from all sides with scarcely a shot fired. Serb fighters respected NATO and Abrams tanks. Notice that peacekeeping requires prior acceptance of a cease-fire, which is based on a balance of military strength between the contending parties, plus sufficient and visible military strength on the part of the peacekeeping forces. Where these conditions obtained, in Bosnia and Kosovo, peacekeeping was moderately successful, but at the price of turning Bosnia and Kosovo into international protectorates requiring peacekeepers for many years. Trying something similar between Israel and the Palestinians could be much more difficult.

Osama bin Laden was born and raised in Saudi Arabia, and most of his funds and many of his recruits come from there. Much of Saudi grade-school education is in the hands of Wahhabi clerics, who teach Qur'an and hatred of all non-Muslims. "Well, of course I hate you because you are Christian," a Saudi professor of Islamic law explained to an American reporter, "but that doesn't mean I want to kill you." Some failed to grasp the distinction. Saudi-funded Wahhabi **madresas** in Pakistan were the religious basis of the Afghan Taliban movement, which we overthrew in

rules of engagement   (ROEs) Instructions to soldiers as to when to shoot back.
madresa   Muslim school, chiefly for memorizing the Qur'an.

2001. John Walker Lindh, the California youth now in jail for aiding the enemy, got his fundamentalist education in one such madresa. Although the Saudi regime sponsors salafiyya, it is itself a target of salafis, because in salafi eyes its Islam is hypocritical and allows Americans on the sacred soil of Arabia.

Washington and Riyadh both sense doom but neither knows what to do. Some top Saudis now speak of cutting ties with Wahhabism, but the House of Saud, based on Wahhabism, does not dare. Said one Saudi journalist, who had been an extremist in his youth: "We have to develop a modern, tolerant, and inclusive interpretation of faith." Some speak of reforms leading to democratization, but they also understand that reforms would embolden salafi revolutionaries. As Tocqueville said of the period just before the French Revolution: "The most perilous time in the life of a bad regime is when it seeks to mend its ways."

Washington can see no reasonable alternative on the horizon. Whatever comes after the House of Saud is bound to be worse, likely an Osama. Leaning on Riyadh to reform or seriously stop terrorist activity and fund-raising could destabilize the Kingdom. So we both did nothing. It worked for half a century, some reassure us.

But it had stopped working by the Iraq War, which Saudi Arabia opposed out of fear of further regional and domestic destabilization. Almost all Saudis, like Arabs everywhere, denounced the war. Arabs do not like seeing brother Arabs attacked, even if they feared the secular and tyrannical regime of Saddam Hussein. In 1990 and 1991, Riyadh let us use Saudi territory to attack Iraq; in 2003 it did not. The U.S.-British attack had to mass in little Kuwait. Quietly, the Saudis did let us use the Prince Sultan airbase (built and run by Americans) to direct the air war in 2003, but not to launch strikes from there. The Saudi government quietly requested that all 5,000 U.S. military personnel be withdrawn after the Iraq War in 2003. Secretary Rumsfeld had no trouble honoring this request. The feeling of estrangement was mutual.

The Saudi regime is weak and frightened and has very mixed feelings toward us. They genuinely and correctly fear mass uprisings. The Saudis have always been ambivalent about U.S. bases. They like U.S. security guarantees but worry that U.S. personnel on their soil feed fundamentalist rage against the regime. They want us "over the horizon" on ships and carriers. Now they will find out which is riskier, a U.S. presence or U.S. absence.

We, too, face a "presence or absence" question in the Persian Gulf. Do U.S. forces calm or raise tensions? Will the situation take care of itself? What kind of regimes will we tolerate there? Elected Osamas? Regimes that simultaneously sell us oil and fund terrorists? Are there any circumstances in which we would do to Saudi Arabia what we have done to Iraq—invade, occupy, and attempt to democratize? Are we equipped, militarily or psychologically, for that? As George Kennan noted long ago, "Imperialism is not our dish."

WHAT NEXT FOR U.S. POLICY?

Is the 2003 Iraq War a template for further U.S. actions in the Middle East? Rumors swirled after that war that we would soon invade Syria and depose the sister Baathist regime that had ruled there for decades. Other rumors were that we would go after Iran, which likely was building nuclear weapons. Would further U.S. invasions have been wise? It was perhaps good that we had to pause and put Iraq back together to understand that security is not simply a matter of winning wars but of establishing stable governments.

According to some reports, the neo-cons in the Bush administration viewed war with Iraq as simply a first step to establishing a major and long-term presence in the region. We would set up semipermanent U.S. bases in Iraq—which was in no position to complain—and vacate our bases in unreliable Saudi Arabia. Then we would not have to ask anyone's permission for U.S. military action throughout the region. Extremists would know that U.S. power was just in the next country. That might also encourage Saudi Arabia, Syria, Iran, and other regimes to turn to democracy.

Almost instinctively, few Americans liked that picture, especially if that put us in the midst of peoples seething with hatred of America. America, born in a revolt against an empire, does not like to see itself playing empire. Empires are bad; free and independent peoples are good. The Cold War was one of the few times we kept U.S. forces overseas for decades, and that was to defend willing allies.

The problems of a U.S. empire emerged a century ago. We took the Philippines in 1898 but got a bad conscience when we had to crush an insurrection of Filipino patriots against us. The war officially ended in 1902, but conflict continued until 1913. We told the Filipinos we had come to liberate them from Spanish tyranny, but then we decided to stay. The Philippines, thought Teddy Roosevelt and his fellow imperialists (the neo-cons of their day), would be a splendid base for U.S. commerce and power in Asia. By 1907 even Roosevelt saw the mistake: First we had to fight to keep the Philippines, then we would have to defend the Philippines, and growing Japanese power already loomed on the horizon. We had acquired a vulnerability. Lightly garrisoned and nearly forgotten between the wars, the Philippines were easy pickings for the Japanese in 1942. Empires cost money, troops, and a shift of attention from domestic affairs to overseas affairs.

ISLAMIC RAGE AND U.S. RESPONSE

Muslims have been getting beaten by the West for centuries. The Moors were pushed back in Spain over eight centuries until expelled in 1492. The Turks were pushed back in the Balkans over two centuries until confined to their little corner of Europe in 1913. Then, after defeat by the West in World War I, the Ottoman Empire and Caliphate were terminated. Osama bin Laden referred to this end of the last Muslim empire as a terrible tragedy the West had inflicted on the entire community of Islam. The British and French occupied Arab lands and treated them as colonies. Then Israel, a branch of Europe in Muslim eyes, repeatedly beats Arab armies, occupies more and more Arab land, and crushes Palestinians who complain about it. And finally the United States twice makes quick work of little Iraq, killing thousands of civilians as "collateral damage." Is there no end to the humiliation? This is the psychological self-portrait of Arabs and to a certain extent of Muslims as a whole: always the defenseless victim. Now, everything Muslims felt about

Conflicts

CATCHING TERRORISTS: NO ONE IN CHARGE

Is the United States organized to fight terrorism? 9/11 revealed that U.S. agencies were not talking to each other and had no overall plan to fight terrorism. The Federal Bureau of Investigation is not supposed to operate overseas, where it has no powers of arrest. (Some FBI agents representing the Justice Department staff embassy positions to coordinate crime-fighting with host countries.) The FBI is generally unequipped with foreign-language and area skills to make sense of underground movements. Before 9/11, the FBI paid little attention to terrorism. It ignored its own field agents who urgently signaled that Arab visitors were taking flying lessons for dangerous purposes. As critics said after 9/11, the FBI catches bank robbers.

The Central Intelligence Agency, on the other hand, is loaded with area and language expertise but has no legal power to arrest anyone or even carry out operations inside the United States. The CIA is not a law-enforcement agency and does not share information with other agencies. Its mission is to prepare intelligence reports from secret sources for the president and a handful of other top officials—and not for anyone else, for that might reveal its "sources and methods" and get its informants killed. The CIA attempts to penetrate foreign organizations with its own informants. (This is terribly difficult with al Qaeda, as it recruits from kinfolk and neighbors who know each other personally.) The Immigration and Naturalization Service (INS) and Customs Service are our front line against terrorism, but they are underfunded and overburdened. Two years after 9/11, there was still no single computer system or data base by which the FBI, CIA, INS, and local police could share information.

The U.S. armed forces are superbly trained and equipped to destroy hostile countries but not to catch small groups of hostile characters. They too are not law-enforcement agencies, and using them as a heavily armed police force invites tragedy, like crushing a gnat with a bulldozer. Top civilian officials sometimes think that the Army or Marines can be used as police, but military officers, knowing what can go wrong, generally oppose such misuse. As of now, no U.S. department or agency is set up to catch terrorists, a task that falls between stools.

Crusaders, Mongols, and British imperialists is focused against the United States. We do not really deserve it, but can we escape it?

Muslims will have to lose the self-pity and rage in order to progress. Some realize the fault is in their authoritarian regimes, soaring populations, and faltering economies. And it is possible to outgrow this rage. Other ex-colonial lands had similar grudges, but they faded. India had some justifiable anger against British imperialists, who finally left in 1947, as they had agreed to do. During the Cold War, Indian intellectuals transferred their rage against Britain to the United States, the new English-speaking power that wished to arrange the world to suit its commerce and its values. This showed up in Indian policies of socialism at home and neutralism abroad. After the founding Congress party was voted out of power and as India gained self-confidence and self-respect through economic growth, this pointless hostility faded. Now a newly capitalist India (big-growth industry: computer operations) has excellent relations with the United States. An unspoken factor pulling the two together: Both face Islamic terrorism.

Some coordination and centralization came with the new Department of Homeland Security, but the FBI and CIA are not part of it. Ironically, the CIA was set up in 1947 precisely to centralize intelligence data and remedy the problem of Pearl Harbor. We had considerable intelligence before Pearl Harbor, but it was scattered on various desks. If State, the Army, and the Navy had put all their information on one desk, the pattern of Japanese activity would have been clear. Unfortunately, intelligence functions tend to proliferate and scatter over time, as each department wants its own, specialized information.

What is needed is a new, small agency—perhaps part of Homeland Security—that draws on the intelligence capabilities of all other agencies and has the policing capabilities to track down terrorists. It will have the weapons and training of Special Forces, the area expertise of the CIA, the detection capabilities of the FBI, and the law-enforcement powers of police. It will be a sort of international SWAT team with language skills. Chances are we will see this in fanciful television dramas long before we see it in operation.

We will also need an important element that the Bush neo-cons have scorned: international law. What will give this imaginary SWAT team permission to operate on foreign soil? To send armed men into another country without permission is an act of war. The world urgently needs to develop a body of terrorism law that most countries accept. The United States must take the lead here, and, yes, even sign treaties that are binding on us. We rejected the International Criminal Court, thinking it would bring frivolous anti-U.S. charges against our soldiers. One administration neo-con argues that no treaty binds us; we may do as we wish. The problem here is that if the United States is not bound by a treaty on terrorism law, few other countries will be. Reciprocity is the basis of international law. Fortunately, precedents are at hand: centuries-old laws on piracy. As Israeli Attorney General Gideon Hausner pointed out in the 1961 Eichmann trial, pirates may be tried and hanged by whoever catches them. Their crimes are the concern of all, not just one country. In our day, terrorism equals piracy.

India, of course, has only a Muslim minority and started life as a democracy under the highly developed Congress party of Gandhi, but potentially Muslim lands could undergo a similar transformation. It will not happen easily or automatically. Steps need to be taken. Muslims must reject the extremist versions of Islam that are being offered as the answer to their problems. An angry return to an imaginary past and hatred of all things non-Muslim will only make their condition worse. A thousand years ago, Islam was a vibrant, growing culture, far ahead of Christian Europe in science, medicine, commerce, architecture, and tolerance of other religions. Muslims have a proud past they could refer to. The narrow, bitter past offered by the salafis goes back to the fourteenth century, when Islamic civilization was already starting to decline after the Mongol conquest of Baghdad in 1258. They have got to accentuate the positive in their own civilization.

Can the United States play any role in this process? Intervening with troops may be an occasional unfortunate necessity, but we must not make a habit of it. Every time we do, we reinforce the Muslim sense of humiliation and victimization, which leads to more rage, much of it against the United States. Economic examples are much better. Indeed, it was the incredible growth of Japan, South Korea, Taiwan, Hong Kong, and Singapore from poverty to world-class prosperity that chipped away at the self-confidence of Communist regimes, whose citizens increasingly asked: "If we are the wave of the future, then why are we so damn backward?" The ultimate weakness of Islamic extremism is that it cannot put food on the table. When the rage subsides, Islamic revolutionaries realize this fact, as they have in Iran.

One example of a Muslim country that modernizes into prosperity and democracy will be worth more than America's vast military strength. Encouraging that to happen is a worthwhile U.S. goal. As economist Paul Krugman points out, no one has been able to predict the next lands of rapid economic growth; it is always a surprise. Famed Swedish economist Gunnar Myrdal penned his pessimistic *Asian Drama: An Inquiry into the Poverty of Nations* in the 1960s. Scarcely was the ink dry when several Asian countries began to take off. (He underrated the growth of manufacturing for the world market.) The Muslim world may surprise us.

If we are not careful, we could turn current U.S.-Islamic antipathies into a new Cold War. Already, some Americans speak of it as such: a long, bitter, ideological struggle in which Islam is the new Soviet Union. If that view ever gets planted—and some on both sides are busy planting it—your generation will know the fears and frustration of the Cold War, which our generation waged and eventually won. It was not a pleasant thing; it cost millions of lives in wars that now appear absurd and squandered vast resources in weapons systems that, if used, could have destroyed the planet. Let us not go through anything like that again.

How to prevent it? Keep your rage in check. We are certain to be hit with more horrifying terrorist strikes. Al Qaeda will attempt many attacks, some small and some on the scale of 9/11. Furthermore, there are other Islamist organizations beyond al Qaeda that could follow in its footsteps. The Palestinian Hamas organization may expand its suicide bombings beyond Israel; the United States would be the natural target. We will have to be on guard for decades and must organize for it immediately (see box on pages 322–323). U.S. homeland security does not have nearly the funding to safeguard America. A major weakness: the thousands of containers that come in by ship every day.

But we must not lapse into indiscriminate rage against Muslims, for that plays into the hands of the terrorists. By invading Muslim lands on suspicion of terrorism, we convince more Muslim youths to join a jihad against us. Rage can be contagious: We catch it from Islamic extremists and sneeze it back to the whole region, which is exactly what the terrorists want. The extremists, following the revolutionary theory of "the worse, the better," try to create maximum chaos out of which they suppose they will be the net winners. They may be terribly mistaken and simply end up with a destroyed, impoverished region. No one can be sure where this cycle of the rage of one fueling the rage of the other will end up.

America must be well armed but remember that force of arms alone cannot settle this problem. From time to time we will have to take military steps, but they must be carried out calmly and always with an eye on the aftermath. Remember, we won the Cold War not by fighting but by waiting. Eventually, our

Soviet adversary collapsed under pressure of its own faulty economic system. Many Americans were frightened of the Soviet Union during the long Cold War, but history always was on our side, and it is now. Our generation made it; yours will, too.

CONCLUSIONS

World War II brought the United States into the Middle East in a major way. The region's oil—especially that of Saudi Arabia, with whom FDR established personal ties in 1945—and founding of Israel pulled the United States into the affairs of the Middle East. We may wish to stay out but cannot. U.S. policy toward Israel and the Arabs was even-handed until Nixon, who resupplied Israel in the 1973 war. Europe turned first neutral and then hostile toward Israel. NATO simply does not operate in the Middle East. Israel likewise abandoned its early neutrality between Moscow and Washington and turned sharply to America. U.S. Marines have been in Beirut twice, in 1958 and 1982–1983, when they were blown up by a truck bomb.

Bush junior, looking at the intense U.S. involvement in the Middle East of previous administrations, wished for less U.S. involvement but soon put the United States more deeply in the region than ever. Neo-cons in the Bush administration especially favored U.S. involvement, but this led to U.S. unilateralism with few allies.

Saudi Arabia is the great prize of the region, but it is showing signs of unrest and instability as it denies any problems. Much Islamic terrorism originated in the Wahhabi faith of the kingdom, including Osama and fifteen of the nineteen 9/11 skyjackers. Constantly afraid of mass anger, Saudi Arabia did not let U.S. forces use Saudi soil for the 2003 war and asked U.S. forces to leave after the war.

The United States faces major Middle East policy choices. How many and how long should we keep troops there? Can we meld several U.S. agencies—which communicate little with each other—into an effective antiterrorist force? Are we willing to make and adhere to new international laws against terrorism? How can we best handle Islamic rage directed against us? If we turn to rage ourselves, we may be creating a new and long-lasting Cold War.

FURTHER REFERENCE

Brown, L. Carl, ed. *Diplomacy in the Middle East: The International Relations of Regional and Outside Powers*. London: I. B. Tauris, 2001.

Brzezinski, Zbigniew. *The Choice: Global Leadership or National Insecurity*. New York: Basic Books, 2004.

Cordesman, Anthony H. *Saudi Arabia Enters the Twenty-First Century: The Political, Foreign Policy, Economic, and Energy Dimensions*. Westport, CT: Praeger, 2003.

Hemmer, Christopher. *Which Lessons Matter?: American Foreign Policy Decision Making in the Middle East, 1979–1987*. Albany, NY: State University of New York Press, 2000.

Hinnebusch, Raymond, and Anoushiravan Ehteshami, eds. *The Foreign Policies of Middle East States*. Boulder, CO: Lynne Rienner, 2002.

Miglietta, John P. *American Alliance Policy in the Middle East, 1945–1992: Iran, Israel, and Saudi Arabia*. Blue Ridge Summit, PA: Rowman & Littlefield, 2002.

Moller, Bjorn, ed. *Oil and Water: Cooperative Security in the Persian Gulf*. London: I.B. Tauris, 2001.

Potter, Lawrence G., and Gary G. Sick, eds. *Security in the Persian Gulf: Origins, Obstacles, and the Search for Consensus*. New York: Palgrave, 2002.

Quandt, William B. *Peace Process: American Diplomacy and the Arab-Israeli Conflict since 1967*. Berkeley, CA: University of California Press, 2001.

Telhami, Shibley. *The Stakes: America in the Middle East*. Boulder, CO: Westview, 2003.

Index

A

Abbasids, 45–49, 53
Abbas, Mahmud, 131, 133
Abbas (Shah), 157, 175
Abdo, Geneive, 238
Abdullah I (of Jordan), 207, 208
Abdullah II (of Kuwait), 218
Abdallah III, 219, 220
Abel, 1
Abraham, 70
Abu Bakr, 41, 46
Abu Mazen, 131
Abu Nidal Organization, 110
Aburish, Said K., 205
Achille Lauro, 282
Afghan Arab, 284
Afghanistan, 256–261, 265, 276, 283–290
Aflaq, Michel, 215
Ahmad I, 219
Ahmad, Feroz, 154
Ahmad (Shah), 180
Aisha, 43, 46
Ajami, Fouad, 308
Ajax, Operation, 186
Al Aqsa Martyr's Brigade, 117, 129, 282
Albright, Madeline, 236, 237
Alexander the Great, 26, 27, 71
Algeria, 97, 284, 295
Algiers Accords, 217
Ali ibn Abu Tayyid, 38, 39, 41–45
Aliyah, 78

Allenby, Edmond, 81, 82
Amir, Yigal, 279
Andersen, Roy R., 17
Anderson, Terry, 232
Anglo-Iranian Oil Corporation (AOIC), 185, 186
Ansar al-Islam, 275
Aqaba, Gulf of, 93, 98, 104, 115, 193, 196
Arab League, 198, 214, 219, 220
Arab Legion, 93
Arafat, Yassir, 109, 117, 121, 122, 128, 131, 132, 135, 282
Araki (Ayatollah), 234
Arfa, Hassan, 172
Archetype, 12
Arif, Abdul Rahman, 216
Arif, Abdul Salam, 213, 215
Armed Forces Union, 145
Armenians, 68
Armitage, Richard, 243
Armstrong, William H., 35
Aruri, Naseer, 135
Aryan, 23
Al-Assad, Hafez, 275
Ashkenazim, 76
Assyria, 19, 21, 22, 25
Aswan Dam, 100, 101, 106
Ataturk, Mustafa Kemal, 68, 137–142, 154, 160, 295
Atta, Muhammad, 263
Ayyubid, 52
Aziz, Tariq, 247

B

Baath, 215, 217, 270, 273, 294, 320
Bab al-Mandab, 193
Babylon, 19–22, 72, 74
Al-Badr, Muhammad, 202
Badr Khan, 158
Baer, Robert, 308
Baghdad Pact, 200, 201, 213
Baha'I, 176, 299
Bahrain, 173, 231, 267, 295, 296
Baker, James, 247, 248
Bakhash, Shaul, 189, 238
Bakhtiar, Shahpour, 224–226
Al-Bakr, Hasan, 216, 217
Balfour Declaration, 82, 84
Balkans, 57, 58, 60, 64, 65, 79
Bamban, Robert, 35
Banani, Amin, 189
Bani Sadr, Abul Hasan, 166, 227, 228,
   230, 235, 236
Barak, Ehud, 111, 121, 131, 133
Barlas, Asma, 308
Bar Lev Line, 106, 107, 111
Barzani, Idris, 166, 168
Barzani, Masoud, 166, 168
Barzani, Mustafa (Mullah), 162–166, 213
Batatu, Hanna, 221
Bay'a, 42
Bazargan, Mehdi, 227–230
Bayar, Celal, 142
Bedillo, Jose, 289
Bedouin, 11
Begin, Menachem, 86, 114–116, 121,
   278, 282
Beheshti (Ayatollah), 166
Ben Gurion, David, 86, 88
Bergen, Peter L., 291
Berlin, Treaty of, 158
Bidlisi, Sharaf Khan, 172
Bickerton, Ian J., 111
Bill, James, 17, 189, 238
Bin Ladin, Osama (Usama), 80, 138, 212,
   236, 258–261, 276, 283–286, 289, 290,
   302, 306, 318–321, 325
Bin Ladin, Salim, 283

Binder, Leonard, 189
Al-Bitar, Salah al-Din, 215
Black, Anthony, 54
Black September, 109, 282
Blair, Tony, 263
Bosphorus, 24, 32
Bowden, Mark, 291
Braude, Joseph, 277
Bremer, L. Paul, 269
Brinton, Crane, 226
Bronze Age, 2, 19
Brown, L. Carl, 325
Brown, Peter, 35
Bruinesen, Martin van, 172
Brzezinski, Zbigniew, 317, 325
Bunche, Ralph, 115, 135
Bush, George H. W., 120, 153, 169, 241,
   244–247, 251, 252, 256, 273, 276, 280
Bush, George W., 121, 131, 134, 153,
   237, 251, 254, 256, 261, 263, 266, 275,
   277, 301, 312, 314, 315, 318, 325
Byzantium, 25, 31–35, 50

C

Cain, 1
Calendar, 6, 41
Camp David, 113, 115, 122, 131, 132,
   135
Canaan, 70, 71, 89
Capitulations, 61
Carey, Roane, 135
Carter, James E. ("Jimmie"), 113, 115,
   123, 135, 222, 223, 229, 230, 242, 258
Carthage, 23, 27, 28
CENTCOM, 4, 173, 242, 243
Central Treaty Organization (CENTO),
   200, 201
Chalabi, Ahmad, 209
Chaldiran, 157, 174
Charmoy, Francois Bernard, 172
Cheney, Richard (Dick), 244, 265
Churchill, Winston (Sir), 181, 183
Ciller, Tansu, 149, 151
Clark, Wesley K., 277

Clash of Civilizations, 300, 301
Clemanceau, Georges, 84
Cleopatra, 30
Clinton, William J., 113, 121, 131, 236, 252, 287, 288, 292, 301, 314
Cohen, William, 317
Committee of Union and Progress, 67, 68, 138
Constantine, 30–32
Constantinople, 32, 34, 35, 50, 57, 58, 64
Constitutional Revolution of 1906, 178, 179, 181
Cordesman, Anthony H., 277, 325
Council of Guardians, 234, 235
Cottam, Richard W., 190
Cox, Percy (Sir), 219
Cronkite, Walter, 115
Crusades, 15, 33, 34, 50, 51, 74, 83
Crystal, Jill, 221
Cyprus, 147, 148

D

Dardanelles, 23, 24
Dayan, Moshe, 311
Dead Sea, 3
Deir Yassin, 97
Demirel, Suleiman, 146, 148
Democratic Party (Turkey), 143–146, 154
Dervis, Kemal, 151, 152
Dhimmi, 16, 68, 74
Dulles, Allen, 186
Dulles, John Foster, 100, 186, 201, 264

E

Eagleton, William, Jr., 172
Eaton, Charles Le Gai, 54
Ecevit, Bulent, 147, 148, 151
Eden, Anthony, 101
Egypt, 19, 26, 27, 29, 52, 80, 83, 93, 97, 99–101, 103–109, 113–116, 123–125, 134, 150, 194, 199, 200, 202, 203, 212, 245, 284, 287, 295, 297, 304, 307, 310, 313, 317

Egyptian Islamic Jihad, 100, 287
Ehteshami, Anoushiravan, 326
Eisenhower, Dwight David, 100, 102, 201, 202, 264, 310
Erbakan, Necmettin, 146, 147, 149–151
Erdogan, Recep Tayyip, 151, 152
Erzerum, Congress of, 138
Eshol, Levi, 104
Esposito, John L., 205
Etzioni-Halevy, Eva, 135
Evin, Ahmet, 69
Expediency Council, 234, 235

F

Faisal I of Iraq, 207–209
Faisal II of Iraq, 210, 211, 213
Faluja, 93
Fall, Bernard, 280
Farouk (King), 93, 99
Farouk-Sluglett, Marion, 221
Farouk Sluglett, Peter, 221
Farsi, Jalal ad-Din, 228
Fatah, 109, 110
Fatima, 41, 45
Fatimid, 46, 49, 50, 52
Faw (Fao) peninsula, 206
Fazilet Party, 151, 152
Ferdowsi, 26, 54
Fertile Crescent, 7, 70
Franks, Tommie, 267
Free Officers Movement, 93, 200
Free Party, 141
Freud, Sigmund, 22
Fromkin, David, 90
Fukuyama, Francis, 301
Furtig, Henner, 254

G

Gabriel, Richard, 35
Al-Gailani, Rashid Ali, 211
Gallipoli, 81
Ganji, Manouchehr, 238
Garner, Jay, 269

Gaza Strip, 96, 97, 99, 100, 109, 111, 116–118, 122, 123, 128–131, 134, 313
Gellner, Ernst, 304
Gemayel, Bashir, 110
Gerges, Fawaz A., 308
Gerner, Deborah J., 308
Ghareeb, Edmund, 172, 254
Ghazi (King), 210
Gibbon, Edward, 35
Gilan Republic, 179, 180
Glaspie, April, 241–243
Globalization, 301, 307
Golan Heights, 109, 124
Goldschmidt, Arthur, Jr., 17
Goldstein, Baruch, 279
Goltz, Thomson, 69
Gopin, Marc, 135
Gorbachov, Mikael, 120
Gordon, Haim, 135
Gordon, Rivca, 135
Gray Wolves, 146
Great Bitter Lake, 198
Great Rift, 3
Green Line, 118
Gul, Abdullah, 152
Gulf Cooperation Council, 296
Gulf War, 120, 135, 153, 154, 168, 169, 240–249, 254, 259
Gush Emunim, 118

H

Hadith, 40
Haganah, 84, 92, 97
Haifa, 210
Halabjah, 168, 272
HAMAS, 117, 129, 130, 133, 135, 282
Hammurabi, 20
Hamsa, Khidhir, 254
Hannibal, 28
Haram es Sharif, 122
Hashemites, 197, 201, 207, 273
Hashmi, Sohail H., 308
Hatshepsut, 21
Hekmatyar, Gulbuddin, 283
Held, Colbert C., 17

Hellenes, 72
Hellespont, 24
Helms, Christine Moss, 205
Hemmer, Christopher, 325
Henze, Paul B., 154
Heper, Metin, 69, 154
Herzog, Chaim, 111
Hilberg, Raul, 90
Hill and Knowlton, 245
Hijra, 39
Hinchcliffe, Peter, 112
Hinnebusch, Raymond, 326
Hittite, 19–22
Hizballah (Hezbollah, Hezballah), 111, 123, 279, 280, 282, 283, 314
Holden, David, 205
Hoogland, Eric, 239
Hormuz, Strait of, 193, 232
Hostage Crisis, 228–230
Hourani, Albert, 54
Hoveyda, Feredoun, 239, 291
Howath, David, 205
Hudaybiya, 40, 43
Hunter, Shireen T., 308
Hunter-gatherer, 1, 5
Huntington, Samuel, 137, 300, 301, 305, 307, 308, 316
Husayn ibn Ali, 43, 44, 47
Husayn-McMahon Correspondence, 81, 207
Husayn, Sharif, 197
Hussein of Jordan (King), 104, 105, 200, 244
Hussein (Husayn), Saddam, 80, 100, 105, 120, 153, 167, 189, 212, 216, 217, 231, 233, 240–247, 249–254, 261–264, 267–273, 275, 277, 280, 285, 292, 294, 297, 298, 302, 320
Al-Husseini, Hajj Amin, 84, 211
Husyer, Robert, 225

I

Ibn Khaldun, 83
Ibn Taymiyah, 53
Ijtihad, 48, 299

Ikhwan, 196, 219
Illiteracy, 14
Imset, Ismet G., 172
Incirlik, 153
International Atomic Energy Agency
    (IAEA), 246, 251
Inter Services Intelligence Directorate
    (ISI), 258, 276, 283
Intifada, 117, 120, 123, 135
Inönü, Ismet, 142, 143, 145, 146, 154
Ionia, 23, 25, 26, 30
Iran, 123, 150, 151, 155–157, 160,
    162–167, 173–189, 201, 214, 220,
    222–238, 259, 294, 295, 307, 309, 310,
    316, 317, 321
Iran Air 655, 233
Iran Contra, 232
Iran-Iraq War, 167, 168, 231–233, 240
Iraq, 82–84, 97, 107, 120, 153, 155, 156,
    164, 165, 167, 168, 172, 173, 189, 196,
    197, 201, 204–217, 220, 230, 231, 233,
    240–244, 246–254, 256, 261–277, 285,
    292–295, 297, 301, 302, 305, 307, 309,
    316, 318, 320, 321
Iraq War, 153, 206, 254, 261, 263–267,
    314, 317, 320
Iraqi Petroleum Corporation, 214, 216
Irgun, 84, 86, 97, 114, 278
Iron Age, 21, 23
Iskandar, Adel, 308
Islam, 12, 36, 52, 53, 80
Islamic Republic Party, 227, 228, 230
Ismael, Tareq Y., 291
Israel, 70–72, 74, 79, 83, 88, 89, 91–99,
    102–105, 107–111, 113–115, 120,
    122–127, 129–135, 169, 203, 247, 261,
    265, 275, 279, 283, 294, 295
Istanbul, 35, 58, 64, 66, 295, 309
Izadi, Mehrdad R., 172

J

Jabir I, 217, 218
Jabir III, 220
Jacobson, Eddie, 89
Jangal Movement, 179

Janissary, 59, 60, 62, 63, 66
Jansen, Johannes J. G., 54
Al Jazeera, 306, 307
Jerusalem, 73, 74, 78, 81–84, 87, 93–96,
    105, 108, 113, 115, 120, 125, 126, 128,
    129, 131, 132, 135, 157, 278, 313
Johns, Richard, 205
Johnson, Chalmers, 260, 277
Johnson, Lyndon Baines, 104, 147, 248,
    266, 310
Jordan, 83, 84, 93, 97–99, 104, 105, 109,
    124, 125, 130, 134, 196–198, 200, 213,
    214, 267, 288, 295, 317
Judea, 71, 74, 89, 96
Justice Party, 146, 148
Justice and Development Party (AK
    Party), 152, 154
Justinian, 32, 33

K

Kabba, 37, 40
Kamil, Husayn, 253
Kaplan, Lawrence, 277
Karbala, 44, 47
Karbaschi, Gholam Hossein, 236
Karine A., 123, 237
Karlowitz, Treaty of, 295
Karzai, Hamid, 261
Kashani, Abdul Qasem, 185
Kavakci, Merve, 152
Keddie, Nikki R., 239
Kennan, George F., 268, 320
Kepel, Gilles, 291
Kerr, Malcolm, 314
Khadije, 38
Khadduri, Majid, 221, 254
Khalidi, Rashid, 90
Khamenei, Ali, 234–237
Khan Yunis, 100
Kharijites, 44
Khatami, Muhammad, 235–238
Khobar Towers, 237, 318
Khoeiniha, Mohammad Musa, 229
Khomeini, Ruhollah, 45, 166, 188,
    223–229, 233, 234, 238

Khoury, Philip S., 17
Kimmerling, Baruch, 136
King David Hotel, 86, 278
Kinross, John Patrick Douglas Balfour
  (Lord), 69
Kinzer, Stephen, 190
Kissinger, Henry, 113, 120, 165, 312, 317
Klausner, Carla L., 111
Klinghofer, Leon, 282
Koestler, Arthur, 86
Kolleck, Teddy, 132
Komala, 161
Koran, 13
Kostiner, Joseph, 17
Kristol, William, 277
Kurdish Democratic Party-Iran, 161
Kurdish Democratic Party-Iraq, 168, 169,
  272, 280
Kurdistan Workers Party, 151, 272
Kurds, 141, 150, 153, 155–172, 174, 189,
  209, 213, 216, 250, 266, 269, 271, 272,
  277, 301
Kurmanji, 156
Kutschera, Chris, 172
Kuwait, 153, 173, 194–196, 202, 204,
  207, 214, 217–220, 231–233, 240–249,
  252, 254, 262, 265, 268, 295, 296, 320
Kuwaiti Oil Company, 219

L

Lacy, Robert, 205
Landau, Jacob M., 154
Laqueur, Walter, 90
Latham, Aaron, 172
Latrun Heights, 93, 95
Lausanne, 139, 153
Lawrence, T. E., 81, 194, 195
League of Nations, 82, 86, 209, 271
Lebanon, 80, 108–111, 114, 123, 208,
  231, 279, 282, 283, 293, 295, 311, 314,
  315
Lehi, 84, 86, 278
Leiden, Carl, 17
Lenczowski, George, 190

Lewis, Bernard, 17, 69, 83, 154
Levant, 7, 51
Libya, 115, 150, 284, 294, 295, 307, 309
Likud, 118, 120, 122
Lindh, John Walker, 320
Lipset, Seymour Martin, 316
Little, Douglas, 255
Locke, John, 6
Long, David E., 17
Lyons, Jonathan, 238

M

Makey, Sandra, 190
Madrid Conference, 120, 135
Mahabad, 160–163, 184, 213
Mahdi, 52
Maimonides, Moses, 74
Al-Majid, Ali Hasan (Chemical Ali), 167
Major, John, 251
Mamluk, 52, 53
Mandaville, Peter G., 308
Mandelbaum Gate, 94
Manila Air, 288
Mardin, Serif, 69
Marr, Phoebe, 221
Marsh Arabs, 273
Marx, Karl, 83
Massoud, Ahmad Shah, 260
Maude, Stanley, 206
McMahon, Henry (Sir), 81, 82
Mehmet the Conqueror, 35, 59
Meier, Golda, 107
Menderes, Adnan, 142, 144, 145
Menemen, 141
Mesopotamia, 10, 11, 18, 20, 21, 70, 72,
  82, 206
Messiah, 74
Migdal, Joel S., 136
Miglietta, John P., 326
Miller, Aaron David, 205
Miller, Judith, 221
Millet, 59
Milton-Edwards, Beverley, 112
Moller, Bjorn, 326

Mongols, 49, 53, 56, 57
Montazeri, Husayn Ali, 234
Montreux Convention, 24
More, Christiane, 172
Morocco, 97, 275, 289
Mossadeq, Muhammad, 183–186, 223, 224, 316
Motherland Party (ANAP), 148, 151
Mottale, Morris M., 255
Mu'awiyya, 43
Mubarak I, 194, 218
Mubarak, Hosni, 241, 245
Muhammad, 36–41, 302
Muhammad I, 218
Muhammad Ali of Egypt, 80, 192, 193, 217
Muhammad Ali (Shah), 178, 179
Muhammad, Khalid Shaykh, 287
Muhammad, Qazi, 161–163, 171
Mujahedin-e Khalq, 167, 230
Murden, Simon W., 308
Murphy, Emma C., 136
Muskie, Edmund, 230
Muslim Brotherhood, 100, 284
Mu'tazilism, 48, 49
Muzaffar (Shah), 178
Mylroie, Laurie, 221
Myrdal, Gunnar, 325

N

Nader (Shah), 175
Nafziger, George F., 54
Naser-ed-din (Shah), 178
Nasreddin (Mullah), 66
Nasser, Abdul Gamal, 19, 80, 93, 99–104, 106, 199–203, 212, 213, 215, 284, 310
Nateq-Nuri, Ali Akbar, 235
Nation Party, 144
National Front, 185, 224
National Pact, 138, 311
National Order Party, 146, 147
National Unity Committee, 145
Nationalist Action Party, 146, 148, 151
El-Nawawy, Mohamme, 308

Neolithic, 1, 19
Netanyahu, Benjamin, 134, 279
Nikitine, Basile, 172
9/11, 256, 260, 261, 263, 276, 288, 306, 314, 318, 322, 324, 325
Nixon, Richard M., 106, 108, 114, 164, 189, 204, 222, 264, 311, 312, 325
North Atlantic Treaty Organization (NATO), 147, 316, 317
North, Oliver, 232
Northern Alliance, 260
Norwich, John Julius, 35

O

Ocalan, Abdullah, 151, 169–171
Olson, Robert, 172
Oman, 195, 196, 203, 267, 295, 296
Omar, Muhammad (Mullah), 260, 287
Onassis, Aristotle, 140
Oren, Michael B., 112
Organization of Petroleum Exporting Countries (OPEC), 187, 204, 241, 244
Oslo, 118, 120–122, 135
Ottoman Public Debt Authority, 67
Ottoman, 26, 34, 35, 56, 58, 59, 61–65, 67, 68, 78, 80–83, 85, 89, 137, 138, 154, 157, 160, 174, 191–195, 206–208, 210, 217–219, 273, 294–296, 309, 321
Ozal, Turgut, 142, 148–150, 153, 241

P

Pahlavi, Mohammed Reza, 183–189, 203, 222–226, 228, 229
Pahlavi, Reza I, 160, 179–181, 183, 225
Pakistan, 258, 259, 261, 276, 283, 284, 295, 297, 304
Palestine, 71, 74, 78, 83–87, 89, 90, 91–93, 95, 97–99, 102, 107, 109, 111, 113, 116, 117, 120–135, 205, 208, 210, 211, 265, 278, 280, 282, 287, 302, 313, 314, 317, 319, 321
Palestine Authority, 121, 123, 132, 133

Palestine Liberation Organization (PLO), 109, 117, 120, 128, 129, 133, 282
Palestine National Covenant, 120
Palestinian Islamic Jihad, 117, 282
Palmach, 93
Patriotic Union of Kurdistan (PUK), 167–169, 272
Pavis, Timothy J., 221
Pearl, Daniel, 304
Peel Commission, 85, 124
Peled, Yoav, 136
Peleg, Samuel, 136
Peloponnesian War, 25
Persia, 23, 25–27
Phalange, 110
Phoenicians, 22, 23, 25
Pike Commission, 165
Pishavari, Ja'afar, 184
PKK, 151, 169–171
Pollack, Kenneth M., 112, 277
Pope, Hugh, 154
Pope, Nicole, 154
Potter, Lawrence G., 326
Powell, Colin, 243, 249, 263, 264, 266
Praetorianism, 59, 60, 305
Progressives, 140, 141
Public Broadcasting System, 255
Punic Wars, 23, 28

Q

Qadaffi, Mu'ammar, 150
Qadir, Abdul, 158
Al-Qaeda (Qaida), 100, 237, 260, 261, 263, 269, 270, 275, 276, 282, 283, 287–290, 302, 318, 324
Qajar, 175, 176
Qasim, Abdul Karim, 213–215, 219
Qassemlu, Ahmad Kazem, 166
Qatar, 173, 195, 196, 267, 295, 296, 306, 307
Qavam, Ahmad, 184
Quant, Willim B., 326
Qur'an, 13, 37, 38, 41, 42, 48, 66, 299
Qutb, Sayyid, 284

R

Rabin, Yitzhak, 121, 122, 279
Rafsanjani, Ali Akbar Hashemi, 234
Rahman, Omar Abdul (Shaykh), 287
Rajavi, Masoud, 230
Ramadan, Taha Yassin, 254
Al-Rashidi, 194–196, 199, 218
Reagan, Ronald W., 230, 232, 242
Refah Party, 149, 151, 152
Reich, Bernard, 17
Reid, Richard, 289
Republican Peasants National Party, 146
Republican Peoples Party (RPP), 140–147, 152, 154
Rex Cinema, 223
Rice, Condoleeza, 314
Riley-Smith, Jonathan, 55
Roosevelt, Franklin D., 183, 198, 199, 204, 285
Rosenwein, Barbara H., 55
Rubin, Barry, 291, 308
Rubin, Judith Colp, 291, 308
Rumsfeld, Donald, 263, 264, 266, 317
Rush, Alan, 221

S

Sabra, 109, 110
Sachar, Howard M., 90
Sachedina, Abdulaziz, 308
Sadat, Anwar, 80, 106, 108, 114–116, 122, 123, 125, 126, 302, 313
Safavid, 173, 174
Safire, William, 166
Sa'id, Muhammad, 184
Said, Edward W., 17, 90
Al-Said, Nuri, 209, 213
Ibn Said, Qabus, 203
Saladin (Salah ad-Din), 50–52, 99, 157, 212
Salafiyya, 286, 302, 307, 320
San Remo Conference, 208
Sargon the Great, 20
Al-Saud, 218–220, 287, 302

Ibn Saud, Abd-al Aziz, 194–199, 204, 285
Ibn Saud, Abdallah ibn Abd-al Aziz, 307
Ibn Saud, Bandar ibn Sultan ibn Abd-al Aziz, 241, 244, 245
Ibn Saud, Fahd ibn Abd-al Aziz, 205, 307
Ibn Saud, Faisal ibn Abd-al Aziz, 201–205
Ibn Saud, Muhammad ibn Abd-al Aziz, 205
Al-Saud, Muhammad ibn, 191–192
Ibn Saud, Saud ibn Abd-al Aziz, 199–203
Saudi Arabia, 98, 173, 191–205, 214, 232, 237, 244, 245, 247, 249, 259–261, 266, 268, 275, 282–285, 288–290, 294–297, 302, 304–307, 309, 315–321, 325
Saunders, J. J., 55
SAVAK, 186, 189, 222
Schlessinger, James, 312
Schliemann, Heinrich, 19
Schultz, George, 314
Schwarzkopf, Norman, 242, 243, 249, 250
Segev, Tom, 90
Seibert, Robert F., 17
Seleucid, 72
Seljuks, 33, 49, 50, 53, 56, 57
Sephardim, 76
Settlements, 118, 119
Sevres, Treaty of, 159, 208
Shafir, Gershon, 90, 136
Shahname, 158
Shainin, Jonathan, 135
Shakak Tribe, 160
Shamir, Yitzhak, 86, 278, 282
Sharafkandi, Sadeq, 167
Sharafname, 158
Shari'a, 48, 53, 66
Sharon, Ariel, 92, 95, 99, 110, 111, 118, 122, 128, 131, 134
Shatilla, 110
Shatt al Arab, 163–165, 231
Shawcross, William, 277
Shin Bet, 121
Shipler, David K., 136
Shriteh, Taher, 135
Sick, Gary, 239, 326
Simko, Ismail A., 160, 161, 171
Sinai, 101, 106, 109, 114, 116, 123

Sivas, Congress of, 138
Smith, Charles D., 291
Sorani, 156
Stein, Jeff, 254
Stein, Leslie, 90
Stereotype, 12
Stern, Jessica, 290, 291
Stout, Chris E., 291
Sudan, 115, 260, 282, 286, 294, 295
Sulayman, 59–61
Suez Canal, 100, 102, 105–108, 111, 124, 153, 193, 213, 219
Sullivan, William, 223, 225
Al-Suwaidi, Jamal S., 238
Swain, Joseph Ward, 35
Sykes-Picot, 81, 84, 207
Syria, 98–100, 109, 110, 124, 125, 155, 156, 169, 170, 199, 205, 208, 213, 214, 245, 266, 267, 275, 295, 321

T

Taba, 121, 132
Taher (Shaykh), 158
Talib, Sayyid, 208
Taliban, 259–261, 276, 287, 319
Talibani, Ibrahim Ahmad Jalal, 163, 169
Tanzimat, 66, 67
Telhami, Shibley, 326
Temple Mount, 122
Tessler, Mark A., 90
Thatcher, Margaret, 244, 245
Theodora, 33
Thomas, Baylis, 112
Tiran, Strait of, 102, 104, 193
Torah, 72–74
Trucial States, 195
True Path Party, 148
Truman, Harry S, 89, 162, 184, 200, 310
Tudeh Party, 183, 186, 223, 230
Tunisia, 97, 295
Turkes, Alparslan, 146
Turkey, 137–155, 168–171, 182, 201, 214, 244, 250, 266–268, 272, 293–295, 313, 317

Turkish Straits, 23, 24, 64, 193
Tutweiller, Margaret, 242

U

Ubaydallah (Shaykh), 158, 159, 171
Umar, 41, 32
Umayyad, 43–46
United Arab Emirates (UAE), 173, 195, 196, 267, 295, 296
United Arab Republic (UAR), 100, 213, 215
United Nations (UN), 86–88, 90–92, 95, 97, 102, 103, 114, 115, 125, 135, 246, 247, 251–254, 262–265, 277, 279, 298, 310, 313, 319
USS *Cole*, 275, 280, 288
USS *Quincy*, 198
USS *Stark*, 233
USS *The Sullivans*, 288
USS *Vincennes*, 233
U Thant, 103, 104

V

Vahit-ed-Din (Sultan), 139
Vance, Cyrus, 230
Velayat-e Faqih, 188, 228, 234
Viorst, Milton, 308

W

Wagner, John G., 17
Al-Wahhab, Muhammad ibn, 191–192

Walton, Mark W., 54
Watt, W. Montgomery, 55
Weapons of Mass Destruction (WMD), 251, 262–266, 269, 270, 276
Weber, Max, 83, 294
West Bank, 96, 97, 99, 102, 105, 109, 111, 117, 118, 122–124, 126, 128–131, 134, 135, 279, 280, 313
Westwood, John, 112
White Revolution, 186
Williams, Paul, 291
Wilson, Woodrow, 159
Wittfogel, Karl, 10
World Trade Center, 287–289
Wyman, David, 90

Y

Yazid, 43
Yemen, 95, 97, 100, 173, 196, 202, 275, 284, 288–290, 295
Yergin, Daniel, 190
Young Turks, 67, 68
Yousef, Ramzi, 287, 288
Yu, Dal Seung, 190

Z

Zaher, Muhammad (Shah), 257
Zahidi, Dariush, 190
Zakariya, Fareed, 297
Al-Zawahiri, Ayman, 287, 289
Zealots, 73
Zurcher, Eric J., 154

S0-ARV-986

To provide accurate medical information for lay-people, to heighten awareness about low back pain, and to change attitudes and behavior of the medical profession, corporate world, and those who are directly affected by lower back problems and challenges.

YOUR LOWER BACK

YOU ARE NOT ALONE!

Warren J. Potash
Michael J. Gratch, M.D.
Andrew M. Star, M.D.
Richard A. Goldberg, D.O.

A Patient and His Doctor Answer Questions and Present Exercises to Help You Manage Your Lower Back

For educational purposes only.   Every effort has been made to ensure that the information in this book is medically accurate.   This book is not technical and is not for use in diagnosing or treating individual problems.   Those areas are the domain of a qualified physician.   Every person can benefit from the authors' experiences with low back pain.   **Never** use this book for self-diagnosis, just for information.

Printed in the United States of America
printing number
1 2 3 4 5 6 7 8 9 10

Warren J. Potash, Dr. Michael J. Gratch, Dr. Andrew M. Star, and Dr. Richard A. Goldberg, coauthors.

Your lower back: a patient and his doctor answer questions and present exercises to help you manage your lower back / by Warren Potash ... [et al.].
    p. cm.
Includes bibliographical references and index.
Preassigned LCCN: 93-92564.
ISBN: 0-9636076-3-4

    1. Backache–Popular works.   2. Lumbosacral region–Care and hygiene.   I. Potash, Warren.

RD771.B217Y68 1993   617.564
                                QBI93-1019

Edited by Lenna Holt
Front cover design and illustrations by David Ben-Yaacov
Back cover design and inside page design by Bonnie Burgemeister
Electronic publishing layout by Digitalight, Jenkintown, PA
Printing by Arcata Graphics, Fairfield, PA

Your Lower Back may be purchased for corporate, educational, or sales promotion usage.   When requesting information or writing to the authors of ***Your Lower Back***, please address all correspondence to: Paragon Communications, Inc., P.O. Box 457, 720 Greenwood Avenue, Suite 102, Jenkintown, PA 19046.

ACKNOWLEDGMENTS

Special thanks to my wife, Millie, and to our children, Jordan, Marc, and Elizabeth. Without my parents, Rosalie and Irvin Potash, *who knows what might have been?* Millie's parents, Gert and Bob Sherman, were always there to provide much-needed support.

A special thanks to Dr. Benjamin Williams and the staff of Atwood Library at Beaver College; to Andras Spiegel, Bob Martin, and Audrey Cross for all of their contributions.

Warren

We would like to thank our wives for putting up with the long hours of our normal work days and the additional hours of work to make this book a reality. We would like to thank our children for understanding that it takes hard work and dedication to complete a project and it does not allow a lot of time for play. Thank you to the staffs of Paragon Communications, Abington Orthopaedic Specialists, and the Abington Back Institute for juggling our schedules so that we could sometimes see each other face to face. The staffs of Jefferson Medical College Library, the Connelly Library at LaSalle College, the Van Pelt Library at the University of Pennsylvania, and the Abington Free Library all gave immense help along the way.

David Ben Yaacov receives our gratitude for his excellent illustrations within this text.

Last, but by no means least, Lenna Holt was a tremendous help, not only with the editing, but with her many recommendations and ideas.

Warren J. Potash

Michael J. Gratthay

Andrew Star

Freha

With low back problems, as with most medical problems, no two are exactly the same. The information provided in this book can help in the active management and care of the lower back, but **only a physician experienced in the treatment of lower back problems is qualified to diagnose your individual medical conditions**. **Never** use this book for self-diagnosis, just for information.

Every attempt has been made to ensure the accuracy of the information in this book; however, there still remain differences of opinion about the care and treatment of some back problems. The purpose of *Your Lower Back* is to provide general information, but it does not reflect all opinions or options available.

This unique publication has relevance for anyone interested in up-to-date information on low back pain and special exercises for being active in lower back care. The information on the lower back does not apply to those who are 18 years or younger because they usually have not reached their adult height.

TABLE of CONTENTS

INTRODUCTION *13*

PROLOGUE by Warren Potash *17*
    A patient's perspective

STARTING OUT *23*
    How should I use *Your Lower Back*?
    What is the purpose of this book?
    Is this one of those *feel good* books?
    Why is it so important to educate people about the lower back?
    What role does attitude play?
    Why me?
    How can another person's experience help me manage my lower back?
    What is meant by the lower back?

BACK PAIN: WHAT IS THE MAGNITUDE OF THE PROBLEM? *29*
    How many people suffer from significant low back pain?
    What are the odds of recovering from low back pain
        without treatment?
    What are the odds that the pain will come back?
    Do lower back problems primarily affect men or women?
    Why do many people think that their lower back problem
        occurred for no apparent reason?
    What responsibility have the general public and industry taken
        in caring for the lower back?

ANATOMY *35*
    Why should I learn about the structure of my spine?
    What is the spinal column?
    What are the discs?
    How does the spine move?
    What is the function of the ligaments?
    What are the central and peripheral nervous systems?
    What about the muscles?
    How does the anatomy of the spine influence
        back problems?

CAUSES OF BACK PAIN *49*
    What are the causes of back pain?
    What is idiopathic low back pain?
    What is a herniated disc?
    What is spinal stenosis?
    What is a compression fracture?
    What is spondylolisthesis?

TABLE of CONTENTS

PHYSICIANS   53

What is a physician?
How do I know if I need to consult a physician?
Who are the physicians that treat spine problems?
What is Board Certification?
How should I choose a physician?
What should I expect from a physician?
How can I describe my pain to my physician?
When should I seek a second opinion?
Who is the best qualified physician to perform surgery?
What should I ask a potential surgeon?

THE DIAGNOSIS   65

What is the primary diagnosis?
What information is important in the history?
What types of questions are commonly asked?
What should a physical examination include?
What technologies are available to help with the diagnosis?

TREATMENT   75

How do I choose the best treatment for my back problem?
What types of treatment methods are available?
How should I start treating my back problem?
How do I know when I have gone too far in treating my back problem?
Shouldn't I just stay in bed until my back pain gets better?
Are there any times that bed rest is prescribed for a back problem?
I really am afraid to do anything strenuous. Can't you just give me
    a pill or crack my back?
Why is exercise beneficial for the lower back?
If my doctor recommends bed rest, should I run to another doctor?
What medications are available for low back pain?
What is the role of medication in treatment?
What is physical therapy for my back problem?
How do I choose a good therapist?
What are the roles of ultrasound and electrical stimulation?
What about salves, balms, and lotions?
How about heat or ice?
What are *alternative approaches*?
What is spinal manipulation?
If I choose to have my spine manipulated, what should I do?
Will acupuncture help my back pain?
Will spinal injections help my problem?
Is there a basis for *hands-on* therapy?
What is a back school?
What about surgery for low back pain?

THE AGING SPINE   99

Is low back pain in the geriatric age-group similar to that in
    younger individuals?
What about nerve problems in the elderly?
Are lower back problems in the elderly treated
    like those in young people?

ERGONOMICS   105

What is ergonomics?
How does ergonomics affect my life?

LIVING WITH A LOWER BACK CHALLENGE   107

How important is attitude in dealing with lower back problems?
How active should I be?
Is general physical fitness important for lower back problems?
How can I effectively manage time with a lower back challenge?
Is weight important?
Are there any tips for traveling?
How do I stay comfortable while flying on an airplane?
How can you drive with a minimum of discomfort?
What is the proper way to get in and out of the car?
How long should I sit at one time?
How should I sit?
Is there a standing position that is most effective?
What is the proper way to bend, lift, and carry packages?
Are certain positions better for sleeping or lying down?
Is firm bedding recommended?
What can I do if my lower back gets tired and sore at night?
Can my sex life be affected by low back problems?
Is relaxation important?
Will a whirlpool or hot tub help my back?

PREGNANCY AND YOUR LOWER BACK   119

Is back pain during pregnancy normal?
What hormonal changes are occurring?
What structural changes are occurring?
Are there other causes for pain?
What can I do about low back pain during my pregnancy?

CUMULATIVE TRAUMA   121

What is cumulative trauma?
How do cumulative trauma disorders usually occur?
What are some examples of CTDs?
Are there other risk factors for back pain?
Are there solutions for cumulative trauma?
How can I help decrease CTD injuries in the workplace?

TABLE of CONTENTS

PERSONAL EXPERIENCE FROM A FELLOW BACK PAIN SUFFERER   131

Maybe it's me; maybe it's in my head!
How did friends react?
What did my children think?
What were the best times?
What were the worst times?
What about self-esteem?
What did I tell my children?
How did I feel when I woke up in the morning?
How do I view the world after this experience?
    Has my outlook changed?
The business world - how did associates react?
Perceptions as a back pain sufferer
Why did I write *Your Lower Back* with Dr. Gratch,
    Dr. Star, and Dr. Goldberg?

A PRIMER ON EXERCISES FOR THE LOW BACK   141

Take charge!
How important is exercise for the lower back?
Is exercise important even if I am considering surgery?
How should I feel when I exercise?
What is the difference between *warming up* and stretching?
What is *cross-training*?
How much exercise does the lower back need?
What types of exercises should I choose?

EXERCISES   147

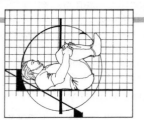

STRETCHING
    Pelvic Tilt
    Double Knee to Chest
    Single Knee to Chest
    Leg Extension - Advanced
    Trunk Roll
    Cat and Camel
    Prayer Stretch

STRENGTHENING
    Partial Sit-Up or Stomach Crunch
    Bridging
    Abdominal Stabilization with Arm Movements
    Abdominal Stabilization with Arm and Leg Movements
    Hands and Knees Balancing
    Functional Squat
    Hip Extension
    What is *cooling down* after exercise?

OTHER TYPES OF LAND-BASED EXERCISES
  Machine-Based Exercise
  Free Weights
  Aerobics
  Water Exercises
    Can water exercises be effective for those with lower back pain?
    What does water do?
    Can my whole body benefit from water workouts?
    Can water exercise be useful after surgery?
    Should you stretch first?
    Is special equipment used in water workouts?
    Is swimming good?
    What are the types of water exercises?

TRAINING ZONE   *163*
  What is my training zone?
  I am sore when I start working out. How will I know
    when to stop?

EPILOGUE by Millie Potash   *165*
  A spouse's perspective

GLOSSARY OF MEDICAL TERMS   *175*

REFERENCES CITED AND BIBLIOGRAPHY   *185*

INDEX   *189*

THE NEUROSURGEON THAT WARREN Potash had consulted said to *lie down flat for at least 18 hours a day for 2 weeks.* In November 1985, Warren did not realize that his life was about to change forever. Over the next 4 years he experienced some of the best and some of the worst that medicine had to offer. Although people initially felt sorry for him, they soon changed. They lost confidence in the way he was coping and ultimately he began to lose confidence in himself. How many times did he ask himself, *Is this pain all in my head? Am I crazy?*

Fortunately, his long journey had a happy ending. His problem was diagnosed and treated, and he was able to return to a normal life. Along the way he learned a great deal about his back – and about himself. He learned that even though his surgery was successful, he will always have a back problem and will always need to actively pursue keeping his back healthy. He learned that physicians do not always have the answers and that individuals with back problems must actively participate in their own care. Becoming active participants means exercising several times a week and avoiding certain activities. In certain situations, it may even mean learning to live with soreness and pain.

The authors had a single purpose in writing this book: to save the readers from the prolonged learning process that Warren had to endure before he could come to terms with his back problem. For Warren, like most, this process did not result in complete cure, so he had to learn how to live with a problem that many other people also face every day. Literally millions of people in the United States experience low back pain. For some the pain may be incapacitating; and like Warren, they may lose their job, their friends; some may even lose their family.

Many have questions: What is causing my low back pain? How do I choose a doctor? Will surgery help me? Should I see a chiropractor? They ask, but they may have difficulty getting straight answers. The authors wrote **Your Lower Back** to provide up-to-date and accurate information about low back problems. This collaborative effort involves a patient who has lived through a debilitating back problem and three doctors who treat back problems on a daily basis. If you do not suffer from low back pain, then you probably know someone who does. *Your Lower Back* will help you to understand both the condition and those who live with its pain.

Unfortunately, even if the best health care were available to everyone, low back problems would continue to affect millions of people. Knowledge about back pain has been rapidly improving in recent years, but a great deal is still left to learn. In the United States low back pain is more than just a medical problem; it is an industry. People with back pain spend billions of dollars on various treatments, and insurance companies spend billions on disability payments for back pain sufferers. The individual sufferer can easily feel lost amid the barrage of information from practitioners and special interest groups. *Your Lower Back* should help back pain sufferers in more critically questioning the information they are given and in asking the questions for which they desperately need answers. Critical questioning should not be confused with hearing only what you want to hear. Some information about back pain is unpleasant; and there are very few fast or simple answers. Back pain is a lot like gray hair: Almost everyone gets it, very few like it, and nobody knows a cure for it.

Each author has his own reasons for wanting to be involved with *Your Lower Back*. For Warren, who had suffered for years before finding an answer, it is a way to prevent anyone from suffering as he had. He was encouraged by his wife, Millie, who had suffered along with him. For the doctors, *Your Lower Back* is a way to begin to educate people about becoming actively involved in diagnosing and treating their back problems. A great deal of ignorance and misinformation abound on the topic of the lower back. One physician, or even several, cannot educate large numbers of people by answering questions, one by one, in the office. *Your Lower Back* gives those in pain a head start by offering timely information on back pain before they consult a physician. Beyond basic information about the back, the book helps educate people to gain realistic expectations about their conditions. If they are already seeing a doctor, they can become better informed patients.

Your Lower Back will not solve everyone's problems. It is not a self-diagnosis book. If it helps people understand more about the back ... how the back is constructed, how it can be injured, how everyone can stretch and strengthen the back, what happens to the back with age ... then this book will have fulfilled its mission. If it convinces people to take a more active role in making themselves better rather than expecting a pill or an operation to solve their problem, then *Your Lower Back* is a success.

To the best of the authors' knowledge, *Your Lower Back* is the first book of its type to be coauthored by a nonmedical person with a low back problem and his doctor. The authors hope that a layperson's perspective combined with the physicians' knowledge will benefit the maximum number of people. Even if only a few are helped, *Your Lower Back* will have achieved its purpose. The book uses a question-and-answer format. As a result, readers can study the book from cover to cover or choose only the sections that interest them. A practical exercise section is also included which presents a variety of ways to stretch and strengthen the back.

A patient's perspective

THE YEARS HAVE PASSED, 5 years since my back surgery and 7½ years since I could not get out of bed. To borrow a phrase from Dickens, *it was the best of times and it was the worst of times.* I believe that I knew some good times, even though my life and the lives of those closest to me were altered by a medical problem that went undiagnosed for almost 2½ years. In some ways it seemed like an out-of-body experience, almost surreal. Had I really gone through all of this? Why didn't I do things differently? What was the purpose of this? I was not sure that the doctors believed me; I really didn't care. I had no financial incentives to be inactive since my disability insurance paid nothing. The doctors could tell me it was in my head; I knew it was not.

I learned an important lesson in my youth: Do not ask, *Why me?* It is a useless question since it has no answer. The lesson continues: Be thankful for what you have, particularly your health. Loss of health is not new to me. When I was 8 or 9 years old, I was speaking to my grandmother in our living room when she fell over from a stroke. She was rather young for a stroke, and I had known her very well because she and my grandfather lived with us. She had always been kind. Why her? On that day I learned that there is not always an answer, and there is no sense in looking for one.

I've had my share of personal challenges. Luckily for me, I've also had my share of successes. I have always found strength from within myself and from my family; this time was no different. The challenge was greater; but when my back pain began in November 1985, I did not know that it would change my life so drastically. During the first week, while I was on muscle relaxants and painkillers, I told my wife, Millie, *I'll beat this!* I had no idea how long that would take.

That same month, I was referred to a doctor who was known as the *doctor's doctor*, the physician to whom most doctors would refer their own families. I really believe that because of his reputation, subsequent doctors were afraid to disagree with him. I'm not so sure that they **really** took the time to diagnose me. This doctor initially prescribed bed rest for 2 weeks. I was given muscle relaxants and pain-relievers. Over the next few weeks, I was grateful that I could at least begin to move around as the pain subsided. The doctor told me *to lie in the sun for a few weeks.* Fortunately, Millie and I had a neighbor with a house in the islands, so we spent a week resting and trying to heal my back. At my request, my doctor referred me for physical therapy. I seemed to make some progress, but a sneeze or rapid movement could cause spasms of pain that might last for days. After 6 months, my doctor admitted me to a hospital for a myelogram. He told me that I had a disc problem, then added that surgery would not help me. He recommended a corti-sone injection, one of many injections that I tried. However, I continued to experience frequent episodes of severe pain that came without warning ... from even minimal exertion.

After 2 years of this problem, while in and out of physical therapy, I was examined by another doctor because I needed a prescription to continue my physical therapy. That doctor told me that I should never have surgery. He had seen me over a 1-year period during this portion of my physical therapy. I remember explaining that if he had what I had, he wouldn't be able to practice medicine. I decided not to see him again. During the first 2 years of my illness, I also sought opinions from several other physicians, but none had anything further to offer.

Finally, in November 1987, after over 2 years of pain, I made arrangements to be evaluated by another physician, a neurologist, while I was traveling to the Washington, D.C. area. This physician was the first to tell me that I had a condition in my lower spine called spondylolisthesis. In my case, this condition appeared to be caused by two small cracks in the bone where the last vertebral bone attaches to the sacral part of the pelvis. The physician also showed me that this crack had appeared on my first x-rays, in November 1985.

In December 1987 after my diagnosis was finally made, I was sent back to the original doctor (the *doctor's doctor*) who had treated me. As it happened, he and the Washington, D.C. physician who diagnosed my spondylolisthesis had trained together after medical school. Because of scheduling and the

Christmas season, 6 weeks passed before the *doctor's doctor* told Millie and me that he disagreed with the physician from Washington and that I had no significant problem; he added that it was probably all in my head. The next morning I had my fifth or sixth epidural steroid shot.

After 10 weeks and another consultation, this time with a rheumatologist, I met Dr. Gratch. He agreed with the physician who had told me that my spondylolisthesis was significant. He took the time to explain the importance of this problem, described my options for treatment, and explained the chances for success. Surgery was scheduled for April 20, 1988. No other doctor had spent as much time with me as Dr. Gratch did. We reviewed my files and he also explained his thoughts on why most of the other doctors did not see how a spinal fusion would be likely to correct the problem. He told me which exercises to concentrate on prior to surgery, and scheduled an appointment to meet Millie; some 2 hours later I left.

My confidence was surging; I thought we finally had the answer. I figured that if my problems were in my head, now was the time to trick myself into getting better. But I couldn't. By the time April 20 came around, I was prepared, but hurting big time. I could not be on medication prior to the surgery, and I was in spasm. Hot showers, hot baths to relax were all that I was allowed.

The surgery started around noon; by the time I first saw a clock in the recovery room at 2:50 p.m., all 2½ years of lower back and leg pain had gone ... replaced with the normal pain from the surgical incision. When I was brought to my room and saw Millie and my mother, I told them that the pain was gone. They probably thought that I had lost my marbles, but it really happened that way. Within 24 hours, I was able to stand and be measured for a back brace. I progressed well but finally *hit the wall* 7 or 8 days after surgery. I was trying to do too much, too soon.

The summer of '88 was the hottest in the history of the Philadelphia area, and I had to wear the brace until October. I was allowed to take it off while walking in the pool for 15 minutes and when showering and lying down. The pool and shower were a sheer joy. I continued to make progress physically, but many obstacles had yet to be overcome. Throughout this time of rehabilitation and recovery, I was trying my best to retain a positive mental attitude. However, the pressure of being unable to earn a living was constantly on my mind.

This story is not written to scare anyone; I know I am the exception, not the rule. But, in understanding my past, you may appreciate how powerful a statement my wife made about 15 months after the surgery: *With your knowledge of the lower back, it would be a shame not to write a book, so no family would ever again have to go through what we did.* I can also hear my daughter at age 5 saying: *I don't 'member you ever running around, just lying down.* The surgery ended one journey, but it started me on another.

Trying to get back into the business world has not been easy; but with financial help, I am starting to see the light at the end of the tunnel. Our family is intact. It has been quite a ride, but we all made it through together, sharing the sorrow and the joy. Maybe my religious beliefs gave me the strength to endure. Prior to my back problems, when things were going my way, I was told that my good fortune was due to my faith in God. How foolish, I thought. I had always believed, but I never expected good fortune in return for my religious devotion. Looking back, I can now see that my faith in God and the support of my entire family helped me get through my low back problem.

My family and I have weathered a tremendous storm that has transformed our lives. We hope that revealing what we endured will lessen the suffering of others.

Warren J. Potash

How should I use Your Lower Back?

THIS BOOK CONTAINS USEFUL information for your daily life. Skim the book first, look at the illustrations, review the exercises, and scan the glossary. The question-and-answer format is designed to allow you to rapidly find the information that will help you immediately. But, you will probably want to explore the book in more detail. You can also use it as a reference source, particularly if you are already receiving advice or treatment for a lower back problem.

The authors have gathered the most current information concerning the low back. Their personal experiences may offer insight into concepts or problems that have been troubling you. This resource is valuable, but is not a substitute for qualified medical opinions about your particular problem.

What is the purpose of this book?

THE PERSONAL EXPERIENCE OF a low back pain sufferer plus the collective experience of several physicians who specialize in low back problems give the reader a starting point for learning about low back problems. Those with minor problems or simple questions may never have to go beyond the information in *Your Lower Back*. However, others will use this book as a source of information that supplements the advice of physicians, therapists, friends, and others. Only you can make the final decisions about your particular case, but sound advice from qualified professionals will help you make those decisions.

This book **does not substitute** for your relationship with your doctors; it supplements their role. Consultations with physicians are often brief; patients may forget to ask all of their questions. Often, it is hard to remember all of the details, even when the explanations have been excellent. This book can provide more complete background information and become a starting point for further questions.

Is this one of those feel good books?

NO, THE AUTHORS DO not pretend to have the answer for everyone. The road to recovery has very few shortcuts and often involves long periods of hard work. Sometimes an individual's problems may not have an answer; moreover, certain information about back problems is unpleasant. *Your Lower Back* combines answers to commonly asked questions with advice for the average person with a back problem. Much of the information is based on common sense and supported with up-to-date medical information.

With this book, you can become **active** in caring for your low back disorder. Passive *feel good* treatments may play a role, but passive treatment alone is not an effective long-term solution. Active involvement includes actively learning about your problem, actively deciding on the course of treatment, and actively participating in exercises even when you do not feel well. Warren Potash found out firsthand how difficult it can be to take action. However, through persistence and a positive attitude, he has contributed to the success of his surgery and rehabilitation.

Why is it so important to educate people about the lower back?

BACK PAIN IS EXTREMELY expensive in terms of financial cost as well as physical suffering for back pain patients and their families. About 80% of people over age 35 have - or have had - back problems of some kind. Researchers estimate that, in the United States, more than $60 billion each year goes towards expenses for low back pain, and that amount is for **first-time occurrences only**. Whatever the number of people, many feel better fairly quickly without invasive action by a physician or healthcare professional. Less than 2% ever need surgery, and only another 1% is disabled to some degree. The majority of back pain sufferers live with their problem without ever understanding much about it.

Over the past 10 years, knowledge about the diagnosis and treatment of low back pain has dramatically improved. This improvement is due to our increased ability to make a diagnosis with the aid of new sophisticated tests. Help has also come from treatment centers which specialize in problems unique to the low back. Also, specialized medical societies have formed to advance the diagnosis, treatment, and rehabilitation of back disorders. From all of these efforts, **active rehabilitation** for low back disorders has been developed to bring the patient a more active role in therapy. Research has shown that these active approaches are important for the rehabilitation of low back problems.

Prior to this book, many of these new concepts in spine care did not reach the general population, nor have recent advances reached all levels of the healthcare community. By reviewing the concepts in this book, the average person can begin to learn more about back problems and take an active role in the treatment and prevention of low back pain.

Having experienced the debilitating effects of delayed diagnosis and treatment, Warren Potash has had to become an expert in his own low back care. If he had not taken an active role in his care and had not continued to seek answers, he still might not have known that surgery could correct his underlying medical condition, a spondylolisthesis, a crack in his fifth lumbar vertebra that allowed it to slip forward onto the first sacral vertebra. More importantly, being motivated to exercise and be active every day has allowed him to return to a productive fulfilling life.

What role does attitude play?

IF YOU HAVE SIGNIFICANT back problems, you will more than likely have some discomfort on and off for the rest of your life. Over 5 years have passed since Warren Potash had surgery and he still has soreness and occasional pain. However, it is manageable and Warren's attitude helps a great deal. Morning soreness, some discomfort during the day, and evening aches and pains can occur. However, they do not have to be the focus of daily life. Taking control of low back pain can keep it from controlling you.

Why me?

Falling into the trap of feeling sorry for yourself can be self-defeating emotionally. Like worrying, it is useless unless it can bring change. The *Why me?* attitude is nonproductive. It is also very frustrating and does not help in dealing with the problem. What does help is learning how you can help alleviate the soreness and pain in your back; while you are doing this, you will take charge of your own problem and stop feeling sorry for yourself.

How can another person's experience help me manage my lower back?

This book can help you learn from the practical experience of a fellow back pain sufferer, from one layperson to another, supplemented with the medical expertise of Dr. Gratch, Dr. Star, and Dr. Goldberg. First, you need to determine what will work for you. If you grasp information that you did not previously understand, you can begin to improve your low back pain.

What works for one person may not, or does not, necessarily work for another. You need to be patient. The trial-and-error method is important in the rehabilitation of low back pain. This book offers suggestions on taking care of your low back pain. Still, each person's pain and response to treatment are different, so you must seek an **individualized program** with the aid of a competent healthcare professional.

What is meant by the lower back?

WHEN HEALTHCARE PROFESSIONALS SPEAK of the low back, or lower back, they refer to the lumbar vertebrae, the sacrum, and the coccyx. Most people have 5 individual lumbar vertebrae numbered L-1 to L-5, although it is common to have as few as 4 and as many as 6. The lumbar spine sits directly on top of the sacrum, which is the portion of the spine that makes up the back of the pelvis. Most lower back problems occur in the lower part of the lumbar spine where it connects to the sacrum. The coccyx is the bottom tip of the spine, and like your appendix, is not of much importance to you unless it causes pain or problems.

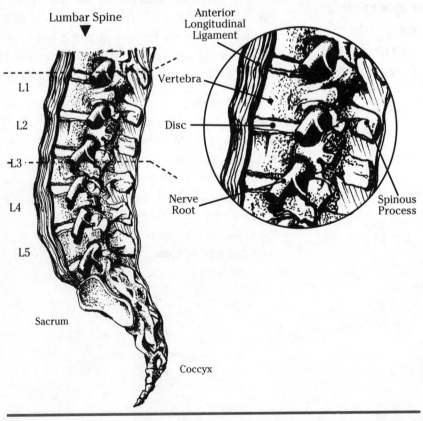

Lumbar Spine

Anterior Longitudinal Ligament

L1

L2

L3

L4

L5

Vertebra

Disc

Nerve Root

Spinous Process

Sacrum

Coccyx

How many people suffer from significant low back pain?

FOUR OUT OF FIVE American adults, 80%, will at some time experience back pain that is significant enough to miss work (Andersson, Svensson, and Oden 1983). In the United States, back pain is the leading cause for visiting a physician (Caruso and Chan 1986). Since about 5% of the population develop low back pain each year, this translates to about 10,000,000 people who are looking for ways to relieve their pain each year (Frymoyer and Cats-Baril 1991).

As bad as back pain is for the individual, it may be worse for corporate America, where back pain is a leading cause of absenteeism and lost productivity (Cypress 1983). Employers generally treat workers with back pain as damaged goods that they would like to discard. Unfortunately, most studies have shown that workers with low back pain have only a 50% chance of ever returning if they are absent from their jobs for 6 months. By 1 year the chance of returning approaches 0% (Andersson, Svensson, and Oden 1983). As a result, many workers' compensation insurance carriers will not even bother trying to rehabilitate a person who has been out of work for 1 year, and some carriers use 6 months as the cutoff. Between 70% and 90% of total costs relate to those with disability, either temporary or permanent (Snook and Jensen 1984; Spengler et al. 1986).

What are the odds of recovering from low back pain without treatment?

LOW BACK PAIN WILL usually resolve on its own whether or not a person seeks medical treatment. On average, 70% will be pain-free within 6 weeks (Kahanovitz 1991). Within 3 months after the onset of pain, 90% will have recovered and all but a few percent will be better by 6 months. **Since most low back pain gets better on its own**, it is wise to be skeptical of popular methods that advertise success in treating this condition. The easiest problems to treat are the ones that go away on their own. Thus, in the case of low back pain, any form of treatment is 90% effective after 3 months since the person would have improved anyway. At 1 year, only 1% will still complain of low back pain.

What are the odds that the pain will come back?

UNFORTUNATELY, BACK PAIN IS so common that the likelihood that a person will suffer another episode of pain is very high. Of the many theories on causes for the pain, none have gained general acceptance. One thing is known: **aging of the spine is inevitable**. Signs of wear and tear are commonly present in the discs, joints, and bones by the age of 30 (Frymoyer and Cats-Baril 1991). Even teenagers with worn discs are not uncommon. Everyone seems to experience aging of the spine, and most people experience some back pain. Fortunately, the majority of people have brief episodes of pain that do not interfere with their lives very much.

The impact of modern living on this problem is not completely known. However, out-of-shape, overweight, overtired modern adults are probably not helping their backs. The people who do the least exercise during the week often compound the problem by engaging in very strenuous activity on the weekend. These *weekend* or *vacation warriors* often end up with back injuries. Some modern vices, such as smoking, also seem to have a negative impact on the back by increasing the likelihood of degeneration and injury (Kelsey et al. 1984).

Do lower back problems primarily affect men or women?

THE SPLIT IS ALMOST 50-50.

According to the American Academy of Orthopaedic Surgeons in a report on musculoskeletal conditions, impairments to the musculoskeletal system occur in approximately 124 out of 1,000 persons. Back or spine impairments are the most frequently reported subcategories and represent 51.7% of musculoskeletal impairments.

The primary site of pain is the lower back, 85.1%; another 7.9% report middle back pain, and 7.0% report upper back pain. Lower back pain is represented by a slightly higher percentage of total back pain in men (88.4%) than in women (81.8%).

Why do many people think that their lower back problem occurred for no apparent reason?

AS WITH MANY OTHER injuries or medical conditions, individuals may not feel anything while the process is occurring; but when the process is complete, they really feel it! Pain from a fall that results in a fractured spine is obvious; however, most people do not have such obvious causes for their pain. For the vast majority, the causes of back pain are subtle minor injuries that occur over a long period of time. For example, people who are engaged in strenuous activities commonly have back pain. People who sit for long periods of time very commonly have pain. In both situations, the persistent insult to the spine may ultimately become serious enough to produce severe back pain. The pain may seem to have started suddenly, but **repetitive insults** to the spine over a long period of time have really caused the problem. Unfortunately, the individual who previously felt well always looks for some dramatic event that caused the pain and rarely realizes that the injury has developed over a long period.

What responsibility have the general public and industry taken in caring for the lower back?

THE PAST YEARS HAVE brought surprisingly little effort in this direction. Recently, the public has been growing more aware that, in addition to the obvious harm to the individual, back pain is extremely expensive for society. As this awareness has grown, basic principles have arisen regarding low back pain treatment:

1. Prolonged periods of inactivity are detrimental to the treatment of routine low back pain and only delay recovery (Deyo, Diehl, and Rosenthal 1986).

2. Emphasis should be on **return of function** rather than on complete elimination of pain. Most people can accept a tolerable level of pain as long as they have strength and endurance to carry out normal life activities. They should not wait for all of the pain to resolve before increasing activities, particularly since the development of safe back exercise programs.

3. Good communication among the patient, the healthcare providers, and the insurers is an important part of having a good outcome. Injured workers do not seem to fare well when their employer does not seem to care about them. The worst results occur when those that are injured are just sent home from work and told not to return until they are healed. They do not like being an anonymous number in a ledger. In particular, those injured at work respond much more favorably when their employers' representatives and healthcare providers frequently communicate with them in a caring manner (Hanson and Merritt 1988).

4. Back injury prevention, including analysis of ways people perform their jobs, has finally become popular. Employers know that it is much better for them to prevent an injury than to pay for treatment, in view of both total economic cost and employee satisfaction.

Why should I learn about the structure of my spine?

IF YOU ARE GOING to take care of your lower back, you should understand the anatomy of the spine. Once you have learned the anatomy, you will appreciate the delicate balance that exists in a healthy spine. Diseases, aging, or injury can upset this balance and lead to chronic problems, including pain. An appreciation of how the spine can fail will help you understand why certain types of treatment are successful and why a complete solution may not be possible in some cases.

A knowledge of the anatomy of the structures that support the spine should also help you understand why spinal exercise rehabilitation programs can be beneficial. Through this understanding, you can gain more confidence in all aspects of the treatment program.

Learning about a back problem can be intimidating, particularly when you are forced to learn at a time when you are in pain. If you understand the basic structure of the spine, your physician can better help you understand your specific problem and teach you what to do about it. After referring to the glossary and reviewing the illustrations of the anatomy, you may also want to consult with your family physician, a spine care specialist, or a qualified physical therapist in order to have these concepts explained further. For more detailed understanding, you may want to track down anatomy textbooks at your library.

What is the spinal column?

THE SPINE USUALLY CONSISTS of 26 separate bones (7 cervical, 12 thoracic, 5 lumbar, the sacrum, and the coccyx) that are stacked one on top of the other. They are held together by soft tissue supports, the ligaments, the discs, the joint capsules, and the muscles. The properties of this dynamic structure will change with age and injury.

Each section of the spine has natural built-in curves that add to its dynamic stability. The cervical and lumbar spines have a natural lordotic curve, which gives them a gentle backward curve when viewed from the side. The thoracic spine has a natural kyphotic curve, which gently bends forward when viewed from the side. Certain disease processes that affect the lumbar spine may interfere with these natural curves. A common example is scoliosis, which results in curvature of the spine to the side. Aging or disease can also interfere with the flexibility of these regions of the spine. Depending on the particular disease, abnormally increased or decreased flexibility can result.

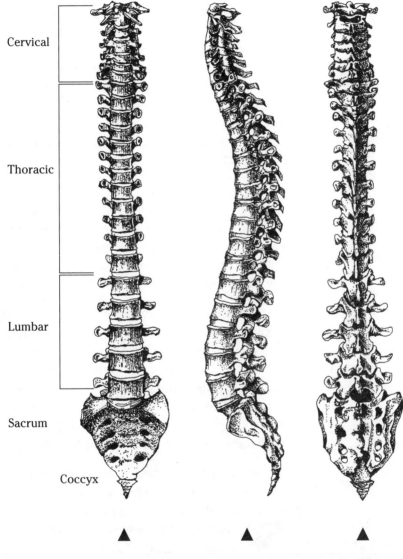

Cervical

Thoracic

Lumbar

Sacrum

Coccyx

Spinal Column -
Anterior View
*Looking at the
front
of a person*

Spinal Column -
Lateral View
*Person turned
facing
the right side*

Spinal Column -
Posterior View
*Looking at the
back
of a person*

What are the discs?

BETWEEN EACH LUMBAR VERTEBRA is a disc. The disc is the primary supporting structure of the lumbar spinal column. The disc consists of two distinct parts: a gelatinous center and a firm, fibrous covering. The gelatinous center is called the nucleus. This nucleus, when young, has the ability to hold or retain water. In fact, in the teenage years, it is approximately 90% water. The outer fibers are called the annulus fibrosis. These interweaving annular fibers are similar to the rings of a tree.

The disc contains microscopic nerve fibers that can sense pain. Therefore, disease states and repetitive injuries to the disc can readily be the source of back pain. However, many other areas are possible sources of pain in the lumbar spine.

The natural degenerative changes that occur with aging also affect the disc. Repetitive, everyday injuries can cause peripheral tears of the discs. Since the water content of the disc decreases slowly with time, the disc can slowly collapse. Degenerative disc disease, however, is a natural aging process and, even when present, is not necessarily the source of low back pain.

Nucleus

Herniation

Annulus Fibrosis

Herniated discs, which are common disc problems, occur when a portion of the annulus weakens and the gelatinous center, the peripheral annular fibers, or both push backwards and press on a nerve in the spinal canal, resulting in sciatica. Fortunately, 90% of these individuals do get better with time and conservative treatment (Weber 1983).

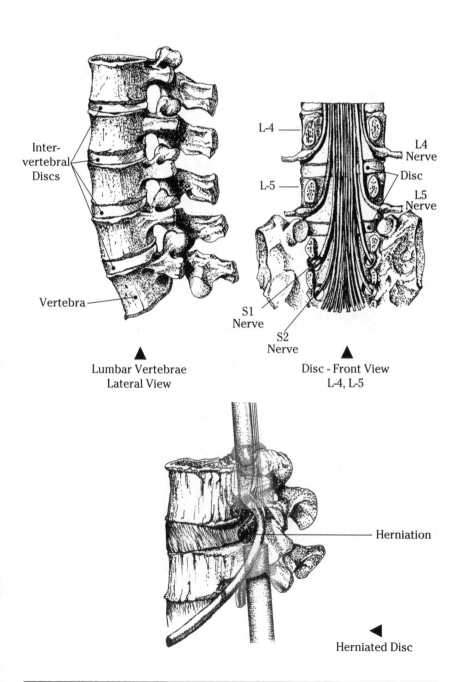

Inter-vertebral Discs

Vertebra

Lumbar Vertebrae
Lateral View

L-4

L-5

L4 Nerve

Disc

L5 Nerve

S1 Nerve

S2 Nerve

Disc - Front View
L-4, L-5

Herniation

Herniated Disc

How does the spine move?

▲

Spinal Column -
Lateral View

THE SPINE HAS MANY functions, which include supporting the weight of the body and protecting the spinal cord. However, at the same time, the spine must be mobile enough to allow for bending and twisting as each person goes about daily activities - and it is. The vertebral bones are connected in a way that permits controlled motion while also providing strength and support for the body's weight.

The connections between the vertebral bones are the keys to the motion of each area of the spine. Each vertebra is connected to the one above by one disc and two joints. The discs are pliable and allow for a certain amount of motion. Joints are areas of the body where two bones actually touch. The surfaces of the bones within the joints are smooth and covered with soft cartilage. The cartilage provides padding to keep the bones separated. The shape of the joints determines the directions that the bones can move. Fibrous capsular ligaments that cover these joints prevent the vertebral bones from separating as the spine moves.

What is the function of the ligaments?

LIGAMENTS ARE FIRM, FIBROUS bands that hold the skeleton together but also allow some movement between the bones. Anyone who follows professional sports acknowledges the importance of ligaments of the knee. Tearing a ligament in the knee results in instability and has often meant the end of a successful professional sports career.

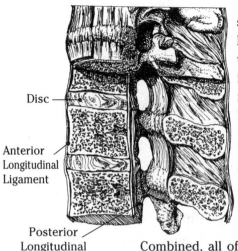

Disc

Anterior
Longitudinal
Ligament

Posterior
Longitudinal
Ligament

Posterior
Longitudinal
Ligament

Anterior
Longitudinal
Ligament

Ligaments of the spine serve the same function by holding the vertebral bones together. Major ligaments include the anterior longitudinal ligament and the posterior longitudinal ligament, which basically run as continuous bands from the top to the bottom of the spine along the vertebral bodies. Other shorter ligaments include those that cover the joints of the spine. Combined, all of these ligamentous structures provide tremendous strength to prevent excessive movement of the vertebral bones. This role is particularly important when one considers that the major nerves of the body run within the spine, and excessive uncontrolled movement could damage these delicate nerves.

Certain disease states can affect the ligaments as well. The ligament is a dynamic structure that can slightly lengthen and contract with stress. It should then return to its normal length. When that stress goes beyond the ligament's strength, the ligament can fail. It can fail from severe acute stress or it can fail over time from repetitive stresses. The weakened ligament is unable to support the spine, which leads to an unstable spine. If the instability is not severe, strengthening the secondary supports (the muscles) through an **active rehabilitation program** may control this instability.

What are the central and peripheral nervous systems?

THE CENTRAL NERVOUS SYSTEM consists of the brain and spinal cord. All signals from the brain must pass through the spinal cord in order to reach the muscles and cause movement. If this vital link is broken, the individual will experience paralysis. The spinal cord is an extremely sensitive structure that can be damaged by very minor trauma. Fortunately it is encased within the strong bony spine to protect it from injury. In the normal adult, the spinal cord runs from the brain to approximately the first lumbar vertebra, L-1. The nerves remaining in the spinal canal below L-1 are all peripheral nerves and are not as sensitive to injury and compression as those in the spinal cord. Also unlike the nerves in the spinal cord, the peripheral nerves have a much greater ability to recover from injury.

L-1

L-5

5th Lumbar Nerve

Coccyx

At the level of each disc within the spine, small nerves separate from the main nerve bundle and pass through holes in the bone out to the body. These nerves can be compressed by external pressure, whether from ligament, bone, or disc. The situation allows very little room for error since the space available for the nerves is small. For example, a disc may herniate and press on the nerves within the spine. This pressure is responsible for the sciatica (pain down the leg) which occurs with disc herniations. Small nerve branches also provide sensation to the ligaments, discs, and joints of the spine, so almost any structure in the spine can produce pain.

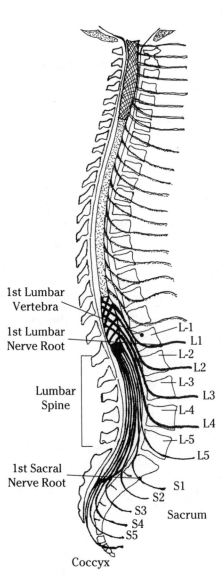

1st Lumbar Vertebra

1st Lumbar Nerve Root

L-1
L1
L-2
L2

Lumbar Spine

L-3
L3
L-4
L4
L-5
L5

1st Sacral Nerve Root

S1
S2
S3
S4
S5

Sacrum

Coccyx

L1 to L5, S1 to S5 are the nerves exiting the Lumbar & Sacral Spines

Since each nerve that exits the spine travels to a different area of the body, the surface of the body shows the nerve distributions. This road map of nerve distributions is referred to as a **dermatome chart**. By comparing a person's complaints of numbness or pain with the dermatome chart, physicians and other healthcare providers can often determine which nerves are being pinched or compressed.

It is important to understand the close relationship between the nerves and all of the supporting structures of the spine. The vertebral bodies, ligaments, muscles, and discs provide protection and support as the major nerves travel through the spine from the brain to the most peripheral parts of the body.

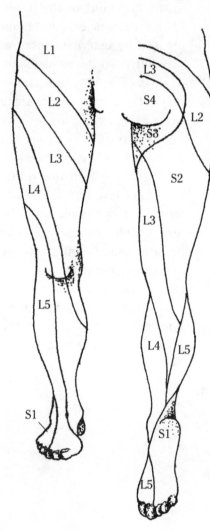

What about the muscles?

MUSCLES ACT LIKE ENGINES within the body; they provide strength for movement. Among the many muscles that act together to support the spine are the muscles of the abdomen, lower back, and legs. Unlike bones and joints, the muscles can lengthen and shorten in response to stress. In addition, muscles have the ability to be strengthened through exercise.

Each group of muscles must act in harmony with other groups in order for the spine to function properly. For example, in order to bend forward, the muscles behind the spine must relax while those in front of the spine must tighten. When injury or disease affects the spine, this delicate balance may be disrupted. This condition may become even worse when exercises that strengthen only one or two muscle groups lead to an imbalance between groups of muscles. A **balanced exercise program** can improve the strength of all of the muscle groups and restore the effectiveness of the muscles as stabilizers of the spine.

Although the muscles of the thighs and legs may seem far removed from the lumbar spine, their strength and weakness can have a profound effect on back rehabilitation. The major muscles of the thighs all originate, in part, on the pelvis. Tightness of these muscles can rotate the pelvis, requiring the lower back to compensate. The stress of movement will then transfer from the hips and legs to the spine, which has less strength to accommodate this degree of pressure. One of the most common muscular problems in the lower extremity is tight hamstrings (muscles behind the thigh). A person with tight hamstrings who bends forward flexes the spine instead of the hips, thus increasing the likelihood of a back injury.

How does the anatomy of the spine influence back problems?

MOST PEOPLE HAVE HEARD of disc herniations, but all of the parts of the spine can become injured or diseased. The ligaments that hold the spine together can become stretched or partially torn from a sudden back injury. Anyone who has had a sprained ankle is familiar with this problem since sprains are caused by stretched or torn ligaments. When this problem develops in the spine, it shows as persistent back pain associated with movement.

Another common problem occurs from wearing away the cartilage padding in the joints of the spine. This process is similar to the one in the knee or hip joint ... commonly called arthritis. Unlike the hip or knee joints, where arthritis can be treated by artificial joint replacement, the technology to perform spinal joint replacements has not yet been developed.

Each spinal component is exposed to the ravages of time, and most will degenerate as the body ages. In many cases, this process is painless, but for others pain may develop. It is quite easy to diagnose an arthritic knee since the knee joint is physically separated from the rest of the joints of the body. However, the spinal joints, discs, and ligaments are stacked one on top of the other and are quite deep below the surface of the body. This stacking and location can make it extremely difficult to diagnose which specific worn disc, torn ligament, or arthritic joint is causing the pain. As a result, patients are often labeled as having *spinal arthritis, degenerating disc, or bulging discs* without knowing which of the many structures is causing the pain.

The role of spinal exercise programs becomes obvious once the anatomy of the spine is understood. Spinal exercise will not grow new discs or new cartilage on the surfaces of the joints, and it will not repair torn ligaments. **One of the prime effects of exercise is to strengthen muscles**. Since the muscles of the back, abdomen, and thighs are also supporters and stabilizers of the spine, strengthening these muscles can help protect the injured spinal structures. In other words, protecting the discs, ligaments, and joints from injury involves transferring some of the stress to the muscles and away from the spine. In addition, spinal rehabilitation programs **emphasize stretching exercises** that restore mobility to parts of the body, such as the legs, as a way to decrease stress on the spine.

What are the causes of back pain?

THE SPINE IS A very complicated structure made up of many different tissues, all of which can cause pain. The tendons, ligaments, muscles, bones, and discs can react to injury by producing a feeling of pain. What distinguishes the spine from other organs is that large nerves pass through it, then extend into the arms and legs. Painful conditions in the spine can therefore produce a feeling of pain in these other areas.

Some of the more common painful conditions in the spine include idiopathic low back pain, herniated discs, spinal stenosis, and compression fractures.

What is idiopathic low back pain?

IDIOPATHIC LOW BACK PAIN refers to pain in the back from unknown cause. This most common form of low back pain will affect the majority of people who are reading this book. Most people with idiopathic low back pain will show degenerative changes within the spine, including bulging discs, loss of disc thickness, degenerated spinal joints, and thickening of the spinal ligaments. However, since these types of degenerative changes occur both with and without pain, it is impossible to say for sure that these changes are the causes of the pain. In fact, idiopathic low back pain probably comes from any one, or all of these structures. Physicians hope to identify the source more specifically in the future.

Patients with idiopathic low back pain usually experience the majority of their pain within their backs, with only occasional radiating symptoms in the buttocks or thighs.

What is a herniated disc?

A HERNIATED DISC REFERS to protrusion of some material that is normally part of the intervertebral disc. The material pushes out from between the vertebral bodies and extends into the spinal canal. The difference between a bulging disc and a herniated disc is based strictly on size. When a piece of the disc actually comes out and presses on a nerve, it is clearly a herniation.

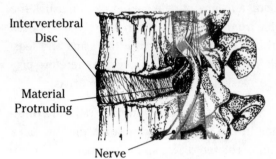

Intervertebral Disc

Material Protruding

Nerve

People with herniated discs usually experience pain that extends into the lower leg below the knee. Some associated back pain may occur, but the major complaint is usually of pain in the buttock and leg. Numbness, tingling, and weakness often are associated with this condition. The herniated disc is one of the few spinal problems that respond well to surgery; but even in this situation, the majority of patients can treat the condition with appropriate rest and exercise.

What is spinal stenosis?

SPINAL STENOSIS REFERS TO narrowing of the canal containing the nerves within the spine. It can occur at any age, but is most common in older patients. In these patients, the ligaments within the spine thicken and calcify, the bones and joints enlarge, and bone spurs may form. All of these enlarged structures in combination encroach on the spinal canal and place pressure on the nerves.

Spinal stenosis can also occur in younger patients who have genetically small spinal nerve passages or in certain genetic diseases that prevent the spine from forming normally.

People with spinal stenosis commonly complain of aching pains in one or both legs, particularly with standing or walking. Pain is usually relieved by sitting, but can be worse with lying down in bed, so sleeping can be difficult. Unlike disc herniations, which occur suddenly, spinal stenosis is the result of a slow degenerative process and usually progresses gradually. The pain can commonly switch from one side to another or disappear for periods of weeks to months.

What is a compression fracture?

COMPRESSION FRACTURES OCCUR WHEN pressure on the spine crushes the vertebral body. When the fractures occur in young people, they usually are the result of a severe injury. However, they are most common in older people who have soft spines from osteoporosis. In these people, simply bending or twisting can cause collapse of one or more spinal vertebrae. The fractures usually cause back pain that lasts for 8 to 12 weeks. Although a wide variety of options are available for treatment, the fractures are basically treated by allowing the vertebrae to heal on their own. The loss of height of the vertebra is never regained, but the pain usually will resolve.

What is spondylolisthesis?

THIS CONDITION IS PRESENT in approximately 5% of the general population. Many of those afflicted never know that they have it since it often has no associated pain.

Spondylolisthesis refers to slipping of one section of the spine forward or backward. One common type, which is associated with a crack in the back of the spine, allows the spine to slip forward. Surprisingly, these cracks can occur without a severe injury such as a fall. Certain individuals may have been born with a weakness in the back of the spine that allows these cracks to occur quite easily. This condition is close to Warren's heart, since it was the primary medical condition causing his lower back problem.

Spondylolisthesis may require no treatment if it is not associated with pain. In those individuals who do have pain, the majority may be successfully treated with education and rehabilitative exercises. In a minority of cases, surgery is required to restore stability to the spine, as was necessary for Warren.

Do you have **tight hamstrings**? Are you unable to touch your toes while standing, without bending your knees? And without much discomfort? Although many conditions can cause these symptoms, they could be a sign of spondylolisthesis. But don't worry ... even if you have this condition, proper education about exercise, stretching, and body mechanics can lessen your chances for future problems.

What is a physician?

WHEN THE WORD PHYSICIAN is used in this book, it refers to a qualified physician who is familiar with the diagnosis and treatment of low back problems. Trying to find a *qualified* physician can sometimes be confusing for the patient, who is first faced with choosing from among the many different types of practitioners. If you have a mild problem, then a family doctor or general practitioner is certainly **qualified**. For initial evaluation and treatment, these generalists may even be better than the specialists, because the general physician knows your medical history and will be aware of other problems (such as kidney stones) that may be causing your pain. Specialists in back problems are very helpful for the treatment of pain that is disabling or long-lasting, as well as for the treatment of more serious problems. Ideally, the specialists and your general physician should work together.

Although the physicians you choose may offer excellent advice, they will not be the only ones giving recommendations. Your friends, your spouse, your children, and complete strangers will also be giving you suggestions - if they haven't already. You may want to listen to all of their well-meaning advice, but remember that **your problem may be quite different from theirs**. You need to be evaluated by a competent professional so that appropriate treatment can be chosen for your individual problem.

How do I know if I need to consult a physician?

FOR SEVERE PAIN, YOU probably should seek medical help immediately. If the pain or soreness continues for an extended period of time or recurs, you should also seek consultation with a healthcare professional. You never know whether the pain is the result of normal wear and tear or signals something more serious. A qualified medical evaluation, including a history of the problem, physical examination, and appropriate tests, is required for proper treatment.

Who are the physicians that treat spine problems?

MANY DIFFERENT PHYSICIANS TREAT low back pain. Each type of physician provides a particular level or type of expertise depending on background and training. The traditional *M.D.*, who provides the majority of standard medical care in the United States, is also referred to as an *allopathic physician*. This physician is different from the osteopathic physician (or *D.O.*). Because these words are unfamiliar to many people, it is easy to become confused when seeking and choosing a physician. People may confuse osteopathic physicians with orthopaedic surgeons since the words sound alike. What is even more confusing is that some chiropractors advertise themselves as orthopaedic chiropractors. Before choosing an expert for your particular problem, it is worthwhile to review the training of the various types of physicians and nonphysicians who treat back problems.

Allopathic Physician: This physician is the traditional *M.D.*, who has usually attended 4 years of college and 4 years of medical school. At one time, these practitioners would then complete a 1-year internship to become a general practitioner. At present, however, most medical doctors complete a residency training of 3 to 5 years. Residencies are carefully monitored programs, usually completed at large teaching hospitals, where the doctor gains a great deal of experience in one area of medicine. Residencies must gain approval from the American Board of Medical Specialties and are subject to review every few years. Typical residencies include internal medicine, pediatrics, orthopaedic surgery, and family practice. In order to complete a residency, the physician usually must pass written tests as well as submit to an evaluation by the physicians on the faculty of the teaching program.

Osteopathic Physician: The training of the osteopathic physician or *D.O.* is very similar to the training of the allopathic physician. Both complete 4 years of undergraduate college, but one applies to osteopathic school, the other to traditional medical school. The curriculum at osteopathic medical schools contains the same general topics, including anatomy, physiology, and pharmacology, as the curriculum at an allopathic school. However, the osteopathic schools also teach manipulative therapy. At the end of 4 years of osteopathic school, the osteopathic physician usually will complete a residency in order to specialize in a particular area such as internal medicine, rehabilitation medicine, or orthopaedic surgery.

Orthopaedic Surgeon: This M.D. or D.O. has completed an approved orthopaedic surgery residency after graduation from medical school. Residencies of this type include 5 years of training in management of bone and joint disorders, for example, nonoperative treatment and extensive surgical training. In order for a residency to be approved, the teaching program must include classroom teaching as well as practical experience in the operative and nonoperative treatment of spine disorders.

There is no difference between the *orthopaedist* and *orthopaedic surgeon*. Both refer to someone who has completed an approved residency in orthopaedic surgery.

Neurologist: This M.D. or D.O. completes an approved residency in neurology, which is a nonsurgical specialty. Neurologists are experts in the diagnosis and medical treatment of disorders of the brain, spinal cord, and nerves.

Neurologic Surgeon: This M.D. or D.O., commonly referred to as a **neurosurgeon**, completes an approved neurologic surgery residency, which teaches about disorders of the brain, spine, and peripheral nerves.

Rehabilitation Physician (Physiatrist): This M.D. or D.O. completes a rehabilitation residency. Rehabilitation physicians specialize in the rehabilitation of many medical problems and illnesses – including strokes, injuries, postoperative weakness, and many others. Unlike orthopaedists or neurosurgeons, their training does not include surgery, but they are experts in nonoperative treatment of spine problems.

Rheumatologist: This M.D. or D.O. usually completes a residency in internal medicine and then a fellowship in rheumatology. Of interest to those people with low back problems, rheumatologists are experts in the diagnosis and treatment of arthritis and related disorders.

Spine Surgeon: A spine surgeon is an orthopaedic surgeon or neurosurgeon who has chosen to specialize in spine surgery. Some of these practitioners have completed additional spine surgery training after their residencies. This additional period of training is usually referred to as a *fellowship*. Although these fellowships are not currently monitored by a certifying agency, a prospective patient can readily evaluate the physician's credentials by finding out where the fellowship was completed. If it was sponsored by a large teaching hospital with a good reputation, then the individual probably has special expertise in this area.

Many highly qualified spine surgeons have not completed fellowships, but have chosen to intensify their work in this particular area of medicine. Here, referral from other physicians and reputation can be helpful in evaluating a physician.

Alternative Practitioners: A large number of *alternative practitioners* are available for the treatment of back pain. They include chiropractors, reflexologists, and acupuncturists. Among these alternatives, chiropractic care is the most popular; in fact, in the United States, the number of visits to chiropractors exceeds the number of visits to orthopaedic surgeons for treatment of back pain (Collins 1992). These other practitioners and treatment options are discussed later in the **Treatment** section.

What is Board Certification?

BOARD CERTIFICATION IS A physician accreditation process that is intended to ensure a high level of competence in a selected specialty. Most allopathic or osteopathic physicians attempt to become Board Certified in their specialty once they have completed residency training. This certification usually involves written and oral examinations as well as personal references from other physicians who are practicing within the same specialty. Physicians who satisfy the American Board of Medical Specialties requirements become certified in their specialty. Most practitioners must periodically recertify. **NOTE:** It is not necessary to become Board Certified to practice a particular medical or surgical specialty.

How should I choose a physician?

YOU SHOULD START WITH your family physician or the specialist who has been treating you. If you are in an HMO or similar health plan, you must start with your primary physician. That doctor's diagnosis determines whether you will be referred, if at all.

Starting with your family physician or internist is a good way for anyone to approach this problem. Most family physicians have a reasonable understanding of low back basics, although some are better informed than others.

It is important for you to be in regular contact with your physician regarding your pain. If the pain does not improve, your family physician may choose to send you to a specialist or you may choose that course on your own.

Numerous subspecialists have a strong interest in spine care. Orthopaedic surgeons, neurosurgeons, neurologists, physiatrists (doctors of physical medicine and rehabilitation), and rheumatologists are certainly qualified specialists in the care of the lower back. Subspecialists within these groups include spine care specialists, but many people can find appropriate treatment from a general orthopaedist, neurosurgeon, or physiatrist. However, if your problem becomes complicated, if it seems that no one can find an answer, if your doctors cannot agree on treatment, or if you want an additional opinion, it is worthwhile to seek out someone with additional expertise in treating spine problems.

An important question to ask the specialists is whether they are Board eligible or Board Certified. Most specialists, at your request, will provide you with information on their training and background. You should ask these specialists whether they subspecialize in the care of the spine. Another important question is whether they are members of special spine societies that emphasize the care of the spine. Also of interest is whether they have taken any special training or fellowships in diseases of the spine. **NOTE:** If you choose to see a spine surgeon for your problem, it does not mean that you will be treated with surgery. The majority of patients who are evaluated by spine surgeons are treated successfully without surgery.

Off and on for almost 2½ years, Warren saw several physicians before his real problem was diagnosed. It is hoped that your situation will not be as frustrating as Warren's, but you can prevent delays in diagnosis by seeking the care of a qualified physician and being persistent in your quest for a cure. You should follow up with the physician's suggestions, and keep the physician informed of your progress.

What should I expect from a physician?

PERHAPS THE MOST IMPORTANT quality in a physician is the ability to listen to your problems. Most physicians agree that the correct diagnosis can usually be found just by carefully listening to what the patient has to say and asking appropriate questions. Your physician should then perform a thorough physical examination. Diagnostic studies, including x-rays, laboratory tests, bone scans, CAT scans, and MRIs are not necessary for every back problem. You should not judge a physician on the ability to order tests.

Regular follow-up visits with your physician are important in order to monitor your response to treatment, and you need to gradually establish a plan for your long-term care. As you progress, an **active**, not passive **rehabilitation program is very important for long-term success**. If, in spite of treatment, you do not improve, you should speak to your primary physician about a referral to a qualified spine care specialist.

Except on a **rare** occasion, surgical approaches are not necessary within the first 6 to 8 weeks of treatment. Beware of a physician who recommends early surgical intervention, unless you have a significant, progressive neurologic problem or the pain is so severe that you cannot tolerate it.

How can I describe my pain to my physician?

DESCRIBING THE LOCATION, QUALITY, and intensity of your pain to the physician is important. The doctor needs your help to make a diagnosis and this includes listening to your answers as well as asking appropriate questions. The doctor can also get a measure of your pain by using a scale of 0 to 10, with zero being no pain and ten being the most severe pain. Many physicians also use a pain drawing to learn the exact location and type of pain that the patient is experiencing. The patient marks a standard line drawing of the human body with symbols that indicate the location, intensity, and type of pain being experienced.

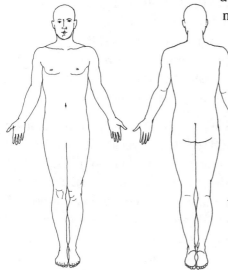

Mark the areas on the drawing where you feel pain. Use appropriate symbols.

Ache !!!!!   Numbness #####   Pins & Needles ^^^^^
Burning +++++   Stabbing*****

When should I seek a second opinion?

WHEN YOU ARE IN pain, it is easy to become impatient, but remember that most back pain resolves on its own within a few weeks. It is certainly appropriate for a physician to proceed slowly with testing or treatment for an otherwise healthy person with only occasional back pain. However, when a physician continues passive treatment for many weeks without a reasonable treatment plan, it is probably time to seek a second opinion.

As previously mentioned, your physician needs to listen to your complaints and provide reasonable treatment options. It is very important that you feel comfortable with your physician. Beyond being treated by someone who is well qualified, you must be able to get answers to the questions that you feel are important. There is also nothing wrong with choosing another physician just because you do not feel that you are getting along well. Choosing a physician is a little like choosing a friend; it is inevitable that some personalities just do not mesh together well.

You will also want to seek a second opinion if you think that the physician is pushing you toward surgical intervention too quickly. Most surgeons feel very comfortable when a patient decides to obtain a second opinion if surgery is being considered. Your family or treating physician can refer you to a spine care physician for a second opinion.

Who is the best qualified physician to perform surgery?

WHEN DEALING WITH LOW back problems that do not improve with conservative treatment, for example, herniated discs, spinal stenosis, spondylolisthesis, and lumbar instability, the opinion of a qualified spine surgeon is important. Whether that surgeon is an orthopaedic surgeon or a neurosurgeon is not important.

What should I ask a potential surgeon?

- Do you specialize in spine care?

- Are you fellowship-trained in spine surgery?

- Are you Board eligible or Board Certified?

- Are you a member of any specialty societies for care of the spine, such as the North American Spine Society?

- Will you continue to care for me if my pain persists after surgery?

- Do you believe in rehabilitation and physical therapy postoperatively?

- Is rehabilitation easily available to me through your practice or by referral?

- Will you be the doctor who actually performs the surgery?

What is the primary diagnosis?

IN ORDER FOR A physician and patient to develop a rational treatment plan, they must first discover the cause for the back problem. In medical terminology, the cause of the pain is called the *primary diagnosis*. For example, a person may present to the physician with a complaint of stomach pain, and appropriate testing determines that the cause of the problem is an ulcer. In this case, the **primary diagnosis** would be a gastric ulcer. The treatment for the condition would then be directed toward healing the ulcer rather than just treating the pain with analgesic medication. This example is a very simple one, but it illustrates that successful treatment involves treating the underlying cause rather than just the symptoms.

The majority of patients with lower back problems will find it very difficult to find the primary diagnosis. Why? Because almost everyone who presents with back pain has some degree of deterioration involving the spine. For example, bone spurs, bulging discs, narrowed discs, and degenerated joints are seen on x-rays and scans. Several studies have shown that the amount of degeneration in the spine may not be related to the amount of pain. In addition, the spine consists of many discs, joints, and bones, any of which can be the cause of pain. Unfortunately, the source of the pain is not measured directly by any scan. As a result, most cases of back pain remain undiagnosed other than the working diagnosis of generalized degeneration, arthritis, or disc deterioration, all of which represent approximately the same thing.

Even though the majority of people with back pain will be found to have nothing more than normal spinal aging, Warren's experience highlights the importance of carefully searching for the cause of the pain. Several doctors told him that his problem came from disc deterioration and that surgery would not be helpful. When the crack in the back of his spine was finally diagnosed, the situation reversed. Surgery was appropriate and he could finally begin the process of recovery.

In order to establish the correct diagnosis, physicians use various sources of information, for example, interviewing the patient about the problem (called taking a history), then performing a physical examination and a variety of tests such as x-rays and MRI scans. With some patients, for example, a young person with mild, brief episodes of pain, a simple history and physical examination are all that is necessary. In other cases, more extensive testing is indicated, as it was for Warren.

What information is important in the history?

THE HISTORY OF YOUR lower back pain is the single most important piece of information that your physician or healthcare professional can have. Information about your present problem is vital; however, your past medical history, past back history, prior operations, allergies, family history, and other system complaints are also important. The answers to questions on all of these topics help your treating physician or healthcare professional formulate a diagnosis and subsequent treatment plan.

What types of questions are commonly asked?

IS YOUR PAIN AGGRAVATED by activity? By sitting, by standing? By rest or by walking? Is it relieved by rest? Does it awaken you from sleep at night? Are you stiff in the morning when arising? Are car rides a problem for you?

Where is the pain located? Is it in your back or does it radiate into your buttock or down your leg? Do you have pain when you cough or sneeze? Do you have any numbness or tingling? Do you have any change in bowel or bladder function?

Is your work affected? Are your activities of daily living affected?

What prior treatments have been performed? Have you gone through physical therapy? Have you used a support? Have you used a car seat? Have you tried lumbar epidural steroid injections? What medications are you taking? Have you tried a chiropractor? Have you gone through acupuncture?

Were any x-rays, CAT scans, EMGs, myelograms, or MRIs taken? If so, what did they show? It is important to bring along all reports AND films on your first visit. Was there any prior surgery performed? If so, who did the surgery and when? Can you get the operative reports for the surgery?

These questions hit some of the important areas that need thought before your initial visit with your doctor or healthcare professional. Most times a diagnosis can be made just from the answers that you provide.

NOTE: Be fully honest with the examiner. Honesty with the examiner gives you the best chance for a proper diagnosis.

You should not be afraid of what the examiner may find. The **cause** of your low back problem is critical in planning for successful treatment and long-term success.

What should a physical examination include?

THE SECOND MOST IMPORTANT part of an evaluation for low back pain is the physical examination. It is natural to be nervous during the examination, but an awareness of what the examination includes, and why, may help to make the experience more pleasant.

The patient should be wearing only a gown to allow full examination of the low back and legs. The physician is there to be helpful so it is important to be cooperative. This doctor should be viewed as a partner who will help you find the best solution for your back problem.

A neurologic evaluation is an important part of a back examination, since back problems can be associated with injury to the nerves that pass through the spine. Sensory examination ordinarily using pinprick or light touch, deep tendon reflex examination (done with a reflex hammer), and motor strength testing of both lower extremities are the most common tests. The circulation to both lower extremities should also be evaluated because vascular disorders there can mimic problems coming from the low back. Neurologic tension signs will be checked by raising the leg in order to stretch the nerves. If you experience pain that extends into the leg, you have a high likelihood of nerve compression.

Examination of the joints of the lower extremities is also an important part of a back evaluation. Arthritis of the hips can mimic or accentuate back problems, and the physician often can discover the problem simply by testing the motion of the hips and knees.

The examiner should carefully press (palpate) the lower back to try to discover any areas of tenderness. Examination of range of motion of the back, assessment for any curvature of the spine, and palpation for muscle spasm are also included in a thorough examination.

Other areas of the body may also be examined, depending on the particular problem.

What technologies are available to help with the diagnosis?

AFTER THE HISTORY AND physical examination are completed, your physician may want to perform diagnostic tests to complete the evaluation. These studies are only an adjunct to the diagnosis and treatment of low back pain; the history and physical examination are **key** to the diagnosis. The studies are done to confirm the suspected diagnosis and to rule out other unusual causes of low back pain. Each examiner has a preference about which test to order and whether they are indicated at all. Many times these tests will be performed over a period of several visits to a physician, so nothing is wrong if your particular physician does not suggest all of these tests on the first visit. The order of the tests listed next does not imply that these tests should be done in any particular order. Remember that **every low back problem is unique** and should be approached accordingly.

X-ray: A plain x-ray still remains the cornerstone of diagnostic imaging. It is relatively low in cost, it usually can be done in the examiner's office or nearby, and it also can be reviewed immediately. However, the limitations should be kept in mind. An x-ray shows only bone. The physician can make conclusions from an x-ray, but it does not show soft tissue. Also, frequent x-rays are not usually necessary since most low back problems do not show rapid x-ray changes. Exceptions do occur, however.

MRI: The greatest advancement in diagnostic testing in the last 7 years is high-quality **M**agnetic **R**esonance **I**maging (MRI). This type of scan visualizes tissues with a magnetic field recording that uses high-speed computers to provide very clear images of the spine and other tissues. Although this study is expensive, it is the **single best image** of the lumbar spine. There are no needles, no dyes, no injections (except for special circumstances), and no standard x-ray exposure. MRI is very effective for visualizing soft tissue disorders. It is highly effective for the diagnosis of disc disease, tumors, infection, spinal nerve compression from stenosis, and nerve disorders. Most physicians would agree that, in the majority of cases, this test provides the most information.

Although some concern exists about long-term exposure to magnetic fields on a daily basis, it is generally believed that no harmful effects result from MRI scanning. Claustrophobia can be a problem since the space for the patient inside the machine is limited; however, using faster computers has decreased the time to complete a scan.

One area of confusion regarding the MRI scanner concerns the way that the scans are performed. The machine is quite large and the entire body is placed within it; however, the machine is unable to study the entire body, or even the entire spine, during one scan. MRI scans for low back problems produce pictures of only the lumbar vertebrae and the top of the sacrum. Many people wrongly assume that a larger area is examined and are disappointed to find that each scan usually includes only about 6 inches of the spine. The procedure is handled this way because a scan of even this small area requires 30 to 45 minutes, and each area of the body that is scanned requires different computer settings in order to provide clear pictures. Therefore, when your physician orders a scan, you need to understand, specifically, what parts of your body are being examined.

CAT Scan: Computed Axial Tomography, or CAT scans are also excellent for studying the lumbar spine. The CAT scan is somewhat less expensive than an MRI, but it does not provide quite the same information either. This study is performed using a computer-guided x-ray tube, so the patient receives significant radiation exposure. The CAT scan provides high-quality, cross-sectional images of the spine. For evaluating injuries to the bones themselves, these images sometimes can be even more accurate than the MRI scan; but MRI shows the discs and nerves more clearly. When a CAT scan is performed right after a myelogram, it can also become very effective for evaluating nerve problems since the dye remaining within the spine outlines the nerves.

Myelogram: Myelograms are an invasive procedure that can be done in an outpatient setting, and they are often followed by a CAT scan. The myelogram used to be the *gold standard* of spine diagnosis; but with high-resolution MRI, it is now a secondary test in the diagnostic workup of low back disorders. It does require an injection of dye, usually performed by a neuroradiologist, and it does expose the patient to significant radiation.

Electromyelogram and Nerve Conduction Study: An electromyelogram (or EMG) and a nerve conduction study (or NCS) are electrical studies done by specialists in physiatry or neurology. In the care of back pain and sciatica, these studies are used to determine whether a nerve in the back is pinched or irritated. The cause may be a herniated disc which directly impinges on, stretches, or chemically irritates the nerves. Pain is typically referred down one or both legs. During an EMG, the examining physician stimulates nerves directly to see how they conduct electrical current. The doctor also inserts needles into the affected muscles to determine whether the nerve that innervates (supplies) the muscle is damaged. By utilizing these two techniques, the physician can determine which nerve is injured and how recently the injury occurred. This information is used by the doctor to provide a prognosis for recovery. Unfortunately, EMG results can sometimes be confusing, particularly in cases where there are underlying diseases (such as diabetes) or prior surgery that may affect the response of the nerve to EMG testing.

Bone Scans: A bone scan is a procedure that starts with an injection of a radioactive material that attaches itself to bone. This material goes to areas that are either actively breaking down bone or making new bone. It highlights areas of fracture, tumors, infections, and arthritis ... but is often unable to tell one from another. The scan can be a useful adjunct in the workup of low back pain. It is moderately expensive and takes about 3 hours from the time the radioactive material is injected until the picture is taken.

Laboratory Testing: Blood tests are often requested during the evaluation of low back problems. Analysis of blood specimens can demonstrate signs of infection, tumors, calcium deficiency, or certain forms of arthritis.

*How do
I choose
the best
treatment
for my back
problem?*

AT THE PRESENT TIME, many treatment alternatives are available for the person with a back problem. Unfortunately, choosing the best alternative can be very difficult. Society places great value on high-tech solutions and fast answers, which may not always be the best approaches. Many of these treatment methods generate such high revenue that the groups providing these services are tempted to ignore less expensive and potentially better alternatives.

Ideally, a treatment modality should be inexpensive, very successful, free from side effects, and readily available. In such a situation, your **knowledge is power**: the more that you know about a problem, the more likely you are to make an appropriate choice. Just by reading books like this one, you are making yourself a more educated consumer and beginning to take charge of your own back problem. For many people, the exercises and advice available in a book may be enough to let them control their own back problems.

Again, this book gives **general advice** that is applicable to most back pain sufferers. For a particular condition or situation, you should seek competent medical advice. **Never** use this book for self-diagnosis, just for information about the low back.

What types of treatment methods are available?

THREE CATEGORIES OF TREATMENT methods are available for the back pain sufferer:

- Noninvasive and readily available without a doctor's prescription. Examples include heating pads and self-help books.

- Noninvasive and available through a healthcare provider. Examples include physical therapy, chiropractic, and braces.

- Invasive and available from qualified physicians. Examples include surgery, injections, and medication.

Particularly with regard to treatment, the medical terms *invasive* and *invasiveness* are good choices of words. Invasive or invasiveness refers to the extent that a procedure intrudes on or potentially harms an individual. When you choose a back treatment method, start with the **least invasive treatment**. You should progress to more invasive treatment methods only if the problem persists and shows a high likelihood of improvement with the more intrusive and potentially harmful procedure. **NOTE:** The more invasive procedures tend to invade your bank account to a greater extent as well.

The three methods just listed have been simplified in order to illustrate a point. Actually, all treatment methods are somewhat invasive, so it is really a matter of degree. For example, a heating pad, which is generally felt to be noninvasive, is a frequent cause of serious burns when people fall asleep before they turn off the heat. Similarly, all medications are invasive to a greater or lesser extent depending on their side effects.

How should I start treating my back problem?

IF YOU ARE ONE of the millions of people who suffer from occasional back pain, you may not need to go any further than reading this book ... and perhaps others on the topic. Occasional back pain sufferers have episodes severe enough to keep them from normal activities only once or twice a year. These people may occasionally wake up with back discomfort, but it rapidly subsides. They may have some mild aching in the thighs, but most of their pain is directly in the back. A day or two of rest; mild medication such as aspirin, Tylenol™ (acetaminophen), or ibuprofen; and application of ice or heat usually lead to rapid recovery.

One suggestion that may reduce the frequency of these back episodes is to begin a **standard program of exercises** in order to improve **flexibility, strength, endurance, and posture**. Careful attention to proper lifting techniques should help reduce the number of injuries. **Adequate rest** is also important. Another is avoiding the **weekend** or **vacation warrior** syndrome, in which an individual tries to make up for an entire week of inactivity in one free day on a weekend. Aerobic exercise also improves overall fitness and well-being. For other significant health problems, such as obesity or heart disease, a family doctor should provide consultation before the start of any strenuous exercise program.

How do I know when I have gone too far in treating my back problem?

WHILE IT IS APPEALING to treat your own back problem, certain warning signs should not be ignored. Frequent episodes of pain are the most common reason for seeking medical advice. Particular danger signs are pain that prevents you from sleeping for more than a day or two or pain that persists while you are at rest. Weakness or numbness in the legs for more than a brief instant can be a reason to seek medical attention. Back pain caused by a serious accident such as a fall from a height should always be evaluated by a physician. Other associated symptoms, such as stomach pain and lightheadedness, may be signs that this low back pain is not routine.

Recognizing most of these danger signs is just common sense. A good place to start is **always your personal or family physician** because that person **knows you best** and can rule out other potential medical problems.

Shouldn't I just stay in bed until my back pain gets better?

ACTUALLY, STUDIES HAVE SHOWN that return to normal function can be slower if you spend too much time resting after a back injury (Deyo, Diehl, and Rosenthal 1986). The current recommendations for ordinary low back injuries usually include only a day or two of rest to decrease the level of pain. Immediately after, the approach calls for gradually increasing activities until normal in order to avoid the stiffness, weakness, and deconditioning that accompany prolonged rest.

Are there any times that bed rest is prescribed for a back problem?

ONE OF THE COMMON causes of back pain and sciatica (pain extending from the back to the lower leg) is a herniated disc. In this situation bed rest may be prescribed for up to a few weeks to try to reduce the inflammation and associated pain. But, be aware that some practitioners tell all of their patients with back pain that the problem is caused by a herniated disc. The best insurance against unnecessary bed rest and its consequences is to see a qualified practitioner for advice about your particular problem.

I really am afraid to do anything strenuous. Can't you just give me a pill or crack my back?

PATIENTS MUST TAKE AN **active role** in their treatment process. Passive treatment modalities are those in which patients do not actively participate. In other words, they wait for someone else to do something to them in order to solve their problem. These treatments may include application of heat, cold, electrical stimulation, spinal manipulation, and traction, among others. Although these types of treatment reduce pain for the first few days after a back injury, most qualified healthcare providers recommend a rapid transition to a more active approach. Long-term use of passive modalities is often very expensive through a healthcare provider, and gives the patient little benefit beyond the first week or two.

Active treatment methods, in which the patients **actively** participate in their treatment, seem to be a better solution for those with long-term back problems. The benefits of active treatment are both physical and emotional.

Physically, strength and endurance can be built through active exercise programs, and usually without an increase in pain. In addition, frequent exercise reassures patients that activity is possible, and self-reliance increases when patients find that they can help treat their own problems.

Why is exercise beneficial for the lower back?

REGULAR SENSIBLE EXERCISE IS beneficial for most adults, but particularly for those who have back problems. The components of an exercise program and the types of exercise chosen depend on the individual. The goals of exercise include:

- Muscle tone and general fitness,

- Reasonable flexibility, and

- Aerobic conditioning.

Each of these elements is important in an exercise program. The *weekend warriors* do no exercise during the week and then get involved in strenuous sports over the weekend. They are a good example of what not to do. Inactivity during the week allows their backs to stiffen and weaken. On the weekend, or during a vacation, they spend hours playing sports and subject their backs to a tremendous amount of strain. Without adequate reserves of endurance or flexibility all it takes is one jolt too many or one awkward position to injure their backs.

Unfortunately, a frequent treatment for people who injure their backs is prolonged periods of rest, often recommended by misinformed but well-intentioned healthcare providers (Deyo, Diehl, and Rosenthal 1986). Often neglected is the rehabilitation phase that should be associated with recovery. The back pain sufferers just resume normal activities when they feel better. This approach leads to the *anniversary effect:* each subsequent injury causes further weakening and stiffening of the back. Back pain sufferers gradually become afraid of all exercise because they experience injury again and again. Unfortunately, they are the ones who should be carefully increasing their exercise programs to improve their endurance.

Although no generic set of exercises will benefit everyone, the back exercises in **Your Lower Back** are standard and will benefit most people, including those without any significant back problems and those who have minor difficulties. The exercises are not a substitute for seeking out medical professionals, including physicians and physical therapists, for advice about a specific problem.

Aerobic activity is also important in an exercise program because it promotes cardiac fitness as well as producing a sense of well-being in those who are physically fit. Aerobic exercise is one of the healthiest ways to reduce stress and cope with the challenges of modern living.

If my doctor recommends bed rest, should I run to another doctor?

THE EVIDENCE WOULD SEEM to indicate that bed rest is no longer advisable. In some situations, bed rest is still useful for the treatment of back problems, but its usefulness is decreasing. A doctor who recommends a trial of bed rest for a particular problem should be quite willing to explain the reasons for choosing this course of action. If the doctor does not offer a good explanation, then a second opinion would be totally appropriate.

What medications are available for low back pain?

EVERYONE WHO HAS HAD low back pain is looking for a magical cure, and most seek medication as a simple answer. It is much easier to take a pill every day than to set aside time for exercise. Unfortunately, all drugs have side effects and not everyone responds well to them.

Several categories of medication are available for the treatment of back pain.

Anti-inflammatory medication: Two groups are nonsteroidal drugs and steroids.

Nonsteroidal drugs. These agents are the largest and most profitable class (for the pharmaceutical companies) of medications for back pain. They work by blocking certain chemicals that the body produces in association with inflammation. Since most pain is associated with inflammation, these medications may help by reducing inflammation. In practice, they are moderately effective pain-relievers. The most well known of these drugs is aspirin. Ibuprofen, which no longer requires a doctor's prescription, is also readily available even at most supermarkets. Many prescription medications in this class are in common use, but they are very expensive and may be no more effective than aspirin or ibuprofen.

Some people may be surprised to learn that aspirin has a very long list of side effects, some of which are very serious. All of these anti-inflammatory drugs share many side effects, the most common being stomach irritation, adverse interactions with other drugs, and kidney damage. Those who use these medications over a long period, or plan to combine them with another medication, should consult their physician and pharmacist.

Steroids. These medications, which include cortisone and prednisone, have very powerful anti-inflammatory actions. They also have many side effects; for example, they induce a sense of euphoria that may be responsible for part of their pain-relief action. Some individuals with serious medical problems that are not related to the back do need to take these medications for prolonged periods. However, long-term use is always associated with complications, including weakening of the bones, fluid retention, weight gain, and many others. Because of the serious side effects, many of which are irreversible, steroids should be used only when absolutely necessary to treat severe inflammation, and then only for the shortest possible duration.

Analgesics. These medications are prescribed only for the relief of pain. One of the most common, acetaminophen (Tylenol™), is a moderate pain-reliever with few side effects at low doses. At high doses, it can cause severe liver damage, so even this medication requires care about dosage.

Most people think of narcotics when they think of pain-relievers. This group of medications includes codeine, Vicodin™ (hydrocodone), Percocet™ (oxycodone), Demerol™ (meperidine), and morphine. The distinguishing characteristic of these medications is that they lose effectiveness after only a brief period - and they are **addictive**.

Muscle-relaxing drugs. The most well known of these medications is diazepam (Valium™). Whether these medications are useful for relieving muscle spasm is controversial, but it is well known that they cause drowsiness since many of them are used as sleep-inducers.

Psychotropic drugs. These drugs, which include tranquilizers and antidepressants, are being used more frequently for chronic pain. They have a very long list of potentially serious side effects, so **caution** is the key word.

Although not exhaustive, this list of medications features those that are most commonly prescribed. None of these medications is perfected for long-term use even though the anti-inflammatory medications are often used that way. The hope is to make back pain sufferers better consumers by helping them make more informed choices.

What is the role of medication in treatment?

IN SPITE OF THE extensive number of available medications, they really have limited use for long-term problems. A back pain sufferer should keep aspirin, Tylenol™ (acetaminophen), or one of the nonsteroidal anti-inflammatory medications available for intermittent use. If continuous use is necessary, then monitoring by a physician is essential. Narcotics provide only short-term relief of severe pain. A very important responsibility of the healthcare provider is to **educate** the back pain sufferer about the limitations of medication. Unfortunately, some physicians find it easier to prescribe a narcotic than to educate a patient about why it is a bad idea to use these medications continuously.

The other medications listed have specific uses for certain conditions, and back pain sufferers should take them only under **close observation** by a physician.

What is physical therapy for my back problem?

PHYSICAL THERAPY FOR BACK problems can take many forms depending on the philosophy and training of the physical therapist as well as the instructions of the physician. Depending on where you live, a physical therapist often may not be able to start treatment until a physician evaluates the back problem. In most situations of patient referral to physical therapists, the physician refers the patient and writes a prescription for the type of therapy.

Under ideal circumstances, when a physical therapist meets a back patient for the first time, the therapist performs an evaluation similar to a physician's evaluation. The therapist's evaluation will include a careful survey of flexibility in many planes of motion, posture, specific muscle group strengths, and other areas. This information helps the physical therapist design a physical therapy program that meets the patient's particular needs. The therapist also takes into consideration the general health, age, and medical problems of the patient.

Physical therapy encompasses a wide range of options, including active and passive modalities. Passive modalities include electrical stimulation, application of heat or ice, ultrasound, manipulation, and many others. Active modalities are primarily exercises but many different options are available here too. One patient's problem may be best suited to simple stretching exercises each morning upon awakening, whereas another may visit a well-equipped health club several times a week to *pump iron*. In each case, the physical therapist provides specific instruction on how to do the exercises, often followed by a period of training in the physical therapy facility to be sure that the patient is doing the exercises properly. In some cases, patients may require a longer period of training to build up the confidence and endurance to continue exercising on their own.

How you perform the exercise is most important. You will not gain the desired fitness from incorrect practice; and, quite possibly, the incorrect exercise can lead to additional physical problems. **Practice makes perfect; perfect takes practice.**

How do I choose a good therapist?

AS WITH ANY SPECIALIST, some physical therapists are better than others. Just because the physical therapy center has *back* or *spine center* in its title does not mean that the center is using the most up-to-date techniques. Perhaps friends with similar problems can recommend a physical therapy center; certainly, physicians in the area can. Another approach is to call or visit the center and ask about the qualifications of the therapists. Ask other patients whether their therapist was actively involved in their exercising or whether aides provided most of the treatment. Aides or assistants may help with the exercises, but the therapist should be in charge and actively involved in treatment. Perhaps you can find out what percentage of the patients being treated have low back problems. If the therapists are primarily treating low back problems, they should have additional expertise.

Do not stop being a good consumer once the therapy sessions start! Therapy for back problems will include some limited use of passive modalities such as heat and ultrasound. However, routine back pain treatment should also involve a rapid transition (within a week or two) to an active exercise program. Most physical therapy centers charge for each modality that is used. A therapist could easily generate a very large bill by using an excessive number of passive modalities for a prolonged period of time. The average patient with a low back problem should move from physical therapy to a home exercise program within 6 weeks.

Trust in the therapist is important, and most are honestly trying to be helpful; but if you think that the therapist is taking advantage of you, perhaps it is time to choose another therapist or center.

What are the roles of ultrasound and electrical stimulation?

ULTRASOUND IS A METHOD of applying energy that penetrates deeper into the body than warmth from a heating pad can reach. The beneficial effect should be an increased flow of blood to the injured part. The ultrasound applicator is a small electric device shaped like a microphone. It may be a useful adjunct to an exercise program by reducing pain and temporarily increasing the ability of the muscles to exercise.

Electrical stimulation can be applied to the body surface in several ways. Depending on which type of current is applied, energy may penetrate deeply or may just stimulate the skin surface. Electrical stimulation is a common pain-reducing device for chronic pain patients. Small portable battery-operated Transcutaneous Electrical Nerve Stimulation (TENS) units are available for long-term use at home. These units are believed to work by overloading the body's pain centers with enough stimulation to block further transmission of pain. Other types of electrical stimulation devices are used to reduce swelling or even induce deep muscle contractions.

What about salves, balms, and lotions?

HERBAL REMEDIES HAVE BEEN used for thousands of years by people suffering from pain. Many of these topical applications are counterirritants that stimulate nerves within the skin to overload the nerve pain centers and block some of the pain from the back. Other remedies claim to increase blood flow to the region. Although it is difficult to prove that they have any specific value, these types of remedies have such widespread acceptance that they are hard to resist. With such types of treatments, back pain sufferers can control their lives and gain the sense that they are doing something for themselves. The treatments also continue to enjoy great acceptance because they are inexpensive and have very few side effects.

These types of treatments have little downside risk, so they are *worth a try*. If they provide even short-term relief, they may be valuable.

How about heat or ice?

WHEN ANY PART OF the body is injured, ice is commonly used to reduce swelling and inflammation. In fact, the generally accepted treatment for any injury is rest, ice, compression, and elevation, easily remembered as **RICE**. For a back injury, compression or elevation would be difficult, but ice and rest are still of value. Many people find that applying ice after exercising reduces the inflammation that is associated with exercise.

Heat, on the other hand, will not reduce inflammation and may even increase it. Still, heat seems to have value in loosening stiff muscles in preparation for activity by increasing circulation to the painful area.

A common routine that works well for most people is to use heat to loosen up; for example, in the morning or before exercise. Ice is very useful after stretching and exercising as a way to reduce the aftereffects.

One important rule to remember when using ice: **Do not place ice directly in contact with the skin**. Wrapping the ice in a towel or using commercially prepared reusable ice packs works well. The commercially prepared variety is very convenient; when you finish using it, you can just toss it back in the freezer until the next time you need it. The commercially prepared ice packs also avoid the dampness associated with melting ice. If you want to try an inexpensive alternative, you can wrap frozen vegetables in a towel. Ice should be applied for up to 20 minutes at a time, with at least a 20-minute rest period between applications. If you have a skin condition or circulation impairment, **do not** use ice except under a physician's guidance.

The major risk associated with using heat is **skin burns. Never** go to sleep while using an electric heating pad. Personal comfort should be your guide in determining how long to use the heat. Hot water bottles are safer than heating pads (dry heat), although less convenient. Some prefer devices such as hydroculators (moist heat) that are immersed in boiling water, or electric hydroculators. To avoid the possibility of burning yourself when you fall asleep, you should try to find heating pads or electric hydroculators with a trigger switch that turns the unit off when the pressure is released.

The trick is to know your body and develop the program that works for you. If ice helps when you are in severe pain, but heat is better on a day-to-day basis, then use that combination. Some patients prefer a program using ice alternating with heat at 20-minute intervals. Be open to suggestions from physicians and therapists, **but find and use what works for you!**

What are alternative approaches?

THE MANY *ALTERNATIVE APPROACHES* for the treatment of low back pain include chiropractic, reflexology, acupuncture, acupressure, biofeedback, and many others. The term *alternative approaches* indicates that they are outside the traditional treatment provided by an M.D. or D.O., but in some regions these approaches are very popular. Each treatment has its advocates and detractors. Warren has tried some of these treatments without success, but it is difficult to generalize from only one case.

This type of treatment will continue to be available. Not surprisingly, many back pain sufferers seek these alternatives when traditional methods do not cure them or when they do not want to take responsibility for their own problem by using active techniques like those discussed. Many doctors do not like some of these options. Patients who are interested in these options should discuss them with their treating physicians. For a few patients, sound medical reasons eliminate these options; but for most people, they are safe, if not always effective solutions.

What is spinal manipulation?

Spinal manipulation refers to pulling or twisting the back to place pressure on the joints of the spine - a technique which is commonly performed by chiropractors, physical therapists, and osteopaths. Some practitioners feel that manipulation moves the vertebral bones and joints slightly beyond their normal range of motion. The most vocal supporters of this treatment are chiropractors, many of whom contend that diseases are caused by subluxations or small malalignments of the joints within the spine. At one time the chiropractic community contended that all types of disease, including such conditions as diabetes, were caused by these subluxations, but most no longer support such claims. There remains little proof for the subluxation concept of disease, even for spinal problems. Critical reviews of radiographs by orthopaedists and radiologists have failed to disclose these subluxations.

Regardless of the lack of scientific foundation for chiropractic, many back pain sufferers are convinced that manipulation is beneficial. Several studies have shown that manipulation reduces the number of days of pain after some patients' back injuries. Usually these effects are limited to a few days less pain for those patients who are manipulated compared to those who are not. Some conservative chiropractors and therapists believe that their manipulation techniques restore motion to the joints in the spine. Others suggest that the *hands-on* nature of manipulation promotes healing for psychological reasons.

In summary, manipulation is another option available to those who seek relief from their spinal pain. It may have value for relief of acute pain for a short time; but at best, relief comes only a few days sooner than it would have occurred anyway. Claims that manipulation will strengthen the spine, correct curvatures, or prevent disease have little scientific basis; and treatment can be quite expensive over a prolonged period of time. Still, many spine pain sufferers will continue to undergo frequent manipulations. It is tempting for the patient to allow the spinal manipulator to *solve my problem.* **Unfortunately, this approach can place the patient into a passive role and transfers the burden for solving their spine problem onto someone else.** If you choose manipulation as part of your treatment, **you still should be involved in some active forms of treatment** like those that are outlined in this book. By continuing to be an active participant in your care, you will have the **best** opportunity for success.

If I choose to have my spine manipulated, what should I do?

IF YOU HAVE PERSISTENT back pain, you should first be evaluated by a qualified physician. In most cases your personal or family physician is the best place to start. Many times back pain results from problems other than those in the spine. During your first visit, a physician can evaluate whether these other causes (kidney stones, inflammation of the pancreas, diverticulitis, and many others) are present. In this way, people with potentially more serious or more urgent medical conditions will avoid being manipulated as if they just had ordinary back pain.

Choose a qualified practitioner for the manipulation. Chiropractors are most commonly sought for manipulation, but osteopathic physicians perform this procedure as well. These osteopaths also have had a conventional medical education, so they are probably more knowledgeable about general medical conditions. Many physical therapists are also qualified to perform manipulation.

Avoid any practitioner who uses fear to get you into long-term and frequent manipulation. In other words, if the practitioner says that you have a severe problem that needs to be manipulated 4 times a week for a year, seek another opinion. Back pain sufferers should also beware of practitioners who require frequent x-rays during their treatment. Although there are sound medical reasons why an occasional patient may require frequent x-rays, **repeated full spine x-rays may unnecessarily increase radiation exposure**. If a practitioner even suggests frequent x-rays, seek an additional opinion from a qualified spine physician.

Will acupuncture help my back pain?

MOST PEOPLE ARE FAMILIAR with acupuncture from television and magazine reports. Acupuncture treatments involve inserting fine needles into various areas of the body in order to relieve pain. This technique was developed in the Far East and, although not extremely popular, has its practitioners in most metropolitan areas of the United States. According to some experts, acupuncture works by overloading or *burning out* certain nerve centers within the body. With these nerve centers shut down, transmission of painful nerve impulses is blocked.

Spine experts have shown no consensus regarding the use of acupuncture. Although some people are certain that the technique is helpful, researchers have difficulty separating the psychological from the physical benefits. People tend to exhaust most other methods before trying acupuncture, probably because of the unpleasantness that most people associate with needles. Acupuncture is certainly available to those who wish to try it, and not very dangerous, but does not seem to be as popular as many of the other forms of treatment.

Will spinal injections help my problem?

MANY PHYSICIANS RECOMMEND INJECTIONS for the treatment of pain in the back. The most common materials to inject include steroids (cortisone, triamcinolone) and local anesthetics (Novocaine™). The medication is often injected into painful areas, which physicians sometimes refer to as *trigger point injections*. They are commonly performed by many different types of physicians - family doctors and orthopaedists among them. Like many of the pain-relieving modalities, local injections may have a short-term role in supplementing other, more active, treatments. Some physicians will try one or two injections if nothing else seems to help and if appropriate tests show no serious cause for the pain. Some people seem to get significant relief by using injections during their occasional painful episodes; however, they represent a relatively small percentage of back pain sufferers.

Another common alternative is the **Lumbar Epidural Steroid Injection**, or LESI, which involves actually injecting a steroid into the spinal canal. An anesthesiologist usually performs the injection at the recommendation of the treating physician. The procedure takes just a few minutes; a local anesthetic injection into the skin prepares the patient for insertion of a longer needle into the region of the nerves within the spine. When the steroid is injected, it bathes the nerves. Steroids are strong anti-inflammatory medications, and the theory is that the injection reduces inflamed nerves. Usually these LESIs are performed for patients whose symptoms of pain extend into the lower legs because of nerve compression. Although use of these injections is somewhat controversial, many physicians consider them useful as temporary relief, but not for frequent use. According to some physicians, use of these injections in chronic pain patients may improve their participation in aggressive exercise programs to rehabilitate their backs.

Is there a basis for hands-on therapy?

TRADITIONAL MEDICAL TREATMENTS HAVE shown a positive effect from hands-on procedures. The *laying-on of hands* has always been associated with promotion of good health, and most patients feel neglected if their healthcare providers perform only cursory *hands-on* examinations. *Hands-on* treatment can have the positive, though short-term, psychological effect of restoring confidence by attending to a patient's needs. Most *hands-on* treatments such as manipulation seem to have only short-term benefits.

The problem with *hands-on* treatment is that it is primarily passive. In other words, the practitioner does the work while the patient rests. As attractive as it may be to let someone else do the work toward your long-term health, a more active approach is best. For this reason, **most back specialists have been moving toward short-term passive treatment with rapid progression to a program where the patient is a more active participant**. In this way, the back pain sufferer takes charge of the treatment and is responsible for its success or failure.

What is a back school?

BACK SCHOOLS WERE FIRST developed in Sweden to educate people about the function of the back and the techniques for promoting good back health (Forsell 1981). A back school does not describe a building, but rather an education program that is most often taught by physical therapists. Usually presented in a classroom format, the program uses visual aids such as slides to emphasize the points being taught.

Most back schools attempt to teach anatomy, posture, function of the spine, and lifting techniques. By better understanding the function of the spine and learning how to protect it during day-to-day activities, patients should be better able to function in spite of their back problems.

What about surgery for low back pain?

SURPRISINGLY, SURGERY IS THE answer for very few back pain sufferers. For Warren, diagnostic evaluation led to a solution that has provided increased function and less pain. Combined with rehabilitation, this solution has allowed him to get back to a normal life. Although many back pain sufferers seek medical help with the expectation that surgery will be the answer, it usually is not. **Greater** than 90% of people with back problems **never** need surgery. From another perspective, surgery has little to offer these patients. Unfortunately, surgery is often viewed as the fast solution, particularly by a patient who has lived with pain for a long time. Even in successful cases, the surgery is often just the first step toward recovery. In the United States, approximately 1 person per 1,000 population has had lower back surgery (Porkas, Graves, and Dennison 1978).

The many different types of surgery offered to people with back problems include simple disc removal, fusions, vertebral body reconstructions, as well as other procedures. The details of such surgery are beyond the scope of this book.

Is low back pain in the geriatric age-group similar to that in younger individuals?

MOST PEOPLE LOOK FORWARD to the *golden years* of retirement as a time for rest and enjoyable activities. Unfortunately, these years can also be a time for a new spectrum of back problems. Elderly individuals may still experience the disc herniations and muscle strains that are more commonly associated with younger people. However, older people witness not only the results of aging upon the spine, but also the aging of other organs that affect the spine.

As time passes, everyone experiences osteoporosis in one way or another. **Osteoporosis** is a condition of aging that weakens the bones by slowly absorbing them. Women are affected earlier than men because women lose hormonal stimulation of the skeleton at menopause. Exercise and an adequate lifetime intake of calcium seem to slow down the process of osteoporosis. Although not usually painful, the results of this condition can be osteoporotic spines that are weak and can develop painful crush fractures (compression fractures) from a minimal injury. The square-shaped vertebral bones literally become compressed or crushed, often to less than half of their original height. This experience can be very painful and may last for 3 months or more. Not uncommonly, an elderly individual may develop these types of fractures from merely bending over. The bent-over appearance, sometimes associated with later life, is often caused by compression fractures that occur in several vertebrae.

Arthritis of the spine is also commonly associated with older individuals. By the age of 70, approximately 75% of people will have significant x-ray evidence of degenerative changes in the discs and joints of the spine (Butler et al. 1990). Flexibility of the spine decreases, and often the spine bends forward in the upper back because of a combination of disc deterioration and loss of height of the bones as a result of multiple compression fractures. Although this degeneration of the spine is a normal part of aging and is not always associated with pain, many people experience frequent pain and muscle fatigue. You will know why this bent-forward position of the spine is tiring if you spend a single day walking in that bent-over position. The muscles of the spine have to work much harder when the spine is bent compared to when the weight of the body is centered over the vertebrae in the normal upright position of the spine.

Causes of back pain in later life are often related to other organs of the body. Older patients more commonly have disorders of the kidneys, prostate, or uterus, for example, and these disorders may refer pain to the spine area. In a small number of patients, pain in the spine may indicate the spread of cancer to the spine from other sources. With all of these visceral conditions as possible causes for back pain, it is easy to understand the importance of a careful medical evaluation in all elderly patients who have persistent spinal pain.

What about nerve problems in the elderly?

WHEN BACK PAIN IS associated with pain that radiates down the leg, particularly into the lower leg, this condition is often called sciatica or radiculopathy. Among the young, this pain usually indicates injury to a spinal nerve by a herniated disc. In older patients, this pain is the result of **spinal stenosis**, which literally means narrowing of the spine. In this condition, the spine does not have enough space for the nerves. With aging, the associated thickening of the bones and ligaments, bulging of the discs, and bone spur formation take up some of the space that the nerves would normally occupy. Certain body positions further reduce the amount of space within the spine, which would not be a problem in a normal spine. But when activities or positions compromise the space within an already narrowed spine, pressure is applied to the nerves, and pain radiates into the areas where these nerves travel. In the case of stenosis in the lower back, these nerves extend into the legs, so the pain extends into those areas.

Stenosis usually develops so slowly that the body can adapt to the loss of room for the nerves. Because of the human body's tremendous ability to accommodate gradual injury, significant symptoms are rare until the process is fairly advanced. Although some people eventually require surgery to make more room within the spine, the majority control their symptoms with rest, avoidance of painful activities, and mild medication. Spinal stenosis may occur in young people who are born with narrow spinal canals, but the condition is most commonly associated with aging, for the reasons just described.

Are lower back problems in the elderly treated like those in young people?

THE TREATMENT OF BACK pain in all individuals takes into account many factors. A person's age is certainly important, but it is not the only consideration. For example, an active 65-year-old person may be healthier, stronger, and more flexible than many inactive 35-year-olds. The category of patients that can be described as *elderly* is very heterogeneous. A 68-year-old person who is still working full-time and engaged in sports activity is very different from a 95-year-old person who lives independently, but requires a cane to walk.

In general, people over the age of 55 to 60 should have more extensive and earlier testing than a younger person would need to rule out a visceral cause for their back pain (for example, internal organ failure or cancer). Medication is also more of a concern since older individuals seem to be more sensitive to side effects. Strong pain-relievers such as narcotics should be used in low doses, if at all, in order to avoid confusion and depression, particularly in the very elderly. Numerous reports have described organ damage, such as injury to the kidneys and stomach ulcers, from the use of even such mild medication as aspirin and ibuprofen. These medications can be used safely, but require careful monitoring.

Exercise is an important part of treatment in the elderly patient, but needs a careful design that avoids injury to bones and joints that are often ravaged by osteoporosis and degeneration. This exercise program is not strictly age-dependent, but is instead individualized based on a careful evaluation that includes measuring such factors as flexibility and strength. Other medical conditions that commonly afflict the elderly, such as heart disease or diminished circulation, must also be considered in the design of an effective exercise program. A physical therapist with experience in treating older patients with back pain can be very helpful. Almost anyone can start with a walking program or a swimming program such as those commonly available at community health centers, which have programs designed for older people. Exercise promotes a sense of well-being, strengthens muscles to reduce fatigue, slows osteoporosis, and helps maintain range of joint motion. If the back problem is severe, then consultation with a physician and physical therapist should result in an individualized program that takes into account many of the factors described.

In summary, treatment of back pain in the elderly usually includes prudent medical evaluation, low-dose mild analgesics or arthritic medications, and careful exercise programs.

A **general rule** for older people with advanced spinal degeneration: Exercise when you can; rest when you must. In other words, take advantage of the days when you are feeling well to exercise. On those days when you are fatigued or when the pain is severe, it is more appropriate to rest.

What is ergonomics?

ERGONOMICS IS THE SUBJECT which deals with the way that people interact with machines. Its primary use today is to provide a comfortable environment for workers while minimizing their risk of injury. The popularity of ergonomics has been driven by corporations and insurance companies who are designing work environments where humans can operate machines safely.

For a job that requires repetitive bending to retrieve an object, ergonomic intervention would involve changing the workstation to place that object at a comfortable level for the person who will retrieve it. Other changes might include floor mats for those standing on hard concrete all day, and machines to lift heavy objects for the workers.

Some groups are finally realizing that society gains more from engineering the workplace to fit the worker and prevent injuries than from trying to rehabilitate people who have already been harmed. **Prevention** is the key.

How does ergonomics affect my life?

ERGONOMICS HAS BECOME A part of everyday life. The design of new cars, new homes, and office furnishings all benefit from ergonomic science. Ergonomically designed seating includes support for the lumbar spine. People understand the importance of ergonomics when they are directly affected by a low back problem or some other medically related challenge. When they are hurting, they appreciate proper seat design for lumbar support, as well as proper desk height, for example.

Redesigning the workplace for human comfort and increased productivity is one way that corporations, large and small, hope to reduce workers' compensation costs, which have been rising faster than employee salaries for the past 20 years (Snook and Jensen 1984). Industry and business will continue to actively support ergonomically designed workplaces. Those that make the investment see how the workplace becomes a safer, more efficient place. Also, employers that stress safety and comfort send an important message to their employees: They care about their employees as human beings.

How important is attitude in dealing with lower back problems?

ATTITUDE IS THE SINGLE most important component of living with a back problem. It is easy to become depressed when you can no longer do the activities that you want to do. If you are unable to work because of pain, it is common to feel that you are becoming a burden to your family since you can no longer provide for them. As upsetting as these problems may be, this is one time in your life when it is important **not to give up**. It is a time to rise to the challenge and try to find a solution to your problems. The first step is to remain calm and be optimistic that you will find a solution.

Part of maintaining this positive attitude includes a willingness to accept the challenge that you face. Most people will have to modify their lives in some way. For some, this change may mean doing a few exercises each morning. For others, it may require a complete change of occupation. There may be a long period of information-gathering from books, medical specialists, therapists, and other sources. There may be a period of trying various treatment methods, and perhaps even trying several different jobs. For some people, as for Warren, there may be the stress of surgery and a long postoperative period of rehabilitation. Life is not always fair, but you will be successful in controlling your problem if you maintain a positive attitude.

How active should I be?

AN ACTIVE PROGRAM IS not for everyone, but be as active as you can. Find a happy medium between fighting your way through pain and surrendering to your painful low back. Use common sense, and search for qualified professionals to help you learn what you should and should not be doing. Activity and attitude go hand in hand with managing your low back challenge. Keep trying for a positive mental attitude.

Is general physical fitness important for lower back problems?

REGULAR AEROBIC EXERCISE PROMOTES a sense of well-being and health. The choice among aerobic exercises needs to be individualized in order to avoid additional injury. For example, an elderly person probably should avoid jogging because of the trauma to bones and joints of the legs and back, which may already be arthritic. For an older person, brisk walking may be a better choice. One reason that people who exercise may feel better is that aerobic exercise is believed to release **endorphins**, which are natural chemicals that relieve pain and make you feel good. Whatever the reason, people who participate in regular exercise seem to have more endurance and fewer disabling painful episodes.

How can I effectively manage time with a lower back challenge?

LIVING WITH A BACK problem without giving up daily responsibilities means that you have to manage your time more effectively. You have to allot time to accomplish all of your normal activities in addition to finding time for proper rest and exercise. Even if you do not feel well late in the day, you can still manage your time effectively so that you can accomplish what needs to be done. Warren has always been able to find time to deal with daily responsibilities as well as to take care of himself. In fact, one benefit of having a back problem is that his time management skills have become better, out of necessity.

Libraries and bookstores have many books on developing effective time management skills.

Is weight important?

SINCE YOUR SPINE IS responsible for holding your body upright, the heavier you are, the more stress you place on your spine. If you weigh 25% more than your ideal weight, each step you take places 25% more weight on your bones and joints. If you think about how many steps you take in 1 day, it is easy to realize why being overweight can damage your spine. Unfortunately, most people find it very difficult, if not impossible, to lose weight and keep it off.

Realistically, not everyone is going to be able to be slim and trim overnight. Dieting is usually ineffective when done too fast, so it is important to make changes slowly. If you can cut down on your fat intake, you will help many parts of your body in addition to your back. Most importantly, worrying about a problem can be counterproductive, so make a few sensible diet changes, increase your exercise to burn more calories, and realize that you do not need to look like a movie star to be healthy.

Are there any tips for traveling?

ABSOLUTELY! BE PACKED AND ready well in advance of a long trip. Make sure that you take along necessary medications, but try not to rely on them. In this way you can travel relaxed and prepared for any situation encountered.

How do I stay comfortable while flying on an airplane?

AIRPLANES CAN BE A very difficult problem, so start early in preparing for your trip. Arrive at the airport well ahead of time. If possible, have someone carry your luggage; otherwise, use a carrier with wheels. You want to get to your destination in good shape and enjoy the activities that you have planned. If you travel by plane on a regular basis for work, try to fly when you are fresh.

In advance, try to arrange for an aisle or a bulkhead seat. On board, notify the flight attendant that you need to get up every 30 to 45 minutes, or so, to stretch. An aisle seat can be very helpful in that respect. Bulkhead seats are also very good, since they generally offer more room. Should your plane have to wait on the runway for an hour or 2 and you need to stretch or get up, explain your situation to the flight attendant. By explaining your situation during boarding, most attendants will be cooperative and understanding of your low back problem

A lumbar support or roll is also a help when traveling. If you do not have one, place an airline pillow behind your low back for support. While supporting your lower back, try bringing your knees up higher than your hips when you are sitting. That position may be difficult to attain, but it can be helpful.

How can you drive with a minimum of discomfort?

WHEN YOU DRIVE ANY distance, adjust the seat so that your knees are higher than your hips. Bring your seat as close to the steering wheel as possible to keep both your knees and hips in proper flexion. Use a back support. Simple inexpensive low back rolls are available, but many people are satisfied with a rolled-up towel placed behind the small of the back. One type of support is shaped like the contoured back of a chair and fits into your car. Ask your healthcare provider for a recommendation if you would like to try one of these. These supports work well, but may seem expensive. For most people, a simple lumbar roll is usually adequate.

NOTE: If you are going to drive for a few hours, stop every 45 minutes to an hour, get out of the car and stretch your lower back, even if it is only for a few minutes. If you do stop 3 or 4 times more on a long trip, it will add only a few minutes to your trip, but will greatly enhance your comfort.

What is the proper way to get in and out of the car?

As YOU ENTER OR leave your car, try to keep your shoulders and hips square, so you do not twist your back. When entering the car, sit down onto the seat with your legs outside the vehicle and your feet on the ground. Then, lift your legs up and turn your shoulders and hips at the same time until you are squarely in the seat. To exit the vehicle, reverse the order. Lift your legs up and then rotate your whole body in unison until your feet are outside on the ground. Then stand up by placing your hands on the door and top of the seat for support.

How long should I sit at one time?

IDEALLY, EVEN A PERSON with no lower back problems should not sit for more than 20 minutes without standing or stretching. Unfortunately it may not always be practical to stand and stretch, but it is almost always possible to shift your position.

While you are working, it is particularly important to change your position every once in awhile. Most people become absorbed in their work and it is easy to forget to change positions. If you work at a desk job, you can stand at your desk and work or, perhaps, lie down for a break. Either will decrease fatigue in your low back.

How should I sit?

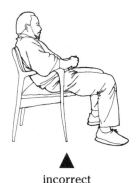

▲
incorrect

SIT WITH YOUR KNEES higher than your hips, making certain that the lumbar spine is supported. This position can be accomplished by having your buttocks situated all the way back in the chair, with a lumbar support inserted in the small of your low back, firmly against the back of the chair or seat. You may have to elevate your legs on a stool. Occasionally try a wedge on the seat so that it tilts your pelvis forward, prompting you to maintain a normal lumbar curve.

▲
correct

Is there a standing position that is most effective?

FIRST, STANDING IN ONE position for long periods of time is not recommended. If you must do that, get a stool so you can place one leg on it while keeping the other leg straight. A 6-inch to 8-inch stool height is best. Then, when you become somewhat fatigued in this position, all you have to do is alternate your legs.

If a stool is not available, stand with one or both knees slightly bent. Try to elevate one leg several inches after awhile.

What is the proper way to bend, lift, and carry packages?

PERFORMING A BIOMECHANICALLY CORRECT squat (see Functional Squat in the **Exercise** section) is the best way to bend and lift packages out of a car. First, you place your feet shoulder width apart and plant your feet firmly on the ground, bending at the knees and hips and allowing your back to flex slightly forward while keeping the spine relatively straight. When lifting packages, try to let your legs perform all of the work. Within a car or other enclosed area, it is sometimes difficult to perform a biomechanically correct squat. Always try to keep the object close to the body to reduce the stress on your arms and back. When trying to lift objects from the trunk of a vehicle, you may have to place a knee or leg on the bumper to give you some support so that you are not lifting with just your back muscles.

Are certain positions better for sleeping or lying down?

AVOID SLEEPING ON YOUR stomach. If you must sleep on your stomach, do away with your pillow. Using a pillow promotes extension of the spine and, thus, increases stress on the lumbar facets and discs. Most people can find a comfortable position on their backs, with their knees slightly bent and one or two pillows under their knees. Others find the fetal position most comfortable: sleeping on your side, with your knees slightly bent and a pillow between them. Head placement should be at the center point between your shoulders supported by one or two pillows.

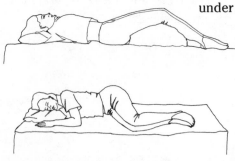

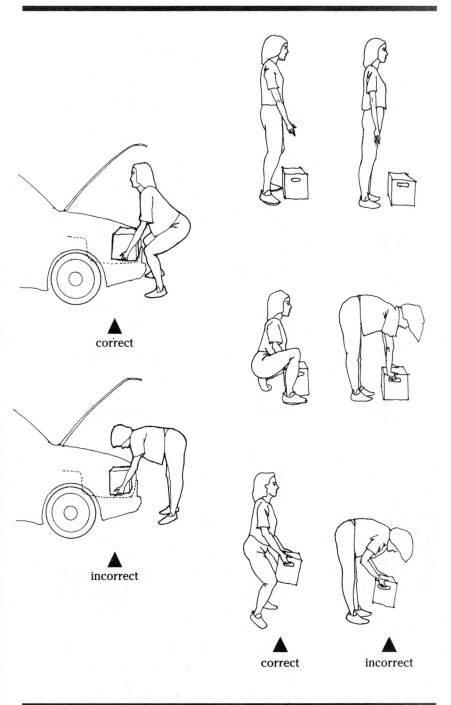

correct

incorrect

correct   incorrect

The spine maintains its natural curves in these positions, which are the most comfortable.

Is firm bedding recommended?

MOST PHYSICIANS RECOMMEND A *firm mattress*. However, this description can be very misleading. A firm mattress is one that supports the spine when a person is lying on it. It does not need to feel as hard as a rock when you lie on it. A well-designed mattress can have firm innersprings, but you can choose padding on the top if you are more comfortable with this softer effect. Unfortunately, what makes a good mattress is often something that you cannot see when you buy it. The mattress must continue to provide support for the spine and not rapidly develop bumps or soft areas, but hard is not necessarily better.

The best advice is not to emphasize a bargain price. At a store with a good reputation, you can ask which mattresses provide the best guarantees and have had the fewest problems. Then *test-drive* the various choices to find one that not only feels comfortable but also provides effective support.

What can I do if my lower back gets tired and sore at night?

WHEN YOU ARE TIRED and fatigued, perform your **stretching exercises**. Stretching decreases stress and allows the muscles to elongate and relax. If hot packs, cold packs, or heating pads help, use them. These modalities have no downside if you use them according to proper instructions, and they may make you feel more comfortable. For acute back problems, some doctors recommend ice or cold packs for approximately 24 to 48 hours to decrease inflammation. In practice, some people seem to do better with heat right away. Experiment and find what works for you. Also, a small dose of an anti-inflammatory medication such as ibuprofen or an analgesic such as Tylenol™ (acetaminophen) may be helpful.

Can my sex life be affected by low back problems?

IN TERMS OF WARREN'S experience, an active sex life is possible, even with a low back problem. But you must take precautions. The sensual pleasure of sex can make a bad day good ... low back pain or no back pain. Using common sense, he and his wife were able to find spine-safe positions that allowed both to feel stimulated and avoid anxiety about Warren's low back problem.

If you have severe pain, then avoiding sex during this time is probably a good idea. If your pain level does not increase during intercourse, then the positives may outweigh any negatives. With low back problems, a back rub has never felt better. This time can be pleasurable for both partners as they explore new ways of touching and feeling that provide mutual satisfaction.

Millie and Warren found that if they made a joint effort and communicated their feelings, safe ways of having intercourse were very satisfying to both the affected and unaffected partner.

Is relaxation important?

ALL PROBLEMS SEEM TO be made worse by anxiety and tension. When you have back pain, it is natural to worry about your health and your ability to live a normal life. In addition to being a cause of stress, back pain typically feels worse when you are under stress. Education about your back can reduce your anxiety, but relaxation techniques are also very helpful in coping with this problem.

Try to pace yourself throughout the day in order to reduce your stress level. At the end of the day, try taking a 10-minute break in a quiet room, resting in a comfortable position. This break is a time to relax and decrease stress from work.

Will a whirlpool or hot tub help my back?

MOST PEOPLE FIND THAT whirlpools or hot tubs help reduce their back pain. These methods provide warmth directly to muscles and superficial tissues, increasing blood flow, thus helping you relax by decreasing muscle spasm.

Generally you should spend no more than 5 or 10 minutes at a time, and water temperature should not exceed 106°F. When you are using this type of treatment, you will perspire, so you should drink plenty of fluids, but not alcohol.

Pregnancy, skin disease, neuropathy, impaired circulation, and heart disease are all reasons for avoiding a hot tub or whirlpool. If you have one of these conditions and would still like to try a hot tub, be sure to consult your doctor.

Is back pain during pregnancy normal?

YES AND NO. WHILE a woman is pregnant, her body is undergoing several changes, both hormonal and structural. Back pain begins because these structural changes place stress on her spine. Increased stress tends to increase discomfort. However, this pain and discomfort should not be severe.

What hormonal changes are occurring?

ACCOMPANYING CHANGES IN ESTROGEN and progesterone levels, another hormone called relaxin is readying the body for delivery. Relaxin increases elasticity of ligaments, so the pelvis can expand and the pelvic outlet can widen while the baby is being delivered. However, relaxin also acts on all other areas of the body, including the spine. This hormone causes all of the joints and ligaments to become more elastic or flexible.

What structural changes are occurring?

AS THE BABY GROWS, the uterus enlarges, moves forward, and thus shifts the center of gravity forward. This shift in the woman's center of gravity, coupled with added weight, increases the normal lumbar curve and the cervical curve at the same time. These changes combined cause a pregnant woman to lean backward. As she continually arches her back, she may eventually have low back pain.

Are there other causes for pain?

SOMETIMES THE BABY MAY be lying directly on nerves or other structures which refer pain to the leg or the back.

Herniated discs can occur at any time, even during pregnancy. They are quite difficult to treat during this time. Most physical therapy modalities and medications cannot be used for fear of injuring the unborn child. If a woman suspects a severe back problem, such as a herniated disc, she should consult her physician. Physical therapy can still be employed to get through these rough times.

What can I do about low back pain during my pregnancy?

ANYONE WHO HAS SIGNIFICANT low back pain related to pregnancy should be evaluated by a physician, a physical therapist, or both. A formal physical therapy program may not be necessary. However, the physical therapist may teach exercises or mobilization techniques to improve discomfort after just one visit. Typical back pain in pregnancy is very responsive to a mild exercise program and usually resolves without surgical intervention.

What is cumulative trauma?

CUMULATIVE TRAUMA IS GRADUAL injury caused by repetitive minor stress to a part of the body. The stress that causes the injury is usually quite small; and if an individual is exposed to it for only a short period of time, it normally does not cause any harm. A typical example of a person who is exposed to cumulative trauma is a factory worker who is loading small bottles into a carton. Lifting an individual bottle does not cause any harm, but lifting thousands of bottles day after day may result in stress fractures, tendinitis, or other injuries.

Cumulative trauma can affect bones, ligaments, tendons, muscles, and even discs. Injuries due to repetitive trauma are referred to as CTDs, Cumulative Trauma Disorders.

How do cumulative trauma disorders usually occur?

THREE COMMON TYPES OF activity cause cumulative trauma disorders:

- Repetitive movements with little force,

- Less repetitive, more forceful movements, and

- Large loads without movement.

Repetitive Movements, even when manipulating light objects, cause continual stress on muscles, joints, and ligaments. Since the same motion is used each time the task is performed, the affected structures are chronically irritated. Examples of occupations that commonly expose workers to repetitive motions are supermarket checkout and many types of assembly line work.

Less Repetitive, More Forceful Movements are movements that often require pushing or pulling against moderate or high resistance. These actions may include using pliers or other hand tools to manipulate objects.

Exposure to Large Loads occurs when holding heavy weights in one position for prolonged periods of time. When this occurs, muscle fatigue develops. Eventually muscles are injured by impaired blood flow, which affects the supply of oxygen to the muscle and impedes the removal of waste products.

What are some examples of CTDs?

CARPAL TUNNEL SYNDROME IS caused by repetitive motions, awkward hand angles, or postures that injure the nerves of the hand. Typically, patients experience numbness and tingling into the thumb and index fingers of the hand. When carpal tunnel syndrome is severe, it can cause weakness of the hand muscles. Usually symptoms increase with both awkward and antigravity positioning. Symptoms can often be reduced by wearing a splint or injecting the wrist with cortisone. However, when the syndrome persists, surgery is the usual recommendation.

Tennis Elbow or **Lateral Epicondylitis** is painful inflammation of the tendons of the outside portion of the elbow. Although commonly called *tennis elbow*, this condition can result from any activity that requires a forceful grasp with the hands. The muscles around the elbow provide the power for vigorously gripping objects. With repetitive gripping of objects, whether playing tennis or working on an assembly line, repetitive contraction of the forearm muscles provides the grip power. When the force of this contraction overcomes the absolute strength of the muscle, injury occurs at the point where the muscle and the bone connect. Since the involved muscles connect to the bone along the outside of the elbow, the pain and tendinitis occur in this region.

Low Back Pain and **Disc Disease** can also result from cumulative trauma. As discussed earlier, all of the components of the spine are susceptible to injury and degeneration. For example, the disc is much like a jelly doughnut, with a sturdy outside and soft inside. The outside portion is called the **annulus** and the inside portion is the **nucleus pulposus**. The annulus is constructed much like layers in a tree trunk, with overlapping layers of strong fibrous ligament-like tissue. Injury occurring to the annulus over time causes small (micro-) tears in the fibers. As the deterioration progresses through the annulus, degeneration of the disc center also occurs, with loss of hydration (water) and, in most cases, a narrowed degenerated disc. If the individual is unlucky enough to have the tears extend all the way through the annulus before the central soft portion of the disc has degenerated, then the soft jelly portion may be forced out of this weakened area. This condition is a true disc herniation, and the herniated portion of the disc often causes direct injury to a nerve through pressure.

Are there other risk factors for back pain?

BODY MECHANICS IN THIS context refers to an analysis of the stresses that are placed upon the spine during bending, twisting, and lifting. For example, loading dock workers would place much less stress on their spines if they were to lift with their legs rather than bending forward at the waist and lifting with their back muscles. Biomechanically, the human body is basically sound. As long as proper body mechanics are observed, the human body can tolerate a great deal of physical stress. However, back injuries are common when individuals do not lift properly, either because no one has shown them how to lift properly or because their working conditions force them to lift improperly. An example of this second situation would be a mover who brings heavy furniture up winding staircases. Unfortunately, improper bending and twisting are hard to avoid in these situations, so back injuries are quite common. One solution is to **educate** workers in proper body mechanics.

Vibration, from vehicles or machines, increases stress on the axial skeleton. With time, injury to the discs, ligaments, and joints can occur (Panjabi et al. 1986).

Static Posture is another risk factor for back pain. Staying in one place, or maintaining one position for an extended length of time, places stress on the spine so breakdown may occur. Examples include driving long distances and sitting for extended periods of time.

Force and Weight cause injury to the spine as increased load is placed on it. Since people do not directly hold heavy objects with the spine, there is no direct relationship between the amount of weight held and the actual force on the spine. For example, the same 10-pound weight feels much heavier when held at arm's length versus next to the body because of the lever effect. The same lever principle magnifies the amount of stress on the spine. So when you lift objects that are held away from your body, you are increasing the stress on your spine by using improper body mechanics. Therefore, the risk of injury to the spine is related to what amount you lift and how you lift it; the risk is reduced if you use proper body mechanics.

Repetitive Trauma injury results from frequent bending, twisting, and lifting, which cause increased stresses to the spine and related areas.

Other factors that may affect cumulative trauma disorders include production-based incentives; the employee makes more money by making more products. Since everyone is somehow driven by money, almost everyone pushes to the point of injury to make more money. This situation can result in increased activity and decreased rest periods.

Are there solutions for cumulative trauma?

THE ANSWER TO THIS question is yes. However, the best solution for cumulative trauma is **prevention**. Typically, these solutions include rotating jobs to avoid repetitive activities, modifying workstations, and taking frequent breaks for exercises or stretching. **If a cumulative trauma injury develops, early diagnosis and treatment are essential to avoid prolonged disability.** Everyone, including the doctor, the physical therapist, the employer, and particularly the employee, should understand what cumulative trauma means, how they can prevent it, and how they can recognize the early signs of injury. All of them must work together as a team for **education, prevention, and treatment.**

Stretching and Exercise Breaks are important for cumulative trauma education programs. Whether for carpal tunnel syndrome, headaches, neck stress, or low back problems, these breaks need to be scheduled at appropriate time intervals. If possible, these breaks should occur every hour, and the appropriate exercises usually require only about 2 minutes.

Job Rotation is an effective tool that has the potential to increase productivity as well as decrease injury. This solution allows workers to rotate their jobs so they have periods for doing heavy activities and other periods for performing light or mixed activities. The stresses on the body are significantly reduced. This arrangement also requires that employers train people at different positions. Therefore, when people are out of work, productivity does not have to decrease. To be successful, job rotations must be set up by a qualified professional to ensure decreased stresses on the body.

Task Rotation is fairly easy. Typically, jobs are set up so that workers perform one specific task at a time, often for several hours. Instead of constantly performing one job, workers must do other related activities. These tasks may include obtaining equipment or materials for a specific job task, performing that job, and also storing the devices or materials used for the completed product. In this way, one specific job is broken down into several tasks so that employees can take a break from their normal routine. The original position may be redesigned so that heavy manual activities are alternated with lighter activities.

Work Modification solutions typically involve altering the workstation by performing a work risk analysis and reviewing the biomechanics of specific jobs. This analysis helps to identify risk factors that are causing the cumulative trauma. The solution may involve modifying tool design, providing specific tools, or both, for a task to be safely completed. This solution would also require a look at body positioning as a whole, including posture, seating, and other features, to make sure that the job performed is biomechanically sound.

Early Intervention and **Early Treatment** require awareness of cumulative trauma disorders as well as education and training. Ownership, management, supervisory staff, and employees must all be aware of the risks of their individual jobs. Owners, managers, and supervisory staff should receive education in the early warning signs of cumulative trauma disorders. Recognizing the early warning signs means early treatment and prevention of more serious problems. It is easy to identify the cause of the injury if a worker complains of pain after lifting a very heavy object. The work is undoubtedly related to the problem, and immediate medical attention is usually provided. However, cumulative trauma may be more insidious and difficult for either workers or supervisors to identify. An aching back can be a symptom of cumulative trauma or the normal aging process. Proper attention to detail can prevent it from becoming a full-blown work injury. Other examples include pain in the forearm secondary to tennis elbow, or numbness and tingling of the fingers. An easy way to determine whether these symptoms are caused by the cumulative trauma is to move the injured employee to a task that does not require repetitive motion. If the problem subsides, then the cause is obvious. A minor alteration in the pace of work, a slight modification of work, or a change in position may be all that is needed to ensure recovery.

Prevention is the best solution for cumulative trauma disorders. Once most of these problems occur, they are very difficult to treat.

Fatigue occurs to the muscles, tendons, and circulatory system. Rest periods become very important. Throughout each day, people place stress on their ligaments, muscles, tendons, and bones. Normal physical stress is important and helps to maintain strong healthy tissue. However, when the stresses applied are greater than a maximum threshold, fatigue occurs and, eventually, breakdown. The cycle of tissue injury begins. Breaking this cycle requires rest. It would be smarter to give your body rest periods **before** breakdown occurs.

NOTE: Fatigue is one of the major causes of tissue injury.

The best way to prevent cumulative trauma is to pace yourself. Just as marathon runners pace themselves for a race, so you have to pace yourself with your daily activities in the workplace, at home, and during exercise.

Rest periods are a must. Rest periods do not imply that productivity stops, but rather that specific tasks may stop, allowing other duties to be performed. Stretching affected muscles and joints helps flexibility. Changing positions, for example, sitting to standing, or even just placing a stool to rest your leg while you stand, decreases fatigue.

Everyone needs to understand that **each individual** is in control of his or her own destiny. Cumulative trauma disorders **do not** have to occur. **Fatigue is the major cause.** If you rest frequently, alter body position, and modify your tasks, you can avoid these injuries. Employers should continually analyze job tasks and identify the jobs that are causing cumulative trauma to their employees.

How can I help decrease CTD injuries in the workplace?

IF YOUR WORKPLACE DOES not have an in-house engineer and you have noticed that significant cumulative trauma disorder injuries are occurring to your fellow workers or employees, you should have an ergonomic or biomechanical evaluation performed at your site. Professional people trained in ergonomics, biomechanics, or both will come to your place of employment and perform a **work risk analysis** that will enable them to determine which areas are involved and how specific job tasks can be changed to make sure that they are biomechanically sound.

The second component in **preventing cumulative trauma** is **education**. Workers and their employers need to be educated to communicate concerns related to the work environment and the stresses placed on workers' bodies. An additional recommendation may include a cumulative trauma school at the work location to educate employers and employees about safer work methods.

The total program to prevent cumulative trauma can be an enlightening experience. Employers who cultivate involvement of their employees in prevention programs often see a decrease of injuries. Employees soon realize that the employers really do care about workers' health and well-being.

NOTE: A workplace cumulative trauma disorder reduction program should result in reduced injuries, improved attendance, reduced workers' compensation costs, reduced medical claims, and better attitudes and productivity.

Maybe it's me; maybe it's in my head!

MOST ADULTS HAVE FELT a twinge in their low back at one time or another. The repetitive motions of everyday life - straining, twisting, and bending - may take their toll over time. In other words, the normal activities in which everyone participates may ultimately lead to low back injury and pain. In fact, 4 out of 5 adults (80%) experience significant low back pain at some time in their lives.

Suppose that you cannot stand up straight, you cannot bend over to wash, and you cannot brush your teeth in the morning. Perhaps it takes you an hour to get out of bed. What about sneezing and then having severe low back pain? Also, suppose that you cannot sit for even 5 minutes at a time. You may not have been affected in these ways, but I am a living example that it can happen to you. Even though you are otherwise healthy and *in good shape,* you may not be spared.

When my back problem began, I went to several different doctors. The pain was affecting my job, my friends, and my family. Almost every part of my life was touched by this problem; yet I was being told that this problem was *in my head.* Well, my problem was not in my head; and **if you are having pain like mine** (severe low back pain with pain down the legs [sciatica]), **you should not assume that it is in your head either.** If one doctor tells you that nothing can be done, then get a second opinion. Even if you are unlike me in that surgery cannot help you deal with your back problem, you should be able to help yourself by learning about your back. You need to learn about:

- Exercises to stretch and strengthen your back,

- Activities or positions to avoid because they may injure your back, and

- Warning signs of more serious problems that should be medically evaluated.

You need to consult a doctor or a healthcare professional if your low back pain affects your productivity and daily function. Low back soreness should be a warning sign. If you have recurring pain, you should probably seek medical treatment. Persistent and recurrent bouts of low back pain or sciatica (pain down your leg) are examples of problems that need qualified medical treatment.

Reading **Your Lower Back** may encourage you to look forward to functioning and being productive on a regular basis. If you need additional help coping with this problem, your doctor can recommend psychologists or psychiatrists. Many people resist this alternative because of the mistaken belief that only *crazy people* see psychiatrists. On the other hand, a surprise is that more people do not need this type of help, particularly those who have spent their whole lives being active and then, suddenly and without warning, experience severe pain and a major lifestyle change. Those people who do not seriously consider this alternative may lose an excellent opportunity to learn how to deal with their physical or emotional pain.

How did friends react?

IN MY CASE, THEY whispered that I had suffered a nervous breakdown. The rumor was understandable, but also untrue. I went from being active 18 hours a day to spending most of the day in bed.

As my condition persisted, people who had initially been supportive began to avoid me. Fortunately, a few close friends hung in and supported my family and me. Millie and I were very fortunate to meet people that accepted my new limitations.

In fairness to those that stayed away, a *quick-fix society* does not deal well with long-term problems. Why should a medical problem be different, especially when you are only 35½? Maybe spending time with an ill person reminds people of their own vulnerability. I was tired all the time from the persistent pain. It hurt too much even to do simple tasks. After a short time it seemed that very few people were interested in hearing about my problem anymore, but I had a need to speak about it. Millie and my mother listened; I thank God that they were there whenever I needed to speak.

What did my children think?

WHEN THEY WERE AGES 10, 7, and 5, it was very hard to tell. My oldest son, Jordan, went about his business and still rarely talks. My middle son, Marc, to this day checks on me and worries that I will do too much. Elizabeth, our youngest child, never talks about my back problems. Over the past 2 years I have finally been able to take her to the playground and actually play softball or basketball, her favorite. I do have to be careful not to overdo it. I can't jump too well, nor should I. I lost a lot of hamstring flexibility after the surgery.

While I was recovering from the surgery, we had to move in order to save money, as well as to be on one floor. Millie and I took the time to explain to each child what was happening and why - to the best of our combined abilities.

They know that life is not fair. I found out with my grandmother; they found out with their father, firsthand. We discuss our concerns with them and try to be honest about much that we do not understand. All in all, we came through this in good shape. They are aware of how fortunate it is to be healthy. We never took our health for granted before and, after this experience, we could not forget this lesson.

What were the best times?

I HAD ALMOST ALWAYS attended my children's school plays and major events; but like most working fathers, I sometimes found it difficult to take the time off. When my back problem began, I had plenty of time to attend school functions and I could be home when our children arrived from school. My wife was working. I probably spent more time with my children over those 3½ years than any father in the world. It's a shame that I wasn't pain-free and independently wealthy, but no one has it all. Also, and just as important, I watched Millie mature although I was not happy with the circumstances that caused this growth.

What were the worst times?

MILLIE AND I HAD lived a fairy-tale life together. In some ways, the fairy tale continues to this day when we think about what we have experienced together. We met and were engaged in 10 days; we both knew what we had found. We have always been, and continue to be, best friends and lovers. We still have a very special and meaningful relationship. Then again, we really work at it each day. However, I was frustrated by my persisting condition and, while Millie never lost faith in me, I felt that I had let her and the children down. She felt that we must have done something wrong to be in this predicament. I suggested that we were being given some kind of test with no rational explanations.

We supported each other, but the feeling of letting my family down did not go away. In the evening, I would hurt and had to lie down in bed; as a result, I missed a lot of time with the children and Millie, and those times can never be recovered. During my illness, Millie did not want to do things without me. Fortunately, my parents took the kids to places where I would have wanted to go, but couldn't.

Worse than feeling that I was letting down the people who were closest to me was knowing that I needed to rely on others to do things for me.

What about self-esteem?

I FOUND IT VERY difficult to feel good about myself when I watched my old world falling apart. However, I am strong-willed and knew in my heart that I would eventually eat the bear. That bear would **never** eat me.

It still upsets me that I could not provide certain experiences for Millie, Jordan, Marc, and Elizabeth. Still, Millie and I believe that our love for each other, a ton of family support, and honesty with the kids have helped pull us through. It was a constant struggle: my mind-set versus the circumstances that seemed beyond my control. But we persevered, and we feel that we are winning.

You can **never give up!**

What did I tell my children?

MILLIE AND I TOLD them age-appropriate information and answered any and all questions. We tried to give them information that they could understand and would not find confusing. We also tried not to give too much information, just what they needed to know. They may have sensed Millie's and my frustration, but I can remember only a few instances when I lost it.

They seem to understand that life offers no guarantees and that, without our savings, we might not have been able to get through the first 3½ years in one piece. We told them that when you cannot work, you have less money to spend on discretionary items. They know that I cannot do what I used to do physically, and they also understand how important it is to keep on believing.

No matter how bleak a situation looks, the sun will come up tomorrow. And no matter what life brings each day, you must look for the rays of sunshine that are always there.

Sometimes you must look really, really hard. Also, laughter in your life is terrific medicine.

These conversations with the children and Millie's and my experience may turn out to be one of those lessons of life for all time. Discussing your feelings with loved ones is the best way to get through good and bad times for us. **Never** close the lines of communication.

How did I feel when I woke up in the morning?

I ALWAYS WONDERED WHETHER the pain and soreness would be gone. How long would it take to get through the first part of the day? Could I bend to get washed? Lots of questions were in my mind, and many concerned my family.

Fortunately I am not one to worry too much. I truly believe that needless worrying usually makes things worse ... and never makes them better. If worrying led to constructive action, I would worry like crazy. But it is usually paralyzing. If it eats you up inside, then you are only hurting yourself.

How do I view the world after this experience? Has my outlook changed?

I HAVE ALWAYS VIEWED a half glass of water as half full, not half empty. Today, I probably tend to be more skeptical or cynical, but just moderately.

This back pain was not the first medically related challenge that I had faced. The first time was quite different, however. Millie was 6 months pregnant with our oldest, Jordan, and a grapefruit-size mass was discovered in my stomach. An estimated 1-hour surgery became 4 hours; but after 1 to 2 months I was working and feeling pretty good. It was scary, but I was able to function each day after a reasonable time period.

Millie came down with double pneumonia and was hospitalized for 2 weeks. Lots of scrambling occurred, but after several months she was all right.

These challenges explain why we never took our health for granted. My early experience with my grandmother's stroke had left its mark in a vivid memory of how quickly someone can be incapacitated.

The back problem was different. I didn't look very different. What was hurting me could not be found for a long time. Even when discovered, it could not be treated with medication and did not go away. It just lasted and lasted.

Because of my experience, I do not have a lot of respect for the legal and insurance industries. I feel that they discriminated against my family and me. I understand how they try to box you into a corner and how they challenge the little guy. But when you are truly disabled and they ignore you, it is a bitter pill to swallow. It was criminal that in spite of proper coverage, we were never able to collect 1 cent for this truly disabling condition.

I used to be prudent and careful. Now, I am doubly careful with a dash of healthy skepticism.

The business world - how did associates react?

THEY TREATED ME AS though I were a leper ... damaged goods! What I had accomplished in the past meant little, if anything. They did not give me time to get well. Many in the business world believe that only wimps get sick or incapacitated for any length of time. What can you do for me today, not yesterday or tomorrow? These reactions had to be dealt with.

I took time off for vacations, but not too much time for sickness. Yet, when I became incapacitated, I was accused of faking it. Relationships in business, and out of business, are more important to me now. They were always important; but if I sense a one-way street, no reciprocity, I'll bail out early.

Perceptions as a back pain sufferer

HAVE YOU EVER FELT that a knife was in your back and the more you tried to relax, the more the knife would twist? Add pain and numbness down your legs. That's how my back pain felt.

You try to bend down, but you can't. You can't get in or out of a car. You can't sit down with your family to have dinner or to relax at the end of the day.

You may be able to sit long enough to go somewhere; but when you get there, you cannot enjoy yourself - or you have to leave - because you're in too much pain to stay any longer.

You lose control of your life when you cannot function.

The pain is all you really think about. How did it get there? Why won't it go away? Why can't someone help you?

Are you sleeping in the wrong position? You don't start out in the wrong position; after that, who knows? It's not the bedding. My platform bed is fine.

People feel sorry for you. Who wants someone's pity? Then, after awhile they don't believe you. It isn't what they say; it's how they react or do not react.

Or, a neighbor knows someone who appears to have had what you have; after a few days, maybe weeks, that person was up and about, doing what had to be done.

After awhile it just doesn't pay to discuss these topics with anyone.

Then, when they see you, they ask how you feel. They don't really want to know. They just say it. They don't want to listen. Not everyone; some are sincere and concerned.

Then you need surgery, and people rally around you. Soon, they wonder why you aren't better yet?

So, even if you want to forget about your back, someone is there to remind you. It can really consume you, if you let it.

I didn't and I never will.

Why did I write Your Lower Back with Dr. Gratch, Dr. Star, and Dr. Goldberg?

AFTER WHAT I WENT through and what my family went through, I wanted to point out important concepts about being active in low back care. Then, no one would ever again have to go through my experiences with physical and emotional pain.

Take charge!

THE 40+ AGE-GROUP grew up believing that hurting is the only way to benefit from exercise. Their belief stems from the NO PAIN, NO GAIN theory. Most adults begin an exercise program by doing too much. The day after their first vigorous exercise program, they are so uncomfortable that they are unable to continue.

The first thing you must realize is that you have to take charge. **Consistency** is the key. A **gradual exercise program** means that your back discomfort should gradually lessen. Remember that **gradual** is the important term here, especially if you have not exercised for quite a long time.

Start just by walking and increasing your normal activities. Then start a back-specific exercise program.

You are not in a race. You are changing your behavior and establishing new habits to feel your best each day. An active program should help you feel better on a daily basis, back pain or no back pain. It is never too late to start.

How important is exercise for the lower back?

EXERCISE FOR YOUR LOWER back is as important as exercise for your heart. Most adults in industrialized countries will experience back pain at least once. Again, it is very important to start gradually and then increase your work load. Exercise does not have to be painful.

The exercise program should include:

- A warm-up program,

- Stretching and flexibility exercises,

- Strengthening exercises, including stabilization techniques,

- Mobilization exercises and coordination techniques, and finally

- A cool-down period.

Is exercise important even if I am considering surgery?

ABSOLUTELY! FIRST, RECENT STUDIES have shown that back pain patients who have physical therapy and those who have surgical care typically show similar improvements. Reasons for surgery include severe pain that is intolerable, progressive muscle weakness, progressive sensory loss, or bowel or bladder dysfunction. Other reasons may involve economics, i.e., a loss of income.

Everyone should start an exercise program. These exercises need not be vigorous but should work on those muscles close to the spine. If an exercise program brings no improvement, then surgery may, indeed, be indicated. However, because muscles involved in surgery may have improved during training, recovery is quicker and overall recuperation time is shorter.

How should I feel when I exercise?

IF YOU FEEL INCREASED soreness or pain compared to when you started, **stop immediately**. Understand that some increased discomfort is normal. When your back was hurting, you became inflexible and weak. Thus, the increase in activity may increase your pain. You must be aware of the type or character of the pain. Is it similar to the pain you have had all along, or is it different? Is it typical muscle soreness after exercise, which may be a good sign; or does it feel more like a nerve pain?

Muscular discomfort due to exertion completely resolves, or improves within approximately 2 weeks, after you start an exercise program. If the pain is quite similar to your usual discomfort and is increasing, you should stop performing that specific exercise. Rest and try a different exercise. If the pain returns, consult your physician or physical therapist.

What is the difference between warming up and stretching?

MANY PEOPLE CONFUSE *WARMING UP* and stretching.

A *warm-up* exercise such as riding a stationary bicycle without resistance or walking will increase blood flow and the temperature of your muscles. Then, you can perform stretching or flexibility exercises without injuring yourself. The *warm-up* prepares your body for the stretching or exercising.

Stretching actually increases the elasticity of your muscles, tendons, and ligaments. It promotes increased flexibility, which lets you move freely. When you move more freely, you feel more comfortable within a given range of motion.

As little as 5 minutes of *warm-up* activity may be all that you require before starting your other exercises.

What is cross-training?

USING DIFFERENT MUSCLE GROUPS during successive exercise sessions is referred to as *cross-training*. For example, you could walk on a treadmill 3 days a week and swim 3 different days each week. *Cross-training* reduces boredom, but also combats overuse of bones and joints since different muscle groups are used on different days. *Cross-training* is an effective technique to allow an injured person to exercise effectively, yet minimize the potential for reinjury.

NOTE: Consult your physician before starting an exercise program.

How much exercise does the lower back need?

MANY DIFFERENT EXERCISE PROGRAMS are adequate. Here are a few examples:

- Walking for 20 minutes, several times a week and moving at a steady, but not rapid pace coupled with stretching, flexibility, and endurance exercises can be most effective in lower back care and management over the long term.

- Doing 10 to 15 minutes of stretching and strengthening exercises in the morning, 4 or 5 times a week, with 3 or 4 walks a week can be an adequate program.

- Joining a local gym, or club, may also be helpful and may decrease some of the boredom inherent in a home exercise program. Nautilus machines are typically safe and may be helpful, but the exercise instructor where you work-out should familiarize you with the machinery.

- Using free weights may also be helpful to increase your strength; however, there is a greater chance for injury. Be careful and, again, consult your physician, therapist, or trainer prior to embarking on an exercise routine at your local health spa.

What types of exercises should I choose?

WARNING: Start only those exercises that your doctor permits after you have a physical examination.

WARM-UP

Each morning, but not less than 4 or 5 times per week, spend several minutes as follows:

1. Walk in place, or use an exercise bike or treadmill without resistance or incline for several minutes.

2. Perform ankle pump exercises. Step on a telephone book with the front of your foot, but let your heels hang over the edge. Slowly, go up on your toes and then back down **without** touching your heels to the floor.

3. Do both for several minutes.

NOW YOU ARE READY.

You must breathe during exercises. The rule is: **EXERT = EXHALE.** Inhale during the resting phase of an exercise.

The exercises that follow are typically performed by holding a stretch for **6 seconds** and performing approximately **10 repetitions**. Start off with **one set** a day and increase your sets as much as possible. If this program is too strenuous, decrease your repetitions first; then decrease the time you hold the stretch if you are still having discomfort.

You are not participating in a competition. You will notice results over several months. Just stay with the program, and you can derive benefits for a lifetime.

Many people will work too hard and forget to breathe during exercise. When you begin a program, you should be able to talk or sing while exercising. If you cannot talk or sing, you are working too hard.

The exercises presented represent a basic stretching, strengthening, and endurance program. The Training Zone information in **Your Lower Back** will help you in endurance training.

If you want a more aggressive approach after performing the exercises in **Your Lower Back**, Dr. Gratch, Dr. Star, and Dr. Goldberg recommend that you consult with a qualified healthcare professional; i.e., a physician, physical therapist, or certified trainer, so that person can design a program to meet your personal needs.

NOTE: When the instructions state to hold for 6 seconds; count one thousand, two thousand ... 6 thousand out loud. This will encourage proper breathing during all exercise. Use a second hand or stopwatch to check that you are saying the words for a full 6 seconds.

It is not necessary to perform all of the exercises at the same time. First, select those exercises that you enjoy. As you progress, you may find that adding different exercises makes working out more interesting. If you can do all of the exercises, then go for it, after checking with your healthcare professional before starting.

A **balanced exercise program** will usually provide the best results. If you strengthen the biceps, strengthen the triceps as well. Likewise, when strengthening the stomach muscles, select exercises to strengthen the lower back.

As with all exercise, a *warm-up* and stretching are required before beginning the strengthening and endurance parts of your program. Also, *cooling down* after you exercise is very important. If you are not prepared to do all that is required, you are risking injury and placing your prevention program in jeopardy.

NOTE: Repeat 10 times = 1 complete set.

Stretching

PELVIC TILT

Purpose: To stretch, strengthen, and increase mobility in the small muscles of the lower back.

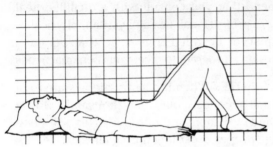

1. Lie on your back with your knees bent, feet flat on the floor, and arms at your sides.
2. Flatten the small of your back against the floor.
3. Your abdominal muscles should be pulling your hips upward.
4. Hold for 6 seconds and relax.
5. Repeat 10 times.

DOUBLE KNEE TO CHEST

Purpose: To stretch the low back, hip, and groin.

1. Lie on your back with your knees bent, feet flat on the floor, and arms at your sides.

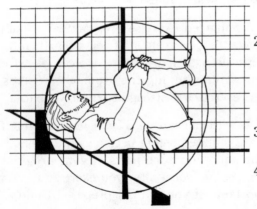

2. Raise knees, one at a time, to your chest, placing your hands in front of your knees or in the bend of your knees.
3. Hold for 6 seconds and relax.
4. Repeat 10 times.

**Starting Position:
This position should
be used for all
exercises unless
indicated otherwise**

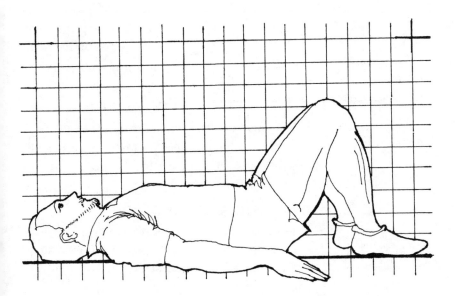

SINGLE KNEE TO CHEST

Purpose: To stretch the low back, hip, and groin; one leg at a time.

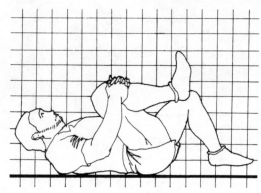

1. Lie on your back with your knees bent, feet flat on the floor, and arms at your sides.

2. Raise one knee to your chest, keeping the other foot planted on the floor.

3. Hold for 6 seconds and relax.

4. Repeat 10 times.

5. Repeat exercise using the opposite leg.

NOTE: Once you can perform the preceding exercises without difficulty, go to the Leg Extension - Advanced.

LEG EXTENSION - ADVANCED

Purpose: To strengthen the low back; proceed only after performing the pelvic tilt, then single and double knee-to-chest exercises as noted.

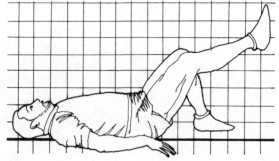

1. Lie on your back with your knees bent, feet flat on the floor, and arms at your side.

2. Raise one knee to your chest, keeping the other foot planted on the floor.

3. Extend the bent leg while the other foot remains on the floor.

4. Hold for 6 seconds and relax.

5. Repeat 10 times.

6. Repeat all steps with the other leg.

TRUNK ROLL

Purpose: To stretch the low and mid-back muscles.

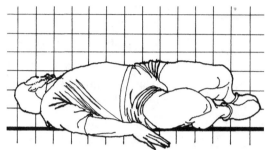

1. Lie on your back with knees bent, feet flat on the floor.

2. **Slowly** drop your knees to the **right** very gently while turning your head to the **left**.

3. Hold for 6 seconds and relax.

4. Return to the starting position and repeat on the opposite side.

5. Do 10 times. Each set includes dropping the knees to the right and then to the left while turning the head in the opposite direction.

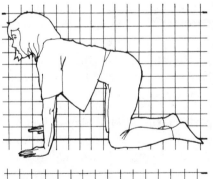

CAT AND CAMEL

Purpose: To increase flexibility and stretch the low and mid-back muscles.

1. Start on your hands and knees with your head parallel to the floor.

2. Position your hands directly beneath your shoulders, with each knee aligned with the hip.

3. Relax and let your back sag in the middle while lifting your chin.

4. Hold for 6 seconds.

5. Lower your head and tighten your stomach muscles to make your back as high and as round as possible.

6. Hold for 6 seconds and relax.

7. Repeat 10 times.

PRAYER STRETCH

Purpose: To stretch the low and mid-back muscles.

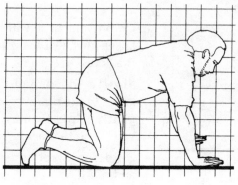

1. Start on your hands and knees, tucking in your chin and arching your back.
2. Hold the stretch for 6 seconds.
3. Slowly sit back on your heels, dropping your shoulders to the floor.
4. Keep your arms as flat on the floor as possible, feeling the stretch in your back.

5. Hold for 6 seconds and relax.
6. Repeat 10 times.

Try to perform all of the exercises comfortably for as many times as indicated. Start the exercises once daily and increase as tolerated. Most of the exercises call for 10 repetitions. If you can't do 10, try 5. If 5 repetitions is still not possible, just try 1.

Try to perform the stretches until you feel stretching or tightness. Do not continue until you feel burning. If you feel burning, drop the repetitions or the degree of stretching. You are probably doing too much. With time and effort each day, you will be able to perform more repetitions with less discomfort and greater effect.

Strengthening   PARTIAL SIT-UP OR STOMACH CRUNCH

Purpose: To strengthen the abdominal muscles.

1. Lie on your back with your knees bent and your feet flat on the floor.

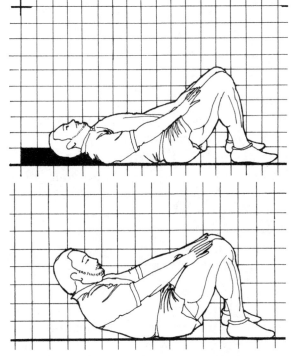

2. Perform a pelvic tilt.
3. Keep your arms straight and advance your hands toward your knees.
4. Focus your eyes on a spot where the wall meets the ceiling. Focusing on a spot forces you to keep your neck still and your head level with your back.
5. Gently lift your shoulder blades off the floor.
6. Hold for 2 to 3 seconds and relax.
7. Repeat 10 times.

Hint: Do not close your eyes when exercising. Your focus should be external, outside yourself. You benefit internally from strengthening your body.

Once you can do this exercise without significant discomfort, cross your arms on top of your chest to perform the partial sit-up exercise. When you are proficient at doing the partial sit-up with your arms across your chest, place your hands behind your head; interlocking your fingers behind your neck, proceed to do the partial sit-up.

These variations will allow you to select different ways of performing a partial sit-up and alleviate boredom. As you become more proficient, these variations will also allow you to increase your abdominal muscle strength.

If you are sore, perform the exercise in the easiest manner. Make certain that your soreness or pain level is no higher than it was at the start of the exercises.

BRIDGING

Purpose: To strengthen the low back, buttocks, and abdominal muscles.

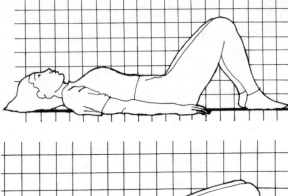

1. Lie on your back with your knees bent.
2. Perform a pelvic tilt.
3. Keep your knees close together.
4. Use the muscles of your buttocks to pull your body off the floor without bending your lower back.
5. Hold yourself in this raised position for 6 seconds; then relax.
6. Repeat 10 times.

ABDOMINAL STABILIZATION WITH ARM MOVEMENTS

Purpose: To mobilize the upper extremities while helping to stabilize and control the lumbar spine and abdominal musculature.

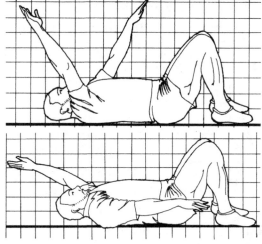

1. Lie on your back with your knees bent.
2. Perform a pelvic tilt and hold.
3. Continue the pelvic tilt while contracting your abdominal muscles.
4. Raise one arm, then the other and keep moving while breathing slowly.
5. Hold the pelvic tilt for 6 seconds; then relax.
6. Repeat 10 times.

ABDOMINAL STABILIZATION WITH ARM AND LEG MOVEMENTS

Purpose: To strengthen abdominal muscles and the small muscles of the low back.

1. Lie on your back with your knees bent.
2. Perform a pelvic tilt and hold.
3. Lift right foot approximately 2 feet off the floor; then bend the right knee while raising the opposite arm over your head.

4. Return to starting position and repeat with the opposite foot and arm.
5. Do one complete set 10 times.
6. Hold your pelvic tilt for 6 seconds, trying to get into a slow and steady rhythm.

NOTE: When beginning this exercise, start with your heel 3 to 4 inches off the floor. Your goal is to lift your foot approximately 2 feet off the floor.

HANDS AND KNEES BALANCING

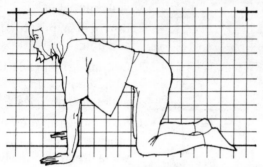

Purpose: To improve balance and strengthen the arms and legs while strengthening the small muscles of the back.

1. Start on your hands and knees, with arms straight and each knee aligned with the hip.

2. Raise one arm and the opposite leg slowly while trying to maintain your balance.

3. Return to starting position and repeat on the opposite side.

4. Do one complete set 10 times.

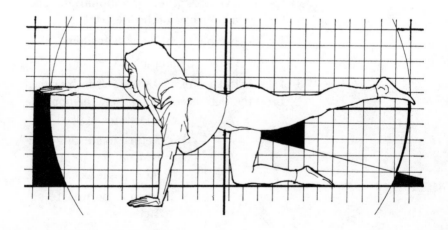

FUNCTIONAL SQUAT

Purpose: To strengthen the muscles of the lower extremities and to encourage good body mechanics.

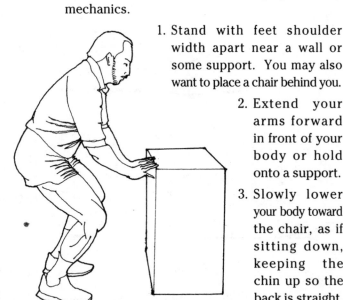

1. Stand with feet shoulder width apart near a wall or some support. You may also want to place a chair behind you.

2. Extend your arms forward in front of your body or hold onto a support.

3. Slowly lower your body toward the chair, as if sitting down, keeping the chin up so the back is straight.

4. Continue to bend your knees and keep your feet flat on the floor.

5. Return to starting position by slowly rising to an upright position.

6. Repeat 10 times.

7. Try to increase the number of sets weekly.

HIP EXTENSION

Purpose: To strengthen the low back, buttocks, and hamstring muscles.

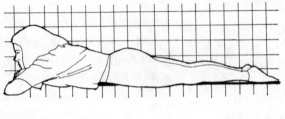
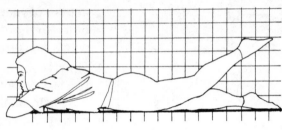

1. Lie on your stomach with your arms folded under your chin.
2. Keep your pelvis flat on the floor and slowly lift one leg off the floor.
3. Hold 6 seconds and relax.
4. Return to starting position and then repeat on the opposite side.
5. Repeat 10 times.

NOTE: Start slowly as with any exercise program. Some muscular discomfort is normal, but pain that radiates from your back down your legs is not. If this kind of pain occurs, **STOP** the exercise immediately. If the pain resolves, try another exercise. Modify your exercise program to those techniques which do not increase your discomfort or exacerbate (sharply increase) your pain.

AGAIN, start slowly!

If 10 repetitions is too many, then try 5. Change the number of repetitions or hold your position longer, to your level of tolerance. Any amount of exercise, even just 1 repetition, is better than none.

What is cooling down after exercise?

COOLING DOWN AFTER EXERCISE, or a *cool-down*, refers to light stretching of the muscles before ending the exercise session.

As with the *warm-up*, the *cool-down* is an essential part of your exercise program. It is another preventive technique to avoid serious injury. The theory is that the *cool-down* period helps remove waste products of vigorous exercise by promoting continued increased circulation. The *cool-down* also continues muscle action, which prevents blood from accumulating in the lower extremities and, thus, prevents an abrupt blood pressure drop.

Do not skip the *cool-down*. It takes only a few minutes.

Practice makes perfect; perfect takes practice.

Other types of land-based exercises

Machine-based exercise

WARNING: Most exercise machines (such as Nautilus™) build the back and abdominal muscles. They are made for healthy individuals of medium height and weight. Consult your physical therapist or doctor before exercising on them.

BE CAREFUL. You must be properly trained. If the staff at the spa or gym do not seem knowledgeable about training or if you already have a back problem, it is always a good idea to consult with a physician or physical therapist before starting.

NOTE: Balance your workouts. Work both the stomach muscles and the back muscles. Mat or floor exercises are generally safer than machine-based exercise, and you can do floor exercises at home at a lower cost.

Free weights

Once you can perform the stretching and strengthening exercises (discussed earlier) without difficulty, you can add ankle or wrist weights to your routines.

Barbells, dumbbells, and similar equipment should be used only with proper body mechanics and technique. A partner or spotter is a requirement for safety, as is an experienced person to train and teach you proper techniques. **BE CAREFUL.**

Aerobics

Low-impact aerobics is relatively safe. As long as you are pain-free, aerobic exercise is an option. If pain returns, try performing water exercises.

Water Exercises

Can water exercises be effective for those with lower back pain?

WATER THERAPY CAN BE extremely effective. These exercises are employed when land-based exercises are too painful. Even if you cannot swim, these exercises are typically performed in shoulder-deep water, low enough to stand in. As with all water-based programs, a **buddy system is the rule**. You should **never** go into a pool without another person present in case you need assistance.

What does water do?

THE BUOYANCY OF THE water reduces stress and weight on your entire body. The water also acts as a shock absorber. At the same time it provides resistance to help strengthen muscles.

Can my whole body benefit from water workouts?

ABSOLUTELY. ARM AND HAND motions should be part of a water program. Alternating activities such as jogging in the water provide a good cardiovascular workout without much weight on your spine. As with **all** exercise, you should work with a certified trainer, a physical therapist, or other professional who knows how to properly instruct you for your individual needs.

BE CAREFUL when you start walking in the water. Proper technique is the critical aspect in avoiding injury.

Can water exercise be useful after surgery?

CHECK WITH YOUR PHYSICIAN. As long as your incision is well healed, water exercise is usually an option. Water exercise can also be used as a transition to land-based exercises.

Land and water exercise programs can be part of an effective *cross-training* program. This varied program alleviates boredom and helps when you are not feeling your best.

Should you stretch first?

ALWAYS STRETCH BEFORE PERFORMING any activity. As previously stated, it is important to warm up, stretch, and cool down. This sequence is also helpful during aerobic workouts and cardiovascular training.

Is special equipment used in water workouts?

YES. HOWEVER, THIS EQUIPMENT is not typically necessary and may be costly.

You may try using specially designed mitts or fins to increase resistance, thereby increasing your work load. If exercising in deep water, wear a flotation vest.

Is swimming good?

SWIMMING IS A GREAT source of aerobic activity and cardiovascular exercise. It provides both an aerobic and anaerobic workout and lets you work your entire body, including your respiratory muscles.

Practice makes perfect; perfect takes practice.

What are the types of water exercises?

THE SCOPE OF THIS book precludes the authors from illustrating all the different types of water exercises. Walking forward and backward in the water (without overdoing it) is recommended for the initial water program. An experienced healthcare professional can develop an advanced program to meet your individual needs.

What is my training zone?

THE TRAINING ZONE IS the heart rate range that you should maintain, but not exceed, during your exercise program. Determine the zone by using the following formula or by finding your age and target heart rate in the chart. Your maximum heart rate is 220 minus your age. Your target heart rate is your maximum heart rate multiplied by 0.6 to 0.8.

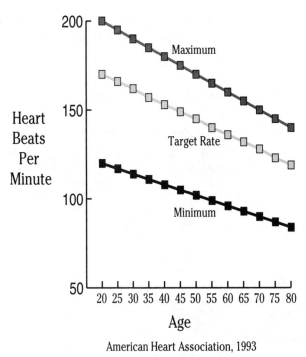

Heart Beats Per Minute — Age

American Heart Association, 1993

TARGET HEART RATE = (220 - AGE) x (0.6 to 0.8)

You should work out somewhere between 60% and 80% of your maximum heart rate. This recommendation applies to any cardiovascular or aerobic training programs. **However, if you have a preexisting heart problem or are over 30 and do not exercise regularly, you should absolutely consult with your personal physician before you start any exercise program.**

I am sore when I start working out. How will I know when to stop?

IF YOU ARE SORE when you start working out, your pain during exercise should go no higher than the level at which you started. **Stop immediately** if this occurs. Rest and try again. If your pain stays at a higher level than when you began, **stop immediately!** If this situation continues for 2 or 3 days, contact your physician about your concerns or tell your physical therapist at once.

BE PATIENT! Just because you are feeling better on a given day does not mean that you can resume all of your normal activities. As you continue to perform your exercises and increase your exercise program, you will have more days when you feel relatively well and are able to accomplish almost anything. Then you should be able to go back to your regular activities of daily living.

A spouse's perspective

WHERE DO I BEGIN? How do I put into words my life, our life, over the past 7½ years? One day we were leading a relatively *normal* wonderful life and the next day we were in a nightmare.

I remember that morning so well. It was the fall of 1985 and we had just come back from a family visit to Massachusetts. It was a long trip with our three children, and we were all exhausted from the drive. We had a lovely night's sleep, but the next morning Warren could not get out of bed. He had had some spasms in the past, but nothing very serious. This time was different. At first we attributed the discomfort to the long drive home and the nights on a sleeper sofa in Massachusetts. This day was the beginning of our nightmare.

I just couldn't believe what was happening to us and our life. Warren went from a healthy, energetic athlete to a man in constant pain. He couldn't work, sit, or find a comfortable position. Our whole life turned upside down in a matter of weeks. When this nightmare continued, it seemed as though we were living someone else's life, not ours.

The first doctor we saw, a well-respected *doctor's doctor*, told my husband to lie flat for 18+ hours a day for a few weeks and gave him enough drugs to turn him into an addict.

This predicament went on for quite awhile. Sometimes I wonder why we let it go on for so long; but after all, we were seeing the top doctor in his field and felt privileged that we were able to see him at all.

Meanwhile, Warren couldn't work. I finally felt ready to go back to work when Jordan, Marc, and Elizabeth were all in school full-time. I was just starting to work part-time. And we had just moved into a new home in the suburbs. It was not only time to help out financially, but also time to get back to the *real world*. Working became a wonderful outlet for me. It allowed me to be with adults and get my brain functioning again on more than the children. Also it gave me a chance to focus on something other than all the problems we were facing.

When I look back now and realize that 2 years went by without the proper diagnosis, it just boggles my mind. Why did it take so long to find the right doctor? What took **us** so long? I don't know. The days and weeks just kept going by, and we didn't realize how many months and years had passed.

Warren's disability affected not only our financial situation but every other situation as well. We were used to just picking up and going. Now we had to plan everything, even going out for pizza.

Warren couldn't shoot baskets, hit tennis balls, or go jogging anymore. If he felt fairly decent and we wanted to go out, or just be with friends in the evening, he had to rest all afternoon in bed. Even so, by 9 p.m., he was so exhausted from the pain that our outings were always cut short.

Before Warren's illness we shared the responsibilities of our three children. He did everything except breast-feed! Now it became my responsibility to be mother, father, chauffeur, disciplinarian. Whatever the role, I had to play it. I was responsible for rearing our children in a loving, caring, supportive household, and I tried to keep our home and family a *normal* one.

Our children did not understand why Daddy was always lying in bed or lying on the family room floor. Why didn't he go to work anymore? Why couldn't he sit with us at the dinner table; why did he stand and eat? Our daughter, Elizabeth, told us a few years later that she didn't remember her Daddy being well; in her mind, he had always been sick. How do you explain all this change to your children when you don't understand it yourself, and especially when they are 5, 7, and 10? I explained Warren's health problems the best way I knew how. I was honest with them and explained the situation in terms that they could understand. We went about trying to keep our lives as close to our normal schedule as possible - with one exception, without Daddy. Jordan, Marc, and Elizabeth became used to our new routines and adjusted beautifully.

By December 1987, when we finally found someone to help us, the idea of surgery was a relief, not a frightening event. It was also comforting to have the doctor explain to me exactly what Warren's problem was and that it definitely was **not** in his head. He took the time to explain the procedure, in words I could understand; and he showed me, on a scale model of the spine, exactly what the surgery would consist of and what I could expect afterwards. We could finally hope to be going back to a normal existence. But we had to wait until April to have the surgery. I didn't realize until this point how important it is to find a doctor who not only makes your husband feel comfortable, but also makes you, the spouse, feel a part of everything. And our doctor surely did this. Whenever I had a question about what was going on, Dr. Gratch would always come to the phone to talk to me and ease my mind.

On the day of surgery, I was able to be with Warren until he was taken down to the operating room. My mother-in-law and a friend sat with me during the 3 hours of surgery. I think that they were more nervous than I was. I had so much confidence in Dr. Gratch that I knew everything would be okay. When Warren was finally in recovery, Dr. Gratch came to see me in the waiting room and sat down to explain exactly what took place during the surgery (with diagrams) and what I could expect during the next few days. I was so amazed that this doctor would take the time and have the patience to talk with me after 3 hours of surgery.

During these years of confusion and upheaval, our family and friends rallied around us. Whenever I needed help with our children or just needed someone to talk to, they were always there. Our friends would come over on the weekend and spend Saturday evenings with us playing games, or just watching television and talking with Warren as he lay on the floor, in front of the fireplace.

No matter what I needed, whether it was help in taking out the trash or carpooling, they were there. But, surprisingly, once the surgery took place and Warren was recuperating, they thought that everything should go back to normal. They didn't understand the constant struggle of trying to get strong and healthy again and the total exhaustion of physical therapy. They didn't understand what was taking so long. Why couldn't he work immediately? Why couldn't we go out on a Saturday evening? One by one, they deserted us. Over the years I rationalized that they weren't really deserting us; they just didn't know how to cope with what was happening. They were tired of listening to Warren's stories about doctors, and they didn't want to hear that no one would hire him. Were they afraid that his problems might rub off on them? I did have one friend who stood by us. She was always there for me to lean on, and I could cry on her shoulder, and she just let me talk and talk and talk. She kept me sane!

When I try to understand how we got through this ordeal, I shake my head in disbelief. Warren and I have always had a very special and close relationship. We were not only husband and wife and lovers, but best friends. We met and married within 7 months, one of those love-at-first-sight romances. We shared everything. But I could not share his pain. I could not feel the pain that he was in constantly, but I could feel the pain of frustration and helplessness. I had to be strong emotionally and physically, for him and for our children. I always had to be *up*. I didn't want Warren to see me depressed and scared and weak. It was very tiring! I felt that I always had to have a smile on my face and a positive attitude. I suffered with intestinal problems from the stress, and sometimes I was so tired of being strong that I sat down and cried.

Some acquaintances and some *friends* thought that Warren was having a nervous breakdown. They believed that he didn't have a back problem; it was all in his head, just a stress-related situation. Do you know what it's like to walk into a room and have everyone stop talking when they see you? I knew that parents at school were talking, but I just had to hold my head up high, be strong, and keep going. I knew that Warren wasn't crazy! How could our *so-called friends* not believe my husband? It was a time of learning for me, a time to learn who our *real* friends were and a time to grow emotionally. I learned a lot about myself during those years. I was a lot stronger than I thought possible and I had grown a lot. I wasn't that cute, naive little girl anymore. I found that I could handle just about anything.

It was not so much that people didn't care anymore; they just didn't understand. Even to this day, they don't understand why we can't just get in the car and drive 6 hours straight. They don't see why we can't go out for dinner on a Saturday evening at 9 p.m. They find it hard to believe that he still gets tired from the soreness he will always have. In the beginning, we couldn't go out for an early dinner without Warren having to stand up 2, 3, or 4 times to stretch. If we attempted to go to the movies, we had to sit toward the back and on the aisle seats so that Warren could get up and stretch. It changes your life and the way you live it. Once he had surgery, everyone thought that our life would go back to normal. It just didn't work that way.

During Warren's recovery, when he was able to start doing things again, Marc, our second-born, was very worried and frightened that Dad would hurt himself. He worried about every move that Dad made. I understood exactly what he was going through because I felt the same way. After surgery, every time Warren moved in bed, or made a funny noise, I jumped. He had to wear a specially fitted backbrace for 6 months. The only time he was allowed to take it off was when he was in bed or in the water. I didn't really sleep for weeks after the surgery. If he had to get up in the middle of the night to go to the bathroom, I sat up in bed to make sure that he was okay and wouldn't fall. Only 2 weeks after the surgery, the doctor allowed him to drive short distances. I wanted to kill Dr. Gratch.

One day when I was at work, Warren came to my office with lunch for both of us, so proud that he could drive and walk up the 20 steps on a 90 degree day. I almost had a heart attack! It took me years to stop feeling frightened every time he did something new. I worried that he would be in a car accident; I worried that he would trip; when winter came, I worried that he would slip on the ice; I worried when he sneezed too hard; I just worried and worried. I have calmed down a lot, but I still get apprehensive when he tries to do too much.

We had to learn to adjust and reset our priorities. It was hard, especially when he looked good physically. People just didn't want to hear about it anymore. We had to become more selfish and do what was good for us. I tried not to ask, *Why us?* It was more a time of going through pure disbelief. This really wasn't happening to us!

It wasn't always easy to be optimistic, to see the light at the end of the tunnel. Warren was almost always optimistic that things would get better; but on the rare occasion when he wasn't feeling well and was feeling depressed, I was there to give support, to listen and say *I love you*, and just to be there with open arms. And when I was having a down day, he was there for me, and he would say, *It's going to be all right*, then hold me in his arms. Jordan, Marc, and Elizabeth were always there for me when I was having *one of those days*. They would give me a hug and a smile to let me know it was okay.

Because of our deep love for each other and our deep religious belief, we knew that things would get better. We just didn't know that it would take so long.

One of the positive effects of our experience (and it wasn't easy to focus on the positive) was the family closeness we now have. When Warren was well and working many hours and traveling, we weren't always able to be together. Then, when we couldn't go out and he wasn't working, we were able to spend quality and quantity time with our children. It gave us a chance to get to know them and learn what they were all about, and it gave them a chance to get to know us. In this day and age of everyone running all the time to keep to schedules and outside activities, we had a chance to slow down and appreciate what we did have. Thank God, my husband is recovering and is young enough to start over again; thank God that we have three healthy, loving, well-adjusted children; thank God for our four healthy parents; for my sister Anita who was always there to listen; and for my sister-in-law Marilyn, who was always just a phone call away as well. And thank God for all the love and devotion that we have for each other. After going through this experience, I can better understand why families break up when they face severe medical problems. It isn't easy to be supportive, feel compassionate, and totally believe in your spouse (or yourself for that matter) all the time. Seeing my husband getting stronger each day and feeling more like himself is still somewhat unbelievable to me. For the longest time I thought that we would never lead a relatively normal life again. We have started going to the movies again and out to dinner; now Warren only has to get up once during the movie; and we have even started taking long rides again.

It **does** get better. We have made new friends who are supportive and have accepted us for who we are and respect the limitations that we sometimes have. Our *true* friends from the past are still with us. And I have learned that you have to have a lot of patience and a lot of faith.

Millie Potash

Sources

- Churchill's Medical Dictionary, 1989

- Dorland's Illustrated Medical Dictionary, 27th Edition, 1988

- Lezlie Martin, RPT, for *Neutral Spine*

- Low Back Pain, Glossary, 1989

- Orthopaedic and Sports Physical Therapy, 1990

- Taber's Cyclopedic Medical Dictionary, 1993

- Webster's 9th New Collegiate Dictionary, 1985

NOTE: Not all of the terms found in this glossary are used in *Your Lower Back*. However, some of the terms listed are used by health-care professionals in discussing low back problems.

Acute - Occurring recently - typically the first few days or weeks of illness or injury.

Ambulation - Moving from place to place; walking; not bedridden.

Analgesic - Pertaining to medication that reduces pain.

Anaphylactic - Immediate and severe allergic reaction.

Annular - Circular appearance.

Annulus - Outer part of the intervertebral disc.

Anterior - Situated in or toward the front.

Anthropometry - Measurements of proportions of the human body, e.g., use of calipers to measure fat on the body.

Arachnoiditis - Inflammatory disease leading to scarring which binds the nerve roots.

Arthritis - Inflammation of a joint; usually accompanied by pain, swelling, and, sometimes, destruction of the bony surfaces.

Arthrogram - X-ray procedure that involves injection of a dye into a joint. The dye outlines structures such as cartilage and ligaments so that they can be seen on subsequent x-rays.

Arthropathy - Any disease affecting a joint.

Arthroscopy - A procedure in which a small telescope (usually 2 mm to 5 mm in diameter) is inserted into a joint to visualize structures such as ligaments, cartilage, and bone. Knees, shoulders, and wrists are commonly examined this way.

Articular - Pertaining to a joint.

Articulation - Pertaining to the junction of 2 or more bones. The process of moving a joint through all or part of its range of motion.

Biofeedback - A process that provides an individual with visual or auditory evidence of the status of an unconscious body function. Used in relaxation techniques.

Biomechanics - Interdisciplinary science that describes, analyzes, and assesses human movement. The study of forces and the effect of those forces on and within the human body.

Buttock - Either of the 2 fleshy, rounded parts at the back of the hips; the rump.

Chemonucleolysis - Treatment of intervertebral disc lesions by injection of a medication into the disc. This was once commonly used in an attempt to dissolve disc herniations, but has become much less common in recent years.

Chronic - Continuing for a long time.

Claudication - Cramping leg pain.

Coccygeal vertebrae - The lowest segments of the vertebral column, comprising 3 to 5 rudimentary vertebrae at the base of the spine; together they form the coccyx.

Contraction - Development of tension within a muscle or muscle group with or without changes in its overall length.

Contracture - Loss of range of motion in a joint. Usually caused by scar tissue within or around a joint or group of muscles.

Cramp - Painful involuntary muscle contraction.

Diffuse pain - Pain that is spread throughout an area of the body. Pain that is in many locations. See also **Pain**.

Disc - Primary supporting structure between vertebrae in the spine. Consists of 2 distinct parts; a gelatinous center called the nucleus and a firm, fibrous covering called the annulus fibrosis.

Disc degeneration - Deterioration of the disc. Loss of the normal structure of the disc results in loss of the flexibility and shock-absorbing function.

Discectomy - Surgical removal of all or part of the intervertebral disc.

Discitis - Inflammatory disease of the disc. Can be caused by infection or injury.

Discogenic - Coming from a disc. Discogenic pain is believed to be caused by injury to a disc.

Discography - Introduction of an x-ray dye into the center of the disc for purposes of identifying the structure of the disc. Usually followed by x-rays or CAT scans.

Dorsal - Related to back, posterior.

Dysfunction - Abnormal function.

Electromyography (EMG) - Recording of electrical output of the contraction of a muscle.

Endorphins - Chemicals that are secreted in the brain or spinal cord and are said to relieve pain.

Endplate - The top or bottom of the vertebra where it joins the intervertebral disc.

Epidemiology - The study of disease (epidemics) among populations.

Epidural - Situated on or outside the dura membrane, which is the membrane covering the brain and spinal cord.

Ergonomics - Science that seeks to adapt working conditions to suit the worker. 2. The study and design of work situations, taking into account the anatomic, physiologic, and psychological variabilities of the people who will work within the given environment.

Etiology - Study of the causes of diseases.

Facets - A joint of the spine. A pair of joints between each 2 vertebrae; essential for spinal stability. A small, smooth area on a bone or other hard surface.

Facet arthritis - Degenerative changes of the facet joints characterized by cartilage thinning and bone-spur formation.

Flexion - Bending over forward, from the waist, as refers to the lower back. A movement that returns the trunk from an extended to a neutral position.

Functional assessment - An evaluation of a person's ability to perform various tasks. This analysis uses tests that involve the whole body versus a single joint.

Fusion - Surgically connecting 2 or more bones together to form one solid unit.

Gluteal muscles - Pertaining to the buttock muscles.

Goniometer - A device used to measure angles. Used to measure range of motion of joints.

Graft - A piece of tissue that is transferred from one area to another. Often refers to bone removed from the pelvis and transplanted to the spine in order to promote a fusion of 2 or more vertebrae.

Hamstring - One of the tendons starting at the back of the knee and extending to the buttock.

Herniated disc - 1. Displacement of nucleus pulposus and other disc components beyond the normal confines of the annulus. 2. Protrusion which may impinge on nerve roots.

    A. **Protrusion** - Displaced material causes a bulge in the annulus, but no material escapes through the annular fibers.

    B. **Extrusion** - Displaced material presents in the spinal canal through disrupted annular fibers, but remains connected to material persisting within the disc.

    C. **Sequestration** - Nuclear material escapes into the spinal canal as free fragments which may migrate to other locations.

Hypermobile - When motion is more than that which is normally permitted by the structures. Excessive movement in a joint when compared to the normal position.

Hypomobile - When motion is less than that which is normally expected.

Idiopathic - Denoting a primary disease of unknown origin.

Iliopsoas muscles - Muscles lying along either side of the spine passing within the pelvis. They are powerful flexors of the hip.

Impairment - Physical and/or psychological limitation.

Inflammatory - Relating to or marked by inflammation, which is the nonspecific immune response to any type of bodily injury.

Instrumentation - Metal rods, screws, or plates commonly attached to the spine during fusions.

Invasive - Involving the penetration of a body cavity or the skin; used especially as a therapeutic or diagnostic procedure. Opposite of noninvasive.

Ischemic - Relating to lack of blood supply.

Job site analysis - Measurement of factors at a given location that influence job task performance.

Job task analysis - Observation and measurement to analyze the components of a worker's job.

Joint - The junction of 2 or more bones.

Kyphotic - Curvature of the spinal column toward the front as seen from the side. Normal in the thoracic spine.

Laminectomy - Removal of the back portion of the spine. Usually used to create more space for the nerves within the spine.

Laparoscope - An instrument introduced surgically into the body for examining and repairing internal organs. Sometimes used in back surgery.

Lateral - From the side. As in lateral view of the spine.

Lesion - Site of an injury, pathological condition, or dysfunction.

Lordosis - Curvature of spinal column toward the rear as seen from the side. Normal in the cervical and lumbar spine.

Lumbar - Pertaining to the 5 vertebrae below the ribs and above the pelvis.

Medial - Towards the middle.

Microtrauma - Very small injury. When it occurs repetitively over time, it can cause serious damage to the body.

Muscle guarding/splinting - Generalized, increased muscular tone as a protective response to pain, dysfunction, or stress.

Musculoskeletal - Pertaining to the muscles or bones of the body.

Nerve - A cordlike structure, consisting of a collection of nerve fibers which convey impulses between the brain or spinal cord and some other region of the body.

Neural foramen - A hole in a bone through which a nerve passes.

Neurology - Branch of medicine that deals with the nervous system and its diseases.

Neuropathy - A disease that involves a nerve.

Neutral spine - That position in which the spine is in its most pain-free state. This position may vary with every person.

Nucleus pulposus - Central, viscous portion of the intervertebral disc.

Orthosis - Orthopaedic device for supporting the spine (e.g., brace or corset).

Osteo- - Bone.

Osteoarthritis - Degenerative arthritis affecting many joints.

Osteopenia - Decreased bone density usually apparent on an x-ray. May be from many causes such as osteoporosis, vitamin deficiency, or cancer.

Osteoporosis - Thinning of the bones which is commonly associated with aging. It results in weaker bones that are susceptible to developing fractures.

Pain - The International Association for the Study of Pain defines pain as the sensory and emotional experience associated with actual or potential tissue damage. Pain includes not only the perception of an uncomfortable stimulus but also the response to that perception. See also **Diffuse pain.**

Peripheral nerves - Those nerves which lie beyond the central nervous system (brain and spinal cord).

Posterior - Situated behind or at the rear.

Primary medical condition - The medical condition that a physician determines to be the most significant medical condition presenting upon evaluation.

Proprioceptive neuromuscular facilitation (PNF) - Form of exercise in which accommodating resistance is manually applied to various patterns of movement for the purpose of strengthening and retraining the muscles guiding joint motion.

Pseudoarthritis - Failure of 2 bones to unite. This may occur after a fracture or attempted fusion.

Psychophysiologic disorder - Physical symptoms that are caused by emotional factors.

Radiating pain - Pattern of pain that follows the path of a spinal or peripheral nerve.

Radicular - Relating to a nerve emerging from the spine.

Radiculitis - Inflammation of a spinal nerve.

Radiculopathy - Abnormality of a spinal nerve resulting in pain, numbness, and/or weakness. Commonly refers to compression of a nerve in the lower back by a disc; results in pain that radiates into the leg.

Radiopaque - Impenetrable by x-rays.

Referred pain - Perception of pain that is felt elsewhere than the site of the (tissue) injury.

Sacroiliac - Relating to the joint between the pelvis and vertebral column (sacrum).

Sacrum - Triangular bone just below the lumbar vertebrae, formed usually by 5 fused vertebrae (sacral vertebrae) that are wedged between the 2 hip bones.

Sagittal - Anatomic plane passing vertically through the body from front to back.

Sciatica - Syndrome characterized by pain radiating from the back into the buttock and into the leg; it is commonly caused by herniation of the intervertebral disc. The term is also used to refer to pain anywhere along the course of the sciatic nerve in the leg.

Scoliosis - Abnormal curvature where the vertebral column bends to the side.

Secondary gain - Any advantage that is produced by being ill. An example is receiving disability payments after an injury.

Segmental instability - Abnormal, excessive motion between two adjacent vertebrae.

Soft tissue - All neuromusculoskeletal tissues except bone and articular cartilage. (Examples are cartilage, ligament, tendon.)

Spasm - Involuntary muscle contraction.

Spinal stenosis - Reduction in the size of the spinal canal. Commonly occurs in older people and can cause pain from compression of the nerves within the spine.

Spondylitis - Inflammatory disease of the spine.

Spondylolisthesis - Slipping of a vertebra in front of or behind the one below. This condition can result from an injury or from an abnormality present at birth.

Spondylolysis - A defect in the back of the vertebra adjacent to the facet joints. This crack in the back of the spine can lead to slipping of one vertebra on another (spondylolisthesis).

Spondylosis - Degenerative disease of both the disc and the facet joints.

Spur - An outgrowth of bone. Usually a protrusion on the surface of the bone.

Stenosis - Narrowing of any canal; e.g., **spinal stenosis** denotes a state of decreased diameter of the spinal canal and the intervertebral foramen.

Strain - Overexertion injury to a muscle.

Subluxation - Partial dislocation of a joint.

Supine - Lying on back, as in supine position.

Symptom - An abnormal feeling, such as pain that a patient experiences in association with an illness or dysfunction.

Systemic - Pertaining to a whole body rather than one of its parts.

TENS - Transcutaneous Electrical Nerve Stimulation - A device which delivers electrical impulses to the skin. Used for relief of pain.

Trauma - 1. Bodily injury, wound, or shock. 2. Painful emotional experience.

Trigger point or **myofascial trigger point** - An irritable site that causes pain when stimulated. Commonly refers to sensitive areas that are injected to relieve pain.

Vertebra - Any of the 33 bones of the spinal column; consists of the 7 cervical, 12 thoracic, 5 lumbar, 5 sacral, and 4 coccygeal vertebrae.

Visceral - Organs within the body, such as the liver and stomach.

Work hardening - Term used to identify a program of exercises designed to rehabilitate injured workers in preparation for return to the workplace. Often includes simulation of normal work activities to allow the workers to gradually increase their work tolerance in a protected environment.

REFERENCES CITED AND BIBLIOGRAPHY

Anderson JA. Grant's Atlas of Anatomy, 7th edition. Baltimore, Williams and Wilkins, 1978.

Andersson GBJ. Epidemiology of spinal disorders. *In* Frymoyer JW (ed): The Adult Spine: Principles and Practice. New York, Raven Press, 1992.

Andersson GBJ, Svensson HO, Oden A. The intensity of work recovery in low back pain. Spine, 8:880, 1983.

Biering-Sorenson F. Low back trouble in a general population of 30-, 40-, 50-, and 60- year old men and women: Study design, representativeness and basic results. Danish Medical Bulletin, 29:239, 1982.

Butler D, et al. Discs degenerate before facets. Spine, 15: 111-113, 1990.

Caruso LA, Chan DE. Evaluation and management of the patient with acute back pain. The American Journal of Occupational Therapy, 40(5):347-351, 1986.

Collins AM. Frequency of Manipulation Procedures by Provider Type for 1990. Ann Arbor, MEDSTAT Systems, March, 1992.

Cypress BK. Characteristics of physician visits for back symptoms: A national perspective. American Journal of Public Health, 73:389-395, 1983.

Detrick JE, Whedon GD, Shoir E. Effects of immobilization upon various metabolic and physiologic functions of normal men. American Journal of Medicine, 315: 1064, 1986.

Deyo RA. Conservative therapy for low back pain: Distinguishing useful from useless therapy. Journal of the American Medical Association, 250(8): 1057-1062, 1983.

Deyo RA. Reducing work absenteeism and diagnostic costs for backache. In Hadler NM (ed): Clinical Concepts in Regional Musculoskeletal Illness. Orlando, Grune & Stratton, 1987.

Deyo RA, Diehl AK, Rosenthal M. How many days of bed rest for acute low back pain? A randomized clinical trial. New England Journal of Medicine, 315: 1064, 1986.

Deyo RA, Rainville J, Kent DL. What can the history and physical examination tell us about low back pain? Journal of the American Medical Association, Vol. 268, No. 6, August 12, 1992.

Deyo RA, Tsui-Wu JY. Descriptive epidemiology of low-back pain and its related medical care in the United States. Spine, 12:264-268, 1987.

Forsell M. The Back School. Spine, 1981.

Frieberg S. Studies in spondylolisthesis. Acuta Chiropractica Scandinavia, p 55 (suppl), 1939.

Frymoyer JW, Cats-Baril WL. An overview of the incidences and costs of low back pain. Orthopaedic Clinics of North America, 22:2, 1991.

Frymoyer JW, et al. Risk factors in low-back pain. An epidemiological study. American Journal of Bone and Joint Surgery, 65:213, 1983.

Hanson TJ, Merritt JL. Rehabilitation of the patient with lower back pain. Rehabilitation Medicine, Principles and Practice. Philadelphia, J.B. Lippincott, 1988, pp 726-747.

Heliovaara M. Body height, obesity, and risk of herniated lumbar intervertebral disc. In Heliovaara M (ed): Epidemiology of Sciatica and Herniated Lumbar Intervertebral Disc. Helsinki, Social Insurance Institution, 1988.

Kahanovitz N. Diagnosis and Treatment of Low Back Pain. New York, Raven Press, 1991.

Keim HA, Kirkaldy-Willis WH. Low back pain. Clinical symposium, CIBA, 32:6, (Illustrations) 1980.

Kelsey JL. In Frymoyer and Cats-Baril: Epidemiology of radiculopathies. Advances in Neurology, 19:385, 1978.

Kelsey JL, et al. *In* Frymoyer and Cats-Baril: Acute prolapsed lumbar intervertebral disc: An epidemiologic study with special reference to driving automobiles and cigarette smoking. Spine, 9:608, 1984.

Kelsey JL, et al. *In* Frymoyer and Cats-Baril: An epidemiologic study of lifting and twisting on the job and risk for acute prolapsed lumbar intervertebral disc. Journal of Orthopaedic Research, 2:61, 1984.

Mandell P, et al. Low Back Pain. Thorofare, NJ, Slack, Inc., 1989.

Martin L, RPT. General information for back school participants. Spine, 5(3):337, 1991.

Miller JAA, Schmatz C, Schultz AB. Lumbar disc degeneration: Correlation with age, sex, and spine level in 600 autopsy specimens. Spine, 13:173-178, 1988.

Muller EA. Influence of training and inactivity of muscle strength. Archives of Physical Rehabilitation Medicine, pp 449-462, 1970.

Nachemson AL. The lumbar spine - An orthopaedic challenge. Spine 1:59, 1976.

National Health and Nutrition Examination Survey data, NHANES II. Musculoskeletal conditions in the United States. Park Ridge, IL, American Academy of Orthopaedic Surgeons, February, 1992.

National Institute for Occupational Safety and Health. Proposed national strategies for the prevention of leading work-related diseases and injuries, Part I and Part II. The Association for Schools of Public Health, 1986 and 1988.

Netter FH. The CIBA Collection of Medical Illustrations, volume 1, Nervous system, part 1, Anatomy and physiology. Summit, NJ, CIBA Pharmaceutical Company, 1982.

Orthopaedic and Sports Physical Therapy. Edited by James A. Gould. St. Louis, C.V. Mosby, 1990.

Panjabi MM, et al. In vivo measurements of spinal column vibrations. Journal of Bone and Joint Surgery, 68-A; 5:695-702, 1986.

Pope M. Measurements of intervertebral space disc heights. Spine, 2:282-286, 1977.

Porkas R, Graves EF, Dennison CF. *In* Frymoyer and Cats-Baril: Surgical operations in short-stay hospitals: United States, Series 13, No 61. Hyattsville, MD, DHEW Publication (PHS) 82-1722, 1978.

Robinson R. The new back school prescription: Stabilization training, Part I. Spine, 5(3):341, 1991.

Rutkow IM. In Frymoyer and Cats-Baril. Orthopaedic operations in the United States 1979 through 1983. American Journal of Bone and Joint Surgery, 68:716-719, 1986.

Snook SH, Jensen RC. Cost. *In* Pope MH, Frymoyer JW, Andersson G (eds): Occupational low back pain. New York, Praeger, 1984, pp 115-121.

Spengler DM, et al. Back injuries in industry: A retrospective study. I: overview and cost analysis. Spine, 11:241-245, 1986.

Svensson HO, Andersson GBJ. Low back pain in 40-47 year old men: I. Frequency of occurrence and impact on medical services. Scandinavian Journal of Rehabilitation Medicine, 14:47, 1982.

Weber H. Lumbar disc herniation: A controlled prospective study with ten years of observation. Spine, 8:131-140, 1983.

Boldface page numbers indicate illustrations

Abdominal stabilization exercises, 155-56, **155**
Absenteeism, from back pain, 29
Acetaminophen, 77, 84, 85, 117
Active treatment
      to control spine instability, 42
      for pain management, 107-8
      versus passive treatment, 24, 60, 79-80, 93, 97
      for rehabilitation, 25-26
Acupressure, 91
Acupuncture, 57, 91, 94-95
Aerobic exercise, 81, 108, 160
Aging
      effect of, on disc, 38
      effect of, on spine, 30, 36, 47, 50, 51
            arthritis, 100
            osteoporosis, 99
            spinal stenosis, 101-2
            treatment of, 102-3
Airplane travel, 100
Allopathic physician, training of, 54-55
American Academy of Orthopaedic Surgeons, 31
American Board of Medical Specialties, 55, 58
Analgesics, 84
Anatomy. *See under* Spine
Anesthesiologist, 96
Anesthetics, local, 95
Anniversary effect, 81
Annulus fibrosis, 38, 123
Anterior longitudinal ligament, 41
Antidepressants, 84
Anti-inflammatory medication, 117
      nonsteroidal, 77, 82-83
      steroids, 83
Arthritis, 46, 47, 69, 100
Aspirin, 77, 82, 85
      side effects of, 83, 102
Attitude, role of, in pain management, 24, 26-27, 107

Automobile travel, pain management tips for
    driving, 111, **111,** 124
    getting in and out of car, 112

Back pain. *See also* Personal experience of back pain
    causes of, 30-32, 49
        compression fracture, 51
        difficulty in diagnosing, 65-66
        in the elderly, 100
        herniated disc, 50, **50**
        during pregnancy, 119, 120
        spinal stenosis, 50-51
        spondylolisthesis, 51-52
    during exercise program, 142-43, 158, 164
    lower
        cost of, 25
        from cumulative trauma, 123
        diagnosis and treatment of, 25
        and gender, 31
        idiopathic, 49
        persons who suffer from, 29
        recovery from, without treatment, 30
        treatment of, 32-33
        and worker absenteeism, 29
    middle, 31
    recurrence of, 30
    upper, 31
Back school, 97
Back support
    while driving, 111
    while flying, 110
Bed rest, effectiveness of, 78-79, 82
Biofeedback, 91
Blood tests, 73
Board certification, 58, 59
Body mechanics, and cumulative trauma, 124, 125
Bone scans, 73
Bone spurs, 50
Breathing during exercise program, 145, 146
Bridging exercise, 154, **154**

Bulging disc, 49
    difference between, and herniated disc, 50
Burns, skin, 90

Carpal tunnel syndrome, 122
Cartilage, 40
    wearing away of, 46
Cat and camel exercise, 151, **151**
CAT scan, 71-72
Central nervous system, 42-44, **43**
Chiropractors, 54, 57-58, 91
    spinal manipulation by, 92-93, 94
Coccyx, 28, **28,** 36
Communication, importance of, in back injury recovery, 33
Compression fracture, 51, 99
Computed Axial Tomography, 71-72
Cool-down period, 147, 159
Cortisone, 18, 83, 95
Cross-training, 144, 161
Cumulative trauma disorders (CTDs), 121
    activities causing, 121
        forceful movements, 122
        holding heavy loads, 122
        repetitive movements, 121
    and body mechanics, 124
    decreasing injuries in workplace, 130
    examples of
        carpal tunnel syndrome, 122
        disc disease, 123
        lateral epicondylitis, 122-23
        low back pain, 123
        tennis elbow, 122-23
    and force and weight, 125
    and production-based incentives, 125
    and repetitive trauma, 125
    solutions for
        early diagnosis, intervention and treatment, 126, 127-28
        education, 126, 127-28
        exercise, 126
        job rotation, 126

Cumulative trauma disorders *(continued)*
        prevention, 125-26, 128, 129
        rest periods, 128-29
        task rotation, 127
        work modification, 127
   and static posture, 124
   and vibration, 124

Deep tendon reflex examinations, 68
Degenerative disc disease, 38
Dermatome chart, 44, **44**
Diagnosis
   patient history, 66-68
   physical examination, 68-69
   primary, 65-66
   tests for, 69-70
        blood tests, 73
        bone scans, 73
        CAT scan, 71-72
        electromyelogram (EMG), 72-73
        Magnetic Resonance Imaging (MRI), 70-71
        myelogram, 72
        nerve conduction study (NCS), 72-73
        x-ray, 70
Dieting, 109
Disability, and back pain, 29
Disc, 38, **38, 39**
   bulging, 49
   difference between herniated and bulging, 50
   effect of aging on, 38
   effect of cumulative trauma on, 123
   herniated, 38, **39,** 43, 50, **50,** 101, 123
        during pregnancy, 120
        treatment of, 79
   loss of thickness in, 49
   parts of, 38, 123
Disease, effect of, on spine, 36
Double knee to chest exercise, 148, **148**
Driving, 111, **111,** 124
Drugs. *See* Medication.

Education
       back school, 97
       to decrease cumulative trauma disorders, 130
       importance of, in dealing with back problems, 75
Elderly. *See* Aging
Electrical stimulation, 88
Electromyelogram (EMG), 72
Endorphins, 108
Ergonomics
       definition of, 105
       and prevention of back injury, 105
       in workplace, 105, 106
Estrogen, 119
Exercise program, 80-81
       aerobics, 160
       balanced, 45, 147
       breathing during, 145, 146
       cautions for, 145, 159, 163
       cool-down period in, 147, 159
       cross-training in, 144, 161
       and cumulative trauma, 126
       difference between warming up and stretching, 143
       discomfort/pain during, 142-43, 158, 164
       for elderly, 102-3, 108
       examples of adequate, 144-45
       free weights in, 145, 160
       goals of, 80
       gradual, 141
       importance of, 141
       instructions for, 146-47
       machine-based, 144, 159
       parts of, 142
       during pregnancy, 120
       to reduce frequency of back pain, 77
       role of spinal, 47
       starting position, **149**
       strengthening exercises in, 47, 153-58, **153-58**
       stretching exercises in, 47, 116, 148, **148**, 150-52, **150-52**
       and surgery, 142
       training zone in, 163

Exercise program *(continued)*
  warm-up activities in, 145
  water exercises in, 160-62

Fatigue
  and cumulative trauma, 128-29
  and pain management, 116-17
Fellowships, 57, 59
Force/forceful movements, and cumulative trauma, 122, 125
Fractures, compression, 51, 99
Free weights, 145, 160
Functional squat exercise, 157, **157**

Gender, and occurrence of back pain, 31

Hamstrings, effect of tight, on back, 46, 52
Hands and knees balancing exercise, 156, **156**
Hands-on treatment, benefits of, 92, 96
Heat treatment, 89, 91
  for pain management, 116-17
  risks with, 76-77, 90
  whirlpool for, 118
Heavy loads, and cumulative trauma disorders, 122, 125
Herbal remedies, effectiveness of, 88-89
Herniated disc, **39,** 43, **50,** 63, 101
  causes of, 38
  difference between, and bulging disc, 50
  during pregnancy, 120
  treatment of, 79
Hip extension, 158, **158**
Hot tub for pain management, 118

Ibuprofen, 77, 82, 117
  side effects of, in elderly, 102
Ice treatment, 77, 89, 91
  caution with, 90
  for pain management, 116-17
Idiopathic low back pain, 49
Invasiveness of treatment, 76-77

Job rotation, as solution to cumulative trauma, 126
Joints, 40

Kyphotic curve, 36

Lateral epicondylitis, 122-23
Leg extension exercise, advanced, 150, **150**
Ligaments, 46
      anterior/posterior longitudinal, 41
      disease states affecting, 41-42
      function of, 40-41
      thickening/calcifying of spinal, 49, 50
Local anesthetics, 95
Lordotic curve, 36
Lower back, 28, **28**
Lumbar Epidural Steroid Injection (LESI), 96
Lumbar instability, 63
Lumbar spine, 28, **28, 39,** 105
      lordotic curve of, 36

Machine-based exercise, cautions for, 159
Magnetic resonance imaging (MRI), 70-71
Manipulation therapy, 55
Mattress, choice of, for pain management, 116
Medical opinion, seeking second, 62
Medical terms, glossary of, 175-83
Medication, 77, 117
      analgesics, 84
      anti-inflammatory, 82-83
      for elderly, 102
      muscle-relaxing drugs, 84
      narcotics, 84
      psychotropic drugs, 84
      role of, 85
Morphine, 84
Motor strength testing, 68
Muscle-relaxing drugs, 84
Muscles, 45-46
      effect of, on back rehabilitation, 46
      tight hamstrings, 46, 52

Musculoskeletal system, impairments to, 31
Myelogram, 18, 72

Narcotics, 84, 102
Nautilus machines, 144, 159
Nerve conduction study (NCS), 72
Nervous systems, 42-44
Neurologic surgeon (neurosurgeon), 56
Neurologist, 56, 59
Nonsteroidal drugs, 77, 82-83
Nucleus, 38
Nucleus pulposus, 38, 123

Orthopaedic chiropractors, 54
Orthopaedic surgeon (orthopaedist), training of, 56
Osteopathic physician, 54, 94
        training of, 55
Osteoporosis, 51, 99

Pain drawing, to describe pain to physician, 61, **61**
Pain management
        attitude in, 107
        and bending, lifting, and carrying packages, 114, **115**
        and fatigue, 116-17
        getting in and out of car, 112, **112**
        importance of relaxation in, 117-18
        and level of activity, 107-8
        role of attitude in, 26-27
        and sex life, 117
        while sitting, 112-13, **113**
        while sleeping
                bedding, 116
                position, 114, **114**
        while standing, 113, **113**
        time management for, 108-9
        travel tips
                while driving, 111, **111**
                while flying, 110
                for packing, 109

and weight control, 109
whirlpool/hot tub for, 118
Passive treatment, versus active treatment, 24, 60, 79-80, 93, 97
Patient history, 66-68
Pelvic tilt exercise, 148, **148**
Peripheral nervous system, 42-44
Personal experience of back pain, 17-22, 131-32
 best times, 17, 134
 effect of, on outlook, 13, 137-38
 feelings upon awakening, 137
 informing children, 136-37
 perceptions as sufferer, 139-40
 reactions of business associates, 13, 138-39
 reactions of children, 133-34, 167, 170-72
 reactions of friends, 13, 133, 168-70
 reasons for writing book, 13, 140
 self-esteem, 13, 135-36
 wife's perspective, 165-74
 worst times, 135
Physiatrist, 56-57, 59
Physical examination, 68
 examination of joints in lower extremities, 69
 neurologic evaluation, 68-69
Physical fitness, importance of, 108
Physical therapy, 85
 active/passive modalities, 86
 choosing therapist, 87-88
 evaluation in, 85-86
 for older patients, 103
 for pregnant women, 120
 spinal manipulation in, 94
Physician(s)
 allopathic, 54-55
 board certification of, 58, 59
 choosing, 58-60
 consulting with, 54
 describing pain to, 61
 expectations from, 60-61
 finding qualified, 53-54
 neurologist, 56, 59

Physician(s) *(continued)*
    osteopathic, 54, 55, 94
    physiatrist, 56-57, 59
    rehabilitation, 56-57, 59
    rheumatologist, 57, 59
    and seeking second opinion, 62
    surgeons
        neurologic, 56, 59
        orthopaedic, 54, 56, 59
        questions to ask when choosing, 63
        spine, 57
Posterior longitudinal ligament, 41
Posture
    and cumulative trauma, 124
    sitting, 113, **113**
    standing, 113, **113**
Prayer stretch exercise, 152, **152**
Pregnancy
    back pain during
        causes of, 119, 120
        treatment of, 120
    hormonal changes during, 119
    structural changes during, 119
Prevention of back injury
    and cumulative trauma, 125-26, 128, 129
    and ergonomics, 105-6
    importance of, in workplace, 33
Primary diagnosis, 65-66
Production-based incentives, and cumulative trauma, 125
Progesterone, 119
Psychotropic drugs, 84

Radiculopathy, 101
Reflexology, 57, 91
Rehabilitation physician, 56-57, 59
Relaxation, importance of, for pain management, 117-18
Repetitive trauma, 121, 125
Rheumatologist, 57, 59
RICE, rest, ice, compression, elevation for injury, 89

Sacrum, 28, **28**
Sciatica, 38, 43, 101
       treatment of, 79
Scoliosis, 36
Sensory examination, 68
Sex life, and pain management, 117
Single knee to chest exercise, 150, **150**
Sitting
       duration of, 112, 124
       position for, 113, **113**
Sit-up, partial, 153-54, **153**
Sleeping
       bedding for, 116
       position for, 114, **114**
Smoking, and back pain, 31
Spinal arthritis, 46, 47, 100
Spinal cord, 42, **42**
Spinal injections, 95-96
Spinal joints, degenerated, 49
Spinal manipulation, 92
       choosing qualified practitioner for, 94
       evaluation for, 93
Spinal stenosis, 50-51, 63
Spine, 36, 37, **40**
       anatomy of
              anterior view, **37**
              and central nervous system, 42-44, **43**
              cervical, 36
              coccyx, 28, **28,** 36
              curvature, 36
              discs, 38, **38, 39**
              function of ligaments, 40-42, **41**
              importance of understanding, 35
              influence of, on back problems, 46-47
              lateral view, **37**
              lumbar, 28, **28,** 36, **39,** 105
              movement of, 40
              muscles, 45-46
              and peripheral nervous system, 42-44
              posterior view, **37**

Spine *(continued)*
  sacrum, 28, **28,** 36
  spinal column, 36, **37**
  and stability, 36, 41-42, 45, 47
  thoracic, 36
 effect of aging on, 30, 36, 47, 50, 51, 100
  arthritis, 100
  osteoporosis, 99
  spinal stenosis, 101-2
  treatment of, 102-3
 effect of disease on, 36
  kyphotic curve of thoracic, 36
  lordotic curve of lumbar, 36
Spine surgeon, 57
Spondylolisthesis, 19, 20, 26, 51-52, 63
 treatment of, 52
Standing, position for, 113, **113**
Static posture, and cumulative trauma, 124
Steroids, 95, 96
 side effects of, 83
Stomach crunch exercise, 153-54, **153**
Strengthening exercises, 47
 abdominal stabilization
  with arm and leg movements, 155-56, **155**
  with arm movements, 155, **155**
 bridging, 154, **154**
 functional squat, 157, **157**
 hands and knees balancing, 156, **156**
 hip extension, 158, **158**
 partial sit-up/stomach crunch, 153-54, **153**
Stretching exercises, 47, 116
 cat and camel, 151, **151**
 difference between, warm-up activity and, 143
 double knee to chest, 148, **148**
 leg extension - advanced, 150, **150**
 pelvic tilt, 148, **148**
 prayer stretch, 152, **152**
 single knee to chest, 150, **150**
 trunk roll, 151, **151**
Subluxations, 92

Surgery, 97-98
conditions responding to, 50, 52, 63
early intervention by, 61
and exercise program, 142, 161
types of, 98

Task rotation, as solution to cumulative trauma, 127
Tennis elbow, 122-23
Thoracic spine, kyphotic curve of, 36
Time management, for pain management, 108-9
Training zone, determining, 163
Tranquilizers, 84
Transcutaneous electrical nerve stimulation (TENS), 88
Trauma
cumulative. *See* Cumulative trauma disorders (CTDs)
repetitive, 121, 125
Travel tips
for driving, 111, **111**
for flying, 110
for packing, 109
Treatment
active versus passive, 24, 60, 79-80, 93, 97
acupuncture, 94-95
alternative approaches/practitioners, 57-58, 91
back school, 97
bed rest, 78-79, 82
choosing best, 75
for elderly, 102-3
hands-on therapy, 92, 96
heat versus ice, 89-91, 116-17
individualized program for, 27
medications for, 77, 117
analgesics, 84
anti-inflammatory, 82-83
for elderly, 102
muscle-relaxing drugs, 84
narcotics, 84
psychotropic drugs, 84
role of, 85

Treatment *(continued)*
      methods available, 76-77
      physical therapy, 85-88
      during pregnancy, 120
      principles of, 32-33
      salves, balms, and lotions, 88-89
      self-treatment, 77
      spinal injections, 95-96
      spinal manipulation, 92-94
      surgery, 97-98
      ultrasound and electrical stimulation, 88
      when to seek professional, 78
Triamcinolone, 95
Trigger point injections, 95
Trunk roll exercise, 151, **151**
Tylenol^{TM}, 77, 84, 85, 117

Ultrasound stimulation, 88

Vibration, and cumulative trauma, 124

Warm-up activities, 145, 147
      difference between, stretching exercises and, 143
Water exercises, 160
      benefits of, 161, 162
      buddy system in, 160
      equipment used in, 161
      stretching before, 161
      after surgery, 161
      types of, 162
Weekend warrior syndrome, 30-31, 77, 80-81
Weight control, and pain management, 109
Weights, free, 145, 160
Whirlpool
      for pain management, 118
      reasons for avoiding, 118
Worker absenteeism, 29
Workers' compensation
      rehabilitation coverage by insurance carriers, 29
      rising costs in, 106

Work modification, as solution to cumulative trauma, 127
Workplace
    decreasing CTD injuries in, 130
    ergonomics in, 105-6
Work risk analysis, 130

X-rays, 70, 94